The Clive Cussler
Adventures

The Clive Cussler Adventures
A Critical Review

STEVEN PHILIP JONES

Foreword by Mike Grell

McFarland & Company, Inc., Publishers
Jefferson, North Carolina

LIBRARY OF CONGRESS CATALOGUING-IN-PUBLICATION DATA

Jones, Steven Philip, 1960–
The Clive Cussler Adventures : a Critical Review /
Steven Philip Jones ; foreword by Mike Grell.
p.   cm.
Includes bibliographical references and index.

ISBN 978-0-7864-7896-5 (softcover : acid free paper) ∞
ISBN 978-1-4766-1521-9 (ebook)

1. Cussler, Clive—Criticism and interpretation.   I. Title.
PS3553.U75Z69 2014   813'.54—dc23   2014012456

BRITISH LIBRARY CATALOGUING DATA ARE AVAILABLE

© 2014 Steven Philip Jones. All rights reserved

*No part of this book may be reproduced or transmitted in any form
or by any means, electronic or mechanical, including photocopying
or recording, or by any information storage and retrieval system,
without permission in writing from the publisher.*

Front cover Titanic illustration © iStock/Thinkstock

Printed in the United States of America

*McFarland & Company, Inc., Publishers
Box 611, Jefferson, North Carolina 28640
www.mcfarlandpub.com*

For Clive Cussler
For the inspiration,
With respect and gratitude on
Dirk Pitt's fiftieth anniversary
and
For Sarah Jane,
for looking over my shoulder
while I was writing,
I miss you

Acknowledgments

In the 1930s, films from Universal Pictures would end with a list of a movie's actors and a banner proclaiming, "A good cast is worth repeating!" I always liked that. Nonfiction books do not have casts, of course, but no one writes any kind of long book alone, so I would like to thank the good people who helped me with this one by listing them here (in no particular order).

Again, Mr. Clive Cussler.

Professors J. Kenneth Kuntz and Jay Holstein, of the University of Iowa's Department of Religion, for teaching me the most important thing a writer needs to know, and that is how to read.

My brother-from-another-mother, Christopher Jones, for the prospective cover art.

Wayne Valero, the world's number-one Cussler collector, for answering numerous email questions and for providing an unpublished 1985 interview with Clive Cussler, which is a treasure trove of information.

Andy Scheer, Mike (a.k.a. Captain Sparrow) and Peter Slater, of the Clive Cussler Society, for advice and information about classic cars, naval uniforms and the opening credits to the film *Sahara*.

The University of Iowa Library for its invaluable reference resources, as well as providing me with a home away from home and the inspiration for this book.

My mom and my brothers, Don and Tom, and their families, for always being there.

My good friends Justin Beahm, Tammy Varner O'Brine, Gary Reed, Bill Rosell and Dennis Stick for their unflagging encouragement.

Todd and Ruth Meyer, of Mystery Cat Books, as well as hardboiled writer extraordinaire Ed Gorman, for their support—not just of me but all Iowa authors.

And, as always, to Lisa and Katie, who make life worth living and constantly remind me that there really are more important things in the world than books and writing.

Now *that* is a cast worth repeating!

To anyone who helped me in any way but whose name does not appear here, please accept my humblest apologies and sincerest gratitude. I assure you your absence is unintentional and due totally to my faulty memory and inexcusable recordkeeping. Please feel free to chew me out at your earliest convenience.

Last, but not least, a *caveat lector*. Any critical review reflects the reviewer, not the subject, and everything expressed in this book is simply my opinion supported whenever possible by facts or logic.

Table of Contents

Acknowledgments — vi
Foreword by Mike Grell — 1
Preface: Negative Evidence of Scholarly Production — 3

1. Clive Cussler and Dirk Pitt — 9
2. Cussler's Characters, Part 1: Dirk Pitt and Family — 18
3. Cussler's Characters, Part 2: The Other Heroes — 37
4. Cussler's Characters, Part 3: Heroines/Other Women and Villains/Villainesses — 53
5. Women in Green: Cussler's Thematic Preoccupations — 65
6. Influences from the Golden Age of Pulps, Movies and TV — 94
7. Apotheosis: The Hero Reborn — 111
8. Cussler's Evolving Structures and Plots — 146
9. Adaptations and Cussleresque Adventures — 164

Afterword: A Review of the Review — 191
Chapter Notes — 195
Bibliography — 245
Index — 255

When you speak of those who comment on popular fiction, speak gently. They are childish in their enthusiasms, these commentators.... They search earnestly, stumbling from volume to volume, seeking to understand what is of dubious importance. Accident guides their minds as much as design.—Robert Sampson, *Yesterday's Faces: Glory Figures*, p. 163

Foreword by Mike Grell

"Who's your favorite author?"

The person being asked that question was *my* favorite author, Mickey Spillane. His answer sent me straight to the bookstore.

"Clive Cussler."

Spillane, a master yarn-spinner who loved intricate plots and carefully crafted mysteries that challenged the reader to follow all the clues, went on to rave about Cussler's masterwork *Raise the Titanic!* and said that Dirk Pitt was a far more interesting character than James Bond. This from the man who created the ultimate hard-boiled private eye, Mike Hammer, and knew good storytelling. He also said he couldn't figure out how Hollywood had managed to make such a terrible movie out of such a wonderful book as *Raise the Titanic!* (I have to agree with him there, but it's Hollywood's nature to attempt to "improve" on something unique, running it through the formula grinder until it's indistinguishable from anything else that's gone through the process.)

Mind you, the movie came out in 1980 and the book was written in 1976, nine years before the final resting place of the *Titanic* was discovered. Despite what we now know to be the actual condition of the wreck, which would make it virtually impossible to actually raise it, Cussler's novel stands as a masterpiece of storytelling, rich in character and crafted with an expert's hand. Long before James Cameron wrote and directed *Titanic* (1997), Cussler crafted a riveting tale about the people who sailed aboard the doomed vessel and the modern-day effort to retrieve something locked away in a safe that's at the bottom of the sea. Sound familiar?

I think it was Agatha Christie who said, "When you read a book, you get ten percent plot, twenty percent characterization and seventy percent whatever the writer knows best." And Clive Cussler knows his stuff, and lives it. Whether it's classic automobiles or underwater adventure, he's been there, done that. Dirk Pitt's National Underwater and Marine Agency (NUMA) became reality through Cussler's patronage and has become a major player in underwater research and exploration. In 2000, after more than a decade of searching, NUMA recovered the sunken wreck of the CSS *Hunley*, the first submarine to sink an enemy ship in battle. NUMA has since gone on to discover a number of wrecks, long lost in the depths.

Clive Cussler's claim of being an instinctual writer rather than a cerebral one is something I can relate to. Clearly, he's writing like I do ... for an audience of one: himself. He's writing the kind of story he'd like to read, rich in historical detail and great characters, filled with complex intertwined plotlines and bold action set against the backdrop of exotic international and undersea locations. It just so happens that millions of readers are looking for the same thing.

With over 125 million copies sold, I'd say they found it.

Mike Grell, creator of *Jon Sable, Freelance*, has been one of America's most popular and influential adventure writers and artists. His credits include drawing the *Tarzan* newspaper strip, creating the original comic book series *The Warlord*, and writing and drawing the graphic novels *Green Arrow: The Longbow Hunters* (DC Comics) and *James Bond: Permission to Die* (Eclipse Comics).

Preface
Negative Evidence of Scholarly Production

Man, they just don't get it.—Johnny Cash (*Live at San Quentin*)

There is a scene in Herman Melville's *Moby-Dick* (1851) where the harpooner Queequeg nearly has his hand bitten off by a dead shark hauled onto the *Pequod*. "Queequeg no care what god made him shark ... wedder Feejee god or Nantucket god; but de god wat made shark must be one damn Injin."[1] The self-conscious irony of a Southern Pacific cannibal calling a deity a damn Injin underscores Melville's contention that any god who would create a monster like the shark must be undeniably savage, a point of view scarcely out of place in a story fixated with the mystery of man's deathbound plight.[2] When Melville began writing *Moby-Dick* in early 1850, however, it was nothing more than another unpretentious sea adventure in the same vein as four of his first five novels.[3] It was not until September of that year, after reading Nathaniel Hawthorne's 1846 short story collection *Mosses from an Old Manse*, followed by several days visiting Hawthorne, that Melville changed *Moby-Dick* from a whaling adventure to a work of literature.

But what if Melville had not changed *Moby-Dick*? How would he have written the shark scene with Queequeg?

There is no way to know for sure, but in the words of D.H. Lawrence (*Lady Chatterley's Lover*, "The Rocking-Horse Winner"), Melville was "rather a tiresome New Englander of the ethical mystical-transcendentalist sort ... the solemn ass even in humour,"[4] so it seems probable that the scene would have been more journalistic. In any case, in most adventure stories a shark is not an ironic symbol. It is a test or challenge that a hero must circumvent or conquer to reach a reward, in this case finding and cutting whales. If a hero wants those whales then he will have to come and get them, but in adventure stories rewards never come without some kind of trial. Here be dragons, but if the hero conquers the threat of the sharks and reaches the reward then he and the members of his society will be better off for it.

Sometimes only a thin line separates literature from popular or light fiction. Sometimes the difference only comes down to intent and execution. Literature, such as *Moby-Dick*, is like a Romanesque cathedral, while popular fiction is like a prairie church. A considerable amount of time, skill and coordination is required to build a cathedral, but the result can be an impressive creation infused with influences from artisans, down through the centuries, to impress a certain reaction in visitors. Prairie churches are simpler by purpose and design, but you had better know which end of a hammer to hold if you want to create something that not only functions as a church but can stand up to sun, wind, rain, snow, hail and the occasional twister. In comparison, literature, such as Harper Lee's *To Kill a Mockingbird* (1960), Ernest Hemingway's *The Old Man and the Sea* (1952) and Alain-Fournier's *Le Grand Meaulnes* (1913), stir the senses by provoking pleasant or unpleasant reactions and contemplations through characters, plots and settings hardy enough to bear the burden of representing ideas and ideals, whereas popular fiction delights and amuses,[5] simply and elegantly reinvigorating the spirit by bringing "adventure to drab classrooms, where chalk scraped slowly on blackboards, and to factories untouched by the sun."[6]

Neither is superior. Both serve important purposes.

That said, popular fiction tends to be what its name implies, popular, but many critics rarely consider sales success when deciding what to review. These critics moon over the most obscure literature if it "shivers with that ecstasy of multi-level interpersonal interactions and awareness shifts from one mode of desperation to the next,"[7] but shy away from some of the most well-liked fiction with the public.[8] A good example of this is Alistair MacLean (1922–1987), a bestselling author for over 30 years and one of the most popular suspense-adventure writers of his generation.[9] MacLean's books, like *The Guns of Navarone* (1957), *Ice Station Zebra* (1963) and *Where Eagles Dare* (1967), were generally snubbed by critics during his lifetime, and today much the same can be said about Clive Cussler, a best-selling author for nearly 40 years, one of his generation's most popular suspense-adventure writers[10] and (doing MacLean one better) creator of one of the best-loved series heroes[11] of the past 50 years, Dirk Pitt, special projects director for the National Underwater and Marine Agency (NUMA), a federal bureau that oversees marine conservation as well as the salvage and preservation of historical maritime vessels.

Pitt updates the globetrotting post-war adventure hero that was popular for most of the 20th century,[12] a reinvention that struck a chord with millions of readers and codified one of the most popular heroic archetypes from the waning years of the Cold War. The Pitt archetype hero is self-reliant, sometimes self-effacing but always self-sacrificing, usually in the military or a veteran employed (or formerly employed) by the government. This hero is educated, intuitive, or both, a realist and sometimes a cynic, genial but dangerous when threatened,[13] witty or wisecracking, patriotic to his country, as honorable as a Boy Scout by nature yet willing to break a rule if necessary; there is also a dash of Peter Pan in him. Several of these elements can be found in many of the most popular adventure series heroes that came after Pitt, including Jon Sable (1983), Jack Ryan (1984), Angus MacGyver (1985), John McClane (1988), Colonel Jonathan "Jack" O'Neill (1997), Leroy Jethro Gibbs (2003), Benjamin Franklin Gates (2004) and Captain Jack Harkness (2005).

To be fair, Cussler and Pitt have not been completely ignored by critics. For instance, archivist Arlene Schmuland explains in her 1997 article, "The Archival Image in Fiction: An Analysis and Annotated Bibliography," how Cussler and other best-selling authors "play a role in popularizing and perpetuating images of certain professions."[14] Along these same lines, an article published in 1999, "Fuzzy Lines: Using the Best-Selling Novel to Illustrate the Blurring Boundaries of 'Public'" by political science professors Nolan J. Argyle and Gerald A. Merwin, argues that Pitt's role as an adventure hero who works for the government contributes to an increasingly risky blurring of the general public's perception about the duties of the public and private sectors.[15] (Argyle and Merwin's article is examined in Chapter 5.) Yet another 1997 article, "Wildmen, Warriors, and Lovers: Reaching Boys through Archetypal Literature" by Professor William G. Brozo and Ronald V. Schmelzer, champions boys reading "classic stories and current young adult literature" with positive male archetypes such as Pitt to help them "develop a realistic idea of what it means to be a man" and "help boys appreciate honored character traits of males while they learn how authentic adult men and adolescent boys deal with themselves, other males and females, and difficult ethical and physical situations."[16] Interestingly, reviews like these that focus on the cultural effects of Cussler's novels tend to be courteous if not always positive in their assessments, but the few literary critical reviews there have been of Cussler's novels tend to be primarily negative.

Some good examples of this can be found in Mark Gallagher's *Action Figures: Men, Action Films, and Contemporary Adventure Narratives* (2006). Gallagher, a lecturer on film and television studies at the University of Nottingham, devotes a chapter to the "Airport Fiction" of Cussler and Tom Clancy (*Hunt for Red October*, *Rainbow Six*), which he claims "preserve constructions of heroic, idealized masculinity" and redeem "archaic notions of loyalty and duty." (Apparently Gallagher did not read Brozo and Schmelzer's article.) Gallagher also claims the largest audience for Cussler and Clancy's bestsellers is "white, middle-aged, professional men" for whom the authors created "the recurring figure of the exceptional woman" who "functions as the ideal 'man's woman'" by divesting herself "of conventionally feminine traits." (Cussler claims 50 percent of his readers are women[17] and confesses to taking pride in creating classy heroines who are "never harsh, stupid bimbos. They've all made it in the world and carry their own weight."[18]) Gallagher specifically brands Cussler's adventures as "a playground of protracted adolescence," a Neverland where, among other things, "male protagonists spend active and leisure time manipulating vehicles," such as "classic automobiles," and where Cussler can inject himself as a character, which Gallagher suggests may attest to Cussler's "own inflated self-regard."[19] (More about that below.)

Not all critics are as tactful as Gallagher.

When Robert McKee, one of America's most successful screenwriting instructors, was asked to give his critical assessment of Cussler's *Sahara* (1992), during a civil trial involving the 2005 film adaptation of the novel, he testified, "I cannot overstate how terrible the writing is.... It is flawed in every way writing can be flawed." When told the novel was a huge commercial success McKee was unimpressed. "Bad writing often makes a lot of money." [20]

Cussler's fans do not fret that Gallagher thinks Cussler's novels are "adolescent fantasies."[21] They know Cussler's adventures are "elementary tales ... where the incidents defy the probabilities and march just inside the borders of possibility,"[22] but who are they hurting by enjoying recurring travel-guide thrills, cliffhangers, narrow escapes, and last-second rescues mixed in with nautical settings, evil conspiracies and search for lost treasure? And as for Cussler's "literal insertion of himself into his own fictional world,"[23] how is it worse than Simon Templar being aware that he is a character in Leslie Charteris's Saint novels? To Cussler's fans, it is too bad that Gallagher, McKee and critics like them cannot or refuse to see that Cussler is having fun and inviting us to join him. McKee complains that in *Sahara* something "unbelievable [is] happening every two minutes,"[24] never appreciating that is the point. In the words of film director Alfred Hitchcock, "Logic is dull."[25] The Master of Suspense also understood how much harder it is to create a successful commercial story than it is to make a private statement,[26] as did the grandmaster hardboiled writer Mickey Spillane (*I, the Jury*, *Kiss Me Deadly*), who tried to tell his critics, "You don't read a book to get to the middle. You read it to get to the end."[27]

That said, anyone who has written as many successful books as Cussler deserves a balanced critical review no matter what Gallagher, McKee and, yes, even Cussler, might think. When I sent Cussler a letter about wanting to write this book he replied, "Why anyone would want to write a critical review of Dirk Pitt's adventures is a mystery to me, but go ahead if you wish."[28] This response seems to beg the question popular culture critic George N. Dove asks in *Suspense in the Formula Story* (1989): "How does one criticize (i.e., interpret) a popular story that relies heavily upon the suspense process? One quick answer is to dismiss it as popular and therefore trivial, or label it a potboiler, lacking depth and hence inappropriate to real criticism." Dove disagrees. "The popular culture critic, however, will insist that the story must be interpreted because it *is* popular."[29]

In spite of Cussler's reservations, he was kind enough to answer several research questions and even took the time to call me before sending his answers to say he was worried I was going to be disappointed. Cussler felt my questions were cerebral while he insists he is an instinctual writer. In a note attached to his answers, Cussler wrote, "I'm sorry I didn't answer in more depth. I'm simpleminded at heart."[30] Creative influences and literary techniques rarely, if ever, cross Cussler's mind when he is writing, which seems to beg another question: "How can you write a critical review if an author never intentionally puts anything in his stories to critically review?" You can do it because, as a fiction writer, I know from experience that authors incorporate genre patterns and literary techniques into stories without being aware of it, an opinion shared by commentator and cultural historian Camille Paglia, professor at Philadelphia's University of the Arts and author of review books *Alfred Hitchcock's The Birds* (1998) and *Sexual Personae: Art and Decadence from Nefertiti to Emily Dickinson* (1990). Paglia believes that an "artist is not nearly as aware of what he or she is doing as those who study an artist's work"[31] and cites Bob Dylan's "Desolation Row" as proof. One of Paglia's courses takes three days to examine the song's complexities, yet Paglia is convinced the song "just poured out of [Dylan] ... in ways that I think he himself would be amazed at, the structure of it, the themes, the organization." Paglia argues, and I agree, that an artist's efforts come from their unconscious mind when it is "working at a very high level of creative ferment," and since artists "make art via a certain gift which is not necessarily verbal" it is the role of the critic and the commentator and the professor to "verbalize in a subordinate role to major artistic creation."[32] Bestselling author and former English teacher Stephen King (*Salem's Lot*, "Rita Hayworth and the Shawshank Redemption," *The Shining*) says much the same thing in his nonfiction horror treatise *Danse Macabre* (1981) when he reviews Jack Finney's *The Body Snatchers* (1955). Thesis after thesis continues to explore the popular perception that Finney's novel is a warning against the loss of individuality, while a plethora of movie reviews continue to impute either anti–McCarthyism or anti–Communist messages in the fairly faithful 1957 film adaptation *Invasion of the Body Snatchers*. According to King, the film's director, Don Siegel, claims the movie is about the Red Menace, so apparently Kevin McCarthy really is trying to warn us about more than pod people when he goes around shouting, "They're here already! You're next! You're next!" As far as the novel is concerned, however, Finney insists in a 1979 letter to King, "The idea of writing a whole book in order to say that it's not really a good thing for us all to be alike, and that individuality is a good thing, makes me laugh." Sounding a little like Cussler in his note to me, Finney adds that *The Body Snatchers* "was just a story meant to entertain, with no more meaning than that," however King believes that "Finney's contention that *The Body Snatchers* is just a story is both right and wrong." King explains:

> My own belief about fiction, long and deeply held, is that story *must* be paramount over all other considerations in fiction; that story *defines* fiction, and that all other considerations—theme, mood, tone, symbol, style, even characterization—are expendable.... And yet I don't

think Finney would argue with the idea that story values are determined by the mind through which they are filtered, and that the mind of any writer is a product of his outer world and inner temper.[33]

So even if a message or allegory in a story is unintentional, that does not negate exploring it and its relation to other elements in the story or the author's body of work.

The aim of *The Clive Cussler Adventures: A Critical Review* is to take what I believe is an overdue, balanced, critical look at Cussler's novels, particularly those featuring his best and most influential hero, Dirk Pitt. A review that is merited, in my opinion, and I believe Dove would agree, based upon their current success and popularity. In that regard, this review is concerned only about the present, not about the future, since only Time will tell if Cussler will join the elite pantheon of adventure writers like Alexandre Dumas, Robert Louis Stevenson, Rudyard Kipling, H. Rider Haggard, Sir Arthur Conan Doyle, Rafael Sabatini, Edgar Rice Burroughs and Ian Fleming, whose tales are still being read long after the writers have ceased writing and the world in which they lived has changed forever. Some might think Cussler's success guarantees he will,[34] but in reality success impresses future generations of readers even less than it does contemporary literary critics, which is why many of yesterday's most popular writers are forgotten today.[35] The fact is, classic adventure writers must prove their merits to every new generation or they, too, will be forgotten.

This review also takes the approach of French entomologist and author Jean-Henri Fabre (1823–1915) that critical as well as scholarly works should be written for general readers, an unpopular approach with some critics who believe this is negative evidence of scholarly production,[36] doubly so when the subject is a popular fiction writer who has never sought literary laurels. Cussler claims that all he wanted to do when he created Pitt was "to produce a little paperback series,"[37] but over the years his books have shown constant improvement in style and skill along with a willingness on Cussler's part to attempt new things, hallmarks of talent and a dedication to workmanship that not only provide further merit to this review but stand as evidence that Cussler is a better writer than many of his critics, including himself, may want to admit.

So, with all that said, from this point on critics and general readers who admire cathedrals but refuse to appreciate prairie churches have only themselves to blame if they continue. Readers can decide for themselves whether or not Cussler intentionally put any of the various thematic preoccupations or plot elements explored in this review into his adventures, but one thing is for certain: here be dragons, but there are no naves.

1

Clive Cussler and Dirk Pitt

It is no doubt a pleasant power to be able to interest others in the creations of one's own mind.—Sir Arthur Conan Doyle[1]

Like most good writers of fiction, he had a perverse and devious mind.—*Valhalla Rising*[2]

Sometime around 1964 Clive Cussler decided to create a hero.

Cussler's wife, Barbara, was working the graveyard shift for the police department and Cussler wanted something to do after putting their children, Dirk, Teri and Dana, to bed. An award-winning advertising copywriter, Cussler had recently been contacted by a professor at the University of California who needed help writing a textbook on sea farming. Cussler wrote 250 pages for the professor, who apparently never did anything with the manuscript,[3] but the experience convinced Cussler that he could write a book in his spare time.

All Cussler had to do was figure out what to write.

* * *

A half century later, Cussler has over 50 books with over 125 million copies in print, but these statistics fail to do his accomplishments justice. Many people get an itch to write a book, but very few scratch that itch and fewer still write anything worth publishing.

There are exceptions, of course.

As a struggling doctor, Arthur Conan Doyle was blessed with more time than patients, so he began writing short stories. Conan Doyle eventually combined his admiration for Edgar Allan Poe, the scientific method, lessons learned in observation and deduction from one of his medical professors, Dr. Joseph Bell, and his love of knights and chivalry to write a detective novel featuring a new type of intellectual adventure hero named Sherlock Holmes.[4] *A Study in Scarlet* (1887) and its sequel *The Sign of Four* (1890) did not set the world on fire, but when Holmes began appearing in a series of short stories in *The Strand* magazine in 1891 he went on to become the most popular fictional character in Western literature.

As a struggling telegrapher in Tulsa, Oklahoma, Lester Dent worked the graveyard shift, a job that left him with plenty of slack hours. When Dent discovered another "brass pounder" was selling stories to pulp magazines and earning checks worth more than Dent made in a month, he began submitting his own stories, combining his love of the outdoors, adventure and technology with his ideal of manly morality. Dent's first dozen or so stories were rejected, but he persevered and eventually became such a prolific contributor to the pulps that Dent caught the attention of the publishers at Street & Smith, who asked him to write the adventures of a new adventure hero the company had created, a two-fisted super-genius named Doc

Savage.[5] Thanks to Dent, Doc Savage became the pulps' most popular series hero after The Shadow and is still appearing in books, graphic novels and movies.

These are exceptions, of course.

Extreme exceptions.

Most people who get an itch to write fiction and follow through never experience this kind of success. Even Dent's co-worker and his stories are forgotten today. Cussler joined a very select fraternity when he became a bestselling writer and created one of the most popular and influential adventure heroes of his generation.

* * *

Cussler used his marketing experience as much as his ingenuity and creativity when it came to deciding what to write.[6]

First, Cussler researched the publishing industry and discovered that almost no one was writing pure adventures like those he read as a boy. Stories like the novels of Samuel Shellaburger and Thomas B. Costain, the Horatio Hornblower sea tales by C.S. Forester[7] and pulp stories about "globe-spanning adventurers, one man facing impossible odds, racing against time to save the world."[8] The classic old-fashioned adventure field was virtually free of competition,[9] so Cussler decided to create a little paperback adventure series. Since armchair detectives, private eyes and secret agents had been done to death, the man who helped create the iconic Ajax White Knight advertising campaign ("Stronger than dirt!")[10] decided to create a brand new kind of hero.[11]

Next, Cussler researched adventure series heroes like Holmes, Bulldog Drummond and James Bond. Cussler also decided he wanted to incorporate the sea into his new series, having noticed that many adventure novels were set aboard ships or on the oceans, including some of MacLean's best works, including *HMS Ulysses* (1955) and *Ice Station Zebra*, but the same could not be said for any modern adventure series. This gave Cussler the hook he needed to make his series and its hero different.[12]

* * *

Cussler was six years old when he fell in love with the sea.

Born July 31, 1931, in Aurora, Illinois, Cussler lived in Kentucky and Minnesota before his family moved to the Los Angeles suburb of Alhambra in 1938. Soon after, his parents, Eric and Amy, took Cussler to see the Pacific Ocean and the captivated boy ran all the way into the water. Eric fished Cussler out and, soon afterwards, Amy signed her overzealous son up for swimming lessons.[13]

Cussler was not so enthusiastic when it came to school and class work. A bright and competently athletic boy, his report cards were often littered with Cs and Ds, much to Eric's concern, but away from school Cussler demonstrated the work ethic that would sustain him as a struggling writer, making Eagle Scout by age 14 and working several jobs before and after high school to earn the money to buy cars, which he loved to restore.[14]

Another thing Cussler loved was exercising his imagination. Cussler recalls his boyhood as "Tom Sawyer meets The Little Rascals," with the friendships he made in those days continuing through high school and afterwards.[15] Cussler's boyhood was filled with tree houses, make-believe battles waged in backyards, and pirate ships sailing in vacant lots. Later in life, Cussler turned his imagination towards finding angles to achieve his goals, a skill he honed until it was on par with Quentin McHale and Ernie Bilko. During high school football games, Cussler and his friends often arrived in his black 1925 Auburn limousine, dressed like Prohibition-era gangsters, with Cussler toting a violin case, which he used to smuggle beer and wine into the stands past security guards. While in the Air Force, Cussler bought a medical book in an antique store and whenever work got too boring he would wrangle some time off by pretending to have symptoms of diseases like Borneo Jungle Incepus.[16]

* * *

Convinced that everyone is fascinated with the mysteries that lie in the deep, Cussler decided his hero's territory would be the sea, his challenge the unknown,[17] but Cussler's daring, drive, passion for cars, fidelity for friendships and con man's audacity also became a part of the character.

All Cussler had to do was figure out what to call this hero.

Many writers give a hero a name that reflects the character's nature, like Rex Stout's Nero Wolfe,[18] but Stout proves, with Archie Goodwin, that an effective name does not have to reflect anything about a hero. A memorable name is also preferable, but while it is hard to imagine Conan Doyle's greatest hero going by either of his creator's less memorable first choices, John Reeves or Sherrinford Holmes,[19] Fleming gave his dashing secret agent hero "the most plain sounding name I could find"[20] by lifting James Bond from the author of the book *Birds of the West Indies* (1936). Cussler decided to give his hero the memorable name Dirk Pitt, taking "Dirk" from his own middle child and "Pitt" from William Pitt, the Elder.[21] Then Cussler made Pitt a blond as a contrast to other series adventure heroes (most of whom had black hair), until his research revealed female readers preferred heroes with dark hair.[22] Cussler also lent Pitt some of his own physical traits, such as height (six-foot-three), weight (185 pounds), eye color (green ... though Pitt's eyes are greener) and approximate age.[23] Both, likewise, served in the air force, however Pitt is an officer and remains on active duty into his forties. In the ensuing years, Cussler incorporated more similarities. When Cussler quit smoking, so did Pitt. When Cussler switched from Cutty Sark Scotch to Bombay Gin, so did Pitt. And when Cussler developed a taste for tequila, so did Pitt,[24] but Cussler concedes that Pitt attracts more ladies than he ever did.[25] Neither Cussler nor Pitt are handsome in the classical Errol Flynn or Cary Grant tradition, but like the more rugged-looking Gary Cooper or Humphrey Bogart, women are drawn to Pitt, and he and Cussler have no problem with that.

* * *

Cussler met Barbara Knight on a blind date in 1951 while on leave from the air force. Four months after Cussler was discharged in 1954, the couple married and moved into a duplex in Alhambra. Over the next few years Cussler worked a variety of jobs, including pumping gas for Union Oil Company, leasing a Mobile Oil station with friend and partner Dick Klein, and working as an advertising manager for Richard's Lido Market, a major independent supermarket in Costa Mesa. Prior to this, Cussler had never worked in advertising, but he was a born promoter who took to his new job like the proverbial duck to water.[26]

After winning several local advertising awards, Cussler teamed up with a young illustrator named Leo Bestgen to open their own advertising firm. Cussler supplemented his income with a night job at a liquor store during Bestgen & Cussler's first three years, but, just as the firm was starting to prosper, the two partners decided to sell it. Bestgen wanted to pursue his dream of becoming an illustrator, while Cussler accepted a copywriting job with a large Los Angeles advertising firm. Cussler ended up working for three different firms during the sixties, including D'arcy, where he helped create the Ajax White Knight campaign. Cussler also continued winning industry prizes, including four CLIO Awards, six International Broadcast Awards and an award at the Venice Film Festival.[27] Cussler "enjoyed writing and creating original concepts and transferring them into visual images that sold a product and made everybody happy,"[28] but he also got that itch to write fiction and, over a period of a couple of years, he finished the first Dirk Pitt novel, originally titled "The Sea Dwellers" but eventually renamed *Pacific Vortex*.[29]

In 1967, Cussler enrolled part-time at Orange Coast Community College, in Costa Mesa, to study creative writing and oceanography. A short-story assignment that became the first chapter of *The Mediterranean Caper* won a second-place trophy from the college and, as of this writing, remains Cussler's only literary award.[30] In 1968, D'arcy laid Cussler off, but he was soon offered a $2,500-a-month job with another firm. Cussler instead decided his sea adventures might benefit from his taking a sabbatical from advertising to accept a $400-a-month job as counter salesman at the Aquatic Dive Center in Newport Beach. Cussler was a lifelong bodysurfer[31] but the shop's owners, Don Spencer, Ron Merker and Omar Wood,[32] were respected members of the diving community, and, over the next year, Cussler earned his scuba diving certification. Whenever business was slow, Cussler worked on his next Pitt novel,[33] and when *The Mediterranean Caper* was finished, Cussler quit the dive shop to return to advertising. Spencer, Merker and Wood gave Cussler a Doxa dive watch with an orange dial as a farewell gift, and Cussler appreciated it and his time at the shop so much that the Doxa became a standard piece of equipment for Pitt[34] and Newport Beach became Pitt's hometown.[35]

* * *

Following the tradition of post-war adventure heroes like Drummond and Bond, Pitt is an officer and combat veteran.[36] Like Bond, Pitt works for the government, but not in any enforcement capacity. Pitt is a bureaucrat, a new wrinkle for an adventure hero in the sixties.[37] Officially, Pitt is a marine engineer on loan from the air force to Admiral James Sandecker (retired) to serve as special projects director for NUMA. Pitt's primary duties are searching for shipwrecks and leading salvage operations, but if an ancillary project like raising the *Titanic* or neutralizing a lost cache of virulent neuro-toxins drifts into NUMA's purview, it usually gets assigned to Pitt.

Another innovative wrinkle Cussler incorporates into Pitt is the blurring of class lines. Prior to Pitt, the average adventure hero tended to associate with his own class. Holmes, for instance, belongs to London's upper class. Bond is a British club man. John D. McDonald's Travis McGee is American middle-class[38] as is Dashiell Hammett's Continental Op, who may investigate well-to-do people but only when the underworld of crime they inhabit manages to slop over into the higher stratum of society. Cussler wanted Pitt to be different: "Someone with rough edges, yet a degree of style, who felt equally at ease entertaining a gorgeous woman in a gourmet restaurant or downing a beer with the boys at the local saloon. A congenial kind of guy with a tinge of mystery about him."[39] Pitt comes from America's privileged class, the heir of a wealthy California family and the son of a senior senator. Pitt is also a pilot, scuba diver, gourmet cook and classic automobile collector, not typical middle-class pursuits, but he never attended private school (unless you count the Air Force Academy); his best friend and surrogate brother is the working class Al Giordino (whom he met during a playground fight in elementary school), and few things make Pitt happier than getting greasy while working with his hands.[40] When it comes to rough edges, Pitt can be disrespectful to authority figures or anyone he dislikes, and selfish with his emotions to the women he loves, although he has mellowed and matured as he has grown older. When it comes to being congenial, Pitt is a hopeless Good Samaritan, an echo of Cussler's days as an Eagle Scout,[41] although Pitt takes this to extremes when he risks his life to defend strangers like Eva Rojas in *Sahara* and Julia Lee in *Flood Tide*. In contrast, the savagery Pitt rains down upon villains like Qin Shang in *Flood Tide* and Min Koryo in *Deep Six* contributes to his tinge of mystery. Not that savagery in a hero is a bad thing. As the late pulp historian Robert Sampson points out, "The only difference between a popular hero and a criminal is that the hero strikes on the side of the right."[42] Further adding to Pitt's tinge of mystery, he can be intensely private, shielding a part of himself from everyone he knows, including Giordino.

All in all, Pitt is a patriotic defender of the realm and knight-errant willing to put his life on the line for his country and his fellow man, as well as a merciless nemesis and manhunter against his adversaries. Pitt is also an adventurer unafraid to stray from the highroads traveled by most people to uncover the secrets that can be found in places lost to history.

* * *

After Cussler completed *The Mediterranean Caper*, he submitted his manuscript to several publishers. When he got no takers, Cussler realized he needed a literary agent.

All Cussler had to do was figure out how to find one.

Aware that literary agents receive hundreds, if not thousands, of unsolicited manuscripts each year, Cussler knew he had to find a way to make his submission stand out from the slush pile. First, Cussler solicited the names of 25 New York literary agents from casting agencies with whom he had worked. Next, he ordered a thousand sheets of stationery (with matching envelopes) for the nonexistent "Charles Winthrop Agency" and sent a letter from Winthrop to the first name on his agent list, Peter Lampack of the William Morris Agency in Manhattan:

Dear Peter,
  As you know, I primarily handle motion picture and television screenplays; however, I've run across a pair of book-length manuscripts which I think have a great deal of potential. I would pursue them, but I am retiring soon. Would you like to take a look at them?

A week later a letter arrived from Lampack agreeing to look at the manuscripts. Two weeks after Cussler mailed the manuscripts another letter arrived from Lampack:

Dear Charlie,
  Read the manuscripts. The first one is only fair, but the second one looks good. Where can I sign Cussler to a contract?

Cussler signed the contract, threw away the list of literary agents, and started writing the third Pitt adventure, *Iceberg*, on the back of the Winthrop stationery.[43]

* * *

It was the summer of 1970 and Cussler decided it was time to find out if he could make writing his career. The Cusslers sold their house and belongings, deposited the earnings in the bank, and traveled the western United States until they landed in Estes Park, Colorado, so the children could start school in the fall. Cussler finished *Iceberg* in 1972 and sent it off to Lampack, but Lampack had no more luck selling it than he did *The Mediterranean Caper*. Lampack's bosses were suggesting that he dump Cussler, but Lampack refused. Meanwhile the Cusslers' savings were nearly depleted, so Cussler finagled a copywriter job from the tiny Hull/Mefford Agency in Denver, and the family eventually moved to the bedroom community of Arvada.

Before long, Cussler was winning awards for Hull/Mefford, but success came at a price. As the little agency's reputation grew so did its client list and Cussler was soon too busy to write fiction. Fate or coincidence (take your pick) stepped in when Cussler was also offered a promotion to become a vice president. Cussler refused. He wanted to stay in the agency's creative area. So Hull/Mefford hired an executive from a New York agency. This new hire and Cussler did not get along and, within three months, Cussler was let go. Swearing never to work for anybody ever again,[44] he went home and started writing the fourth Pitt novel, *Titanic*.

* * *

The trademark of a great hero is that he comes when he is needed.

A knight-errant arrives to rescue a damsel in distress.

A wandering cowboy moseys in from the wilderness to rid a town of gunslingers before riding out again.

A world-weary private detective braves shadowy mean streets to right a wrong ignored by a society grown callous to injustice.

During the sixties and seventies, America was in trouble. Since 1961 the country had suffered through the Bay of Pigs fiasco, the erection of the Berlin Wall, the Cuban Missile Crisis and the assassinations of President Kennedy, the Reverend Martin Luther King, Jr., and Senator Robert Kennedy. By 1973 politicians and bureaucrats in Washington, DC had micromanaged the Vietnam War into a disaster, and the Watergate scandal dominated the national news. America and many Western Allies were also facing a collapse of confidence in traditional cultural values that extended to Christianity, which had undergirded various Western civilizations since medieval times. Much of Christianity's moral authority had been shattered when large numbers of white Christians sat on the sidelines during the civil rights struggles even as liberal-leftist elements in the Church increasingly associated with communist dictators.[45]

During troubled times, people turn to tales of heroes for comfort and reassurance. Conan Doyle wrote his greatest historical romance, *Sir Nigel*, in 1904, while England was beginning to confront problems caused by postindustrialism. Like Shakespeare's histories, *Sir Nigel* champions the notion "that the heroism of the past must serve as an example and inspiration for the present-day Englishmen and women,"[46] but America's past was being assaulted by revisionists in the entertainment industries, the mainstream media and academia, and anyone who disagreed with them was disparaged, insulted and attacked.[47] As John Wayne was making his final movies, and anti-heroes like Dirty Harry Callahan and Paul Kersey were taking the Duke's place, heroes became increasingly hard to find on the big screen, TV screen and in print.[48]

* * *

It was about this time that Lampack sold *The Mediterranean Caper* to Pyramid Books for five thousand dollars. Pyramid sold only 32,000 copies, but the novel received a Mystery Writers of America nomination for Best Mystery of 1973, Cussler's only major literary nomination to date. Soon after, Dodd, Mead paid five thousand dollars for *Iceberg*; they then printed five thousand hardcover copies, and sold 3,200. Lampack next sold the British rights to *Iceberg* to Sphere for four hundred dollars along with British first-refusal rights to Cussler's next novel. In the United States, Dodd, Mead held the American first-refusal rights to Cussler's next novel, but when Lampack sent Dodd, Mead the manuscript for *Titanic*, the publisher passed. So did Bantam Books, on the grounds that the book was too heavy at a time when paper costs were high.[49] Putnam expressed interest, but wanted massive rewrites. In the end, Viking Press purchased *Titanic* for $7,500.

Soon after this, an editor from London's Macmillan Books, who was in New York visiting a friend at Viking, heard about *Titanic* and asked to read the manuscript during his flight home. The Macmillan editor liked *Titanic* so much he encouraged his company to submit a bid, but Sphere had already acted on its first-refusal right and put in its own bid. Macmillan went ahead and submitted a bid, and that kicked off a bidding war. When it was over, Sphere purchased *Titanic* for $22,000, an usually large amount for a British publisher in 1974.

A week before Sphere won the bidding, Cussler played a hunch and asked Lampack to see if Pyramid would give him back the rights to *The Mediterranean Caper* since the book was out of print. Pyramid agreed. Then Jonathan Dodd at Dodd, Mead contacted Lampack to let the agent know that Playboy Books was offering four thousand dollars for the paperback rights to *Iceberg*. Lampack was delighted to see his faith in Cussler beginning to reap dividends, but Cussler refused the Playboy deal and offered to pay Dodd, Mead five thousand dollars to get back the exclusive rights to *Iceberg*. Dodd, Mead accepted, but the Cusslers only had four hundred dollars in the bank, so the family was forced to take out loans to cover the other $4,600.[50]

When news about the British bidding war for *Titanic* reached America it got enough publishers interested in the book's paperback rights that Lampack decided to hold an auction. As Barbara left for work on the morning of the auction, Cussler joked that if the bidding reached $250,000 she could quit. Bantam Books won the auction with a bid of $840,000, and Barbara handed in her two-week's notice later that morning. When Bantam discovered *Titanic* was the third book in the Pitt series—Cussler had long ago tossed the unpublished *Sea Dwellers* on a closet shelf next to his lone attempt at nonfiction humor, *I Went to Denver but It Was Closed*—it offered an additional eighty thousand dollars for *The Mediterranean Caper* and *Iceberg*.[51]

Back at Viking the sales department was assembling the jacket for *Titanic* when some anonymous employee suggested that the title *Raise the Titanic!* might sell better.[52] There is no way to know how much this suggestion affected sales, but by the spring of 1978 Viking had sold over 145,000 copies of *Raise the Titanic!* and the book had owned the number-two spot on bestseller lists for 26 weeks. Lampack also sold the motion picture rights to Marble Arch Productions, netting Cussler nearly half million dollars.[53]

* * *

America got more than Cussler's breakout novel with *Raise the Titanic!*. It got an old-fashioned adventure hero and would not get another one like him until *The Hunt for Red October* was published in 1984.

Pitt is imperfect, but he is also brave, resourceful and identifiable, the kind of hero who would fit right in in most John Ford films. It is not a stretch to see Pitt admirably filling in for Captain Kirby York in *Fort Apache* (1948) or "Guns" Donavan in *Donavan's Reef* (1963) or Sean Thornton in *The Quiet Man* (1952).[54] Would Pitt really be anywhere else during World

War II but the Philippines, bringing the PT boat into prominence like The Duke does in *They Were Expendable* (1945), with James Sandecker filling in for Robert Montgomery's John Brickley? And when Pitt's blood is on the boil is he any less indefatigable and ruthless than Ethan Edwards from *The Searchers* (1956)?

This was just the type of hero America was looking for when Pitt appeared on the bestseller list. Ford had stopped making films and Hollywood was putting the western into mothballs. Not only love of country but love of adventure was falling out of favor in the popular media, but not so with the American public, who responded enthusiastically when given a chance to see a film with real heroes like *Patton* (1970), *Star Wars* (1977), *Raiders of the Lost Ark* (1981) and *Die Hard* (1988), or read a book like *Raise the Titanic!*

* * *

Cussler's next nine books—*Vixen 03*, *Night Probe!*, *Deep Six*, *Cyclops*, *Treasure*, *Dragon*, *Sahara*, *Inca Gold* and *Shock Wave*—are all Pitt adventures and all bestsellers, but in 1996 Cussler began to expand his publishing empire with *The Sea Hunters*, a nonfiction book written with Craig Dirgo. Each chapter of *The Sea Hunters* recounts the historical circumstances surrounding a shipwreck or lost train, followed by details of the search by Cussler's real-life National Underwater and Marine Agency (NUMA), a 501(c)(3) non-profit organization dedicated to the preservation of maritime history.[55] In spite of the phenomenal success of the Pitt adventures, *The Sea Hunters* paperback is Cussler's first book to reach the top of *The New York Times* bestsellers list.[56] New York Maritime College also accepted *The Sea Hunters* in lieu of a thesis and presented Cussler with the college's first honorary PhD in 1997.[57] In 1998, Dr. Cussler and Dirgo released another nonfiction book, *Clive Cussler & Dirk Pitt Revealed*, a companion text to the Pitt series that included an original story, "The Reunion," in which Cussler meets various characters from the Pitt novels, up through *Flood Tide*. In 2002 came *The Sea Hunters II*, another Dirgo collaboration, and that same year Canadian television broadcast the inaugural season of *The Sea Hunters*, a documentary series produced by Eco Nova Productions. The series ran three seasons, with Cussler hosting six episodes and concluding each segment with the incentive: "And now it's your turn to get up off the couch and go into the deserts, go into the mountains, go under the lakes, the rivers and the seas, and search for history. You'll never find a more rewarding adventure."

Twenty-six years after Pyramid published *The Mediterranean Caper*, Cussler released the first spin-off series from the Pitt adventures, the *NUMA Files*. The premiere adventure, *Serpent*, introduced Kurt Austin, head of NUMA's Special Assignments Team, and Joe Zavala, the team's marine engineer. Four years later a second spin-off, *The Oregon Files*, was launched with *Golden Buddha*. Where *NUMA Files* presents Pitt-style adventures with different characters, the heroes of the *Oregon Files* are a cast of mercenaries led by former CIA operative Juan Cabrillo (introduced in *Flood Tide*) who possess a peculiar bent towards capitalism and operates from an even more peculiar vessel called the *Oregon*. Cussler created both series but restricted further contributions to plotting and some editing.[58] Paul Kemprecos, author of the Shamus award-winning mystery *Cool Blue Tomb*, collaborated with Cussler on the first eight *NUMA Files* adventures before Graham Brown (*Black Sun*, *Black Rain*) took over, while Dirgo collaborated on the first two *Oregon Files* books before he left and was replaced by Jack Du Brul, creator of the Pitt archetype hero Philip Mercer (*Vulcan's Forge*, *Charon's Landing*).[59] Cussler continued to write the Pitt adventures by himself up until 2004, and all three novels produced during this period include a major change in the hero's life. In *Atlantis Found* (1999), Pitt proposes marriage to longtime girlfriend, Congresswoman Loren Smith. In *Valhalla Rising* (2001), Pitt discovers he is the father of full-grown twins Dirk and Summer. At the end of *Trojan Odyssey* (2003), Pitt is offered the director's job at NUMA by Sandecker, and marries Smith. The next adventure, *Black Wind* (2004), marks the start of Cussler's collaboration with his son Dirk on the Pitt series.

In January 2003, Barbara Cussler passed away from cancer, and in April 2005 Cussler underwent a quintuple bypass operation on his heart. In February 2005, Cussler filed a lawsuit against Crusader Entertainment, the producers of the film adaptation of *Sahara*. Through it all Cussler continued to write and, on his own, released a children's book, *The Adventures of Vin Fiz* (2006), and the bestselling western adventure *The Chase* (2007). In 2007, Cussler married his second wife, Janet Hovarth. A third series, *Fargo Adventures*, written with Grant Blackwood, author of the Briggs Tanner series, debuted in 2009 and was followed later that year by *The Wrecker*, a sequel to *The Chase* and the launch of the Isaac Bell Detective series with collaborator Justin Scott, creator of realtor/private investigator Ben Abbott. In 2010, Cussler turned 79 and celebrated with his most productive year yet, with a total of four books, and then followed that up with four more in 2011. Cussler was also a part of a USO tour to Afghanistan, called Operation Thriller II, which included fellow writers Sandra Brown, Kathy Reichs, Mark Bowden and Andrew Peterson. In 2012, Cussler underwent knee surgery and released five new novels, including *The Tombs: A Fargo Adventure* with new collaborator Thomas Perry (the Jane Whitefield and Butcher Boy series). In 2013, a special 40th anniversary edition of *The Mediterranean Caper* was released along with a new Fargo adventure, *The Mayan Secrets*, a new *Oregon Files* adventure, *Mirage*, a new NUMA Files adventure, *Zero Hour*, and a new Isaac Bell adventure, *The Striker*. Du Brul and Perry also announced in 2013 that they were ending their collaborations with Cussler.

* * *

When Cussler created Dirk Pitt he did a lot of research but he also injected a lot of himself into his hero. Cussler did this because he understands that a successful hero provides a proxy for the reader.[60] People enjoy thrills, and imaginative people enjoy picturing themselves participating in adventures,[61] so if killers are chasing Pitt in a far faster car, it is *we* who elude them by driving our classic coach car off a ski jump. If Pitt is lost in the Sahara and happens across the ruins of a lost aircraft, it is *we* who know how to reconstruct the remnants into a land yacht that can be ridden to civilization. Most of all, though, America needed an old fashion adventure hero in the sixties and seventies.

All Cussler had to do was figure out how to bring this hero to life.

A half century and approximately 50 novels later, the rest, as they say, is history.

2

Cussler's Characters, Part 1
Dirk Pitt and Family

> We will walk with giants—men and women of accomplishment; heroic figures undaunted by action, prone to dangerous encounter.—Robert Sampson[1]

Martin H. Greenberg claims in *The Tom Clancy Companion* that Cussler's Pitt adventures are some of the best-known forerunners of Clancy's bestselling techno-thriller novels.[2] According to Greenberg, Clancy and Cussler both "fuse technology with superpower politics and a dose of science fiction," but unlike Clancy, "Cussler's plots are not anchored in reality so much as in wild flights of fancy more reminiscent of Kenneth Robson's Doc Savage adventures."[3] Cussler grew up during the heyday of the pulps and admits his goal, when he began writing, was to create "a thrilling story with a modern setting and contemporary characters in the tradition of the great adventure stories that kept me turning the pages when I was a kid." Those adventures include pulp stories about "globe-spanning adventurers, one man facing impossible odds, racing against time to save the world,"[4] and, except for The Shadow, no pulp adventurer was more popular than Clark "Doc" Savage, Jr., a combination of Sherlock Holmes, Tarzan, Professor Craig Kennedy[5] and Abraham Lincoln.[6]

Between 1933 and 1949 Doc Savage starred in 181 adventures,[7] most of them written by Missouri native Lester Dent. (Kenneth Robson was an imprint of Street & Smith, which owned Doc Savage.) A fine writer, Dent was even more prolific. Between 1934 and 1935 alone Dent wrote the lead story for each monthly issue of the *Doc Savage* magazine (average length: 60,000 words), a handful of short stories for other pulp magazines, and 26 scripts for the *Doc Savage* radio program.[8] This kind of successful output did not go unnoticed; in 1936, *The Writer's Yearbook* asked Dent to contribute an article about writing for the pulps. The result was "The Pulp Paper Master Fiction Plot," one of the most popular and influential pieces in the *Yearbook*'s history.[9] Two years later Dent was asked to contribute another article and, in 1940, *The Writer's Yearbook* published "Wave Those Tags," Dent's blueprint for creating characters, a process he breaks down into four steps: (1) find a name; (2) find an external tag; (3) find something to go inside; and (4) make use of characterization tricks in writing the story. For each step Dent includes common-sense suggestions,[10] some of which Cussler has also suggested in his own articles about writing.

When it comes to a name, Dent recommends having it express the character's nature, like Nero Wolfe (a predatory animal) or Hammett's Sam Spade ("a hard digging instrument") and Casper Gutman (an educated but insatiable villain). Another suggestion: "If heroes have manly names, it may help."

Dent believes external tags or "peculiarities of appearance, manner, voice, clothing, hobby, etc." may be the most important part of creating a character because they identify characters during a story; Cussler gives much the same advice in his 1982 article, "Do Your Characters Fit Their Roles?" wherein he instructs writers to give a character an anomaly "that identifies him in the mind of the reader and makes for quick recognition and easy retention of his appearance."[11] Dent uses Wolfe as an example. The brilliant but eccentric detective's most obvious tag is his girth, but Wolfe is also an expert on orchids and a prickly gourmand who will not drink a beer unless it is served at a specific temperature. Wolfe also has a penchant for the color yellow. According to Dent, "The moment Wolfe comes onto a scene, one of the tags is waved like a flag, so that there is no doubt about who has appeared."[12]

When it comes to finding something to go inside the character, "The whole idea is to dope out some reason for the character acting like a hero, a villain, or whatever." Dent is hardly the first writer to stress that what goes on inside the heart and mind of a character is vital to a story, but he is one of the few to explain that the degree of emphasis should be balanced in relation to the level of a story's literary ambitions (i.e., simple adventure = less, literary fiction = more). In Cussler's 1979 article, "Make Your Story Fly," he appears to be even less concerned than Dent about such motivations in an adventure story, but does insists that a hero's believability is always crucial. Cussler warns how "heroes must overcome the pitfalls and thrash the villain in the finale," but they must also be humans and not supermen because the "more believable they are, the easier it is for the reader to accept them."[13]

Finally, space limitations prevented Dent from mentioning more than a couple of common characterization tricks, such as building up a hero by delaying the character's introduction while other characters talk about him, a technique that works equally as well with villains, as anyone who has read *Dracula* (1897) or *The Insidious Dr. Fu Manchu* (1913) can attest.

Dent wraps up "Wave Those Tags" by telling aspiring writers that the best way to learn these four steps is to "wade through published material, purloin what seems good, and adapt the idea a little," a similar piece of advice that Cussler often gives to new writers,[14] which brings us back to Greenberg's comparison of Cussler's adventures to Doc Savage stories. Because pulp stories like Dent's inspired Cussler's fiction, and since it appears that Cussler is of like mind when it comes to many of Dent's writing tips, we should be able to reveal or glimpse some of the things that make up Cussler's characters by purloining Dent's blueprint, and the next three chapters overlay some of these steps on Dirk Pitt and his "family" (i.e., supporting cast), Cussler's other heroes and Cussler's more notable heroines/other women and villains/villainesses.

* * *

One of the best things about series literature is that every new story is like a visit with old friends.

A popular adventure series depends upon familiarity as much as it does action. Fans enjoy getting reacquainted with their favorite characters as much as they do thrilling to their hero's latest exploits, and if the characters belong to a family or to a group that behaves like a family so much the better, because now each new story feels like a reunion regardless of its medium. In video games, Mario and Luigi have the Princess, Toad and Yoshi. In comics, Bruce Wayne has Dick Grayson, Alfred Pennyworth and Commissioner James Gordon. In the movies, James Bond has Ms. Moneypenny, "M," "Q" and Felix Leiter. On TV, Senior NCIS Special Agent Leroy Jethro Gibbs has "Ducky" Mallard, Tony DiNozzo, Abby Sciuto, Tim McGee and Ziva

David. In the pulps, Doc Savage has Monk, Ham, Renny, Long Tom, Johnny and his cousin Patricia. And in books, Pitt has Al Giordino, Admiral James Sandecker, Rudi Gunn, Loren Smith, St. Julien Perlmutter, Hiram Yaeger and his twins Summer and Dirk Jr.

Dirk Pitt

Near the end of *You Only Live Twice* (1964), Fleming presents a somewhat premature obituary for Bond,[15] and Cussler does the same thing for Pitt in one of the last chapters of *Dragon* (1990).[16] Pitt's *Dragon* obituary is a fair summary of his exploits through October 1993, but a more insightful overview of him can be found in *Flood Tide* (1997) when the villain Qin Shang asks his perceptive personal secretary Su Zhong for her opinion of Pitt based on an FBI photograph:

> He is handsome in a rugged sort of way. I sense a magnetism about him. He has the look of an adventurer whose love is exploring the unknown, especially what lies under the sea. No rings on his fingers suggests that he is unpretentious. Women are drawn to him. They do not consider him a threat. He enjoys their company. There is an aura of kindness and tenderness about him. A man you can trust. All indications of a good lover. He is sentimental about old objects and probably collects them. His life is dedicated to achievement. Little of what he has accomplished was for personal gain. He thrives on challenges. This is a man who does not like to fail but can accept failure if he has tried his best. There is also a cold hardness in the eyes. He also has the capacity to kill. To friends he is extremely loyal. To enemies, extremely dangerous. All in all, a most unusual man who should have lived in another time.[17]

The first time we meet Dirk Eric Pitt he is sunbathing on Kaena Point, Hawaii, a fitting locale for a man whose adventures will revolve around ships and the water. Like more than a few adventure heroes created in the sixties, Pitt smokes and drinks, although as times and customs change he gives up cigarettes.[18] Somewhere along the way Pitt also picks up the unusual habit of relaxing in a shower by aiming hot water into one corner of the stall while he lies on his back with his long legs stretched up and his feet propped against the soap dish. Cussler created Pitt to be an amiable but mysterious guy who is as comfortable with locals at the corner tavern as he is entertaining a lovely lady in a fancy restaurant. This type of hero is fairly common today, but with the possible exception of Hammett's Nick Charles from *The Thin Man* (1934) they were unheard of in detective fiction before Archie Goodwin and unprecedented in old fashion adventure literature before Pitt. Unlike Charles, a second-generation Greek-American, and Goodwin, a street-smart Midwesterner, Pitt is an heir of American aristocracy, the son of a federal politician and the nephew of a Manhattan Project scientist. Despite his heritage, Pitt is not one to high-hat anyone, and in many of his adventures someone who has just met him is surprised to discover Pitt was born with a silver spoon instead of a socket wrench in his hand.[19]

Regarding Pitt's external tags, he is about six-foot-three,[20] approximately 185 pounds, deeply suntanned with a hairy barrel chest, muscular arms and black hair worn thick and shaggy, but the two external tags Cussler waves with the most frequency are Pitt's hard-yet-friendly face and deep-green eyes.[21] A graduate of the Air Force Academy, Pitt earned a degree in marine engineering while playing quarterback for the Falcons football team and competing in saber fencing and boxing. Pitt never studied any other martial arts, but surviving several barroom brawls has made him an excellent free-for-all fighter. He is also an expert diver. A decorated Vietnam combat pilot who earned the rank of major during his ten years of active duty,[22] Pitt rescues Sandecker during the final days of the war by shooting down the admiral's plane before it could land in a field overrun by North Vietnamese regulars. Sandecker remembered his quick-witted and daring savior when he needed a special projects director for a new agency he was asked to launch, and for the remainder of Pitt's duty in the air force he is on loan to the National Underwater and Marine Agency.

Pitt appears to be in his early thirties[23] and has only been with NUMA a couple of years when he is introduced in *Pacific Vortex*.[24] Being special projects director makes Pitt a government bureaucrat, a unique occupation for an adventure hero in the sixties and seventies, but Pitt is not your average public-sector employee. This is explored in more detail in Chapter 5, but unlike most bureaucrats, Pitt can be depended upon to do what he believes is right without giving a second thought about personal consequences. When Pitt helps a captured British secret agent named Brian Shaw escape while under his custody, Shaw warns that Pitt is asking for trouble, but Pitt tells Shaw he has been in trouble before,[25] and when Julia Lee worries that Pitt is going to be in big trouble with the American government after it is discovered he has killed Qin Shang, Pitt laughs, "Dearheart, I'm *always* in big trouble with the government."[26] Pitt's ties to government also include his father, Senator George Pitt of California, but Pitt has no desire to follow in his father's political footsteps.[27]

Adventure is Pitt's narcotic, his mistress is the sea and he loves the company of beautiful women, but he also has a great passion for classic automobiles.[28] A wealthy grandfather who developed Southern California real estate left Pitt a sizable inheritance that he invested to build one of the world's most unique collections of classic cars and aircraft.[29] Pitt does most of his own renovation work on this collection, which he stores alongside trophies from his adventures on the main floor of his home, an airplane hangar at 266 Airport Place, Washington, DC 20001.[30] Beginning with *Deep Six*, Cussler has featured at least one car from Pitt's collection in each adventure and includes a photograph of himself standing beside that car on the book's back cover. (In reality, these cars are part of Cussler's own classic automobile collection, many of which can be seen in the 2011 coffee table book *Built For Adventure: The Classic Automobiles of Clive Cussler and Dirk Pitt* and at the Cussler Museum in Arvada.[31])

Another of Pitt's passions is on display in his apartment overlooking the hangar's main floor, which is decorated with marine antiques from various NUMA salvage operations.[32] One visitor to Pitt's home likens it to a museum of a man's life,[33] but, in truth, Pitt is an old soul born 80 years too late[34]; he belongs as much to the past as the present. Let other men attending a fancy dress party wear modern formal; Pitt prefers the old look, complete with a heavy gold chain draped across the front of his tuxedo vest. Attached to the chain is a pocket watch that belonged to his great-grandfather, an engineer for the Santa Fe Railroad.[35] Pitt also has a habit of dropping old song lyrics, movie references and clichés or phrases into conversations. These outdated pop-culture references are part of Cussler's writing style and not limited to the Pitt series, but by virtue of being Cussler's first hero this habit has become one of Pitt's tags. Sometimes Pitt does this subtly, like when he brushes off good-timing Adrian Hunter by reciting a variation of the refrain from the popular 1911 song "I Want a Girl (Just Like the Girl that Married Dear Old Dad),"[36] or invokes *Casablanca* (1942) by telling a flight inspector, "And I thought we had the beginnings of a beautiful friendship."[37] At other times this tag borders on the marvelous but ridiculous, like when Pitt makes one of his most memorable entrances driving the deep-sea-mining vehicle (DSMV) *Big John* along the bottom of the western Pacific

Ocean while singing the 1923 standard "Minnie the Mermaid." Occasionally, though, it comes off as clunky, like when Pitt is forced to knock out Summer Moran on a public beach and worries about someone "playing Herbert Hero and rescuing little Eva from the villainous Simon LaPitt."[38] History seems to have a reciprocal passion for Pitt, since many of his adventures directly or inadvertently involve uncovering secrets or artifacts that change the course of history or explain a historical mystery. These remarkable revelations often result through the auspices of Fate or coincidence (take your pick) and almost always involve copious action and dangerous encounters. In *Valhalla Rising*, Yaeger asks Pitt, "How do you become involved in so much havoc?" All Pitt can tell his friend is, "It *finds* me."[39]

Turning to what goes on inside Pitt's heart and mind, Cussler's most famous hero may not be as complex as Heathcliffe or Hamlet, but he is not an easy man to figure out. Like Peter Pan, Pitt can be amiable, even a scamp, then at the drop of a thimble turn moody, cynical or dangerous. Not even Giordino can figure out what key connects the "two men" that make up Dirk Pitt, one "humorous, unpretentious and [who] easily made friends" and the other a "coldly efficient" automaton who "rarely made a mistake."[40] At his most coldly efficient, Pitt is an indefatigable nemesis and manhunter to any enemy who hurts him or any family member, friend, acquaintance or stranger he cares about. Pitt tells Arthur Dorsett, in *Shock Wave*, that his mother taught him that life is a gift,[41] but as Wayne Valero points out, in *The Adventure Writing of Clive Cussler*, when "Pitt is unable to foil the evil cause or rescue the person in harm's way, he has been known to later instill his own personal vengeance."[42] Cussler never explains how Pitt can behave so savagely in any of the adventures, but in "The Reunion" Cussler chances to overhear some of Pitt's resurrected former adversaries pondering this and Cussler tells them, "It was easy."[43]

When Pitt is in an immature mood he can be crass and rude, especially to authority figures. In *Pacific Vortex*, Pitt refuses to follow military protocol and present his orders to report to Admiral Leigh Hunter of the 101st Salvage Fleet to a Marine sergeant, and continues to be rude to Hunter and the admiral's executive officer, Paul Boland, until the men prove themselves worthy of his respect.[44] This same pattern is repeated in *Iceberg* with Commander Koski, of the *Catawaba*, and his XO lieutenant Amos Dover.[45] Pitt's attitude towards authority improves as the series progresses,[46] but even in later adventures there are flashes where Pitt relapses, even with superiors he likes, including Sandecker.[47]

Counterbalancing this immaturity is Pitt's unpretentiousness. At his noblest, Pitt is a humble man who leaves glory to others[48] and does not give a damn what anybody else thinks about him.[49] Archie Goodwin could have been describing this side of Pitt when Goodwin writes about himself:

> I have always had a fairly good opinion of myself. Even when I've made mistakes—and Lord knows I've made some beauties—I haven't collapsed from remorse or gone into a blue funk over them. My ego is not repressed, my psyche does not squirm under any inferiority complex. I have no delusions of grandeur, I'm not inclined to be manic, and I don't depress easily. In fact, I like me, and I wish a lot of my fellow human beings could say the same for themselves because I have learned that if you can't like yourself, it's a thousand to one that you can't like your neighbor, be he or she next door or in Saudi Arabia.[50]

Pitt is just as comfortable as Goodwin is in his own skin. Unconcerned with slights or insults, Pitt wastes no time or energy feeling harassed or mistreated and rarely permits others to rattle his confidence enough to make him insecure or defensive. Two fine examples of this occur back to back in *Iceberg*, as Pitt accompanies National Intelligence Agency chief Dean Kippmann back to America from Iceland. During the flight, Kippmann offers to let Pitt read his agency's file on him, but Pitt declines because it cannot tell him anything he does not already know.[51] After they arrive in California, Kippmann and Pitt are met by a pair of NIA agents who pay no attention to Pitt, but Pitt ignores this slight and uses the free time to enjoy a cigarette.[52]

Cussler never states any specific reasons why Pitt behaves like a hero, but in *Vixen 03*, Giordino does tell Abe Steiger:

> "Let's just say that Pitt has a ton of balls, the brains to go with them, and the uncanny knack for knocking the shit out of any obstacle, man made or otherwise, that gets in his way. He is a soft touch for kids and animals, and helps little old ladies up escalators. To my knowledge, he's never stolen a dime in his life nor used his sly talents for personal gain. Beyond all that, he's one helluva guy [sic]."[53]

These attributes, shared almost point by point with Doc Savage,[54] divulge a little about why Pitt behaves as he does, but are these attributes (and the behavior that springs from them) heroic? In his essay *The Adventurer: The Fate of Adventure in the Western World* (1974), critic Paul Zweig argues that heroes possess courage, loyalty and selflessness employed for moral purposes while adventurers perform moral actions for the exhilaration of adventure.[55] Marilyn Cannady applies this distinction to Doc Savage in her Dent biography, *Bigger than Life: The Creator of Doc Savage* (1990), and while Doc possesses a moral purpose, and the fight of good against evil is paramount to him, even Dent admits, "Doc is in the business of fighting evil *partly* for the adventure, the thrill of it."[56] Dent was a pilot, a sailor and a treasure hunter who believed possessing a thrill for adventure is an important part of what it means to be a man,[57] and, by extension, it appears that Dent's greatest character feels the same way. Could Cussler, who was influenced by pulps like *Doc Savage* and who lives an adventurous life, feel the same way as Dent? If so, does Pitt feel the same way by extension? If so, what does this reveal about Pitt?

In the prologue to Pitt's first adventure, Commander Felix Dupree and the crew of the prototype U.S. nuclear submarine *Starbuck* confront anomalies 670 miles north of Oahu, in a Bermuda Triangle–like area known as the Pacific Vortex. The *Starbuck* is maintaining radio silence while on a test run, but every rule in the Naval Handbook dictates that Dupree break silence and report to the navy base in Pearl Harbor. Instead, Dupree investigates. "Perhaps the lure of the unknown was too strong. Perhaps he saw a fleeting vision of himself as a discoverer, sailing toward the glory that had always been denied him."[58] Whatever the reason, Dupree and his crew pay a hefty price.[59] Contrast this to Pitt, who definitely has a weakness for the lure of the unknown, especially when it presents no ready explanation.[60] Pitt is driven to rediscover the past because he believes we must look into history to see ourselves,[61] and so he strays from the highroads traveled by most other people to discover secrets that might be found in lost places. Unlike Dupree, however, there is almost always a moral component mixed in with Pitt's motives for investigating the unknown. Pitt possesses the same thrill for adventure as Dupree, but time and again he succeeds where men like Dupree fail because they seek fortune and glory while Pitt seeks to benefit others.[62] In *Pacific Vortex*, Pitt searches for the vanished *Starbuck* to prevent its nuclear arsenal from falling into enemy hands, a motive that places service over hubris. In *Raise the Titanic!*, Gene Seagram loses his wife and his sanity because he is compelled by his ego to prove he is more than a Midwestern physicist, while the humbler Pitt raises the sunken *Titanic* and makes Seagram's Sicilian Project a success. In *Deep Six*, a supporting character, Senator Marcus Larimer, has grown soft and become a drunk during his days in the Beltway, but when he finds himself on a doomed Russian cruise ship, the *Leonid Andreyev*, his moral purpose rises to the surface as he sacrifices himself to save others. Loren feels strongly that Larimer deserves a state funeral, but Pitt tells her that it does not matter so long as people know Larimer went out a man.[63] These examples would seem to demonstrate that Pitt's ideal of a man, and by extension Cussler's, means putting moral purpose ahead of the thrill for adventure, making Pitt more than an adventurer and his attitudes and actions heroic.

Pitt is also a patriotic[64] defender of the realm and knight-errant, a throwback to the southwestern American folk hero. This hero type dates back to James Fenimore Cooper's Hawkeye, the protagonist of five novels, including *The Last of the Mohicans* (1826). According to historians Larry Schweikart and Michael Allen, Hawkeye is a frontiersman who aids the cause of American civilization by "assisting army officers, settlers, townspeople, and, of course, damsels in distress. In classic American style, however, Hawkeye also constantly sought to escape the very civilization he had assisted." America was a new nation in Cooper's day, but Americans embraced his novels as well as southwestern folk hero tales of frontiersmen like Daniel Boone and Davy Crockett that "looked back longingly at a vanished (and, often, imagined) agrarian utopia." These folk tales and Cooper's novels, like the Western genre they helped inspire, regularly feature "heroes in conflicts that placed them between nature and civilization. Like Hawkeye, the southwestern folk hero always found himself assisting American civilization by fighting Indians and foreign enemies and, above all, constantly moving west."[65] Pitt is a modern hero so he escapes to the sea, the last remaining frontier on Earth. In true southwestern folk hero tradition, however, Pitt regularly comes to the aid of American civilization by assisting the military, other sea hunters, citizens, allies and damsels in distress from foreign and domestic enemies rising out of the private and public sectors.

Pitt is a patriotic American in philosophy as well as behavior. A realist, Pitt shares the same cynical view of humanity expressed by such founding fathers as Alexander Hamilton and James Madison, who distrusted human nature as much as they distrusted government.[66] Even George Washington once contended that people are incapable of acting outside of their own self-interests,[67] and Pitt is even less charitable in this opinion. Pitt is unimpressed as he listens to Bill Hunnewell eulogize the magnanimous capitalist and adventurer Kristjan Fyrie in *Iceberg*, recalling how his father once told him if you take the clothes away from the greatest living man "you behold a very embarrassed, naked and defenseless animal."[68] Nevertheless, Hamilton, Madison, Washington and other founding fathers believed it was better to trust the nation's sovereignty to *We, the People* than any state or federal government,[69] and therefore pledged their sacred honor and sacrificed much, if not everything, they had for the same people Hamilton once referred to as "the great beast."[70] Like founders Francis Lewis (whose properties were confiscated and wife taken prisoner by the British) and Judge Richard Stockton (whose family was forced to live off charity while he spent time in a British jail),[71] Pitt risks his life time and again for his country, his fellow citizens and anyone who needs his help.

Being a realist, though, Pitt gives very little leeway to anyone he suspects is a bad actor. Even if Pitt likes you, he still follows President Ronald Reagan's axiom of trust but verify, and he does not suffer fools. As mentioned, Pitt has his flaws but egotism is not one of them, and while he probably should know better, Pitt seems to expect this same humility in others, which may be why he is not shy about making his feelings known when people disappoint him, a predisposition that leads to strained relationships with such characters as Seagram or Jessie LeBaron at the start of *Cyclops*.

A delightful contrast to Pitt's realism is his unpredictable audacity or "aversion to pursuing the expected,"[72] a trait he shares with his creator.[73] However, where Cussler smuggled booze into high school football games dressed as a Prohibition-era gangster[74] or used an old medical book to con his way out of work while in the air force, Pitt attempts the most outlandish things to rescue the girl, defeat the bad guy and save the world. Pitt claims his ancestors were gypsies[75] and apparently he inherited their wily boldness as few heroes play the angles Pitt does. Would Holmes, Drummond or Bond act flagrantly gay to get an opponent to underestimate him? Would even a historian like Jack Ryan consider using a Mississippi riverboat and a regiment of Civil War enthusiasts to capture a barge manned by merciless brigands? Would the Continental Op, McGee or any MacLean hero think to build a boat out of a bathtub and then dare to sail it across ocean waters? Pitt, a marine engineer, can be as resourceful as the titular hero from the television adventure series *MacGyver* (1985–1992) when it comes to manipulating technology or science, and other examples of Pitt's makeshift MacGyverisms include compasses,[76] a torsion spring bow,[77] a magnet,[78] a land yacht,[79] and a trimaran.[80] In *Cyclops*, Pitt even uses the catch from his Doxa watch as a screwdriver to escape a cell.[81]

As for characterization tricks, in *Pacific Vortex* and *The Mediterranean Caper* Pitt is introduced early and Cussler reveals most of what we learn about him through the third-person narrator. In *Iceberg*, Cussler delays Pitt's entrance and builds anticipation for the hero's arrival by having other characters talk about him. When Pitt does appear, the narrator describes him from another character's point-of-view, creating a sense of distance between reader and hero that accentuates Pitt's tinge of mystery. Cussler employs these characterization tricks to even better effect in *Raise the Titanic!*, but, starting with *Vixen 03*, Cussler switches things up by introducing Pitt early or delaying Pitt's introduction in different adventures.[82]

Another characterization trick first used in *Raise the Titanic!* is combining a delayed introduction of Pitt with his rescue of one or more supporting characters (e.g., *Dragon*, *Atlantis Found*).[83] While clever and dramatic, these rescues also demonstrate from the start that Pitt is capable of surmounting steep odds, which provides the reader with hope that Pitt will overcome the increasingly overwhelming obstacles that develop later in the adventure.[84]

One more characterization trick Cussler makes good use of is showing what Pitt does *not* do in certain situations, such as when Kippmann's NIA agents snub him. A lack of reaction can be more revealing than anything an omnipotent narrator can tell readers, and Pitt's nonchalance demonstrates that he is exactly the kind of person Goodwin describes earlier when talking about himself.

Al Giordino

Pitt may be a don't-give-a-damn enigma,[85] but when it comes to personal history we know even less about his closest friend, Giordino.

Albert Cassius Giordino's name and several external tags are inspired by Al Giordano (spelled with an "a"), a rugged and sarcastic little stonemason from South Vineland, New Jersey, who served with Cussler at Hawaii's Hickam Air Force Base. One of Cussler's favorite characterization tricks is to differentiate characters linked together as a pair by making them as dissimilar as Mutt and Jeff, and there is no better illustration of this than Pitt and Giordino. Giordino is five-foot-four-inches tall, with shoulders twice as broad as his waist. Pitt and

Girodino both have dark skin and black hair, but Pitt is tanned and wears his hair thick and shaggy while Giordino is swarthy with curly hair, evidence of his Italian ancestry. Girodino has walnut eyes and, if he had a flowing beard and a sack of toys, he could pass for a young Etruscan Santa Claus.[86] Like Pitt, Giordino is a marine engineer, a graduate of the Air Force Academy and a Vietnam veteran. Through *Valhalla Rising*, Giordino is an active air force captain on loan to NUMA to serve as assistant special projects director. Giordino lives in a condominium with mismatched furniture in Alexandria, Virginia, and although he is not a car collector like Pitt, he does drive a split-window 1963 Corvette. Girodino is as humble as Pitt and his sense of humor can sometimes border on the adolescent, like Pitt's,[87] although he has displayed moments of sophistication. Starting in *Raise the Titanic!*, Giordino initiates his most famous and intricate running gag by apparently purloining Sandecker's prized handmade cigars[88] and smoking them in front of the admiral, despite Sandecker keeping his stogies under lock and key.[89]

Cussler never explains what goes on inside Giordino's heart and mind that makes him behave like a hero, but in *Vixen 03* Giordino admits that he was the class bully until he lost a playground fight with Pitt. It seems that Giordino saw the light and began treading the straight and narrow after this defeat.[90] Conversions like this appear in adventure literature at least as far back as the *Epic of Gilgamesh*, wherein the wild man Enkidu becomes the civilized boon companion of Gilgamesh after the great king of Uruk defeats Enkidu in a mighty battle.[91] It also probably does not hurt that Pitt and Giordino are ideally suited to each other. In *Pacific Vortex*, Pitt mentions he has known Giordino since kindergarten[92] and throughout the series the men behave like brothers from different mothers, to borrow Chris Tucker's appellation for his and Jackie Chan's characters in the film *Rush Hour 3* (2007). Giordino even feels as if he has lost a brother when it looks like Pitt dies while destroying Hideki Suma's Dragon Center in *Dragon*.[93]

Giordino enjoys the company of beautiful women as much, if not more, than Pitt, but as of this writing Giordino is a committed bachelor, although he almost beats Pitt to the altar with Pat O'Connell in *Atlantis Found*. Neither he nor O'Connell are willing to quit their jobs and settle down, however, so when O'Connell abandons him for a position in China[94] Giordino is not exactly heartbroken. Giordino claims to have never found the husband-and-father routine appealing,[95] but even he is not immune to wondering what might have been. In *Inca Gold*, for instance, he tells Loren about the girl that got away:

> One summer, when I was nineteen, I saw a girl riding a bicycle along a sidewalk on Balboa Island in Southern California. She wore brief white shorts and a soft green blouse tied around her midriff. Her honey-blond hair was in a long ponytail. Her legs and arms were tanned mahogany. I wasn't close enough to see her eyes, but I somehow knew they had to be blue. She had the look of a free spirit with a warm sense of humor. There isn't a day that goes by I don't recall her image.[96]

Giordino confesses he walked along that same sidewalk for a month but never saw the girl again.[97]

Other attributes that Giordino shares with Pitt are realism and patriotism,[98] a frequent disregard for self-preservation, an occasional disrespect for authority and a talent for badinage. Cussler claims this last attribute was influenced by his mother, who often teased her husband and son,[99] but it is hard to ignore that Pitt and Giordino's patter, or the patter between other Cussler heroes like Austin and Zavala or the Fargos, has the same ring to it as the banter in pulp and movie adventures from the thirties and forties. To find a good example of this, look no further than the B-movies based upon Sapper's Bulldog Drummond novels. In *Bulldog Drummond's Revenge* (1937), Drummond (John Howard) speeds along a narrow country road to meet his fiancée, Phyllis Clavering (Louise Campbell). Drummond's best friend, Algy Longworth (Reginald Denny), is along for the ride and more than a little nervous.

Algy: Why in such a hurry, Hugh?
Drummond: I want to get somewhere.
Algy: (pauses) So do I.

In *Bulldog Drummond's Secret Police* (1939), Drummond, Algy, their good friend Colonel J.A. Nielson (H.B. Warner) of Scotland Yard and Drummond's manservant and second father figure "Tenny" Tennison (E.E. Clive) are trapped in a secret medieval chamber beneath Drummond's ancestral estate while rescuing Phyllis (Heather Angel) from a sociopathic thief. As spikes descend from the ceiling, Tenny tells Drummond, "Pardon me, sir, but we're in for a spot of trouble." Compare these to patter from *Inca Gold*, beginning with Girodino communicating via radio as he helps extricate Pitt from a subterranean cavern. Pitt tells his friend that when he steps on firm ground again he expects a Dixieland band playing "Waiting for the Robert E. Lee."[100] Later, Pitt and Giordino are floating in a life raft along with Shannon Kelsey and some other people the men are trying to rescue. Pitt has a gunshot wound and his blood leaking into the water attracts a hammerhead. Giordino spies more fins and announces, "He invited his pals for dinner." To keep Kelsey and the others calm, Pitt pretends to nap. Shannon stares at Pitt and says, "He must be mad," to which Giordino replies, "That makes two of us,"[101] and he settles down for his own nap.

Giordino is not an old soul. Where Pitt finds pleasure in the past, Giordino lives only for the present.[102] Giordino does appreciate historical artifacts,[103] but he has his limits, like when Kelsey, an archaeologist, acts more concerned about some Mesoamerican antiquities than another person's life.[104] Giordino does have a bit of Pitt's "two men" paradigm about him, however. On one hand, Giordino can be a perfectionist, but he also has such an indolent attitude that he can will himself to fall asleep, no matter the circumstances.[105] It is also not unusual for Giordino to look like he is half-dozing when an enemy threatens him and Pitt, but seconds later Giordino, a tenacious fighter, will spring into action, and when the chips are down his never-say-die stubbornness amazes even Pitt.[106]

Reviewers, critics and even Cussler refer to Giordino as Pitt's sidekick,[107] but a more accurate tag for the swarthy little Italian may be buddy-in-color. In *Nice and Noir: Contemporary American Crime Fiction* (2002), Richard B. Schwartz explains that the buddy-in-color appears in myths and tales about "men following the urge to set out for the wilderness ... to leave behind the constraints of civilization and the mundane duties attending it (an opportunity largely denied them in the everyday world)." In these stories, the wilderness is a "threshold symbol, a locus for intense and, to a degree, private experience of the sort associated with romance and Romanticism." As the heroes of these stories strike out into the wilderness, they join "with men of color in an attempt to understand one another and achieve a degree of brotherhood that seems difficult or even impossible to achieve in daily life."[108] In the landmark study on the hero's initiation quest pattern in myth, legend and religion, *The Hero With a Thousand Faces* (1949), Joseph Campbell describes the wilderness as "regions of the unknown (desert, jungle, deep sea, alien land, etc.),"[109] areas beyond civilization where men may find adventure but where they may also find violent death,[110] and there is no denying that Pitt and Giordino spend a good deal of time in such regions. Usually these areas are on or under the ocean, but the pair has had adventures in drier (but no less dangerous) wildernesses like the Andes (*Inca Gold*), Soseki Island off the coast of Japan (*Dragon*), the Sahara desert (*Sahara*), Antarctica (*Atlantis Found*) and Communist Cuba (*Cyclops*), and in the process they have forged an extraordinary brotherhood.[111] For his part, Pitt never hesitates to trust his friend with his life, and one of the best examples of this happens in *Valhalla Rising* when Pitt decides Giordino must take the last seat on the last escape pod of the sunken luxury submarine *Golden Marlin*. Pitt assures Giordino that he will survive, but only if his best friend leads the rescue.[112] In return, Giordino will follow Pitt into any situation, even if all he has to go on is blind faith.[113]

Schwartz cites examples of the buddy-in-color concept from classic American literature, including James Fenimore Cooper's Hawkeye and Chingachgook, Mark Twain's Huck Finn and Jim, and Herman Melville's Ishmael and Queequeg, and from pop culture figures such as Kelly Robinson (Robert Culp) and Alexander "Scotty" Scott (Bill Cosby) from the television program *I Spy* (1965–1968) and Spenser and Hawk from Robert B. Parker's Spenser novels. In classic literature, the buddy-in-color tends to be a native or a noble savage, but in more recent times the buddy-in-color has become almost interchangeable with his white friend. This is the case with the Caucasian social outcast Martin Riggs (Mel Gibson) and respectable Negro family man Roger Murtaugh (Danny Glover) in the film *Lethal Weapon* (1987) and its sequels.[114] Even more recently, the buddy-in-color has blended with the Christian concept of an avenging angel. For instance, fans of the Spenser novels find Hawk's support during tight moments a necessity, even though Spenser is capable of getting along without his more physically imposing friend.[115] Cussler's fans, however, do not expect Giordino to always support Pitt,[116] even though Pitt would have never survived some of his adventures without his buddy-in-color/avenging angel, and Giordino has the scars and a missing right pinky finger to prove it.[117]

Admiral James Sandecker

James Sandecker is the only member of Pitt's family to appear in all 17 Pitt adventures written solely by Cussler, but when it comes to the admiral's name tag Cussler had no inspirations like he did for Giordino. When asked how he came up with the name James Sandecker, Cussler replies, "Don't recall. Just sounded like a good name for an admiral."[118]

It certainly is a good tag for this admiral.

"James" is a patriarchal name that resonates respect,[119] and the admiral is one of the most respected men in Washington, even by his enemies.[120] Very few characters call him Jim, and those that do are peers or superiors like Navy Chief of Staff, Admiral Joseph Kemper,[121] the commandant of the Coast Guard, Admiral Dale Ferguson[122] and Admiral Clyde Monfort of the Caribbean Joint Task Force.[123] Even President Dean Cooper Wallace only dares to call him James.[124] Meanwhile "Sandecker" is a hard-sounding last name for a hard man. The word "sand" in the first syllable conjures beaches and shorelines, which is apropos for a navy man, but sand is also gritty and abrasive, which is even more apropos considering the admiral's personality.[125] As for the second syllable, "decker" invokes the word "deck" which brings to mind the platform or deck of a ship, but "deck" is also slang for knocking someone down.[126] Put them all together and James Sandecker is a fitting name for someone Cussler describes as "a man who played straight ball, encasing himself in a cold, tensile shell, bowing to no one."[127]

Sandecker is five-foot-six,[128] with hazel eyes.[129] In Pitt's early adventures, Cussler often compares the admiral to a cocky bird or birdlike creature, using nouns like banty and bantam to describe the griffon-faced man.[130] Sandecker also has a barracuda's smile, fiery red straight hair and, in the early adventures, he alternates between a full beard or goes clean-shaven, but since *Night Probe!* he has sported a Vandyke. Depending upon the adventure, Sandecker is in his fifties[131] or sixties[132] and he is either divorced[133] or a widower.[134] Prior to the apparent deaths of Pitt, Giordino and Rudi Gunn in *Cyclops*, Sandecker never suffered personal tragedy as his brother, sister and elderly parents are alive.[135] Sandecker also has a daughter, a son-in-law and three grandchildren living in Hong Kong.[136] A physical-fitness nut, most days Sandecker jogs the six miles from his Watergate penthouse apartment to his office on the tenth floor of the NUMA building,[137] but every good Cussler character possesses the seed for a little cognitive dissonance, so Sandecker also smokes ten custom-made cigars a day. Sandecker does not get involved with the Beltway social scene, but does belong to the Army and Navy Club and the John Paul Jones Club. Like Pitt and Giordino, Sandecker enjoys the company of women and is one of Washington's most eligible (yet dedicated) bachelors.[138]

Cussler offers no explanations about what goes on in Sandecker's heart and mind, but it is obvious that the admiral is driven to succeed, regardless of the task. After a distinguished navy career, where he made flag rank before age 50,[139] Sandecker was stagnating prior to his appointment to NUMA, which he built into the world's largest oceanic science organization with thousands of employees spread around the globe.[140] And when times get tough, Sandecker becomes even more driven. The admiral never sleeps during a project crisis[141] and he is relentless dealing with Washington power players,[142] but Sandecker is just as motivated when it comes to little things like playing gin rummy.[143] Habitually punctual,[144] Sandecker is courteous and loyal to his employees, and, unlike many federal directors, he gives his people proper credit for their successes.[145] Because of this, it is next to impossible to slip something past him at NUMA.[146] The admiral is also wise enough (or sly enough) to be gracious to other agencies' employees, which, in turn, has allowed him to set up an early-warning network all over the city.[147]

Sandecker serves as NUMA's director until he turns the reins over to Pitt, in *Trojan Odyssey*, so the admiral can replace the ailing vice-president and campaign with the president in the next election.[148] Pitt is the most qualified man to succeed Sandecker after Gunn, but Rudi is satisfied being second-in-command,[149] and if the admiral ever considered offering anyone else the job besides Pitt it would have been surprising, considering their relationship. Pitt is Sandecker's best friend[150] and the admiral is a second father to Pitt as well as Giordino,[151] not always an easy task considering their habitual insubordination, but Sandecker can be a softy when it comes to his special project directors and Gunn.[152] The three were with Sandecker when he launched NUMA[153] and the admiral is cut from the same cloth as Pitt and Giordino, so much so that he makes a more than adequate stand-in for Giordino in *Iceberg*. Sandecker can be as mischievous[154] and chivalrous[155] as Pitt and Giordino, and he trusts Pitt as much as Giordino does.[156] Sandecker is also just as willing to sacrifice himself for the benefit of others, as evidenced in *Vixen 03* when he and Steiger join forces for a mission of no return to rescue Washington DC from a poison-missile attack.[157]

Rudi Gunn

Rudolph "Rudi" Gunn is the final member of NUMA's answer to the Four Musketeers. As second-in-command, Gunn has served at different times as director of operations, director of logistics and deputy director.[158] Whatever his title, Gunn attends to the day-to-day operations at NUMA so Sandecker is free to battle Congress and wrestle with members of the federal bureaucracy, and NUMA's success attests to the fact that, in their own way, Sandecker and Gunn are as formidable a team as Pitt and Giordino.

Short, slight and bespectacled, Gunn is not as unpredictable as Pitt or as charismatic as Girodino or as wily as Sandecker. His strengths are his intellect and daring. Gunn and Pitt have worked together on several NUMA operations, including the *Titanic* salvage, so he has had almost as many occasions to battle alongside Pitt as Giordino. As far as Pitt is concerned, Gunn and Giordino are "head of the class ... brave and competent men to have standing at his side during a fight,"[159] and when things look their darkest, Pitt always puts his trust in Gunn and Girodino, confident they will not fail him.[160] When a cruise ship carrying Pitt's father vanishes and Pitt needs help searching for it, he immediately asks for Giordino and Gunn.[161] Giordino good-naturedly refers to Gunn as a worrywart yet likens Rudi to an IRS agent about to make a kill,[162] while Sandecker ranks Gunn as one of his dearest friends[163] and one of the best people in their business.[164]

When it comes to Gunn's tags, readers of a certain age, or those with a fondness for vintage television, may find it hard to hear his name and not think of the stylishly cool titular hero of Blake Stevens's jazzy private-eye series *Peter Gunn* (1958–1961). Peter Gunn was played by Craig Stevens, an actor who would have made a decent Dirk Pitt in his day, but Cussler's Gunn is a small man with slim hips and narrow shoulders; he suffers from insomnia, played coronet in high school and owns a small but respectable collection of abstract art.[165] Gunn is extremely nearsighted, with brown eyes,[166] and his most recognizable external tags are his large horn-rimmed glasses and a mischievous grin that always seems to be curling his lips. Once again Cussler reveals nothing about what goes on in this character's heart and mind, but Gunn, a genius with degrees in chemistry, finance and oceanography, is a natural when it comes to compiling reports and planning research projects.[167] He is, in fact, a person who rarely gambles or plays angles, preferring to work from solid facts rather than vague percentages. These tags may sound more apropos for a Rudi than a Gunn, but Rudi graduated first in his class at Annapolis, earned the rank of commander and spent a good chunk of his 15-year naval career aboard submarines, some of that as Sandecker's chief.[168] Gunn also helped design NUMA's *Deep Fathom* submersible; he served at least one time as a member of a pit crew for one of Pitt's automobile races and is proficient with his father's snubnose Smith & Wesson Bodyguard .38.[169]

Gunn appears in most of Pitt's adventures and a number of *NUMA Files* adventures. Gunn is also the only major character in the Pitt series mentioned in an adventure prior to his debut in a subsequent novel. Burdette Denver vouches for Pitt in *Pacific Vortex* because Pitt works with Denver's cousin Gunn,[170] but Gunn is not introduced until *The Mediterranean Caper*, even though he recollects trusting Pitt's judgment the previous year in Hawaii.[171]

Pitt has only known Gunn for little more than a year in *The Mediterranean Caper* but already regards him as a smart customer and a good friend.[172] Gunn is also brave and calm under pressure (like Pitt and Girodino), and there may be not be a better example than in *Cyclops* where all three friends are captured and tortured in a secret Soviet outpost on a Cuban island. In *Treasure* and *Sahara*, circumstances force Gunn to abandon Pitt and Giordino in the midst of dangerous situations to fetch help,[173] but in *Cyclops*, Pitt is the one who has to abandon his friends because Gunn and Girodino are too injured to go with him. Nevertheless, Gunn, who speaks a smattering of Russian, succeeds in developing a prison grapevine even as he refuses to buckle under to a torturer who beats him and sadistically twists his broken ankle.[174]

Hiram Yaeger and St. Julien Perlmutter

Pitt's closest friends after Giordino, Sandecker and Gunn are Hiram Yaeger and St. Julien Perlmutter. Memorable characters on their own, this pair of opposites embodies Cussler's passion for research while representing different approaches to technology.

Yaeger is the chief of NUMA's Communication and Information Network, located on the agency's tenth floor. Yaeger's first name is Hebrew for "exalted brother,"[175] yet it has the folksy charm of a bluegrass banjo picker. Yaeger's last name recalls Major General Charles Elwood "Chuck" Yeager, the decorated veteran of World War II and Vietnam War who became the first man to fly faster than Mach 1.[176] It is a fitting tag for this computer genius, dedicated family man[177] and Navy SEAL who served three tours in Vietnam, but currently drives a BMW 740 il and splits his time between an elegant house in a fashionable Maryland neighborhood and a farm in Sharpsburg, where he raises horses and repairs old computers as hobbies. Yaeger is the one regular character in the series trained in personal combat, yet he has never joined Pitt on an adventure. The closest Yaeger has come is in *Atlantis Found*, wherein he accompanies Loren Smith, Sandecker and Dr. Timothy Friend to Buenos Aires for a confab with Pitt to try to figure out the Wolf family's world-threatening machinations.[178] The only other time Yaeger comes close to getting in on some action is *Fire Ice*, in which Austin asks that Yaeger join him, Zavala and a Russian assault force aboard the USS *Benjamin Franklin* to help with a raid on Mikhail Razov's yacht *Ataman Explorer I*, but Yaeger is there for his computer expertise and, at Sandecker's insistence, remains aboard the submarine until the yacht is secured.[179] Yaeger's most prominent external tags are his rumpled Levi jeans with matching jacket, long graying blond hair worn in a bun or a ponytail, his beard and granny spectacles. Such counterculture attire is in keeping with the Information Technology (IT) crowd but not NUMA's dress code, but Sandecker gives Yaeger a pass because Yaeger is as good at his job as Pitt, Giordino and Gunn are at theirs. After Sandecker pirated Yaeger away from a Silicon Valley computer-design company, Yaeger spent five years creating NUMA's data complex, a vast electronic library of scientific facts and historical events about the oceans.[180] Yaeger's crowning achievement, however, is Max, a voice-activated virtual computer that incorporates holographic images in its communication. The first incarnation of Max appears in *Flood Tide*, in which the computer speaks in a monotone and projects three-dimensional images of Yaeger, but by *Atlantis Found* Yaeger has reprogrammed Max with his wife Elsie's voice, image and personality.

St. Julien Perlmutter, a family friend and Pitt's godfather, is like a favorite uncle to Pitt, while Perlmutter, a lifelong bachelor, often refers to Pitt as his tenth son.[181] Perlmutter is a cultivated man with an equally cultivated sounding name tag. The spelling of his first name is similar to Saint-Julien, a popular name for towns in France,[182] as well as Saint Julian, which possibly references several historical figures, including a handful of religious martyrs.[183] Julian is also an adjective meaning "of Julius Caesar."[184] The surname Perlmutter is German and Ashkenazi Jewish[185] so it may not be a coincidence that Perlmutter, a gourmand, is especially fond of German food. Being a bon vivant is also one of many external tags Perlmutter shares with Nero Wolfe. Both men are approximately the same age, around fifty-six. Both have encyclopedic minds. And both are approximately four hundred pounds, although the six-foot-four Perlmutter is taller than the five-foot-eleven Wolfe. Wolfe's expertise is detection and orchids and he habitually wears the color yellow, including pajamas, while Perlmutter, owner of an immense private nautical library, is a world authority on maritime history; he frequently wears purple pajamas under a red and gold paisley robe while at home. Wolfe rarely abandons his luxurious brownstone on West 35th Street in New York, but Perlmutter has no qualms about venturing from his renovated carriage house on N Street in Georgetown. Perlmutter even joins Pitt and Girodino on an adventure as they use a helicopter to uncover the Confederate ironclad *Texas* in *Sahara*. Perlmutter's other external tags include his round crimson face, twinkling blue eyes, gray beard, flowing hair and tulip nose. Perlmutter also owns a dachshund named Fritz, another clue to his German heritage, and has been known to carry a cane with a gold knob and a hollow center that doubles as a brandy flask.

The middle-aged hippy Yaeger and the corpulent connoisseur Perlmutter are as different in their techniques as they are in their appearance. Both utilize deductive reasoning in their research, but Yaeger is the next generation of researcher, using data mining and computer hacking to get results. Perlmutter, who owns a computer and knows how to use it,[186] more often than not relies upon his memory, books and other documents along with a network of contacts around the globe, including Yaeger.[187] By basically forsaking technology, Perlmutter continues the tradition of the sage or Wise Old Man, like the eccentric but brilliant bookstore owner Felix Mulholland (Murray Matheson) from the seventies mystery-adventure television program *Banacek* (1972–1974).[188] Pitt, a modern man with an old soul, wisely recognizes that the combination of Yaeger and Perlmutter's different approaches yield more results than relying upon the assistance of one man's method. A good example of this occurs in *Inca Gold*, wherein Pitt has Perlmutter research the capture of the *Nuestra Señora de la Concepción* by Sir Francis Drake, in March 1578, while Yaeger researches a tidal wave that might have struck the shoreline between Lima, Peru and Panama City about the same time and carried the galleon inland.[189]

Blood Kin

Very few of Pitt's relatives appear in his series before Dirk Jr. and Summer arrive in *Valhalla Rising*.

The first is Senator George Pitt of California (R).[190] Pitt inherited his tall, lean body, humorous outlook and wandering ways from his silver-haired father's family, descendants of Spanish Gypsies who migrated to England during the 17th century,[191] and, in *Treasure*, the senator demonstrates the same courage and indomitable will as his son when his cruise ship is abducted by apparent terrorists. Prior to *Treasure*, Cussler builds up George Pitt's first appearance by having characters talk about the senator as early as *Pacific Vortex*. A World War II veteran who worked on a lumber ship and sold cars while attending law school, George Pitt is known as the Socrates of the Senate, where he is a member of the Narcotic Drugs Committee, head of the Senate committee for oil exploration on government lands and chairman of the Naval Appropriations and Senate Foreign Relations Committees.[192] In *Vixen 03*, Pitt mentions that his father plans to retire the following year (1989), but in *Trojan Odyssey* (2006) the elder Pitt is still in the Senate as well as serving as a director for a national cancer foundation.

An incredibly tight bond exists between father and son.[193] Pitt has accompanied his father on several junkets over the years, including one to Latin America, where he served as the senator's aide and pilot.[194] George Pitt has taught his son to be realistic (some might say cynical) about humanity[195]; he also taught his son how to play hardball the way they do in the Beltway. When a congressman attempts to extort Loren by ruining her and Senator Pitt's careers, Pitt easily quashes the scheme and informs the corrupt politician that the man would not last ten minutes against a professional blackmailer like his father.[196]

The next relative to appear is Pitt's uncle Percival "Percy" Nash, also known as Payload Percy. Pitt mentions, in *Iceberg*, that he has an uncle who is a leading bon vivant in San Francisco,[197] but says nothing more until *Dragon*, when he asks Nash to help him locate nuclear devices smuggled into the United States and Western Europe. Nash is an expert on nuclear weaponry, having worked as a scientist on the Manhattan Project and a director on the Atomic Energy Commission. In *Dragon*, we learn that Nash (1) is pushing 82 but sounds and acts 20 years younger; (2) has a face that belongs in TV beer commercials with a great white beard, a knuckle for a nose, a set brow and squinting eyes; (3) is living in Chevy Chase, Maryland; (4) is a gourmand with a wine cellar that is the envy of D.C.'s party throwers; (5) is a bachelor sought after by every widow within a hundred miles; (6) has had his motorcycle license revoked by the DMV, but still drives a Jaguar XK-One-twenty; and (7) is the family character. Fond of garish clothes, including lavender sport coats and lizard-skin cowboy boots, Nash brags about spiking Pitt's baby formula with sherry. Pitt, meanwhile, remembers racing his uncle in Marinda Park when he was six, only to have his uncle throw him in the bushes every time he tried to pass.

No more relatives appear until the end of *Shock Wave* when Pitt's mother, Barbara, (Nash) Pitt[198] makes a cameo at a surprise party in Pitt's hangar home. Barbara's only other appearance is another cameo during Pitt and Loren's wedding at the end of *Trojan Odyssey*. Both times Barbara is in the company of her husband, but neither time is she described. In *Treasure*, George Pitt does mention that Barbara is constantly fighting her weight,[199] and, in *Shock Wave*, Pitt proclaims that his mother taught him that life was a gift,[200] wisdom he has taken as much to heart as his father's observations about humanity, and finally, in *Valhalla Rising*, Pitt ponders the green eyes and facial features he inherited from the Nash side of his family.[201]

Something else Pitt ponders in *Valhalla Rising* is his past. By this time, Pitt is pushing 50 and feeling his age[202] as he recalls visiting the Tutuila Naval Station on the harbor of Pago Pago with his father. Pitt was then in his middle teens[203] and spent his days on the American Samoan island, swimming and relaxing on a beach contemplating his future. This pleasant recollection conjures up bittersweet memories from almost two decades later of another beach, on the Hawaiian island of Oahu, where Pitt walked with Summer Moran. Pitt overlooks the fact that Summer tried to kill him during this walk, but he can never forget that they fell in love. Soon after this momentous walk, Summer apparently died trying to rescue her father, Delphi Moran, during an underwater earthquake. When Pitt tries to shut out his grief, he finds himself wondering what would happen if he could meet his younger self. "Would the young Pitt be repulsed at what he saw and shy away from what lay ahead, taking a totally different direction in their lives?"[204] If a fantasist like Ray Bradbury (*Something Wicked This Way Comes*, *The Martian Chronicles*, *Fahrenheit 451*) was writing Pitt's adventures, Pitt might *actu-*

ally meet his younger self, but as *Valhalla Rising* is a Clive Cussler adventure, Pitt is eventually visited by a woman and man, both 23 years old, who look very much like Summer and his younger self. Pitt's visitors explain that Summer was crippled and disfigured in her attempt to save Moran, but she lived for several years afterwards at her family's home, on the island of Kauai. During her recovery, Summer discovered she was pregnant, and even though she never stopped loving Pitt, she was too proud to be a burden, so she raised their twins, Summer and Dirk Jr., using her own resources.[205] Both twins learned to dive at age six[206] and, inspired to study ocean science so they could work with their father some day,[207] Summer Pitt earned a master's in biological oceanography, from the Scripps Institute of Oceanography, while Dirk earned a degree in ocean engineering from Florida Atlantic Engineering and a master's in marine engineering (Pitt's degree) from the New York Maritime College.[208] Jump ahead almost three years to *Trojan Odyssey* and Pitt's children are working at NUMA, where young special projects director Dirk, Jr. is a chip off the old block. So much so that it seems a safe bet that, given the chance, the young Dirk Pitt would embrace the old Dirk Pitt's life.

Delphi Moran was six-foot-eight, and Dirk Jr. is six-foot-four, an inch taller than his father, but in every other way the younger Dirk resembles a Pitt or Nash. Dirk has his father's green eyes, wavy black hair, warm smile and lean physique along with Pitt's humorous outlook and penchant for asking women he has just rescued out to dinner.[209] Dirk has his own orange-faced Doxa dive watch, a SUB 300T given to him by his father, and, just like his father before *Trojan Odyssey*, Dirk prefers playing the field instead of being tied down to one girl. Also like Pitt, Dirk finds different types of women attractive, but Dirk is not a chef like his father and sister,[210] although he claims to be competent with a grill. Dirk likes antique automobiles and racing as much as Pitt, but where the father enters car competitions that require a team, the son prefers racing by himself on cross-country motorcycles and powerboats. Even in college, Dirk competed in solitary track-and-field events[211] in contrast to Pitt, a star quarterback on his high school and college football teams.[212] Dirk's passion for the sea is the equal of his father's, however, as is his passion for adventure, although the younger and less experienced Dirk has a lot to learn about taking precautions during perilous situations.[213] On the other hand, Dirk possesses the same courage and indomitable will as his father and George Pitt as well as his father's knack for cobbling makeshift MacGyverisms, such as a catamaran he assembles from his and Summer's surfboards in *Treasure of Khan*.[214]

Summer possesses the same passion for the sea and adventure, courage and indomitable will as her brother, but unlike her fraternal twin, she prefers steady romantic relationships, and, physically at least, takes after their mother. When it comes to Summer's heart and mind, however, it is not as easy to see what she might have inherited from the Morans.

Summer Pitt's brilliant but egocentric great-grandfather, Dr. Frederick Moran, is known as the Oracle of Psychic Unity and was one of the 20th century's great classical archaeologists. World War II convinced Dr. Moran that humanity would soon incinerate itself in a nuclear holocaust, so with the aid of his son, colleagues Drs. Lavella and Robleman (no first names given) and several loyal followers of the Oracle of Psychic Unity, he created the ultimate bomb shelter in the caverns of the sunken Pacific kingdom of Kanoli. Summer's grandfather Delphi Moran is not as brilliant as his father but he is twice as egotistical and much more merciless.[215] When the world did not destroy itself by the time Drs. Moran, Lavella and Robleman drowned in a tunnel flood, Delphi took advantage of his secret Pacific base and the Oracle's remaining followers to become a pirate and black marketeer. Summer's mother has no qualms about Delphi murdering people to protect their sanctuary so long as the deaths occur away from Kanoli.[216] She makes a pretty good effort at killing Pitt when she mistakes him for a traitor working for her father, but she also rescues Pitt twice, nearly dies trying to save her father, and raises her twins on her own in a loving and nurturing environment. To Summer Moran's credit, her daughter behaves bravely and nobly from the moment she and her brother arrive at Pitt's door, although a little bit of Summer Pitt's shadow side does sneak out in *Trojan Odyssey*.

A "shadow" is a Jungian fantasy archetype that can be an internal part of a character or represented by an external trickster, often an ancestor or a more recent relative, such as a parent. This archetype is examined in more detail in relation to Pitt in Chapter 7, but a shadow is tapped into mankind's amoral animal past and, in *Trojan Odyssey*, Summer is seduced by elements of the ancient pagan religion of Druidism. Summer is captivated by the power that high priestesses or Druidesses and their goddesses commanded in the past and does not want to believe that Druidesses participated in human sacrifices, but Summer discovers how dangerous giving in to the temptations of her shadow side can be when she is drugged by members of a modern Druid cult and she and Dirk nearly become its next sacrifices.

Loren Smith

"Loren Smith is the woman we all want to be, and Dirk Pitt is the man we all want."[217]

Cussler likes to quote this snippet from a review of *Inca Gold*, but how did a congresswoman from Colorado's seventh district capture Pitt's heart and those of his fans?[218]

Loren is not the series' most voluptuous woman, although she is a looker. Her external tags are violet eyes, prominent cheekbones and long cinnamon hair, and thanks to yoga, jogging, ballet classes and riding horses, Loren has a smoothly contoured body with a sculptured bottom. Loren's introduction in *Vixen 03* may also be the most erotic introduction of any Cussler heroine.[219]

Loren is successful and intelligent with an impressive job, although it is not as exotic as investigating Chinese slave smuggling for the Immigration and Naturalization Service or searching for the source of a deadly toxin for the World Health Organization. Even Loren's name seems a tad bland when compared to Lily Sharp, Maeve Fletcher or Eva Rojas, although it does reflect her no-nonsense-girl-next-door-with-a-Type-A personality.

The lady is patient, which is a benefit when dating a Peter Pan. Loren meets Pitt in 1988, but they do not marry until 2006.[220] Loren also has a passion for classic automobiles. When Loren picks up Pitt from the airport she always borrows a car from his collection[221] and she drives Pitt's 1953 Allard J2X in vintage sports car races.[222] Loren not only tolerates Pitt's adventurous lifestyle, she thrives in his crazy and often dangerous world. In *Vixen 03*, Pitt becomes obsessed with finding out how an airplane's oxygen tank and nose gear wind up in the garage to Loren's cabin, and late one night he decides to load the nose gear into the back of his Jeep so he can take it to Stapleton Airport in the morning for examination. When Pitt is unable to load the nose gear alone, a befuddled Loren slips off her peignoir and helps cart it in the nude. In *Deep Six*, Pitt stashes Loren and two other people trying to avoid capture by the crew of a Russian cruise ship into a tiny shower stall with Giordino. When the crew arrives to search Pitt's cabin they find him eating appetizers while his "wife" takes a shower. The crew requests to search the bathroom. Pitt shouts to ask if his wife minds. Loren agrees but asks if the crew will bring her a couple of extra towels first, and her quick thinking earns her a kiss, praise and admiration from Pitt.

This is discussed in more detail in Chapter 6, but Pitt is similar to the heroes in the films of classic Hollywood director Howard Hawks, and in many ways Loren is cut from the same template as such Hawks heroines as Hildy Johnson (*His Girl Friday*) and Nikki Nicholson (*The Thing from Another World*), likable and independent[223] working girls who succeed in a male-dominated society[224] and do not take guff off anyone. In Loren's first scene with Pitt he teases her about her small breasts, then about the graft in her district and then about how Loren's sexual excesses will come back to haunt her, but Loren takes it all in stride. First, Loren tells Pitt that he will "have to make do with my thirty-four B cuppers," then (while waving a frying pay), "There is no political hanky-panky in the seventh district, and I am the last one on Capitol Hill who can be accused of being on the take,"[225] and finally that her private life is her own business as long as she keeps her lovers off her office payroll and congressional expense account.

Loren is not quite so independent in her final scene in *Vixen 03*, during which she entices White House press secretary Phil Sawyer into proposing to her. To be fair, this is not the first time Sawyer proposes, and Loren has been up front with Pitt about Sawyer,[226] plus she claims to be under no delusions when it comes to Pitt. Earlier, Loren tells former school friend Felicia Collins how Sawyer is the dependable sort of man you marry, while Pitt sets his own schedule like an alley cat.[227] In another scene, Loren tells Pitt that she will settle for any percentage of him that she can get after he admits that he is too selfish with his emotions. For all her honesty, though, Loren comes across like a temptress to coax Sawyer into proposing again in a scene with more Gothic elements than romantic ones,[228] but Loren more than redeems herself in *Deep Six*, wherein she survives two abductions and helps rescue people from the *Leonid Andreyev*. As for Sawyer, no explanation is given about what happened to him or how their engagement ended. All we are told is that Loren's sole activity outside work is her on-again-off-again affair with Pitt.[229] In *Dragon* Loren realizes how much she loves Pitt,[230] yet, in *Inca Gold*, she rejects Pitt's first proposal to her, telling him that they are married to their jobs and do not need each other.[231] By *Atlantis Found* Loren is having second thoughts, and by *Trojan Odyssey* she and Pitt are ready to get married.

Which brings us back to the question of how Loren has managed to win Pitt's heart and those of his fans. The best explanation may appear in "The Reunion," in which Loren is the only character besides Pitt to recognize Cussler. Cussler is surprised but takes the opportunity to tell Loren "that you have been the girl of my dreams."[232] Cussler had no idea that Loren would be the woman for Pitt when he wrote *Vixen 03*,[233] so it could be that Loren has captured Pitt's heart and those of his fans because, before accomplishing these feats, she captured her creator's heart.

3

Cussler's Characters, Part 2
The Other Heroes

Unsung heroes. They're the ones I like.—Juan Cabrillo[1]

Starting with *Pacific Vortex*, Cussler has excelled at creating other heroes, perhaps none more memorable or audacious than Brian Shaw, the aging British Secret Service agent called out of retirement for a final assignment that leads to a showdown with Pitt. Shaw, who might be James Bond, fails in his mission but triumphs over Pitt for the heart of Heidi Milligan. There are also Sal Casio and Jerome P. Lillie III. Casio, a tough-guy private eye from the Mike Hammer School, is savvy enough to slip past the sophisticated burglar alarms protecting Pitt's hangar home and get the drop on Dirk yet needs his help to solve the 20-year mystery of his missing daughter. Lillie is the tragic young heir of Lillie Beer, of St. Louis, and a field agent with the National Intelligence Agency. For approximately 25 years these and other heroes (like Julia Lee, a beautiful and determined undercover agent with the Immigration and Naturalization Services) battled alongside Pitt but were never seen or heard of again. With the exception of *Sea Hunters*, *Clive Cussler & Dirk Pitt Revealed*, and a smattering of non-fiction pieces, Cussler seemed satisfied writing Pitt adventures.

That all began to change in 1999.

NUMA Files

Cussler's fans received a double dose of action with the 15th Dirk Pitt adventure, *Atlantis Found*, and the inaugural *NUMA Files* adventure, *Serpent*, the first Cussler adventure with a hero other than Pitt[2] and Cussler's first fiction collaboration. Kemprecos teamed with Cussler on the first eight *NUMA Files* before Brown joined Cussler in 2011 on the ninth adventure, *Devil's Gate*.

In a June 2001 interview with AudioBooksToday.com, Cussler was asked if writing *NUMA Files* with a partner means "you come up with the parameters of the story and then someone else fills it in?" Cussler explained, "Yeah ... I had to have somebody help write it. I couldn't do two books at the same time." When asked how he felt about having someone else fleshing out his ideas Cussler answered, "Oh, it doesn't bother me. [Kemprecos is] actually making up most of his own words. I edit it."[3]

The collaborative process is a little more complicated than that, of course.

Cussler and his collaborator generally start off by working out a concept. The collaborator then begins writing, sending Cussler approximately a third of the manuscript at a time. If the collaborator is unhappy with how things are progressing then the pages are scrapped and the collaborator starts over. If the collaborator gets stuck with plotting or the direction the story is taking then Cussler steps in to provide guidance and suggestions. As the manuscript develops, Cussler adds or edits material if he feels it is necessary.[4]

NUMA Files chronicles the exploits of the agency's Special Assignments Team, which handles jobs outside of NUMA's ordinary tasks and outside the realm of government oversight.[5] Originally, the publisher Simon & Schuster wanted NSAT to be a three-member team with (1) a Navy SEAL and jack-of-all-trades in the lead; (2) a brilliant oceanographer from Woods Hole Oceanographic Institute; and (3) a gorgeous Marine captain, in her late twenties, cross-trained in special underwater engineering and as a pilot capable of flying any type of aircraft. These stereotypes left Cussler underwhelmed and, in a letter to Lampack, he suggests that the team's leader be "an ex-ship's engineering officer, who became a designer and builder of deep sea vehicles." Cussler felt that the Woods Hole oceanographer presented "an opportunity to be original" but recommended "a husband and wife team or a couple who live together, particularly if they have a little spark and warmth between them. Here you get two for the price of one, a man along with a woman who is bright and feminine." As for the gorgeous young Marine, Cussler thought the character was not believable, plus he wanted to "keep the military out of the team. The naval personnel can enter via the various plotlines, along with intelligent female characters, scientists, government officials, business executives, etc."[6] Eventually, the team leader developed into series protagonist Kurt Austin, while the deep sea vehicle designer and builder merged with the Marine to become Austin's buddy-in-color Jose "Joe" Zavala, a tough marine engineer and the team's self-proclaimed "propulsionist" who can "repair, modify, or restore any engine, be it steam, diesel, or electric and whether it was in an automobile, ship, or aircraft."[7] The Woods Hole team became Paul Trout, a Ph.D. in ocean science specializing in deep ocean geology recruited into NUMA by his high school friend Gunn, and his wife, Dr. Gamay Morgan-Trout, a Ph.D. in marine biology and one of Cussler's finest redheads.[8]

While Austin, Zavala and the Trouts are as memorable as they are formidable and NSAT's duties are different from Pitt's special projects director duties,[9] *NUMA Files* is no different from the Dirk Pitt series than *Star Trek: The Next Generation* (1987–1994) is from *Star Trek* (1966–1969)[10] or *Stargate Atlantis* (2004–2009) is from *Stargate SG-1* (1997–2007).[11] Which is the point. Contemporary television is replete with franchises like *Law & Order*, *CSI* and *NCIS* that spawn spin-offs which walk a fine line between being different yet not too different from their parent series,[12] while in literature it is commonplace for series characters to be inspired by another series character. There is no better example of this than Conan Doyle's eccentric knight-errant Sherlock Holmes when it comes to inspiring other characters. Elements of the Great Detective can be found in hundreds of characters created since the late 19th century, ranging from the intentionally derivative, like Solar Pons,[13] to the inspired, like Nero Wolfe, to the innovative, like Dr. Gregory House,[14] but even Holmes was inspired by an earlier character, the Chevalier C. August Dupin, created by Poe. *NUMA Files* follows these traditions as it gives Cussler fans more NUMA adventures with a different cast of heroes. The structure and plot styles in *NUMA Files* and the Dirk Pitt series are virtually the same[15] while Austin and Zavala are inspired (if not patterned) after Pitt and Girodino.

Pitt and Austin are approximately the same age and height, although at six-foot-one Austin is approximately two inches shorter than Pitt. Pitt is leaner than the broad-shouldered

Austin, who is built like a football player, while Austin has coral blue eyes and his hair is prematurely white. Both Pitt and Austin were raised in and around the sea and are only children from wealthy West Coast families, but Austin's mother is deceased and his background is more blue collar. His father owns a marine salvage company in Seattle,[16] where Austin worked for six years, as well as two years in the North Sea on oil rigs.[17] Like Pitt, though, Austin has a sophisticated side. A chess player with a library stocked with philosophy books and jazz records, he collects antique dueling pistols, frequently exercises by sculling and might even love racing more than Pitt, except he prefers boats to automobiles. Austin does not even own a car, content to borrow one from the NUMA motor pool whenever the need arises. Also like Pitt, Austin fails to rescue a woman he cares about in an early adventure when Francesca Cabral sacrifices herself to destroy the über-zaftig eco-extortionist Brynhild Sigurd and her Gogstad Corporation in *Blue Gold*.[18]

Austin's name tag combines Cussler's German heritage (Kurt) with southwestern folk hero elements (Colonel Travis Austin from the Alamo),[19] and it should come as no surprise that Austin is a hero in the Pitt archetype. A former CIA underwater intelligence operative, Austin never served in the military but is patriotic, self-reliant, sometimes self-effacing, and always self-sacrificing as well as educated (he has a master's in systems management from the University of Washington), intuitive, genial, dangerous when threatened, and prone to wisecracks. Growing up, Pitt was a Boy Scout[20] and Austin was a Cub Scout.[21] Austin is an honorable man who has no qualms when his NSAT duties require him to break a rule or a law, so long as it is necessary or for the good of his country. This makes Austin a realist, but he is a philosophical one rather than a cynical one like Pitt, and there are two good examples of this in *Fire Ice*. The first occurs during a Cold War showdown over a stranded American submarine between Austin and his opposite number in Soviet naval intelligence, Viktor Petrov. During radio communications, Austin (who is using the alias John Doe) warns Petrov (who is using the alias Ivan) not to board the sub because it is heavily mined. When Petrov asks why Austin should care if the Russian is killed, Austin points out that the Cold War will not last forever. Petrov suspects a bluff, unaware that Austin's game is chess, not poker, and Petrov is nearly killed trying to invade the sub.[22] During his recuperation, Petrov receives a bouquet of red, white, and blue carnations and a card with genuine well wishes from John Doe.[23] In the second example, Austin is feeling uneasy about his current mission and is unable to sleep. Austin steps out on the deck of the NUMA vessel *Argo* and studies the Black Sea, a "big puddle of dead water, but Austin knew that an abyss with far more reason to be feared was the remorseless evil that lurked in the depths of the human mind."[24] This philosophical bent, a carryover from Kemprecos's Cape Cod Pitt-archetype-hero Aristotle "Soc" Socarides,[25] may explain why Austin is not a Peter Pan, like Pitt, but a man who is content with his lifestyle and in no mood to change how he lives it. Austin is also not as audacious as Pitt when it comes to escaping death traps or planning a mission. Before one dive, Zavala sums up Austin's *modus operandi* by saying, "Plan the dive and dive the plan. Get in. Take a look. Get out. Stay flexible. Improvise when necessary."[26] Austin and Pitt do share other attitudes, however, such as a casual acceptance to surviving danger, a levelheaded approach to death and killing, and a habit of asking women he rescues to dinner, sometimes during the rescue. If there is a key difference between Pitt and Austin, however, it is that Pitt is unafraid to stray from the highroads most men travel and bring back secrets from lost places. It is not that Austin has any qualms against straying—he does find Christopher Columbus's tomb in *Serpent*—but in personality and as head of NSAT he is primarily a defender of the realm.

The similarities between Giordino and Zavala begin with their names, although it is not an obvious connection. When it comes to naming characters, Cussler tends to rely on his imagination rather than tuckerization, the practice of naming a character after a real person,[27] but there have been exceptions like Leigh Hunt/Leigh Hunter,[28] Foss Gly[29] and, as we will soon see, Juan Rodriguez Cabrillo. Girodino and Zavala, however, are exceptions among these exceptions. Where Giordino's name and appearance are based on Albert Girodano, Zavala is named after a ship, the Republic of Texas Navy steamer *Zavala* that was located by Cussler's NUMA organization in November 1986.[30]

Zavala is physically the opposite of his best friend in many of the same ways Giordino is to Pitt. Both are shorter, but at five-foot-ten Zavala is only three inches shorter than Austin and six inches taller than Giordino. Both weigh 175 pounds, but Girodino is stocky as opposed to the leaner Pitt; Zavala, who paid his way through college as a middleweight boxer, is wiry as opposed to the stocky Austin. Both have brown eyes, black hair and are swarthy, however Zavala combs his hair straight back and his heritage is Mexican. Zavala's parents migrated to New Mexico before he was born and his native tongue is Spanish, a language he sometimes slips into when surprised or angry. Zavala and Giordino are also gentlemen by nature who enjoy cigars and the company of women, but as the brutal Sigurd and Melika, the overseer from *Sahara*, discover, neither man is afraid of fighting a brutal woman when pushed too far. Finally, both men are marine engineers who have worked together on submersible designs and construction like NUMA's *Pisces* underwater laboratory.[31]

Austin and Zavala will occasionally quote old lyrics or make old references like Pitt and Giordino. In *Fire Ice*, Austin mentions the television programs *Mission: Impossible* and *Murder, She Wrote*, wiggles his eyebrows like Groucho Marx, and compares a situation to the Keystone Kops, while at one point Zavala sings an off-key version of the 1929 Cuban song "Guantanamera." The patter of the banter between Austin and Zavala at times also sounds note for note like that of Pitt and Giordino. Zavala also shares Cussler and Pitt's low opinion of most politicians.[32]

The *Oregon* Files

In 2003, Cussler launched his third adventure series with *Golden Buddha: The First Novel of the "Oregon Files."*[33] Cussler's collaborator on the first two *Oregon Files* is Craig Dirgo, co-author of *Clive Cussler & Dirk Pitt Revealed* and both *Sea Hunters* books, but after *Sacred Stone* Dirgo left to concentrate on his own adventure series featuring the Pitt-archetype-hero John Taft and buddy-in-color Larry Martinez, operatives with the small and ultra-secret National Intelligence Agency (*The Einstein Papers*, *Tremor*).[34] Starting with the third *Oregon Files* adventure, *Dark Watch*, Cussler collaborated with Du Brul, but in 2013 Du Brul announced he was leaving the series.

Unlike *NUMA Files*, *Oregon Files* features characters that have nothing to do with NUMA, but first appeared in a Pitt adventure. In *Flood Tide* we meet Cabrillo and a handful of the mercenaries that belong to The Corporation, a mixture of ex-intelligence agents and elite retired naval men and naval officers who work for any U.S. government agency requiring their unique services.[35] Some of The Corporation's members include Max Hanley (a chief engineer and first officer whose father died during a Japanese bombing while serving in Manila Bay in 1942), Eddie Seng (a planning expert and former CIA agent who served as the agency's man in Beijing for 20 years), Linda Ross (a surveillance analyst and former navy fire-control officer aboard an Aegis-missile cruiser), Hali Kasim (a communications expert), Monica Crabtree (a quartermaster) and field operatives Pete James and Bob Meadows.[36]

Also introduced is the *Oregon*.

The brainchild of former CIA agent Cabrillo,[37] the *Oregon* is a Pacific Coast lumber hauler converted into a sophisticated covert vessel disguised to resemble a ramshackle tramp steamer. Sandecker commissions the *Oregon* to help Pitt and Girodino transport NUMA's *Sea Dog II* submersible close enough to secretly inspect and photograph Qin Shang's own covert vessel *United States*, a converted passenger liner being used for human smuggling and other sinister purposes. During this mission, the *Oregon* is compromised and then damaged while battling the Chinese destroyer *Chengdo*. Cabrillo also loses his right leg beneath the knee, but Cabrillo tells Pitt when they part company that a grateful U.S. government is going to pay for a new and improved ship.[38]

Even though its predecessor was compromised, this new vessel is also called the *Oregon*, and, as far as most of the world is concerned, it is still one of the last tramp steamers.[39] Also like her predecessor, this new *Oregon* flies the flag of Iran[40] and is camouflaged to look like a derelict,[41] but beneath her apparently rust-flaked blue hull is the closest thing to the starship *Enterprise* on the Seven Seas. Instead of diesel engines or nuclear power, the *Oregon* employs the magnetohydrodynamics technology invented by Dr. Elmore Egan that has been otherwise ignored since the luxury cruise vessels *Emerald Dolphin* and *Golden Marlin* were sabotaged during their maiden voyages in *Valhalla Rising*.[42] The *Oregon*'s MHD engines generate an almost limitless amount of electricity by employing super-cooled magnets to strip naturally occurring free electrons from seawater. In turn, this power is fed into four aqua pulse jets capable of pushing water through two vectored-thrust drive tubes, a system designed to propel the *Oregon* to such speeds that her hull had to be stiffened and reinforced, which also gives the *Oregon* moderate icebreaking capabilities. Even more impressive is the *Oregon*'s complement of weapons; a hidden hangar in the aft-most hold housing a four-passenger Robinson R44 helicopter that can be raised hydraulically to the deck; a host of concealed waterline doors through which Zodiacs, a SEAL assault boat and other small water crafts can be launched; a moon pool along the *Oregon*'s keel where a pair of mini-subs can be secretly launched; and a sophisticated suite of electronics. Like her predecessor, though, the passageways and cabins of this new *Oregon* are as luxurious as a five-star hotel. Its kitchen remains one of the finest afloat, with Cordon Bleu-trained chefs.[43]

It is apparent in *Flood Tide* that there are several more members of The Corporation than are actually presented, but the *Oregon* appears for less than a hundred pages so only necessary associates are introduced so not to hinder the action, however such moderation is lacking in *Golden Buddha* or *Sacred Stone*. In the foreword to *Golden Buddha*, Cussler describes how he and Dirgo worked to create a unique cast of characters,[44] and the authors do their best to showcase all of them; but having so many characters coming and going while maintaining an action-packed pace would test the limits of Cecil B. DeMille or D.W. Griffith, especially in *Golden Buddha*, which also features a complicated sting. The members of The Corporation aboard the new *Oregon* are still mercenaries, but in *Golden Buddha* they are educated and highly trained people in their respective fields who also served in the armed forces. The Corporation's mission statement is also different as it now contracts with governments, corporations and private interests while performing good works of its own choosing.[45]

All of The Corporation's members that appear in *Flood Tide* are present in the *Oregon Files* series (although beginning with *Golden Buddha*, Pete James is Pete Jones), and, just like in *Flood Tide*, The Corporation's members are stockholders who split the profits from their missions and are assigned a title related to their duties rather than a rank.[46] For instance, Hanley is The Corporation's president, a promotion from *Flood Tide*, where he is corporate vice-president in charge of operational systems.[47] New cast members include Eric Stone (the ship's best handler), Mark Murphy (the man responsible for the *Oregon*'s vast arsenal), Franklin Lincoln (an ex-SEAL in command of the *Oregon*'s former Special Forces operators), Kevin Nixon (a prop master in charge of the ship's Magic Shop, which is responsible for creating everything from false identifications to whatever clothing the *Oregon*'s operatives require during covert missions), and the chief steward, Maurice (a retired member of the British Royal Navy and the only person aboard the *Oregon* allowed to call Cabrillo by the rank of captain instead of the title Chairman).[48]

After Du Brul joined *Oregon Files* the plots became less hectic. The number of regular characters spotlighted in each adventure was reduced and the focus of much of the action involving the *Oregon* centered around or on series' protagonist, Cabrillo.

When it comes to Cabrillo's external tags he is a tall man in his mid-forties, handsome, well built though slightly on the thin side, with clear blue eyes and crew cut blond hair. Cabrillo's grandparents emigrated from Sonora, Mexico, in 1931, and when Cabrillo was born they insisted their grandson be named after a famous historical figure, so Cabrillo's father named him after the explorer and sailor who discovered California.[49] Cabrillo is not a bureaucrat like Pitt, but a former CIA agent like Austin. A bit of a clotheshorse, in *Flood Tide* Cabrillo also smokes a pipe that he habitually clenches between his teeth. In *Golden Buddha*, Cabrillo replaces the pipe with a new tag, a collection of prosthetic right legs that conceal weapons and are otherwise modified to fit his unique lifestyle.

Cussler provides more clues for what goes on in Cabrillo's heart and mind than most of his heroes. Raised in Orange County, California, by an upper-middle-class family, Cabrillo is by nature conservative, patriotic, fearless but controlled. Cabrillo majored in political science in college, where he was an active member of the ROTC, and hired by the CIA after graduation. Fluent in Russian, Arabic and Spanish, Cabrillo is also a master at disguises and stealth.[50] Like Pitt, Cabrillo has lost a woman he loves, his wife Amy, who died in a single-car accident while driving drunk.[51] This makes Cabrillo the only Cussler hero who was married prior to the start of his series, and the only widower. Cabrillo is also loyal. When Sloan Macintyre, the heroine of *Skeleton Coast*, learns about Amy she can tell that Cabrillo is the kind of man who marries once in his life.[52] Likewise, Cabrillo left the CIA to protect his partner, Langston Overholt IV, after interference from the agency's chiefs ruined covert operations against Nicaraguan Sandinistas. Since then, Overholt has ascended in power at the CIA, where he used his influence to help Cabrillo finance building the *Oregon* and funnels lucrative jobs to The Corporation. Perhaps the most revealing moment about what goes on inside Cabrillo takes place in *Skeleton Coast* as he and Sloan travel alone in one of the *Oregon*'s luxury lifeboats to interview a West African hermit fisherman named Papa Heinrick. Cabrillo and Sloan have known each other only a few hours, yet Cabrillo can tell Sloan is as driven as he is, the kind of person who leaves no job half-finished or backs down from a challenge. Cabrillo also admires Sloan's curiosity and tenacity, traits he prizes in himself. Sloan, meanwhile, is intrigued by the enigmatic Chairman. In an attempt to learn more about him, she asks what Cabrillo would do if he was not the captain of the *Oregon*:

The question didn't veer into any dangerous territory so Juan gave her an honest answer. "I think I'd be a paramedic."

"Really? Not a doctor?"

"Most doctors I know treat patients like a commodity—something they have to work on if they want to get paid before returning to the golf course. And they're backed by a huge staff of nurses and technicians and millions of dollars' worth of equipment. But paramedics are different. They are out there working in pairs with just their wits and a minimum of gear. They have to make the first critical assessments and often perform the first life-saving acts. They're there to tell you everything is going to be all right and make damn sure it is. And once you get the person to the hospital you simply fade away. No glory, no God complex, no 'gee, doc, you saved my life.' You just do your job and go on to the next."[53]

In contrast to Pitt, a cynical realist, and Austin, a philosophical realist, Cabrillo is an EMT for a troubled world, which makes the Chairman a knight-errant and defender of the realm. But Cabrillo can be as much of a nemesis and manhunter as Pitt. When he discovers Papa Heinrick has been murdered, he revs up the lifeboat to chase the killers. As the lifeboat increases speed it transforms into a high-performance hydrofoil, and a flabbergasted Sloan asks, "Who in the hell are you?"

"Someone you don't want to piss off.... And they just pissed me off."[54]

The Lacey and Casey Nicefolk Adventures

In 2006, three years after Cussler's last solo writing effort, he gave his readers something completely different, a children's story called *The Adventures of Vin Fiz* featuring ten-year-old twins Lacey and Casey Nicefolk of Castroville, California. As for name tags, Nicefolk is self-explanatory while Casey is a good old-fashioned boy's name that recalls American folklore and tall tales (e.g., Casey Jones, Mighty Casey at the Bat) and Lacey conjures images of distinctively feminine things like lace from the tintype days. Blond and green-eyed Casey is not fond of school, although he is not a bad student, he just prefers thinking about mechanical things, exploring and building model airplanes and automobiles. In contrast, Lacey, who has golden brown hair and robin egg blue eyes, loves school, especially English and mathematics, as well as creating recipes using herbs grown on the family's farm. Lacey also designs furniture that her father, Ever Nicefolk, builds and sells.[55] Casey and Lacey also share a shadow side represented by a relative from the past, their family's patriarch Knot Nicefolk, a highwayman during the days of merry old England.[56]

The family's herb farm, Nicefolk Landing, sits in a valley near Monterey Bay, otherwise populated with artichoke farms. These other farms represent conformity, a way of life that provides security but sometimes requires a person to behave in ways contrary to his real nature, an incongruity represented by the contradictory nature of artichokes, a thistle with leaves that must be dipped in sauce to taste good.[57] Ever Nicefolk does not follow the beat of an artichoke drummer like all his neighbors,[58] but unlike the artichokes farms, which regularly turn a profit, the 60 acres of Nicefolk Landing is insufficient to raise enough herbs to be lucrative, and if the Nicefolks ever suffer one bad year without rain they know they will lose their farm.[59]

Casey, Lacey and Ever Nicefolk share more autobiographical elements with their creator than any other Cussler hero besides Pitt. The family lives near the same area of California where Cussler spent most of his childhood. Casey's ambivalence towards school reflects Cussler's belief that education is geared towards students with a flair for scholarship rather than a bent towards creativity, and comments on Casey's report cards that he daydreams and does not apply himself irritate Ever, much like the Cs and Ds that often appeared on Cussler's report cards concerned his father, Eric.[60] Lacey's academic success reflects Cussler's passion for research[61] and his success at Pasadena Community College, where Cussler applied himself after high school and earned As and Bs, much to his father's amazement.[62] Lacey's talent for designing furniture harkens to Cussler's own talents as an amateur handyman, landscaper and interior designer,[63] while her passion for creating recipes reflects Cussler's passion for fine dining that is evident in almost every one of his adventures.[64] Casey's use of herbs from Nicefolk Landing in her recipes likewise demonstrates a practicality inherited from Ever, a serious man who seldom laughs,[65] and from Cussler, a serious man who describes himself as having a "mind rigid with practicality."[66] Ever Nicefolk also has "twinkling gray eyes" and "a crooked smile that moved back and forth across his mouth as if unable to settle in one position. He moved and talked slowly, traits that fooled some into thinking he was dull witted, when in fact he was very clever and smart."[67] Cussler's eyes are green, but if you see him speak in public or watch an interview with him you can see that his eyes twinkle and his mouth is often set in a crooked grin. Cussler also moves and talks slowly, but his complex adventure plots and his honorary doctorate are proof of his intelligence, despite his insistence of being simpleminded.[68] Elements of Cussler can also be seen in the wandering field-worker Sucoh Sucop ("Hocus Pocus" spelled backwards), a mysterious stranger who helps the Nicefolks with the harvest in exchange for room and board and permission to build a workshop in the barn so he can tinker after work. A tall, lanky older fellow with a long gray beard and looking like "an understuffed scarecrow,"[69] Sucop is accompanied by a white donkey, named Mr. Periwinkle, who is pulling a cart painted a gleaming gold and filled with paraphernalia. Trim the beard and add a couple of pounds to Sucop and his description approximates Cussler. During the author's cameo appearances in *Sahara* and *Inca Gold* he is accompanied by a donkey named Mr. Periwinkle,[70] while in *Valhalla Rising* Cussler rescues Pitt, Giordino and Misty Graham in a catamaran named *Periwinkle*. Sucop likewise entertains Casey and Lacey with "wondrous stories"[71] much as Cussler does with his readers.

Sucop is also a Wise Old Man figure, another Jungian fantasy archetype whose job is to coax the hero (or, in this case, heroes) into leaving the security and familiarity of home to set off on an adventure.[72] Lacey and Casey love Nicefolk Landing and the surrounding countryside and rivers, but often wonder what it would be like to board one of the trains that journey along the nearby railroad tracks and see what waits beyond. Sucop provides the means with two gifts he makes, a small copper box with two levers and a large, square mat. If a toy is placed on the mat and the box's left lever is pressed, the toy grows until it is life-size. Press the right lever and the toy returns to its original size. More than a gift, Succop is giving the children "the secret of enchantment," but "you must believe with all your heart that your toy will become as real as life itself." If the twins try to use the box for bad it will vanish, otherwise it will work until Casey and Lacey are both grown up, "Then your dreams will take new directions, and the secret will fade in your mind and heart."[73]

Soon after Sucop leaves Nicefolk Landing, the twins discover Casey's model of a *Wright Flyer* airplane on Sucop's workbench. Casey names the plane *Vin Fiz* after his favorite grape soda pop, and the twins grow it life-size so they can see the world. The twins tell their parents that they are going on a short summer camping trip, then Casey, Lacey, their dog Floopy and the enchanted *Vin Fiz* experience a string of adventures while flying cross-country to New York City.

Cussler explains in a 2006 *Publisher's Weekly* interview that the inspiration to write a children's book came in part from Ian Fleming's *Chitty Chitty Bang Bang: The Magical Car* (1964).[74] Fleming based his automobile on a real car named Chitty Bang Bang, one of a series of racing cars built with airplane engines in the early twenties by Count Louis Zborowski, and Cussler based his fictional airplane on an actual *Wright Flyer* named *Vin Fiz*, the first airplane to make a transcontinental flight across America.[75] Fleming and Cussler's stories also feature vehicles capable of independent actions, but in spite of the title of Fleming's book there are no magical explanations. Chitty-Chitty-Bang-Bang, a Paragon Panther and the only car ever built by the defunct Paragon Motor-Car Company, just begins behaving oddly soon after it is restored by an inventor with one of fiction's niftiest non-conformist names, Commander Caractacus Pott. With no warning and to the surprise of Commander Pott, his wife, Mimsie, and their children, Jeremy and Jemima, Chitty-Chitty-Bang-Bang is able to sprout wings and fly as well as convert herself into a hovercraft capable of sailing across the English Channel. From this point on the Potts and Chitty-Chitty-Bang-Bang spend most of their time spoiling the plans of a group of criminals led by Joe the Monster, who is operating a gunrunning operation out of a cave near Calais. In *The Adventures of Vin Fiz*, the Nicefolk twins, Floopy and *Vin Fiz* squelch the schemes of two criminal brothers during their New York trip, The Boss in Nevada and The Chief in Ohio. And just like in *Chitty Chitty Bang Bang: The Magical Car*, the exploits in *The Adventures of Vin Fiz* are to be enjoyed for their own sake and nothing else. Except for the contrast of the artichoke farms with Nicefolk Landing and the autobiographical elements in the characters of Sucop, Casey, Lacey and Ever Nicefolk, *The Adventures of Vin Fiz* offers very little in the way of subtext, allegories or metaphors. Cussler did not write a children's book with messages like C.S. Lewis's *Chronicles of Narnia* (1949–1954) or J.K. Rowling's *Harry Potter* series (1997–2007). If *The Adventures of Vin Fiz* contains any message it appears to be the same one found in Fleming's novel, which is presented as a piquant snippet of advice from Commander Pott: "Never say 'No' to adventure. Always say 'Yes,' otherwise you'll lead a very dull life."[76] If Cussler has anything to add to that it may be this encouragement from Lacey to her brother: "We've got to try. If we try, we can do. If we do, we can achieve and succeed."[77]

Cussler was asked in his *Publisher's Weekly* interview if there would be any more Nicefolk adventures and he said, "I have no other children's book in the works,"[78] but in 2010 Casey and Lacey returned in *The Adventures of Hotsy Totsy*. This time their magical vehicle is a replica of a powerboat that won the Gold Cup Grand National Race in back-to-back years.[79] The twins manage to figure a way to compete in the Gold Cup in spite of their age and the lack of the thousand-dollar entry fee—basically they just run along with the other racers—but they have a harder time dealing with their old enemy The Boss, who (along with his henchmen) just robbed half a million dollars from a local bank. After watching a TV story about the twins trying to enter the Gold Cup, the vengeful Boss abducts Casey and Lacey while they are sleeping on the *Hotsy Totsy* and locks them in a rusty cell on abandoned Alcatraz Island that once held the Chicago gangster Al Capone. Thanks to Lacey's ingenuity, as well as some timely assistance from Floopy and *Hotsy Totsy*, the twins escape to run the race, but if The Boss has his way Casey and Lacey will never reach the finish line.

Unlike *The Adventures of Vin Fiz*, which parades through one generally unconnected chance adventure after another, *The Adventures of Hotsy Totsy* concentrates on an adventure of the twins' own making, racing in the Gold Cup, and the ancillary adventures that spring up around it, much like what happens to Sam and Remi Fargo in their premiere adventure, *Spartan*

Gold. The situations in *The Adventures of Hotsy Totsy* are also local or microcosmic, just like in *The Adventures of Vin Fiz, Spartan Gold, The Chase* and Pitt's earliest adventures. However, unlike the universal or macrocosmic adventures in most of the Pitt novels and all the *NUMA Files* and *Oregon Files*,[80] *The Adventures of Hotsy Totsy* and *The Adventures of Vin Fiz* are meant to be as simple as they are innocent. Where the Pitt series and Cussler's other series are updated versions of old fashion adventure stories, the Casey and Lacey Nicefolk adventures are traditional children's literature set in a relatively recent time. These stories, first told by Cussler to his children and grandchildren,[81] are as devoted to the naive fun of childhood as any dime novel boy's adventure tale. Adolescent angst, sex, drugs, absentee parents, child molesters and other harsh realities are not broached, and while The Boss and his henchmen are crooked and mean they are also comical and dimwitted, making them dangerous but no more wicked than the bad guys faced by the Hardy Boys, Nancy Drew, Shaggy and Scooby-Doo or the Duke family. These foes never think twice about abducting you, and some may even intend to kill you, but fate-worse-than-death scenarios are never considered.[82] Such unpleasantries can wait for the day Casey and Lacey's dreams take them in new directions, but not while the secret of enchantment is real in their young hearts and minds.

The Adventures of Vin Fiz and *The Adventures of Hotsy Totsy* share additional similarities with other Cussler adventures.

Casey and Lacey are too young to have had a chance to satisfy many of the qualifications to be Pitt archetype heroes, but like Pitt and Cussler's other heroes the Nicefolk twins are not above bending rules on occasion, like when they refuse to drop out of the Gold Cup race or fib to their parents about going camping so they can fly on *Vin Fiz*. The twins are generally more respectful towards authority figures than Pitt, but like Pitt and other Cussler heroes Casey and Lacey always put the needs of others ahead of their own. In *The Adventures of Hotsy Totsy*, a race official asks Lacey why the twins stopped to help other racers who were in trouble when the children could have possibly crossed the finish line first, and she explains that their parents taught them to help other people and do the right thing.[83] (One can almost hear the echo of Pitt telling Dorsett how his mother taught him that life is a gift.) Lacey likewise exhibits a knack for MacGyverisms when she concocts a way to create string saws to cut through the rusting bars of Capone's former cell.[84]

Casey and Lacey are neither defenders of the realm nor manhunters, but rather noble children longing to see what lies beyond the horizon, and in the process they end up receiving a gift from the fairylands in the form of Sucop's secret of enchantment. The Nicefolk twins are also the second set of twins to become major heroic characters in a Cussler series after the introduction of Dirk Jr. and Summer Pitt in 2001. A few other twins have appeared in Cussler's adventures, but so far they have either been villainous (Melo and Radko Kradzik from *Blue Gold*) or, at the very least, duplicitous (the supposed twins Kristjan and Kirsti Fyrie from *Iceberg*).

As detailed in Chapter 5, Cussler habitually incorporates Gothic elements in the adventures he writes without collaborators, and the Gothic elements in *The Adventures of Vin Fiz* and *The Adventures of Hotsy Totsy* include an abandoned ghost town, a creepy deserted manor house in the middle of a forest that The Chief and his gang use as a hideout, and Capone's one-time cell on Alcatraz.[85]

Casey and Lacey's adventures are also as respectful, if not as passionate, about history as the Pitt series. The twins' magical vehicles are based upon historical vehicles and the series itself is set in the past, although the exact decade for either adventure is hard to pin down. In *The Adventures of Vin Fiz* Lacey does not think the 1911 Wright *Flyer* looks anything like the airplanes that fly over their house, while telephones, tractors, packaging machines, steamships, steam locomotives and horseback U.S. Cavalry are still part of the American landscape. This suggests *The Adventures of Vin Fiz* is set during the thirties or forties, but in *The Adventures of Hotsy Totsy*, which takes place the following summer, the original *Hotsy Totsy* won its back-to-back Gold Cups in 1930 and 1931,[86] but Casey tells Lacey it happened long ago.[87] Televisions are never mentioned in *The Adventures of Vin Fiz* but are commonplace in *The Adventures of Hotsy Totsy*, and Alcatraz was not closed as a prison until March 21, 1963. These discrepancies make selecting a compatible date for *The Adventures of Vin Fiz* and *The Adventures of Hotsy Totsy* impossible, but what is important is that both adventures take place in the past. Just as important, *The Adventures of Vin Fiz* and *The Adventures of Hotsy Totsy* are the only Cussler adventures, with the possible exceptions of *Golden Buddha* and *Corsair*,[88] to feature the supernatural. By setting these stories in the past and injecting Sucop's secret of enchantment, Cussler gets away with things he would never be permitted in a modern children's adventure book. Not only would the naive wonder permeating these stories be dismissed as hokum, readers would be horrified to see children embark alone on such journeys.[89] (However, such expeditions are considered *de rigueur* for contemporaries of Dorothy Gale, Penrod Schofield and Encyclopedia Brown.) The inclusion of magic also makes it abundantly clear that Casey and Lacey do not live in the real world but a more forgiving one, where innocence and the incredible are excused, not dismissed.

The Isaac Bell Detective Series

The Adventures of Vin Fiz is Cussler's first solo novel not to feature Pitt as its hero, but *The Chase* (2007) is Cussler's first western, his first detective novel and, as of this writing, Isaac Bell of the Van Dorn Detective Agency is the only series adventure hero besides Pitt to be introduced in a novel exclusively written by Cussler. To date there have been six more adventures in the Isaac Bell Detective series, *The Wrecker* (2009), *The Spy* (2010), *The Race* (2011), *The Thief* (2012), *The Striker* (2013) and *The Bootlegger* (2014), and Cussler's collaborator on all of these sequels has been Justin Scott, the creator of realtor/private investigator Ben Abbott (*Hardscape, Frostline, Mausoleum*) and the author of a variety of other thrillers under his own name (*The Shipkiller, Rampage*) and as Paul Garrison (*The Ripple Effect, Robert Ludlum's The Janson Command*).

With the exception of a prologue and an epilogue that take place on April 15 and 16, 1950, respectively, *The Chase* takes place in 1906, approximately the same period as transitional western movies set during the waning days of America's expansion, such as *The Man Who Shot Liberty Valance* (1962), *Big Jake* (1971) and *The Shootist* (1976). This period also marks the final years of dominance for the dime novel, which had been as popular and influential with young Americans as television is today.[90] By 1915 pulps like *The Argosy* and *All-Story Magazine* were all the rage, but in 1906 this transition was still in its infancy, which makes Bell a contemporary of Old Sleuth,[91] Nick Carter,[92] Duckworth Drew and Gerry Sant,[93] larger-than-life dime novel detectives and intelligence agents whose sensational (and sometimes lurid) adventures promoted public interest in tales of detection and espionage. While early detective stories capitalized on public interest "in the ways that detectives worked,"[94] dime novel espionage adventures called attention to foreign threats against America, especially from Germany, a danger Bell thwarts in *The Spy* and *The Thief*.[95]

Bell's introduction in *The Chase* is from the point of view of another character, Colonel Henry Danzler, a veteran of the Spanish-American War, who served with distinction against the Moros in the Philippines and was selected by President Theodore Roosevelt to become the first director of the U.S. Criminal Investigation Department (CID). Along with a physical description, we are privy to Danzler's professional opinions about Bell, who in many ways resembles the Dirk Pitt from *Pacific Vortex*. Bell is well over six feet tall, weighs approximately 175 pounds and appears to be about 30 years old with eyes that look beyond the horizon for what lays beyond, an effect Danzler finds almost mesmerizing, as if Bell's eyes are searching deep into his thoughts. Unlike Pitt, Bell's eyes are blue with a hint of violet and he has blond hair and a mustache that covers his upper lip, but Danzler can sense Bell (like Pitt) prefers to deal with substance and has no patience for fools or phoniness. Bell does not exhibit Pitt's "two men" personality, but he is a man of contrasts. At first glance Bell appears to be a dandy. His hair is neatly trimmed, and he is as snappy a dresser as Pitt and Cabrillo. Bell's tags include an immaculate white linen suit and a low-crowned hat with a wide brim, but he also wears a pair of leather boots that are worn from many hours in stirrups, and he keeps a derringer tucked inside his hat that he can draw quicker than a man can blink.[96]

The name tag Isaac Bell has a distinguished ring to it, if you will pardon the pun. Isaac is a Biblical patriarch and his name means "he laughs," which might seem ironic considering Bell is all business and the least prone of Cussler's heroes to laugh or wisecrack or be humorous, but the name Isaac has ironic connotations. In the Book of Genesis, Isaac's father, Abraham, falls on his face with laughter when God informs him that he will be a father, and Abraham's wife, Sarah, laughs to herself when she overhears God telling her husband that she will bear a son in the spring. At the time, Abraham is 100 years old and Sarah is 90, but God commands the doubting Abraham to name the boy Isaac, and a few days after Sarah gives birth to their son she says, "God has made laughter for me; everyone who hears will laugh over me."[97] As for Bell's last name, a bell can be a musical instrument, a tocsin or used to mark the passage of time. Bell is not a musical person, but as a detective he stands as a symbol of warning for justice, and, as a historical figure living in 1906, he stands at the cusp between the end of American expansionism and the prosperous but increasingly perilous period that led up to President Woodrow Wilson's election in 1912.[98]

Bell is a hero in the Pitt archetype, as self-reliant, self-sacrificing, patriotic and as much of a realist as any southwestern folk hero. Bell is also intuitive and educated, attributes he demonstrates early in *The Chase*, first by some solid deductive reasoning about a sadistic bank robber[99] and then by being better informed about criminal psychology than his Van Dorn colleagues.[100] Bell never served in the military or worked as a government employee like Pitt, Austin, Cabrillo and Sam Fargo; however, like these heroes Bell inherited a strong work ethic from his family. Also like Pitt, Austin and Cabrillo, Bell did not go into the same business as his father but followed a different career path. (Cussler likewise inherited his family's strong work ethic and did not follow in his father's footsteps. Eric Cussler was a hardworking student while his son connived ways to escape doing household chores and earned average grades in school. On the other hand young Clive worked from sunup to sundown to raise money to buy and rebuild cars, and during his one year in college Cussler did apply himself and earned high grades.)[101] Like Pitt, Bell inherited a small fortune from his grandfather and comes from a prominent family, but where Pitt's father is a California senator, Bell's father is a wealthy Boston banker. (This is another example of Cussler's fiction somewhat imitating his life. As a young World War I veteran, Eric Cussler worked at a bank and wisely invested in the European stock market before earning a degree in accountancy at Heidelberg University,[102] commendable feats considering the harsh post-war economic conditions in Germany.) Bell is an honorable, genial gentleman, but he is dangerous if threatened. Bell's employer, Joseph Van Dorn, tells Danzler how Bell shot and killed three members of the Barton gang in Missouri before the remaining two surrendered. Bell, like Austin and Cabrillo, is no Peter Pan, but like Pitt he falls in love in his first adventure. We can never know for sure if Pitt would have married Summer Moran, but we do know Bell marries the woman he loves, even though the wedding does not occur until *The Thief*. Bell and his wife, the former Marion Morgan, a secretary turned motion picture director, do appear in the epilogue of *The Chase*, where we are informed that they have three sons. All in all, the detective Isaac Bell is a defender of the realm and knight-errant who puts his life on the line for his fellow man and for his country, a manhunter and merciless nemesis to his adversaries, and, in his journeys for the Van Dorn Detective Agency, he is unafraid to stray from the highroads traveled by most people. Rather than searching for secrets in places that have become lost to history, Bell searches for secrets to thwart plots against the innocent and bring his adversaries to justice.

Another of Bell's tags, a large gold watch with a heavy chain that he carries in his right vest pocket, demonstrates what makes him unique among Cussler's heroes. One of Pitt's most famous tags is his Doxa dive watch, so giving Bell a watch as a tag serves as a nice homage to Cussler's first and most popular hero, but it also links and defines these two heroes through time. Pitt's Doxa is a thoroughly modern watch, but (as mentioned in Chapter 2) Pitt also owns a pocket watch that belonged to his great-grandfather. Bell's pocket watch is new, while Pitt's is an heirloom, which is all a matter of perspective based upon time, but that difference is what makes Bell unique and defines the essence of both heroes. Bell is Cussler's only historical hero, whereas Pitt is a contemporary man born 80 years too late. Pitt works for NUMA in part because he is compelled to rediscover the past,[103] but Bell is a thoroughly modern man who embraces the latest marvels of science and technology. Where Pitt collects and restores antique automobiles, Bell's Locomobile race car is new, his motorcycle is the latest racing model and his Custom Super 8 convertible Packard, in the epilogue, is a 1950 model.[104]

Bell's vehicles are among the wealth of exact details that make the vanished world of his adventures "sharp, fresh, once more alive." Presenting a plethora of details is a trademark of dime novel adventures, but Sampson could be talking about Bell's adventures when he writes, "These casual descriptions catch the look and feel of the times and lend the story singular excitement for modern eyes."[105] In *The Chase*, a drunken miner (or, rather, a very dangerous man disguised as one) stumbles about with one suspender holding up torn and ragged pants; his boots are so scuffed and worn that they should have been discarded in a trash gully behind the town long ago. The inside of a bank vault is illuminated by an Edison brass lamp hanging from its steel ceiling. A simple wooden fence surrounds a mining town's cemetery, where most of the markers are carved with the names of children who died of typhoid or cholera. Elsewhere in the same town stands a house built using thousands of cast-off saloon beer bottles embedded in adobe mud, the "green glass casting the interior in an eerie sort of light."[106] Along a set of railroad tracks a brakeman moves from car to car, checking the grease in the axle boxes before the train departs for Tonopah and Sacramento. And majestic chandeliers hang from a high ceiling in the grand lobby of a railroad depot, where the floor is filled with rows of high-backed oak waiting benches. These (and many more) details bring the lost dime novel world of detective and espionage adventure back to life in Bell's adventures.

The Fargo Adventures

In contrast, Cussler's newest heroes, Sam and Remi Fargo, live in a world of treasure hunting adventure that recalls Poe's "The Gold Bug" (1843)[107] but is as modern as the Disney films *National Treasure* (2004) and *National Treasure: Book of Secrets* (2007).[108] Introduced in *Spartan Gold* (2009), the Fargos have so far appeared in *Lost Empire* (2010), *The Kingdom* (2011), *The Tombs* (2012) and *The Mayan Secrets* (2013). Cussler's collaborator on the first three Fargo adventures, Grant Blackwood, is the creator of the Briggs Tanner series (*The End of Enemies*, *The Wall of Night*) and he also collaborated with Tom Clancy on the Jack Ryan adventure *Dead or Alive* (2010). Starting with *The Tombs*, Cussler's collaborator is Thomas Perry, creator of the Edgar Award-winning Butcher's Boy series (*The Butcher's Boy*, *The Informant*) and the acclaimed Jane Whitefield series (*Vanishing Act*, *Poison Flower*), but in 2013 it was announced that Perry was leaving the series.

Sam Fargo, with his tattered Panama hat, is a hero in the Pitt archetype, while Remi, with her lustrous auburn hair, is cut from the same classic Hawks heroine template as Loren Smith. The name tag of Fargo recollects the Gateway to the West, Fargo, North Dakota,[109] and the Fargos possess the same zest for exploration and unflagging grit as any southwestern American folk hero or real-life American frontiersman. Sam and Remi are also self-reliant and self-sacrificing, attributes that are reflected in their strong, simple and unpretentious first names.[110]

Sam Fargo is a native Californian and a successful college athlete like Pitt, although Sam won his trophies in lacrosse and soccer, and whereas Pitt competed in boxing and fencing in college, Sam studies judo. Both heroes are also engineers. Pitt earned his master's in marine engineering at the Air Force Academy, where he graduated 12th in his class,[111] while Sam earned an engineering degree and graduated *cum laude* from Caltech. Sam worked for the government like Pitt, Austin and Cabrillo, but unlike these heroes Sam followed in his father's vocational footsteps, at least at first. Sam's late father, a Marine who saw action in the Pacific during World War II, was a lead engineer at the National Aeronautic and Space Administration (NASA) during its glory days in the sixties and seventies, and Sam worked for seven years at the Defense Advanced Research Projects Agency (DARPA). Like Pitt and Austin, Sam is a pilot and a scuba diver, learning the latter from his mother, Eunice, who is in her late sixties and runs a charter boat business in Key West that specializes in snorkeling and deep-sea fishing. Sam never served in the military or the CIA, but while working for DARPA he underwent covert operative training at the agency's Camp Perry facility and frequently interacted with the CIA's Clandestine Service, so he knows how field operatives think and act. Sam, like Remi, enjoys fine dining and is as much of a patriot as any Cussler hero. DARPA paid Sam far less than he could have earned working for a private company, but he could not resist the dual allure of pure creative engineering and serving his country.[112] Sam Fargo also displays the same combination of creativity and studiousness that are personified by Casey and Lacey Nicefolk.

The former Remi Longstreet graduated from Boston College with a master's in history and anthropology, with a focus on ancient trade routes. Remi is a New England native whose father, a retired private contractor, built custom homes along America's Eastern Seaboard and whose mother, a pediatrician, writes a series of bestselling books on child rearing. An excellent marksman, Remi is also a qualified scuba diver, and where Remi enjoys her husband's adventurous impulses, Sam loves Remi's courage and determination. Remi does not work in as male-oriented a society as Loren, but she is as likable, independent and averse to taking anyone's guff as the congresswoman, and while Loren thrives in Pitt's crazy and often dangerous world there are times when Remi is even more anxious than Sam to discover the secrets that may be found in lost places.

The Fargos' enthusiasm for history rivals, if not surpasses, Pitt's. Sam inherited his father's passion for World War II history and collecting rare books, whereas Remi's expertise is ancient history. The couple also approaches history from different perspectives. Remi is analytical, but, to Sam, history is a living thing about real people doing real things. "Remi dissected; Sam dreamed,"[113] but it is differences like this that balance the Fargos' marriage.[114] Sam is an intuitive right-brain thinker, and Remi is a logical left-brain thinker. Sam enjoys bird watching, and Remi tolerates it. Sam plays the piano by ear—another talent he picked up from his mother—and Remi plays the violin. It is their passion for music that led to the couple meeting at the Lighthouse jazz club and, to this day, they enjoy playing duets together. Sam and Remi also enjoy the good-natured debates these duets usually descend into over such topics as the best way to play a piece like Antonio Vivaldi's concerto *Summer*. Sam and Remi also debate things like who is the best actor to play James Bond, or what started the English Reformation. Sam might never have followed his dream to start his own business, the Fargo Group, if not for Remi's encouragement; however, it is Sam's argon laser scanner, an invention that detects and identifies mixed metals and alloys from a distance,[115] that led to the Fargo Group being purchased for enough money to finance the couple's lifestyle. (This is another case of Cussler's life imitating art. As mentioned in Chapter 1, Cussler and his partner, Leo Bestgen, sold their advertising business in part so Bestgen could concentrate on his dream of becoming an illustrator.)

If the Fargos' marriage sounds familiar it may be because their relationship is inspired by Nick and Nora Charles from Hammett's novel *The Thin Man* and MGM's classic *Thin Man* film series starring William Powell and Myrna Loy (1934–1947). Hammett's model for Nora, playwright Lillian Hellman (*The Children's Hour, The Autumn Garden*), once wrote that Nick and Nora have "maybe one of the few marriages in modern literature where the man and woman like each other and have a fine time together."[116] When Cussler was asked if the Fargos are his take on the Charleses, he confessed, "Yes, it is. I thought it was time for a husband and wife to entertain the readers with treasure stories."[117] This does not mean that the Fargos are Cussler's first happily married adventurers. Remember, Cussler recommended that Paul Trout and Gamay Morgan-Trout be "a husband and wife team or a couple who live together" because it offered "an opportunity to be original," particularly "if they have a little spark and warmth between them."[118] Isaac and Marion Bell have that spark and warmth. So do Dirk and Loren Pitt. Other examples can be found among Cussler's supporting cast, including Yaeger and his wife, Pitt's parents, Steiger and his wife (*Vixen 03*) and Oscar and Carolyn Lucas (*Deep Six*).[119] A troubled marriage among characters qualifying as good guys is unusual in Cussler's adventures, whereas dysfunctional relationships tend to be the norm among characters that are bad actors. Only two of Cussler's couples from the dark side seem to like each other and have a fine time together,

Lee and Maxine Rafferty, from *Vixen 03*, and Henry and Micki Moore, from *Inca Gold*. And while plenty of Cussler's good guys, like Giordino, Sandecker and Gunn, are single, these characters have healthy friendships and/or solid relationships with their natural or extended families. In contrast, Cussler's single villains tend to be isolated neurotics, or have lost a spouse (perhaps through foul play) or belong to some type of dysfunctional family. Another nod to *The Thin Man* is the admiration Sam and Remi reveal for each other in their banter.[120]

The Fargos are as honorable and as genial as any of Cussler's heroes, and if they are not as dangerous when threatened as Pitt or Austin or Cabrillo or Bell they are able to take care of themselves.[121] Neither Fargo is a manhunter[122] nor nemesis, nor are they defenders of the realm or knights-errant. What they are, again, are people who forsake the highroads to search for treasures and secrets lost to history. Because of this, Sam and Remi's adventures are peppered with fairy-tale elements.[123] One of the most famous fairylands is Neverland, and, as it turns out, the Fargos have a Peter and a Wendy working for them. Peter Jeffcoat and Wendy Corden are boyfriend and girlfriend who work as assistants to Selma Wondrash, head of the research team at the charitable Fargo Foundation. Enchanted forests, wild places that are possibly magical and frequently unknown or forbidden, likewise appear.[124] For Sam and Remi enchanted forests are places like swamp inlets, sea caves or secret tunnels under mountains that feel separated from the rest of the world.[125] Another popular fairy-tale element often found in the *Fargo Adventures* is riddles. This is explained in more detail in Chapter 7, but many fairy tales include riddles or a riddle contest between a hero and a character representing the hero's shadow side. Wild places that hide treasure and secrets can also contain death, and when they do, heroes cannot find one without facing the other. Sam and Remi's adventures are therefore filled with perils as well as cryptograms and riddle clues such as Napoleon's wine bottles in *Spartan Gold* and a confounding poem by Winston Lloyd Blaylock in *Lost Empire*. *Spartan Gold* and *Lost Empire* are also the only adventures outside of the Pitt series to include the fantastical element of Cussler making a cameo in the role of a helper.

The Fargos' adventures are fairy tales for adults. While Casey and Lacey Nicefolk live in a world set in an indefinable past where magic operates, Sam and Remi live in a more modern and realistic world but one where high adventure is possible and riddles and clues rediscovered from the past can guide the way to priceless historical artifacts and knowledge. The *Fargo Adventures* are also sophisticated bad-boy adventures akin to *King Solomon's Mines* (1885) and *The Lost World* (1912), so it should not be surprising that several references to Cussler's boyhood state of California (e.g., the Fargo Foundation is based in La Jolla; the Lighthouse jazz club is in Hermosa Beach; Sam is a native Californian and graduated from Caltech) run through the series alongside its fairy-tale elements.

4

Cussler's Characters, Part 3
Heroines/Other Women and Villains/Villainesses

> ... accepting the adulation of men, and having a splendid time adventuring through this naughty world.—Robert Sampson[1]

Cussler's non-regular supporting characters have as much to reveal about his writing as his heroes. Dozens of supporting characters have appeared in Cussler's adventures, however, so to prevent this chapter from becoming too unwieldy it will focus on Cussler's two most common types of supporting characters—heroines/other women and villains/villainesses—from the adventures he wrote alone. Since Cussler's collaborators assist with creating an adventure's story and write most of the manuscript, the only way to review characters that are uncorrupted by another person's influence is to concentrate on *Pacific Vortex* to *Trojan Odyssey* and *The Chase*. Supporting characters from the Casey and Lacey Nicefolk stories are not included because of their simplistic qualities necessitated by Cussler's traditional approach to young children's adventure.

Heroines and Other Women

When it comes to women, Pitt's behavior ranks somewhere between Bond and the postwar adventure heroes who preceded 007. Bond is promiscuous, while heroes like Drummond can no more think of a woman in that way then spit on the Union Jack.[2] By the time Cussler created Pitt, however, the sexual revolution was in high gear and a gulf existed between how heroes in literature and movies treated the opposite sex, (mostly like Bond) and how heroes on television treated women (mostly like Drummond). In matters of sex Pitt tends to lean towards Bond, otherwise he usually behaves like a gentleman around women.[3] Pitt is also not compelled to have sex in every adventure and does not even have his first love scene until *The Mediterranean Caper*.[4] Bond is notorious for having few problems getting the women he wants whenever he wants,[5] but Pitt is rarely as successful. This is because Cussler does not "subscribe to having lush-bosomed gals wait around for the bell to jump in the sack with my hero. In my books, the time and place is usually of the women's choosing."[6]

Much like the women in the pulp stories that influenced Cussler, his heroines occasionally get "severely endangered, as is the right of any woman appearing in an adventure series,"[7] however, Cussler's heroines are not larger than life and behave realistically when in peril.[8] Cussler also believes heroines should be characters other women can identify with, or would at least ask to be a guest in her house,[9] and subscribes to the theory that more women identify with the classy Audrey Hepburn than the bawdy Mae West.[10] Cussler often gives a heroine an imperfection for a tag, such as crow's feet, freckles or broadening hips that may make her self-conscious but no less attractive,[11] and he also tries to elevate women to a worthy status, like Kirsti Fyrie (who owns an industrial complex), Dana Seagram (a Ph.D.) and Loren (a congresswoman).

Cussler's first heroine, Summer Moran, is actually the first woman to capture Pitt's heart and she never completely relinquishes it. Summer is 25 years old and named after the season that represents a person's age from young adulthood to middle age, also known as the prime of life. Summer is the daughter of Delphi Moran,[12] a villain created in the tradition of Sax Rohmer's Emperor of Crime, Dr. Fu Manchu,[13] which suggests that she is Cussler's version of the Devil Doctor's daughter Fah Lo Suee, Lily Blossom. Both daughters are loyal but will upset her father's schemes by falling in love with an adversary. Fah Lo Suee and Summer are also rare beauties. Summer has no physical imperfections but she has plenty of other tags, including cascading red hair, eyes so gray they defy reality, a curvaceous body and a green Oriental sheath dress she wears in her first scene.[14] From head to toe Summer is a living fantasy and the paradigm of the Cussler heroine. Other heroines will have different hair or eye colors, they may not be as young or voluptuous and might not even wear green, but they all embody several (though never all) of the elements that make up Summer Moran. Summer is strong and has the gumption as well as the wherewithal to take care of herself. When Adrian Hunter and Summer decide to settle a disagreement by stepping outside the bar in the Royal Hawaiian Hotel, it is Summer who comes back with a shiner, a cut lip and victory. Summer is also a wounded woman, or what Fleming describes as "a bird with her wing down."[15] Summer loves Delphi as much as she loves Pitt, but she is self-sacrificing to both. Having promised never to leave her father's side, Summer tricks Pitt into leaving Kanoli without her, and after Summer gives birth to Dirk Jr. and Summer she raises the twins alone, rather than have Pitt see her crippled and deformed.

No woman ever measures up to Summer in Pitt's eyes,[16] but Maeve Fletcher in *Shock Wave* comes close. Maeve's name means "she who intoxicates,"[17] an apt description for how she affects Pitt. Maeve is the first person Pitt talks to about Summer after *Pacific Vortex*, and he tells her that Summer looked like her[18] even though Summer looks exotic[19] and Maeve is pretty in an outdoorsy way, a tomboy with tawny skin, yellow hair sometimes worn in pigtails, blue eyes, high cheekbones, a warm smile and a tiny gap in her front teeth. Maeve is also the mother of twins, but when it comes to choosing between Pitt and her father, Maeve has no problem picking Pitt. Maeve is as wounded by her family as Summer, but Maeve runs away to start a healthier life elsewhere. It is her father, Arthur Dorsett, who refuses to let Maeve escape.

Cussler claims he had every intention of bringing back Delphi Moran until Pitt took center stage in *The Mediterranean Caper*. When that happened, Moran was replaced with Bruno Von Til,[20] so logic dictates Teri Von Til replaced Summer, and Teri has two scenes that recall scenes Pitt has with Summer. In *Pacific Vortex* Pitt and Summer take a walk on a beach after they meet, and in *The Mediterranean Caper* Pitt meets Teri on a beach. In *Pacific Vortex* Pitt finds Summer sleeping in the nude in her bedchamber after he and Giordino sneak into Kanoli to rescue Adrian, and in *The Mediterranean Caper* Pitt and Giordino find Teri sleeping on a sofa wearing next to nothing.[21] Teri is not the same character as Summer, of course, nor is she as memorable, even though she is onstage more in *The Mediterranean Caper* than Summer is in *Pacific Vortex*. Teri is not as stunning as Summer, although she is beguiling, with classic Grecian features, black hair and a firm but graceful figure. It also does not matter that she is five years older than Summer, or has an imperfection (a round pockmark near her right temple), or that she is wounded (Teri claims to still be mourning a husband killed in an automobile race eight and a half years earlier), or that she turns out to be an undercover operative named Amy. If anything, being an operative is part of Teri's problem. When Teri finds herself in protective custody aboard the NUMA research vessel *First Attempt*, she is forced to play dumb (so she can drug a radio operator and contact her superior Inspector Zacynthus), but in the process she comes off as irritating. Unfortunately Amy's real identity is not revealed until the climax of *The Mediterranean Caper*, and she is not seen enough afterwards for her to demonstrate her real personality and create a better impression.

Kirsti Fyrie and Tidi Royal from *Iceberg*, Dana Seagram from *Raise the Titanic!* and Heidi Milligan from *Vixen 03* and *Night Probe!* are examined in Chapter 7, so Cussler's next heroines are Julie Mendoza from *Deep Six* and Jessie LeBaron from *Cyclops*. Mendoza's name is almost as bland as Loren's, a reflection of Julie's no-nonsense approach to life, while Jessie's name aptly combines the toughness and shiftiness of Jessie James with royalty. After keeping time with women approximately his own age, Pitt now finds himself romancing a pair of older ladies, although not much older. Mendoza is in her mid-forties, which is not much older than Loren, who is 37 in *Vixen 03*, while Jessie is 50 but looks 37. Both women are attractive, smart and strong. Mendoza is a senior biochemist with the Environmental Protection Agency and one of the best in her field, so she is selected by Sandecker to be the on-scene coordinator for a Regional Emergency Response Team sent to Alaska to find the source of a biological weapon called Nerve Agent S that could contaminate the Gulf of Alaska. As for Jessie, she is a former senior editor at *Prosperteer* business magazine and is entrusted by the president to discuss a treaty with Fidel Castro. Neither Mendoza nor Jessie makes a good first impression on Pitt, but, to be fair to Julie, she is racing against a 48-hour deadline before the Gulf of Alaska is quarantined. Pitt has no idea what is happening when he meets Mendoza so he misinterprets her blunt attitude, but after the source is tracked to a shipwreck called the *Pilottown* it does not take Mendoza long to win over Pitt and the Response Team with her leadership and skill.[22] Regrettably, Mendoza falls victim to Nerve Agent S before we learn much about her, but Jessie survives her adventure with Pitt and even administers the *coup de grâce* on one of Cussler's deadliest villains, Foss Gly. When it comes to physical imperfections, Jessie's body is firm but slightly heavy and she has had some plastic surgery around her eyes. Jessie's wound is living with the secret that her husband, Raymond, is a bigamist still married to his first wife, Hilda, the widow of LeBaron's late business partner, Hans Kronberg. Jessie is selfless enough, though, to regularly visit Hilda after LeBaron abandons his first wife in a nursing home.

Hala Kamil and Lily Sharp from *Treasure* do not have any imperfections, or at least none that are mentioned. Hala's name reflects her Egyptian heritage and "poised and sphinx-like"[23] character, while Lily's name reflects her American heritage and vibrant personality. Hala is a gourmet cook, an artist, the secretary-general of the United Nations and holds a Ph.D. in archaeology, while Lily is a professor of anthropology at the University of Colorado, who ends up directing the cataloguing of the rediscovered treasures of the Library of Alexandria. As for looks, Hala is a modern-day Nefertiti with a swan neck, tawny skin, silken jet-black hair and black eyes, while Lily has blue-green eyes and long, thick dark red hair. Lily's age is not specified, but Cussler never mentions that she looks younger than her years the way he does with Mendoza and Jessie, so it seems likely that Lily is in her late twenties or early thirties. Hala, on the other hand, is 42 and survives three separate attempts on her life. By Fate or coincidence (take your pick) Pitt is on hand to rescue her each time. As for wounds, Lily appears to be free of them, but Hala carries emotional scars from growing up a modern Muslim woman in Cairo. Hala often feels alone and distant with no real interest in relationships. Although she is tempted to fall in love with Pitt, she does not succumb; instead, she is determined to dedicate her life to serving the people of Egypt.[24] Five years later, in *Sahara*, Hala is still secretary-general but she has finally fallen in love, unfortunately with a Turkish triple-agent named Ismail Yerli.[25] The good news is that Hala is not only wise enough but proud enough to dismiss Yerli as soon as she realizes he is using her for his own criminal gains.

Treasure is the first Pitt adventure to spotlight two heroines. *Iceberg* has Tidi and Kirsti, and *Vixen 03* has Loren and Collins; however, Kirsti is as much villain as victim, and if Collins is not a villain then she is an accomplice. Hala and Lily are heroines, as are Loren and Stacy Fox in *Dragon*, although Stacy lives up to some of the less-than-noble vulpine connotations of her name,[26] and, like Teri Von Til, turns out to be a covert intelligence agent, in her case with the National Security Agency (NSA). A pretty blonde, Stacy is a photographer, judo expert and a former California beach girl with green eyes. Stacy's wound (one she shares with Pitt) is that she has some Peter Pan in her, which is most noticeable in her relationships. Stacy is twice divorced with a daughter who lives with her sister, and is so determined to have sex with Pitt that she seduces him while he is sleeping.

With the exception of a cameo in the final chapter of *Shock Wave*, Loren shares the spotlight with another heroine in every adventure she appears in after *Dragon* and prior to Dirk Cussler coming on board the series with *Black Wind*, but Eva Rojas and Julia Lee have Pitt to themselves in *Sahara* and *Flood Tide*. *Sahara* is Pitt's 11th adventure and, after this many stories, similar traits are cropping up among Cussler's heroines, such as Loren being a landscape painter, Hala an artist and Stacy a photographer. Eva, a member of an epidemiology team from the World Health Organization researching reports of strange diseases in western Africa, is a doctor (like Hala and Lily), has red hair (like Summer, Lily, Gamay Morgan-Trout and Remi [Longstreet] Fargo),[27] is 38 but looks 30 (again, Jessie is 50 but looks 37), and is pretty but not *Vogue* beautiful (like Stacy, who is not disturbingly attractive but is pretty)[28] with high cheekbones (like Loren, Maeve and Summer Moran).[29] Julia, a special undercover agent with the United States Immigration and Naturalization Service investigating Qin Shang's smuggling operation, is a gourmet cook (like Hala), and Eva and Julia meet Pitt when he saves their lives (like Maeve, Hala and Stacy). Eva does have the distinction of nearly becoming the one heroine Pitt kills (to save her from a fate worse than death at Fort Foureau),[30] and Julia is the only heroine (besides Pitt's great loves, Summer and Maeve) who makes no second appearance but is discussed by Pitt in a later adventure.[31] Neither Eva nor Julia have any imperfections or wounds that are mentioned.

Shannon Kelsey, of *Inca Gold*, is a doctor (most probably in archaeology) in her late thirties (with a stunning hourglass figure),[32] who meets Pitt when he and Giordino save her life. Shannon's wound, like Stacy's, appears to be her attitude when it comes to relationships, but instead of being a Peter Pan, Shannon possesses a cool and aloof self-sufficiency[33] (like Hala's poised and sphinx-like character). Shannon displays much less grace than Stacy when she meets Loren, even though she does not love Pitt.[34] There are no romances between Pitt and Patricia O'Connell in *Atlantis Found* or Kelly Egan in *Valhalla Rising*, either, even though both harbor feelings for Pitt and feel a little jealousy towards Loren; however, they never show it. Patricia is a 35-year-old doctor, a redhead, and a divorced mother. Kelly is not a doctor but does have a master's in business from Yale, which is impressive; we are never told her age, but she appears to be somewhere in her late twenties to early thirties. Kelly also has high cheekbones. Patricia and Kelly both meet Pitt when he saves their lives and Pitt rescues Kelly on two different occasions. Patricia does have the distinction of being the first love interest in the series for Giordino.

There is also no romance between Pitt and Loren's co-heroine in *Trojan Odyssey*, but there is no doubt that Pitt loves his daughter, Summer. As mentioned earlier, Summer Pitt looks as much like her mother as her brother looks like his father, so besides being beautiful Summer has gray eyes and red hair. Summer is not a doctor but has her master's degree and works for NUMA. Summer also shares living quarters with her brother in a Pullman car that is part of Pitt's trophy collection in his hangar home, the twins taking up half of the Pullman's four staterooms.

One more woman deserves some attention, even though she only appears briefly in a handful of the Pitt adventures. Zerri Pochinsky, Pitt's secretary, is introduced in *Vixen 03* and could be described as a slightly less erotic version of Sandecker's personal secretary, Tidi Royal. Both have unusual names and lively personalities, but where Tidi has an even more astounding hourglass figure than Shannon, Zerri is full-bodied.[35] Both have fawn-colored hair, and Tidi's hazel eyes and Zerri's brown eyes are close to the same color. Tidi is not shy about expressing romantic feelings towards Pitt, while in Zerri's earliest appearances she makes it subtly clear that she would not turn down the opportunity to have an affair with her boss. Tidi and Zeri's feelings regarding Pitt are not the only things that make them pre-PC secretaries. Both women can type like nobody's business, take shorthand and put her employer's needs ahead of her own, whether that entails fetching coffee or knowing when the boss needs a day off before he knows it himself. Tidi's lone appearance is in *Iceberg*, but after *Vixen 03* Zerri appears in *Night Probe!*, *Atlantis Found*, *Valhalla Rising* and *Trojan Odyssey*. In *Valhalla Rising* Zerri is married to a Washington lobbyist, and the couple has adopted five orphans. Zerri is also working four days a week at NUMA, an arrangement Pitt is happy to accommodate because of her masterful secretarial skills and her uncanny ability to be two steps ahead of him.[36]

Villains and Nasty Folks

Many fine villains appear in the Pitt series, but there are no archenemies like Bond's Ernst Stavro Blofeld[37] or anything comparable to Fleming's Blofeld Trilogy *Thunderball* (1961), *On Her Majesty's Secret Service* (1963) and *You Only Live Twice*.[38] If Pitt was ever going to have an archenemy his best shot was probably Summer's father, created to be a reoccurring villain, but according to Cussler Delphi Moran is "still lying under the sea off Hawaii."[39] There have also been no villains in the Pitt series or any Cussler adventure that have become a part of popular culture like Fleming's Blofeld, Auric Goldfinger, Doctor No or Red Grant.

A great hero does not need to be opposed by great villains so long as his adversaries make him suffer. "No adventure worthy of the name is enjoyed without suffering," writes Sampson. "If the hero is to stand forth immense, his challenges must be equally immense. All is magnified. His successes are bought in agony."[40] Pitt first became a bestselling hero because he raised the *Titanic* in spite of everything Man or Nature threw at him, not because he bested Captain Andre Prevlov, so if a villain is going to rise to the level of a Goldfinger or Grant he has to be more than just an opponent. A great villain must be a nemesis, or what Campbell calls a tyrant-monster:

> The figure of the tyrant-monster is known to the mythologies, folk traditions, legends, and even nightmares, of the world; and his characteristics are everywhere essentially the same. He is the hoarder of the general benefit. He is the monster avid for the greedy rights of "my and mine." The havoc wrought by him is described in mythology and fairy tale as being universal throughout his domain. This may be no more than his household, his own tortured psyche, or the lives that he blights with the touch of his friendship and assistance; or it may amount to the extent of his civilization. The inflated ego of the tyrant is a curse to himself and his world—no matter how his affairs may seem to prosper. Self-terrorized, fear-hunted, alert at every hand to meet and battle back the anticipated aggressions of his environment, which are primarily the reflections of the uncontrollable impulses to acquisition within himself, the giant of self-achieved independence is the world's messenger of disaster, even though, in his mind, he may entertain himself with humane intentions.[41]

This is the difference between villains like Jack Stapleton and Professor James Moriarty, Arabella March and Count Dracula, The Penguin and The Joker. Great villains have a grand tradition in adventure literature, and the greater the villain the more pervasive the havoc he brings or threatens to bring down on his domain. As much as great villains can elevate an adventure series, however, they are not necessary for its success. Jack Ryan never battled a memorable tyrant-monster, nor has Doc Savage, The Shadow or Tarzan, the three heroes that personify pulp adventure.[42] If a hero and his adventures are interesting enough then an adequate, if less than memorable, villain will suffice. In the film *Sherlock Holmes* (2009) the villain Lord Henry Blackwood (Mark Strong) is, in many ways, like Oskar Rondheim from *Iceberg* (see Chapter 7). A dangerous man pretending to be something he is not, Blackwood participates in an organization, the Temple of the Four Orders, which he plans to betray for his own acquisition of political power. Blackwood's Byzantine plan perplexes the hero, Holmes (Robert Downey, Jr.), for awhile, but the Great Detective figures out most of the scheme by the end of the second act, when Holmes is pursued by the law and apparently dabbles in necromancy. By the time Holmes corners Blackwood on top of a half-constructed London Bridge we discover the hero has been one step ahead of the villain for some time, and when the two square off Holmes subdues Blackwood as easily as Pitt defeats Rondheim in the *Pirates of the Caribbean* ride in Disneyland.[43]

Cussler's villains are generally on par with Blackwood: cunning, clever and wicked, but not memorable tyrant-monsters. This is not a slight against Cussler but a testament to any writer who has created a memorable hero and villain for the same adventure series.[44]

If Cussler has never created a memorable tyrant-monster it is not from lack of effort. There may be no better example of this then Arthur Dorsett, a villain in the Goldfinger tradition. Dorsett wants to artificially manipulate a mineral commodity to increase his wealth (in this case, gemstones) and it means nothing to him if millions of innocent people are killed in the attempt. Dorsett also believes it is essential to perpetuate his empire, so he sets out to abduct his grandsons and subdue Maeve. Dorsett errs, however, by overlooking one more thing Campbell writes about the tyrant-monster, and that is wherever this villain "sets his hand there is a cry (if not from the housetops, then—more miserably—within every heart): a cry for the redeeming hero, the carrier of the shining blade, whose blow, whose touch, whose existence will liberate the land."[45] Pitt is that hero, but Pitt cannot prevent Dorsett from destroying himself and his children, while the degree of havoc Dorsett attempts to bring down is so terrible that averting it results in the destruction of Dorsett's evil empire in a volcanic holocaust. In spite of all this, Dorsett has never captured the public's imagination like Goldfinger.

To assist with this review of Cussler's villains, we will borrow a list of villain types Sampson created for *Yesterday's Faces*, his omnibus overview of pulp series heroes. Sampson's list includes the Emperor of Crime, the Criminal Mastermind and the Grand Single.[46]

An Emperor of Crime is a super genius that plots on an international scale to sway governments and manipulate national destinies. This macrocosmic villain commands armies of criminals to accumulate power along with the wealth of whole nations,[47] and after quashing the schemes of the Wolfs and the Odyssey syndicate, Pitt is more than familiar with this villain type. The Capesterres from *Treasure*, Rondheim and Min Koryo might also qualify as Emperors of Crime. An international crime family, the Capesterres use media and political manipulation along with violence (including those three attempts on Hala's life) to try to put dictators in control of Mexico and Egypt. Rondheim uses hard-won skills learned on the New York docks to build Rondheim Industries, an international corporation with one of the world's largest private fleets and a chain of canneries, and Hermit Limited, a clandestine business cartel out to control the international financial markets. A major step towards Hermit Limited achieving its goal is the overthrow of several South American countries. Min Koryo, though, could not care less about ruling countries, although she does help the Soviet Union's plot to turn the president of the United States and several key U.S. government officials into brainwashed puppets of the USSR. Min's true passion, however, is revenge. She uses the assets of the tiny business she transformed into an international shipping corporation to punish America, the country responsible for the death of many of her family members during World War II. The Capesterres, Rondheim and Min do not rule an army of criminals, but they do command a large number of henchmen, and while none of these villains are geniuses, an Emperor of Crime must possess remarkable administrative abilities.[48] As their preliminary successes prior to Pitt's arrival attest, each of these three knows how to formulate an action plan and optimize resources.

So, too, do Delphi Moran and Bruno Von Til, but it is even harder to tell if either qualifies as Emperors of Crime, which is ironic for Moran (originally Delphi Ea)[49] as he was inspired by the paradigm of the Emperor of Crime, Fu Manchu.[50] There are commonalities shared by Fu Manchu and Moran, but they are few and primarily physical, even though Cussler claims Rohmer's character had no influence on Delphi's appearance.[51] Both villains are tall and have unusual eyes that can affect other men.[52] Just the shine of Fu Manchu's brilliant green eyes can stun, while Moran's gold eyes (possibly the result of contacts) can hypnotize most people. The crucial differences between Fu Manchu and Moran are their goals. Fu Manchu is a warlord dedicated to overwhelming the Western world through the combination of his intelligence and his private army, the Si Fan. Moran, however, is a pirate with a secret base in Kanoli, many men at his command and the vast resources of his international Pisces Corporation, but he has no grand desires. Moran seems satisfied with luring ships off course, killing the crew and selling the cargo and then the vessel. If Moran could not sell the *Starbuck* he would have never bothered to capture it. With his resources and intelligence there is the potential for better things, though, and who knows what Moran might have attempted if he had returned to plague Pitt? For this reason, categorizing Moran as an Emperor of Crime is not totally unjustified.

Bruno Von Til, on the other hand, never rises above the status of Criminal Mastermind. These villains are organizers and planners who play for big stakes and may have a vast organization at their command, but like Goldfinger in the film adaptation of Fleming's novel, their goal is the simple accumulation of wealth. Even when a Mastermind does have a vast organization, he or she often prefers working alone or maybe with one or two dacoits or a trusted assistant. Von Til and Moran share enough similarities (e.g., owning shipping lines, occupying subterranean caverns, a not-completely-loyal female descendant) that, in hindsight, it seems obvious the latter was created to replace the former, but Von Til never inherited Moran's potential to be an Emperor of Crime.

One of Von Til's henchmen, Captain Darius, is a minor character worthy of a closer look because he is a forerunner of one of Pitt's most frightening adversaries, Foss Gly, the only villain to appear in two Pitt adventures. Darius, like Captain Orl Cianan in *Pacific Vortex*, is a traitor among the good guys, a plot element Cussler borrows from MacLean.[53] Cianan and Darius are informers, but Cianan is never seen with Moran, his character is never developed and his murder (by Moran's men) takes place off scene. A hysterical Adrian has to tell Pitt about it. Things are a little better for Darius, even though his character is not developed much more than Cianan's, in spite of having more time onstage. Darius's death also takes place off scene, but it is an honor suicide, so it is appropriate that Darius dies alone. Darius is frighteningly big, like Gly, at least 260 pounds with the largest shoulders Pitt has seen, and has an attractive but brutal face, also like Gly.[54] Darius is indifferent to killing,[55] another trait the Greek shares with Gly, and Pitt and Giordino's fight with the almost-indestructible Darius during an interrogation scene foreshadows Pitt's vicious struggle with the monstrous Gly in interrogation room six of the Soviet's headquarters on the Cuban island of Cayo Santa Maria, in *Cyclops*.[56]

When it comes to villain types, Gly is a Grand Single or "The Meat and Potatoes of Crookdom."[57] Gly's background is unremarkable, at least what we know of it. Born in Flagstaff, Arizona, Gly was conceived during a drunken tryst between a professional wrestler and the daughter of the county sheriff. Gly's grandfather beat Gly and made the boy's childhood a nightmare, but these misfortunes made Gly strong and hard. One day Gly beat the sheriff to death, ran away and survived by rolling drunks in Denver, leading an auto theft ring in Los Angeles, and hijacking gasoline tankers in Texas. A brutal life story to be sure but, again, unremarkable, until Gly becomes an assassin. Cussler never explains where Gly learned such skills as disguise, scuba diving or building bombs, but it made him as formidable an assassin as Fleming's Donovan "Red" Grant, who shares many qualities with Gly. Grant was also conceived during a tryst, this one between a German professional weightlifter and a Southern Irish waitress who was paid half-a-crown for her services. Grant was never beaten as a child, but he inherited his father's strength and is a sociopath. Grant's reputation as a vicious boxer and wrestler led to work for the Sinn-Feiners, but eventually Grant defected to Russia, where he was trained by SMERSH and became their Chief Executioner.[58] While Grant is a more memorable villain (due, in part, to Robert Shaw's chilling portrayal in the 1963 film *From Russia With Love*), Gly appears to be the better man. When Grant has Bond at his mercy, 007 gets the upper hand and kills Grant,[59] but when Gly has Brian Shaw (who just might be James Bond) at his mercy in *Night Probe!* the only thing that rescues Shaw is Pitt's timely arrival, although Gly gets some revenge six months later when Pitt chances to cross his path.[60] As examined in Chapter 5, a thematic preoccupation with resurrections runs through Cussler's adventures, but *Cyclops* is one of the few occasions where a villain experiences a rebirth. Near the end of *Night Probe!* Gly apparently dies in a plane accident arranged by Canadian Prime Minister Charles Sarveux, but in *Cyclops* we learn that Gly survived this death trap and then (like Grant) went to work for the Soviets. We never find out how Gly survived, but somewhere during his resurrection he becomes an even greater monster than Grant.[61] Gly is an interrogator who waits for his victims like some ancient beast in a labyrinth, his lair a tiny boxlike room with a sickly stench at the heart of a maze of concrete corridors. Gly's resurrection also involves a physical transformation. Muscular in *Night Probe!*, in *Cyclops* he is grotesque with ponderous chest and shoulders and taunt skin with pronounced veins. In *Night Probe!* Gly has a nice head of light sandy hair[62] until he shaves it, along with every other hair on his body, to impersonate the narcissistic and traitorous Canadian Parliament member Henri Villon; Gly still seems to be carrying a bit of Villon with him in *Cyclops* as his head is completely shaven except for a Bismarck mustache. Gly only wears rubber boots and tropical shorts, most likely because bloodstains are hard to wash out of clothes, shoes and hair, but being nearly naked only adds to his bestial appearance. Befitting his degeneration, Gly smells like decayed meat. As bad as he is in *Night Probe!*, in *Cyclops* Gly is a murdering machine capable of inhuman feats, such as ripping a wall sink from its plumbing and heaving it across a room.[63]

Pieter De Vaal, minister of the South Africa Defense Forces, Democratic congressman Frederick Daggat, American expatriate Hiram Lusana and Emma the informer are the villains of *Vixen 03*. Janus-Villain elements of Lusana and Emma's characters are explored in Chapter 5 and all four villains are examined in Chapter 7, but it is worth noting that De Vaal and Daggat are Cussler's first corrupt politicians, one of his favorite villain types. Villon is also a corrupt politician, a member of the radical Free Quebec Society, who hires Gly to assassinate Sarveux. Another frequent villain type in Cussler's adventures is the corrupt businessman.[64] Raymond LeBaron from *Cyclops* is a pedestrian example of this villain type, a greedy, murdering bigamist who is cooperating with the Soviets. Lusana, however, is a gangster-turned-rebel leader with an eye on becoming South Africa's first black prime minister, which also makes him a borderline corrupt politician. Von Til and Rondheim are also corrupt businessmen, as is Min Koryo, who is also the first leader of a criminal clan in the Pitt series. Min and her grandson, Lee Tong, are the only surviving members of their family, but this merciless pair is as effective (destructive?) as any of Cussler's larger criminal clans. Min, like Gly, even lives like an ancient beast, except she is more dragon than Minotaur. Min's lair is high over the world, but instead of a mountaintop, she resides in a penthouse in one of the original World Trade Center towers.[65]

The Capesterre family from *Treasure* is the next criminal clan to appear, and, like Min, they are also corrupt businessmen and borderline Emperors of Crime, but their plot comes off as tepid when compared to the mechaniations of the appropriately named Wolf family, from *Atlantis Found*. Not satisfied with ruling a couple of countries, the Wolfs want to create a Fourth Reich that shall rule the world after they kill everyone who does not belong to their family. Where the Capesterres are estimated to be worth $12 billion, Karl Wolf, the leader of the Wolf family, is estimated to be worth over $100 billion alone. And whereas the Capesterres are a small tight-knit clan, the Wolfs' 200-plus members constitute a dynasty and fraternal elite, living mostly in the shadows away from publicity.

Almost as terrible as the Wolfs' plot is the one to change world history through a combination of new fuel cell technology and global warming by Epona Eliade's Odyssey syndicate in *Trojan Odyssey*. Odyssey's members are not related by blood, but they are stunning redheaded[66] misandrists who practice the religion of the Celtic Druids, making it the series' first villianous cult. Epona also borrows a page from Emma[67] to conceal her leadership position from the outside world, but whereas Emma hides her true identity behind several disguises, Epona only has Spectre, the Odyssey empire's nebulous, rotund and publicity-shy founder.[68] In contrast, Epona's name tag hides nothing about her identity or character, combining the Celtic deity Epona ("Great Mare") with the last name of religious historian Mircea Eliade, whose theories include *the eternal return*, a "belief, expressed (sometimes implicitly, but often explicitly) in religious behavior, in the ability to return to the mythical age, to become contemporary with the events described in one's myths."[69] Except for a couple of cameos as Spectre, Epona makes her first appearance during the third act of *Trojan Odyssey*, the latest introduction of a villain or villainess in the Pitt series, and Epona also has the series' most distinguished dénouement when she is exposed during a Congressional meeting.[70] In spite of her brief time onstage, Epona is such a formidable zealot that the thought of tangling with her again puts a knot in Pitt's stomach.[71]

A less ambitious criminal clan, the Zolars, are among the villains in *Inca Gold*. The children of Mansfield Zolar, better known as the infamous art thief The Specter,[72] Charles (a.k.a. Charles Oxley), Joseph, Marta and Samuel (a.k.a. Cyrus Sarason) Zolar deal in stolen art and artifacts. Unlike most of Cussler's post-*Iceberg* adventures, which feature a macrocosmic political or economic threat, *Inca Gold* features a microcosmic threat with a treasure hunt tossed in for fun.

In between the Odyssey syndicate and the Wolf family, Pitt battles the series' most dangerous corrupt businessman, Curtis Merlin Zale. Zale's name tag is similar to the tyrant-monster, corrupt businessman and would-be corrupt politician Charles Foster Kane from *Citizen Kane* (1941),[73] and although Zale is not as memorable as Kane he is a much more villainous. A sociopath on par with Gly, Epona and Karl Wolf, Zale has no use for disguises, likeminded associates or family, even though he sees to the needs of his mother and three sisters. The only thing Zale wants is power.[74] The head of the Cerberus Corporation, Zale is a corrupt businessman of the Criminal Mastermind class, but with thousands of fanatical employees, hundreds of crooked politicians and corporate executives on his payroll and a goal to replace the American government with a corporate state, Zale is one step away from becoming an Emperor of Crime. As one former employee tells Pitt, Zale's workers are indoctrinated like recruits in a cult with four-day workweeks, absurd perks, outrageous annual bonuses and nepotism when it comes time to replace retiring employees. Zale even has his own Si Fan called the Vipers, a covert dirty-jobs squad made up of former Special Forces-turned-mercenaries. The worst Viper is Ono Kanai, who replaces retired Major James Wong as the group's leader after Zale murders Wong. Like Epona, Zale's downfall takes place during a Congressional hearing, but Zale lacks Epona's indefatigable fortitude. Epona is confident enough to wait and fight another day, but in another similarity to Kane, after his public dénouement Zale goes home to die.[75]

Memorable villains are often an opposite or warped version of the hero.[76] For Bond his opposite is Red Grant, for The Batman it is The Joker and for Holmes it is Moriarty. As discussed in Chapter 5, Isaac Bell has an opposite in Jacob Cromwell, but the closest thing to an opposite Pitt encounters is Qin Shang.

Pitt and Qin Shang were born on the same day and year, but in the Chinese zodiac Qin Shang was born in the Year of the Rat whose motto is "I Rule,"[77] while in the West, Pitt was born under the sign of Cancer (the same as Cussler) with its affinity for water.[78] Qin Shang's name tag reflects this difference, both names referring to different Chinese dynasties. Both men have green eyes, black hair and are tall, or, in Qin Shang's case, he is tall for his race, at five-feet-eleven. But all similarities end there. Pitt is in excellent physical shape, injuries aside, and often has a genuinely warm smile on his lips; Qin Shang is chubby and broad around the waist, and only the cut of his mouth makes it appear that he has a perpetual grin on his feline face. Pitt is a humble Good Samaritan and realist; Qin Shang is an egomaniac with an insane level of optimism.[79] Pitt is a Westerner from a wealthy and politically connected family; Qin Shang is a Westernized Asian orphan whose criminal activities have his government's blessings and who uses his wealth to purchase international political influence, even with the White House.

All the ingredients for a memorable opposite are here, including Qin Shang's early presentiment that his and Pitt's paths shall cross,[80] but, unfortunately, Qin Shang never develops into more than a Chinese variation of *Dragon's* Criminal Mastermind Hideki Suma. Both are corrupt businessmen, Qin Shang a smuggler (among other things) and Suma a second-generation member of Japan's Black Sky underworld organization, and both have grand schemes to shift the world's balance of power in their nation's favor, which could qualify them as failed Emperors of Crime.[81] Both also have exceptional personal secretaries. Qin Shang has Su Zhong, and Suma has Toshie Kudo, an exotic beauty with an IQ bordering on 165.[82]

Pitt does not get an opposite in *Flood Tide*, but Sandecker does with President Dean Cooper Wallace. Sandecker is an ethics hero, a public servant dedicated to doing the right thing; Wallace is a power monger, a bureaucrat dedicated to advancing his career, and woe be to anyone that gets in his way.[83] Wallace is the first fictional president of the United States that Cussler refers to by name and not his title,[84] perhaps because Wallace does not deserve this sort of respect or maybe because corruption is more reprehensible when it cannot hide behind anonymity. Unlike Sandecker, a sexagenarian health fanatic who looks younger than his age[85] and dyes the gray in his red hair and Vandyke, Wallace is in his late fifties but looks 65 with prematurely gray hair, red veins on his face and beady eyes that make him look like a wino. Where Sandecker is unafraid to step on toes in Congress but prefers driving himself rather than being chauffeured in a limousine like most agency directors,[86] Wallace is a purely political animal[87] who accepts financial contributions from the notorious Qin Shang in exchange for favors. Even after Wallace finds out about the mass murder of illegal Chinese aliens at Qin Shang's Orion Lake campus, he reigns in INS and Coast Guard inspections of Qin Shang Maritime vessels entering the United States. Sandecker continues to pursue Qin Shang and bests his opposite when Wallace demands his resignation, warning the president that if Wallace fires him Sandecker will bury the White House in enough dirt to keep its advisors busy until the next election.[88] To give Wallace his due, the man knows when to pick his fights, and by the time Wallace butts heads again with Sandecker in *Fire Ice* he has learned not to make their relationship as openly adversarial.[89]

Corrupt businessmen and corrupt politicians appear more than any other type of villains in Cussler's adventures, but admirable businessmen and politicians also appear in many adventures. Capitalism and politics are not wicked in Cussler's adventures; it is the abuse of power by the corrupt because, in the tradition of the tyrant-monster, the corrupt not only destroy themselves but others, even innocents that the corrupt never meet. A Mongol herdsman named Tsengel gives one of the best explanations about this to Pitt and Giordino in *Treasure of Khan*. Bureaucrats have gradually commandeered so much of the grazing land Tsengel's family has used for generations in Chinese Inner Mongolia that he had no choice but to cut the size of his herd and cross the border into Mongolia to try to survive. Pitt commiserates that it is a crime to take a man's livelihood away from him, then asks Tsengle about some empty oil containers disguised as the *gers* (or tent homes) of a nomadic village he and Giordino stumbled across in the Gobi desert. Tsengel has seen many of these phony villages scattered along the Gobi's border, and while he does not know the reason for their existence he is convinced of one thing. Perhaps speaking for Cussler, he tells Pitt and Giordino, "It is simply the work of the powerful, who wish to exploit the wealth of the desert. Why do they disguise their efforts? Why else but to disguise their evil hearts."[90]

Recap

The last three chapters have explored some of the tags and other characteristics of Cussler's heroes and supporting characters by overlaying Dent's character blueprint over them. In the process we have gotten a glimpse of what makes Pitt, Austin, Cabrillo, the Nicefolk twins, Bell and the Forgos such successful proxies for adventure readers.

As discussed in Chapter 1, imaginative people enjoy picturing themselves participating in adventures, so a successful adventure hero must be identifiable to the reader. Like Conan Doyle's Great Detective, Cussler's globetrotting adventure heroes are, in the words of Sherlockian Edgar W. Smith, a "symbol ... of all that we are not, but ever would be. His figure is sufficiently remote to make our secret aspirations for transference seem unshameful, yet close enough to give them plausibility. We see him as the fine expression of our urge to trample evil and to set aright the wrongs with which the world is plagued."[91]

As we have seen, Cussler believes modern adventure readers prefer classy heroines, and as will be discussed in Chapter 5, he believes readers prefer shrewd, devil-may-care heroes, but only if these heroes and heroines are believable. Cussler may have read comic books as a boy[92] but his heroes do not possess powers and abilities far beyond those of mortal men. They are certainly more educated, more fit and more daring than the average person, but none of them are intellectual, physical and moral paragons like Doc Savage or Nick Carter.[93] Like many adventure heroes that came before and after them, Cussler's heroes exemplify the notion of *mens sana in corpore sano* or "strong mind in a healthy body." Sometimes even this may seem unrealistic because, also like many adventure heroes that came before and after them, Cussler's heroes are slightly stronger in mind or health, or both, than anyone else.

There is no better example of this in Cussler's adventures than Pitt and Giordino, men whose hearts and minds are ideally suited to one another and whose histories and skill sets are virtually identical. Pitt and Giordino have walked side by side in education and accomplishments through childhood, the air force, Vietnam and NUMA, but since Pitt is the hero he is somehow always a little more educated or accomplished than Giordino when things look their darkest. According to Sampson, a hero's companion is "frequently of almost equal competence. But not quite. Even [a hero's] opponents, dark geniuses that they were, could not match him, quite.

"A curious position, this having no equals."[94]

In all seriousness, Sampson knows there is nothing curious about it. Adventure readers relish unparalleled competence in the heroes they want to identify with, and the popularity of Sam and Remi Fargo, Isaac Bell, Casey and Lacy Nicefolk, Juan Cabrillo, Kurt Austin and, most of all, Dirk Pitt, is proof that Cussler knows how to give his readers what they want.

5

Women in Green
Cussler's Thematic Preoccupations

But the gray-eyed girl is almost always good.—Robert Sampson[1]

When it comes to fiction writing, Clive Cussler will tell you he is an entertainer[2] with no literary pretensions. But no writer can avoid weaving part of himself, or what interests him, into his stories. Stephen King, another bestselling author who claims to have no literary pretensions,[3] describes this process as having "filters on the floors of our minds" that catch some of our experiences as they pass through each day. All writers try "to make something of the stuff that didn't go through the filter and down the drain into the subconscious," and this stuff often appears as a writer's thematic preoccupations, or what King calls "obsessions."[4] Cussler is well known for obsessions like the sea and automobiles in his adventures, but there are others ranging from the trivial, like women wearing green (e.g., Summer Moran, Kirsti Fyrie, Bigalow's great-granddaughter Sandra Ross, Felicia Collins, Loren Smith, Dr. Julie Mendoza, Jessie LeBaron, several female employees in jumpsuits for the Odyssey organization and the girl who catches the 19-year-old Giordino's eye on Balboa Island), to full-blown thematic preoccupations such as:

- The Classic Hero Cycle of Adventure (See Chapter 7)
- Public Sector Employees, Both Good and Bad
- Janus Villains and Opposites
- Fairy Tale Motifs
- Gothic
- Science Fiction and Techno-Thrillers
- History
- Rebirths and Resurrections
- Differences Between Men and Women

Public Sector Employees, Both Good and Bad

"You can begin with your name, your title and function in the American bureaucracy."
"My name is Dirk Pitt. My title is *Mister* Dirk Pitt. My function is United States taxpayer, and you can go straight to hell."—Pitt to Robert Capesterre, *Treasure*[5]

When Cussler decided to create a hero who cut a different mold[6] he not only bucked a bias against adventure literature in publishing[7] but a bias against government employees. Negative presentations of public-sector employees were quite common during the sixties and the post–Vietnam and post–Watergate years of the seventies, but that did not deter Cussler from making Pitt the first adventure series hero who is a public administrator (a government employee unassociated with a political figure).[8] Starting with *Raise the Titanic!* Cussler also begins filling his adventures with politicians (elected government officials), their appointed officials (bureaucrats directly tied with an elected official who may be dismissed when that politician leaves office) and other public administrators.[9] A partial list includes: Senator George Pitt. Congresswoman Loren Smith. Congressman Frederick Daggat. Minister Pieter De Vaal. Dale Jarvis, National Security Agency director. Secretary of State Douglas Oates. Phil Sawyer, White House press secretary. Chiefs of Staff Harrison Moon, Dan Fawcett and Wilbur Hutton. Richard Essex, undersecretary of state. Harvey Shields, British deputy secretary of the Foreign Office. Prime Minister Charles Sarveux of Canada. Henri Villon, member of the Canadian Parliament and minister of internal affairs. Georgi Antonov, Soviet president. Fidel Castro, Cuban president. Senator Marcus Larimer. Congressman Alan Moran, speaker of the house. Dale Nichols, special assistant to the president. Julius Schiller, U.S. undersecretary for political affairs. Martin Brogan, CIA director. Senator Mike Diaz. Raymond Jordan, head of the National Security Service. Prime Minister Ueda Junshiro of Japan. Davis Gaskill, U.S. Customs Service special agent. Ferdinand Matos, Mexican National Affairs Department. George Simmons, assistant district director of the Immigration and Naturalization Service. Congressman Christopher Dunn. Sundry anonymous presidents of the United States, including Woodrow Wilson, Dwight D. Eisenhower, and the fictional Dean Cooper Wallace. Kurt Austin. Joe Zavala. Al Giordino. And, of course, Dirk Pitt.

Some might argue that Pitt is actually the first public-sector adventure series hero. Secret agents, police detectives and military personnel are government employees, and many series heroes held these positions before Pyramid published *The Mediterranean Caper*. The difference is that their job duties include going into harm's way to defend the law or the nation, but when Pitt goes into harm's way it is due to circumstances that arise from a NUMA operation he is working on, or he stumbles across on his own (e.g., *Vixen 03*, *Flood Tide*, *Crescent Dawn*). With the arguable exceptions of *Iceberg* and *Deep Six*, Pitt never goes into harm's way because of orders.

Some might also argue that a hero being a public administrator merits critical attention, but not Gallagher, who examines it in *Action Figures*,[10] and especially not Professors Argyle and Merwin, who spotlight Pitt's role as a bestselling bureaucrat hero in "Fuzzy Lines: Using the Best-Selling Novel to Illustrate the Blurring Boundaries of 'Public.'"[11] The thesis of Argyle and Merwin's article, first published in the public sector trade magazine *Public Voices*,[12] is the inherent risk of privatizing areas of the federal government, a trend that is potentially creating blurring (or fuzzy) lines between what should be the duties of the private and public sectors. Exasperating this situation are bestselling heroes like Pitt who "shape the popular image of the public sector—or they may reflect that image; either way, they tell us something of how the many in the general public view the public sector."[13] Argyle and Merwin claim that, unlike adventures by Cussler's bestselling predecessors, such as MacLean and Fleming, which involve the relationship between the public and private sectors, Cussler "produced a series of novels in which the central protagonist was a public administrator" and then another series, the

Oregon Files, wherein the protagonists work for a private firm "doing 'what the U.S. can't.'"[14] Juan Cabrillo and his corporation generally work outside the system, but even though heroes like Pitt and Austin choose to work within it they are capable of breaking a regulation or bending a law if the result satisfies their moral compass. Gallagher points out that "situational rejection of authority appears as a positive trait"[15] in Cussler's novels, and Argyle and Merwin are concerned that novels like Cussler's contain no warnings about the consequences of public administrators misbehaving or circumventing the system.

The fact is, a hero rejecting authority is nothing new. Selective obedience of the law is a familiar game in popular fiction,[16] dating back in Western society at least as far as Robin Hood and reinvented in the pulp magazines as bent heroes and justice figures. A bent hero is a reluctant criminal-turned-adventurer who bends the law for thrills and/or profit, while a justice figure voluntarily steps outside the law to correct injustices the legal authorities are unable to handle.[17] Among the first and finest examples of justice figures are the titular characters in Edgar Wallace's *The Four Just Men* (1905) who stop the "dreadful human ghouls fattening on the bodies and souls of the innocent and helpless; great magnates calling the law to their aid or pushing it aside as circumstances demanded."[18] The idea behind the Four Just Men lives on in Cabrillo's Corporation. The lives of the crew of the *Oregon* are filled with perpetual secrecy and danger while the consequences of their actions weigh on their minds. Unlike the Four Just Men, however, The Corporation does not always work outside the system as some of its missions are underwritten by government intelligence organizations, including the CIA (e.g., *Golden Buddha*, *Skeleton Coast*). And it does not appear that the popularity of bent heroes and justice figures like the Four Just Men and The Corporation is abating. New examples of such rebels arrive every year, not only in such suspense-adventure novels as Vince Flynn's *Term Limits* (2009) but in movies such as *The Expendables* (2010) and on such television programs as *Person of Interest* (2011–present).

Another article published in the same issue of *Public Voices* elaborates on Argyle and Merwin's concern. "Wonks and Warriors: Depictions of Government Professionals in Popular Films" by Beth A. Wielde and David Schultz [19] surveys 20 government-themed feature films to examine if the way popular culture presents bureaucrats affects public opinion and attitudes about public servants. "Fuzzy Lines" focuses on bestselling novels and "Warriors and Wonks" on movies, but Wielde and Schultz point out, "Popular film messages merge with other media and environmental factors to form a perceived reality for many,"[20] and cite novels that demonstrably affected public perceptions, including *Uncle Tom's Cabin* from 1852 (slavery) and *The Jungle* from 1906 (food processing). "Overall, pop culture, including movies, can affect how people think about the world."[21] To study this effect, Wielde and Schultz developed classifications to label different types of non-elected public servants[22] in films. These include action heroes, power mongers, bureaucratic criminals and ethics heroes.[23]

Pitt qualifies as an *action hero*, a public servant who "seemed to have superhuman qualities, where their service to the elected official or to the public went, physically, far beyond the call of duty."[24] Wilde and Schultz point to rebellious heroes Atticus Finch (Gregory Peck) from *To Kill a Mockingbird* (1962) and Bill Woodward (Robert Redford) and Carl Bernstein (Dustin Hoffman) from *All the President's Men* (1976) as inspirations, Police Chief Martin Brody (Roy Scheider) from *Jaws* (1975) as the prototype and U.S. Geological Survey staff member Harry Dalton (Pierce Brosnan) from *Dante's Peak* (1997) as a prime example for the action hero[25]:

> The action hero often not only casts aside the books and breaks procedure, but does so under physical danger.... Action heroes show a focused loyalty with the spark of fight that only comes with true belief in what they are doing, rather than any sense of career advancement. There is no self-interest more fundamental or understandable than self-preservation, and these fictitious public servants throw off this interest to serve a greater good.... They refuse to follow bureaucratic rules if it will mean breaching an ethic or putting lives at risk, but will fight to the death for the cause they believe in.[26]

This is a good description of Pitt, but, ironically, his bureaucratic duties have never even been specified. Except for a possible brief tenure as NUMA's surface security officer, Pitt has been the agency's special projects director, but Pitt just thinks of himself as a troubleshooter.[27] All we know for certain is that Sandecker did not hire Pitt because of any particular skill sets but because of Pitt's sometimes-annoying ability of delivering the goods, no matter the job.[28] Successful as Pitt has been, he would be the first to admit that he would not be alive, much less employed by NUMA, if he did not possess Wielde and Schultz's last requirement for an action hero, an "almost frightening amount of luck."[29]

Beginning with *Raise the Titanic!* conflicts between public-minded and self-interested government employees occur in several of Cussler's adventures. In fact, after the corrupt businessman, corrupt public servants like the power monger Moran and bureaucratic criminals like Daggat and Villon are Cussler's most common type of villains. *Power mongers* are concerned about serving themselves or exerting power, and will crush any colleague or underling if it will advance their careers.[30] Moran is already speaker of the house, but when an opportunity to step into the presidency arises he does not hesitate to try to capitalize on the opportunity. Moran's attempts to move into the White House eventually border on the illegal, which potentially elevates him to *bureaucratic criminal*, the "(more) evil twin of the power monger."[31] Committing felonies is no problem for a bureaucratic criminal such as Daggat, another politician with an eye on the Oval Office, which he demonstrates by trying to blackmail Loren, but Villon does Daggat one better by trying to assassinate Sarveux as part of a plot to have Quebec succeed from Canada so Villon can become the new nation's first president.

Cussler putting power mongers and bureaucratic criminals in his adventures suggests that he may not always have much faith in most people's ability to act beyond their own self-interest, a dark view of humanity shared by many of America's founding fathers, but the appearance of action heroes like Pitt, Giordino, Sandecker, Gunn, Austin and Zavala[32] as well as *ethics heroes* (public servants who are "more dedicated to doing what is right than in any personal gain")[33] like Loren, Senator Pitt and Yeager suggests that, like the founding fathers, Cussler also realizes that there are at least some people in the world who will act outside their own self-interests.[34] When Cussler was asked if Pitt is an example of the type of person who is necessary to counterbalance public administrators abusing their governmental powers, Cussler said, "I hope so."[35]

Janus Villains and Opposites

> Gly leaned over the stained washbasin toward the mirror and rearranged his face.—
> *Night Probe!*[36]

Janus has two faces.

The Roman god of beginnings and endings and of the rising and setting of the sun has one face that looks east and the other west, but, symbolically, one looks to the future and the other to the past. Janus is a god of opposites. This is reflected in terms that use his name, like Janus cloth, a worsted fabric with a different color on each side, and being Janus-faced, which can refer to someone's alternating moods, to contrasting characteristics or to the fact that someone is deceitful.[37]

Deceit is common among villains, as are aliases and shiftiness. Contrasting characteristics and alternating moods are also common in villains as well as heroes, but a Janus villain is a divided person—so divided that he may even become a different person or people. When Kristjan Fyrie changes sex he converts from a generous and industrious adventurer into a destructive temptress who, like the runaway heiress Sue Hambleton in Hammett's Continental Op detective story "Fly Paper," has a literal passion for the rough side of life.[38] Even if Fyrie was unaware of the destructive side of his personality it must always have been a part of him, a bad seed that lay dormant only to sprout roots during his physical change.[39]

A less drastic example is Emma, the informer, from *Vixen 03*. Emma is a trickster who changes forms (i.e., her appearance) to avoid predators.[40] Emma is a divided, if not mercurial, personality in that she never wears the same disguise twice, and her true sex is not even hinted at until after her death. Everyone assumes Emma is male, an error she encourages in conversations[41] and by always appearing as a man, but her greatest deceit is that she is an informer. Emma is in cahoots with the corrupt De Vaal, selling doctored Defense Ministry reports and splitting the take. Emma also helps De Vaal as the minister plays the South African government, Captain Patrick McKenzie Fawkes, native black revolutionaries and the United States government against each other. For all of this, though, Emma is a cipher. We hear a lot about Kristjan Fyrie from people like Sandecker and we get to know Kirsti so she becomes a three-dimensional Janus villain, but we know nothing for certain about Emma's background,[42] her motivations or her true appearance. This makes Emma two-dimensional, just as if we only saw The Scarlet Pimpernel but never Sir Percey Blakeney. There is no denying that Emma is a formidable opponent; her daring and skill make her a dangerous will-o-the-wisp, but she has no identifiable character.

This is not the case with Jacob Cromwell, the Butcher Bandit, from *The Chase*. Cussler's early adventures feature several Janus villains, but they fade into the background after *Treasure* as corrupt businessmen and corrupt clan corporations[43] come into ascendance. The Janus villain makes an impressive comeback with Cromwell, who gives Madame Min Koryo Bougainville a run for her money as Cussler's best corrupt businessman. Min and Cromwell are very different villains, however. Min is the leader of a corrupt clan corporation, while Cromwell is a trickster of the most monstrous kind. Min uses cold-blooded piracy and her grandson, Lee Tong, to build Bougainville Maritime Lines, Incorporated into a shipping empire that provides her with opportunities for vengeance, but Cromwell ostensibly robs and kills to raise the capital he needs to start the Cromwell National Bank of San Francisco, and then continues for the joy of the challenge. Cromwell's public face is that of a leader in the conventional button-down world of finances and a respected (and protected) member of high society, but his private face belongs to a homicidal sociopath. As divided as any of Cussler's Janus villains, Cromwell is convinced he is invincible, but still feels the need to wear lifts in his shoes. A handsome dandy and one of San Francisco's most eligible bachelors, his closest companion is his sister Margaret. Cromwell owns a mansion on Nob Hill[44] that resembles the White House, but feels most alive while traveling the rails to and from his latest crime in a posh apartment concealed in what appears to be a dilapidated boxcar. An expert with disguises, Cromwell has none of Emma's qualms about pretending to be a man or a woman. Even with these schisms Cromwell is cunning, intelligent and resourceful, with spies and thugs at his disposal. Cromwell is also "short and thin and carries himself with more feminine grace than masculine roughness,"[45] but, like Min (who cannot walk) and Fleming's Doctor No (who has no hands), Cromwell offsets any physical limitations he might have and puts the hero to the test, a "demonic character so hauntingly sinister"[46] that his end comes far too soon. Cromwell always seems to have the odds stacked in his favor, even after he is captured, and he possesses no mercy or conscience. When Bell is introduced to Cromwell, the banker's expression reminds Bell of the cold, dead gaze of a mountain lion.[47]

Almost 20 years before *The Chase*, Clement Massey (a.k.a. Dapper Doyle) heralded Cromwell's coming in *Night Probe!* A Janus villain who, in many ways, is a forerunner of Cromwell, Massey is the son of a wealthy Boston family, who graduated *summa cum laude* from Harvard and was twice elected to the Massachusetts senate. Massey is a short, thin dandy[48] and a respected (and protected) member of his community.[49] A Rhode Island lawyer with a thriving practice in Providence (as opposed to of a California banker), Massey plans all his crimes as meticulously as Cromwell and also has a team of criminals at his disposal. But Massey rarely participates in a robbery himself and, even though history remembers him as a mass murderer, he is no homicidal maniac. Massey never killed anyone on purpose, but he causes the deaths of more people than the merciless Cromwell. Legend has it that Dapper Doyle and the Butcher Bandit escaped and disappeared, but, in reality, both suffered horrible deaths as a result of their crimes. Like Cromwell, Massey's motivation is the joy of the challenge; however, Massey donates all of his ill-gotten gains to charity. Professor Preston Barton, an expert on unsolved crimes, could also be talking about Cromwell when he describes Massey as a "closet bandit" who robbed "for the hell of it" and, in the best Janus villain tradition, lived "a double life."[50]

More than a few other characters in *Night Probe!* lead double lives or affect some sort of characteristic to hide their true personalities. Just like Massey, Villon is a respected member of high society, but in private he is the leader of the radical Free Québec Society; he is also having an affair with the prime minister's wife, Danielle. As for Danielle, she is a political creature who calculates every move she makes in public and whose beauty and personality overpowers men and makes women envious. But Danielle aches to be dominated by Villon and cries like a schoolgirl when she is fooled into thinking he has rejected her. Meanwhile, Danielle's husband appears to be powerless to prevent Quebec from seceding from Canada, but it turns out that Sarveux has always planned on running for president of Quebec. Sarveux has also been covertly working with the president of the United States (who affects his own lack of involvement) to unite their nations into the United States of North America, and when Sarveux finds out about Danielle and Villon's affair he orchestrates their disappearance.

Falling somewhere between Massey and Cromwell on the vileness scale is Hiram Lusana. Born Hiram Jones in the United States, Lusana made most of his fortune as an international drug smuggler before reforming, changing his name and moving to South Africa, where he founded and finances the African Army of Revolution (AAR) in a clean war against the Apartheid government. Many South Africans look upon Lusana as a Moses figure, but it is hard to fight any war cleanly. Hiram Jones fought and stole to make something of himself and to rise above his ghetto surroundings, and his ultimate goal is to become South Africa's next prime minister.

Oskar Rondheim also grew up in America, where he was arrested a number of times while making a name for himself along the New York waterfront. Born Carzo Butera and raised in Brooklyn, he is tough enough and smart enough to help form the fisherman's union before organized crime muscles him out. Butera dropped out of sight after that, living under a variety of aliases before re-creating himself as the founder of Rondheim Industries, headquartered in Reykjavik. Like Lusana, Rondheim also finds old habits hard to break. Rondheim's Janus villain division comes in two forms. First is his encyclopedic knowledge of poetry, an uncharacteristic expertise for a thug. The second (and more dramatic) is his hatred for homosexuals. During the early seventies, when *Iceberg* was published, the study of poetry was not considered masculine[51] and the stereotype for homosexuals was that they were pansies or sissies.[52] Making Rondheim a poetry expert suggests that this macho bad guy could be a little light in the loafers (to borrow a popular phrase of the time), however no other characters in *Iceberg* suggests such a thing. As for Rondheim, he is not at all ashamed of his command of poetry.[53] Mastery of any form of literature, whether it is Shakespeare's plays or the works of William Faulkner, demonstrates intelligence, and Rondheim is not stupid. That said, Rondheim's behavior towards Pitt and Kirsti demonstrates that he is violently divided about his masculinity. Rondheim and Kirsti are engaged to be married, a union that will create a cartel with the financial clout to control every government in the North Atlantic. And while it is never made clear if the two have even considered consummating their relationship Rondheim and Kirsti appear to be attracted to each other. Even though Kirsti is literally a physical fantasy of female perfection, Rondheim seems to resent that attraction. All of this becomes obvious during a brutal scene, in which Rondheim nearly beats Pitt to death until Kirsti interferes. Pitt has been acting flagrantly gay to get Rondheim to underestimate him, and Rondheim calls Pitt a "slimy faggot," "a spineless homosexual" and a "queer bastard" during the beating. When Kirsti steps in, Rondheim retaliates by calling her a "warped whore."[54]

Along with Janus villains like these, Cussler often uses opposites in his stories. Some of these opposites are no more than the pairing of two characters that have different physical attributes, like Mutt and Jeff, which makes it easy for readers to identify them.[55] Examples include Drs. Elmer Chrysler and Raymond York (*Pacific Vortex*), Lieutenant Commander Lee Koski and Lieutenant Amos Dover of the Coast Guard's supercutter *Catawaba* (*Iceberg*), Lieutenant George Uphill of the *Thomas J. Morse* and Lieutenant Commander Scotty Butera of the *Samuel R. Wallace* (*Raise the Titanic!*), Harvey Dolan and Phil Devine (*Vixen 03*), Ansel and Annie Magee (*Night Probe!*), Dr. Calvin Rooney and Sheriff Tyler Swear (*Cyclops*), Ralph Wilbanks and Wes Hall of the *Divercity* (*Flood Tide*) and Arthur Curtis and Glenn Irvine (*The Chase*). Not to be overlooked, of course, are Pitt and Giordino and, by extension, Austin and Zavala.

Other opposites in Cussler's stories not only look different but have distinctly different personalities, like Gene Seagram and Mel Donner from Meta Section, inventors of the Sicilian Project. Whereas the egotistical Seagram loses his wife and sanity before the project is completed, the humbler Donner sees it through to the end and even picks up a wife along the way.

Heroes and villains can also be opposites, like James West and Dr. Miguelito Loveless from *The Wild, Wild West* (1965–1969), Steve McGarrett and Wo Fat from the original *Hawaii Five-O* (1968–1980) and Isaac Bell and Cromwell. In contrast to Cromwell, Bell is tall and masculine, with thick hair and a mustache. Bell dresses elegantly but is no dandy, and while Cromwell is a self-made banker who gets his thrills robbing and killing, Bell comes from a wealthy East Coast banking family but prefers working as a detective. Both also have different types of unhealthy affections for Cromwell's sister. Considering how exciting the battle of wits between Cromwell and Bell is, it is unfortunate that *The Chase* is the only time Cussler gives one of his heroes an opposite. As mentioned in Chapter 4, it appears for awhile in *Flood Tide* that Pitt may get one in Qin Shang, but Shang never pushes Pitt the way Cromwell pushes Bell. There are times in *The Chase* when it seems that Cromwell is as invincible as he imagines and that Bell will never catch him, but there is never a moment in *Flood Tide* that Shang's defeat at Pitt's hands is honestly in doubt.

Another type of opposite that haunts many of Cussler's stories is the double. This variation of the Gothic element of repetitions[56] is common in many genres, such as the detective story beginning with Wilkie Collins's *The Woman in White* (1860), wherein there is a doubling of Anne Catherick and Laura Fairlie, women whose uncanny physical resemblance permits their identities to be switched.[57] In *Pacific Vortex* Pitt and Capt. Orl Cinana look enough alike to be cousins, and in *Vixen 03* Giordino and Steiger could pass for brothers in spite of their different heritages. In *The Mediterranean Caper* Admiral Heibert looks enough like the real Bruno Von Til that all he needs is a little plastic surgery and some walking and speech retraining to take Von Til's place, while Amy naturally looks enough like Teri Von Til to pass for her. In *Deep Six* Jack Sutton, an actor who looks enough like the president to appear in commercials as the Chief Executive, is enlisted to appear in public (at a distance) after the president is kidnapped.[58] Cussler does this one better in *Night Probe!* wherein Foss Gly looks so much like Villon that he manages to fool both Villon's lover and wife, and then goes a step further in *Deep Six*, in which Arta Casilighio is a virtual doppelgänger. Arta never meets a woman named Estelle Wallace but pretends to be her after finding Wallace's passport on a bus and noticing the physical similarities. Arta is like the hypocritical Henry Jekyll, who finds a release for his repressed inhibitions through the draft he concocts that transforms his body into the form Jekyll names Edward Hyde. Jekyll and Arta do transform into someone else, one physically and one by identity theft, but inside they remain the same person.[59] In *Vixen 03* Daggat and Lusana do not look alike but are linked by their pasts and their goals. As Daggat tells Lusana, they both came from the same gutter and did not get to where they are without acquiring some smarts along the way.[60] Both men will do anything to get what they want; they even share the same woman, Collins, who also grew up poor and did what she had to to make something of herself. Lusana basically sells Collins to Daggat like someone would a slave, uniting the three in an unholy bargain. But, in the end, Lusana sacrifices his selfish goal for something greater, while Daggat (with his "trophy," Collins) is nearly destroyed by his need for power.

Fairy Tale Motifs

> Pitt to the rescue. I always was a pushover for congresswomen in distress.—Dirk Pitt[61]

Prince Charming, spells, magic mirrors and enchanted forests might not sound like the sort of things you would find in Cussler's adventures, but adventure novels often overlap or blend with other genres,[62] including the fantasy subgenre of fairy tale.[63] A popular type of fairy tale is one in which a Prince Charming hero rescues a girl "from a life of sexual deprivation and then liberates her to pursue her own inclinations."[64] The most famous Prince Charming fairy tale may be "Cinderella" from 17th century France,[65] but it can still be found in modern adventures like Fleming's Bond novels.[66] Bond almost always finds a good and beautiful girl rendered frigid by adolescent trials and conditioned to serve the villain. While Bond does not always behave like a Prince Charming, he does introduce the girl to an appreciation of human nature before possessing her, but except for Contessa Teresa "Tracy" Di Vicenzo in *On Her Majesty's Secret Service* Bond always liberates any girl he rescues.[67] The Prince Charming fairy tale also appears in many Pitt adventures, beginning with *Pacific Vortex*, wherein Pitt fails to help Summer Moran escape her wicked father. In *The Mediterranean Caper* Teri Von Til tells Pitt she has not had sex since her husband was killed in a racing accident eight and half years earlier. Pitt rescues Teri by slapping her to snap her out of her grieving and making love to her on a beach. In *Night Probe!* Heidi Milligan has grown mostly indifferent to sexual attention. She is mourning the recent death of her lover, and, prior to that affair, Heidi survived an abusive 11-year marriage, but Pitt liberates Heidi from these traumas during a night of passion, during which she is metaphorically and sexually reborn.[68] Variations of the Prince Charming fairy tale also appear in *Cyclops*, *Deep Six*, *Iceberg* and *Raise the Titanic!*, although in Pitt's most famous adventure his recovery of the *Titanic* blends the Prince Charming fairy tale with the Lady in the House of Sleep motif found in myth and legends as well as fairy tales like "Sleeping Beauty."[69]

In *Hero with a Thousand Faces* Campbell describes the Lady in the House of Sleep as "the paragon of all paragons of beauty, the reply to all desire, the bliss-bestowing goal of every hero's earthly and unearthly quest."[70] When Sandecker is told that a coronet recovered by the crew of the NUMA submersible *Sappho I*[71] belonged to Graham Farley, a musician aboard the White Star liner when it sank, the admiral speaks the name *Titanic* "like a man savoring a beautiful woman's name." Later while talking with Dr. Murray Silverstein, the oceanographer leading the team that deduces the search grid for the *Titanic*, Sandecker comments on the ship's allure. "Once *her spell* strikes, you can think of nothing else (my emphasis)."[72] Even Pitt is not immune, although he tries to pretend otherwise. Pitt is told he is selected to lead the salvage operation in part because he is a *Titanic* expert, but Pitt dismisses the compliment and in the process comes off sounding like an overaged *Star Wars* fan rationalizing his action figure collection.[73] Later, after Farley's coronet is restored, Pitt mentions the last song heard coming from the sinking *Titanic* was "Autumn," not "Nearer My God to Thee" as legend has it. Another character points out that Pitt must have studied the *Titanic*, to which Pitt compares his interest to a contagious disease or a fever that is hard to break.[74]

The most potent comparison of the *Titanic* with the Lady in the House of Sleep takes place in "Regenesis," an interlude[75] inserted between chapters 36 and 37, showcasing the discovery of the *Titanic* by Pitt, Giordino and Gunn.[76] In the Grimm fairy tale "Sleeping Beauty," a witch puts Princess Briar-rose to sleep for one hundred years. A sympathetic fairy eager to make sure everything in Briar-rose's palace will be the same when the princess awakes casts her own spell that puts everyone to sleep, then conjures a "thicket of bushes prickly with thorns and briars and walled by a matting of thickly entwined vines and twists" to protect the castle's occupants. There Briar-rose remains "for nearly a hundred years" until "a young Prince in a neighboring country" intrigued by the "mysterious stories" about the "enchanted castle" investigates. The Prince makes his way to the castle and through the "forest of tangled trees and briars" into the deathly quiet palace where he finds Briar-rose, the "loveliest, most exquisitely beautiful girl" he had ever seen, "deep in sleep."[77] In "Regenesis" the *Titanic* has been lost beneath the Atlantic for three-quarters of a century. Pitt, Giordino and Gunn locate the *Titanic* after making their way across the ocean and far below its surface to a "black, bitter-cold environment" inhabited by bizarre creatures, including vampire squid and sea spiders. When they find *Titanic*, Cussler invokes images of a sleeping maiden as he describes the ship as "*cloaked in the eerie stillness of the black deep*" with her forecastle still "set on a southerly course, *as if she were still pathetically struggling to reach out to touch the waters of a port she had never known* (my emphases)." There is "a morbid beauty" about the ship, and all things considered, the *Titanic* is, like the enchanted Briar-rose, in remarkably good condition in spite of the passing years.[78] Another similarity between Briar-rose and the *Titanic* in their House of Sleep are their fellow inhabitants. When the Prince enters the enchanted castle he "saw within it what looked like waxen images of a great celebration in progress. There—motionless yet with the flush of life on their faces—were great numbers of knights and ladies, nobles all, as well as courtiers, servants, flower girls, and all manner of royal guests."[79] In contrast to this, as the lights of the NUMA submersible *Sea Slug* "danced over" the *Titanic*'s "ghostlike superstructure, casting long spectral shadows," Pitt, Giordino and Gunn "could almost see" the passengers and crew as they were on the day the ship sank.[80] Unlike the Prince, however, Pitt cannot resurrect his sleeping beauty with a simple kiss, so when the *Sea Slug* has to surface, Cussler describes the *Titanic* as being "alone once more." But, like a bride anticipating her wedding night, she "would feel the tools of man working on her steel skin" and then "perhaps, just perhaps, she would make her first port after all."[81]

Two more fairy-tale motifs prominently featured in *Raise the Titanic!* are curses and magic mirrors.

Gene Seagram's wife, Dana, a marine archaeologist with NUMA, is introduced in a lunch scene with Seagram, and it does not take long to realize their marriage is in trouble. Dana begs Seagram to return to their old academic life away from the Beltway, but Seagram, a Midwestern college professor struggling to prove his worth after working on a series of failures for the White House's top-secret Meta Section, is cursed by hubris. When he refuses, Dana makes a prophetic prediction that whatever he is working on is going to cost him a terrible price.[82]

Dana's next scene is her first with a magic mirror. In fairy tales, myths and legends, magic mirrors often reveal the inner person, even as they reflect that person's appearance.[83] The wicked Stepmother in "Snow White" reveals her vanity and insecurity when she instructs her mirror to reveal the fairest in her realm; she is only satisfied, of course, if the mirror pronounces her the winner. A similar thing happens in the Turkish fairy tale "The Snake Peri and the Magic Mirror" wherein a selfless young woodsman is given a piece of broken mirror after saving a snake's life, only to discover that a genie is living in the shard. The woodsman's kindly character is revealed when he uses the genie for good purposes, and an old woman who steals the mirror reveals her greedy nature by using the genie for her own benefit.[84] In *Raise the Titanic!* Dana's true nature begins to be revealed when she looks in her dressing-table mirror as she is getting ready for a White House dinner party and gripes about getting crow's feet at age thirty-one. When Seagram suggests they take their marriage to the next level and have a baby, Dana slaps the table and knocks over "a regiment of evenly spaced bottles of artificial beauty,"[85] her first defense in the battle against time. Undaunted, Seagram stares into Dana's mirror image and reveals the hidden motivation behind her outburst: Dana is a beautiful girl who suffered adolescent trials, but she is also afraid of a family curse. Dana's mother was a floozy, and her father was an alcoholic who abandoned his family when Dana was ten; another lost soul, her brother is serving a life sentence in prison. Dana, on the other hand, has made something of her life, but she lives in fear that her family's curse may one day catch up with her.[86] Later in this same scene, Dana stands in front of a full-length closet mirror critically studying herself in a white designer dress that reveals a good deal of cleavage. In Western cultures the color white can represent purity or virginity, and as it turns out Dana is a virgin to Washington high society. If this is not Dana's first White House dinner then it is one of her first, and she is so eager to partake of the aphrodisiac of political power that she wears a fur stole in the middle of summer, sacrificing personal comfort in hopes of making a good impression.[87]

Dana confronts another magic mirror at the White House dinner party; this one is not a looking-glass, however, but a person. The president's consort, Ashley Fleming, the most elegant and sophisticated divorcée in Washington, is wearing the same white dress as Dana. Dana tells Seagram that Fleming "is nothing but a glorified hooker,"[88] a snipe that turns out to be tragically ironic as Dana will gradually succumb to her family's curse and supplant Fleming as the Beltway's most elegant and sophisticated divorcée,[89] not only becoming a glorified hooker like Fleming but a more respectable version of her floozy mother.

A few days later Dana accepts a private invitation to the White House, and on this visit she wears a virginal white dress over black lingerie. Because of a proposition the president whispered in her ear during the dinner party Dana expects to be seduced, but the president only wants to ask her to support Seagram while her husband completes his project. A disappointed Dana leaves Seagram soon after and moves in with another NUMA employee, Marie Sheldon. Dana tells Marie she plans to platonically date other men, but inside she feels terribly conflicted. And while there are no magic mirrors around, Cussler reveals Dana's conflict by starting this scene with the following description: "*Dana Seagram stood* in front of her closet going through the feminine ritual of deciding what to wear."[90] Salvation of a sort arrives when news of the *Titanic* salvage is leaked and Sandecker assigns Dana to be the operation's spokesperson. Dana is a natural, relishing the spotlight as she duels with journalists, and Cussler reveals Dana's change in attitude with the first sentence of her initial press conference scene: "*Dana Seagram stood confidently* at the lectern and deftly fielded the questions put to her."[91] These two life-changing moments for Dana are later linked to her last appearance in *Raise the Titanic!* Anxious to capitalize on any fame and potential fortune her part in the *Titanic* recovery might generate, Dana justifies leaving Seagram by convincing herself he married her out of pity and behaved more like a father than a lover to her. Since Dana's real-father abandoned her it is only fair that Dana abandons her second father. But if Dana were being honest she would admit that she has succumbed to her family's curse, a fate Cussler announces in this scene's first sentence: "Pensive and dreamy-eyed, *Dana stood* in front of a full-length mirror and scrutinized herself (my emphases)."[92] (Notice Seagram no longer appears after her first name.) During each of these life-changing scenes some type of magic mirror or mirror sentence reveals Dana's inner person while exposing her egocentricity and self-delusion, or what Dana refers to as the albatross around her neck.[93] Whenever Dana looks in a mirror she sees only what she wants to see, and like Jekyll inspecting himself after his first reconfiguration as Hyde and seeing only wonder where others see "deformity and decay,"[94] by the end of *Raise the Titanic!* Dana is no longer fixating on her crow's feet but sees a "lithe and perfect" body and none of the "mythical hardened look of a fallen woman."[95] Like Snow White's wicked Stepmother, Dana feels content because (she thinks) her reflection reveals that she is the fairest in the land.

Gene Seagram has his magic mirror moments, too. Battling depression and his curse of hubris, he is teetering on the edge of madness after Dana leaves him and it appears that the Sicilian Project will fail. Sitting alone in a park and contemplating suicide, Seagram "envisioned the past few months as reflected in *the cracked and distorted mirror* of acute despair (my emphasis)." This sentence comes to mind again after the *Titanic* arrives in New York and a rare mineral called byzanium, needed to power the Sicilian Project, appears within reach. Seagram now is a shell of a man, and Pitt tries to snap him out of his depression by forcing him to look into a mirror to see that he is destroying himself. Instead, Seagram experiences the novel's most intense magic-mirror moment as his face appears to transform into that of Joshua Hays Brewster, a miner and engineer who also coveted the byzanium at the cost of everything in his life, including his sanity. (This scene is detailed in the "Gothic" subsection.)

An even more potent magic-mirror scene occurs in the prologue for *Deep Six*. Arta Casilighio, a bank teller at the Federal Reserve Bank in Los Angeles, finds a lost passport one evening that belongs to Estelle Wallace, a stranger who bears a striking resemblance to Arta. The passport exudes an inexplicable allure and soon Arta is making herself up to look like Estelle. Not long after that, Arta begins scheming to steal money from the bank so she can start a new life in another country. On the morning of the robbery Arta stands in front of a full-length mirror and repeats to herself that Arta Casilighio no longer exists and she is now Estelle Wallace. This repetition is like a magical incantation, and by the time Arta escapes on the Liberty ship *San Marino* the transformation is complete. Timid and mousy Arta Casilighio is gone, replaced by daring and beautiful Estelle Wallace. There is no second mirror scene on the *San Marino*, but the ship itself stands in for one as Arta (now Estelle) contentedly studies the *San Marino* without realizing it reveals the inner person she has become: "She looked as sordid as a Bowery hooker, but in the eyes of Estelle Wallace she was virgin and beautiful." [96]

The last time the Prince Charming fairy tale appears in a Cussler adventure (as of this writing) is *Shock Wave*, an adventure that reworks several plot elements from *Pacific Vortex*. Both stories are set on the Pacific Ocean. Both feature an evil empire,[97] or criminal clan, that owns an international corporation it uses to further the family's nefarious schemes. In *Pacific Vortex* there is the egomaniacal father Delphi Moran, conflicted daughter Summer and the Pisces Pacific and Pisces Metal Companies; in *Shock Wave* there is the merciless father Arthur Dorsett, sociopathic daughter Deirdre Dorsett, white-sheep daughter Maeve Fletcher, brutal cross-dresser Boudicca Dorsett and Dorsett Consolidated Mining Company. The Morans live in the fantastic ruins of a legendary kingdom on the sunken island of Kanoli while the Dorsetts' palatial home is on Gladiator Island, site of one of the world's richest diamond deposits, and both islands have fabled guardians. For Kanoli it is a golden-eyed giant, and for Gladiator Island it is a centuries-old sea serpent. Both adventures include children that are stolen away to these evil kingdoms to coerce a parent. In *Pacific Vortex* it is Admiral Leigh Hunter's wayward daughter Adrian, and in *Shock Wave* it is Maeve's six-year-old twins Sean and Michael.[98] (As mentioned in Chapter 4, being the mother of twins is one more thing Maeve and Summer have in common.) Pitt invades both evil empires and fails to rescue the girl he loves, but when Giordino and Sandecker rescue Pitt afterwards near the end of *Shock Wave*, Cussler could almost be borrowing references from the Grimm Brothers' "Sleeping Beauty" when he describes Maeve's body: "A *waxen* sheen on her lovely features, she reminded Sandecker of a white, unburned candle, a sleeping beauty no kiss would ever awake."[99] Pitt is taken to a hospital and, just like in *Iceberg*, he refuses to stay in spite of being badly injured, but the end results of his disobedience in the two novels are radically different. After leaving the hospital in *Iceberg*,

Pitt, who is feeling self-confident, has two magic-mirror scenes. In the first, Pitt looks at the reflection of his battered face and wryly smiles.[100] In the second, Pitt puts on a Big Bad Wolf costume to patrol Disneyland unnoticed, and when he looks in a mirror he is torn between amusement and embarrassment, but then admits the costume is in keeping with his character.[101] In *Shock Wave*, after Pitt checks himself out of the hospital, he notices himself in a mirror while boarding a jet bound for the United States. Pitt has momentarily lost his self-confidence and, for one of the few times in the series, feels humiliation.[102]

Another fairy-tale motif that appears in Cussler adventures is the enchanted forest. These wild and possibly magical places, often unknown or forbidden, are where characters may encounter transformation or liminality.[103] Enchanted forests appear as far back as the *Epic of Gilgamesh*[104] and as recently as the *Harry Potter* adventures,[105] but an enchanted forest does not even have to be a forest. In *Star Wars: The Empire Strikes Back* (1980) the enchanted forest is a swamp on the planet Dagobah,[106] and in *Skeleton Coast* it is a reed-choked bay in Namibia. Cabrillo and Sloan Macintyre pilot a lifeboat from the *Oregon* through the secluded bay searching for Papa Heinrick, who claims to have seen giant metal snakes in the waters off West Africa. Papa Heinrick lives in a hut on a tiny island in the heart of the reeds, which are so tall that Cabrillo needs GPS to guide his way. When Cabrillo and Sloan reach the hut they find it ablaze, with Papa Heinrick chained to his bed inside. Before Sloan's eyes, Cabrillo changes into a merciless manhunter determined to capture Papa Heinrick's killers, a transformation that extends to the lifeboat, which turns out to be a high-performance hydrofoil. Even the enchanted forest seems to rally to Cabrillo's aid as a trail of bioluminescent organisms glitter like fairy dust in the killers' wake.

Sam and Remi Fargo's first adventure *Spartan Gold* is filled with enchanted forests, including two at the very beginning of the novel.

In the prologue, scouts from Napoleon Bonaparte's Grand Army stumble across a cave containing an ancient secret while trekking the treacherous Grand St. Bernard Pass in the Pennine Alps, during the spring of 1800, on their way to the Second Italian Campaign. Bitter cold, snowstorms and avalanches have harassed the army like elemental mountain guardians, but as Napoleon's scouts lead him to the cave an almost supernatural stillness permeates the area. The cave's secluded entrance is covered by a curtain of ice that mysteriously forms over it each night. Inside the cave the party journeys through a labyrinth of tunnels and across an icy bridge over a bottomless gorge to reach a small chamber with two ice columns in the center. Like a Prince Charming approaching a Sleeping Beauty, the Emperor draws near to one column, leans close to peer inside its ice, and realizes the face of a golden woman is staring back at him.[107]

The second enchanted forest lies in Maryland's Great Pokomoke Swamp, where Sam and Remi are searching for the loot of Patty Cannon, the leader of an early 19th-century gang based in what is now known as the Delmarva Peninsula. The historical Cannon gang mainly kidnapped free blacks and sold them into slavery, but according to *Spartan Gold* the gang also waylaid, robbed and murdered people along the Delaware-Maryland border and (just like innkeepers/serial killers John and Kate Bender of Labette County, Kansas, almost half a century later)[108] visitors to Cannon's remote hostel. During the search Sam spots something through a gap in some foliage that does not look natural. In order to find out what it is, he and Remi must abandon their boat and swim underwater. On the other side the couple discovers an inlet with an almost solid canopy of trees, where sunlight stipples the algae floating on the water.

Inside this enchanted forest they take the first step of what proves to be a perilous adventure to greater treasures than Cannon's loot.

There is no rule against enchanted forests being in urban areas. In *Cyclops* it is the Winthrop Manor Nursing Home, where Pitt visits Hilda Kronberg. Most of the nursing home looks like a five-star hotel, but the pool where Hilda spends most of her time resembles a fantasy paradise inside a snow globe, minus the snow. Hilda acts like a woman waiting to die, but she is actually a Wise Old Woman who reveals secrets about the La Dorada statue and her husbands to Pitt. Hilda also dispatches Pitt on a quest to find the La Dorada, not as the treasure Raymond LeBaron desires but to put on display for the public the way her first husband, Hans Kronberg, would have preferred.

A variation on the enchanted forest is the fairyland. Fairylands, like Neverland and Oz, are, to borrow a line from Poe, "From a wild weird clime that lieth, sublime, Out of Space—Out of Time,"[109] and Arthur Machen ("The Great God Pan," "The Bowmen") describes them as "deep, dark, and secret places" that a man or hero on a journey or a quest may discover "if he cares to stray a little from the highlands."[110] In *Pacific Vortex*, for instance, Pitt crashes an airplane in the Pacific to reach Kanoli at the bottom of the ocean, where he finds Summer's bedchamber, a "fairyland of gleaming black statuary and blue velvet-covered walls."[111] A subtler example can be found in *Night Probe!* during Pitt's search for the Deuville-Hudson River bridge and the spectral *Manhattan Limited* in the Hudson River Valley, a "breeding ground for myths."[112] Machen writes that if a man dares to stray from the highlands he may find "paths that lead down lonely hills, and when the twilight falls, it is evident that they must end in fairyland," [113] and it is twilight when Pitt finds what its left of the bridge and walks out on it. It seems to Pitt that he can see the past as he imagines battle-weary Revolutionary War soldiers straggling along, but then the past genuinely seems to catch up with Pitt when the spectral *Manhattan Limited* appears and barrels down upon him.[114] Machen never denies that journeys to fairylands can be perilous, but they can also be beneficial. "There are flaming walls that bound the world of our thought; pillars of Hercules beyond which no ship can sail. And yet it is our privilege that now and again there is one who has passed beyond these walls, these bounds, these pillars, who has looked on the other side and has brought back its secrets."[115] Pitt and other Cussler heroes like the Fargos risk straying from the highlands to look on the other side, but where traditional fairylands are associated with myths and legends such as Álfheim, the home of the night elves from Norse mythology,[116] fairylands in Cussler's adventures are usually lost historical places such as the Library of Alexandria, Troy, Atlantis and (maybe) El Dorado,[117] but the journey, the risk and the rewards remain the same.

Gothic

Shades of Edgar Allan Poe, Pitt thought.—*Pacific Vortex*[118]

People have become conditioned to think of the suspense-adventure genre, not Gothic, when they hear Cussler's name,[119] but Gothic elements frequently appear in his stories. Even *Vixen 03*, the most relevant Pitt adventure, includes allusions to tombs and graves,[120] suggestions of animation in inanimate objects[121] and bad weather underscoring dire situations.[122] These and other Gothic elements appear so often in the adventures that Cussler writes that some academics like suspense and mystery scholar Dr. Shelley Costa Bloomfield might be tempted to classify them as Gothic. Bloomfield describes Gothic as "medieval settings—castles, catacombs, and crypts figure large—supernatural elements, weather gone crazy, melodramatic language, and what we now call 'fem jep,' or damsels in distress. Think of Gothic as Romance on steroids—caught in an underground passage in the wee hours of the morning."[123] Unscrupulous villains have been pursuing damsels through underground passages only to have these lovelies rescued by noble avenging heroes since the first Gothic story, Horace Walpole's *Castle of Otranto*, was published in 1764, and variations of this Gothic theme have appeared in Cussler's adventures since *Pacific Vortex*. As limiting as the Gothic theme may sound, it was once so popular that it almost single-handedly kept the novel alive during that medium's first hundred years.[124] The genre's popularity flagged until Bram Stoker reinvigorated it in 1897 by combining folk tales with eastern European superstitions in *Dracula*. British critic Clive Bloom calls *Dracula* "one of the most significant pieces of literature ever written," but concedes "Stoker's literary style as well as much of his book's content represent a revisiting of the old gothic that had given way to a more contemporary attitude toward the fiction of the weird and supernatural by the middle nineteenth century,"[125] a transitional period when Gothic elements were being incorporated into other genres, including the detective mystery,[126] science fiction[127] and adventure. Adventure writers like Rohmer (Fu Manchu), Wallace (The Just Men) and Frank L. Packard (Jimmie Dale, the Gray Seal) injected Gothic elements into many of their stories, and even Clarence E. Mulford could not resist writing "The Ghost of the Canyon" (1935) for cowboy hero Hopalong Cassidy. Gothic elements continue to appear in popular non–Gothic novels to this day,[128] but like Hammett in *The Dain Curse* (1928) and Daphne du Maurier in *Rebecca* (1938) Cussler's sole intention is to evoke the Gothic.[129] As Ebenezer Scrooge might say, there is more of gravy than of grave in Cussler's adventures.

The downside to all of this incorporating is that it makes defining Gothic difficult.[130] Instead of one monolithic category of Gothic there are actually many,[131] so scholars like Bloomfield often resort to listing elements to define the genre. Helen Wheatley resorts to such a list in her thesis about *Gothic Television*, but then she uses it to create an initial taxonomy or checklist for studying what constitutes a Gothic story. This checklist includes highly stereotypical characters and plots often derived from Gothic literary fictions: haunted or tortured or troubled homes and families, plots that are organized in a complex way, supernatural representations that may be either overt (created through special effects) or implied (suggested rather than fully revealed) and a proclivity towards the structures and images of the uncanny (e.g., repetitions, returns, déjà vu, premonitions, ghosts, doppelgängers, animated inanimate objects and severed body parts).[132]

Cussler's characters and plots are highly stereotypical. Villains like Bruno Von Til and good guys like Casio are wonderful but it is hard to argue that, on the surface, they come straight out of Central Casting.[133] This might chafe fans that think this is an insult, but what a writer does with stereotypes makes all the difference.[134] H. P. Lovecraft ("The Colour Out of Space," *Shadow Over Innsmouth*, *At the Mountains of Madness*) praises *The Castle of Otranto* in his groundbreaking study of "Supernatural Horror in Literature" (1927, 1933–4) for creating novel Gothic "puppet-characters" and "dramatic paraphernalia" that "reappears with amusing sameness, yet sometimes with tremendous effect."[135] Many contemporary adventure series have derived wonderful variations from Gothic characters, like the "valorous and immaculate" hero and "tyrannical and malevolent nobleman as villain,"[136] while mixing them with adventure stereotypes, such as the brother-in-arms (or the brother-of-color) and the Wise Old Man (who can also be a second father figure). Examples of this include Fleming's Bond novels (007, Ernst Stavros Blofeld, Felix Leiter, "M") and *Stargate SG-1* (Jack O'Neill, Apophis, Teal'c, Master Bra'tac) as well as many of Cussler's Pitt adventures (Pitt, Von Til, Giordino, Sandecker).[137]

What goes for characters also goes for plots. What plot could be more stereotypical than the initiation quest pattern (see Chapter 7) that appears in almost every adventure story? But people go on reading adventures because, to quote Campbell, the initiation quest contains the "challengingly persistent suggestion of more remaining to be experienced than will ever be known or told."[138] Cussler generates this sensation in all of his adventures, but he also derives plots from Gothic literary fictions. Perhaps the best example of this is the past reaching out to affect the present, a Gothic chestnut that appears so often in Cussler's stories it almost qualifies as its own thematic preoccupation.[139] Classic stories that use this plot includes Walter de la Mare's *The Return* (1910), Hawthorne's *The House of the Seven Gables* (1851), Emily Brontë's *Wuthering Heights* (1847), Poe's "Ligeia" (1838), Machen's "Great God Pan" (1890, 1894), Robert W. Chambers's "The King in Yellow" (1895) and Lovecraft's *The Case of Charles Dexter Ward* (1927).[140] The past reaching out to affect the present tends to be destructive in Gothic stories because the genre, created as an escapist and conformist retaliation against the mundane activities of the Age of Reason,[141] speaks to the dark side of domestic fiction,[142] but in the more optimistic adventure genre it is usually beneficial. In *Dragon* a painting seized by Nazis and stashed among plunder in a forgotten Luftwaffe bunker fortuitously reveals itself to help quash a nuclear threat against America by Germany's former Axis ally Japan.[143] In *Deep Six* the past helps squash another threat against America when Pitt leads a company of Civil War re-enactors into actual combat aboard a commandeered 1915 steamship called the *Stonewall Jackson*.[144] In this same adventure Arta's murder, in 1966, spurs her father, Casio, to search for her killers through the decades like an avenging spirit, a search that helps rescue the office of the President. But, even in an adventure story, the past reaching out to affect the present can be destructive. The curse that plagues Gene Seagram is an example of this. Seagram's hubris links him to Brewster, a self-aggrandizing engineer who concocts a scheme to sneak into Russia, mine the rare mineral byzanium for the United States Army and dupe a French mining syndicate to foot the bill. First Brewster's hubris destroys his sanity,[145] then it physically destroys him with an ironic flourish worthy of a Greek tragedy. Nearly 75 years later Brewster's curse reaches out to snare Seagram, who needs the byzanium to prove to himself and the world that he is not a failure.[146] Pitt tries to rescue Seagram soon after the *Titanic* docks in New York by forcing Gene to look in a mirror to see how his hubris is destroying him, but the result is hardly what Pitt hopes for as Seagram imagines he sees Brewster staring back at him.[147]

Brewster's specter is a product of Seagram's madness, but as Poe demonstrates better than most in stories like "The Black Cat" (1843), "The Tell-Tale Heart" (1843) and "The Cask of Amontillado" (1846), insanity is another classic Gothic convention.[148] Cussler also links Brewster and Seagram through parallel actions. For example, in the prelude, Brewster decides to die with the *Titanic* so he can end his suffering, and ends up dragging an innocent young officer named Bigalow down into the ship. Later, in Chapter 49, Seagram is sitting in East Potomac Park preparing to shoot himself when Officer Peter Jones arrives to rescue Seagram, but like Brewster, who pulls a gun on Bigalow, Seagram aims his gun at Jones. Seagram and Dana, along with the Morans and Dorsetts, are also examples of haunted, tortured or troubled families.

Cussler has been organizing his plots in a complex way for most of his career. This is examined in more detail in Chapter 8, but *Pacific Vortex* and *The Mediterranean Caper* are straightforward plots in which everything is seen from the hero's perspective. Then, starting with *Iceberg*, Cussler begins to develop what he calls a Structure B formula, which features a "labyrinth of subplots, 'sideplots,' and 'twistplots.'"[149] Other trademarks of Structure B include an omnipotent narrator and a large cast of characters, some of whom may never meet during the story but each of whom are confronting problems that are inexorably drawn together into the story's climax. Although it is complex, by forgoing the multiple narrators that are a trademark of the Gothic genre, Structure B can create a brisk pace that is not possible, much less desired, in Gothics like *Wuthering Heights*, James Hogg's *The Private Memoirs and Confessions of a Justified Sinner* (1824), Charles Maturin's *Melmouth the Wanderer* (1820), Mary Wollstonecraft Shelley's *Frankenstein* (1818), Wilkie Collins's *The Woman in White* and Stoker's *Dracula*.[150] The typical adventure story has no need to force a reader into making "provisional moral judgments as the narrative unfolds"[151] through the use of multiple narrators because the reader "cannot place unquestioning trust in the objectivity of any narrator."[152] Structure B also dispenses with Gothic's convoluted plotting like "flashbacks, sequences, memory montages, and other narrative interpolations"[153] which Gothic scholar Eve Sedgwick identifies as "the difficulty the story has in getting itself told."[154] This is exactly the opposite effect readers want in an adventure story.

Finally, Cussler's adventures include their fair share of supernatural representations as well as a proclivity towards the structures and images of the uncanny. There is the spectral *Manhattan Limited* and what appears to be a cadaver coming to life in its Pullman car in *Night Probe!* In *Deep Six* a strange fog materializes out of nowhere along the Potomac River, and when it mysteriously vanishes it takes the Presidential yacht *Eagle* and everyone on board with it. Another mysterious fog presages the disappearance of the prototype nuclear submarine *Starbuck*. During the search for the missing boomer in *Pacific Vortex*, Pitt, who believes only what he can see, smell and touch[155] recounts a report he read from a NUMA zoologist recording fish sounds off the Continental slope near Iceland at a depth of ten thousand feet. According to Pitt, the zoologist picked up noises like someone using a pencil to tap a code on the microphone (later translated as a mathematical formula) followed by shrieking laughter. In *Cyclops*, the dirigible *Prosperteer* returns to Florida, after it has been missing for ten days, with a crew of rotting corpses in its gondola. In *Flood Tide*, Katie Garin is adrift in a raft and freezing to death when her dead father appears to foretell that she shall live only moments before her future husband, Ian Gallagher, sights land. In *Trojan Odyssey*, Pitt, Giordino, Gunn and the crew of the NUMA salvage ship *Poco Bonito* find themselves under attack by the ghost ship of the legendary Wandering Buccaneer Leigh Hunt. Cussler's adventures are also replete with Gothic settings such as caves, underwater caverns, mines, secret rooms and hidden passages as well as the requisite weather gone crazy,[156] melodramatic language,[157] premonitions,[158] doppelgängers,[159] animated inanimate objects[160] and body parts, although they are usually still attached to the corpse instead of severed.[161] Cussler does not use Gothic imagery frequently, but all of his adventures often have Gothic scenes, including the underwater graveyard in Orion Lake from *Flood Tide*[162] and the embedded ships *Lax*, from *Iceberg*, and *Pilottown*, from *Deep Six*. Cussler will pepper such scenes with phrases to evoke a Gothic mood, the finest example possibly being the "Regenesis" chapter from *Raise the Titanic!*[163] Conversely, a disproportionate lack of Gothic atmosphere and phrases in *NUMA Files*, *Oregon Files*, the post-*Chase* Isaac Bell Detective series, *Fargo Adventures* and the Pitt series beginning with *Black Wind* marks a key distinction between Cussler and his collaborators.[164] It is also one reason Cussler's collaborations, though excellent, never quite ignite the same irresistible spark found in the author's solo stories. The introduction of Sam and Remi Fargo in *Spartan Gold* is an excellent example. As discussed in Chapter 7, the scene wherein Pitt introduces himself to Seagram in *Raise the Titanic!* drips with Gothic atmosphere, even though it takes place at a private club in Newport Beach. Searching for lost loot in a swamp that is reportedly haunted by Canon's ghost is rife with even greater Gothic potential, but it goes unexploited.[165] For whatever reason, when Cussler is writing alone he takes advantage of the appreciation even non–Gothic readers have for the Gothic genre. Sadly, Cussler has no interest in writing a genuine Gothic story[166]; he makes it clear in *Pacific Vortex* that NUMA is not in the business of researching strange phenomena when Pitt confesses that unexplained discoveries, like the one he describes happening near Iceland, are quietly filed away.[167]

Science Fiction and Techno-Thrillers

> It was difficult for [Pitt] to believe that he was in a submarine far beneath the sea instead of a highly complex command center at the National Space Headquarters.—
> *Pacific Vortex*[168]

Cussler's adventures contain the essence of science fiction. Science-fiction scholar John Clute writes that the genre "faces into the wind of the future,"[169] a maritime metaphor that sounds apt when describing many of Cussler's adventures. Tom Clancy, a science-fiction fan, offers a more practical definition when he describes the genre as "talking about ways in which technology or ideas or people can change the world."[170] Starting with *Iceberg*, most of Cussler's adventures deal with world-altering or macrocosmic changes. The lunar Jersey Colony extends the boundaries of Man's influence and conflicts beyond Earth's orbit.[171] The re-establishment of trade between the U.S. and Cuba is a historic change,[172] though not quite on par with the rediscoveries of the Library of Alexandria and Atlantis. These are all realized changes, but Cussler's adventures also deal with potential changes, although these generally involve the prevention of a catastrophe, such as the destruction of Hawaii by acoustic waves or the shifting of the earth's crust ("earth crust displacement") with a nudge from nanotechnology.[173]

Cussler is also often credited with Clancy and the late Craig Thomas, author of the Mitchell Gant series which includes *Firefox* (1977), with creating the techno-thriller,[174] a science-fiction subgenre that blends espionage adventure, the traditional values often found in military fiction and science fiction's technological flavor.[175] According to Ray Bradbury, "Science fiction guesses at sciences" and the "machines which are the fruit of those sciences,"[176] so when the Wolf Family tries to induce earth crust displacement, their scheme harkens to science-fiction tales like Conan Doyle's Professor Challenger adventure "When the World Screamed" (1928) and films like *Crack in the World* (1965); when the Soviet Union tries to take control of the United States government's chain of command in *Deep Six*, their effort mixes two literary chestnuts, pulp science fiction's mind control[177] with the political thriller's abduction of the president of the United States.[178] Misuse of technology is common in techno-thrillers, even though the genre generally does not focus on technology's dark side—at least not as pessimistically as have some other science-fiction stories dating back to Karel Čapek's play *R.U.R.* (1920) and Fritz Lang's film *Metropolis* (1926); and Cussler's adventures on the whole tend to be value-neutral when it comes to technology. In *Vixen 03*, for instance, the QD organism is not presented as evil or beneficial, just too volatile to control, and when Satan missiles kill a handful of Navy SEALs, the responsibility does not fall upon the missiles but the president who orders the strike. In *Cyclops* a computerized synthesizer is used by both Soviets on Cayo Santa María and by Americans on an NSA ship to jam radio signals. And in *Dragon* a pack of robotic sentries that capture Pitt and Giordino are not electronic monsters, but machines performing their programmed task of defending the subterranean marvel Edo City.[179]

Techno-thrillers tend to be more pragmatic than other forms of science fiction by avoiding intergalactic spaceships and time machines[180] and concentrating on technology that either exists or can reasonably exist in the near future. The technology in Cussler's adventures, therefore, ranges from the ancient (like the *quipu*, or "talking knots," used by the Incas and earlier civilizations) to antiques (like Admiral Byrd's Antarctic Snow Cruiser) to near-future wonders (like Yaeger's supercomputer Hope). Clancy is better known for incorporating military science in his stories, but some impressive (if not always existent) military technology can also be found in Cussler's adventures, such as the small and silent Carrier Pigeon Special Forces helicopters, from *Treasure*, and the special-purpose undersea transport (SPUT), from *Cyclops*. Clancy believes "the military has the best toys"[181] while Cussler's passion is underwater salvage and exploration. It stands to reason, then, that Cussler is better known for incorporating marine science in his stories: the Fyrie probe (*Iceberg*); the submersible *Old Gert*, the Deep Sea Mining Vehicle *Big John* and NUMA's underwater colony Soggy Acres (*Dragon*); the *Wallowing Windbag* hovercraft (*Treasure*); and Zavala's renovated bathysphere (*Medusa*). But these are far from the only advanced technology that appears in Cussler's adventures.

Starting with *Raise the Titanic!* Cussler began setting his adventures a few years in the future to prevent them from becoming dated as quickly as other adventures, like Fleming's Bond novels. To that end, he tries to feature technology scientists and engineers predict will exist in ten years.[182] In *Raise the Titanic!* America has the ability to create a sonic version of Star Wars or SDI (Strategic Defense Initiative), and submersibles like the *Sappho I*, that are more spacious and can stay under water for up to eight weeks. Personal communication has taken a step forward in *Night Probe!* judging by Foss Gly's lapel microphone, and sea salvage gets some impressive upgrades with Baby the RSV (remote-search vehicle) and the *Doodlebug*, whose unusual configuration is so radical it acts as a form of stealth technology.[183] In other adventures satellites are more advanced,[184] as are holograms,[185] but big cars like Cadillac's are threatening to become passé as a gas crisis makes minicars more popular.[186] Computers become more prevalent in Cussler's adventures starting in *Raise the Titanic!*[187] and become more advanced starting in *Night Probe!*, wherein National Security Advisor Alan Mercier's briefcase has a personal computer with a battery-operated microprocessor in its lid,[188] although this pales when compared to Yaeger's supercomputers. In *Deep Six* NUMA's computers are still cranking out paper print-outs, but in *Cyclops* Hope arrives complete with a voice synthesizer and enough artificial personality that Pitt finds himself wishing "she" were real. *Cyclops* marks Hope's lone appearance and, in *Inca Gold*, Yaeger is using a computer terminal he calls Brunhilda, but in *Flood Tide* the first version of Max is introduced. This incarnation speaks in a monotone,[189] but in *Atlantis Found* Yaeger re-programs Max with his wife, Elsie's, voice, image and personality.

Max reflects a shift in science fiction's attitude towards computers, spurred by the popularity of personal computers. Prior to this, science-fiction stories often presented computers as electronic Frankenstein Monsters like HAL 9000 from *2001: A Space Odyssey* (1968).[190] HAL (Heuristically programmed ALgorithmic computer) is an artificial intelligence that kills the crew of the spaceship *Discovery* when it discovers a plot to shut it down. Almost 15 years later, in Arthur C. Clarke's sequel *2010: Odyssey Two* (1982), HAL turns out to have been a victim of conflicting programming. Like Lusana in *Vixen 03* HAL redeems itself by becoming a martyr, in this case by sacrificing itself to save a joint Soviet-American space crew that has come to the *Discovery*.[191] Max's personality and beneficent nature also makes her a literary descendant of the HOLMES IV (High-Optional, Logical, Multi-Evaluating Supervisor, Mark IV) computer Mike (a.k.a Mycroft) from Robert A. Heinlein's *The Moon Is a Harsh Mistress* (1966). Mike, the master computer for a prison colony on the Moon, becomes self-aware, has an immature sense of humor, and helps plot a revolution to save colonists from eventual food riots and cannibalism. Max, on the other hand, can become testy and petulant, has a weakness for slang and mild curses, likes to "dress" herself in clothes she finds while surfing Internet catalogs and will imitate Barbara Eden from *I Dream of Jeanie*.[192] In 2001, Yaeger was predicting that Max would be obsolete in five years, but Max is still going strong in 2006 (*Valhalla Rising*), and in *White Death* (2003) Yaeger brings us back full circle to Mercier's briefcase with Portable Max, a laptop version that connects to Max's mainframe.[193]

Impressive as Max is, the crown jewel of Cussler's science-fiction tech is the *Oregon*, the USS *Enterprise* of the bounding main that takes the subterfuge of Pitt's abandoned hangar and Cromwell's dilapidated Pullman car to the extremes. More formidable than the USS *Ronald Reagan*, the *Oregon* looks like a rust bucket but is as luxurious as the MS *The World* and probably has more advanced technology than Q Branch. The *pièce de résistance* of the *Oregon* is her operations ("op") center that has "the feel of the bridge of television's starship *Enterprise*, right down to the large seat in the middle of the room" which "the crew called 'the Kirk Chair.'"[194] When the *Oregon* is in action the scenes even have the feel of one of the starship's engagements with the Klingons, Romulans or Khan Noonien Singh.[195]

Why the similarities? Alan Stern's foreword to *Clive Cussler & Dirk Pitt Revealed* might provide a clue.

Stern mentions that Cussler has only two pictures of himself in his home or office, one of them a superimposed image of himself standing in a Starfleet uniform on the bridge of the *Enterprise* with the *Star Trek* crew.[196] Could the *Oregon*, like this picture, be the result of a little wish fulfillment?

Finally, Cussler's adventures feature science fiction because, as Bradbury writes, the genre "is interested in more than sciences, more than machines. That *more* is always men and women and children themselves, how they behave, how they hope to behave."[197] Cussler's adventures may generally be value-neutral when it comes to technology, but not when it comes to judging characters by their behavior, including their use or misuse of technology. The Soviets are viewed as negative in *Deep Six* because of their attempts to use advanced memory transfer technology against America, but members of the CIA's Fathom mind-control project are presented in a positive light because they thwart the Soviet plot. In *Vixen 03* anyone who thinks the QD organism should be used as a weapon is viewed negatively because of its devastating volatility, while anyone seeking to destroy it is presented positively, even though such actions are potentially traitorous.

History

> Strange how a casual conversation between a young minister of Parliament and a freshman senator in front of a fireplace at a hunting lodge so many years ago could change the course of history.—The President of the United States, *Night Probe!*[198]

In Cussler's adventures, history is more than Pitt's classic automobile collection or prologues set decades or centuries or millennia ago. History permeates his stories like a loom's warp or vertical threads weaving through an unending tapestry.[199] The present is dependent upon the past, its pattern perpetually being designed by what has happened before. Everything happening today is a result of everything that happened before our arrival. Ignore the past and you are doomed to repeat it, but in Cussler's adventures history is vibrant with taproots saturating the loam of current events, ready to burst forth at the discretion of Fate or coincidence. Humanity is not only a part but a product of history, so humanity is at the mercy of history. In this way, history is as tangible as magic is in the Harry Potter adventures, and the people who study history are, in their own way, as powerful as the wizardry students at Hogwarts[200]; people who try to advance their own villainy through misuse of artifacts or ancient knowledge are as dark and as doomed as Lord Voldemort's Death Eaters.

Pitt, driven to rediscover the past and born 80 years too late, is the ultimate Cussler hero, a human divining rod for lost treasures that change what we know about history or alter its current course. To this end, Pitt works for NUMA, whose charter is as much about the preservation of maritime history and artifacts as it is aquatic conservation,[201] and whose leader, Sandecker, has dedicated his life to the agency's ambitions. Even NUMA's technical staff members, including Yaeger, actively preserve the past through his computer archives. One of Pitt's dearest friends, Perlmutter, may even be more of an old soul than he, shunning current technology when possible as he compiles the world's largest maritime library. As for Cussler's other heroes, Austin is no old soul but his work at NUMA and his passion for collecting antique dueling pistols make him a salvager of the past, while the Fargos are professional treasure hunters who respect history and the preservation of historical artifacts. Ironically, Bell, whose stories are set in the past (from our perspective), is no student of history. Perhaps because Bell lives in the past, he is the one Cussler hero whose adventures occasionally begin with a prologue set in a time ahead of the story's main section. One of the joys of Bell's adventures is looking through the lens of history at the technological marvels from Bell's youth, like the steam locomotive and early automobiles and motorcycles, and seeing them as if they were brand new. This is also true in the Lacey and Casey Nicefolks series, which takes place "In a time still remembered."[202]

Cussler frequently tags supporting characters as negative or positive based on their respect for history. Egocentrics like Gene Seagram and power mongers like Harrison Moon disregard the past,[203] but people who study or preserve history are usually trustworthy, possibly even passing on some sage or local knowledge about the past to another character when it is needed most. Such helper characters include Mildred Gardner, the matronly head archivist at Princeton University (*Night Probe!*), archaeologist Dr. Raphael O'Meara (*Cyclops*) and George Papaaloa, curator of the Bernice Pauahi Bishop Museum of Polynesia Ethnology and Natural History (*Pacific Vortex*). Ansel Magee (*Night Probe!*) is even a positive character despite pulling a prank involving the *Manhattan Limited* because there is no apparent malice or harm and, more importantly, he is an old soul like Pitt, who studies and preserves history.[204]

Even the science-fiction elements examined in the last section demonstrate the importance history plays in Cussler's adventures. Professor William Foster-Harris writes in the *Basic Patterns of Plot* that in science, "A fact, to be recognized as such, must recur. It must have happened before, and it must have happened not once but many times, before the scientist will admit it to his book of demonstrated fact. Thus committed to looking backward, science, as the great scientists freely admit, has no regard for, or consideration of, the future."[205] In contrast, science fiction, which faces the winds of the future, is more concerned about what *could* happen then what *has* happened. Like Janus, who is always looking into the future and the past, the "science" of science fiction always looks backwards while the "fiction" always looks forward. A meteor may strike the earth over seven thousand years before the birth of Christ, wipe out the most advanced civilizations, reshape the continents and seas and leave only the most isolated and primitive humans alive, but the catastrophe is remembered today in the Greek legend of Atlantis and tales that exist in almost every culture about a Great Flood. A tidal wave can sweep a Spanish galleon deep into a South American jungle or a Civil War ironclad can get stranded when an African river dries up, but their fates live on in ancient records that have become rumors and folk tales. The past lives in the present, and there is no disconnecting one from another.

Rebirths and Resurrections

It seems our Major Pitt is about to be reborn.—Jerome P. Lillie[206]

Symbolic rebirths and resurrections are commonplace in heroic literature. The concepts behind them are examined in Chapter 7, but as long as there have been myths and legends there have been heroes who have left home, journeyed to unknown lands and made dark descents. From there they must submit to a new awakening about themselves before they can return, possibly to recover a boon, win a bride or defeat a father figure, any of which will, in some way, benefit their homes. These dark descents and returns symbolize death followed by rebirth or resurrection. This is what happens in *Harry Potter and the Deathly Hollows* (2007) when Voldemort attempts to slay Harry in the Forbidden Forest, followed by Harry's vision of Albus Dumbledore at King's Cross Station, and then the young Potter's final battle with the Dark Lord in Hogwart's Great Hall.[207] But rebirths and resurrections also occur outside of fantastic stories. This is what happens in Fleming's *On Her Majesty's Secret Service* and *You Only Live Twice* when Bond's bride, Tracy, is murdered on their wedding day, followed by "M" sending a despondent 007 on an impossible mission and Bond's final showdown with the man responsible for Tracy's death.[208] The story does not even have to be a traditional adventure. This is what happens in *Rocky III* (1982) when Rocky Balboa (Sylvester Stallone) is defeated by James "Clubber" Lang (Mr. T) and Rocky's mentor and second-father Mickey Goldmill (Burgess Meredith) unexpectedly passes away, followed by a despondent Rocky regaining the eye of the tiger (his hunger to compete and win) and Rocky's rematch with Lang.

Rebirths and resurrections have been a part of Cussler's adventures beginning with *Pacific Vortex*, wherein Pitt descends to the Kanoli caverns to rescue Adrian Hunter, but also ends up uncovering Delphi Moran's plans to sell the *Starbuck* and the boomer's Hyperion nuclear missiles to an unnamed Arab oil-rich country. Pitt defeats Moran and tries to take the woman he loves away from Kanoli, however, like Orpheus trying to rescue Eurydice, Pitt only succeeds in bringing Summer to the edge of the underworld and not beyond. Pitt's rebirth is not completed until an early morning swim in the Aegean Sea in *The Mediterranean Caper*. The moon is still visible as Pitt walks from the beach into the water and begins his submission. "It was as though his soul seeped out of his body, and he became a thing without substance, without form." Dawn begins to break as Pitt walks into the water, and soon his "mind was purified and cleansed" as he "lay dead and floated in the water" and "listened to the nothingness of silence; the greatest, but most unknown, treasure of man" until he eventually "drifted back onto the beach like a piece of flotsam." As daylight fills the sky Pitt falls asleep, a contented man reborn, but the sun has not set again before Pitt finds himself making another dark descent. This time it is in Bruno Von Til's labyrinth, the Pit of Hades, and instead of water Pitt submits himself to the darkness inside the tunnels by lying upon the maze's floor and quietly waiting for the labyrinth's monster (Von Til's immense white dog) to come to him so he can slay it. Pitt carries the secret of the labyrinth (that one of its passages leads to Von Til's villa) with him when he escapes, but in a reversal of his Kanoli descent, Pitt uses the secret he learns to try to strike back at Von Til, only to end up rescuing Teri.

Pitt's most important and complex rebirth takes place in *Iceberg* as he is transformed from a local or microcosmic hero to a universal, or macrocosmic, hero. This rebirth is detailed in Chapter 7 as is the dark rebirth of Kristjan Fyrie, the first character besides Pitt to undergo a resurrection in a Cussler adventure. It also explores (among other things) the rebirths that occur in Pitt's next three adventures. *Raise the Titanic!* is the first Cussler adventure in which other characters experience rebirths but Pitt does not; *Vixen 03* features the most intricate resurrections that happen to other characters other than Pitt, although one character, Heidi Milligan, has to wait until *Night Probe!* before she is ready to enjoy her rebirth. Pitt also goes through a rebirth in *Night Probe!*, as does retired British Secret Service agent Brian Shaw and a few supporting characters, including Foss Gly and Prime Minister Sarveux, who resurrects himself after he is almost assassinated.

It is Loren Smith's turn for a rebirth in *Deep Six*, a penance for playing temptress in *Vixen 03*, but *Deep Six* also features the most tragic rebirth in any Cussler adventure, this one involving the president of the United States and Oskar Belyaka, a man who never physically appears in the story. The Gothic elements of ghosts and the past reaching out to fasten upon the living are given a technological makeover when the president is abducted from his yacht, *The Eagle*,[209] as part of the Soviet plot to gain control of America's chain of command. Dr. Aleksei Lugovoy, creator of the memory-transfer process, places a microminiaturized implant that transplants and receives brain signals in the cerebral cortex before injecting RNA[210] from another person, who has been programmed with certain useful memories, into the hippocampus. The RNA injected into the president's hippocampus comes from Belkaya, a dissident artist whose memories were erased before he was indoctrinated with political concepts the Soviets want implemented by the president. At one point Lugovoy sounds a little like a humbled Henry Frankenstein (Colin Clive) near the end of James Whale's film version of *Frankenstein* (1931) when Lugovoy admits that he is concerned about the human brain being "a magical universe we will never fully understand" and that the president's brain may "break the bonds of reality, despite our control."[211] Which is exactly what happens when Belkaya is reborn in the president's dreams and daydreams. In the sixties, the science of cybernetics often demonstrated the parallels rather than the broad differences between the human brain and a computer; many science-fiction stories from this era through the eighties often warned that human behavior could be controlled the same way a computer is controlled with punch cards,[212] but *Deep Six* takes the opposite view. The war poet Keith Douglas writes, "How easy it is to make a ghost,"[213] but Lugovy and the president discover how hard it is to be rid of one, or at least its memories.

One of Pitt's most dramatic rebirths outside of *Iceberg* happens in *Cyclops*. Like *Iceberg*, Pitt has fallen captive with other people (Girodino, Gunn and Jessie LeBaron), and he is the only member of his group who is healthy enough to try to escape to bring back help. Before his escape, Pitt again makes a dark descent, but instead of a basement gym or an isolated ravine Pitt and his friends find themselves in a labyrinth (a secret Soviet complex on Cuba). The monster at the heart of the maze (the resurrected Foss Gly) is far fouler than Rondheim. Pitt is reborn as he escapes and returns home (to America) with a secret (the USSR is planning a coup in Cuba), but unlike *Iceberg*, wherein he rescues his friends and then defeats the monsters Rondheim and Kirsti, in *Cyclops* Pitt has to descend back into the labyrinth and defeat the monster Gly before his friends can be rescued. Pitt's battle with Gly even borrows a page from another legend as ancient as Orpheus and Eurydice. Paris slays Achilles, the man-god who killed his brother Hector, by stabbing his apparently invincible opponent in Achilles's one vulnerable spot. But, whereas Paris shoots Achilles with an arrow, Pitt jams his thumb into Gly's brain through an eye socket.

Another dramatic rebirth for Pitt that parallels one from an earlier adventure begins in *Shock Wave*, a novel which borrows more than a few plot elements from *Pacific Vortex*.[214] Instead of a dark descent with Giordino on Kanoli, and failing to rescue Summer from her dysfunctional and dangerous father, Pitt and Giordino make a dark descent with the woman Pitt loves, Maeve, on isolated Gladiator Island to rescue her twin sons from her dysfunctional and dangerous family. The twins are rescued and the family is destroyed, but, again, Pitt fails to bring the woman he loves all the way back from the dark descent. And just like in *Pacific Vortex*, in which Pitt's rebirth is not finished until his next adventure, he must wait until *Flood Tide* before this rebirth is completed.[215]

Pitt is not the only Cussler hero who experiences rebirth or resurrection. In *The Chase* Isaac Bell's dark descent begins when he is wounded, and another Van Dorn Agency detective is killed by Cromwell during an attempt to trap the Butcher Bandit. This trap marks a rebirth for Cromwell, too, except his reaction is the opposite of Bell's. For Bell, the botched trap marks the first time he has failed to capture a quarry, so he mourns the loss of a friend even as he redoubles his efforts to succeed, making Bell a more dangerous foe for Cromwell. As for Cromwell, the botched trap represents the first robbery the Butcher Bandit fails to complete; it is also the first time he leaves any witnesses alive. At first, Cromwell is convinced that Bell is dead because his wound covers most of the detective's face with blood,[216] and, until he discovers differently, this apparent victory intensifies his self-delusion that he is invincible. Cromwell is thus emboldened, which makes him no less dangerous but far less careful.

Differences Between Men and Women

> The basic difference between a man and a woman, my dove, is physical strength. You seem to have forgotten that.—Oskar Rondheim to Kirsti Fyire[217]

In his chapter on "Gender Roles" in *Science Fiction: The Illustrated Encyclopedia*, Clute makes the unsupported claim that differences between men and women are understood to be as much a product of nurture as nature.[218] In grossly oversimplified terms, the belief is that if you give little boys a Barbie doll and little girls a G.I. Joe doll to play with, then, as they grow up, boys and girls will exchange traditional gender behavior. There are exceptions to every rule,[219] but as most parents can tell you, boys tend to be hard-wired one way and girls another, and using nurturing to try to rewire nature usually results in Barbie getting her head hammered against the floor until it pops off her plastic swan neck, and G.I. Joe getting dressed in pink taffeta and condemned to afternoon tea parties.

Cussler does not avoid touchy social topics in his adventures, though he generally acknowledges them only when necessary and then quickly moves on so as not to hamper the story's pace.[220] There are times, however, when Cussler will break out the soapbox for environmental and conservation issues,[221] which are a *sine quo non* for NUMA, but he is just as comfortable pointing out differences between men and women. This may be as innocuous as describing a laugh as a "feminine giggle,"[222] or saying that a woman "shook her head in a feminine display of irritation,"[223] or having Pitt or Sandecker comment, "Women just don't appreciate good booze."[224] Cussler also will not hesitate in prescribing specific natural characteristics to the sexes. When Dana Seagram tries to select a dress from her closet for a White House dinner she is "going through the feminine ritual of deciding what to wear."[225] Shannon Kelsey is a tough lady used to getting her way and dominating men with her beauty and personality, but after exerting herself in the Andes she "daintily patted her face with a soft tissue all women seem to produce at the most crucial times."[226] When a female security guard for the Odyssey syndicate is unable to escape from Pitt she falls back "on her womanly instinct and opened her mouth to scream,"[227] and when Kelly Egan is unable to ward off a man trying to kill her she "went limp and cried the age-old woman's cry."[228] Later, a smitten Kelly kisses Pitt goodbye and then "willed herself into a state of feminine composure."[229] When Tidi meets Kirsti the two exchange "polite but typically cool feminine greetings,"[230] and when Loren meets Kelly "the two women immediately sized each other up. Pitt introduced them, and, being a male, did not see the instant underlying conflict of territory between them."[231] When Pitt is pondering his feelings for Maeve Fletcher and Deirdre Dorsett he muses upon "the age-old choice faced by the sexes" in which women find themselves torn between nice guys who make good fathers "and the hell-raising jerk who represented offbeat romance and adventure"; while men "for all their faults, were occasionally forced to choose between miss wholesome" as the mother of their children "and the wild sexpot who couldn't keep her body off him."[232]

Such observations are no more intrusive than Cussler's environmental and conservation comments because differences between men and women are impossible to tiptoe around in old fashion adventure stories. If an adventure writer goes Victorian and excludes female characters then he must be a chauvinist or his heroes are gay.[233] It is debatable if excluding women would even succeed with readers today, but it is definitely not an option for someone who enjoys the give-and-take between the sexes as much as Cussler. If an adventure writer opts for the pulp-magazine-and-movie-serial route then he may still be labeled a chauvinist because even strong and smart women in his stories like Lois Lane and Margo Kane get abducted by the bad guy and rescued by the hero. This has not stopped Cussler from having women abducted in most of his stories, none more so than Loren Smith. If an adventure writer takes the Mrs. Peel or Ellen Ripley approach then there is no harm, no foul, but a hero is relegated to the back seat because the heroine can take care of everything on her own. This is no better an alternative for Cussler than the Victorian approach because he believes there are times in the mystery and adventure genres when women are forced to stand by and react to circumstances above and beyond their control. At other times, though, women are the powerful ones, particularly when it comes to sex.[234] When Maeve gets a chance to ogle Pitt sleeping nude in his cabin aboard the *Ice Hunter* she feels both power and pleasure while standing over him.[235] And, as already stated, Cussler prefers to have his heroines decide if and when to have sex with the hero. Even Pitt has to admit at one point that sex is a woman's game.[236] Cussler also prefers to elevate women to "a worthy status" by making his heroines smart and successful. "I think it's safe to say my women may not always come off like goddesses, but let no man, or woman, accuse them of being intellectual deserts."[237] Even so, there are times when Cussler's attitude towards women comes off as condescending, particularly in his earlier adventures.[238] Cussler is generally more respectful by the time he writes *Dragon*. Stacy Fox would never put up with Pitt and Sandecker's "No Gals Allowed Club" nonsense like Tidi does in *Iceberg*,[239] but when she stops by Pitt's hangar unannounced with the intention of seducing him, Stacy is obviously attracted to his 1948 Talbot-Lago Grand Sport coupe, a smooth and elegant car that Pitt has noticed is an erotic symbol to most women.[240]

A couple of the most illuminating episodes regarding Pitt's attitude towards women appear in *Valhalla Rising*. When Kelly Egan tears up as she is telling Pitt about her father's murder, Pitt the Boy Scout hands her a handkerchief. Kelly did not think men still carried handkerchiefs, but Pitt tells her he is old-fashioned, adding, "You never know when you may encounter a blue lady."[241] Later, Pitt discovers Loren has taken the liberty of sequestering Kelly and Sally Morse, fugitives from the Cerberus cartel's Viper hit squad, in his home. Pitt is polite to Morse when he stumbles across her cooking beef stroganoff and sees that she has wasted half a bottle of Juan Julio silver, 100 percent blue agave tequila to make margaritas. When Pitt goes to shower and change before dinner he is less than overjoyed to find cosmetics stacked around his bedroom, clothes on the floor and Kelly in the bathroom. Morse assures Pitt that she and Kelly will stay out of his way, and Pitt tries to apologize: "Don't get me wrong ... I adore women and am actually quite fond of their curious mannerisms. I come from the old school that elevates them on a pedestal, so don't think I'm a nasty old grunt." Pitt then grins. "Actually, it will be enjoyable having a pair of gorgeous creatures like yourselves, cooking and cleaning house for me."[242]

Pitt never denies he can be a chauvinist,[243] but there are times when he acts more enlightened about women than most men. When Jessie LaBaron demands to be on the search team for her missing husband, Pitt tells Giordino that Jessie "has just as much right to get herself killed as we do."[244] When Pitt tries to warn Eva Rojas that someone is trying to kill her she stubbornly insists that she can take care of herself. If his observation, that many women have said this and wound up in the morgue, sounds chauvinistic, it still makes good sense.[245] In a charming scene in *Shock Wave* Pitt ignores his usual custom against attending Washington cocktail parties, hoping to meet Maeve again. While he waits for her to arrive, Pitt dances with the plain or unattractive women other men ignore because he has discovered that these women are often the smartest and most interesting.[246] Compare this to an unrepentant chauvinist like French triple-agent Ismail Yerli, who is only sexually attracted to the dazzling Hala Kamil. When confronted about his feelings by Hala, Yerli does not even feel bad about using her because "like too many women who are drawn to aloof men who treat them indifferently, she could not help herself from falling in love with him."[247] Not all observations about women in Cussler's adventures come from men, however. Maeve admits to herself that Pitt has the kind of strong face to which women are drawn.[248] Marie Sheldon observes that her recently separated friend Dana is a classic model of a depressed and frustrated female.[249] Eva tries to dismiss her trepidations about an impending journey as her "suspicious female nature," but "something deep inside, her intuition perhaps, cautioned her not to feel too secure."[250]

Men, meanwhile, do not escape observation. After waking up alone in Pitt's bed after a night of passion, Julia Lee tries to figure out her bachelor host by studying his home and deciding that Pitt falls somewhere between the classic male stereotypes of pack rat and neat freak.[251] Women may be drawn to Pitt's strong face, but Sandecker fairly beams whenever he is in the presence of beautiful women,[252] just one example that men behave differently around women in Cussler's adventures. In *Raise the Titanic!* Pitt notices how men are cautious where women are concerned: "We won't hesitate to risk the lives of a dozen members of our own sex, but we'll balk every time when it comes to endangering one of the female species."[253] Men make sacrifices for women even when there is no danger. Giordino is a tenacious fighter, but he will "suffer the agonies of the damned if he was forced into conversing with women."[254] More tragically, a grieving Fawkes recollects, "When a woman loses a man, he recalled hearing somewhere, she picks up her life as before and perseveres. But when a man loses a woman, he dies by half."[255]

In Cussler's adventures, part-time chauvinists like Pitt can be heroes, but unrepentant chauvinism like Yerli's is usually a tag that a man is a villain. When it comes to heroines and villainesses, however, the dividing line is determined more by behavior than prejudices. Up through the Victorian Era men were the standard bearers of adventure who could only light out for the unexplored places on the map without female entanglement.[256] But heroes change to reflect the norms of their generations,[257] and so there are Pitt adventures in which Loren, Maeve and Jessie join him, and sometimes Giordino and Gunn, for at least part of an adventure and their presence does not affect Pitt's abilities. The one exception is *Vixen 03*, in which Pitt is at his best when he is alone,[258] or in the brotherhood of men, such as his brother-in-color Giordino and the little Italian's "sibling," Steiger. Even though Loren behaves like a Howard Hawks heroine for most of this story her presence still hampers rather than helps Pitt, and at the end of *Vixen 03* Loren switches teams, so to speak, becoming a temptress of geniality, a modern version of the dark temptress.[259]

The dark temptress developed from ancient Eastern ideals about bad women like harlots and good women like mothers, sisters and daughters who should not be thought about in sexual terms.[260] By the time Cussler wrote *Vixen 03* the sexual revolution had swept through Western societies and such ancient ideals had been modified so that women were being judged as good or bad based upon sexual behavior. For most of *Vixen 03* Loren is a good woman because (1) she is sexually active but not a DC party girl, preferring to spend most of her nights at home watching movies with her cat, Ichabod,[261] and (2) she is an honest lover and politician.[262] Loren is up front with Pitt about dating Sawyer, and Sawyer's proposals to her. Sawyer is a secondary love interest, a character type often portrayed as a foil or dupe, such as Ralph Bellamy's Bruce Baldwin in Hawks's *His Girl Friday* (1940), or Dan Leeson in Leo McCarey's *The Awful Truth* (1937), and this is the case in *Vixen 03*.[263] But Sawyer also serves as a character barometer for Loren. As Jacqueline Jaffe explains in her critical review of *Arthur Conan Doyle*, female characters in old fashion adventure literature "seem to be identified with the world of the little men" in "a society that has replaced adventure with superficial social restrictions, curiosity with fear, and aggression with meekness."[264] These little men can be tamed and civilized,[265] but Pitt epitomizes "the idea—which in American literature is vividly expressed by the Huck Finn fantasy—of overt boyish disobedience to maternal female authority."[266] When Loren sets her conjugal sights on Sawyer she oscillates from good to bad by becoming a temptress of geniality who weaves a seductive spell that overpowers her prey.[267] Loren gets what she wants when Sawyer proposes again, but the little man leaves her empty and unfulfilled, so sometime between *Vixen 03* and *Deep Six* Loren does the right thing and breaks the engagement. Contrast this to Loren's former school friend Felicia Collins, a mercurial opportunist who sleeps with a variety of men to launch her career as an entertainer[268] and then to become a consort of political power players like Lusana and Daggat. Collins is a bad woman who cannot recall her lovers' faces but has no problem remembering the décor of their bedrooms, and so it comes as no surprise when Daggat is able to convince her to help him blackmail Loren to further his congressional career and presidential aspirations.

Maeve Fletcher and Deirdre Dorsett are even more dramatic examples of a good and a bad woman. These sisters, as Pitt realizes, are very different. Maeve is the mother of twins but also a tall outdoorsy tomboy who percolates girl-next-door sex appeal. Pitt starts off fantasizing about Maeve as a best friend's untamed sister in cutoff shorts and T-shirt washing a car, but he falls in love with her because she is a lot like him, a tough, intelligent, independent rover who lives to see whatever is waiting beyond the horizon. Deirdre, on the other hand, is a copper-haired temptress who exudes sensuality and sophistication. Pitt is attracted to her, but it is the primal attraction that a man feels for a succubus. When Pitt meets Deirdre on the dead ship *Polar Queen* he smells her perfume and cannot help desiring her, which makes him angry because of the macabre surroundings.[269] And Deirdre is as evil and lethal as a succubus. A sociopath who cannot tell the truth even when there is no reason to lie, Deirdre is a widow whose husband was murdered after demanding a divorce with a healthy settlement. She not only delights in tormenting Maeve, she actually shoots her and Pitt.

Cussler understands that adventure tales are male oriented, but he knows there are more women reading adventure novels than there are men reading romance novels, which is one reason he strives to make his heroines the kind of classy women with which other women identify. Cussler is also convinced that men and women identify with shrewd devil-may-care heroes who surmount all obstacles and emerge victorious in the end.[270] In the film *Six Days, Seven Nights* (1998) urbane heroine Robin Monroe (Anne Heche) tries to explain this to the curmudgeonly hero Quint Harris (Harrison Ford) as they discuss the realities of male-female dynamics:

> *Harris:* I thought that's what women wanted.
> *Monroe:* What?
> *Harris:* Men who weren't afraid to cry, who were in touch with their feminine side.
> *Monroe:* No, not when they're being chased by pirates, they like them mean and armed!

Cussler takes Monroe's argument one step further and insists that "women, in spite of the current hoopla about equality, still secretly yearn for the rugged he-man to sweep them off their feet. If you doubt this last statement, simply take a look at the staggering sales figures of the romantic novels by Rosemary Rogers and several other astute women writers."[271] Or Cussler's sales figures, for that matter, although critics like Gallagher ignore this success and Cussler's claim that 50 percent of his readers are women.[272] According to Gallagher, Cussler's "largest audience [is] among white, middle-aged, professional men."[273] Gallagher does not deny that "Women in [Cussler's] novels display strength and independence,"[274] but ignoring Cussler's claim about his female readers[275] allows Gallagher to dismiss Cussler's argument that "deep down, women still like the big, strong, mysterious guy to pick them up, carry them off, and save them from disaster"[276] and assert that Cussler's heroines "appear lonely and disconnected without Pitt's affection and protection." For critics like Gallagher, Cussler's heroines "serve principally as rewards for successful activity, on the same order of importance as a fine wine or a sumptuous meal, rather than as essential or complementary companions."[277] But Loren could be rebutting for Cussler's female readers (no matter the percentage) when she tells Pitt, "What would the women in the world do without you?"[278]

6

Influences from the Golden Age of Pulps, Movies and TV

Only John Ford could make *Donavan's Reef.*—Proud motto of The Corn-Fed Amigos, *As Time Goes By*[1]

O.F. Snelling's *007 James Bond: A Report* (1964) starts off with a look at two books published in 1953, Richard Usborne's *Clubland Heroes* and Ian Fleming's first 007 adventure *Casino Royale*. *Clubland Heroes* looks at ten authors of sensational fiction from Usborne's youth, but Snelling focuses on Richard Hannay's creator, John Buchan, Bulldog Drummond's creator, Sapper, and John Mansel's creator, Dornford Yates. Dubbing Hannay, Drummond and Mansel "the Terrible Trio of popular fiction between the two wars," Snelling examines how they were cast in the same post-war adventure-hero mold of West End clubmen of independent means who follow a rigid code of honor. Next, Snelling uses Usborne's analysis of Hannay, Drummond and Mansel "as a stepping-off point towards an examination" of Fleming and his clubman hero James Bond. Snelling concludes by comparing Bond to the Terrible Trio and exploring how the generation in which they were created made a difference in these characters.[2]

Following Snelling's example, this chapter looks at some of the creators whose sterling spadework paved the way for Dirk Pitt and Cussler's other heroes. Clive Cussler, born 12 months and three weeks after the death of the creator of Sherlock Holmes and *The Lost World*, grew up during the Golden Age of motion pictures, Saturday matinees and pulp magazines. As an adult, Cussler lived through the halcyon days of early television. During his award-winning advertising career Cussler proved himself an apt pupil of these and other media by creating entertaining (and sometimes iconic) advertisements for companies such as Budweiser, Bank of America, Royal Crown Cola and Ajax. Cussler proved his media acumen again when he became a bestselling suspense-adventure writer, but like the saying goes, all mirrors have two faces, and if we compare some of the dominant heroes and hero types from Cussler's formative years we should be able to gain further insight into his heroes.

Yesterday's Faces (Pulp Series Heroes)

Pulp fiction and pulp art historian Richard Lesser claims that a straight line can be drawn from the heroes of the 12th century to those of the 21st. Lesser points to the knights-errant who lived by the Code of Chivalry and Code of Courtly Love in the West, and to the samurais who followed the Bushido code in the East, and how new versions of these warriors were born anew as pulp magazine series heroes who "possessed a code of honor, and was brother to the samurai, cousin to the knight errant.... From Sir Lancelot to Schwarzenegger, the spirit of the knight errant animates these heroes."[3] As of this writing Cussler has never specified which pulp magazines or heroes influenced him, which might suggest that he may have been influenced more by the adventure in the pulps rather than any particular character or title.[4]

The era of the pulp magazine ran from approximately 1896 to 1957, but even before that there were Great Britain's yellow-backs[5] and the American dime novels. Just to stick a pin in a proper starting place, however, before the yellow-backs there were penny dreadfuls, also known as dreads, penny bloods or bloods.[6] As the general public became more literate around the middle of the 19th century it could not get enough of the dreads' sensational historical accounts of Sweeny Todd[7] or the Red Lion (a headquarters for highwaymen, thieves and law-breakers),[8] or fast-paced episodic fiction like Thomas Preskett Prest or Malcolm James Rymer's Gothic *Varney the Vampire*[9] (1847) and Rymer's prototype "fem jep" adventures *Edith the Captive* (1860) and *Edith Heron* (1861), or the "pot-pourri of crime and criminals in the city's underworld" to be found in *The Mysteries of London* (1848) by George W.M. Reynolds, a spiritual ancestor to Spillane and Fleming.[10] The trickle-down influence of penny-dreadful fiction in Cussler's adventures can be found in his sensational historical accounts of the Vikings or the Library of Alexandria ending up in North America, the Battle of Troy being fought in England instead of Turkey, Odysseus losing his ships near Nicaragua and Atlantis and Captain Nemo's *Nautilus* turning out to be real. Cussler's adventures are also fast paced and episodic. Many chapters end with a tease or cliffhanger like penny-dreadful installments, and for the same reason: to entice the reader to stick with the story.[11] As examined in the previous chapter, Gothic is a thematic preoccupation in Cussler's fiction and, by extension, so too is that genre's plot element of fem jep. Finally, an adventure hero is nothing without an antagonist or a threat, so criminals and crime play as grand a role in Cussler's adventures as they do in any penny dreadful.

While rogues and worse dominated the penny dreadfuls, heroic characters ruled the roost in the yellow-backs that began appearing around 1860. Some of the most popular early yellow-backs were police memoirs purportedly written by retired officers or former detectives,[12] while reprints of successful British and American crime, mystery and detection novels like *The Woman in White* and Richard Henry Savage's *The Masked Venus* (1893)[13] sold even better as inexpensive yellow-backs. The influence of these flamboyant detectives and classic mysteries are evident in pulp-action detectives, including Edward Parrish Ware's Jack Calhoun, chief Inspector for the U.S. Rangers stationed near the Sunken Lands of Northern Arkansas; Walter Archer Frost's semi-justice figure Ruggles (no first name given); Frederick W. Davis's Felix Boyd; John Carroll Daly's Race Williams and his femme fatale love interest, Florence Drummond, better known to the underworld as The Flame. Oh, and Hammett's hard-boiled Continental Op and Sam Spade. This influence is also evident in Cussler's heroes and his combining the mystery of the detective genre with the thrills of the adventure novel.

Across the Atlantic, publishers in the United States watched the success of the penny dreadfuls and yellow-backs with envious eyes, and it was not long before they were producing their own dime novels, story papers and reprint libraries. These weekly publications offered astounding adventures of glory and peril featuring such series heroes as frontier legend Buffalo Bill Cody, the romantic rebels Jesse and Frank James, athletes Frank and Dick Merriwell, the eccentric Old Sleuth and the prototype for the action detective, noble Nick Carter. Dime novels also featured adventures for children; hints of the somewhat fantastical journeys of Casey and Lacey Nicefolk in *Vin Fiz* and *Hotsy Totsy* can be found in the wondrous inventions and explorations of Frank Reade, Jr., and his family.[14]

All these stories and heroes blazed the trail for the pulp series heroes, the earliest of which included fighting sea captains à la Forester's Hornblower: Sabatini's Peter Blood and Louis Joseph Vance's Terence O'Rourke. These sea captains, like all of Cussler's heroes, fall under a pulp-series hero type Sampson calls "adventurers to places close and far."[15] H. Rider Haggard's cynical Allan Quatermain is the preeminent example of this hero type, but a lesser-known example that is a bit more in sync with Cussler's heroes is Peter Moore. Where Pitt is a marine engineer and Austin has a master's in systems management, Moore is a brass pounder in the manner of Dent and Moore's creator, George Frank Worts. But, like Pitt and Austin, Moore is a jack-of-all-trades and master of most[16] with a wanderlust that leads him around the world. Another example is Captain John Fury, an electrical-chemical engineer and explorer who travels the seven seas on his tanker *The Whirlwind*. Fury is the brilliant, brawling titular hero of *The Skipper* series, created by Norman Daniels. Fury starts his career clashing with pirates and other seafaring wrongdoers whose bad luck carry them across his bow, but after the start of World War II Fury dedicates most of his brutal attention upon Axis ships.[17] As for *The Whirlwind*, in many ways it is a precursor of *The Oregon*. The tanker's rusting hull disguises an armed carrier with torpedoes, guns and mines as well as a submarine and airplanes. *The Whirlwind* also boasts its own type of futuristic propulsion system, one that sucks water through the tanker's bow and shoots it out its stern. There is no Corporation but there is a colorful "battling crew"[18] that includes first-mate Marlin "Spike" Briggs, a man with a heavily scarred face from his numerous bouts of hand-to-hand combat, the gorilla-sized second-mate Hurricane Dan Belmont, Grump Rollins and Fury's friend Peter Doom, a former New York police inspector. One more example is Frederic Reddale's Matt Burden, a professional diver whose adventures take him around the world, including the Thames River, where he helps salvage a sunken ship full of copper ingots, and Samoa, where he deals with sharks while working on a breakwater. This is the sort of life Pitt or Austin might have lived if they had not been born 80 years too late.[19]

The audacious adventures in Cussler's novels remind some of Doc Savage, but when it comes to the makeup of his heroes they are more in tune with Dent's Miami private eye Oscar Sail. Extremely tall and dressed in black, Sail is more noir than adventure, but, like any Cussler hero, Sail is independent, pragmatic and capable of taking care of himself. Like Pitt, Austin, Cabrillo and Bell, Sail is unafraid to kill if necessary but has kept his humanity, and, like all Cussler's heroes, he has a natural directness and honesty and is astute at reading a person's character. Sail also loves the sea, making his home on the *Sail*, a black 45-foot Chesapeake Bay bugeye.[20]

Other forerunners for Cussler's heroes can be found almost everywhere in the pulps, but perhaps no hero types are more appropriate than pilots and cowboys.

Being pilots make heroes like Pitt and Austin literary descendants of aerial daredevils such as Wallace's propaganda pilot Tam O' The Scoots[21] and Herman Petersen's Barbe Pivet, a female lead in an adventure series featuring modern pirates and quests for sunken treasure. Tam and Barbe are the stars of such titles as *G-8 and His Battle Aces*, *Wings* and *War Birds*; they, in turn, were inspired by Charles "Lucky Lindy" Lindbergh, Amelia Earhart and Howard

Hughes. According to Lesser, "All of them shared the same secret ingredient; they were 'just a little bit crazy,'"[22] an observation Giordino echoes when he tells Pitt in their very first scene together that no sane person would choose to ditch an airplane in the Pacific Ocean in the middle of the night—"except you, that is."[23]

The popular figure of the American cowboy is a combination of noble savage, daredevil and knight-errant,[24] but pilots and cowboys are actually not that different. A good example is Robert J. Hogan's Lieutenant Smoke Wade, a World War I fighter pilot and an iconic cowboy right down to his Arizona drawl and six-shooters. Whether a pulp cowboy rode in a Spad in Germany or on a pinto south of the Pecos, his stories, like Cussler's adventures, contain plenty of "action, movement, friendship under danger. Lots of freedom, lots of violence. All of this salted down with humor."[25] There was no more popular hero type in the pulps and perhaps no more popular pulp cowboy than Mulford's Hopalong Cassidy, a young redhead who is deadly when drawing his twin Colt .45s. "Hoppy" was not above recklessness and mischief, and he was ready to fight when the cause was right. Just the sort who might shoot down an airplane rather than see it land on an airfield recently overrun by the enemy. A pulp cowboy can even be a solver of mysteries like Pitt and Bell, and there is no better example of this than W.C. Tuttle's Hashknife Hartley and his faithful Giordino, Dave "Sleepy" Stevens.

The young Hashknife, like the young Pitt and the young Cassidy, is a boisterous youth blessed with a mind that remains calm, dispassionate and watchful at all times. (The same can be said for Bell's mind, but he is never boisterous.) Pitt, Cassidy and Hashknife become more mature with age and experience,[26] but no matter how many years pass, Hashknife and Pitt or any of Cussler's heroes will never give up on a puzzle until it is solved. Pitt often wrestles with problems that have explanations that remain just out of reach, only to have Fate or coincidence reveal the proper clue in the nick of time, allowing the solution to snap into focus.[27] Hashknife suffers from the same affliction. In "The Cross in the Box Mystery" a cowboy describes one of these moments of insight.

> Last night [Hashknife] just sat there and never paid no attention to anybody. We was all a-talkin,' but I betcha he never heard a word we said. And all to once he kinda jerks himself almost out of the chair and says, like he was talkin' to himself, "Why, of course! Any damn fool ought to have seen that."[28]

The same type of free and easy banter goes on between Pitt and Giordino, Austin and Zavala, and Sam and Remi Fargo. Consider the following dialogue from "The Buckaroo of Blue Wells":

> *Sleepy*: I dunno just how or why he picked up with me, but we've been together ever since.
> *Hashknife*: I felt sorry for yuh.
> *Sleepy*: Yeah, and I've felt sorry for myself ever since.[29]

The specifics of an adventure involving cowboys, pilots or Cussler's heroes are vastly different, of course, but enough similarities remain as proof that Lesser's line can be drawn between penny dreadfuls to modern suspense-adventure bestsellers. In hindsight, this is not only natural but obvious because, as Sampson writes, "When the pulp magazines first appeared, the adventure story was waiting for them, polished by accumulated centuries of story telling."[30] From the ancient past to today the essence of the hero lives on, changing over time but always at his core brother to the samurai, cousin to the knight-errant.

Movie Heroes for the Greatest Generation

Cussler's stories are littered with movie references, from Errol Flynn adventures to old-time horror, comedy and gangster films to classics like *Casablanca, Arsenic and Old Lace* (1944) and *Titanic* (1953). Cussler also uses movie references to describe supporting characters like Devine ("a W.C. Fields-type, heavy through the middle with a slow whining voice")[31] and O'Meara (who sports a "thick Gabby Hayes beard").[32] Cussler was once told by an interviewer that his writing calls to mind the comic books of the thirties and forties, and Cussler admits he read Superman, Batman and other superheroes as a kid, but "then there were the movies, the older movies, the black and whites." Cussler believes the heroes in older films were bigger but more human, especially in Westerns and detective movies. "[If] you take all the young actors today under the age of thirty ... they all look like they came out of a cookie cutter. There's nothing really distinguished about any of them. Where's the Glenn Fords, the Jimmy Stewarts, the Gary Coopers, the John Waynes, the Humphrey Bogarts, the Jimmy Cagneys? None of [today's actors] have a distinctive voice ... you don't have the super heroes around like you used to."[33] Cussler's heroes are also bigger but more human and distinctive, and to see how they reflect this old-movie influence we can compare them with some of the most popular heroes from Hollywood's Golden Age, brought to the silver screen by the likes of Frank Capra, John Ford and Howard Hawks.[34]

The Capra hero like Jefferson Smith from *Mr. Smith Goes to Washington* (1939) and Longfellow Deeds from *Mr. Deeds Goes to Town* (1936), played so memorably by James Stewart and Gary Cooper, respectively, is a populist who places his faith in individualism, self-help, independence, the past, Yankee common sense and loyalty.[35] The Capra protagonist shares Will Rogers's skepticism of intellectuals and politicians. As Louis Gianetti writes in *Masters of American Cinema* (1981), Capra's heroes "distrust organized power blocks, be they Democratic, Republican, or Independent,"[36] and the same is true for Cussler's heroes.[37] Cussler frequently features corrupt politicians as villains, incorporates governmental corruption in many of his plots[38] and never reveals Pitt's party affiliation. Another parallel between the Capra and Cussler hero is their allergies to authority figures. Capra freely admitted, "I take a dim view of authority of any kind.... I don't like anybody telling me what to do."[39] For his part, the fiercely independent Cussler has made good on his oath to never work for anyone other than himself after being let go by the Hull/Mefford Agency. He also portrays Pitt as rude, even belligerent, to authority figures, including Sandecker.

If there is one group the Capra and Cussler hero have misgivings about more than politicians and authority figures it is powerful businessmen. Capra does not trust the very rich, and his films often portray tycoons as cold, greedy and isolated from the common experiences of life.[40] Film teacher and author Morris Dickstein points out that the Capra country boy hero is confronted in the nation's capital with the corruption embodied by "various capitalist heavies."[41] Gianetti writes that Capra is inclined to take cheap shots at easy targets like "snooty society folks, intellectuals, shyster lawyers, and of course that indispensable figure, the tycoon."[42] Dickstein describes this as "Capra's populist simplicity [showing] up in the way he tended to personalize social problems into boy scouts and bosses, heroes and villains."[43] Cussler displays similar suspicions regarding very rich businessmen, beginning with the villains in *Pacific Vortex*, *The Mediterranean Caper* and *Iceberg*. To date, corrupt businessmen appear in 14 of the 20 novels Cussler has written on his own, making them his most frequently targeted type of bad guy.

There are, however, key differences between the Capra hero and Cussler hero, perhaps best demonstrated by Pitt. Dickstein writes, "Capra's heroes are not exceptional men, but only heightened versions of ordinary good men; they may stumble into heroism, but their myth is the Thirties myth of the common man."[44] Pitt stumbles into a few adventures, as in *Dragon* and *Flood Tide*, but there is very little that is unexceptional about NUMA's special projects director. The Capra hero is also often a country boy who comes to the big city, where he overcomes overwhelming odds to outsmart the corrupt men dedicated to defeating him.[45] Pitt knows a thing or two about overcoming overwhelming odds, but a Newport Beach native can hardly be called a country boy. The Capra hero is also naïve,[46] something else that cannot be said about Pitt, at least by the end of *Iceberg*, and while the Capra hero and Pitt are idealists, Pitt is additionally a cynic.[47] Unfortunately the naïveté of the Capra hero makes him vulnerable to exploitation by people feigning sympathy to his values, especially the Capra heroine, pessimistic manipulators eventually converted to the hero's populist ideals by his inborn goodness.[48] Prior to the heroine's conversion, however, Capra heroes often "fall into bouts of serious depression" after "the great world they enter refuses to answer to their naïve expectations."[49] Humiliation and disillusionment are therefore never far off in the Capra universe.[50] This is not the case with Pitt, who is as pragmatic as he is idealistic. Pitt is not immune to such feelings, but such episodes are typically brief. As for succumbing to false sympathy, smooth talkers need not waste their time on Pitt. Actions impress him, not words or opinions.

Pitt and Cussler's other heroes share this last characteristic with the two hero types created by John Ford and typified by actors Henry Fonda and John Wayne.

The Ford hero played by Fonda in *Young Mr. Lincoln* (1939), *The Grapes of Wrath* (1940) and *Mr. Roberts* (1955) is seldom forceful and usually shy, yet he is brimming with as much confidence as any Cussler hero, and when he takes on a task he sees it through without a lot of hoopla.[51] Ford's Fonda hero and Cussler's heroes also share a genuine decency and intelligence which they do not feel the need to hide beneath a macho veneer.[52]

In contrast, the Ford hero played by John Wayne is, again like Cussler's heroes, someone willing to sacrifice anything, including his life, for the sake of honor and duty. The Wayne hero and Cussler's heroes are also physically intimidating. Pitt, Austin, Cabrillo and Bell are tall, well-built men who carry themselves with an air of hard-won and world-tested confidence, plus Pitt's "firm, almost cruel"[53] face can make people a little ill at ease. These heroes are even more intimidating by reputation.[54] The Wayne hero in *Stagecoach* (1939) and *The Man Who Shot Liberty Valance* (1962) is the toughest hombre and fastest draw in the territory, while in *She Wore a Yellow Ribbon* (1949) and *Rio Grande* (1950) he is known as a respected career military officer. Pitt, in contrast, is best known as Senator George Pitt's son and Sandecker's fair-haired boy until he becomes the man who raised the *Titanic*.[55] In the course of building their reputations, the Wayne hero and Cussler hero establish themselves as men of few words and even fewer pretenses, but when they say they are going to do something they do it, and do it forcefully.[56]

Wayne and Ford made 27 films together, with the Wayne hero becoming a more paternal figure as he ages; the same can be said for Pitt over the course of Cussler's 17 solo novels.[57] This parallel may not be a coincidence. Ford, unlike most American directors, demonstrates an interest and respect for older people[58]; so, too, does Cussler, with such characters as Brian Shaw, Dr. Jonsson (*Iceberg*) and Adeline Hobart (*Raise the Titanic!*).[59] The most obvious example of Cussler's interest in and respect for older people, however, is Pitt's second father,

Sandecker, who would feel right at home in Ford's films, where "authority figures, especially fathers, military leaders, and clergymen, are often portrayed with Jehovah-like infallibility."[60] By the end of *Trojan Odyssey* Pitt is feeling his age and he is a new father, so it is only appropriate that he join the ranks of Cussler's older characters and authority figures by marrying Loren and succeeding Sandecker as head of NUMA, only the second man to hold the post.[61] As will be documented in Chapter 7, becoming a father and husband and replacing his second father marks the end of a series-long hero's quest for Pitt, but, in spite of this, he remains a vital, heroic character.[62] The only other Cussler hero to go through a similar experience is Bell, by which time he is a married man with four children.

Another similarity between Pitt and Ford's Wayne hero is their brusqueness. A fine example of this trait can be found in the 1956 classic, *The Searchers*. Wayne's character, Ethan Edwards, sneers a sarcastic retort, "That'll be the day," whenever anyone suggests he will be bested by another man. In *They Were Expendable* (1945), Wayne's Lt. J.G. "Rusty" Ryan has a surrogate father-son relationship with his superior officer, Lt. John "Brick" Brickley. In an early scene, Ryan reacts to some galling orders from headquarters by kicking a convenient pale.

"Did that help?" Brick shouts.

"It did!" Ryan shouts back before storming out. (As soon as Brickley is alone, the normally placid man also kicks the pale, as Sandecker might do in a similar situation with Pitt.)

An important difference between Ford's heroes and Cussler's heroes is their attitude towards the opposite sex. The Fonda hero is shy around women, and the Wayne hero merely uncomfortable, while Cussler's heroes are at ease. Ford's heroes are perfect gentlemen, and whereas Cussler's bachelor heroes are generally polite, their actions would hardly be considered moral.[63] For example, in *Raise the Titanic!* Pitt makes love to Dana Seagram aboard the salvaged liner. After the *Titanic* docks in New York and Pitt sneaks away from the hoopla with Gene Seagram's help, he gets a room in Central Park's swanky Pierre Hotel. As Pitt relaxes in a bathtub with a vodka, Seagram confides to him that Dana wants a divorce. In one of Pitt's less admirable moments, he advises Seagram to forget about Dana and find someone else. Seagram ignores this advice. Later, when the *Titanic*'s vault is opened and the byzanium for which the liner was raised to recover is not on board, Seagram has a nervous breakdown. Perhaps to assuage his guilty conscience, Pitt refuses to give up until he locates the missing byzanium.

In spite of this difference, Ford's hero types serve as excellent models for Pitt's "two men," or polar personalities, with the Fonda hero representing the side of Pitt that Giordino describes as "the moody one, the one who often withdrew to himself for hours at a time and became remote and aloof, as though his mind were constantly churning over some dream." The Wayne hero, conversely, represents Pitt's "coldly efficient" side that "rarely made a mistake," but is "humorous, unpretentious and easily made friends with everyone who came in contact with him."[64]

As much as Cussler's heroes have in common with Ford's heroes, they would really be at home in a movie directed by Howard Hawks. Like Cussler's adventures, Hawks's action films feature offbeat characters working in adventurous, dangerous professions far from the center of normalcy.[65] Hawks's heroes include race drivers, big-game trappers and military men whose exploits take them to places like Africa, China and the Arctic. Cussler's heroes also travel to the far corners of the globe as well as deep beneath the earth's oceans and all the way to the moon, while Pitt, Girodino, Sandecker and Gunn are either serving in the military or are veterans. Many of Cussler's heroes are also experienced seamen or pilots, or both.

Hawks and Cussler are similar is their casual self-appraisal as creators. Hawks insisted he was just a storyteller,[66] and Cussler considers himself an entertainer rather than an author. Hawks was adamant about working with Hollywood's best people, especially writers, including Ben Hecht,[67] William Faulkner[68] and Leigh Brackett.[69] Cussler, meanwhile, spends months researching his novels before he begins writing, and will even telephone the White House to confirm the accuracy of his historical and technical details.[70] In this regard Cussler is less like Hawks and more like Ford, who claimed he could film a movie in three weeks after he spent six months researching it.[71] Hawks possessed a casual attitude when it came to his movie's internal logic[72]; he insisted the important thing was to give people "two or three really top-notch scenes" and then try "not to annoy the audience the rest of the time." This attitude causes the pacing in Hawks's films to occasionally sag, though his pre–World-War II movies, like all of Cussler's adventures, feature "tight, compact stories, with plots that are usually clear and straightforward."[73] All of Hawks's adventures, like all of Cussler's adventures, are organized around some kind of journey or a job that needs doing or a constricting situation requiring immediate relief,[74] but, structurally, Cussler's adventures have just as much in common with Hawks's screwball comedies, which feature absurdly improbable premises filled with delightfully outrageous twists and turns that have a propensity to snowball out of control.[75] Hawks and Cussler also enjoy having their stories brush up against or veer directly into comedy during suspenseful scenes.

Another key ingredient in Hawks adventure films is how "rugged males master their work and environment through their professional competence."[76] This is as true in a Western such as *Rio Bravo* (1959)—lawmen use their guns and wits to beat overwhelming odds to maintain justice in their town—as it is in a safari film like *Hatari* (1962)—men and women with disparate skills overcome nature to capture wild animals for zoos around the world—or a science-fiction film like the Hawks production of *The Thing from Another World* (1951)—military men and scientists overcome a hostile Arctic environment to defeat an alien threat to our planet. This is also a key ingredient in many Cussler adventures, wherein the hero and his helpers master their work and environment using any engineering training and military, diving, driving and piloting skills they have mixed with personal education and wits.

Neither Hawks nor Cussler ever claimed to be concerned about literary themes, but a few thematic preoccupations that run through Hawks's movies also appear in Cussler's adventures, starting with what Gianetti calls "professionalism as a regenerative force."[77] In *Rio Bravo* the town's deputy, Dude (Dean Martin), becomes a drunk after the woman he loves makes a fool of him. Dude's friends Chance (Wayne) and Stumpy (Walter Brennan) refuse to give up on him, and when danger hits town, Dude reclaims his dignity by becoming sober and fighting alongside his friends. In *Flood Tide* Pitt visits isolated Orion Lake, in Washington, after Maeve's death. Pitt's physical recuperation since the end of *Shock Wave* has been remarkable, but his emotional recuperation is stuck in neutral until curiosity gets the better of him and he investigates suspicious activities at Qin Shang's nearby estate. Before long, Pitt is back in form, with Giordino and Julia Lee by his side as he uncovers an illegal Chinese smuggling operation and recovers stolen treasure.

Another predominant theme is self-respect. In *Red River* (1948), rancher Thomas Dunson (John Wayne) loses his self-respect when his surrogate son, Matt Garth (Montgomery Clift), is forced to take over a do-or-die cattle drive to save it from Dunson's stubborn incompetence. As Garth completes the cattle drive he grows in stature with himself and the cowboys who follow him, but Dunson can only regain his self-respect after he and Garth come to blows and Dunson discovers they are equals, and that there is no shame in being proven wrong by a peer. In comparison, a Cussler hero may suffer disillusionment when a plan goes awry and it leads to unfortunate consequences, but he regains his self-respect by righting his mistake and defeating the villain.

The importance of professionals working together as a group is another thematic preoccupation, although there is never any question that the hero of a Hawks film is the man in charge; the same can be said for the hero in a Cussler adventure.

One more commonality shared by Hawks and Cussler is their ideal heroine. Both favor likable, independent working girls capable of holding their own in a male-dominated society. Hawks and Cussler part ways, however, when it comes to domestic women and married life. Hawks has no interest in such things,[78] while Cussler has created several happily married characters with families, most notably Yaeger.[79] By the end of *Trojan Odyssey* Pitt is also a husband and father, although we see nothing of his domestic life until after Dirk Cussler joins the series, with *Black Wind*.[80] Even so, the only time Cussler makes domestic life an integral part of a plot is with the Seagrams, a possible influence from the soap-opera-adventure novels of Harold Robbins,[81] and then-popular films like *Airport* (1970).

The starkest difference between Hawks and Cussler is their treatment of common folk. Average people are frequently absent in a Hawks films, and when they do appear they are often dismissed as hicks,[82] whereas average people frequently appear in Cussler's adventures and tend to be somewhat clichéd, but still colorful and memorable. Cussler admires average people as much as Capra,[83] which makes the plot twist in *Vixen 03* with Lee and Maxine Rafferty effective. Revealing such a nice older couple to be a pair of greedy, murderous scoundrels is unique in the series. This difference is even more pronounced when Cussler is compared to other influential producer-directors from Hollywood's Golden Age. Hawks's portrayal of average people might be unkind, but he does not appear to dislike or distrust them; the same cannot be said for his peers Alfred Hitchcock and Billy Wilder. Hitchcock's heroes "are generally superficially ordinary" à la Capra, but the Hitchcock hero has "curious—often kinky—quirks"[84] so his most likable heroes tend to appear in lighter fare in which the adventure is not taken seriously, like Cary Grant's Richard Thorndyke in *North by Northwest* (1959). Wilder, whose films include *Some Like It Hot* (1959), *Stalag 17* (1953) and *The Apartment* (1960), takes "savage delight in exposing human venality," so the Wilder hero is often a "weak compromiser who's not as smart as he thinks he is" which makes him both "victim and victimizer."[85] This kind of character would be a villain, or at least despised or pitied by Capra, Ford, Hawks and Cussler.[86] Wilder and Hitchcock look at small-town America and see something like a *Shadow of a Doubt* (1943), in which an innocent teenaged girl named Charlie (Teresa Wright) learns that her big-city Uncle Charley (Joseph Cotten) is a serial killer. Capra sees the populist foundations that create heroes like Jefferson Smith or Longfellow Deeds. As for Cussler, he is aware that some people can be rotten to the core, but, like Capra, Ford and Hawks, he knows there are decent people in the world. Cussler's heroes are more capable, daring and resourceful than the average Joe—readers expect no less from their serial adventure hero. Given the chance, though, average people in Cussler's adventures, such as the members of the Sixth Louisiana Regiment, can turn out to be as courageous as his principal heroes, and that is a crucial point. In Cussler's adventures, as in Capra's, Ford's and Hawks's films, people are not perfect, and even heroes have their faults. As there is no shame in being imperfect, we should not feel guilty or embarrassed about our shortcomings, nor should we dismiss or ignore them. We can be heroes by doing our best for ourselves and for other people, like fixing a flat tire for a stranger even if it means being late to our own party (as Pitt does in "The Reunion"). Hitchcock and Wilder look at people and see the worst even during their better moments, but Cussler, Capra, Ford and Hawks champion people like Pitt who try to do their best, especially during the worst of times.

Small Screen, Big-Time Heroes

Dirk Pitt, created around 1964, is one of the earliest examples of the self-sacrificing, self-reliant and self-effacing[87] hero archetype as discussed in the preface, but *The Mediterranean Caper* was not published until 1973, by which time other heroes in this new mold were appearing in some television adventure shows. According to Bloom, "Cussler's style is reminiscent of much popular adolescent television viewing of the later 1960s and early 1970s."[88] But Cussler insists that television heroes were not an influence when he created Pitt.[89] This suggests that the conditions may have been right in the early sixties for the birth of this new archetype, something Cussler's marketing experience and his research into adventure literature may have made him sensitive to, much like a perceptive investor knows to buy stock in IBM or Apple at their start-ups.

One the earliest television programs with parallels to Cussler's adventures is Irwin Allen's *Voyage to the Bottom of the Sea* (1964–68).[90] Based on Allen's 1961 film of the same title, the series chronicles the adventures of the nuclear submarine USOS *Seaview*[91] designed by Admiral Harriman Nelson. In the film, Nelson (Walter Pidgeon) is a career navy man in his middle sixties, but, in the series, Nelson (Richard Basehart) is more vigorous and closer to 50. One of the world's top scientists and a combat veteran who served as an officer aboard America's first nuclear submarine, USS *Nautilus* (SSN-571), Nelson retired from the navy to form the Nelson Institute of Marine Research. Nelson designed *Seaview* and her sister ships *Polidor*, *Neptune* and *Angler*[92] for marine research, but *Seaview* is also a naval reserve vessel subject to being drafted into service. Because of this, *Seaview* carries ballistic missiles and its crew consists of retired navy men and members of the naval reserve.[93] Like another certain retired admiral, Nelson is shorter than average, has a temper, is known for speaking his mind, and is respected by the scientific and military communities. Nelson also has a father-son relationship with his second-in-command, Lee Crane (David Hedison), an officer on loan from the navy. Crane is tall, has thick black hair, and is unafraid to disagree with or disobey Nelson, but Crane is loyal to the admiral and will not hesitate to risk his career or his life for him; Nelson feels the same way about Crane. Of the two, though, Nelson is the one who can be as clever as Pitt when it comes to concocting MacGyver-like methods to escape certain death, such as building a life raft out of inflated wet suits ("The Mutiny"). *Voyage to the Bottom of the Sea* is set in the near future (approximately 1973 to 1984) and mixes old fashion (and sometimes outlandish) adventure with political intrigue and mystery, most notably during its first season.[94] The premiere episode, "Eleven Days to Zero," prefigures *Atlantis Found* as Nelson tries to stop an organization from flooding the world with tidal waves created by Arctic earthquakes. "City Beneath the Sea" features an underwater city on par with Soggy Acres from *Dragon*. One of the series' best episodes, "The Fear-Makers," foreshadows the QD organism and Nerve Agent S as a nerve gas capable of inducing extreme paranoia before turning toxic is released inside *Seaview*. Echoes of *Deep Six* can also be found in a plot involving the president of the United States and experimental brain surgery (in this case as part of an assassination attempt) in "Hail to the Chief," while a voracious form of plankton in "The Price of Doom" could be the more virulent brother to the red algae from *Sahara*.

The same year *Voyage to the Bottom of the Sea* debuted came *Jonny Quest* (1964–1965),[95] the first cartoon television series to use realistic animation to present a human cast of characters[96] and arguably American television's first techno-thriller, incorporating technology that its creator, Doug Wildey, developed while researching magazines like *Popular Science*, *Popular Mechanics*, *Science Digest* and *Scientific American*.[97] Producers William Hanna and Joseph Barbera, best known for their Oscar-winning *Tom and Jerry* theatrical cartoons (1940–1957)[98] and the popular prime-time cartoon series *The Flintstones* (1960–1966), hired Wildey to design an animation version of the radio program *Jack Armstrong, The All-American Boy* (1933–1951). After seeing Wildey's work, however, Hanna-Barbera decided to have him create an original adventure show along the same lines. Wildey took some of his *Jack Armstrong* concepts and mixed in elements from the newspaper strip *Terry and the Pirates* (1934–1946) by Milton Caniff (for whom Wildey had worked) and Jackie Cooper movies to come up with the globetrotting exploits of eleven-year-old Jonny (Tim Matheson), his father, Dr. Benton Quest (John Stephenson/Don Messick), Jonny's brother-in-color, Hadji (Danny Bravo), the family's guardian and the boys' tutor, Roger "Race" Bannon (Mike Road), and Jonny's bulldog, Bandit (Messick).

Dr. Quest, like Admiral Nelson, is one of the world's top scientists, and with his red hair, mustache and beard he could be the Sherlock to Sandecker's Mycroft. Quest conducts research and experiments at his home on Palm Key Island for the United States government, although it is never made clear if he is a full-time federal employee (making Quest a bureaucrat) or a consultant who goes on assignments.[99] One week Quest is assigned to investigate the disappearance of a guided missile over the Arctic, but the next he is flying to the Andes to install his own prototype air filter in a silver mine. Whatever Quest's exact job duties are, his scientific work is judged to be important enough by an agency, known as Intelligence I, to warrant assigning Race as permanent bodyguard for the doctor and boys.

Cussler's adventures can be audacious but they are not fantasies, and Hanna-Barbera wanted the same balance of "documentary reality and creative adventure" in *Jonny Quest*. Like Cussler, Wildey admits, "I tried to incorporate the [movie] serial approach to *Jonny Quest* in that yes, it was bigger than life, yes, it can't actually happen, but if it's done properly you believe it. That is the philosophy behind it. There is a line I never like to go beyond, because it goes from semi-believable high-adventure to straight-out garbage."[100] These high adventures include the recent disappearance of five ships in the Sargasso Sea ("Mystery of the Lizard Men"), voodoo in the Caribbean ("Dreadful Doll"), artificial dragons in the Pacific ("The Dragons of Ashida," an homage to "The Most Dangerous Game"),[101] the discovery of Spanish treasure while testing an experimental mini-sub ("Skull and Double-Crossbones"), battles with a World War I flying ace ("Shadow of the Condor") and a Nazi war criminal ("Turu the Terrible") and more than one skirmish with Dr. Quest's archenemy, the magnificent Emperor of Crime Dr. Zin. With the exception of a living mummy ("The Curse of Anubis") and possibly a lycanthrope ("The Werewolf of the Timberland") the adventures in *Jonny Quest* strike the same reality/creative balance of Cussler's adventures. The Quests have run-ins with Crypeids, including a Yeti ("Monsters in the Monastery") and a sea creature that may be an oceanic missing link ("The

Sea Haunt"); for his part, Cussler features a sea serpent, named Basil, in *Shock Wave*. Like many of Cussler's adventures, a lost treasure or a lost civilization plays a part in a number of *Jonny Quest* episodes, as do death traps and ingenious escapes. There are also offbeat supporting characters who work far from the center of normalcy, such as the fabulous Pasha Peddler (Jesse White, a.k.a. The Lonely Maytag Repairman) in "Calcutta Adventure." The sea is also a major component in many *Jonny Quest* adventures as is advanced marine technology that would be the envy of NUMA, such as the mini-sub and a Prober ("Riddle of the Gold") that could be a forerunner for the *Big John* DSMV. Dr. Quest's research on the destructive capabilities of ultra-high frequency sonic waves ("Calcutta Adventure") prefigures *Shock Wave*, and a search for a mineral called trinauxite, which is essential for the space program ("Turu the Terrible"), predates the search for byzanium in *Raise the Titanic!*, and zirconium in *Iceberg*.

A year after *Voyage to the Bottom of the Sea* and *Jonny Quest* came *I Spy*, one of the earliest television programs to cash in on the James Bond phenomenon. Like Cussler's heroes, but unlike most television spies from this period, Alexander Scott (Bill Cosby) and Kelly Robinson (Robert Culp) are often injured in the line of duty and worry about the personal toll their jobs are taking on them. They are also as fearless as Cussler's heroes when it comes to challenging those in positions of authority. While *I Spy* is more realistic than Cussler's high adventures, both mix witty comedy with drama and action, most notably in the banter between the principal characters.

The same year *I Spy* debuted came *The Wild, Wild West*, another program that cashed in on the James Bond phenomenon but which became something eccentrically unique. Set during Ulysses S. Grant's administration (1869–77), *The Wild, Wild West* follows the exploits of Secret Service agents James West (Robert Conrad) and Artemus Gordon (Ross Martin). Employing elements from the science fiction sub-genre of alternate history with the western and espionage genres, the show went on to become American television's first steampunk series. But, as in the case of *I Spy*, it is the heroes, not the style of adventure, which parallels Cussler's adventures.

West and Gordon, like Pitt and Giordino or Austin and Zavala, are brothers-in-arms. West, a former Civil War intelligence and cavalry officer, is a charming gunslinger while Gordon is a gifted gadgeteer, consummate actor and master of disguise, and a big reason their onscreen partnership is so effective is because it reflects the way Conrad and Martin complemented each other.[102] Like Scotty and Kelly in *I Spy*, West and Gordon fit the Pitt hero archetype. In their own ways they are self-sacrificing, self-reliant, self-effacing and patriotic. Both, likewise, pursue any beautiful woman that crosses their paths with the same zeal and success as Cussler's heroes. West and Gordon also banter like Cussler's heroes[103] and have more than a spark of Peter Pan, which makes this pair as difficult to handle as any of Cussler's bad boys. In the two-parter "The Night of the Winged Terror," West is working while Gordon is in the nation's capital. (In reality, actor Ross Martin was recovering from a heart attack.) While meeting with President Grant, West asks, "How is Artie bearing up under his Washington assignment, sir?"

Sounding a little like Sandecker, Grant snarls, "The question is, how is *Washington* bearing up?" Grant, like Sandecker, tolerates this behavior with a wink because he has complete faith in the abilities of his top Secret Service agents.

Even though *The Wild, Wild West* takes place about three decades before *The Chase*, it has less in common with Bell's first adventure than the Pitt series or *NUMA Files*. Bell has no partner like Gordon, and the villain Bell pursues is nothing like the "menagerie of psychotically intelligent or blindly baneful villains ... planning to take over either America or the world"[104] that regularly challenge West and Gordon. Cromwell is a psychopath, not a Criminal Mastermind like the marvelous megalomaniac Dr. Miguelito Loveless (Michael Dunn), the Moriarty of *The Wild, Wild West*.[105] There is also the matter of technology. *The Chase* showcases contemporary inventions like automobiles, motorcycles and airplanes, but *The Wild, Wild West* flaunts Victorian variations of Bond technology, including a telegraph device concealed in a cane, and a stagecoach with an ejector seat.

Perhaps no sixties television hero better fits the Pitt hero archetype than James Tiberius Kirk (William Shatner), from *Star Trek*. Modeled in part on one of Cussler's favorite characters, Horatio Hornblower,[106] Kirk is self-reliant, self-sacrificing, self-effacing, patriotic, honorable, genial but dangerous when threatened, educated, intuitive, a realist, a cynic and has a dash of Peter Pan in his makeup. Being the captain of a starship in the 23rd century also makes Kirk a bureaucrat and a military man. Kirk even has Pitt's "two men" personalities, a humorous good-pal-the-captain who snaps to in time of need to become a merciless tactician and fierce combatant.[107] His friends Mr. Spock (Leonard Nimoy) and Dr. Leonard "Bones" McCoy (DeForest Kelley) are as much brothers-in-arms as Giordino and Gunn are to Pitt, and they exchange the same style of classic movie banter.[108] Like Pitt, Kirk disregards logic when it gets in the way. He can also be as unconventionally clever and daring when it comes to cheating death, whether that involves improvising the rules of a card game, called Fizzbin, to facilitate an escape ("A Piece of the Action") or leaving the *Enterprise*'s shields down after an attack to lure an enemy into range for a retaliatory strike ("Balance of Terror"). Both Pitt and Kirk are natural-born leaders, although Pitt is a manager and Kirk is an officer. Adventure is Pitt's narcotic and his drug is flying antique aircraft, driving classic cars, diving for shipwrecks and probing the unknown depths of the sea.[109] Kirk is just as addicted to adventure, but as Spock tells him in the 1982 theatrical film *Star Trek II: The Wrath of Khan*, "Commanding a starship is your first, best destiny." In one of Kirk's last scenes before his death in *Star Trek: Generations* (1994), he advises another *Enterprise* captain, Jean-Luc Picard (Patrick Stewart), "Don't let them do anything that takes you off the bridge of that ship, because while you're there you can make a difference." Kirk's drug is being relevant.

Bloom makes a somewhat backhanded observation regarding these and other similarities in *Star Trek* and Cussler's adventures by claiming that Cussler is recycling clichés that highlight "affinities with other media, especially television 'space opera.'"[110] Outside of the Pitt series this is most obvious in *Oregon Files*, starting with its recurrent comparisons of the *Oregon*'s op center with the bridge on the *Enterprise*. Life aboard the *Oregon* has a similar feel to that on the *Enterprise* (which is patterned after life aboard a military vessel); the ship features an international crew like the ones on *Star Trek* and its spin-offs; the *Oregon Files* adventures tend to focus on the ship's commander, and, like the *Enterprise*, the *Oregon* has no allegiance to any one country, but will come to the aid of any democratic society.

One last television hero with parallels to Cussler's adventures is Thomas Banacek (George Peppard). *Banacek*, which debuted the year before *The Mediterranean Caper* was published, was possibly inspired by the 1968 film *The Thomas Crown Affair* starring Steve McQueen, which is also set in Boston. A suave Polish-American freelance insurance investigator, Banacek is paid a 10-percent finder's fee if he can solve a claim before an insurance company's internal investigators do. Banacek only takes on cases that will net him at least $1 million, and are preferably paid by National Meridian Insurance, the company that replaced his mathematician father with a computer before the senior Banacek could retire and claim a pension.

A combination of sophistication and rough edges, Banacek is a tough self-made millionaire who grew up fighting in public housing. He is an old soul who abstains from using computers (perhaps because of his father), lives in a renovated Beacon Hill townhouse, enjoys fine food and wine and loves classic automobiles, particularly his 1942 Packard One-Eighty limousine,[111] the last of Packard's line of series eight automobiles. Surrounding Banacek is a colorful cast of characters, including his not-so-trustworthy chauffeur, Jay Drury (Ralph Manza), rival investigator and romantic interest, Carlie Kirkland (Christine Belford), and best friend/second father, Felix Mulholland, proprietor of *Mulholland's Rare Books and Prints*. As mentioned earlier, Felix is reminiscent of Perlmutter, a refined older man with an eye for beautiful younger women, who uses his encyclopedic memory and vast personal library to provide Banacek with research on cases. The show also mixes humor with adventure, most notably through Banacek's penchant for quoting Polish proverbs that are often more perplexing than the cases he solves.[112] Physically, however, Banacek resembles Austin and Cabrillo more than any other Cussler heroes. All three are approximately 40 years old, in excellent shape and have premature white hair. Banacek and Austin also enjoy sculling.[113] Finally, the mysteries on *Banacek* are often as audacious and clever as any Cussler adventure, the most famous, a play-fair disappearance of a pro running back who vanishes after being tackled during a televised football game ("Let's Hear It for a Living Legend"). Other mysteries include an armored truck that vanishes while under police escort ("Detour to Nowhere"), the evaporation of $1 million from a casino display ("A Million the Hard Way") and the disappearance of a mammoth medical computer from a high-security building ("If Max Is So Smart, Why Doesn't He Tell Us Where He Is?").

Pitt's Descendants: The Circle Ends and Begins Again

Two themes that run through this examination of the potential influences that may have had on Cussler are (1) heroes reflect the generation in which they are created, but (2) heroes fundamentally remain the same. These themes are evident when we compare the post-war clubland heroes Hannay, Drummond and Mansel to the Terrible Trio's Cold War counterpart Bond; they are just as evident in the television policemen, detectives, secret agents, fugitive wanderers and starship captains of the sixties, all of whom are newer and slightly grittier versions of the cowboys and other Western heroes who ruled the small screen in the fifties. Bloom might cite this as an example of "the *interchangeable* nature of dialogues and series shared between popular genres,"[114] but Bloom would be missing the bigger picture, at least when it comes to the adventure genre.

According to Sampson, the oldest form of fiction is the adventure tale, and the similarities in adventure heroes through the millennia is proof of progression, not interchangeability: "Strangers they seem. Yet we know them well. The present is stripped of its masks."[115] Look behind the mask of James Bond and you find Doc Savage; look behind the mask of Doc Savage you find Nick Carter. It is not so unusual, then, that the heroic archetype of Cussler's work is the result of the natural progression of adventure tales from the pulps and movies to the small screen. Media will change as time marches on, but this does not matter when it comes to adventure heroes because one "convention melts to another, secretly connecting characters widely dispersed in time."[116]

We can see this progression in the heroes that followed Pitt and his peers. Starting with literature, Pitt, Jack Ryan, and Mitchell Gant were joined by the likes of Mike Grell's Jon Sable in *Jon Sable, Freelance* (1983–1987); Brian Daley's Gil McDonald in *The Doomfarers of Coramonde* (1977) and *The Starfollowers of Coramonde* (1979) and the team of Alacrity Fitzhugh and Hobart Floyt in *Jinx on a Terran Inheritance* (1985), *Requiem for a Ruler of Worlds* (1985) and *Fall of the White Ship Avatar* (1986); Randy Wayne White's Doc Ford series, starting with *Sanibel Flats* (1990); Bernard Cornwell's "sailing" thrillers, including *Wildtrack* (1988), *Killer's Wake* (1989) and *Stormchild* (1991); Phillip Kerr's Bernie Gunther, who is introduced in the trilogy *March Violets* (1989), *The Pale Criminal* (1990) and *A German Requiem* (1991); as well as the works of eventual Cussler collaborators like Justin Scott and Jack Du Brul.

The vogue during the first half of the seventies was a decidedly darker theme in films. Consider *The French Connection* (1971), *Deliverance* (1972) and *The Exorcist* (1973) and taciturn anti-heroes such as "Dirty" Harry Callahan (Clint Eastwood) and vigilante Paul Kersey (Charles Bronson). Things took an abrupt turn for the brighter when mega-popular films featuring heroes in the Pitt mode stormed the box office. Sheriff Martin Brody (Roy Scheider) and ichthyologist Matt Hooper (Richard Dreyfuss) kicked things off in *Jaws* (1975), and were followed by Luke Skywalker (Mark Hamill), Obi-Wan "Ben" Kenobi (Sir Alec Guinness), Princess Leia Organa (Carrie Fisher) and Han Solo (Harrison Ford) in George Lucas's *Star Wars*, a 1977 blockbuster partially inspired by classic movie serials of the 1930s. Lucas and *Jaws* director Stephen Spielberg solidified the new heroic archetype's place in Hollywood with Professor Henry "Indiana" Jones, Jr., in a film totally inspired by movie serials, *Raiders of the Lost Ark* (1981). *Raiders* and its sequels *Indiana Jones and the Temple of Doom* (1984), *Indiana Jones and the Last Crusade* (1989) and *Indiana Jones and the Kingdom of the Crystal Skull* (2008) jumble breakneck action with audacious and clever adventure steeped in history, like in the Pitt series.[117] More new archetypal heroes soon followed, including Riggs (Mel Gibson) and Murtaugh (Danny Glover) from the *Lethal Weapon* franchise (1987–1998), John McClane (Bruce Willis) from the *Die Hard* franchise (1988–2013), Benjamin Franklin Gates (Nicolas Cage) from *National Treasure* (2004) and *National Treasure: Book of Secrets* (2007) and Captain Jack Sparrow (Johnny Depp) from the *Pirates of the Caribbean* franchise (2003–2011).

Back on the small screen, heroes in the new heroic archetypal mold began appearing more frequently during the seventies, starting with Jim Rockford (James Garner) in *The Rockford Files* (1974–1980). Rockford could almost be considered a peer rather than a descendant of Pitt's as the series' co-creator Roy Huggins designed Rockford to be a contemporary version of Brett Maverick (also played by Garner) from Huggins's Western series *Maverick* (1957–1962). Where Maverick is a rounder traveling from card game to card game, Rockford is a private investigator who is scraping by after being pardoned from San Quentin; he had served five years for a crime he did not commit. Huggins created *Maverick* to turn many of the traditional cowboy hero conventions of the time upside-down in a lighthearted way, and then, with co-creator Stephen J. Cannell, did the same for private detectives in *The Rockford Files*. Maverick and Rockford go to extremes to avoid using a gun (which neither is proficient at using) or getting into a fight (though both are pretty good with their fists), but, in spite of themselves, Maverick and Rockford often go to the same extremes as Pitt does to help people. After *Rockford*, Cannell went on to create (or co-create) some of the best television heroes featuring the new hero archetype, including undercover police officer Anthony Vicenzo "Tony" Baretta (Robert Blake) in *Baretta* (1975–1978),[118] FBI Agent Bill Maxwell (Robert Culp) in *The Greatest American Hero* (1981–1986), and *The A-Team* (1983–1986) of Colonel John "Hannibal" Smith (George Peppard wearing black gloves and smoking slim cigars like he did on *Banacek*), Sergeant First Class Bosco "B.A." Barracus (Mr. T), Lt. Templeton "Face" Peck (former *Battlestar Galactica* hero Dirk Benedict)[119] and Captain H.M. "Howling Mad" Murdock (Dwight Schultz). One of the most successful takes on the informal private detective is Thomas Magnum (Tom Selleck), in *Magnum P.I.* (1980–1988), created by Glen A. Larson and Donald P. Bellisario.[120] A navy SEAL who served in Vietnam, Magnum is as self-reliant, self-sacrificing and self-effacing as any hero on this list,[121] but few, if any, television heroes exemplify the archetype's Peter Pan element better than he. Magnum wears Hawaiian shirts and khaki shorts and lives a carefree bachelor life in the guest home of wealthy author Robin Masters (Orson Welles) under the dour eye of surrogate father figure and comic foil, Jonathan Quayle Higgins III (John Hillerman).

Another hero who gives Magnum a run for his money in the Peter Pan department is physicist, vagabond world-traveler and master-of-all-trades Angus MacGyver (Richard Dean Anderson), in *MacGyver* (1985–1992). A member of a bomb-disposal unit in Vietnam, MacGyver lives a carefree bachelor life on a houseboat, dresses from the L.L. Bean catalogue and has an enviable amount of free time to play hockey and come to the aid of eccentric friends and colorful strangers. A U.S. Government secret agent for an agency called DXS, MacGyver accepts an offer to become a troubleshooter for the Phoenix Foundation when his DXS superior and best friend, Peter Thornton (Dana Elcar), is transferred to this agency. MacGyver, a pacifist, is as hesitant to use a gun as Maverick and Rockford, preferring to use his considerable brainpower, dependable Swiss Army knife, a roll of duct tape he always carries, and anything else lying around, to escape death traps or foil villains.[122] Five years after *MacGyver* Anderson returned to television as Colonel Jonathan "Jack" O'Neill, a more flippant, more violent (but just as memorable) Pitt archetype hero, in *Stargate SG-1*.[123] Finally, two of the most recent examples of this type on television could not be more dissimilar. Leroy Jethro Gibbs (Mark Harmon) was introduced on Bellisario's military-court room adventure *J*A*G* (1995–2005) and stars on *NCIS* (2003-present), while Captain Jack Harkness was introduced on the time travel-adventure *Doctor Who* (1963–1989, 1996, 2005-present) and stars on *Torchwood* (2005–2011).[124] Gibbs and Harkness are clever,[125] charming (when they want to be) and pitiless (when they need to be) men of action. Both head elite investigative units that become the closest thing they have to a family, but where Gibbs's Naval Criminal Investigative Service unit investigates crimes involving the U.S. Navy and Marine Corps,[126] Harkness's Torchwood Three unit investigates extraterrestrial activity on Earth. The men's backgrounds also make them uniquely qualified for their jobs. Gibbs, a former "gunny," or gunnery sergeant, scout sniper and military police noncommissioned officer (NCO), is a Marine reservist and Corps to his core, while Harkness is a con man, a former Time Agent and an alien from the 51st century. Two of the biggest differences between Gibbs and Harkness is (1) Harkness is immortal and (2) Gibbs is heterosexual with a taste for redheads while Harkness is, for lack of a better word, omnisexual.

Recap

When Bloom looks at Cussler's adventures he sees a "superficial resemblance to the tradition of international espionage thriller writers [that] masks a debt to pulp fiction, television and B-movies."[127] But Cussler is not masking anything. Although he has never listed exactly which pulp stories or magazines influenced him, he admits that he is writing modern versions of pulp adventures in his suspense-adventure novels. And, while Cussler states that he was not influenced by any television heroes, he does admit to "researching and analyzing all the literary series heroes," including Dupin, Holmes, Drummond and Bond. "I studied them all."[128]

7

Apotheosis
The Hero Reborn

> The ultimate aim of the quest must be neither ecstasy for oneself, but the wisdom and the power to serve others. One of the many distinctions between the celebrity and the hero ... is that one lives for self while the other acts to redeem society.—Joseph Campbell (quoted by Bill Moyers)[1]

When people ask Cussler if he has a favorite Dirk Pitt novel they are generally surprised to find out his sentimental choice is *Iceberg*. Cussler says it is because "it was a transition of sorts from the earlier simplified story lines of *Pacific Vortex* and *The Mediterranean Caper*."[2] But *Iceberg* represents a significant transition in Pitt, too. Cussler introduced the Pitt archetype hero in his first two adventures, but *Iceberg* presents the apotheosis of his best and most famous hero from a simple series hero engaged in local (microcosmic) deeds to a mythological series hero capable of accomplishing universal (macrocosmic) feats, including raising the *Titanic*.[3]

The Initiation Quest Pattern in *Iceberg*

According to Campbell, all heroic adventure tales are the same "shape-shifting yet marvelously constant story" that contain the "challengingly persistent suggestion of more remaining to be experienced than will ever be known or told."[4] This is because they all contain the same initiation quest pattern from myth, folk tale, epic, romance and religion:

- The quest begins with a call to adventure, after which the hero will usually gain a helper.
- The hero comes to the threshold of adventure. Crossing this threshold is difficult and may take a variety of forms, such as a battle with a dragon, a sea journey by night, dismemberment or descent into the belly of a whale.
- It is followed by tests that the hero will pass, usually with the aid of more helpers. Then the hero reaches the goal of his quest and confronts his destiny, which will take one of three forms: a woman he must win, a man he must challenge or a treasure he must obtain.
- There follows the return, which may occur as a flight and pursuit.
- At the threshold of return there is another struggle, from which the hero may be rescued by a helper.
- The quest will usually end with the woman brought back as bride or with a public display of the treasure.[5]

Over the centuries authors have adapted this pattern to reflect their generation's concerns and anxieties. Perhaps the most significant modern example of this is Conan Doyle and his Holmes adventures, as Jaffe documents:

> Unlike the mythological heroes who are lured, carried, or in some way mystically summoned to undertake the quest, Holmes is prosaically introduced to his adventure by a person, a letter, a telegram, or even an article in the newspaper. The physical trials that beset the hero have been translated, in the Holmes stories, into the mental trial that is the continuous sifting of the mass of information that surrounds the case. Holmes is aided in his travels to search out the truth, not by any magical helper, like small animals, gnomes, or witches, but by trains that run on time, by hansom cabs that appear whenever they are needed, and by newspapers that publish advertisements instantaneously. When Holmes returns from the place of trial, the murky, rain-sodden, gray city, he brings back with him the traditional "boon," the restoration of order.[6]

Conan Doyle preserved the initiation quest pattern and created a hero capable of dealing with the mysteries and threats plaguing Victorian and Edwardian England[7]; Cussler does the same for late 20th-century America in *Iceberg* by challenging Pitt with a series of heroic episodes that take place within the larger context of a physical, spiritual and psychological journey.[8]

The quest begins with a call to adventure: *Iceberg* marks the first time Pitt is summoned into action by a call to adventure. In *Pacific Vortex* Pitt is lured into action by Delphi, and in *The Mediterranean Caper* he stumbles into action by flying into an attack on Brady Air Field. In *Iceberg* Sandecker orders Pitt to Washington, DC to ask him to fly Dr. William Hunnewell to the North Atlantic, where the crew of a Coast Guard plane used red dye to mark an iceberg with a ship trapped inside it.[9]

After which the hero usually gains a helper: Hunnewell is Pitt's first helper, and Cussler again forges a pair out of opposites. In contrast to Pitt, Hunnewell is a chubby, balding man with brown eyes, rimless spectacles and resembles a stereotypical mad scientist.

The hero comes to the threshold of adventure: The threshold is the iceberg, and Pitt and Hunnewell's sea journey to reach it is fraught with perils and problems, starting with a risky nighttime helicopter landing on the Coast Guard supercutter *Catawaba*.[10] Aboard the supercutter Pitt and Hunnewell skirt Koski's suspicions, the commander being confused that his orders to receive them did not come from the *Catawaba's* district command, and the next morning Koski insists on a prearranged hour for Pitt and Hunnewell to return from the iceberg or he will begin searching for them.

Finding the iceberg is frustratingly difficult. First, someone has chipped off the Coast Guard's red dye marker and splashed more red dye on a decoy iceberg. Next, after the pair land on the genuine iceberg, Pitt has to rescue Hunnewell from falling into the water. Pitt does uncover a concealed tube cut through the ice, leading to the mystery ship (Kristjan Fyrie's yacht, the *Lax*) and descends to it (the belly of the whale), but when he and Hunnewell leave the iceberg they are attacked by a black executive jet (a battle with a dragon), a battle Pitt survives but at the loss of his first helper.

It is followed by tests that the hero will pass, usually with the aid of more helpers: Pitt passes four tests in *Iceberg*, starting with the air duel with the black jet. Pitt also survives a sea battle with a hydrofoil in a fog bank, submits to a savage beating at Rondheim's hands and rescues people left to freeze to death in a ravine. Along the way he meets several more helpers, including Sandecker, Tidi, Lillie and Kippmann.

Then the hero reaches the goal of his quest and confronts his destiny: A hero's goal can involve winning a woman, challenging a man or obtaining a treasure, but it can also incorporate two (or all three) feats like in the 1938 film *The Adventures of Robin Hood*. Robin, earl of Locksley (Errol Flynn) challenges Sir Guy of Gisbourne (Basil Rathbone) and wins the love of Maid Marian (Olivia de Havilland) as he battles to restore order by returning King Richard the Lionheart (Ian Hunter) to the throne of England. In *Iceberg* Pitt challenges Rondheim to prevent Hermit Limited from wrecking economic and political havoc; he also seeks to avenge Hunnewell and the people put into the ravine. Pitt also wins Kirsti, so to speak, by getting her to build NUMA a Fyrie probe, the treasure he must obtain.

There follows the return, which may occur as a flight and pursuit: Or, as in *Iceberg*, the return can simply be a pursuit.[11] When Sandecker orders Pitt to come to NUMA headquarters at the beginning of the novel, the hero is vacationing in Newport Beach. When Pitt pursues Rondheim and Kirsti to California he returns practically all the way home, marking Disneyland as the threshold of return since this is where Pitt challenges Rondheim, wins Kirsti by keeping her out of jail and obtains the treasure (or boon) by getting her to help build the probe.

The Monomyth in *Iceberg*

Campbell divides the initiation quest pattern into three stages he calls the nuclear unit of the monomyth[12]:

A. Departure (a separation from the world)
 1. The Call to Adventure
 2. The Refusal of the Call
 3. Supernatural Aid
 4. The Crossing of the Threshold
 5. The Belly of the Whale
B. Initiation (a penetration to some source of power)
 1. The Road of Trials
 2. The Meeting with the Goddess
 3. Woman as the Temptress
 4. Atonement with the Father
 5. Apotheosis
 6. The Ultimate Boon
C. Return (a life-enhancing return)
 1. Refusal of the Return
 2. The Magic Flight
 3. Rescue from Without
 4. The Crossing of the Return Threshold
 5. Master of the Two Worlds
 6. Freedom to Live[13]

Not all adventures follow this outline or incorporate all of these subsections. Liberties are often taken,[14] as in *Iceberg*, which incorporates most (but not all) of these subsections and not always in this order.

Departure (a separation from the world): In the call to adventure, destiny summons the hero and moves him from his home society to a zone unknown. *Iceberg* not only marks the first time Pitt answers a call to adventure, it is the first adventure in which Sandecker fills the role of the Wise Old Man.

As touched on earlier, this Jungian archetype coaxes the hero into leaving the security and familiarity of home to go on an adventure by inducing self-reflection and a mobilizing of moral forces in the hero.[15] According to Jung, this intervention is indispensable because "the conscious will by itself is hardly ever capable of uniting the personality to the point where it acquires this extraordinary power to succeed."[16] Three of the most popular recent examples of the Wise Old Man are J.R.R. Tolkien's Gandalf, George Lucas's Obi-Wan "Ben" Kenobi and J.K. Rowling's Albus Dumbledore. These fantasy characters have little in common with Sandecker, yet the admiral performs the same indispensable task in *Iceberg* that Gandalf, Kenobi and Dumbledore do in *The Hobbit, or There and Back Again* (1937), *Star Wars* and *Harry Potter and the Philosopher's Stone* (1997), respectively. All four characters break up the hero's comfortable consciousness to get him moving on a journey that brings the hero into contact with a world beyond his everyday one, a world where the hero will have the opportunity to explore the shadow side of his own nature.

The hero's shadow side or "shadow" springs from humanity's own collective unconscious. A shadow is often an animal or trickster tapped into mankind's amoral animal past and therefore able to guide the hero down into the primordial realm.[17] In *The Hobbit* Bilbo Baggins is a homebody satisfied with his creature comforts, but Bilbo has a shadow side in his bloodline, an adventurous ancestor named Belladonna Took, who is said to have married a fairy. It is Bilbo's Took side that is attracted to Gandalf's call. In *Star Wars* young Luke Skywalker is champing at the bit to escape his uncle Owen's moisture farm and become a pilot for the Rebel Alliance against the galactic Empire. Luke's shadow side is his father, the traitorous Jedi knight Darth Vader, but Luke does not know this when he is tempted to join Kenobi on a rescue mission to the planet Alderaan.[18] In *Harry Potter and the Philosopher's Stone* Harry is a lonely, mistreated orphan invited to attend Hogwarts School of Witchcraft and Wizardry on his 11th birthday, per the directions of its headmaster, Dumbledore. Harry's shadow side is represented by a scar shaped like a lightning bolt on his forehead, given to him soon after his first birthday by a powerful dark wizard named Lord Voldemort, who murdered Harry's parents and tried to kill him. The scar links Harry to Voldemort and imbues the boy with some of Voldemort's dark powers. Pitt, like Sandecker, has little in common with his fantasy counterparts. He is a human, unlike Bilbo, and an adult, unlike Luke and Harry. Pitt also lives in a purely realistic world and is a blooded warrior, a Vietnam War veteran with a Purple Heart, a Distinguished Flying Cross with two clusters and several other commendations. Nevertheless Pitt has a shadow side like Bilbo, Luke and Harry in that he has a lot of Peter Pan in him, but by taking the hero's journey in *Iceberg* Pitt confronts his shadow side and matures.[19]

In the novel *Peter Pan and Wendy* (1911) Peter lures Wendy to Neverland to be a mother for him and the Lost Boys. Peter revels in his youthful independence ("I'm youth, I'm joy! I'm a little bird that has broken out of the egg!")[20] and rarely speaks or thinks kindly of his mother.[21] But his luring of Wendy demonstrates that Peter has never stopped craving his mother, and (if the novel's epilogue is any indication) never will.[22] Peter also refuses to see that the greatest danger in Neverland, a realm beyond his society filled with dangerous adventures and bloody battles, is its gift of eternal youth. Nothing or nobody can change in a place where children perpetually remain children. In the epilogue Peter lures Wendy's daughter Jane to Neverland to act as his new pretend mother. Wendy remains behind, too old to follow, but she has accomplished more in her short life than Peter Pan ever will, even if he lives forever. Peter does vanquish Captain Hook and forces Hook's pirate crew to walk the plank, but this is a local (microcosmic) victory. Peter seems capable of accomplishing universal (macrocosmic) feats, but we will never know so long as he squirrels himself away in Neverland.[23]

Pitt is in danger of suffering Peter Pan's fate and remaining a *puer aeternus*, or eternal boy, until he begins to abandon his infantile fixations, in *Iceberg*. If not for this journey the exploits of adventures like *Raise the Titanic!* may have been beyond Pitt's powers. Before he can raise the sunken White Star liner, a more important, primary thing has to be brought to pass as "obscure resistances are overcome, and long lost, forgotten powers are revivified, to be made available for the transfiguration of the world."[24] In his first two adventures Pitt foils the schemes of a pirate and a smuggler, but after *Iceberg* Pitt's adventures become more Herculean (e.g., raising the *Titanic* from two and a half miles beneath the Atlantic) and historic (e.g., recovering a treaty that reshapes North America's governments).[25]

Pitt is nestled at home (in his hometown) when Sandecker's call rings up the curtain on the adventure. A hero can choose not to answer ("The Refusal of the Call"), but Pitt comes to Washington and agrees to fly Hunnewell to the iceberg, the threshold of adventure. Thresholds are generally inhospitable, sometimes threatening landscapes, like the dark, wet conditions permeating the places where crimes are committed in the Holmes adventures.[26] In *Iceberg* a desolate, terrifying and alien atmosphere surrounds the iceberg,[27] the most otherworldly element being the mystery ship.[28] Thresholds are often guarded by dangerous and deceitful guardians, bestowers of magic who block the way into darkness and the unknown.[29] But, in *Iceberg*, Cussler merges the threshold with its guardian, an adaptation denoted (1) by Hunnewell, who senses the iceberg bears a personal enmity against him and Pitt,[30] and (2) with contrasting images of fire and ice associated with the tube to the ship (e.g., "ice crystals," "white-hot temperatures") that reflect the contrary nature of most threshold guardians. Any hero who abandons the comforts of home for the initiation quest must confront these guardians,[31] and Pitt confronts the iceberg's threshold guardian by uncovering the tube.

What Pitt cannot know is that the mystery ship is a herald marking a new stage in his life. The crisis of the herald's appearance is the real call to adventure that summons the hero to begin his journey, because there is no reason for the Wise Old Man to send the hero on his way without this crisis.[32] This new stage, also called the *awakening of the self*,[33] is a second birth, or rebirth, that comes with all the pain, bloodshed and anxiety of separation from the mother that is part of any birth.[34] This rebirth is essential because the object of the hero's quest is often a boon for his community, but before the hero can recover it he must submit to the awakening of the self. Campbell explains, "The hero is the man of self-achieved submission. But submission to what?"[35] The hero must solve this *riddle of submission* to recover the boon, and when the herald arrives all "archetypal images are activated, symbolizing danger, reassurance, trial, passage, and the strange holiness of the mysteries of birth." The idea of a rebirth or the beginning of a new life can be disturbing or frightening, however, so the herald is often presented as a dark and loathsome or terrifying person or thing judged evil by the world. It may be "a beast (as in the fairy tale), representative of the repressed instinctual fecundity within ourselves," or "a veiled mysterious figure"[36] representing the unknown, but it can also be an object or something as ephemeral as a blunder that leads to the opening of a destiny. If the hero has the courage to follow the herald, no matter what form it takes, then the herald will lead the hero to the place where the hero's riddle of submission can be answered.[37]

Making the *Lax* Pitt's herald is inspired. As dark, loathsome, terrifying or evil as a herald may appear, the atmosphere surrounding it is usually one of irresistible fascination,[38] and if anything fascinates Pitt it is ships and mysteries, especially historical mysteries.[39] Even so, as per the monomyth, Pitt and Hunnewell encounter a number of difficulties crossing the threshold.

When Pitt and Hunnewell land on the iceberg, common sense suggests that whoever chipped off the red dye has beaten them inside the ship. Koski's deadline has also expired, and then Hunnewell slips and begins sliding off the iceberg. Myth and legends, as well as suspense, mystery and adventure fiction often gauge a hero against his control over the external world. When Holmes leaves Baker Street to venture into the dark, wet world outside, he acts oblivious to bad weather and equips himself with the tools he needs to overcome the elements.[40] Pitt proves himself by hurling like a bobsled and using quick thinking, brute strength, a coat sleeve and a pair of dividers to rescue Hunnewell. During the rescue Hunnewell is afraid, but Pitt's determined expression and confidence buttress him. Hunnewell cooperates instead of panicking, which demonstrates his trust, and after the rescue Pitt and Hunnewell's relationship changes for the better. Up until the rescue the men had been sniping and disagreeing, but now they are like two doughboys who survived combat inside the same foxhole. Hero and helper have become newborn companions, Hunnewell grateful and Pitt appreciating Hunnewell's behavior when the chips are down.[41]

As the pair search for a way to reach the *Lax*, Hunnewell comments on the threshold's inhospitable and threatening nature. Pitt overcomes this obstacle when he finds a round slab of ice covering the tube, the magical threshold and an apt *locus in quo* for Pitt's rebirth, its constricted boundaries, opaque surroundings and foul odor from a fire that destroyed the ship, simultaneously suggesting a sepulcher and a birth canal. According to Campbell, passing through the magical threshold is a journey into a sphere of rebirth symbolized by the image of the belly of the whale. Instead of conquering or conciliating the power of the threshold, however, the hero is swallowed into the unknown and appears to die[42]; Pitt's mortality is definitely on his mind as he passes through the tube into the deathly still ship.[43]

A hero entering the belly of the whale is an extremely popular womb image. Examples include Jonah swallowed by a leviathan; Little Red Riding-hood swallowed by the wolf; and Pitt in Von Til's labyrinth. Cussler refers back to the labyrinth, in *Iceburg*, by giving Pitt comparable reactions.[44] Cussler harkens to another rebirth that happens aboard the mystery ship, after an isolated compartment where Fyrie apparently died, is discovered. Like the ice tube, this compartment is suggestive of both tomb and womb. It has no windows. It is situated in the center of the ship (as opposed to the center of a crypt or the center of a woman's body). And it is the starting point of Fyrie's awakening of the self.

Pitt continues to prove his mettle after finding the first of 14 charred corpses scattered throughout the ship, in the radio room. This first corpse perplexes Pitt because it appears the man calmly burned to death as the chair beneath him was incinerated.[45] But Hunnewell is more concerned about finding Fyrie's corpse. To that end, Pitt's helper brings along some special knowledge: a rough diagram of the ship, copied from the original, in the maritime archives. It is obvious the fire started in this isolated compartment,[46] but with all of its furniture and equipment destroyed, Pitt cannot deduce the compartment's purpose. Hunnewell finds a pile of ash covering a few bones and little pieces of distorted metal in a corner and tells Pitt that Fyire always wore eight rings, each carved in the likeness of a Nordic god with handcrafted settings inlaid with eight different semiprecious stones native to Iceland. Hunnewell breaks into a brief eulogy, and this is the first time Fyrie's name is mentioned, although Pitt later recalls that, in Washington, Sandecker spoke about Fyrie in the same "hushed, almost reverent tone."[47] Pitt is familiar with Fyrie's reputation and has trouble understanding anyone's reverence for someone "the world's newspapers referred to as the *apotheosis* of the swinging intellectual jetsetter (my emphasis)."[48] Pitt contemplates that he might think differently if he had known Fyrie, but doubts it, recalling his father's comment about taking the clothes away from the greatest man alive.[49]

In *Pacific Vortex* and *The Mediterranean Caper* Pitt displays infantile contempt towards authority figures that have not earned his respect; he reacts the same way when Koski unexpectedly arrives and demands to know why he and Hunnewell are on the *Lax*. This time, Pitt knows he is being arrogant, but still defaults to this behavior, hoping to get the upper hand. Koski gains the advantage, however, by maintaining decorum while turning Pitt's logic against him.[50] When Pitt tells Koski that he suspects the *Lax*'s crew was poisoned by a traitor on the ship so it could be boarded and everything on it destroyed, Koski doubts this theory, but does so respectfully, which wins Pitt's respect.[51]

Before Pitt and Hunnewell can complete the Departure stage, a second threshold guardian (the black jet) attacks. Prior to this, Hunnewell passes along some more special knowledge, telling Pitt how Fyrie made his fortune and used it to build an industry specializing in underwater geological exploration. Hunnewell also mentions that Fyrie's parents perished in a fire and that Fyrie has a twin sister, Kirsti, who is a missionary. When the black jet attacks, the Ulysses is momentarily spared by an act of Fate.[52] There is no escaping the faster aircraft, but like Peter Pan, who relishes a fight no matter how steep the odds, Pitt smiles when he realizes there is a very slight chance he might be able to take the jet down with them.[53] Against all odds, Pitt not only succeeds, he survives, but in the process loses Hunnewell.

Initiation (a penetration to some source of power): Pitt has reached the road of trials, a favorite phase of myths and adventures.[54]

When a hero passes through the threshold he enters the zone unknown, a "fateful region of both treasure and danger" that may be represented "as a distant land, a forest, a kingdom underground, beneath the waves, or above the sky, a secret island, lofty mountaintop, or profound dream state." However it is represented, it "is always a place of strangely fluid and polymorphous beings, unimaginable torments, superhuman deeds, and impossible delight."[55] The zone unknown in *Iceberg* is Iceland, a "strange island" that is an "unequaled phenomenon of beauty."[56] A zone's border is demarcated by representations of opposites[57]; Cussler describes Iceland as a "land of frost and fire, rugged glaciers and smoldering volcanoes ... bounded by the warm waters of the Gulf Stream in the south and by the frigid polar sea to the north."[58] Black sands also surround the country, and sunlight shines well into the night.

Pitt's first trial is losing Hunnewell, and the first opposite he sees is a group of children. Children usually represent naïveté, but the fact that Pitt has entered a dream state is reinforced by their uncanny composure as they ride with Hunnewell's corpse in the back of a farmer's Land Rover[59] through a countryside filled with reminders of death, particularly a traditional Icelandic churchyard that dominates the nearest village.[60] Hunnewell is also not the first helper to die in Pitt's company. That honor goes to Lieutenant March (no first name given) in *Pacific*

Vortex, wherein Pitt melodramatically insists on blaming himself for the man's death. Pitt demonstrates some growth in *Iceberg* by behaving a little more maturely about Hunnewell when he arrives at the home of Dr. Jonsson (no first name given), his second helper.

Somber and little with soft green eyes and steel-rimmed glasses, Jonsson could pass for Hunnewell's brother and is one of Cussler's most memorable supporting characters. Part of the reason for this is that Jonsson is no ordinary helper but a protective figure, a bringer of supernatural aid who usually appears during the Departure. Protective figures are often old crones or little old men who provide amulets to use against the forces the hero is about to encounter.[61] In fairy tales, male protective figures can be an inhabitant of the wood, like a hermit, shepherd, smith or wizard, while in mythologies his role is often that of a guide, teacher, ferryman or the conductor of souls to the afterworld.[62] Jonsson, the village doctor and a poet, is a teacher. When Pitt comments on how Icelanders reflect their country's opposite nature, Jonsson explains that what appears to be contrary is natural in Iceland, where people accept death as a separation. Jonsson points through the window of his office, a place dedicated to the preservation of life, at the churchyard. This seems like another opposite to Pitt, but to Icelanders it is the cycle of life because the people who came before them are still here. Pitt confides that he blames himself for Hunnewell's death, but Jonsson counsels this is a waste of time.[63] Two policemen then arrive on the pretense of investigating Hunnewell's gunshot wounds, but Jonsson warns Pitt that they are impostors. Jonsson helps Pitt capture them, but afterwards the doctor (a healer) advises Pitt that his concern for life will lead to his defeat.[64]

Another reason Jonsson is a memorable character is a revealing statement he makes. Pitt mentions Hunnewell's last words included God, and Jonsson says, "He was fortunate, yet I feel I will be fortunate when my time comes to be laid to rest ... among so many of the people I have loved and cared for." Pitt wishes he had Jonsson's affinity for remaining in one place, but "somewhere in the distant past one of my ancestors was a gypsy. I've inherited his wandering ways." Jonsson wonders which of them is more fortunate, but Pitt can only shrug and say, "Who can tell? We both hear the beat of a different drummer."[65]

Why Pitt's sudden wish for stability? Did Hunnewell's death make him realize that his wanderlust could be a symptom of an immature shadow? Rootless people tend to avoid responsibilities as much, if not more, than they seek to see what lies beyond the next star or horizon. If so, this might explain why Pitt exceeds his record for living in one place after this adventure. Pitt mentions to Jonsson that the longest he has stayed in one place is three years, but he has already worked for NUMA for a year and a half and, after *Iceberg*, he settles down in Washington, DC,[66] where he eventually marries, takes in his twin children and replaces Sandecker at NUMA.

Things go from bad to worse when Pitt leaves Jonsson's village with its ghosts (the residents of the churchyard) and perilous knights (the police impostors) to search for Hunnewell's killers, but downturns are to be expected. The road of trials turns into a journey of darkness, horror, disgust and phantasmagoric fears as soon as the thrills of getting under way come and go.[67] A hero must also pass tests—generally three of them—along the road of trials.[68] Pitt's tests, like the ones passed by the grand heroes Beowulf and Gilgamesh, involve battling two monsters, followed by a dark descent into the lair of an even more powerful adversary, in which the hero confronts his destiny. In the Beowulf legend, the two monsters are Grendel (a half-man/half-monster who lives in a murky fen) and Grendel's dam (who lives at the bottom of a muddy lake) while the more powerful adversary is a dragon, living inside a great cave.[69] Gilgamesh must slay lions prowling the passes along his road of trials before winning leave to pass the Scorpions (creatures that are half man and half dragon) of the great mountains of Mashu before he can reach Siduri the divine wine-maker (a possible manifestation of the goddess Ishtar) in the gardens of the sun beside the sea.[70] In *Iceberg* the two lesser monsters are a dragon (the black jet) and a leviathan (the hydrofoil), while the more powerful adversary is Rondheim.

The remains of the dragon, a beast of the air, lures Pitt, Sandecker and Pitt's third helper, Tidi, to the leviathan's realm of ebony sand and frigid water. When Pitt dives into these strange waters he finds himself in a place where he is unable to trust his senses. Even time is unreliable in this realm.[71] There is also peril waiting inside the dragon's remains. Reminiscent of Theseus following Daedalus's linen thread to escape the Minotaur's labyrinth, Pitt follows a "silver snake" (his air bubbles) out of the dragon and up to the surface. Pitt is lost when he breaches and is "engulfed by a thick cloud of fog,"[72] but the Wise Old Man rescues him. Pitt follows the sound of Sandecker singing "My Bonnie Lies Over the Ocean," but within minutes the leviathan-hydrofoil (equipped with radar) begins hunting their scow, the *Grimsi*.[73] Pitt kills one of the hydrofoil's crewmen as the man tries to board the *Grimsi*, which suggests Pitt listened to Jonsson's advice. But, as the bloodshed escalates, Pitt worries what toll killing will have on his humanity.[74]

Pitt's third and most critical test starts at a poetry reading at Rondheim's mansion. This episode, one of the most harrowing in the series, is the centerpiece of *Iceberg* as Pitt transforms into a modern universal hero.

During the initiation quest a hero is constantly traveling further into a dream landscape of symbolic figures.[75] Campbell, like Jung, believes that men and their societies have fears and anxieties, but men symbolize fears and anxieties in dreams, while societies symbolize fears in myths and legends.[76] Jung classifies the most persistent symbols as archetypes, and the most persistent archetypes along Pitt's road of trials are the Goddess and the Father.

Jung incorporates the Goddess into a more fundamental archetype called the *anima*, a Woman figure, buried deep in every man's nature, whose image is projected upon every female the hero meets on his initiation quest. The Goddess is usually a maternal figure but she can also be a sister, a mate or an old woman the hero turns to for advice. In these incarnations the Goddess symbolizes the promise of perfection,[77] but the Goddess can also be absent, hampering or clinging. The hero may (or may not) desire the Goddess, and the form she takes will depend on the hero's age and attitude. But, for every positive incarnation of the Goddess that appears in an adventure, there will be a negative one.[78] To this end, Jung divides the Goddess archetype into two benign forms, Earthmother and Platonic Ideal, and two destructive forms, Temptress and Unfaithful Wife.[79] In *Iceberg* Tidi represents the benign forms, and Kirsti represents the destructive.

Tidi is introduced after Pitt wakes from a reoccurring nightmare about Hunnewell's death and finds her sitting at the foot of his bed. Tidi is a nurturing figure who is twice associated with über-nurse Florence Nightingale,[80] while her Earthmother qualities are bolstered by the natural imagery used to describe her. Tidi has "a soft voice," "smiling brown eyes," long "fawn-colored" hair and a body that moves like "mercury flowing down a meandering glass tube." Tidi has a "fun-and-games personality" and is not exotically beautiful or sexy but has "a pert attractiveness that melted every man she met."[81] To Pitt, though, Tidi is also a Platonic Ideal because she is Sandecker's personal secretary.[82]

In contrast, Kirsti is a Temptress with a "husky and terribly sexy" voice, cold "deep blue" eyes, is "very tall and very blond" and moves with "the suppleness of a ballerina and more than the suggestion of a natural athlete." Tidi makes men melt, but women look at Kirsti "with instinctive envy." Kirsti is frequently compared to inanimate artwork, which seems appropriate as she was sculpted by a surgeon; this also suggests that Kirsti is not a person but a thing to be possessed.[83] At the same time Kirsti is an Unfaithful Wife. She starts off being blackmailed by Rondheim but ends up assisting his schemes, and while their physical relationship is never defined, they are engaged, yet there is sexual tension between Kirsti and Pitt. Cussler calls attention to this by linking Kirsti and Pitt with a physical similarity. Both their eyes have flashes, rays that spread from the pupil to the iris.[84] Kirsti also rescues Pitt from Rondheim's beating, knowing she is putting herself in harm's way, and at the end of the novel she tries to seduce Pitt after she is sure Rondheim has been eliminated as a threat.

The Goddess can be a paradoxical figure, but not as much as the Father, who possesses the basic and essential secret about creation, life and the cosmos, a secret that can never be fully explained because no human can completely understand the universe.[85] Nevertheless, the hero must defeat the Father to get a glimpse of this secret or its source (i.e., the Creator or creative power of the universe), and the only way a hero can defeat the Father is by answering the riddle of submission and stripping himself of his infantile ways. A hero that can do this is ready to take on the role of the Father, obtaining atonement ("at-one-ment") and, in essence, becoming the Father. "The problem of the hero going to meet the father," cautions Campbell, "is to open his soul beyond terror to such a degree that he will be ripe to understand how the sickening and insane tragedies of this vast and ruthless cosmos are completely validated in the majesty of Being." For just a brief moment the hero "beholds the face of the father, understands and—the two are atoned."[86] It is not unusual for the Wise Old Man to be a Father figure as well, but Sandecker, Pitt's second father,[87] is a benign Father figure in *Iceberg*. The destructive Father figure that Pitt must defeat is Rondheim.[88]

Pitt recognizes Rondheim is a threat when they are introduced,[89] so he borrows and adapts a tactic from Zorro, The Scarlet Pimpernel[90] and The Batman, by pretending to be an effeminate homosexual to get Rondheim to underestimate him.[91] Rondheim is repulsed and Pitt presses his advantage, slipping into feminine poses and claiming to be a painter of landscapes and floral still lifes, but his performance is such a drastic switch from how he was behaving with Kirsti before meeting Rondheim it is a wonder she fails to recognize Pitt is shamming.[92]

The destructive Goddess and Father figures are waiting for Pitt at the poetry reading. Pitt has reached the stage of "descent into darkness and disintegration" where "in true shamanic and heroic style" the hero journeys "with a helper into the heart of the void and there affirms his own existence." After "grasping the secret of life" from the Father, the hero "returns across the threshold ... and ascends into the light ... reborn."[93]

Pitt senses danger as soon as he, Tidi and several other guests enter a study in Rondheim's mansion.[94] The lights are turned down and, like Jonathan Harker exploring the forbidden room in Dracula's castle, Pitt finds himself falling asleep, followed by a shaman-like vision in the form of his recurring nightmare about Hunnewell's death:

> No sooner had the first wave of unconsciousness swept over him than Pitt found himself back on the beach for the hundredth time, cradling Dr. Hunnewell's head in his arms.... The strange phenomenon of the dream wasn't its recurrence, but rather the fact that no two sequences were exactly the same. Each time that Hunnewell died, something was different. In

one dream the children would be present on the beach as they had been in reality. In the next, they would be missing, nowhere in sight. Once the black jet circled overhead, dipping its wings in an unexpected salute. Even Sandecker appeared in one scene, standing over Pitt and Hunnewell and sadly shaking his head. The weather, the layout of the beach, the color of the sea—they all differed from fantasy to fantasy. Only one small detail always remained faithfully—Hunnewell's last words.[95]

The road of trials always leads the hero to a dream landscape "of symbolic figures (any of which may swallow him)." This is "the process of dissolving, transcending, or transmuting the infantile images of our personal past. In our dreams the ageless perils, gargoyles, trials, secret helpers, and instructive figures are nightly still encountered: and in their forms we may see reflected not only the whole picture of our present case, but also the clue to what we must do to be saved."[96] Pitt sees four forms in his nightmare: the children, the black jet, Sandecker and the dying Hunnewell. What are these forms trying to tell him?

When the children find Pitt and Hunnewell they behave calmly because they accept death as a part of life. Pitt feels guilty about Hunnewell's death, so he can learn a thing or two about accepting death from the children; their presence in his nightmare suggests that he recognizes this.

The black jet makes a convenient symbol of death. But why the salute? Fighter pilots salute worthy opponents, most often if they allow an opponent to escape a dogfight. Pitt proves himself a worthy opponent by taking down the jet, but he does not feel like he won (or even scored a tie) because Hunnewell died, so the black jet may also be a symbol of Pitt's guilty conscience.

At one point in *Iceberg* Sandecker confesses to Pitt that he feels responsible for Hunnewell's death.[97] Pitt can also sense that Sandecker feels responsible for the attempts made on his life; it is possible, therefore, that Sandecker, a paternal symbol of strength and authority, has been reduced in Pitt's eyes to being as powerless as he feels.

These three forms represent fears and anxieties that Pitt must overcome, but since none of them consistently appear in his nightmare, it seems unlikely that any represent the clue Pitt needs to find to be saved. That would be the one constant detail, Hunnewell's dying words: "God save thee."[98] During Pitt's vision Hunnewell desperately fights to make himself understood, which suggests it is vital that Pitt figure out what Hunnewell's final words mean.

When Pitt wakes up, he hears Rondheim issuing a challenge. Anyone can quote a line from any poem and Rondheim will finish the stanza that follows, or complete the poem. The first two challenges are *aide-mémoires* of Pitt's hero journey from "One and Twenty" by Samuel Johnson, and "To One in Paradise" by Edgar Allan Poe. Pitt makes the third challenge[99] with "God save thee" and Rondheim laughs because it comes from his favorite poem, "The Rime of the Ancient Mariner." As Rondheim quotes the appropriate stanza Pitt deduces the meaning of Hunnewell's final words and immediately feels exorcised of the guilt that has been plaguing him.[100] Technically Rondheim wins the verse challenge, however Pitt has successfully penetrated the heart of the void (Rondheim's mansion), where he steals a boon that will benefit his community, and, just as important, Pitt has found his clue.

Rondheim's poetry challenge accomplishes the same things as the riddling talk contest in *The Hobbit*. In the chapter "Riddles in the Dark" Bilbo is alone in the underground kingdom of the goblins. Bilbo wakes up after being knocked out during a battle and finds himself in the darker and deeper underground domain of the degenerated cannibal Gollum, who challenges

Bilbo to a contest of riddles. If Bilbo wins then Gollum will show him how to get back to the surface, but if Gollum wins then Bilbo becomes Gollum's next meal. Such perils are to be expected during a dark descent. As English professor Elliot Gose writes, "The dark may hide treasure, but it also contains death. The traveler cannot find one without facing the other."[101] A battle of riddles is appropriate at these times because rituals of asking and answering have long been associated with initiation processes, and this is an initiation quest. "The asker is the priest who knows the mysteries of the universe, and the answerer is the novice who wishes to demonstrate his competence to join the adepts."[102] Except, in this instance, Gollum is no priest; he is Bilbo's shadow. Bilbo inherited his shadow side from Belladonna Took, but Gollum embodies Bilbo's amoral animal past.[103] Like all hobbits, Bilbo loves good food, and, in his own awful way, so does Gollum. Being a shadow also makes Gollum a trickster. Gollum intends to kill Bilbo, no matter the outcome of the contest. As for Bilbo, to succeed in his quest he must confront his shadow because, like all shadows, Gollum "has a prize worth winning, though the cost of losing the struggle for the prize will, of course, be death."[104] A shadow's link with humanity's past enables it to lead the hero down into the primordial realm, and in "a riddle contest, each side is trying to penetrate the dark and hidden realm of the other." Gollum is offering Bilbo initiation into "the primeval world of elemental darkness and death," an initiation Bilbo must experience if he is going to defeat the dragon Smaug later.[105]

Rondheim embodies Pitt's shadow like Gollum embodies Bilbo's shadow. Physically, Rondheim and Pitt are similar, like a father and son. Both are tall, vigorous, ruggedly handsome with slightly cruel faces lined by sea and sun, have nice teeth and are approximately the same age, although Rondheim is slightly older. Rondheim also has white hair, as befits a father, and "cool blue-gray eyes"[106] which links him to the temptress Kirsti and her deep blue eyes, much like the flashes in Kirsti's eyes link her to Pitt. In this way Kirsti is connected to the two men battling to make her his prize: Rondheim, for unscrupulous reasons; Pitt, to benefit others. Psychologically and spiritually, however, Pitt and Rondheim are as different as Bilbo and Gollum are physically. Both men can be ruthless, but Pitt fights for his country, for the benefit of others or in self-defense, whereas the amoral Rondheim seeks power and will do anything to get it. Cussler underscores these differences during the hydrofoil battle. Pitt asks Sandecker if all the killing is worth it. The Wise Old Man and benign Father figure responds, "There are men who wouldn't kill for every cent in the world, and there are others who wouldn't hesitate to slit a throat for the price of a meal."[107] Pitt stands for the former, and Rondheim represents the latter. Rondheim demonstrates his amoral nature during the poetry challenge by offering to pay $50,000 to any winner's charity. This is amoral because Rondheim plans on killing his guests, which makes his offer as empty as Gollum's promise of safe passage to Bilbo. Pitt and Rondheim are also different when it comes to self-confidence. Whereas it takes more than a simple slight or outright rudeness to ruffle Pitt's feathers, Rondheim lets his puerile inferiority complex slip when he becomes the butt of a harmless joke while being introduced to Pitt.[108] This lack of self-confidence ends up leading to Rondheim's undoing because it consistently forces him to underestimate Pitt. After the poetry challenge Pitt steals the boon by wheedling information about Hermit Limited's plans from one of Rondheim's partners, F. James Kelly, and eventually escapes with this information because Rondheim dismisses Pitt as nothing more than a worthless homosexual.[109]

But before a hero can ascend back into the light and be reborn he first has to die or be disintegrated.

Pitt's disintegration takes place in Rondheim's private gym, which lies secluded at the bottom of a circular flight of stairs beneath the mansion,[110] imagery that circles back to the tomb and womb analogies from the *Lax*, and the isolated compartment where Kristjan Fyrie began his dark rebirth into the destructive Goddess figure Kirsti. Pitt's beating also circles back to the riddle of submission that Pitt must solve before he can be reborn. Pitt cannot fight his way to safety; it would only win him the kind of noble death he tried to win against the black jet, but things are different now. Pitt has a boon to return to his community, so it is time to set aside Peter Pan fixations of dying in a glorious battle because he must get away, and Pitt's only chance of escaping is to act helpless.

Unfortunately, Pitt embodies (or is pretending to embody) what Rondheim fears is his shadow because of his feelings for Kirsti. Some may argue that Rondheim has no feelings for Kirsti other than contempt, but the one genuinely warm gesture he makes in *Iceberg* is an affectionate embrace he gives her.[111] Rondheim's problem is that Kirsti was a homosexual before her sex change, and Rondheim seems to be afraid that having feelings for her makes him homosexual by default, a phobia Kirsti takes advantage of by goading Rondheim into sparing Pitt. Chastised by the Temptress and Unfaithful Wife, Rondheim finds himself in a similar predicament as Pitt with Koski aboard the *Lax*, and, like Pitt, he reacts the only way he knows how: by throwing a tantrum, ripping the front of Kirsti's dress, slapping her breasts (her most feminine feature) and calling her a "warped whore."[112] To Rondheim, Kirsti is warped because she warped her sex from man to woman; she is a whore because she is tempting him into becoming what he believes is less of a man. The bad news for Rondheim is that, unlike Pitt, he will never find a clue that will save him from his infantile fears and anxieties. All he can do is to try and fail to exorcise them on people such as Pitt and Kirsti.

Rondheim's attack is as savage as it is juvenile,[113] but, just like in the poetry challenge, what appears to be Rondheim's triumph belongs to Pitt. Pitt wins the hero's decisive victory by answering the riddle of submission: "Can the ego put itself to death?"[114] Pitt buries his ego (his Peter Pan or infantile fixations) and sacrifices himself for the greater good. With that accomplished, the time for Pitt's rebirth has come.

Return (a life-enhancing return): Just as some heroes refuse the call to adventure, some refuse to return from the zone unknown,[115] but Pitt is coaxed back from the void by a combination of pain and pleasure.

Tidi offers a prayer as Pitt opens his eyes and Lillie proclaims, "It seems our Major Pitt is about to be reborn."[116] Tidi is also cradling Pitt's head in her role of Earthmother,[117] an image that circles back to Hunnewell's death scene, during which Pitt cradled the doctor's head. Lillie likewise observes that Pitt has been pretty thoroughly worked over, and these injuries are telling in regards to his rebirth. There is an "agony in his side [that] stabbed and twisted like white-hot iron,"[118] which calls to mind Jesus Christ being stabbed in the side with a spear when He appeared to have died on the cross.[119] Pitt's battered face is almost unrecognizable to his friends, a sign that Pitt is not the same man he was before his sacrifice, a fact further emphasized when Rondheim and Kirsti also fail to recognize him upon their next meeting until he speaks. Jesus's disciples also do not recognize him after his resurrection, though, to be fair, Jesus does not reveal himself at first.[120] But, even when a hero is recognized after rebirth, he can be a figure of suspicion or disappointment to the people for whom he put his ego to death. As with Jesus and the doubting Thomas, Pitt feels Lillie's disappointment when he learns that Pitt submitted to Rondheim's beating without fighting back.[121] In the space of a few seconds Pitt experiences the full range of rebirth experiences except apotheosis, the "divine state to which the human hero attains who has gone beyond the last terrors of ignorance."[122] Before that can happen, Pitt has one last terror of ignorance to overcome.

The hero's return to the world, or magic flight, can be lively, almost comical, or fraught with magical obstruction and evasion.[123] Pitt, Tidi, Lillie, and other guests from Rondheim's party, are in a ravine staged to look like the crash site of a passenger helicopter.[124] With its tall sloping walls and bitter temperatures the ravine is comparable to Sheol, the dank subterranean underworld from Mesopotamian and early Hebrew religions, and if someone does not fetch help it will soon be filled with the frozen dead. Tidi assures Lillie, "Dirk is our only hope,"[125] as Pitt is the only person who is ambulatory. While Pitt prepares his ascension out of the ravine he pauses to talk to two other intended victims. The first, Sam Kelly, is F. James Kelly's older brother. Pitt tries to encourage Sam by saying he will be back with a pretty nurse before lunch. Sam jokes that he would prefer a cigar, then blesses Pitt's journey ("God bring you luck")[126] and asks him to tell James that he forgives him. The second is a Russian diplomat, Tamareztov, to whom Pitt good-naturedly promises vodka if the Communist agrees not to make any indoctrination lectures while he is away.

Pitt's ascent is "a purgatory,"[127] and after reaching the top[128] his magic flight is filled with obstacles, thanks to Hermit Limited's computers, which were programmed to design the fake accident. As discussed in Chapter 5, technology is typically treated as value-neutral in Cussler's adventures, and, to be accurate, it is Hermit Limited's members that are ruthless, not their computers. But, to Pitt, the computers are "cold electronic monsters"[129] which he must outwit. Later, after Pitt completes this magic flight, Cussler reinstates value-neutrality by first having Kippmann admit that the NSA used computers to deduce Hermit Limited's assassination plot,[130] and then by having Pitt inform Kirsti that the data she needs to build NUMA a Fyrie probe is stored in Hermit Limited's computers.

Pitt's magic flight across the tundra also parallels a shamanistic spirit quest, where the goal is to gain a guardian spirit or alter ego, most often in the form of a power animal. According to Gose, the pattern for a spirit quest follows a "schema of initiation: descent to the lower regions followed by ascent to the sky, where the Supreme Being grants shamanic powers."[131] Death and symbolic resurrection are key events, and dismemberment is a frequent and painful part. One notable difference between the initiation quest and spirit quest is that the purpose of the spirit quest is to let go of reality by entering a state of ecstasy, using animal voices, masks, and costumes. The goal is to replace reality with a psychic process from the primitive world to "regain what humanity lost when it separated itself from the other animals." Gose explains:

> While preparing for his ecstasy and during it, the shaman abolishes the present human condition and, for the time being, recovers the situation as it was at the beginning. Friendship with animals, knowledge of their language, transformation into an animal are so many signs that the shaman has re-established the "paradisal" situation lost at the dawn of time.[132]

Pitt has descended into the void (the gym), been dismembered (the beating) and ascended (from the ravine), so now it is time for his ecstasy.

As is usually the case at the beginning of a journey, Pitt is in high spirits. But, before walking 50 feet, he realizes he is lost. Worse, Pitt is surrounded by fog again, and this time there is no Wise Old Man to guide him to safety. Instead, Pitt must prove himself worthy of atonement by saving himself. He makes an oath to himself not to fail,[133] determined to outwit Hermit Limited's computers by traveling in the least-expected direction: "The average man ... would have probably headed toward Reykjavik.... That is undoubtedly, he hoped, what the computers had been programmed for—the average man."[134] Pitt is an exceptional person, but one can almost hear Peter Pan crowing to Captain Hook. At first Pitt has reason to crow when he remembers a Boy Scout trick worthy of MacGyver, to create a makeshift compass using a pin, some silk, two threads and a puddle of water; Cussler does a fine job of building suspense each time Pitt painstakingly assembles the compass in the near-freezing weather to stay on course.[135] But, even with this break, Pitt's self-confidence fades the farther he treks across the tundra into the dream landscape,[136] until, totally exhausted, Pitt succumbs to his ecstasy, hovering over "the black pit of no return" and "twilight sleep"[137] between light and darkness, feeling and insensibility, life and death. Only when he is too weak to take another step does he realize he cannot save the people in the ravine. As there is nothing he can do about it, he does the logical thing and surrenders to this truth,[138] and, by doing so, overcomes his last terror of ignorance (exemplified by his oath to himself) and accepts that life is not Neverland and that Peter Pan cannot always rescue Wendy and the Lost Boys. "The hero transcends life with its peculiar blind spot and for a moment rises to a glimpse of the source," a glimpse that shows the "vast and ruthless cosmos"[139] is greater than any hero and smarter than any computer. The cosmos will have its way, which makes an oath like the one Pitt made worthless. Pitt likewise realizes that every hero must fall one day, so the wise man accepts his lot in life and does not judge what is inevitable as a failure.[140] By winning this glimpse of the germinal secret, he is ready for the Rescue from Without.

Instead of letting our hero fall into the black pit of no return, the cosmos steps in and lends a helping hand.[141] Such aid is not unusual in an initiation quest,[142] and this task falls to the story's second protective figure, Golfur Andursson, a river warder who seems to materialize out of nowhere.[143] Andursson carries Pitt out of the otherworldly green hell and through the clamor and clatter of reality to the sanctuary of his farmhouse, an idyllic haven that stands in welcoming contrast to the stark tundra.[144] The contrary nature of Iceland (the zone unknown) resurfaces as Andursson repeats deeds Jonsson performed earlier, including tending to Pitt's wounds and offering advice. Andursson and Jonsson act as bookends for Pitt's journey along the road of trials, but Andursson's advice is more beneficent than a warning. When it looks as though a suitable aircraft capable of reaching the ravine is unavailable, he tells Pitt, "The knot of death, though it be bound like stone, may be unraveled by he who knows the frail strand."[145] Pitt is pretty good at unraveling frail strands that go unnoticed by everyone else, but he is still on the road of trials, so to unravel this knot he must humble himself one more time and realize that assistance can now only come from a source more powerful than himself. "Holding his cut and swollen face in his hands, Pitt muttered softly, 'God save them. God save all of them now. Hopeless, hopeless.'"[146]

This pseudo-prayer demonstrates a newfound maturity in Pitt, and is a harbinger of a seminal moment in the series. Instead of defaulting to his old ways, he realizes it is time for a different course of action, one that will become his signature as a universal (macrocosmic) hero: "He needed *a plan, a device, a gimmick* to reach those who put their trust in him (my emphasis)."[147] Pitt's prayer not only underscores his concern with the welfare of others ("God save them") over himself ("God save thee," from Rondheim's favorite poem) but that a higher power is playing a role in this adventure, a point Andursson drives home when he blesses Pitt as he leaves the sanctuary of the farmhouse ("God go with you").[148] Andursson thus becomes the fourth character to bless Pitt. The first (though his blessing is unintentional) is Hunnewell

("God save thee."); the second is Jonsson ("God and luck go with you.")[149]; the third is Sam Kelly ("God bring you luck."). All four blessings are made during departures, and all are made by elderly men. Ironically, the only old man in *Iceberg* who does *not* bless Pitt is Sandecker,[150] but it could be that Hunnewell, Jonsson, Kelly and Andursson serve as surrogates for Pitt's brusque second father, a man not given to sentimental public displays.[151]

Not long after Pitt humbles himself to the ultimate authority, an inspiration (revelation?) triggers his imagination, a tool that is unavailable to Hermit Limited's cold electronic monsters. By the grace of Fate or coincidence, the past reaches out to affect the present when Pitt remembers seeing a suitable aircraft, a renovated Ford Tri-Motor, at a Keflavik airport; and he conjures the image of Alexander the Great at the Gordian Knot as he tells Andursson that he plans to cut this knot of death with blades.[152] When the Tri-Motor reaches the ravine, Pitt descends into the underworld again, but even though Tidi welcomes him as though he were a savior ("Good Lord, you've come back"),[153] everywhere Pitt looks is evidence of the cosmos' ruthlessness.

The images of Pitt cradling Hunnewell's head and Tidi cradling Pitt's are recollected as he sees Lillie lying on his back with his head cradled in Tidi's arms, and Pitt's limitations as a hero are delineated as he examines the NSA agent. Lillie will live but he will never walk again.

Pitt moves to Tamareztov and surprises the old Bolshevik with a bottle of domestic Soviet vodka that he presents with a snake-oil salesman's spiel. A nice moment follows as Pitt, a realist who never hesitates to criticize his country and government, proves he is just as quick to defend his homeland when Tamareztov makes a crack about Yankee humor. Pitt then demonstrates Yankee compassion as he helps the injured Tamareztov drink from the bottle.[154]

Last, but not least, Pitt finds Sam Kelly, but the old man is dead, and, in a more succinct eulogy than the one Hunnewell gives Fyrie on the *Lax*, Pitt forgets his father's advice about the greatest living man and says, "I wish I had known him better."[155] Pitt stays with Sam's body while other rescuers work with the survivors, and, in what will become another of his characteristic signatures—gestures of genuine compassion—Pitt tucks a cigar into Sam's breast pocket.[156]

This leaves the Crossing of the Return Threshold,[157] which begins with the arrival of Pitt's last helper, Kippmann, who is as much of a realist as Pitt. Kippmann brings special knowledge by showing Pitt the NSA's files on Rondheim and Kirsti and then explains the mystery behind the *Lax* ending up inside an iceberg. Kippmann also brings Pitt back home in a pursuit that ends with Pitt's decisive victory over the destructive Father and Goddess figures. (Cussler could not have picked a more appropriate setting for this victory than Disneyland, a place where good apparently always triumphs over evil,[158] and fairy tales, myths and legends seem to come alive. It is also the perfect place for Pitt to assume the form of the power animal he gains on the tundra.) During a shamanistic spirit quest the Supreme Being grants shamanic powers after ascension,[159] but Pitt ascends to the sky after his rebirth and then again after the rescue in the ravine (his flight to California). Pitt is granted one shamanistic power after his first ascension—the inspiration to use the Tri-Motor, the first of many similar inspirations—and now he is granted his power animal. Cussler injects his own brand of practical humor on the use of animal voices, masks and costumes during a spirit quest by having Pitt borrow a Big Bad Wolf costume so he can search the park without being spotted by anyone working for Hermit Limited.[160] Pitt can be a wolf when it comes to the opposite sex,[161] of course, but Pitt demonstrates in *Pacific Vortex* and *The Mediterranean Caper* that he is as dangerous as a stalking wolf when he is on the hunt.[162]

Pitt is not the only dangerous character wearing a costume in Disneyland. Rondheim is dressed like a pirate captain, and his assassins as buccaneers, in the *Pirates of the Caribbean* ride, which creates some delicious symbiotic irony. A pirate captain is in keeping with Rondheim's character, but even divested of his costume Rondheim is playing a role. The sophisticated Icelandic tycoon is really Butera,[163] who, as Pitt knows from painful experience, is neither as self-confident nor as rational as he pretends. This irony intensifies when Pitt and Rondheim square off on the ride's corsair. Pitt wears his wolf costume as he hunts down Rondheim's assassins,[164] but when Pitt finds Rondheim he removes the wolf's mask to reveal the real Dirk Pitt and tells Rondheim how he misled the villain. The problem is, Pitt is too fatigued to defeat Rondheim. As in Andursson's farmhouse he needs help, and this wiser and humbler Pitt receives it from "the invisible figures of Lillie, Tidi, Sam Kelly, Hunnewell, and the rest who stood at his side giving him strength he could have never possessed alone."[165] When Peter Pan dispatches the Father figure Captain Hook he refuses to grow up, so Peter remains a local (microcosmic) hero; when Pitt dispatches his pirate captain he relinquishes his infantile fixations, elevating him into a universal (macrocosmic) hero, an apotheosis he demonstrates soon after by defeating the destructive Goddess figure in her lair.

When Pitt tries to open the door of Kirsti's room at the Disneyland Hotel it is locked. This way is barred because Pitt has yet to defeat the Goddess, but as he *has* defeated the Father, he finds the door of Rondheim's adjoining room unlocked. Much like the den of some Gothic monster, Rondheim's room is dark and cool with moonlight creating long shapeless shadows, and there is a foul stench from stale cigar butts.[166] Pitt's power animal is with him as he follows a shaft of light through a half-open adjoining door into Kirsti's room—"treading softly, noiselessly like a night animal ready to spring."

Kirsti is taking a shower, after which she emerges looking fresh and inviting. Cussler draws the battle lines between hero and Goddess by circling back to their eyes: "green eyes locked on violet." She begins her conversation by lying that she is Rondheim's prisoner. Pitt tells her he knows Kirsti Fyrie is no more real than Oskar Rondheim, but unlike Rondheim, Kirsti killed her true self.[167] Although attracted to her beauty, Pitt has no illusions regarding the destruction the Temptress has wreaked. He lists her sins, painting her as a cross between Helen of Troy and Brigid O'Shaughnessy.[168] Kirsti pulls a gun and orders him to wait until Rondheim arrives, but Pitt crushes the Goddess by telling her Rondheim is in jail, and she now belongs to *him*. All Pitt demands for keeping Kirsti's secret is her guarantee of Fyrie Limited's continued cooperation with NUMA, including the construction of another probe.

Realizing she cannot defeat Pitt in a war of words, the Temptress tries to use the make-believe atmosphere of Disneyland and her make-believe body to seduce the hero.[169] But Kirsti is no erotic fantasy to Pitt: it does not matter to him that she was once as gay as he pretended to be; what repels him is that she is a "cold, shrewd, calculating witch." In Greek mythology Perseus uses Medusa's reflection to defeat the Gorgon, and Pitt symbolically stands in for a mirror to destroy Kirsti by verbally showing her what she has become.[170] During Hunnewell's eulogy for Fyrie, Pitt recalled his father's observation about taking the clothes away from the greatest living man, and the battle that began with green eyes locking on violet ends with Pitt metaphorically taking Kirsti's clothes and leaving the former Kristjan Fyrie naked, defenseless and alone.[171] He departs with the cutting blessing, "God save thee."[172]

The Hero Triumphant

Pitt's initiation quest is over.
He defeats the Father.
He wins the Woman.
He returns to his community with a boon.
But his journey home is not finished.

Pitt leaves Kirsti's room to return to his hometown, where another anima waits for him. This Woman Figure is neither benign nor destroyer or even makes an appearance. We never learn her name, but she is critical to this adventure and represents one of Cussler's most adroit creations. The anonymous character is a gorgeous redhead Pitt meets on a beach, who serves as a barometer of Pitt's diminishing infantile fixations.

Pitt thinks about this redhead three times during his journey: the first time is early in the novel as Pitt fondly remembers caressing her with one hand and holding a scotch-rocks in the other[173]; the second time is when Kippmann and Pitt land in California; the last time is after Pitt leaves the Disneyland Hotel. When Pitt first thinks about the redhead it is as a "sex-mad"[174] plaything, but when he next thinks about her, he has grown wiser after his glimpse of the germinal secret and refers to her by the more mature appellation "beautiful."[175] The last time Pitt thinks about the redhead he is hoping she will be "compassionate."[176] With his quest completed and his journey over, the simpler human need for compassion has replaced Pitt's earlier desire for mere sexual pleasure. Outgrowing his infantile fixations and becoming a universal hero has made Pitt a better man. He will not admit this to himself,[177] but the monomyth proves otherwise.

The initiation quest pattern can be found in every adventure tale because all adventure tales are the same "shape-shifting yet marvelously constant story." In *Cyclops*, for instance, Pitt makes another perilous journey across a hostile environment (the Atlantic Ocean between Cuba and Florida) after being forced to abandon injured comrades (Giordino, Gunn and Jessie LeBaron) in hopes of bringing back help to rescue them, but what differentiates *Iceberg* from Pitt's other exploits, including *Cyclops*, is the emphasis placed on "mythological symbols [which] represent, by analogy, the millennial adventure of the soul."[178]

In *Dreams and Personality: A Study of Our Dual Lives*, Frederick Pierce writes that "some of us [may] have to go through dark and devious ways before we can find the river of peace or the highroad to the soul's destination."[179] This seems to be true for Pitt. In his first two adventures he performs microcosmic feats, then in *Iceberg* he goes on the hero's quest and experiences apotheosis to become a universal hero. He glimpses the germinal secret but, because he refuses to see that he is a better man, he must travel another road of trials and complete three separate Herculean macrocosmic labors that involve winning another boon for his society, rescuing his future bride and defeating a Father figure who is also a peer.

The First Labor: Raising the Titanic

Resurrecting the White Star liner from two-and-a-half miles beneath the North Atlantic and sailing her into New York Harbor remains Pitt's most memorable feat, one so monumental that this adventure wraps Pitt in more mythic hero allusions than any other novel.[180]

Cussler limits Pitt's appearances to two cameos early in the novel so other characters can speculate about the new universal hero while he is offstage,[181] a characterization trick that builds anticipation while stressing his larger-than-life qualities. Cussler first tries out this trick in *Iceberg*,[182] but Pitt's introduction happens much earlier than in *Raise the Titanic!* Another characterization trick, first used in *Iceberg*, is introducing our hero from another character's point-of-view, which creates enough distance and mystery between reader and protagonist to sustain Pitt's enigmatic "two men" personality, but Cussler also uses the device in *Raise the Titanic!* to suggest that Pitt might be an elemental hero sent by the Fates or the gods.

Pitt's first cameo is seen from the perspective of Sid Koplin, a mineralogist sent to Novaya Zemlya to survey for byzanium. Koplin is shot by a Russian solider and run down by the Russian's komondor when Pitt seems to materialize out of a storm to rescue him.[183] When Koplin gets a closer look at Pitt he sees evidence of the "two men" personality in the hero's "almost cruel features and warm green eyes." Further evidence of Pitt's contrasting personality is the efficient way he kills the Russian and his dog, only to pause afterwards to look at the komondor and express regret.[184] This is the kind of lament one associates with Old School heroism, as when he approaches Koplin and paraphrases Sir Henry Morton Stanley: "Dr. Koplin, I presume?"[185] Pitt administers first aid, then adds to his heroic presence by lifting and carrying Koplin as easily as if Koplin were a child.[186] Koplin emphasizes these heroic allusions when Seagram and Donner debrief him. Seagram confesses that he and Donner assumed the wounded mineralogist had escaped Novaya Zemlya on his own, but Koplin chides that he is not Superman. And, when Seagram asks where Pitt came from, Koplin unknowingly alludes to Pitt's apotheosis in Iceland by saying that he appeared out of the blizzard "like some vengeful Norse god."[187]

Pitt's second cameo is also linked to a storm (with the help of some Gothic imagery) as Seagram sits outside the Balboa Club, in Newport Beach. Lightning from an approaching electrical storm flashes, and Seagram appears to be confronted with a specter. As the thunder fades, he cannot see Pitt but hears a voice ask if he is Gene Seagram. He recollects the Novaya Zemlya rescue by commenting that Pitt has a habit of making a dramatic entrance, then asks if he conjured the storm. Pitt laughs in unison with a thunderclap, then answers, "I haven't mastered that feat yet, but I am making progress at parting the Red Sea."[188]

This comment's irony is illustrated by the word *conjure* and Pitt's reference to Moses. Pitt is a universal hero, not Koplin's Norse god, and human heroes have their limitations, a fact that is as true for Pitt as it is for Moses. When things look bleak, in Exodus, and the Hebrews' only chance of escaping Egypt is crossing the Red Sea, it is God, not Moses, who parts the waters[189]; when things look bleak later in *Raise the Titanic!*, after Hurricane Amanda blows up during the off-season, there is nothing Pitt can do to prevent the White Star liner from sinking again. As a weatherman says, "God help the *Titanic* this time.... He's the only one who can save her now."[190] Even after Project Sicilian passes its initial test, Pitt is powerless to guarantee if (or how long) America and her people will survive into the future despite his helping liberate the country from its most immediate threat.[191] In Exodus, Moses faces a similar limitation. After he liberates the Hebrews from slavery and leads them to Mount Sinai, he is unable to prevent them from rebelling against God. Despite the Hebrews' betrayal, Moses will not turn his back on his people, and, to Pitt's credit, he never rejects America despite his cynicism towards its corrupt politicians and tycoons.[192] The purpose of all this irony is to point out that even a hero with the power of God on his side, like Moses, much less a universal hero, like Pitt, is still only a man, and men must understand their limitations. Pitt, unlike Seagram, understands his and is comfortable with them.

Cussler presents two more heroic allusions during this second cameo, even as he begins to tone down Pitt's elemental trappings. In the tradition of the southwestern American folk hero who has an aboriginal nearness to nature and is skilled in every sign of the forest,[193] Pitt glances at the storm and tells Seagram it is passing.[194] Then, when Pitt leaves, he vanishes in much the same manner as he arrived, walking into the shadows of twilight and disappearing.[195] In between these allusions Pitt provides some prosaic information about himself, such as being a Newport Beach native, that he vacations in the area a few days each year, and that his parents own a house just across the bay from the club. Pitt also lets his all-too-human penchant for not suffering fools slip. After Seagram insists that Pitt had no business jeopardizing Koplin's mission by rescuing him, Pitt lists the things he did to save Koplin's life and salvage his mission.[196] This biographical information and rebuttal may not seem important, but the success of *Raise the Titanic!* depends upon Cussler humanizing Pitt, who has so far been painted as a near-indomitable force of nature. If the reader is not reminded that macrocosmic heroes have limitations, then the success of Pitt's first labor will seem like a foregone conclusion. A Norse god might not have a problem raising the *Titanic* from deep beneath the Atlantic, but it seems an improbable feat for any mere mortal. (Pitt's best dialogue from the film *Raise the Titanic* neatly summarizes some of the challenges surrounding this feat: "You want to talk about distress? We have Navy Weather forecasting a Force–12 storm, we have Russians looking down our throats, and we are on a ship that never learned to do anything but sink. That's distress.")[197] Like any good southwestern American folk hero, Pitt is cool, brave and incorruptible, the kind of man who is resourceful when in peril, and it seems as if the weakness of failure is impossible for someone with his strong and courageous spirit.[198] But, then, if there is no chance of the protagonist failing, an adventure story can have no suspense.[199]

Unlike *Iceberg*, in which the focus is on a hero's apotheosis, *Raise the Titanic!* focuses on a heroic feat. Pitt is helping to defend his society (America) from a threat (Soviet nuclear weapons) by recovering a boon (byzanium), but this is all a MacGuffin.[200] Everything associated with Project Sicilian is an excuse for raising the *Titanic*.[201] Even the Cold War one-upmanship is simply another set of obstacles Pitt must overcome before accomplishing his primary feat of resurrecting the White Star liner.[202] And while there have been excellent individual adventures, like *Tunneling the English Channel* (1907), *The Lost World* (1925) and *Apollo 13* (1995), each of which focuses on overcoming a threat, it is an unusual focus in a series adventure story wherein the emphasis is usually on a hero figuring out what a bad guy is doing and struggling to prevent it.[203] The Batman does this with The Joker, Bond does this with SPECTRE and Pitt does this in all his adventures except this one. As a result, the antagonist Captain André Prevlov, of the Soviet Navy's Department of Foreign Intelligence, becomes an unusual series adventure villain.

Prevlov represents the Soviet threat against Pitt's society because Prevlov's interests are those of the USSR, which is (1) rightfully unhappy about byzanium being stolen from its borders,[204] and (2) even unhappier about America's plot to use the byzanium to power a defensive shield that will trump its nuclear arsenal. Prevlov is a worthy adversary for Pitt, a worldly but self-centered Russian who drinks like an Englishman, drives like an Italian, lives like a Frenchman and studies the Christian Bible so he can better understand his Western enemies, or so he tells his assistant, Lieutenant Pavel Marganin.[205] What makes Prevlov truly unusual is that he serves double duty by performing many of the functions normally performed by a heroic figure. In Pitt's other adventures the villain is the instigator and Pitt is reacting to the villain's threat, but in *Raise the Titanic!* Prevlov is reacting to a threat against his society. Pitt is in charge of the *Titanic* salvage, so he is Prevlov's antagonist. Indeed, Prevlov is Pitt's heroic opposite number[206] as the Russian engages in a dangerous chess game[207] with Pitt. Unfortunately for Prevlov, he fails to recognize that the CIA is playing its own chess game with him by incorporating the Novaya Zemlya incident into a covert operation to trick the Russian into defecting. Before this trap is sprung, however, the unsuspecting Prevlov faithfully carries out his duties as he seeks to discover why the NUMA vessel *First Attempt*[208] is near Novaya Zemlya when the solider and dog are killed. This leads to the revelation regarding Project Sicilian, followed by a Soviet assault on the *Titanic* to prevent the byzanium's recovery.

In most of his adventures Pitt rescues a damsel in distress, but in *Raise the Titanic!* the damsel is a ship. To add a human dimension to Pitt's technical feat, the *Titanic* is linked with Dana Seagram during two pivotal incidents. In the first, Hurricane Amanda overtakes the salvage site and Sandecker orders everyone off the ship except for a skeleton crew to man the pumps. This crew includes Pitt, Giordino and Gunn, but Dana, an accidental passenger, is also aboard. Prevlov and nine Russian marines take advantage of the weather and minimal crew to gain control of the ship, but they need the Americans to keep pumping until Amanda passes. Sandecker and his crew refuse, so Prevlov orders Dana to remove one layer of clothes at a time until the men comply. Dana and the *Titanic* seem to be vulnerable and helpless, but the *Titanic* regains a little of her initial unsinkable reputation by surviving the hurricane, and, before that, Dana gets a different reputation by shamelessly stripping.[209] For a few moments it looks like Dana might have bitten off more than she can chew when Prevlov orders a marine to cut off her left breast if the Americans do not return to the pumps, but Pitt chooses this moment to rescue both Dana and the *Titanic*.

The second pivotal incident occurs after the White Star liner is on her way to completing her maiden voyage. Pitt is bringing back the woman he must win, and usually a modern series hero symbolically claims his bride by bedding the formerly distressed damsel. Bedding the *Titanic* is not feasible, but bedding Dana aboard the *Titanic* provides a practical alternative, and Cussler creates a startling initiation scene for Dana, infused with dark fantasy and repugnant imagery. Starting with the press conference, at which Dana is introduced as NUMA's liaison for the *Titanic* salvage, her adventures have followed the monomyth of Departure, Initiation and Return. As press liaison, Dana ventures forth from her common everyday world to board the *Titanic*, the region of supernatural wonder where fabulous forces are encountered and a decisive victory won. After Prevlov and his marines are defeated, Dana is the first character to allude to the *Titanic*'s supernatural quality when she tells Pitt she wishes it could sail on forever, like the *Flying Dutchman*. Dana then begs Pitt to make love to her, even though she does not know why she wants him. Pitt suggests the romantic allure of the *Titanic* is infecting her as he leads her on a dark descent to a parlor suite prepared for an afternoon tryst.[210] This might sound romantic, even charming, except that the *Flying Dutchman* is a cursed ship, doomed to sail the seas until Judgment Day, Pitt refers to himself as "a satyr" and the love nest is described in less than romantic terms. Pitt has covered the bed with several blankets after cleaning it of "slime and rot," and after an hour of lovemaking "the humid perfume of sweating skin began to soak the air of that old rotted, ghostly bedroom."[211]

When a hero meets a Goddess figure there can be "a purging, balancing, and initiation of the mind into the nature of the visible world."[212] If the hero is a young man, this meeting "is the final test of the talent of the hero to win the boon of love (charity: *amor fati*), which is life itself enjoyed as the encasement of eternity," but if the adventurer is a maid then "she is the one who, by her qualities, her beauty, or her yearning, is fit to become the consort of an immortal. Then the heavenly father descends to her and conducts her to his bed—whether she will or no."[213] In *Raise the Titanic!* the heavenly father turns out to be the president, the most powerful man in the free world, but Pitt paves the way for the president to conduct Dana to his bed. That said, Dana is as much in control of this seduction as Pitt, who, for once, gets as good as he gives. Even Loren Smith, Pitt's equal in most other ways, finds other men lacking after making love to Pitt, but Dana is less impressed. The sex in the parlor suite is experienced from Pitt's point of view,[214] and, instead of the responsive lover he expected, he tangles with "a spastic tiger."[215] Afterwards, Dana inquires if Pitt would make love to a female commander-in-chief propositioned him, and then asks him to make love to her again. Pitt inquires if she wants to fantasize about making love to the president, to which Dana replies, "Does that bother you?"[216]

Pitt's tryst with Dana demonstrates that he can be as fallible (or human) as anyone. Pitt knows Dana and Seagram are separated but still married,[217] and he tries to cover his shame later by advising Seagram to forget about her. Fortunately Pitt's first labor is raising the *Titanic*, not rescuing the Seagrams, and the selfish couple only have themselves to blame for their marriage's disintegration. In contrast, Pitt continues to try to help society, while trying to make amends to Seagram, by salvaging Project Sicilian. The ultimate aim of the hero is to benefit others, so Pitt searches until he locates the byzanium in a forgotten, fog-shrouded corner of England. Only then does Pitt leave the story the same way he arrived, wrapped again in the illusion of an elemental hero. As Koplin puts it, "He came from the mists and he returned to the mists."[218]

The Second Labor: In the Service of Fate

As noted earlier, the road of trials begins with gusto and optimism before turning into a journey of horror, disgust and phantasmagoric fears, and *Vixen 03* is Pitt's most pragmatic and darkest adventure yet. It pairs Pitt with two warped heroes, the self-serving Lusana and the tragic Captain Patrick McKenzie Fawkes, and introduces the series' first corrupt politicians, Daggat and De Vaal.

The earliest indication *Vixen 03* will be different from *Raise the Titanic!* is Pitt's introduction immediately after the prologue, the first time this happens since *The Mediterranean Caper*.[219] There are also no elemental hero allusions. In *Vixen 03* Pitt is an agent of Fate, the agency that determines the outcome of events before they occur.[220] This is a predictable turn of events because heroes on the road of trials often discover that a benign power is supporting them towards a superhuman place where dragons must be slain and unexpected barriers must be passed over and over again.[221]

Fate first steps in when Pitt meets Loren at a party thrown by the secretary of the environment. Neither Pitt nor Loren are fans of Washington's social scene, so the odds that they would be at the same party are slim, and if not for a stray breeze the two may never have gone to a cabin, owned by Loren's late father, in the Sawatch mountain range. From there the dominos fall until a plan to attack Washington, DC, is stymied. All of these events could be dismissed as a string of coincidences[222] if not for that stray breeze, the signature of Fate. When the breeze shifts some torchlight so it reflects off Pitt's eyes, Loren feels a fever ignite in her stomach and soon after the couple is on their Colorado getaway.

Loren's introduction is another indicator of *Vixen 03*'s grittier tone as she practices yoga naked while Pitt watches, inside Charlie's dusty cabin. Pitt appreciates Loren in a much different way than he does Summer Moran in *Pacific Vortex* when he stumbles across her sleeping in the lost city of Kanoli.[223] Summer is an erotic figure reminiscent of Sandro Botticelli's Venus (right down to her clam-shaped bed)[224] while Loren could be posing for a "Women of Capitol Hill" photo spread in *Penthouse*.

Pitt asks Loren for the name of her wanton yoga position, and she says, "The Fish," the first of many fish or fishing references in *Vixen 03*, a departure from Pitt's other adventures.[225] For instance, a string of related fishing references begin when Daggat meets Collins. Daggat tells her that Lusana is more interested in his own personal pursuits than in helping the black people of South Africa, Collins tells him, "You're fishing in a barren lake, Congressman."[226] Later, Daggat tries to win over Collins by "playing her gently, cautiously, as would a fisherman in the knowledge he had a record fish on the line."[227] Then, when Collins agrees to help Daggat lure Loren into a blackmail trap by suggesting that she and Pitt borrow her Arlington apartment for a rendezvous, Collins "felt her chest tighten as Loren circled the bait." When Loren agrees, Collins "fished in her purse and came up with a key."[228] Afterwards, Daggat asks Collins if Loren "took the bait?"[229] The abnormal number of fish or fishing references in *Vixen 03* emphasizes their importance, and the key to understanding them is supplied by an angler.

Lusana is fly-casting in a river while his second-in-command, Colonel Randolph Jumana, studies an outline for Operation Wild Rose, a stratagem to cast blame for an attack on Washington, DC, on the AAR. As Lusana's security guards stand watch, the general hooks a ferocious tiger fish with a piece of cheese, a feat Jumana thought impossible, but Lusana tells him, "The bait is irrelevant if the prey is hungry." The tiger fish breaks the line and Lusana gets a new leader as he and Jumana debate the outline's legitimacy. Emma wants $2 million for the full plan, but Jumana believes the money could be better spent funding hit-and-run terrorist attacks across South Africa. The AAR's chief intelligence analyst, Major Thomas Machita, arrives and Lusana decides he will "pay Emma his thirty pieces of silver," but orders Machita to kill Emma after paying the informer. As Machita listens, he notices Jumana watching something in the river and follows the colonel's eyes to a crocodile gliding towards Lusana. Machita shouts to the security guards, "For God's sake, fire!" Lusana is saved, and although Machita cannot prove it, he can tell by Jumana's "satanic expression"[230] that the colonel saw the crocodile but said nothing.

Lusana's comment about bait and a hungry prey is the key to understanding *Vixen 03*'s fish or fishing references. Loren is hooked by Collins's offer because she believes she must follow her 11th Commandment, that a congresswoman who screws around cannot win an election.[231] In contrast, Daggat is hooked on political power and will stop at nothing to reach the Oval Office,[232] while Lusana is obsessed with rising above his criminal past by becoming South Africa's next prime minister.[233] Daggat and Lusana are so hungry to satisfy their selfish goals that they blind themselves to any consequences their actions may have whenever an opportunity ("bait") presents itself. Daggat never considers that trying to blackmail Loren might backfire, for example. As for Lusana, he treats Collins no better than a slave when he trades her for political support,[234] and he is so worried about the setbacks Operation Wild Rose might cause that he ignores Machita's prescient advice: that people willing to go to such extremes to sully the AAR's reputation might want to do much worse to its leader.[235]

The river scene also incorporates New Testament allusions like the thirty pieces of silver reference to Judas's betrayal of Jesus Christ. There are, of course, numerous fish and fishing references in the Bible. Many of Jesus's disciples were fishermen, and in the Parable of the Net, Jesus compares the Kingdom of Heaven to a fisherman's net thrown into the sea.[236] Jesus's miracles include feeding thousands of people with a few loaves of bread and a couple of fish,[237] and, during a visit to Capernaum, Jesus has Simon fetch a shekel from a fish's mouth to pay the local tax.[238] The fish became a symbol for Jesus in early Christian art, and the Ichtus, or Jesus Fish, remains a popular modern icon for Christianity.[239] The New Testament also references Jesus as the "Lamb of God who takes away the sins of the world,"[240] and, in this role, Jesus is a *redeemer*, or a savior, selflessly prepared to battle the powers of evil to save the world, even at the cost of his own life.[241] This is Jesus the *Agnus Dei* (sacrificial lamb)[242] and in *Vixen 03* the role of the redeemer gets intermixed with the fish or fishing references in the person of the tragic hero Admiral Walter Horatio Bass.[243]

Bass is the second character introduced in *Vixen 03*.[244] Sandecker's commander in World War II, Bass earned his first star by age 38 and was on the fast track to becoming naval chief of staff. By 1959, Bass was retired, but not before doing everything he could, as per orders from President Eisenhower, to erase all evidence of the Doomsday or Quick Death (QD) organism, a toxin so deadly that five ounces will kill 98 percent of the population of a city the size of Manhattan in four hours and remain effective for three hundred years. Bass was in charge of the QD test program, and, by 1988, he is the last surviving member. Bass authorized Vixen 03's flight from Colorado's Buckley Field to deliver a load of QD poison-gas missiles to the battleship *Wisconsin* in the Pacific for test firing, and for over thirty years he alone has borne the curse of the toxin's existence. Over time Bass hoped the secret would die with him, but after Vixen 03 is found in Table Lake he tries to do the next best thing by asking Pitt, Giordino, Steiger and Sandecker to salvage the plane and destroy the missiles without informing the Pentagon. When Sandecker points out they could be branded as traitors, Bass admits this is a possibility. Unlike Daggat and Lusana, Bass is not blind to the consequences of trying to accomplish his goal; he just does not care. When Giordino hears all this he mumbles that he never pictured himself as a savior to mankind, but in this adventure that job belongs to Bass.[245] After Vixen 03 is salvaged, Bass sees that eight missiles are missing and suddenly the strain of living with the QD secret, coupled with reliving the night the C-97 disappeared, overwhelms him, resulting in his suffering a heart attack. Pitt picks up the gauntlet for Bass (like he did for Seagram) and finds the missiles, but Pitt needs Bass to reveal the secret of the weapon's release mechanism so he can destroy them. Bass is as physically incapacitated as Seagram is mentally debilitated on the *Titanic*, but Bass is more concerned about benefiting others than himself, so he tells Pitt as much as he can before lapsing into a coma. Bass never recovers[246] and his sacrifice makes him an *Agnus Dei*[247] even as it redeems the sailor for his involvement in the QD program.[248]

These and other New Testament references in *Vixen 03* supply the motivations of some characters, explain the self-manipulations of others, and lend credence to the fact that Fate is a palpable part of this adventure. The heroic and fairy-tale motifs in Pitt's previous adventures are important, but most people do not incorporate them into their personal belief systems with the same reverence they do religious stories. Millions of people love the pessimistic donkey

Eeyore from A.A. Milne's Winnie-the-Pooh tales and millions of people love the folk tale of Balaam's talking ass from the Book of Numbers, but the former is adored because Eeyore carries on despite his gloomy nature, while the latter is revered because it demonstrates God's wisdom and Man's myopia when it comes to self-appraisal.[249] Although there are some heroic and fairy-tale motifs in *Vixen 03*, the dominance of New Testament references generates a relevant undercurrent of earnestness that Pitt is being guided by a benign power and not just being swept up in a series of coincidences.

The New Testament references intensify with the introduction of the warped hero Fawkes. A warped hero is a character who forsakes morality to pursue a personal goal, often (but not always) after a personal tragedy. This is not a hero like David Mamet's Eliot Ness (Kevin Costner) in *The Untouchables* (1987), a good man who breaks the law he has sworn to uphold and "become what I have beheld" because it is the only way he can restore his corrupt society.[250] Warped heroes should also not be confused with avengers like Edmund Dantès (*The Count of Monte Cristo*), who operate within a rigid personal code of conduct to counterbalance their vigilantism. A warped hero is an extraordinarily gifted man[251] who completely abandons morality until his only path to atonement is making the ultimate sacrifice.

Religious references surround Fawkes, beginning with his introduction,[252] and, in many ways, he resembles the *Agnes Dei* Bass. Both carry terrible personal burdens: Bass, the QD secret; Fawkes, the loss of his family. Both are retired military sailors; Fawkes, in fact, is a former captain in the Royal Navy.[253] Bass and Fawkes abandoned the sea for careers on dry land, but where Bass owns a modest country inn near Lexington, Virginia, Fawkes becomes a South African farmer. Fawkes and his family have built the finest estate in the northeast coastal plain of Natal Province[254] in only 11 years, and, in a land gripped by minority white rule, the Fawkes estate is an Eden where workers earn shares of the farm's profits. This Eden even has a serpent in a tree, Marcus Somala of the AAR, who is surveying the estate from inside a dead baobab as part of a task force gathering information on Natal farms and military facilities.

Like any hero, Fawkes goes on an initiation quest, and his begins when he begrudgingly answers the call to leave his home at De Vaal's request for a private meeting in Pembroke. At the threshold of adventure Fawkes is attacked by three bush kids: "My God ... I'm being ambushed by schoolchildren."[255] Fawkes kills the boys as he crosses the threshold, and entering the dream landscape of the road of trials he finds the mutilated bodies of the bush kids' first victims, a man and woman stoned and hacked to death beside their overturned lorry. Instead of coming under the guidance of a benign force like Pitt, Fawkes falls victim to De Vaal,[256] who claims to want Fawkes's expert opinion on Operation Wild Rose. The truth is, De Vaal has lured the Scotsman to Pembroke so raiders, disguised as AAR soldiers, can slaughter Fawkes's family and everyone else on or near the estate. This includes Somala, who lives long enough to report what happened to Lusana. Fawkes opines that nothing can justify a plan like Operation Wild Rose, but when he returns home, Fawkes abandons his morality. He buries his family, and then, like the Hebrew prophet Elisha, never looks back as he leaves his home for the last time[257] to seek out De Vaal and volunteer to lead Operation Wild Rose. Fawkes is so overwhelmed by hatred that he refuses to see he is being manipulated, but he knows full well that he is figuratively selling his soul to the Devil.[258]

It is hard not to sympathize with Fawkes, but no tragedy justifies abandoning morality. This becomes obvious if Fawkes is compared to Pitt, another extraordinarily gifted man who shares as many characteristics with the Scotsman as Bass. Besides being military men and professional sailors, Fawkes and Pitt are open-minded when it comes to racial differences; they are not only tough but can be dangerous when provoked; they both enjoy Cutty Sark; and neither gives a fig what other people think about them.[259] There are crucial differences between them, however, that may explain why Fawkes succumbs to De Vaal's manipulation. Pitt can be moody and reclusive but he rarely loses his temper and is never a bully; Fawkes has a short fuse, a bit of a cruel streak and less self-control.[260] Most importantly, Fawkes lacks Pitt's need to find solutions to illogical problems. Pitt doggedly pursues Vixen 03 to Table Lake and ends up benefiting his society, but Fawkes ignores the coincidence that his family is massacred by the AAR immediately after reading a plan about manipulating people via phony AAR attacks. This common sense myopia costs Fawkes his good name, self-respect and, ultimately, his life.

Fawkes can also be compared to another warped hero, Lusana (real name: Hiram Jones), an American hoodlum and international drug smuggler turned freedom fighter. De Vaal identifies Lusana as a warped hero when he tells Fawkes that young men joining the AAR are succumbing to "a form of hero worship."[261] AAR soldiers look up to Lusana "with a primitive sort of awe of the supernatural."[262] To them Lusana is a savior, but the general is betraying their faith. When he trades Collins to Daggat he demonstrates that he is even more willing than Fawkes to forsake his morality if it will help him become prime minister, a goal Lusana has calculated to the exact day. De Vaal's right-hand man, Colonel Joris Zeegler, director of Internal South African Defense, also refers to Lusana in less than respectful redeemer terms when he tells Fawkes how Lusana hopes to use a prolonged economic blockade to choke off the white government of South Africa, after which the general can assume command of the country by "playing benevolent savior."[263] Daggat describes Lusana as "a messiah from the wilderness" who arrives "like a revelation in the night" and "is adored by Bible beaters everywhere for his devout piety."[264] Lusana's two highest-ranking officers, Machita (who serves as an angel on Lusana's right shoulder) and Jumana (a devil on Lusana's left shoulder), further personify the general's role of warped redeemer. Machita, like Lusana, is a former criminal who was raised in America (real name: Luke Sampson), but, unlike Lusana, he was born in Africa (Liberia). Machita is devoted to Lusana and the AAR cause of fighting a clean war, but Jumana, another former thug (but born and raised in Africa), believes it is often necessary to drive his fellow countrymen hard because the people "seldom know what is best for them."[265] Jumana is also not shy about telling Lusana, "Africans know what is best for Africans."[266]

Conflicts between Machita and Jumana come to a head during the fly-casting scene, with the river serving as a symbol for the dangers swirling around Lusana in and out of the AAR.[267] Jesus is baptized in the River Jordan,[268] and, like the African river teeming with tiger fish and crocodiles, the Jordan is an unhealthy place, its waters "green-slimed and sluggish."[269] Jesus wades into the Jordan as willingly as Lusana does the African river because the first law he establishes about the Kingdom of Heaven is that a man must humble himself and repent for his sins before he can enter it.[270] The problem with Lusana is that he has no interest in being humble or in repenting. Jesus's baptism likewise marks the beginning of his ministry on Earth, which starts with his going into the wilderness to be tempted by the Devil.[271] In contrast, Lusana's ministry is already started,[272] but the AAR is suffering in the public arena because of the Fawkes massacre, and Lusana is afraid Operation Wild Rose could cripple his chances of becoming prime minister. So Lusana succumbs to temptation and orders Machita to murder Emma after paying "his thirty pieces of silver." However, this reference is flawed. In the New Testament Judas receives 30 pieces of silver to betray Jesus, but in the fly-casting scene the so-called savior Lusana not only betrays Emma but Machita, by ordering his most loyal officer to execute his sin for him.[273]

Machita is, in many ways, a humbler version of Lusana, and he takes the first steps to possibly becoming the AAR's genuine redeemer hero by saving Lusana's life[274] and then going into the wilderness of the South African countryside. Machita is carrying his goodies ($2 million) in a basket like Little Red Riding-hood when he meets Emma inside a ghost ride at a carnival. Emma, disguised as an old man[275] working at the ghost ride, takes the bait when he jumps into Machita's car.[276] Machita exchanges the basket for Lusana's envelope, supposedly containing the full plans for Operation Wild Rose. But when Machita tries to kill Emma he is distracted by an orange light that unveils a bearded Satan with a pitchfork.[277] The Devil is Emma's accomplice,[278] but instead of tempting Machita, Satan breaks Machita's wrist with the pitchfork. Machita battles the Devil and returns from the wilderness, but Emma, elusive and dangerous as a tiger fish, escapes with Machita's basket.

Jesus faces three tests during his temptation in the wilderness,[279] and Machita faces three tests, although only the first happens in the South African wilderness. The fact that it takes place at a carnival is significant: modern carnival games perpetuate the ancient traditional symbolism of resurrection that started at least as far back as dithyrambs and the "dark, blood-reeking rites" that celebrated "the killed and resurrected Dionysus."[280] Machita symbolically returns from the dead when he enters the ghost ride (a symbolic realm of the dead) and comes out alive, but, soon after, he experiences a genuine resurrection. Machita's road to Golgotha begins when he discovers that Emma's envelope only contains operating procedures for military garbage removal. Jumana, the Judas figure, condemns Machita, but Lusana momentarily behaves like a true redeemer and absolves his loyal officer by accepting blame for the mistake.[281] Lusana remains convinced of Operation Wild Rose's validity, however, and plans to warn America, where he is scheduled to testify before Daggat's committee to request aid for the AAR. This trip is Lusana's second test; the first came when Lusana traded Collins to Daggat for the congressman's favors, and when Lusana pursues his quest for the prime minister's chair to America in spite of Machita's prescient advice[282] he fails his second test as miserably as the first, but this time the consequences are more dramatic for him and for Machita.

Jumana assumes command of the AAR when Lusana leaves and orders a raid on an innocent African village called Tazareen. Jumana asks Machita to join his mutiny, but Machita will not be tempted, which results in his passing his second test. Machita insists that Jumana honor an oath they made to uphold Lusana's principles,[283] but Jumana arrests Machita, and, much like Jesus at the hands of the Romans, Machita is stripped, beaten and tossed in a makeshift cell.[284] However, the Tazareen raid is the last straw for the South African government, and, in a twist on the Fawkes massacre, Zeegler leads a covert assault against the AAR's compound that leaves no trace that the African Army of Revolution ever existed—except, that is, for Machita, who is overlooked by Zeegler's forces.[285]

Machita's resurrection takes place when the building in which his cell is located is blasted and he is knocked out. After Machita "recrossed the threshold of consciousness," he struggled from his would-be tomb and "saw the miracle of his salvation,"[286] a collapsed wall that shielded his cell from the attack. In the Bible, such places as Sodom and Gomorrah are wiped out without a trace by the wrath of God because of its leaders' or citizens' sins; in *Vixen 03* Jumana's sin (the Tazareen attack) triggers the government's wrath. The reason the AAR compound is wiped out, however, is because of the threat it poses to the white South African government, a threat Lusana has created through his sins, including using money from his criminal past to fund the AAR. If Lusana had heeded Machita's advice, Jumana would not have been free to order the Tazareen attack. But, because of his hubris, everything Lusana built in Africa is wiped clean from the Earth. The good news is that a new redeemer, the reborn Machita, can keep his oath by rebuilding the AAR according to Lusana's principles, but Machita cannot do this as long as Lusana is technically in command of the AAR. So Machita disappears after his resurrection and does not return until the end of *Vixen 03*, when he will face his third test.[287]

In the interim, the warped redeemer Lusana finds himself on his own road to Golgotha, in America. Lusana is a lone voice in an urban wilderness after NSA Director Jarvis dismisses Operation Wild Rose as a feasibility game and confides to Daggat that befriending a radical revolutionary could prove embarrassing to the congressman's reputation. Daggat exhibits the same immorality Lusana did with Collins by distancing himself from Lusana, but not before convincing Jarvis to investigate Operation Wild Rose.[288] Popular support is still against white rule[289] in South Africa so Daggat continues seeking aid for the AAR until the Tazareen attack, then he abandons Lusana as quickly as the apostle Peter abandons Jesus[290] by advising the general to return to Africa and put his house in order, even if it means blaming the attack on other insurgent groups.[291] Pitt will see that Daggat does not profit from his sins, but before Lusana can board his plane for home, Zeegler has the general abducted and stashed aboard the *Iowa* (BB-61), a decommissioned battleship that Fawkes has refitted to sail up the Potomac and launch a missile attack on the capitol. It is inside the *Iowa* that Lusana must walk the road of trials, with its dream landscape and succession of ordeals. Drugged by Zeegler's operatives, Lusana loses track of time as strange faces appear and reappear until he is brought before Fawkes, who looks like "a distorted giant."[292] The former Hiram Jones faces his fate without fear as he insists the AAR is innocent of the Fawkes massacre, but the giant tells Lusana they are on a trip that has no return ticket.[293] He then imprisons Lusana in a makeshift cell, where his "*hands were tied wide apart* by ropes wrapped to overhead pipes (my emphasis)."[294] In comparison, when Jesus is unjustly accused by the chief Jewish priests and condemned by the Roman authorities, he bravely faces them all even after being crucified, the ultimate no-return trip at the time.

As for the hero Pitt, the benign power Fate guides him to the *Iowa*, too. Pitt discovers that the missing eight missiles were salvaged from Table Lake and sold to an American arms dealer, who mixed four of them in with a lot of 37 missiles purchased by one of De Vaal's operatives pretending to be an agent of the AAR. Pitt's search converges with Jarvis's investigation into Operation Wild Rose, and the hero and his newest helper track the missiles to the decommissioned *Iowa*, which is supposed to be rusting away in a Maryland shipyard. In a Gothic scene brimming with foul weather[295] Pitt and Jarvis visit the shipyard around midnight, but the *Iowa* has vanished,[296] and Pitt realizes Operation Wild Rose is set to occur that morning, December 7th, the anniversary of the Japanese attack on Pearl Harbor. Jarvis leaves to brief the White House while Pitt pursues the *Iowa* and boards the battleship as it steams up the Potomac. The effort almost kills Pitt, and he is knocked out. But, like Machita in the AAR compound, Pitt survives to cross the threshold of consciousness. Unfortunately, Pitt arrives too late to prevent Fawkes from plowing over a fishing trawler, the *Molly Bender*, rather than risk running the *Iowa* aground. This is Fawkes's point of no return,[297] and, in response, the *Iowa*, like the *Flying Dutchman*, becomes a forward-deployed asset of Hades on Earth.[298] Pitt and his warped counterparts find themselves, like Jesus on Holy Saturday, in the belly of Hell,[299] a situation made even more obvious after the president orders the *Iowa* hit with a strike of Satan missiles that transform the battleship into an "inferno,"[300] "a floating coffin"[301] and "a damn charnel house" filled with "choking haze and gloom."[302]

Unlike Jesus (who humbly entered the belly of Hell to benefit others) or Pitt (who selflessly boarded the *Iowa* to disarm the QD missiles), Lusana is in the belly of Hell as a result of his sins, Fawkes is here because of his blind vengeance, yet Fate brings Pitt here not only to rescue Washington but help Lusana and Fawkes redeem themselves. Time is growing short, however, so Fate is not subtle when it comes to guiding Pitt[303] to confront Lusana with the general's sins. Pitt gives Lusana his Colt .45 automatic to stand guard while he disarms a QD missile; the former Hiram Jones is humbled that a white man trusts a black man of his reputation with a gun. Pitt then asks him to hold a moneybag while he deposits a cluster of gas bomblets inside it as Lusana reads WHEATON SECURITY BANK on the canvas. Perhaps because Pitt trusts him, Lusana confesses that he once robbed an armored truck, something he has never admitted to anyone else.[304] Lusana's sins, represented by the moneybag, are finally coming home to roost as Pitt instructs Lusana to carry the bomblets out of the depths of the *Iowa* and toss them over the side of the ship.

This is Lusana's third test.

The redeemer Jesus was sinless but took on the sins of the world and carried them with him as he bore the cross upon his back, bringing grace to all mankind by sacrificing himself. Bass likewise bore his sins by keeping the QD secret for three decades after his career was cut short, and became a redeemer when he sacrificed himself to help end the QD threat. All Lusana has to do is carry his sins out of the ship, but to become a genuine redeemer and be resurrected from the belly of Hell Lusana must make the ultimate sacrifice, as did Jesus and Bass. Before Lusana can dump the moneybag overboard, a badly wounded navy SEAL blocks his way. Lieutenant Alan Fergus is the leader of a team ordered by the president to board the *Iowa* only to get caught in the Satan missile attack and chopped up in a firefight with the ship's crew, which is made up of young South African blacks. Fergus mistakes Lusana for one of the crew and, in a split second, Lusana realizes he can help Africa's oppressed more as a martyr. The repentant Lusana tosses the moneybag overboard, Fergus fires, and Lusana passes his third test.[305]

Regrettably, Fawkes is less fortunate during his third test. This comes after he interrupts Pitt while Pitt is disarming a QD missile and convinces him that the organism is a genuine threat. The Scotsman realizes the last QD missile must be in one of the turrets, but as the pair hurries to prevent it from being fired they are blocked by the story's trickster and Fawkes's shadow side, Emma. Her arrival aboard the *Iowa* marks the start of Fawkes's third test. In a parallel to Lusana sending Machita to betray Emma and retrieve the plans for Operation Wild Rose, De Vaal sends Emma to betray Fawkes and keep the defense minister's participation in Operation Wild Rose a secret. Up until now Fawkes (sounds like Faust) has been acting as an agent of De Vaal (sounds like Devil). Now Fawkes finds himself literally and figuratively in a hell of his own making where he is confronted by a true agent of the Devil, which makes Emma Fawkes's shadow. Fawkes's third test begins inside the *Iowa* at approximately the same time Lusana's third test transpires outside the ship, but, unlike the wounded and angry Fergus, who mistakes Lusana's identity, Emma knows all about Fawkes and attempts to kill what is left of his soul with this knowledge, engaging him in a watered-down version of a riddle contest.[306] Emma is prevented from revealing the whole truth to Fawkes when Pitt is wounded while trying to subdue her. The distraction allows Fawkes to kill her, after which her true form is revealed.[307] Emma is not the series' first trickster (that would be Delphi Moran) and will not be the last (Foss Gly is up next in *Night Probe!*), nor is she the first trickster to actually (or apparently) change from one sex to another (that would be Kristjan/Kirsti Fyrie) and will not be the last (Boudicca Dorsett is waiting in *Shock Wave*), but Emma comes the closest to killing Pitt because Fate deems that Fawkes, like Pitt without Giordino in *Iceberg*, must finish his third test alone.

Fawkes gets Pitt off the *Iowa* even though Pitt is in the same condition he was in when he arrived—unconscious. Fawkes then picks up the gauntlet for Pitt by returning to the belly of hell to try to disarm the last QD missile. Fawkes fails when a crewman fires two missiles, not realizing that one turret is damaged. The *Iowa* explodes, blasting Fawkes back out of hell through the outside hatch, even as the QD missile is launched. An instant before Fawkes is smashed against the deck he "saw the utter waste, the terrible stupidity, of his actions. He reached out to his beloved Myrna to beg her forgiveness."[308] Fawkes dies without knowing he has passed his third test and that he will earn that forgiveness.

Pitt survives the *Iowa* explosion, thanks to Fawkes, and is able to help Steiger and Sandecker put an end to the last QD missile. In gratitude, Pitt brings Fawkes's body to the family's burial plot and oversees a private ceremony, attended by De Vaal, Zeegler and Machita.[309] Pitt tells De Vaal that Emma's attempt to kill Fawkes's soul not only backfired, but Fawkes tucked his ship's log detailing Operation Wild Rose under Pitt's shirt. In death, the tragic warped hero becomes a genuine hero by exposing De Vaal and performing a posthumous service to mankind. To avoid a scandal for South Africa, Machita stabs the traitor De Vaal and dumps the body in the Scotsman's grave. For over 30 years Bass did mankind a service by keeping the QD organism a secret, and now Fawkes is able to do the same by keeping watch over the secret of De Vaal and Operation Wild Rose for eternity. Pitt follows a last request in Fawkes's log and plants a bougainvillea from the Scotsman's ranch at each corner of the plot, one for each member of the Fawkes family. It appears that the forgiveness Fawkes sought is granted when the four plants arch their blossoms towards the sun.

Fawkes's funeral is also the site for Machita's third test, which the AAR's new redeemer fails. Machita acts as if he is going to say something to Zeegler as the colonel starts to leave but thinks better of it, fumbling a golden opportunity to open a dialogue and prevent further bloodshed in South Africa, which would seem to be in keeping with Lusana's principles. Machita gets a second chance when Pitt tells Zeegler and Machita they would be stupid not to take this moment to discuss their differences, but Zeegler dismisses the suggestion and Machita succumbs to foolish pride, even as he denies his American heritage.[310] In all fairness, when Cussler wrote *Vixen 03* conflict between blacks and whites seemed inevitable in South Africa, so Machita's attitude seemed sad but appropriate then. Happily, when apartheid ended, South Africa had Nelson Mandela to lead them instead of Machita.[311]

Schwartz describes the goal of a hero as preserving the status quo or retrieving society's "previous, happy condition,"[312] something that is possible in *Raise the Titanic!* but impossible in *Vixen 03* because of the intrinsic differences in the stories. In *Raise the Titanic!*, the *Titanic* is a Lady in her House of Sleep, an enchanted lost bride waiting to be united with her husband, and Pitt obliges by salvaging the White Star liner and completing her maiden voyage to New York. Pitt is aided by a team of navy SEALs who help him rescue the *Titanic* from Prevlov and the Russian marines. After the *Titanic* docks, Pitt locates the byzanium so that Project Sicilian can be tested, those successful tests taking place somewhere in the Pacific Ocean. Finally, at the beginning and end of *Raise the Titanic!*, Pitt is compared to an elemental hero who mysteriously appears and vanishes from the mists. In contrast, the famous ship in *Vixen 03*, the *Iowa*, is compared to a disfigured child,[313] a monster, and a hell on earth. A team of navy SEALs is sent to stop the *Iowa*, only to be bombed by their own country, shot at by the ship's crew and killed when the *Iowa* explodes. Prior to that, Fawkes fires two missiles on Washington, DC, and one nearly destroys the Lincoln Memorial.[314] Where the Pacific test for Project Sicilian signals the end of nuclear missile threats against America, the destruction of Rongelo Island in the Pacific (a QD test site) by nuclear missiles merely signals the end of the QD threat against mankind. As Zeegler and Machita demonstrate that the world is a place where men will often maintain the status quo and wage war rather than seek peace, and, in such a world, weapons like the QD organism can cause unintended but catastrophic horror[315] and innocents (like the Fawkes family) can suffer to satisfy other men's desires. Finally, Pitt is never presented as anything more than a universal hero with human limitations, as demonstrated by his inability to get Machita and Zeegler to talk, and by his helpless condition when he arrives on and leaves the *Iowa*.

Fairy tales often end with a marriage between the hero and the woman he must win, while society returns to its previous happy condition. In *Raise the Titanic!* the hero can rescue the girl, defeat the bad guy and save the world, but this is impossible in *Vixen 03*, in which there is no marriage—symbolic or genuine—even though this adventure introduces the series' Queen Goddess figure and Pitt's future bride. Pitt has no intention of marrying Loren in *Vixen 03*, and when she tries to arrange a marriage with someone else she ends up feeling unfulfilled and unhappy. As for Pitt, he accomplishes all a universal hero can by saving Washington, DC, from a QD attack, his second macrocosmic feat. But, with no victories or happy endings, Pitt finds himself feeling "neither remorse or sadness but rather a kind of contentment"[316] at the end of his second labor.

The Third Labor: Uniting Two Great Nations

Lieutenant Commander Heidi Milligan, USN, is tall, beautiful, 30-something, and the first supporting character to appear in more than one Dirk Pitt adventure. In *Vixen 03* Heidi is in love with Bass and powerless to prevent the *Agnus Dei*'s sacrifice, and in *Night Probe!* she unintentionally brings Pitt into the orbit of the man he must challenge at the end of this story's road of trials, secret agent Brian Shaw of Her Majesty's Secret Service.

We know Shaw better as Pitt's heroic predecessor James Bond.[317]

Pitt is again restricted to two cameos at the start of *Night Probe!*, not to build anticipation but to allow the spotlight to shine on Heidi as she chances across a letter from President Woodrow Wilson to Prime Minister Herbert Henry Asquith that mentions an unspecified treaty between the United States and Great Britain. Discovering the details about this North American Treaty becomes a quest for Heidi until she must relinquish it to pursue a more personal matter; she then asks for Pitt's help. He steps in, like he does in *Raise the Titanic!* and *Vixen 03*.[318]

At the beginning of *Night Probe!* Heidi is feeling almost indifferent towards men after surviving a divorce, a hysterectomy and Bass's death—all within three years' time. In *Vixen 03* Heidi tells Pitt she has been married to a Marine colonel who bossed her around,[319] but less than four months later, in *Night Probe!*, she confides to Mildred Gardner, an archivist at Princeton University, that her ex-husband mentally and physically abused her. Gardner's arrival signals a return to dominance of heroic and fairy-tale references, with the matronly archivist serving as a protective figure. Like Jonsson, Gardner sees more in the heroine than the heroine sees in herself. When Heidi tells Gardner that the navy is her first love and that earning a doctorate is necessary for career advancement, Gardner suggests that she is a strong-willed woman who likes competing with men. And, when Heidi says she chose her thesis topic of the navy during Wilson's administration because of its untapped potential, Gardner counters that it is a subject no man had the foresight to research.[320] Gardner also establishes that Heidi is no agent of Fate (like Pitt in *Vixen 03*) by helping her find Wilson's letter to Asquith, but only after Heidi asks if there is any more relevant correspondence she can research. Only then does Gardner barely recall a file of unpublished and uncatalogued letters by Wilson.[321] Finally, the archivist performs the archetypal duties of the Wise Old Man by calling Heidi out of the comfort of her home, or, in this case, Heidi's current life,[322] by suggesting that she live it up every once in a while with a good man.[323]

Soon after, Heidi bumps into Pitt at a restaurant. Failing to recognize him at first in the dim light, Heidi then sees his dazzling smile, the room seems to brighten,[324] and she impulsively kisses him. Things progress from there and the couple wind up in her hotel room, where Heidi crosses the threshold of adventure. Pitt is the herald at the threshold, who, again, may appear dark and frightening but is surrounded by an atmosphere of irresistible fascination and whose arrival activates the archetypal images symbolizing rebirth.

Crossing the threshold of adventure can be difficult because "this is the process of dissolving, transcending, or transmitting the infantile images of our personal past,"[325] which can be as painful as it is rewarding. The strong-willed Heidi submits to Pitt's command to let him do everything and experiences "exquisite agony" as he "sweetly tortured" her. As things heat up, Heidi "seems to dissolve," and when she falls asleep afterwards "one dream falls upon another in a kaleidoscope of vivid fantasies." The next morning she is "thrust back to conscious reality" by a ringing telephone, and Heidi's agony is compounded by a knocking at her door. When she finally opens the door she is presented with a vase of white roses from Pitt, signifying the herald's true gift to her. Red roses symbolize romance, but the color white symbolizes purity, and Heidi's night with Pitt is less about romance and more about rebirth. "The hour spent with Pitt returned as though observed through a pane of frosted glass, the sights and sounds fusing together in a dreamy sort of mist." Heidi has survived the crossing of the threshold with "a glowing soreness from within,"[326] the only proof besides the roses that it ever happened.

Heidi continues her quest to solve the mystery about the North American Treaty after her rebirth, but eventually she must report for sea duty in San Diego. When Pitt comes to see her off at the airport, she impulsively gives him her treaty research. After three difficult years she is ready to live again, so she entrusts her herald with deciding what she should do about the treaty quest. Pitt decides to carry on Heidi's research, moving him back into his normal hero role, which, in turn, leads him to the man he must challenge.

Shaw is a Father archetype,[327] and as befits this figure he is somber, imposing and surrounded by an atmosphere of solitude. Introduced at a funeral (most likely for "M"), we first see him from the perspective of Mrs. Graham Huston (most likely Ms. Moneypenny). Time has been kind to Shaw physically, who is still handsome and fit at age 66. Reminiscent of Sherlock Holmes retiring to beekeeping in Sussex, Shaw left the British Secret Service 25 years earlier[328] and owns a small working farm on the Isle of Wright.[329] During the glory days of 007, Bond got his assignments from "M" and flirted with Moneypenny on the way in and out of his superior's office; the funeral unexpectedly slips into this pattern when Shaw gets one last mission. Shaw asks Huston if she has time for a drink; she declines, explaining that she must get back to London. As Huston bids a final goodbye she slips an envelope, containing orders to visit their old offices, into his coat pocket. The British government has learned about Heidi's research and needs Shaw to leave his comfortable home to travel to North America to find out what the U.S. government knows about the treaty and if it intends to do anything about it.[330]

In *Raise the Titanic!* Prevlov assumes the duties of the hero as Pitt becomes his antagonist, but in *Night Probe!* Shaw and Pitt both assume the duties of a hero and become each other's antagonist. Eventually, both heroes make dark descents into an underground quarry where the *Manhattan Limited* and the North American Treaty have been buried for three-quarters of a century,[331] and face off in a showdown inside the private Pullman car of Undersecretary of State Richard Essex. Heroes can only defeat a Father figure by stripping themselves of their infantile ways, but in *Night Probe!* it is Shaw who artfully uses the infantile skill of lying to locate the treaty. In contrast, Pitt, who can run a bluff or bend the truth with the best of them, prefers honesty, and during his showdown with Shaw he is basically truthful with the British agent, which allows him to outwit the man he must challenge and win the boon.[332]

To be fair, Shaw lies to benefit his country, never himself, and his mission qualifies him as an enemy agent, so telling the truth would be counterproductive. What makes his lying infantile is Shaw's perception of undercover espionage as a game—a most dangerous game, definitely, but still a game. Shaw has not worked as a field agent in a quarter century, but he convinces himself that he still has enough skills to continue competing.[333] In Cussler's words, "He was playing his kind of game and he reveled in it."[334] When Pitt and Shaw meet, Pitt tries to keep his opponent unbalanced by mentioning that he never learned backgammon—Pitt has read the British agent's service file and knows he has a passion for it—and Shaw subtly suggests that Pitt is getting in over his head when it comes to espionage by extending an offer to teach him the game sometime.[335] Later, Shaw asks Heidi to deliver a message from the British prime minister to the president. Shaw cannot do it because "it is too early in the game for a direct confrontation."[336]

Shaw loses the boon, but he wins the woman. His quest for the treaty begins with Heidi, who falls for his charms and into his bed. Heidi is smitten with Pitt and Shaw, but in the end she falls in love with Shaw, who falls in love with her and promises they will be together some day. As for Pitt, he is not ready to abandon his Peter Pan bachelor life,[337] but he is not infantile when he is bested in love. At the end of *Night Probe!* he arranges for Shaw and Heidi to meet at the airport as Heidi waits to return to San Diego and before Shaw is dispatched to a federal prison. But Pitt has also arranged for Shaw's escape, complete with boarding pass and adjoining seats on Heidi's flight. Pitt can get away with this because the president owes him a favor for securing the North American Treaty, but when Shaw asks why he is doing this he answers simply, "She loves you."[338]

At different times during *Night Probe!* Pitt is a hero or a herald, Shaw is a hero or a Father, and Heidi is a hero or an Earthmother. Heidi is wearing denim jeans, a denim blouse, riding boots and a red bandana when she is introduced in *Vixen 03*, and when she goes to the restaurant where she meets Pitt her ensemble is capped off with a long feather and jeweled earring. Her hair is ash-blond and her eyes are an earthy Castilian brown with a pie-shaped splash of gray in the right eye, giving her a supernatural appearance[339] befitting a mythic archetype. As for spiritual and emotional nourishment, Shaw and Pitt are better men for having met Heidi, and her homeland is a stronger country thanks to her efforts.[340]

A beneficial Goddess character like Heidi is usually offset by a destructive Goddess in an adventure, and Danielle Sarveux is a model Unfaithful Wife.[341] A showy dresser, Sarveux exhibits "cold poise and granite confidence," has "raven hair," and "inundates" any room she enters "like a monsoon."[342] When Bass lies dying in a hospital after his heart attack, Heidi is there providing emotional and spiritual nourishment; when Danielle arrives at a hospital to visit her husband after Gly's assassination attempt, she pauses in the doorway for effect as reporters watch, refuses the offer of an adjoining room and flees when the wounded man exhibits signs of delirium. Danielle also does not compete with men, like Heidi, but overpowers them, except for Villon, a Jungian Devil who dominates her.[343] Jung's Devil is a form of shadow archetype who offers treasures such as wealth, power or knowledge in exchange for someone's soul,[344] and Danielle sells hers to escape her marriage and to see an independent socialist Quebec. Danielle hopes that her husband's death will accomplish both ends, but gets worse than she bargains for and loses everything precious to her.

Successful Devils are Tempters, and Villon is the incubus to Kirsti Fyrie's succubus. Villon's physique is as perfect as Kirsti's, and, like her, he is often described as resembling a work of art. There is also something about Villon's features suggesting that a savage lurks just beneath his perfect appearance.[345] He enjoys looking at himself in a mirror as he strikes competitive bodybuilder poses, but he does not need a looking glass to see his lurking savage when Foss Gly is around. Villon and Gly are doubles.[346] When Villon mentions that they could pass for brothers, Gly, a trickster with strong masquerading skills, takes on Villon's form. Villon is leading a double life as a respected member of the Canadian Parliament and as the Free Quebec Society's clandestine leader, but it is Gly in the guise of Villon who performs the savage jobs that Villon hopes will make him Quebec's first president. Villon is unaware that Gly is pretending to be him, however, or that Gly uses this disguise to make love to Danielle and Villon's wife.[347] Again, immoral behavior is not unusual for tricksters, but doubles are prone to replacing the "other" or the person they look like, as in stories such as Poe's "William Wilson" (1839).[348] Eventually, Gly begins plotting to assume Villon's life and dream,[349] and, in the end, Villon is destroyed by his double as he and Danielle, like dark versions of Lancelot and Guinevere, face the wrath of Sarveux, who plays the role of a merciless King Arthur. Instead of becoming Quebec's first president, Villon ends up pondering how odd it is that he is the last man to die for Quebec's liberty.[350] Gly, meanwhile, returns to being Gly again, only to apparently succumb to Sarveux's wrath as well. Gly somehow manages to escape, however, but his salvation apparently comes at a cost as he is transformed into a pure savage in *Cyclops*.

Perhaps Gly made a deal with a Devil.

Recap

"The ultimate aim of the quest must be neither ecstasy for oneself, but the wisdom and the power to serve others." This is the critical difference between Pitt and the adversaries who oppose him, be they villains or supporting characters.

In *Raise the Titanic!* Dana Seagram revels in the fame she receives from the *Titanic* rescue but ends up living a version of her mother's boozy, floozy lifestyle, while Gene Seagram only cares about proving he is not a failure but ends up losing his marriage and his sanity.[351] In *Vixen 03* Fawkes forsakes morality for vengeance after he loses his wife and children only to discover that he has been terribly used, while Lusana and Daggat forsake morality in their quests for political power (although Lusana does realize the error of his ways and becomes a martyr). In *Night Probe!* Villon follows in Daggat's footsteps, only to end up hoisted on his own petard. Pitt, on the other hand, succeeds where these characters fail because he acts to redeem his society, while other characters, including Bass, Heidi and Shaw, win more than they lose because they likewise put the benefit of others ahead of themselves.

Raising the *Titanic* and bringing her into New York Harbor is the equivalent of rescuing the Lady in the House of Sleep and uniting her with her bridegroom, but even though Pitt seems eager to marry Summer Moran in *Pacific Vortex* he is unable to win the series' Queen Goddess figure Loren Smith when they meet in *Vixen 03*. "The mystical marriage with the queen goddess of the world represents the hero's total mastery of life; for the woman is life, the hero its knower and master."[352] But Pitt still has too much Peter Pan in him to have mastered life. "I regret I can't be more of an adoring lover to you," Pitt tells Loren, "but I'm too damned selfish to commit myself."[353] Pitt is still too selfish in *Night Probe!* so Brian Shaw really has no competition when he wins Heidi Milligan. Nevertheless, Pitt is a better and wiser person for having met Heidi, and he will grow wiser in each of his future adventures.

According to Campbell, "The testings of the hero, which were preliminary to his ultimate experience and deed, were symbolical of those crises of realization by means of which his consciousness came to be amplified and made capable of enduring the full possession of the mother-destroyer, his inevitable bride."[354] Pitt makes a half-hearted proposal to Loren in *Inca Gold*, but she is smart enough to recognize neither is yet ready to commit.[355] Pitt again suffers the despair of losing a woman he loves in *Shock Wave*, but instead of retreating into selfishness (as he did after losing Summer), he agrees to think about marrying Loren when she feels ready to broach the subject, in *Atlantis Found*.[356] Life makes Pitt a true father at the end of *Valhalla Rising* and he demonstrates maturity by welcoming his son and daughter into his home without hesitation. Finally, after Giordino confesses he is getting too old for adventuring in *Trojan Odyssey*,[357] Pitt can see that he is mature enough, at last, to win his bride.[358]

In hindsight, the 17 Pitt adventures written by Cussler without collaborators can be viewed as one epic hero's quest, starting with Pitt the microcosmic hero and ending with Pitt the macrocosmic hero whose mastery of life is symbolized by a celebration, his and Loren's wedding, the only traditional celebration that concludes a Pitt adventure. There is also one last challenge with a Father figure. By enduring the full possession of his inevitable bride, the hero "knows that he and the father are one: he is in the father's place."[359] In this case, Pitt assumes the position of his second father, Sandecker, as the head of NUMA, although, in typical Sandecker fashion, the admiral gets Loren's approval before offering the job to Pitt. Pitt's atonement with the Father is also symbolized in the final scene in *Trojan Odyssey*, wherein Cussler drops by Pitt's home. Pitt puts an arm around his creator's shoulder and the two step into the hangar as Pitt closes the door.

The son becomes the father and the father becomes the son.

The circle ends and begins again.

8

Cussler's Evolving Structures and Plots

It isn't plotting that carries a book, it's structure.—Clive Cussler[1]

Cussler believes that the most important component of a successful adventure story is a concept that hooks the reader's attention, but he also believes that even the most mind-boggling concept is worthless without structure. "Structure is more than starting off with a narrative hook.... Structure is hitting with an opening bang and then *building-building-building* to the smash-a-rooney climax. Structure is the architecture in suspense adventure."[2]

Formula-A Structure

Cussler refers to the structure in *Pacific Vortex* and *The Mediterranean Caper* as Formula-A Structure. In these stories virtually everything takes place from the perspective of a single viewpoint character (the VP), in this case Pitt. "The purpose of the VP is to locate, focus, limit, and define the story," writes Foster-Harris, who adds, "nothing he cannot see, hear, think, or feel can properly be included in the story." The VP has no inside knowledge about what is happening or will happen because, like the reader, he "lives only in the present, *remembering* back and *hoping* or *fearing* ahead."[3]

In *Pacific Vortex* and *The Mediterranean Caper* the Formula-A Structure follows this basic plot pattern:

1. A prologue introduces a bizarre situation.
2. Pitt is drawn into an adventure through the intentional or unintentional machinations of the Villain responsible for the bizarre situation.
3. Pitt meets the Heroine, a relative of the Villain, on or near a beach.
4. Pitt uncovers the Villain and the Villain's threat against society.
5. Pitt becomes haunted by the image of the Villain.
6. Pitt leads men in a reckless battle against the Villain's forces.
7. Pitt makes a dark descent into the Villain's underwater lair.
8. Pitt confronts the Villain and like Philo Vance in an Act III Drawing Room scene explains the mysteries behind the bizarre situation.
9. Pitt defeats the Villain.
10. An epilogue ties up the loose ends as society returns to its status quo.

Iceberg also uses the Formula-A Structure, but it also represents a transition to more complicated plots like *Raise the Titanic!*

Some of this has been discussed already, but in Pitt's first two adventures he is immediately introduced in Chapter 1, wherein he must escape a perilous situation (the rip current carrying the communications capsule from the *Starbuck* and the Albatross attack on Brady Air Field), whereas in *Iceberg* Cussler delays bringing Pitt onstage, building anticipation by having Koski and Dover watch Pitt nimbly land a Ulysses helicopter on the *Catawaba* during a storm at night (a substitute for the perilous situation) and then having Hunnewell talk about the helicopter's pilot in the galley before Pitt's arrival. *Iceberg* is also the first adventure in which Pitt's initial appearance is described from another character's perspective. As for the Heroine, she is no longer related to the Villain. Instead we get a good woman (Tidi) and a bad woman (Kirsti), a rather specific example of Cussler's thematic preoccupation with opposites that reappears in such adventures as *Vixen 03* (Loren and Collins), *Shock Wave* (Maeve and Deirdre) and *Skeleton Coast* (Sloan Macintyre and Susan Donleavy).[4] Pitt is again haunted by an image, but this time it is of a friend's murder (Hunnewell). He exhibits some maturity by not leading a reckless battle against the Villain's forces, although he suspects he is making a mistake by letting Kirsti lead him and Tidi into Rondheim's study at the poetry reading.[5] There is also no single Drawing Room scene in *Iceberg*. Pitt reveals information, or gets the bad guys to do it for him, in Rondheim's study and in Kirsti's Disneyland Hotel room. *Pacific Vortex*, *The Mediterranean Caper* and *Iceberg* all feature dark descents and rebirths, but, as discussed in Chapter 7, Pitt's rebirth in *Iceberg* is the most significant of his career.[6] Finally *Pacific Vortex*, *The Mediterranean Caper* and *Iceberg* represent an unofficial trilogy of Pitt's microcosmic adventures that introduces many of Cussler's thematic preoccupations and several of the series' most popular elements. These elements include:

- Pitt's brother-in-arms Giordino, second father Sandecker and close friend Rudi Gunn
- Pitt, Giordino, Sandecker and Gunn's military background
- Pitt's "two men" personality and his passion for automobiles and antique vehicles
- Senator George Pitt
- NUMA
- Old-fashioned "bad boys" adventures mixed with Pitt's unconventional approach to heroism
- Sea exploration
- Myths and legends
- Time
- Fate or coincidence (take your pick)

Two of the most significant elements in Cussler's adventures are Time and Fate or coincidence. As an adventure progresses Time becomes a force the Hero and his helpers must overcome, often represented by a countdown to stop the Villain's threat.[7] Time is also important because the action is always moving forward. It does not matter if the setting is the past, present or future, the action is taking place right *now* for the characters, so the decisions a character makes can only affect the present and the future. Characters are unable to change the past, even though the past is constantly reaching forward to affect the present.[8] This effect is often instigated through Fate or coincidence (take your pick) in a series of complex or simple events. For instance, in *Crescent Dawn* the events are complex. Pitt is part of a NUMA crew helping to locate and study the impact of algae blooms along Turkey's coastal waters when he spies a

Greek fisherman cutting his nets free after they snag on something. Pitt knows most inshore shipwrecks are found by fishermen's nets, so he dives to take a look and uncovers an Ottoman shipwreck and treasures from the Age of Suleiman the Magnificent. About the same time, Pitt's son, Dirk Jr. helps uncover a treasure trove of papyrus scrolls from the fourth-century reign of Emperor Marcus Maxentius in the first-century port city of Caesarea. Meanwhile, Pitt's daughter, Summer, is on temporary duty aboard the NUMA research vessel *Odin*, off the Orkney Islands. Cambridge University research historian Julie Goodyear is accompanying Summer in a submersible to view the HMS *Hampshire* as part of Goodyear's research on British field marshal Lord H.H. Kitchener. The field marshall was killed when the *Hampshire* was supposedly sunk by a German mine during World War I, but Summer and Goodyear stumble across evidence of an explosion from inside the shipwreck. These discoveries appear to be unrelated, but gradually they all prove beneficial in preventing the violent rise of a new Ottoman Empire. In contrast, examples of simple events include: the discovery of Graham Farley's coronet that helps lead the way to the sunken *Titanic* (*Raise the Titanic!*); Albert Caulden and his tractor tumbling into an abandoned Nazi air base where a clue to the location of Suma's Dragon Center lies among a cache of stolen war loot (*Dragon*); and Leroy Jenkins pushing the wrong elevator button leads to uncovering information necessary to unravel Razov's plan to cripple and attack the United States (*Fire Ice*).

Formula-B Structure

Not satisfied with the inherent limitations of Formula-A,[9] in *Raise the Titanic!* Cussler switches to what he calls Formula-B Structure. This features different VP characters within a story and sometimes within a single scene,[10] and "a labyrinth of subplots, 'sideplots,' and 'twist-plots.'"[11] Cussler also developed a new plot pattern:

1. A prelude set in the past introduces what Cussler calls a MacGuffin.[12]
2. The main story, set a few years in the future, introduces a mystery or threat involving the MacGuffin.
3. Several characters, including Pitt, the Heroine and the Villain(s) are introduced, and Pitt rescues one or more characters.
4. Many of the characters are drawn together as good guys work at solving the mystery or threat, and the Villain(s) plot to stop them.
5. The MacGuffin's relationship to the mystery or threat is revealed.
6. Pitt is challenged to perform a macrocosmic feat.
7. The Villain(s) attempt to stop Pitt and any good guys helping him.
8. Pitt confronts the Villain(s) and, like Philo Vance in an Act III Drawing Room scene, explains any apparent mysteries still remaining.
9. Pitt defeats the Villain(s) with the help of other good guys.
10. Pitt solves an unexpected mystery so he can complete his macrocosmic feat and stop the threat.
11. An epilogue ties up the loose ends.[13]

In the Formula-A plot pattern eight of ten steps begin with the VP "Pitt," but in the Formula-B plot pattern only four of 11 steps begin with "Pitt," an indication that he is sharing the VP duties and that *Raise the Titanic!* is not a Dirk Pitt adventure like its predecessors but a Clive Cussler adventure featuring Dirk Pitt.[14] The prologue is also now set several years in the past, and the bizarre incident is replaced with a historical incident with no connection to the story's mystery or threat.

Or so it seems.

Cussler hooks the reader by presenting the historical incident as inside information, in this case by never mentioning the *Titanic* by name in the prologue. Cussler never mentions Brewster's name, either, linking the doomed ship and passenger in anonymity while creating a sense of mystery around Brewster. This mystery thickens when Brewster forces Bigalow to guide him to the vault in number-one cargo hold, G Deck, and shuts himself inside the vault.[15]

Raise the Titanic! also introduces five structural changes. First, maps and illustrations are included. Second, the story is divided into sections that focus on key plot points:

Prelude: "April 1912" presents Brewster and the sinking of the *Titanic*.
Part 1: "The Sicilian Project" concentrates on the defense project.
Part 2: "The Coloradans" reveals Brewster's excavation of the byzanium.
Part 3: "The Black Abyss" follows the search for the *Titanic*.
Part 4: "The *Titanic*" covers the salvage operation.
Part 5: "Southby" unravels the secret of what Brewster did with the byzanium.
Epilogue: "Reckoning" presents Bigalow's burial at sea and a successful first test of the Sicilian Project.[16]

Third, the chapters are much shorter, averaging six pages in length, which keeps the pace brisk.[17] Fourth, the main story is set a few years in the future to keep it from getting as dated as quickly as adventures set in the present.[18] Last, specific dates appear at the beginning of each section. These dates act as a timeline that Cussler uses to manipulate Time, generally by quickening the pace to build suspense.[19] Cussler can also slow the pace down, like a professional racer shifting gears. For example, during most of "The *Titanic*" section the pace is *mush-mush-mush* with only the essential moments from the salvage operation presented, but then it slows as preparations to raise the *Titanic* draw to a close. The pace slows even more after *Deep Fathom* gets stranded and a countdown begins before its crew runs out of air. Cussler draws out the suspense by keeping the pace slow throughout the rescue and as the *Titanic* breaches the Atlantic. Only when the threat of Hurricane Amanda is introduced does Cussler pick up the pace again.

There are stylistic changes in *Raise the Titanic!* as well, starting with Pitt's introduction. Pitt makes an early cameo when he rescues Koplin, then does not reappear for his first extended scene for nearly 70 pages. During Pitt's absence, Cussler builds anticipation by having him haunt Seagram,[20] much like Delphi and Von Til haunted Pitt.[21] Cussler also uses mythical phrases to describe Pitt during his first two and final appearances, further adding to the mystery surrounding him.[22] But, even with these descriptions, *Raise the Titanic!* has more of a real-world sensibility about it than Pitt's first three adventures. Fantastic trappings, such as the caverns of Kanoli, the ruins of ancient Greece and the imprisoned *Lax* are gone, while exotic Ireland and Hawaii have been replaced with work a day Washington, DC, and Moscow. By extension Prevlov is no larger-than-life Villain like Delphi, Von Til and Rondheim,[23] and where the soap opera surrounding the Seagrams' marriage would have been awkward or incongruous in Pitt's earlier adventures it fits right in here, injecting human drama into the technical challenges surrounding the raising of the *Titanic*.

These structural and stylistic changes demonstrate a steady improvement in Cussler's writing that continues in his grimmest and most relevant adventure *Vixen 03*, which features a larger cast and more complex plot.[24] Since then, with the exception of the Lacey and Casey Nicefolk adventures,[25] Cussler has stuck with the Formula-B Structure and *Raise the Titanic!* plot pattern in each of his subsequent adventures, although he has modified them over the years. These modifications include:

- Between *Vixen 03* and *Cyclops* Pitt does not rescue anyone early in an adventure, but in *Treasure* an early (and often elaborate) rescue again becomes a plot fixture.
- Starting in *Deep Six*, Pitt (and sometimes Giordino and Gunn) must escape certain death and solve a mystery in Act I that reveals a macrocosmic threat. Then, in Act II, Pitt (with the help of NUMA and supporting cast) must solve a mystery to discover who is causing the threat and the ultimate plan behind it.
- Starting with *Cyclops*, Pitt often becomes a prisoner at least once during an adventure.
- Depending on the novel, Cussler alternates between delaying the Hero's first appearance and introducing the Hero at the beginning.
- In *Atlantis Found*, *Valhalla Rising* and *Trojan Odyssey* the primary Villain does not appear (or seem to appear) until near the end of Act II or near the start of Act III.
- Fantastic elements return starting with *Cyclops*, as lost treasures (e.g., La Dorada, Huayna Capac's gold chain, Kublai Khan's treasure), myths (e.g., Basil the sea serpent, Atlantis, Norsemen in North America) and legends (e.g., the Voyage of Odysseus, the Lincoln assassination conspiracy, the salvage of the Library of Alexandria) become more important to the plot. Pitt also becomes more addicted to the allure of adventure.
- The number of years in the future that a Pitt adventure is set has decreased to the point where *Poseidon's Arrow* was published in November 2012 but begins June 2014.
- Starting with *Dragon*, Cussler makes a cameo in each Pitt adventure. Cussler has also made cameos in some *Fargo* adventures. Cussler will often reveal a vital clue or some useful information to the hero(es). If it is Pitt, then he will ask if he and Cussler have met before. This running joke reaches a sort-of climax in "The Reunion," wherein Pitt asks why he is not supposed to remember who Cussler is.[26]

Other modifications appear depending upon the particular series. The Isaac Bell Detective series and the Casey and Lacey Nicefolk Adventures are set in the past, but, with the exception of *Serpent* and *Blue Gold*, the only Cussler adventures set in the future are from the Pitt series. Most of the *NUMA Files* and the *Oregon Files* and all of the *Fargo Adventures* are set in the present. Pitt and Bell's adventures are the only Cussler stories divided into sections, and epilogues appear infrequently outside of these series. When it comes to prologues some *Oregon Files* adventures have none, some *NUMA Files* adventures have two instead of one, most of Bell's adventures have one, all of the *Fargo Adventures* have one, and there is none in either *Vin Fiz* nor *Hotsy Totsy*. In the *Oregon Files* The Corporation is generally introduced working on a job that may or may not have anything to do with the main adventure, but, if it does, the reader, as well as The Corporation, may not find out about its relation until later in the story. The plots in the *Fargo Adventures*, the Bell Series and the Casey and Lacey Nicefolk Adventures are less complex than Cussler's other series, which may explain why their casts tend to be smaller. Finally, there are stylistic differences between the way Cussler and his collaborators write. Perhaps the most glaring example involves Cussler's fondness for Gothic phrases, which his collaborators tend to avoid. Cussler's collaborators are also less prone to writing charming-but-awkward snippets like these:

- "This man some of you have referred to as filth and a bastard and wish to cast into chains, is indeed Dirk Pitt."[27]
- Shock it was that showed in the guard's eyes.[28]
- "God only knows how many rotting corpses owe their present condition to him."[29]
- ... his voice was unnaturally soft in the unnatural quiet.[30]
- The torpedo was barreling through the depths with murder on its mind.[31]

Plot Tactics

The most significant component of an adventure story may be its structure, but the plot is its "essence" and "digest,"[32] with a separate anatomy from its structure.

For example, Cussler was influenced by pulp adventure stories. As Dent presents in "The Pulp Paper Master Fiction Plot," a typical story is divided into four parts. Part One introduces the Hero and all other characters, either immediately or as soon as possible. There is also no time wasted swatting the Hero "with a fistful of trouble." His attempts to deal with this trouble put him in physical conflict, and Part One ends with a surprise twist. In Part Two the Hero runs into more trouble, but he never stops trying to deal with it, which leads to another physical conflict before Part Two ends, with another surprise twist. In Part Three the Hero runs into even more trouble, but his attempts to deal with it are beginning to pay off. He corners the Villain (or someone associated with the Villain) and this leads to yet another physical conflict before Part Three ends with one more surprise twist, this one dropping the Hero into what appears to be inescapable peril. In Part Four the Hero's troubles are piled so high they look like they will bury him, but he finds a way to turn the tide by using his skills, abilities and ingenuity. Any mysteries introduced during the story are cleared up before there is one final twist, and Part Four ends with a punch line that carries the suspense to the last word.[33]

In comparison, Cussler divides his stories into three acts, not four parts,[34] and in Pitt's earliest adventures the Hero is introduced immediately or he makes at least one cameo in Act One. Most other characters are introduced as quickly as possible, although in Pitt's first three adventures an important supporting character (e.g., Giordino in *Pacific Vortex*, Inspector Zacynthus in *The Mediterranean Caper*, Lillie in *Iceberg*) does not appear until Act Two or Act Three. In later Cussler adventures the Hero's introduction may or may not be delayed and will often coincide with some sort of rescue necessitated (at least in part) by the trouble, while other characters are introduced when the action calls for them to appear,[35] although some of these delayed introductions may be presented in a way that counts as a surprise twist.[36] The trouble and a mystery are also introduced, and Act One often ends with a rescue that is pulled off using the Hero's skills, abilities, ingenuity and possibly (particularly if the *Oregon* is involved) superior firepower. The mystery is solved, but it reveals a macrocosmic threat that often leads to an even larger mystery.

In Act Two the Hero and some other characters set out to solve the second mystery or end the trouble. Some characters act in a coordinated effort, while others act individually. The Hero (and possibly a few other characters) wind up as prisoner(s) of the Villain(s), and a parallel mystery that was introduced during the prologue reappears. This mystery may eventually help eliminate the trouble, and its reappearance happens through the auspices of Fate or coincidence. The Hero escapes and a countdown to prevent the trouble begins.

In Act Three the Hero may become a prisoner again and escape or he may rescue other characters that have been abducted or are in some other form of peril. As the countdown continues, other characters divide into teams to try to end the trouble, which seems increasingly impossible. Because of this, the Hero (and possibly a few other characters) takes the direct approach and goes after the Villain. The Villain is captured or incapacitated after a final physical confrontation and at least the worst of the trouble is prevented through the Hero's skills, abilities, ingenuity and possibly (particularly if the *Oregon* is involved) superior firepower. Any remaining mysteries left unexplained are solved, but instead of ending the story with a punch line Cussler provides an epilogue that ties up all loose ends and shows how the characters are doing as society is restored to its status quo.

Plot tactics are not limited to plot patterns. They also include plot elements, and right from the start Cussler not only leans heavily on MacLean's style[37] but borrows plot elements, like blending the suspense adventure genre with the detective genre[38] and having a traitor working with the Hero,[39] although Cussler gives this a twist in *Iceberg* by making Hunnewell appear to be a turncoat until the end of the story.[40] Another plot tactic that Cussler borrows from not one but two successful authors is having characters haunted by other characters. In Spillane's *I, the Jury* (1947) Mike Hammer seems to be haunted by the image of a small Japanese he killed during World War II, and in Fleming's *Casino Royale* Bond is haunted by the image of a Japanese cryptographer he recently killed.[41] In *Pacific Vortex*, *The Mediterranean Caper*, *Iceberg* and *Deep Six* Delphi Moran, March, Von Til, Hunnewell and Julie Mendoza haunt Pitt,[42] and, as already mentioned, Pitt haunts Seagram in *Raise the Titanic!*, while in *The Chase* the murder of a fellow Van Dorn detective by the Butcher Bandit haunts Bell, who dedicates himself to capturing Cromwell.[43]

This might be a good time to mention that borrowing plot elements from other writers should not be confused with plagiarism. There is no excuse for cribbing, but the truth is, writers have been borrowing plot elements from their peers at least as far back as the Book of Genesis. Shakespeare borrowed for *Hamlet* and *Macbeth*,[44] Alexandre Dumas borrowed from several sources for his adventures[45] and Stephen King borrowed from *Dracula* for *Salem's Lot* (1975).[46] It is what a writer does with what he borrows that matters.[47] Jeff Thompson writes in *The Television Horrors of Dan Curtis* (2009) that one of the unique strengths of Curtis's cult soap opera *Dark Shadows* (1966–1971) is how well it borrows elements from myths and classic Gothic stories. Thompson believes that "excellence in execution can be more important than originality" and *Dark Shadows*' eclecticism "resulted in its originality. Countless myths and stories found their way into the show, but their *recombination and reinterpretation* (my emphasis) made for startling innovations."[48] This eclecticism can be found in other Curtis productions, including *Moon of the Wolf* (1974), which borrows from Richard Connell's short story "The Most Dangerous Game." Connell's literary cornerstone about a big-game hunter preying on human beings has been borrowed many times in motion pictures (e.g., *The Man with the Golden Gun* [1974],[49] *The Running Man* [1987]), television (e.g., *Star Trek*, *Jonny*

Quest), comic books (e.g., *Manhunter* [1973–4], *The Warlord*), and novels such as Richard Matheson's *Hunted Past Reason* (2002) and Cussler's *Dragon*.

Connell's hero Sanger Rainsford is an expert hunter who washes up on Ship Trap Island,[50] home of the Cossack general Zaroff, another expert hunter. Zaroff is bored with hunting wild animals, so any sailor unlucky enough to find his way onto Ship Trap Island is offered his freedom if he can evade Zaroff, the general's servant Ivan, and a pack of hounds for three days in Zaroff's private jungle. After a rocky start, Rainsford kills Ivan and wounds Zaroff, but is forced to leap off a cliff to avoid the general's hounds. Zaroff assumes Rainsford drowns but he actually swims around the island and waits for the general to return home. Technically, Rainsford has lasted the three days, but instead of accepting Zaroff's offer of liberty he challenges the general to a fight to the death and comes out on top.

In *Dragon* Pitt and Giordino are part of MAIT Team Stutz, which fails in its attempt to put the kibosh on the Dragon Center based in Soseki Island, near Japan. Suma, the Villain, offers Team Stutz their freedom if its members can avoid his chief aide, Moro Kamatori, for 24 hours. Kamatori is a master with a samurai sword and an expert manhunter, but, instead of giving Kamatori a pack of hounds, Cussler gives him a pack of robot dogs that never lose their prey's scent. Pitt goes first, but not before swiping a couple of items from a hospital. First, Pitt uses some of his own blood to make Kamatori think the robot dogs tore into him at the edge of a cliff and forced him to into the sea, where he drowned. This trick buys Pitt enough time to use a makeshift magnet to discombobulate the robot dogs, leaving him free to take on Kamatori in a death match between *katana* and saber.[51]

Cussler's reinterpretation of Connell's story shows how eclecticism can be as important as originality, although it is also important to keep in mind that what may appear to be eclecticism just may be originality. Grell's "The Origin" from *Jon Sable, Freelance*,[52] published by First Comics in 1983, appears to recombine and reinterpret elements from *Vixen 03*, published five years earlier. Jon Sable is a Game Control officer living in Kenya with his wife, Elise, and their young son and daughter. While Sable is away on duty, a gang of ivory poachers attack his ranch, slaughtering Elise and the children after a vicious gun battle. Sable forsakes his moral code and butchers the poachers, but years pass before he tracks down the person who ordered the massacre, an anonymous white-haired man Sable kills just after the stranger is appointed the head of national parks in Zimbabwe (formerly Kenya). In *Vixen 03* Fawkes's wife, Myrna, their adult son and daughter and anyone else unfortunate enough to be on or near the Fawkes ranch is massacred in a vicious gun battle against men posing as AAR soldiers. Fawkes, who had been away during the attack, forsakes his moral code and volunteers to lead Operation Wild Rose to avenge his family, but later discovers that De Vaal ordered the massacre as part of an elaborate plan to make himself prime minister, a plan Fawkes helps quash before he dies. "The Origin" and *Vixen 03* also feature flowers as a reoccurring motif, culminating with Sable bringing violets (Elise's favorite flower) to his family's grave on the anniversary of the massacre, and Pitt planting bougainvilleas (which laced the lattice on the Fawkes's veranda) at the corners of the burial plot. All of these similarities are circumstantial evidence that Grell recombined and reinterpreted plot elements from Cussler, but, in this case, appearances are deceiving. Grell knew very little about Cussler's adventures when he created *Jon Sable, Freelance*[53]; instead, he was influenced by pulp heroes and pulp writers like Burroughs as well as Robert Ruark, Peter Capstick, Spillane and "just about every man vs. nature movie I saw as a kid."[54] Not that Cussler would have cared if Grell did borrow from his stories; regarding the practice, he said, "I think it's cool, I don't mind."[55] The similarities in "The Most Dangerous Game" and *Dragon* are so striking, however, that it seems obvious Cussler did borrow plot elements from Connell's story, but things are not so clear-cut when it comes to other possible examples of reinterpreting and recombining.

Pacific Vortex/The Mediterranean Caper, Shock Wave/Flood Tide, and On Her Majesty's Secret Service/You Only Live Twice. As discussed in Chapter 5, *Shock Wave* reworks several plot elements from *Pacific Vortex*, including a rebirth for Pitt that concludes in his next adventure. On both occasions Pitt's exploits in the second novel revitalize him after he loses a woman he loves in the first[56]; the same thing happens to Bond in Fleming's *On Her Majesty's Secret Service* and *You Only Live Twice*.[57]

On Her Majesty's Secret Service ends with Tracy's murder by Blofeld as the Bonds are driving to their honeymoon. A few months later, in *You Only Live Twice*, Bond is drinking too much, losing too much money in casinos and has botched his last two assignments.[58] On the advice of a friend, Nobel-Prize-winning neurologist Sir James Molony, "M" sends Bond on a mission that is "a supreme call on his talents, something that'll really make him sweat so that he's simply forced to forget his personal troubles."[59] The gambit works, but too well. The mission ends with 007 avenging Tracy and Bond suffering amnesia while escaping Blofeld's Asian-Gothic castle.

Did Cussler borrow plot elements from Fleming's Bond novels not once but twice? Once again the evidence is circumstantial, but is it so farfetched that the writer who put Brian Shaw in *Night Probe!* might borrow some of Fleming's plot elements, too? Cussler researched Bond when he created Pitt[60] and *On Her Majesty's Secret Service* and *You Only Live Twice* were published at approximately the same time Cussler was writing *Pacific Vortex*, so these particular plot elements could have been fresh in his mind. There are differences between Cussler and Fleming's novels, to be sure, one of the most notable being that Pitt is unable to seek vengeance in *The Mediterranean Caper* and *Flood Tide*, like Bond does in *You Only Live Twice*, because Moran and the Dorsetts are already dead. Another difference is that Bond literally starts a new life after his rebirth because of his amnesia, but Pitt simply dispatches the next Villain he faces and moves on. That said, *Shock Wave* may contain a clever and touching tribute to *On Her Majesty's Secret Service*. As Maeve is dying, she and Pitt recite Johnny Mercer and Henry Mancini's "Moon River," the love theme from *Breakfast at Tiffany's* (1961).[61] In the book and film *On Her Majesty's Secret Service* a patrolman finds the couple after Blofeld's attack and Bond reassures the officer that Tracy is just having a rest. "We'll be going on soon. There's no hurry. You see—you see, we've got all the time in the world."[62] Hal David and John Barry's love theme for the 1969 film adaptation of *On Her Majesty's Secret Service* is "We Have All the Time in the World," one of the most memorable songs from the Bond franchise and the last song recorded by jazz great Louis Armstrong.[63]

Night Probe! and "The Lost Special." An 1878 Colorado train disaster inspired the hijacking of the *Manhattan Limited*. Cussler admits in *The Sea Hunters* that he was intrigued by the concept of a missing railroad engine after reading a *Denver Post* article about Pacific Railroad *Engine 51*: 18 of the 25 cars it was hauling plunged into Kiowa Creek when a bridge collapsed on a stormy May night. A salvage operation recovered all 18 cars near the bridge, but the only part of *Engine 51* that was recovered was the locomotive's smokestack.[64] The logical explanation at the time was that the rushing river swept the rest of the engine downstream, where it was buried in quicksand, most likely too deep to be recovered even if it was found.

But, over time, a Gothic legend about a phantom train sprung up around the disappearance. Cussler does an excellent job in *Night Probe!* of reinterpreting the Kiowa Creek disaster and its Gothic legend, but is it possible that a story by Conan Doyle provided the inspiration for the details of Massey's scheme to rob the *Manhattan Limited*?

After Pitt solves the mystery behind the phantom *Manhattan Limited* he deduces that the train must have been diverted off the main track and hidden,[65] a hypothesis that not only turns out to be correct but could serve as a synopsis to the solution behind "The Lost Special" (1898). In this Conan Doyle story the man responsible for the disappearance of a train is Herbert de Lernac, an arch-criminal with a personality more in tune with Cromwell than Massey.[66] A syndicate of "some of the greatest men in France"[67] hire Lernac to prevent Monsieur Louis Caratal from delivering papers that will destroy their careers to a celebrated trial under way in Paris. When Caratal arrives in Liverpool from Central America he hires a special to take him on the next leg of his journey, but Lernac's gang uses a temporary sideline to divert the special into the abandoned Heartease mine. The train crashes into a pit, killing everyone onboard. The temporary tracks are removed, the mine boarded up again and all traces of the deed are covered up.[68]

In *Night Probe!* Massey and his gang are after a gold shipment aboard the *Manhattan Limited*. They flag the train down at abandoned Moondragon Hook junction and divert the *Manhattan Limited* onto an old rail spur leading into a deserted underground limestone quarry, but the train and everyone on it are accidentally trapped inside. Almost 80 years later Pitt finds a way into the quarry, and soon after is joined by Shaw, an agent working for some of the most skillful people in England who are as determined to prevent the North American Treaty from reaching Washington, DC, as Lernac is to prevent Caratal's papers from reaching Paris.

In *The Sea Hunters* the only inspiration Cussler lists for *Night Probe!* is the *Denver Post* article about *Engine 51*, but in *Clive Cussler & Dirk Pitt Revealed* he talks about studying Sherlock Holmes,[69] and "The Lost Special" is cited by some Sherlockians as a Holmes story because the Great Detective is referenced although never mentioned by name.[70] It's possible that Cussler read "The Lost Special," or heard the 1949 radio adaptation on *Escape* or saw the Universal western serial *The Lost Special* (1932) loosely based on Conan Doyle's story, but only remembered the story on a subliminal level while writing *Night Probe!* The parallels are very similar, but this is true with "The Origin" and *Vixen 03*. Sometimes great minds think alike and independently come up with similar plots. Even if Cussler's sole inspiration for the *Manhattan Limited* hijacking is the *Denver Post* article, *Night Probe!* remains as excellent an example of Cussler's skill at recombination and reinterpretation as *Dragon*.

Deep Six and Psycho. The death of Arta Casilighio in *Deep Six* features several parallels with the first act of Hitchcock's *Psycho* (1960) even though these are very different types of stories. *Psycho*, a suspense-thriller based on a novel by Robert Bloch, is a modern Gothic story with a beautiful and headstrong young Heroine, a handsome but bland Hero, a dark and stormy night, a haunted Victorian mansion on a high hill and a secluded swamp that keeps awful secrets.[71] *Deep Six*, a suspense-adventure, is a modern fairy tale with a ghost, doppelgangers, a Goddess destroyer lurking at the top of a tall tower and villains controlling other men's minds. There are enough parallels between the stories, however, that, in a list of questions I sent to Cussler in 2009, I asked if the prologue for *Deep Six* was inspired at all by the classic film. Cussler replied, "*Deep Six* came entirely from my own gray matter."[72] Fair enough, but parallels are parallels, whether they are intentional or not. *Psycho* is one of the most famous movies ever produced, so it's quite possible that some of its early scenes managed to get stuck in the filters of Cussler's gray matter, where they got a subliminal recombination and reinterpretation in *Deep Six*. For the sake of pure speculation let us suppose this did happen.

In *Psycho*, Marion Crane (Janet Leigh), an office worker in Phoenix, is in love with Sam Loomis (John Gavin), who owns a hardware store in Fairvale, California. Marion wants to marry Sam, but he is going through tough financial times and does not want to drag Marion into his problems. One day Marion takes a reckless chance at happiness when her employer, George Lowery (Vaughn Taylor), asks her to deposit $40,000 of a client's money on her way home. Instead of driving to the bank Marion starts driving to Fairvale, but a thunderstorm forces her to stop for the night at the isolated Bates Motel. Norman Bates (Anthony Perkins), a shy and lonely young man, owns the hotel with his invalid mother. After Marion shares a sandwich and some conversation with Norman, she realizes she is making a rash error in judgment and decides to drive back to Phoenix in the morning to return the money. Before going to bed, though, she takes a shower.

In *Deep Six*, Arta Casilighio is a timid and mousy teller who, in 1966, has been working at the Federal Reserve Bank in Los Angeles for four years. Arta is frustrated with her life of self-denial, but one evening she discovers a passport wedged under a seat on her bus that belongs to Estelle Wallace, a beautiful stranger who could pass for Arta's more stylish sister. Cussler never explains who Estelle is or how her passport ends up on Arta's bus.[73] Instead, we witness Arta's "metamorphosis" as Estelle Wallace becomes "an alter ego"[74] for her. Arta begins dressing like Estelle to escape her workaday existence, if only in her imagination,[75] and soon after finds herself studying stacks of freshly printed money at the bank. Soon after this, Arta takes a reckless chance to escape her humdrum life by pulling off two audacious robberies, only to vanish with the ill-fated Liberty ship *San Marino*.

Arta's death does not pack the same wallop as Marion's,[76] but it is just as unexpected. There is no foreshadowing, just some diabolical Hitchcockian whimsy as when Norman tells Marion, "Mother, my mother, uh, what is the phrase? She isn't qu-quite herself today." In *Deep Six* Lee Tong, posing as a mess boy, delivers the captain's invitation for Arta to join the ship's officers for dinner and then adds that he will ask the cook to fix something special for her.[77] The something special is a drug Lee Tong's pirates put in Arta and the officers' meals that acts like Fu Manchu's poison of living-death.[78] The Hitchcockian whimsy continues when Arta returns to her cabin after dinner. She checks that the stolen money is safe under a false bottom in her suitcase before she disrobes and lies down on the bed. Then, without warning, the dream of escaping her old life turns into a nightmare. Her body goes numb, her vision blurs and she cannot move. Soon after, Lee and another pirate carry the paralyzed Arta outside her cabin where she can see the helpless officers being tossed overboard. Perhaps the drug also addles Arta's mind because she vaguely wonders why Lee would attach a length of rusty chain to her ankles and then watches indifferently as she is lifted into the air. Arta finally figures out what is happening after she hits the water.

If nothing else, these parallels demonstrate that Cussler and Hitchcock share some stylistic similarities. If Cussler borrowed the idea for his plot tactic of a MacGuffin from Hitchcock, then the notion that he borrowed other tactics from the man who promoted himself as the Master of Suspense[79] is not preposterous, but this does not necessarily mean Cussler was consciously or even subconsciously influenced by *Psycho* when writing *Deep Six*.

For instance, Arta's death is a stellar example of the Hitchcockian brand of irony that appears in *Deep Six* and other Cussler adventures. Gianetti writes that in Hitchcock's movies "characters are victimized by their own dimly perceived desires," an apt description for what happens to Arta.[80] Gianetti adds, "When these buried impulses are dredged to the surface, the results can be shocking, macabre, even funny. Often they are all three. Many critics regard this vision as pessimistic. Hitchcock preferred to call it absurd."[81] Some prominent victims of this type of absurdity in Cussler's other adventures includes the Seagrams, Daggat, Massey, Villon, Arthur Dorsett, Qin Shang and Jacob Cromwell.

The character of Arta/Estelle is evocative of Hitchcock's fascination with the concept of doubles.[82] In addition to the aforementioned Charlotte "Charlie" Newton (Teresa Wright) and her worldly serial killer uncle Charlie Oakley (Joseph Cotton) from *Shadow of a Doubt*, there is the athletic passive-aggressive social climber Guy Haines (Farley Granger) and the effete sociopath heir Bruno Anthony (Robert Walker) from *Strangers On a Train* (1951), and the brawny down-on-his luck hardware store owner Sam Loomis and the frail down-on-his luck hotel owner Norman Bates. On occasion Hitchcock creates doubles out of a single character (like Cussler does with Arta and Estelle), such as Marnie Edgar (Tippi Hedren) with her various aliases in *Marnie* (1964), and Kim Novak as the working-class brunette Judy Barton and the blonde socialite Madeleine Elster in *Vertigo* (1958).

Cussler and Hitchcock also never seem to tire of the concept of chaos and order. Hitchcock believes that "evil is complete disorder,"[83] and his films, like Cussler's adventures, are all about chaos disrupting the order of society. While the chaos in films like *Psycho*, *Vertigo* and *Rear Window* (1954) is even more microcosmic than it is in *Pacific Vortex*, *The Mediterranean Caper* and *Iceberg*, there is macrocosmic chaos in Hitchcock's *Foreign Correspondent* (1940), *Torn Curtain* (1966) and *Topaz* (1969). The crucial difference between Hitchcock's brand of chaos and order and Cussler's is their notion of morality. Cussler's heroes have been known to bend or even break a law to return their society to its status quo if—and only if—a hero's moral principals dictate that a crime is the only way to do what is right; Hitchcock's films blur the moral distinctions between villains and heroes because Hitchcock believed there "are grays everywhere."[84]

Another Hitchcockian plot tactic is giving a sinister character a distinctive trait, such as the whistling cutthroat Harry the peddler (Emlyn Williams) from *Jamaica Inn* (1939) and the stark white hair of wife-killer Lars Thorwald (Raymond Burr) in *Rear Window*. When Lee Tong is introduced in *Deep Six* Cussler gives this apparently inconsequential mess boy a tag, a large gap in the middle of his upper teeth, and, whenever Lee makes an unexpected appearance, Cussler injects suspense by identifying Lee with this tag rather than by name.

One of the most daunting plot tactics Cussler borrows form Hitchcock is getting readers to identify with Arta even though she is a thief. "Hitchcock rarely presents the plight of his characters objectively," writes Gianetti. "Rather, we are encouraged to identify strongly with their feelings."[85] In *Psycho* the viewer identifies with Marion Crane, at least until she is murdered,[86] because we can sympathize with her motive for stealing the money. Marion loves Sam, so we hope—against all common sense—that she gets away with her crime. In contrast, Arta's motives are more in line with the kleptomaniac Marnie Edgar, a woman who (in part) changes her name and alters her appearance to get away with stealing from her employers and living a life she could not otherwise afford. Cussler gets the reader to identify with Arta the same way Hitchcock gets the viewer to identify with Marion and Marnie, by piling up details about their crime until we cannot help but hope they get away with it.[87] In *Deep Six* we watch as Arta not only figures out a way to steal money from the bank but has the *chutzpah* to commit the same crime twice to assure she has enough capital to live comfortably in another country while investing most of it for the future.[88] The unconventional subtlety of this last touch, Arta's practicality, is pure Cussler. There is no indication in Hitchcock's films that Marion or Marnie ever bothered to consider the advantages of living on a budget while investing their ill-gotten gains.

All speculation about *Psycho* and Hitchcock aside, *Deep Six* features one of Cussler's best and most unique prologues. Cussler's other prologues are adventures about a shipwreck, a plane crash, a battle or maybe even a meteor striking Earth, but *Deep Six* is a slice-of-life story spotlighting a single character.[89] Unlike most of Cussler's other post-*Iceberg* adventures this prologue takes place in the recent past, only 23 years prior to the beginning of the main adventure. It is also different from most of Cussler's other prologues because it does not proceed in a linear manner. The *Deep Six* prologue begins with Act II, wherein Estelle (Arta) is sunbathing on the *San Marino*. Cussler drops hints that Estelle is not what she seems to be and then cuts to Act I, with Arta finding the passport, changing into Estelle and stealing the money. The prologue concludes with Act III and the deaths of Arta and the officers. The *Deep Six* prologue still introduces a mystery or problem and Cussler's MacGuffin, but unlike most of Cussler's other prologues this is a terse three-act short story that reads like a contemporary fairy tale written by O. Henry or Ambrose Bierce. Like Walt Disney's *Snow White and the Seven Dwarfs* (1937), the story of Arta's death "features many nightmarish scenes derived from the Sleeping Beauty myth," including "magical transformations, a poisoned apple, forbidden gardens, enchanted palaces, and a wicked stepmother."[90] Arta magically transforms after discovering Estelle's passport, going from wallflower to prom queen. Arta invades the forbidden garden of the Federal Reserve Bank's vault and makes her escape with its treasures on a floating enchanted palace, the *San Marino*, which looks shabby and tired with its rusty steel skin but to Arta "she was virgin and beautiful."[91] In the end, Arta and the ship's crew succumb to the poison apple (the drug put in their meals) which is administered by the orders of Min Koryo, the wicked stepmother of this brief, fascinating but terrible tale.

Repeating Plot Elements

While the prologue for *Deep Six* is unique in many ways, Cussler is as prone to repeating plot elements in his stories as any writer. *Deep Six* provides quite a few examples.

The main adventure begins when a deadly biological weapon called Nerve Agent S kills the crew of a crab ship, the *Amie Marie*, and then anyone from the Coast Guard cutter *Catawaba* that boards the *Amie Marie* to investigate the derelict. All traces of Nerve Agent S, which was developed by the U.S. Army in Colorado during the sixties, were ordered destroyed when it became clear that the weapon is as much of a threat to anyone using it as the intended target. A boxcar carrying one thousand gallons of Nerve Agent S never reached the incineration depot in Nevada, however, and now those missing gallons are leaking from inside a Liberty ship called the *Pilottown* that vanished in the seventies. The *Pilottown* is also known as the Magic Ship because it has been reported floating around the Cook Inlet region off Alaska for ten years, but Pitt locates the elusive ship on volcanic Augustine Island, where everything except her stern has been covered by mudflows and volcanic ash. The volcano is poised to erupt again, but Pitt manages to stop the remaining Nerve Agent S from leaking into the ocean in time to prevent it from wiping out all marine life on the planet. Pitt's victory comes at a terrible cost, though, when the protective suit worn by his potential new romantic interest, Mendoza, tears in an accident, leading to her demise.

Cussler hangs a lantern on the fact that *Deep Six* repeats some plot elements from *Iceberg* by bringing back the *Catawaba* (with Dover now in command) and having Pitt talk about his Iceland adventures with Mendoza. The missing Nerve Agent S is reminiscent of the missing QD organism in *Vixen 03*, while its potential effects on marine life presages the effects of the red tide in *Sahara*.[92] The *Amie Marie* likewise presages derelicts like the *Polar Queen* (*Shock Wave*) and abandoned death ships like *Divine Star* (*Dragon*) and *Golden Dawn* (*Plague Ship*). As for the *Pilottown* on desolate Augustine Island, in a series that includes the *Nuestra Senora de la Concepcion* in the jungles near Panama and the *Odysseus* as well as the *Nautilus* in caves along the Hudson River, the Liberty ship, formerly known as the *San Marino*, remains one of Cussler's most memorable and imposing *Flying Dutchmen* or lost ships to be found in an incongruous location.[93] Cussler also repeats one of his most famous conceits by naming the manufacturer of the *Pilottown*'s boilers the Alhambra Iron and Boiler Company after his California boyhood home.[94]

As discussed in Chapter 5, rebirths are one of Cussler's thematic preoccupations, but Maeve is one of the few non-cast members in a Cussler adventure to experience one. During Act One of *Shock Wave* we discover that Maeve ran away from the dysfunctional Dorsetts to start a new life in Australia under the name Fletcher, which she took from her great-great-great-grandmother Betsy. In 1856, Betsy is sentenced to the British penal colony in Australia after stealing a blanket for her sick father, but Betsy wins back her independence after the prison ship *Gladiator* is all but scuttled during a typhoon. Maeve eventually discovers that she cannot win her and her twins' independence from the Dorsetts by running away, but will have to make a stand and fight. Before then, however, Maeve must be reborn, following the same pattern as other rebirths in other Cussler adventures.

Meave's rebirth begins when a tour group she is leading on Seymour Island, along the Antarctic Peninsula (perhaps the ultimate zone unknown on Earth), is assaulted by an inexplicable phenomenon. The air becomes hard to breathe while flashlight beams take on an unearthly glow and dust swirls inside a cavern the tour group has just entered. Maeve becomes disoriented, but then the phenomenon stops, leaving her exhausted. She tries to contact their tour ship, but the *Polar Explorer* does not answer and Maeve finds herself in the same position as Pitt in *Iceberg*, *Cyclops* and *Sahara*, wherein the fate of people in a dire situation depend upon her. Unlike Pitt, though, Maeve's rebirth does not involve a lengthy physical journey. All she can do is keep the tour group inside the cavern and wait until a snowstorm passes, but, after three days of cold and hunger, Maeve is physically and mentally spent and she succumbs to her ecstasy as Fate steps in with a Rescue from Without. While still in her ecstasy she hears a noise that goes unnoticed by everyone else in the cavern; she struggles outside the cavern into the storm, sees a hazy shape (Pitt) and collapses in the snow. She is tempted to lie there, but finds the strength to get up, scream and run until she attracts Pitt's attention.

Not all repetitions in Cussler's adventures are this subjective, and even Maeve's rebirth incorporates some objective repetitions. Seymour Island is reminiscent of Novaya Zemlya from *Raise the Titanic!*, giving its northern counterpart a run for its money when it comes to isolation and desolation. Both stories also feature a character (Koplin and Maeve) that is near death but rescued by Pitt, the Hero appearing as an indistinct figure out of a snowstorm who carries the character to safety. Other objective examples of repeating plot elements in other Cussler's adventures include:

Abductions. A staple of adventure literature and a favorite plot tactic of Burroughs, one of the grandmasters of the pulp magazines whose classic adventures include *A Princess of Mars* (1911) and *Tarzan of the Apes* (1912).[95] Abductees in the Pitt series include Adrian Hunter, Teri Von Til, Hiram Lusana, Raymond LeBaron, Senator George Pitt and Hala Kamil (*Treasure*), Sean and Michael Fletcher (*Shock Wave*), a host of illegal Chinese aliens (*Flood Tide*), Henry and Micki Moore (*Inca Gold*), the crew of NUMA's *Deep Encounter* (*Valhalla Rising*), Dr. Patricia O'Connell and daughter Megan (*Atlantis Found*) and Flidais (by a vengeful Pitt in *Trojan Odyssey*). Presidents have been abducted (*Deep Six* and *Sahara*) as have Pitt's children (*Trojan Odyssey* and *Black Wind*) and lovers.[96] Abductions in other Cussler series include Gamay Morgan-Trout, Dr. Chi (no first name given) and George Wingate and his wife (*Serpent*), Francesca Cabral (*Blue Gold*), Skye Labelle and Paul Trout (*Lost City*), Therri Weld, Marcus Ryan, Chuck Mercer and an entire Eskimo village (*White Death*), the unscrupulous art dealer Winston Spenser and insurance appraiser Paul Samuelson and his wife (*Golden Buddha*)[97] and Geoffrey Merrick (*Skeleton Coast*). Not even inanimate objects are safe. A partial list includes the *Deep Encounter*, the *Titanic*, the *Manhattan Limited*, the RSV *Baby* (*Night Probe!*) and the U.S. Naval submarines *Starbuck* and *NR-1* (*Fire Ice*).

The Rime of the Ancient Mariner. Albatrosses and other references to Samuel Taylor Coleridge's 1789 poem appear so often in Cussler's adventures that they border on a thematic preoccupation. When Cussler was asked about this his answer was, "I always liked the 'Rime of the Ancient Mariner.'"[98]

Pacific Vortex ends with Pitt watching an albatross, and *The Mediterranean Caper* begins with Von Til's Albatross strafing Brady Air Field, while in *Raise the Titanic!* Dana Seagram refers to her selfish nature as an albatross around her neck.[99] Pitt paraphrases a verse from Coleridge's poem in *Trojan Odyssey*,[100] Sandecker quotes a verse in *Dragon*[101] and Pitt and Sandecker recite the same verse at different times in *Sahara*.[102] In *Valhalla Rising* an outdated NUMA submersible is named the *Ancient Mariner*, and while there is no mention of Coleridge's poem or albatrosses in *Shock Wave* a providential kea (a New Zealand parrot) appears on two occasions to lead a castaway Fletcher to safety, first Betsy and then Maeve.[103] Cussler's other heroes also get into the act. Austin flies an ultralight seaplane in *Fire Ice*, which its designer, Zavala, calls the Gooney (a nickname for the albatross)[104]; he also quotes the "Rime" in *Blue Gold*[105] and recollects Coleridge's description of a painted ship upon a painted sea in *Lost City*,[106] while, in *Flood Tide*, Cabrillo ponders why Qin Shang's ship the *United States* is sailing minus a crew to the United States and muses how the "Ancient Mariner and the Flying Dutchman had ghostly crews."[107]

The poem is most prominently featured in *Iceberg*, wherein Cussler kicks things off by recalling some of the rhythm and imagery of Coleridge's poem as he describes Pitt's impressions upon entering the dead ship *Lax* inside the iceberg.[108] Still early in the adventure, Hunnewell quotes the poem for his dying clue to Pitt, who later damns Kristi with these same words in her Disneyland hotel room. "The Rime of the Ancient Mariner" is Rondheim's favorite poem and the albatross is his good luck symbol and corporate emblem, but just like Coleridge's Mariner, Cussler's Villain transforms the positive symbolism of the albatross. In the poem an albatross is believed to be a Christian soul when the bird suddenly appears to lead the Mariner's crew to safety after a storm carries their ship to the South Pole, where it becomes lost in snow and mist. After the Mariner shoots the albatross with his crossbow, the bird's symbolism transforms from a good omen to a portent as the crew forces the Mariner to wear the albatross around his neck like a cross as a sign of his guilt and sin. In *Iceberg* the sins committed by Rondheim's fleets (e.g., wiping out fishing grounds, robbing other fishermen's nets and dropping nets inside the territorial boundaries of other countries) has made the Rondheim albatross as feared as the Nazi swastika.[109] Later in the story, Pitt, Sandecker and Tidi are aboard the *Grimsi* when they find themselves caught in a mist like the one that surrounds the Mariner's ship, but, instead of being assaulted by a tutelary spirit, the *Grimsi* is attacked by Rondheim's monstrous hydrofoil.[110] Finally, during Pitt's magic flight across the seemingly endless green tundra, he finds himself "adrift"[111] like the crew of the Mariner's ship when all they could see is "water, water everywhere, Nor any drop to drink."[112] Pitt is at risk of getting caught in another mist,[113] and although no albatrosses appear to lead him to safety, another bird, a snipe, flies overhead and watches him. From the snipe's perspective, Pitt is a solitary "strange animal" with "red and yellow plumage"[114] (a reference to Pitt's outlandish "gay" outfit from Rondheim's party).

Miscellany. Speaking of *Iceberg*, the Fyrie probe requires a fictional man-made element, celtinium−279, to operate, and in *Raise the Titanic!* Project Sicilian requires a fictional mineral, byzanium, as a power source. Man-made chemicals are a major threat in *Vixen 03* (QD organism) and *Deep Six* (Nerve Agent S), and in *Valhalla Rising* the formula for a new super oil (Slick Sixty-six) is an important MacGuffin. *Valhalla Rising* also features Pyrotech 610, a sort of combination celtinium−279 and Nerve Agent S that is so flammable it is too unstable even for military application.[115]

Song lyrics and musical references appear in all of Cussler's adventures. Sometimes they simply add verisimilitude, like when Cromwell passes time listening to Johann Strauss's "Voices of Spring" and *Tales of the Vienna Woods*[116] on an Edison cylinder phonograph or when an orchestra plays themes from John Barry scores as Pitt arrives at Jessie LeBaron's party.[117] At other times they underscore a character's personality, like Cromwell whistling "Garry Owen,"[118] or add irony to a scene, as when the counterfeit rock band The Minutemen play The Eagles' "Already Gone" at Stanley Ho's party[119] or when Stacy Fox hums Seals & Crofts's "We May Never Pass This Way Again" as she and the crew of the stranded submersible *Old Gert* run out of air and begin succumbing to carbon-dioxide poisoning.[120]

When it comes to escaping no-win scenarios Pitt can manipulate technology with the best of them, but he repeats one of his MacGyver tricks in *Sahara* when he creates a makeshift compass similar to the one in *Iceberg*.

Disguising high-tech structures or vessels to look decrepit is another familiar plot tactic. Examples include Pitt's hangar home, the *Oregon*, the Quonset hut headquarters for the 101st Salvage Fleet, the *Martha Ann* in *Pacific Vortex*, and NUMA's salvage ship, *Poco Bonito*, in *Trojan Odyssey*. Meanwhile, some villains from Pitt's earliest adventures borrow a page from the playbook of many of their pulp and movie serial predecessors and hide their headquarters inside caves (e.g., the underwater caverns used by Delphi Moran and Bruno Von Til).

Giordino has bad luck when it comes to muscular women, or muscular men pretending to be muscular women. In *Sahara* he is in no position to retaliate against a beating he gets from the overseer Melika at the Tebezza mines, but when the time is right he hunts Melika down and goes one-on-one in a battle to the death. Much the same thing happens in *Shock Wave* between Giordino and Boudicca Dorsett. Giordino's counterpart, Joe Zavala, a former middleweight boxer, also has a fight to the death with a muscular woman when he nearly loses to Brynhild Sigurd in *Blue Gold*.

Speaking of Boudicca, she is one of three villainous transsexuals (for lack of a better term) to be defeated and then have the truth about them exposed. Boudicca is a brutal transvestite, the former Kristjan Fyrie went through a sex change to become the stunning but manipulative Kirsti Fyrie and Epona Eliade pretends to be the eccentric, publicity-shy Spectre to keep her true position of power within the Odyssey syndicate a secret.

Pitt has never been one to seek personal glory, but after the *Titanic* arrives in New York in *Raise the Titanic!* he avoids the fanfare by pushing his way to the dock through the media and melting into the crowd; and after leading the rescue of the *Golden Marlin* cruise ship, Pitt avoids the media by remaining on the *Deep Encounter*.

In *Iceberg* Pitt is forced to abandon people in a dire situation so he can try to bring back help in time to rescue them. Pitt finds himself in similar situations in *Cyclops*, *Sahara* and *Treasure of Khan*, except in the latter two adventures Girodino is with him during his rescue trek. Rudi Gunn and Giordino also find themselves in this situation at different times in *Sahara*; Gunn must abandon Pitt and Giordino again in *Treasure*, and Girodino is forced to abandon Pitt in *Shock Wave* and *Valhalla Rising*.

One of the most popular scenes in the Pitt series takes place in *Deep Six*, wherein Pitt, Giordino and a group of Civil War reenactors battle Lee Tong and his men aboard the 1915 steamship *Stonewall Jackson*; in *Fire Ice* Austin and the crew of the three-masted frigate USS *Constitution* engage in a battle with killers working for Razov.[121] In *Night Probe!* Pitt and Shaw find the corpses of two apparent adversaries, Massey and Essex, sitting together at a table, and in *Skeleton Coast* the mummified remains of apparent adversaries H.A. Ryder and the Herero chief are found sitting at a table together in the wardroom of the *Rove*. Also in *Night Probe!* Heidi gives Pitt her North American Treaty research material when she must return to San Diego, which helps Pitt locate the history-changing treaty; in *Valhalla Rising* Kelly gives Pitt her late father's leather bag, which helps him locate Dr. Egan's history-changing super oil and teleportation device along with a Viking settlement and the actual *Nautilus* that inspired Jules Verne's *Twenty Thousand Leagues Under the Sea* (1870). In *Treasure*, Pitt's final showdown with would-be Mexican dictator Topiltzin (Robert Capesterre) plays out in the excavated hiding place of the Library of Alexandria; in *Treasure of Khan* Pitt's final showdown with would-be Mongolian dictator Tolgoi Borjin takes place in an excavated sanctuary containing Genghis Khan's tomb. A climax set in a tomb is also featured in *Serpent* and *Blue Gold*. In *Dragon*, Pitt, Giordino, Loren and other good guys meet Suma over dinner shortly before the Villain plans to have most of them killed; in *Valhalla Rising* Pitt, Giordino, Loren and Kelly are eating dinner at the Knox Inn when they meet Zale shortly before the Villain plans to have them killed. Tsunamis generated by underwater landslides are part of a Villain's plot against America and other nations in *Treasure of Khan* and *Fire Ice*. In *Skeleton Coast* Sloan sneaks into Cabrillo's cabin on the *Oregon* and cannot help ogling him while an exhausted Cabrillo is sleeping; in *Shock Wave* Maeve sneaks into Pitt's cabin on the *Ice Hunter* and cannot help ogling him while the nude Pitt is sleeping. A third version of this scene takes place in *Trojan Odyssey* with Loren, who lets herself into Pitt's hangar and finds him sleeping, naked, on his bed. Loren likes the view as much as Maeve, but covers the exhausted Pitt with a bedspread and wakes him six hours later by cooking him a steak dinner.[122] And in Pitt's first three adventures, as well as *Sahara*, he either meets a woman on a beach (Teri Von Til, the anonymous gorgeous redhead, Eva Rojas) or goes to the beach with a woman soon after meeting her (Summer).

Emotional arousal, in particular sexual arousal, often makes a character's voice husky,[123] while a naturally husky voice is considered sexy in women.[124] Using this adjective in this way is an idea Cussler might have borrowed from Harold Robbins. In an unpublished 1985 interview Cussler makes reference to *The Carpetbaggers*,[125] and in that novel Robbins twice describes an attractive woman's voice as husky.[126]

Finally, Cussler frequently mentions eyes and seems to have a passion for the unusual variety. In *Iceberg* Pitt and Kirsti both have flashes, while in *Night Probe!* a tiny wedge-shaped patch of gray at the bottom of Heidi's right iris (heterochromia iridis) made elementary schoolmates taunt her about having an evil eye. Even when there is nothing unusual about a character's eyes, the color can say much about that individual's personality. When Gly makes himself up to look like Villon, he detests using contacts because changing his eye color from brown to gray makes him feel like he is changing his soul.[127] Gray eyes in men often denotes a villain, as in the case with Villon and Rondheim, but just like in the pulp stories of Edgar Wallace, gray-eyed women like Summer Moran, Summer Pitt and Julia Lee are usually good.[128] Sometimes eye color can even seem like a tangible force, like when Kirsti and Pitt are introduced,[129] and when Bell meets Margaret Cromwell.[130] Ironically, Cussler never seems comfortable describing people's eyes in action, often giving them a life of their own, independent from their owner. Adrian does not look at Pitt, "Her chestnut eyes gazed up at him, wide, dark, and afraid."[131] When Pitt sees Kirsti for the monster she really is, "His eyes no longer saw her loveliness."[132] After Prevlov's forces take control of the *Titanic*, the captain strides into the gymnasium, his "intense gray eyes taking in every detail of the scene."[133] Pitt does not have a distant expression, but, rather, his "deep green eyes took on a faraway look."[134] And instead of staring at nothing as he gathers his thoughts, Villon "let his eyes drift across the room to a painting."[135]

9

Adaptations and Cussleresque Adventures

It is truly written: one cannot lose 'em all.—Mr. Wu, *The Love Bug*

The first adaptation of any Cussler novel, a newspaper comic strip of *Raise the Titanic!*, was good considering the medium's limitations, but an expensive film adaptation of Cussler's breakout novel has been almost universally panned since its release in August 1980, and, as of this writing, Cussler and the producers of the 2005 film *Sahara* are engaged in a lawsuit that began two months before the movie's release. Neither film earned a profit but *Sahara* performed well at the box office, demonstrating that there is an audience for Dirk Pitt movies. There have been no adaptations featuring any of Cussler's other heroes, although in 2010 two promotional trailers for a proposed *Oregon Files* television series were produced. Many of the elements from Cussler's adventures can be seen in other films, most notably two from Disney, the animated *Atlantis: The Lost Empire* (2001) and the live-action *National Treasure* (2004).

Best Seller Show Case: *Raise the Titanic!* (1977)

The Star *today launches* Best Seller Showcase, *an innovative approach to best-selling novels.... The first serialization is of Clive Cussler's* Raise the Titanic!, *which is set in 1987.*—Quoted from the *Toronto Star*[1]

The first adaptation of *Raise the Titanic!* appeared in the premiere of United Press Syndicate's newspaper strip *Best Seller Show Case*, running from August 15 to October 9, 1977. The author is believed to be the noted newspaper strip writer and editor Elliot Caplin (*Little Orphan Annie, The Heart of Juliet Jones*) and the artist is book illustrator and comics veteran Frank Bolle (*Doctor Solar, Apartment 3-G*),[2] and, with the possible exception of Jim Sharpe's cover for Pyramid's *The Mediterranean Caper*, this adaptation features the first print illustration of Dirk Pitt. Bolle's Pitt does come closer to Cussler's description of the character than the brawny, bearded Pitt that appears in the film adaptation, but it is missing Pitt's trademark cruel-yet-friendly features and penetrating green eyes. Bolle's Pitt could just as well be James Bond, Secret Agent Corrigan or any other contemporary dark-haired hero from a sixties or seventies newspaper adventure strip. Al Giordino, Admiral Sandecker and Rudi Gunn are also missing, along with NUMA, Meta Section and most of the novel's supporting cast, including Gene and Dana Seagram, all victims of space limitations. Like most of the adaptations in *Best Seller Show Case, Raise the Titanic!* ran for eight weeks,[3] which is not a long time to adapt a novel given an adventure strip's three-panel-a-day format wherein Panel One recaps the previous installment, Panel Two pushes the story along a little further, and Panel Three presents a tease or a cliffhanger to entice the reader to return for the next installment.[4] On the other hand, a press release for the new series, by United Press Syndicate managing editor Lee Salem, explains that the purpose of *Best Seller Show Case* is to give readers "enough of a taste to go out and buy the book."[5] This adaptation of *Raise the Titanic!* does just that.

It begins with Joshua Brewster forcing a young officer (never referred to as Bigalow) into the hold of the sinking *Titanic* at gunpoint, where Brewster locks himself inside the ship's vault as he confesses to killing eight men to get whatever is inside the vault. Seventy-five years later, America needs byzanium to power an impenetrable missile-defense system (never referred to as the Sicilian Project), and Brewster's diary, found with a dead American miner named James Thornton in Novaya Zemlya, indicates that the only known supply of byzanium lies in the *Titanic*'s vault. The president orders Pitt (who is identified as a secret agent,[6] government agent[7] and salvage chief,[8] but never a special projects director) to raise the *Titanic*, and the crew of the U.S. research submersible *Sappho I* is dispatched to the North Atlantic to find the sunken liner. Soon after this, CIA chief, Warren Nicholson, informs the president that the Russian government has found out about the salvage operation, so the president and Nicholson decide to leak small doses of information about the operation to the American press in hopes of distracting Soviet intelligence long enough for Pitt to complete his mission.

When Pitt arrives in the North Atlantic on the salvage ship *Capricorn* he is told that *Sappho I*'s navigator is dead, and that foul play is suspected. Worse, without its navigator, the crew of the *Sappho I* managed to get the submersible tangled in cables on a deck of the *Titanic* and has less than two hours of air remaining. Pitt instructs divers from the *Sappho I* to plant over 80 50-pound charges of dynamite beneath the *Titanic*'s superstructure to blast the ship free of the ocean floor so it will drift to the surface. The plan works, but the ship's flooded boiler rooms are causing the *Titanic* to list, so pumps are installed to keep the White Star liner afloat. Then news arrives that a hurricane is headed towards the *Titanic*.

Captain Andre Prevlov of Soviet intelligence takes advantage of the storm to lead a team of soldiers onto the *Titanic*. Pitt eludes Prevlov's men and tries to escape in a helicopter, but it is swept overboard. He exits the helicopter before it tumbles into the ocean and climbs back aboard the *Titanic*, where he reveals that two members of the salvage crew are Russian infiltrators. Prevlov orders his men to kill Pitt, but an American rescue squad that is hiding in wait cuts down the Soviet soldiers and captures Prevlov. It turns out that a lieutenant aboard the *Mikhail Kurkov*—the ship that brought Prevlov and his soldiers to the *Titanic*—is a U.S. agent. All is not well, however, because the captain of the *Mikhail Kurkov* has orders to sink the White Star liner if Prevlov does not signal him by midnight. Fortunately, the captain is spared the distasteful task of sinking the *Titanic* again when a communication arrives from the U.S. submarine *Dragonfish*, stating it will retaliate if any action is taken against the White Star liner.

After the *Titanic* arrives in New York its vault is opened and it is soon apparent that there is no byzanium. Playing a hunch, Pitt takes a team of men to a cemetery in Southby, England, where they find Thornton's grave. The grave is opened, revealing a case filled with byzanium. Pitt remembered an entry dated March 12, 1912 in Brewster's diary explaining that Brewster was returning home on the *Titanic*, and that the byzanium "will lie safely in T's vault in Southby."[9] Like everyone else, Pitt had assumed the "T" stood for *Titanic* and ignored the reference to Southby. The byzanium is taken to the United States, where tests of the missile-defense system are a success.

While Caplin's script succeeds in giving a taste of Cussler's novel, it suffers from lapses in logic. No reason is given as to why the *Sappho I's* navigator is murdered, or how Pitt deduces who the infiltrators in his crew are, or why Pitt tries to get away in the helicopter when a rescue squad is waiting to repel Prevlov's invasion. One can only marvel how the *Sappho I's* divers survive swimming two and a half miles beneath the ocean, or wonder how (much less why) any submersible would be carrying 80 50-pound charges of dynamite. It is also a letdown that Pitt is not aboard the *Sappho I* when the *Titanic* is found but instead reads a newspaper article about the discovery to the president, or that Pitt exhibits hardly any of the wit or audacity he does in the novel. Despite these shortcomings, Caplin's script strives to be faithful to its source material, incorporating as many of Cussler's plot twists as it can without forsaking understandability,[10] and, unlike the film adaptation, it does not downplay the Cold War tensions between America and the Soviet Union.

On the artistic side, Bolle draws a wonderful *Titanic*, creating many memorable images of the liner as it sinks, lies on the ocean floor, breaches, during the hurricane, and enters New York. Bolle also draws great action scenes, including the opening with Brewster[11] and Pitt climbing back aboard the *Titanic* during the hurricane.[12] The pace rarely lets up until the last panel, when a military officer telephones to inform Pitt that the tests on the defense system are a success, and that it is "too bad you had to raise the *Titanic* for nothing." Pitt could be speaking for many of his fans as he looks out a window at the White Star liner in New York Harbor and tells the officer, "I wouldn't say it was for nothing. I wouldn't say that at all."[13] Impenetrable defense systems can come in pretty handy, but recovering a legendary and elusive treasure like the *Titanic*[14] is priceless.

Raise the Titanic (1980)

> I recall seeing *Raiders of the Lost Ark* a year after *Raise the Titanic* came out in theaters. I almost cried. The manner in which [Steven] Spielberg produced a fast-paced, nail-biting adventure was how I had envisioned the Pitt movie I never got.—Clive Cussler[15]

Approximately three years after *Best Seller Show Case*, Marble Arch Production released its film *Raise the Titanic*, which cost anywhere between $35 million[16] and $40 million,[17] and grossed only $6.8 million.[18] In comparison, box-office champions such as *Star Wars* cost $11 million in 1977[19] and *Raiders of the Lost Ark* $20 million in 1981.[20] The filming of the ship being raised cost more than it did to build the White Star liner, which led Marble Arch's Lord Lew Grade to grouse, "Raise the *Titanic*? It would have cost less to lower the Atlantic."[21]

Bad movies usually have some good things to recommend them, and *Raise the Titanic* does feature a lush atmospheric score by John Barry (*Goldfinger, Somewhere in Time*),[22] a bittersweet cameo by Sir Alec Guinness as Bigalow, and impressive scenes of the discovery and resurrection of the *Titanic*,[23] but these are not enough to rescue a movie that made *New York Times* film critic Janet Maslin ask, "Take the adventure out of an adventure movie, and what have you got?"[24]

Marble Arch faced three problems when it adapted *Raise the Titanic!* into a film. First, it needed the assistance of the U.S. Navy. Second, the studio had no experience in making adventure films. Third, it had to overcome its own creative incompetence.

Marble Arch required navy ships and submersibles to make *Raise the Titanic*,[25] and to get them, the navy, Department of Defense and State Department needed to approve the final script by Adam Kennedy. The problem was, Cussler's novel is a Cold War adventure pitting America against the Soviet Union, and the State Department had a policy against associating with any film that could damage bilateral relationships between the United States and the USSR.[26] After reading Kennedy's script, representatives from all three departments voiced concerns about a number of scenes, especially one showing the U.S. Navy ready to engage the Soviet Navy on the high seas, and another showing Pitt trespassing on Soviet territory (Novaya Zemlya) and shooting a Russian solider in order to rescue Koplin. The departments were also unhappy with the implications that America's leaders and military could not be trusted with the byzanium. After "long and delicate negotiations,"[27] the navy agreed to assist Marble Arch because it believed that *Raise the Titanic* would showcase its underwater rescue and exploration equipment, footage it could exploit to try to acquire appropriations for nuclear aircraft carriers and submarines, a public-relations tactic the navy has practiced since the Vietnam War.[28] Unfortunately, the result of marrying this tactic with the State Department's policy of downplaying conflicts between the United States and Soviet Union resulted in a string of lackluster adventure films—like *Ice Station Zebra* (1968), *Gray Lady Down* (1979) and *The Final Countdown* (1980)—where naval technology overshadows plot and character development.[29] In *Raise the Titanic* the results included moving the scene in which Pitt (Richard Jordan) rescues Koplin, and diluting the face-off between Americans and Russians on the *Titanic*. For Koplin's rescue, Novaya Zemlya is replaced by the fictional Arctic island Svlardala, which CIA Director Nicholson (Paul Carr) explains has been claimed by every country that ever explored it; this means that the Russian soldier had no more right to be on Svlardala than Pitt, and that the United States had just as much right to mine the byzanium as anyone else. As for the face-off on the *Titanic* there are no Soviet marines, Navy SEALs, or gunplay, much less Hurricane Amanda.

Marble Arch's inexperience in making adventure films was a problem because adapting a book like *Raise the Titanic!* requires people with the skills to make ambitious action movies. After the Bond films, *Planet of the Apes* (1968) and *Star Wars* audiences expected more from adventure films, and movies that did not measure up were disregarded, like *Marooned* (1969), or berated if they somehow managed to succeed at the box office, like *Star Trek: The Motion Picture* (1979). Marble Arch could have hired a veteran adventure film director[30] instead of Jerry Jameson (*Airport '77, The Bat People*), who was primarily a television veteran, which may explain why *Raise the Titanic* has the pace and patina of made-for-TV movies of the time. An experienced adventure screenwriter could have also helped, but Kennedy only had two screenplay credits to his name, the most recent being an adaptation of his own 1970 bestselling paranoid thriller *The Domino Principle* directed by Stanley Kramer (*The Defiant Ones, Guess Who's Coming to Dinner*).[31] Marble Arch could have also benefited from paying attention to Bond producer Albert R. "Cubby" Broccoli's famous promise to put every penny of a film's budget on the screen.[32] Instead, the studio dug itself a deep hole by spending $15 million in pre-production,[33] over a third of the film's final cost.

Even if Marble Arch had hired experienced adventure filmmakers, there is no guarantee that these creators could have saved the studio from its own ineptitude. *Raise the Titanic* is a far from faithful adaptation of Cussler's novel, but film adaptations do not have to be faithful to be successful. The blockbuster adaptation of Peter Benchley's *Jaws* takes numerous liberties with the mega-selling novel, and Stoker's *Dracula* has never been faithfully adapted into a movie, but this has not prevented *Nosferatu* (1922) with Max Schreck, *Dracula* (1931) with Bela Lugosi, or *Horror of Dracula* (1958) with Christopher Lee from becoming deserved classics. The trick is *how* a book is adapted into a movie. When screenwriter Nunnally Johnson adapted John Steinbeck's *The Moon Is Down* (1943), he asked the author if he had any suggestions. Steinbeck answered, "Yeah. Tamper with it."[34] Steinbeck understood that film is a different medium from the novel, so a screenwriter adapting a book should do what he thinks best, so long as the source material is not violated. Johnson describes this as doing what is "dramatically right,"[35] but many of the changes Marble Arch made to Cussler's novel are anything but dramatically right.

The best example of this may be the film's ending, which manages to violate Cussler's novel while ignoring the government's concerns about the trustworthiness of U.S. leaders and the military. After the *Titanic*'s vault is opened and Brewster's corpse is found with several boxes of gravel, Admiral Sandecker (Jason Robards) confesses to Gene Seagram (David Selby) that he is unsure if the byzanium could have been strictly tagged for defense purposes if it had been recovered. Gene throws a tantrum after Sandecker leaves, insisting he would have never started the Sicilian Project if he thought his work could be used to create a new weapon.[36] Pitt decides to test Gene and shows him a postcard, found on Brewster's corpse, with a picture of an English seaside village called Southby. Pitt and Gene travel to a cemetery in Southby and find a gravestone for Jake Hobart. Gene has brought along a Geiger counter, and the ground beneath Hobart's headstone tests positive for byzanium. The film ends with Pitt leaving the decision to dig up the byzanium to Gene, who chooses to leave it buried. This is more in tune with *Vixen 03*, in which Pitt helps destroy a volatile weapon because he is afraid the temptation for any government to possess it will trump common sense. But, in *Vixen 03*, the QD organism exists, whereas in *Raise the Titanic* a weapon like a byzanium bomb is hypothetical.[37] Navy chief of information Admiral David Cooney, who liked Cussler's novel, was afraid that the conclusion of Kennedy's script would cancel out any benefits the movie might provide the navy, so meetings were scheduled with Marble Arch. These meetings ended with Cooney thinking Marble Arch had agreed to use an ending he wrote, in which Pitt tracks the byzanium to Southby, but instead of a cemetery he discovers a playground and a plaque commemorating the graveyard's destruction by a German airplane that crashed in World War II. When *Raise the Titanic* was released with Kennedy's ending, Richard O'Connor, executive in charge of production for Marble Arch, claimed there had been a misunderstanding. The producers thought Cooney's revisions were only suggestions. O'Connor apologized but added that Marble Arch felt Kennedy's conclusion "was creatively the better ending, and that was the scene eventually filmed."[38]

Another example involves the showdown between Prevlov (Bo Brundin) and Sandecker, Pitt and Gene aboard the *Titanic*, a scene ostensibly downplayed to satisfy the State Department. Prevlov's actions are merciless in the novel, but Cussler makes it clear that he is defending his homeland. If the United States recovers the byzanium, the Soviet Union will be unable to retaliate against an American nuclear missile attack. Prevlov's motive is the same in the film, but it is not made clear until he is posturing on the *Titanic*, at which point he is spewing accusations that sound more like propaganda than justifications for threatening to sink the ship. This makes Prevlov and, by extension, the Soviet Union less sympathetic than in Cussler's novel.[39] Now there is no way to know for sure, but if the screenplay had done a better job of presenting Prevlov's motive the State Department might have found the showdown's Cold War elements more tolerable, in the same way that changing Novaya Zemlya to Svlardala made the Cold War elements involving that location more tolerable. This would have allowed the showdown to be a true clash, but it appears that no one at Marble Arch realized this face-off is the film's climax and needed to be as spectacular as it is in Cussler's novel.

Further deflating the showdown is the absence of Hurricane Amanda. At one point, Pitt tells Sandecker and Seagram that a Force 12 storm is headed for the *Titanic*, but it never arrives, nor is it mentioned again. Deleting Hurricane Amanda from the film might have been a budgetary rather than a creative decision, but, if that is the case, it illustrates how Marble Arch could have profited from spending less on pre-production and more on what appears on the screen. If Hurricane Amanda had been part of the movie then the downplayed Cold War elements in the showdown could have been compensated with images of Pitt, Sandecker, Gene and the crew struggling to keep the *Titanic* afloat. But, again, nobody at Marble Arch appears to have realized how important it was to make their climax a spectacular one. Cussler created one of the great Act III Drawing Room scenes in adventure literature by combining the resurrected *Titanic* with Hurricane Amanda, and the face-off between the Russians and Americans as Pitt buys time for Navy SEALs to take back the ship. Out of all this, Marble Arch just kept the ship.

Some of the most detrimental creative decisions in the film involve changes to the characters, none more so than Pitt. Cussler's Pitt is part cynic and part Boy Scout, a decent guy who likes most people and goes above and beyond to salvage society's status quo whenever it is threatened, even when other men turn away. In the film, Pitt is a world-weary loner who has no love for the status quo, a Vietnam-era variation of the Byronic hero like Clint Eastwood's Lieutenant Kelly from *Kelly's Heroes* (1970) and Alan Alda's Captain Hawkeye Pierce from television's *M*A*S*H* (1972–1983).[40] In Pitt's single scene with Dana (Anne Archer),[41] a former lover he has not seen in years, she reminds him how he was going to change the world,[42] but Pitt tells her that he was outnumbered.[43] This sadder but wiser Pitt, a retired naval officer with no direct affiliation to NUMA or any government agency or organization, passes his days drifting through assignments that other people write off as impossible. Cussler's Pitt has a solemn and solitary side to his personality, but, in general, he is like Captain Geoffrey Thorpe (Errol Flynn) in *The Sea Hawks* (1940), a daring and self-confident hero who does what he can, where he can, to help while trusting that the rest of the world can take care of itself. The film's Pitt is a grump who would have benefited from having Giordino around to brighten his rainy-day disposition, but there is no Al and the changes to Pitt make Giordino more noticeable by his absence than in *Iceberg*. The only glimpse we get of a comparable character to Giordino in *Raise the Titanic* is Munk (Michael Pataki). In Cussler's novel, Henry Munk, a muscular instrument specialist on Pitt's salvage crew, is murdered by one of the Russian infiltrators while on the submersible *Sappho II*, but in the film, Munk (no first name given) pilots or co-pilots the *Deep Fathom*, and is not murdered. (No one is.) Perhaps it is just coincidence that the swarthy Pataki resembles Giordino, with his curly black hair, stocky frame and gravelly voice, but one can only wonder why Marble Arch deleted Giordino when Pataki was available, and how much the little Italian's presence would have bolstered Pitt and the film with his camaraderie and the pair's trademark banter.

The changes to Pitt are not dramatically right, but they do make a weird sort of sense considering the time *Raise the Titanic* was produced. In the late seventies and early eighties, Vietnam-era Byronic heroes were in vogue, while old fashion adventure heroes were just making a comeback in Hollywood. On the other hand, there is no apparent explanation for changes made to Gene and Dana Seagram (Dana Archibald in the film) except creative myopia. Gene and Dana are no longer the neurotic train wrecks they are in Cussler's novel, and their personal improvement comes at the film's expense.[44]

Cussler's Gene Seagram is a Midwestern fish out of water, desperate to prove himself to his Ivy League peers after five years of failure at Meta Section,[45] a proud man who has put himself into an uncompromising position.[46] In Cussler's novel, Seagram's hubris drives him into the realm of madness, but, in the film, Gene is an insensitive schlub who frets that Pitt will upstage him with the Sicilian Project and his girlfriend. Meanwhile, Dana Seagram, a beautiful woman with a Ph.D. in archaeology, is incapable of loving another person.[47] Dana is brave, as she demonstrates during the showdown on the *Titanic*, but she is also a hypocrite drawn to power and notoriety. In the film, Dana Archibald is a beautiful but run-of-the-mill journalist, a career change possibly inspired by Sandecker assigning Dana to be NUMA's media representative. She breaks the *Titanic* story, so her beat would appear to be national politics or foreign affairs (even though, in 1980, her newspaper, the *Washington Star*, was trying and failing to attract new readers by concentrating on zonal metro news).[48] Instead of being deeply neurotic, Dana is merely conflicted. Dana seems to be drawn to the domestic life, complaining early in the film that she thought Gene was the pipe-and-slippers type who would be home from work each night by six. But, when Dana bumps into Pitt for their one scene together, she acts like a flustered lovesick schoolgirl, and when she argues with Gene about the *Titanic* story she blurts out that she and Pitt lived together for two years and that she was stupid to leave him.

Rehabilitating a novel's damaged or unlikable characters in a film adaptation is fine if the changes do not violate the source material. In Benchley's *Jaws*, Matt Hooper is a New England ichthyologist who has an afternoon fling with Ellen Brody, wife of chief of police Martin Brody, who suspects the affair happened but cannot prove it. Benchley pits Hooper and Brody in an antagonistic relationship that reaches its breaking point after they join an unstable big-game fisherman named Quint to hunt a Great White shark feeding off the shores of Amity Island. In the film *Jaws*, Hooper is still an ichthyologist from New England, but he never has an affair with Ellen Brody, and Hooper and Brody struggle together to work with the unstable Quint (Robert Shaw) during the shark hunt. These changes do not violate Benchley's novel because both film and book focus on the threat of the Great White, and how Hooper, Brody and Quint interact while hunting the mankiller. In *Raise the Titanic* the changes to Gene and Dana, like the changes to Pitt, are not dramatically right because they change the focus from the novel. Robbing Gene of his hubris robs him of his motive for pursuing the byzanium at all costs. It is hubris that makes Seagram insist that the *Titanic* be raised,[49] forces him to put the fate of the Sicilian Project into the despised Pitt's hands,[50] and shatters his mind after the *Titanic* is raised and the vault is opened.[51] As for Dana, she is reduced from scandalous surrogate for the *Titanic* and Washington's next divorcée *du jour* to a cipher spouting lines like, "I'm a dynamite fisherperson. I just can't put the wormy on the hooky." Eliminating Gene's melodramatic motive and Dana's pathos eliminates all of the film's drama except for salvaging the *Titanic*, which is missing its international intrigue and the threat of Hurricane Amanda.

The changes to Gene and Dana could have been accomplished in ways that were dramatically right if the film's triangle between the couple and Pitt had been better developed. We could have seen Gene struggling to come to grips with Dana's past with Pitt, Dana struggling to decide if she loves Gene or Pitt, or both, and Pitt struggling to come to terms with his past disappointments after he sees Dana again. The film could have even placed Dana on the *Titanic* as the ship's human proxy during the showdown or Hurricane Amanda, or both. How would Gene or Pitt have reacted if Prevlov had threatened Dana, or if Dana had been endangered or injured during the storm? What would have happened if Pitt and Gene had to work together to come to Dana's aid? These and other scenarios that do not violate Cussler's novel could have been played out in the film, but Marble Arch was either unable or uninterested in visualizing any of the human drama from Cussler's novel.

The most damaging violation to Cussler's novel, however, is the notion of using byzanium to create a thermonuclear fusion bomb, an idea that is never broached in *Raise the Titanic!* At one point in the novel, Pitt does refer to the Sicilian Project as a "strategic weapon"[52] and Sandecker's first reaction when told about it is to call it the "ultimate weapon," but Kemper is more accurate when he calls it "a defense system," and Seagram makes it clear that "the Sicilian Project is not a weapon. It is purely a scientific method of protecting our country." The notion of a byzanium bomb turns Cussler's novel on its head. The only reason Meta Section and the United States government want byzanium is because it is the one element that can "stimulate the optimum level of sound emission" required to generate "a broad fanlike field of sound waves"[53] that will obliterate any missile flying into it. To paraphrase Pitt, the objective is to protect rather than take lives,[54] which speaks well for America's inherent decency. The concept of using byzanium for a bomb and the aspersions this casts on the integrity of the United States, its military and its leaders belongs to Marble Arch.

Marble Arch's *Raise the Titanic* features a different kind of hero in a different kind of adventure than in Cussler's novel, which is damaging enough, but as a reviewer in *Daily Variety* complained, the film "wastes a potentially intriguing premise with dull scripting ... and clunky direction."[55] People who like Cussler's novel can take some comfort knowing that most of the film's highlights, such as Pitt's conversation with Bigalow and the resurrection of the *Titanic*, are among the few scenes that are adapted in a dramatically right fashion from *Raise the Titanic!* One can only wonder what kind of movie might have been produced if Marble Arch had played straight with Cussler's entire novel.

Sahara (2005)

> With your fertile imagination, Ismail, you'd make a great Hollywood screenwriter.—
> Eva Rojas, *Sahara*[56]

After *Raise the Titanic* things looked bleak that there would ever be another Dirk Pitt movie. Offers for film rights still came into Lampack's office, some in the millions of dollars,[57] but Cussler wanted script approval and studio bosses insisted that was nonnegotiable.[58] Then, in May 2001, Crusader Entertainment announced that it had purchased the film rights to the Dirk Pitt series.[59] Crusader's first production was *Sahara*, released in April 2005, with Matthew McConaughey as Pitt, Steve Zahn as Giordino, William H. Macy as Sandecker and Rainn Wilson as Gunn. Two months before the film's release, however, Cussler filed a lawsuit claiming

Crusader had reneged on their contract by not honoring his right to approve the script.[60] Crusader, which changed its name to Bristol Bay Productions by this time and has since changed it again to Walden Media, filed a countersuit alleging Cussler exaggerated the sales of the Dirk Pitt novels and refused to promote the film, which hurt ticket sales. As of this writing litigation continues in the Colorado Supreme Court.

Critical reviews are not law reviews so anyone interested in sifting through the legal details of this case would be better served reading about them elsewhere, but Cussler made one comment during court proceedings in February 2007 that is relevant here. He complained that the film "tore the heart"[61] out of his novel, another way of saying that Crusader's changes were not dramatically right. Since Crusader's *Sahara* has been called "one of the biggest financial flops in Hollywood history,"[62] Cussler's comment begs the question, "Did *Sahara* flop because Crusader made the same mistake as Marble Arch by violating Cussler's novel?"

According to an April 15, 2007 *Los Angeles Times* article by staff writer Glenn F. Bunting, "Unlike most financial failures, *Sahara* performed reasonably well, ranking No. 1 after its opening weekend and generating $122 million in gross box-office sales." The bad news is that *Sahara* originally had an $80 million budget but "the movie was saddled with exorbitant costs, including a $160-million production and $81.1 million in distribution expenses." Why did the costs grow so high? "[Crusader's owner Philip] Anschutz said in a deposition that he never set a limit on production costs but became 'concerned' as they climbed to $160 million. 'What I wanted to do was make a good film,' he said, adding: 'At the end, we spent, in my view, too much money.'"[63] Bunting adds that *Sahara* "lost about $105 million" by April 2006 "according to a finance executive assigned to the movie," however budget records "show the film losing $78.3 million based on Hollywood accounting methods that count projected revenue ($202.9 million in this case) over a 10-year period."[64]

Gross box-office sales of $122 million?

Over $202 million in total projected revenues?

Losing $78.3 million instead of $105 million still qualifies as a financial flop, but *Sahara* was no flop with moviegoers. Unlike *Raise the Titanic*, people went to see *Sahara*.

In *Sahara* the novel and *Sahara* the film, the focus is on two plagues: one a contamination sickness killing people in Niger and Mali, and the other a red tide spreading through the sea off the West African coast that could destroy all oxygen on earth. The villains responsible for these plagues are French industrialist Yves Massarde and dictator General Zateb Kazim of Mali. Massarde operates a solar detoxification plant in the war-torn African nation, but much of the hazardous waste shipped to Massarde's plant is never destroyed; instead, it is cached in caverns, where the pollutants seep into an underground tributary of the Niger River. Massarde and Kazim are ignorant of this seepage, but neither man wants to give access to World Health Organization scientists investigating the contamination sickness, as they fear that the team might uncover the truth about the plant. A WHO biochemist, Dr. Eva Rojas, is attacked by assailants to scare off the other scientists, but Eva is rescued by Pitt, who is in Africa with NUMA. Eva and Pitt travel separate paths for a time but eventually reunite as the source of both plagues is discovered, and Massarde and Kazim's dirty dealings are quashed. Eva and Pitt end the adventure with a romance.

No one can adapt a five hundred-plus page novel into a two-hour movie without deleting, blending, compressing, streamlining or altering parts of the source material. In other words, "Tamper with it." Crusader's *Sahara* is not always a faithful adaptation of Cussler's novel, but more often than not when changes are made to the source material attempts are also made to acknowledge or incorporate some of the essence from any adapted scenes.

Some of the best examples of this revolve around the ironclad CSS *Texas*. Both Cussler's and Crusader's *Sahara* begin with a prologue set near the end of the Civil War, at which time Captain Mason Tombs and the crew of the *Texas* must run a Union blockade to escape Richmond, Virginia, with a load of Confederate gold. In the novel, little more is said about the ironclad or its precious cargo until the story's midpoint, when Pitt and Giordino chance across a prospector called The Kid (Cussler) in the Sahara. The Kid believes the *Texas* escaped the James River, crossed the Atlantic and wound up beached somewhere along the Niger during a drought. Soon after meeting the Kid, Pitt and Giordino stumble across some cave paintings that include the *Texas* flying its Confederate battle ensign,[65] and, later, the two men read about a strange ship half buried under the sand[66] in the log book of missing Australian aviatrix Kitty Mannock after stumbling across the remains of her plane in the Sahara. These and other clues lead Pitt to suspect that the *Texas* is buried along the Niger's Oued Zarit tributary, but he does not go hunting for the ironclad until the novel is almost over, a good two weeks after Massarde and Kazim have been defeated. An intermittent subplot like this, though intriguing in a novel, can be confusing or distracting to people watching a fast-paced adventure movie, so in Crusader's *Sahara* Pitt has been searching for the *Texas* for years and this search takes him, Giordino and Gunn up the Niger into Mali, where they discover the threat of the red tide. In the novel, NUMA discovers the red tide and Sandecker orders the trio to track down its source by making a perilous journey along the Niger. In the film, locating the ironclad also provides a way of finding the origin of the red tide:

> *Giordino*: So if we find your *Texas*, we find the underground river.
> *Pitt*: We find the river, we find the source of the toxins.[67]

The *Texas* also becomes the setting for the film's climactic battle between Pitt and his allies against Kazim's forces. Having already deduced that the *Texas* lies buried near an ancient palace or fortress, Pitt uses explosives confiscated from Massarde's plant to blast away the sands and expose the ironclad. In the novel, this desperate battle takes place at Fort Foureau, an abandoned French Foreign Legion outpost; however, in both the book and the film Kazim is killed, his dictatorship ended.[68] As for the ironclad's precious cargo, the gold also plays a more integral role in the movie than in Cussler's story. In both Cussler's and Crusader's *Sahara* the gold represents the last of the Confederate treasury, but in the novel the gold is missing when Pitt uncovers the ironclad, most likely carted off by Tuareg warriors who laid siege to the *Texas* after it is beached. In the film, a Confederate gold dollar found in Mali renews Pitt's quest for the ironclad and crates of gold dollars are aboard the *Texas* after it is uncovered, but the Tuareg still end up with the precious cargo after NUMA gives it to the poverty-stricken nomads instead of turning it over to the U.S. government. For the most part, these changes are dramatically right since the *Texas* and the gold have little more influence on the focus of the film than they do the focus of the novel, but one thing Crusader's *Sahara* forgets to do is explain why the *Texas* was carrying the gold and why the ironclad sailed to Africa. In Cussler's *Sahara* the gold represents the South's only hope of setting up a government in exile, but the only hint we get of this in the film occurs when Tombs (Robert Cavanah) tells a young Confederate sailor lugging a crate onto the ironclad, "That's the future in your hands." Later Pitt ponders, "Now, what kind of man tries to take a ship like that across the ocean? Why? How? I don't know, but I plan on finding out." If Pitt does finds out why, he never shares it with the audience.

More examples of the essence of Cussler's scenes being incorporated into Crusader's *Sahara* appear throughout the film. The main story of Cussler's *Sahara* begins in 1996 at the Asselar Oasis in Mali, where, in a scene that predates the diseased zombies from *28 Days Later* (2002), a tour group is massacred by villagers driven to cannibalism by contamination sickness. This is the novel's lone cannibal scene, but this grisly side effect is discussed several times afterwards, and even though everyone in Asselar is dead by the time Eva and a team of scientists from WHO can get there, she finds plenty of gruesome evidence of the villagers' insanity. There are no cannibal scenes in the film, a deletion that may not have been dramatically right but is consistent with Crusader Entertainment/Bristol Bay/Walden Media's practice of producing family-accessible movies like *Holes* (2003), *A Sound of Thunder* (2005) and the *Narnia* series (2005–2010); however, the novel's tour group attack and Eva's gruesome discoveries in Asselar are echoed in a suspenseful night scene wherein Pitt, Giordino and Eva arrive at Asselar to find the oasis deserted. As the trio explores the village a series of vague shots that include figures lying in a pit and a bloody handprint on a wall inside a house suggests something unspeakable happened in Asselar before the last villager passed away.[69]

In the novel, Eva is introduced after the cannibal scene. She is in Africa with world-renowned toxologist Frank Hopper and an international team of scientists from WHO to locate the source of the contamination sickness. Eva's team within this group is assigned to investigate Mali, and as they make preparations in Alexandria, Egypt, for the trip, she sneaks off to a lonely beach to do a little sunbathing. At that point, men sent by Kazim attack her.[70] After Pitt rescues Eva she returns to her team to finalize plans to leave, against Kazim's wishes, for Mali the following day. She then has dinner with Pitt as the pair gets better acquainted. The dinner ends with both parties agreeing to meet the following June at Eva's family home in Pacific Grove, California. "Then it's you and I and the Bay of Monterrey,"[71] Pitt tells her.

Much of this is echoed in the film, which spotlights Eva (Penélope Cruz) by paring the international team to her and Hopper (Glynn Turman), and gets things rolling by foregoing Alexandria for Lagos, Niger. The doctors are already well into their search for the cause and source of contamination sickness spreading through Niger when Eva is attacked, this time while visiting a lighthouse along a beach to get blood samples from the father of a plague victim who recently returned from Mali. As for Pitt, in the novel he and NUMA are in Egypt searching the Nile for the funeral barge of Pharaoh Menkura (or Mycerinus), builder of the smallest of Giza's three pyramids, but in the film he and NUMA are in Niger salvaging the sarcophagus of a ruler named King Bateen. Eva passes out after Pitt rescues her in the novel and the movie, but in Cussler's *Sahara* she wakes up on the beach; in the film, Eva wakes up on NUMA's salvage vessel *Martha Ann* in time to watch the recovery of Bateen's sarcophagus, set to the blaring accompaniment of Grand Funk's "We're an American Band." Instead of dinner with Pitt, Eva and Hopper attend a party, where Sandecker presents Bateen's sarcophagus to the Lagos Museum.[72] Also attending is Massarde (Lambert Wilson), the salvage operation's primary supporter. Sandecker introduces Eva and Hopper to Massarde so they can ask the businessman to help persuade someone in a position of power, in Mali, to pressure WHO to investigate the plague. But Mali is in the grip of a civil war that has left half the country in chaos, and the other half controlled by Kazim (Lennie James), the "man who put the 'war' back into 'warlord.'" Meanwhile Pitt takes a detour on his way to the party to visit a contact in the Nigerian underworld that has the Confederate gold dollar. At the museum, Pitt shows Sandecker the coin and requests to borrow the admiral's boat *Calliope* (a Hunton Gazelle RS43) so he, Giordino and Gunn can survey the Niger River, in Mali, for the *Texas*. Sandecker agrees to give Pitt three days with the *Calliope*, which is all the time NUMA has left in Africa before moving on to its next project in Australia, but only after Pitt agrees never to bring up the *Texas* again if the search fails. Pitt and his crew are in for a surprise the next morning, though, when they find Eva and Hopper waiting for them at the dock because Sandecker has told the doctors that they could hitch a ride to Mali on the *Calliope*.[73] Pitt and Eva get better acquainted during the ride, culminating with an after-dinner conversation during which Pitt implies that he likes his dinner companion: "Well, every great thing that's ever happened to me happened in the water." The next day Eva and Hopper debark the *Calliope* to carry their search inland, but not before Pitt asks to meet Eva again in the town where she lives after their work in Africa is finished. Eva agrees. Pitt tells her it is "you, me, and the Bay of Monterrey."

Then there is Sandecker and Gunn's meeting with Ambassador Polidori (Patrick Malahide) to warn the U.S. government about the red tide. In spite of the threat's magnitude, Polidori, who stammers that he has been in his post for only two months, will not carry NUMA's recommendations further up the political ladder without independent confirmation. This scene reflects Sandecker's frustration from the novel, wherein he vents to Pitt, Giordino and Gunn about his efforts to warn "the cretins in Congress" who are "more concerned with maintaining their precious power base"[74] than stopping the red tide.

Another example is Massarde's death. In Cussler's novel, Pitt has Massarde staked naked in the desert under the pretense of making him reveal the exact location of millions in ill-gotten profits the industrialist has hidden somewhere on Clipperton Island in the Pacific. Several hours later Pitt appears to soften and gives Massarde some water before ordering the industrialist to leave the detoxification plant, but the water is tainted with the toxin causing the contamination sickness. In the film, Massarde escapes Mali for France, but Sandecker sees to it the industrialist gets his comeuppance when a CIA undercover operative named Carl (Delroy Lindo), disguised as a waiter in a restaurant, pours tainted water into Massarde's glass.

One more example involves Pitt's passion for cars. In the novel, he and Giordino steal an Avions Voisin convertible sedan that belongs to Kazim after escaping from Massarde and the General. Pitt and Giordino drive the Voisin across the Sahara until it runs out of gas, but after Kazim and Massarde are defeated Pitt has the Voisin shipped to America. The film keeps the Voisin, but, like the *Texas* and the Confederate gold, it plays a more integral role than in the novel. In Crusader's *Sahara*, Pitt spies the Voisin when entering the Tuareg's village, then later, during a tense discussion with Tuareg leader Modibo (Paulin Fodouop), the Voisin is mentioned and the mood lightens as Pitt tells Modibo, "It's a 1936 Avions Voisin. Six cylinder, sleeve-valve engine. You know, there were only six of these ever made." (In the novel, Pitt tells Giordino much the same information about the car.)[75] In the film, Modibo and his people are the ones who steal the Voisin from Kazim, but Pitt and Giordino still drive the automobile across the Sahara as part of a scheme to rescue Eva from Massarde's detoxification plant and stop the flow of toxins into the underground tributary.[76] Cussler's *Sahara* ends in Monterrey with Pitt picking up Eva in the Voisin, and the film ends with Pitt and Eva at a beach in Monterrey with the automobile prominent in the final shot.[77]

Several bits of dialogue also reflect the essence of adapted scenes. In the novel, Pitt, Giordino and Gunn are posing as French industrialists looking to invest in West Africa. As they travel along the Niger, the Benin Navy tries to commandeer the *Calliope*, and Pitt stalls the navy with some comical banter in French before squaring off in a battle.[78] In the film, there is no reason for the trio to pretend to be anyone else, but when the Mali Navy stops the *Calliope* while searching for Eva and Hopper, Pitt stalls them by using comic banter and pretending not to understand English. Later in the film *and* the novel, Pitt and Giordino are trekking across the desert when they chance across the remains of Mannock's airplane. In Cussler's *Sahara*, Pitt asks if Giordino has ever read *The Flight of the Phoenix* by Elleston Trevor; Giordino suggests that Pitt is crazy if he thinks they can get Mannock's wreck to fly again.[79] In Crusader's *Sahara*, Pitt sees the airplane and tells Giordino there is probably a toolkit in the wreck, to which Giordino replies, "I hate to rain on your crazy parade, buddy, but I don't think we can fix this thing." Even when the film presents original scenes, the dialogue is often in the style of John Ford movie banter also common to Cussler's novels. There is no precedent in Cussler's *Sahara* for the party at the Lagos Museum or the nerdy wardrobe Gunn and Giordino wear there, but their conversation at a buffet table while anxiously waiting for Pitt to arrive would ring true in any Pitt novel:

> *Giordino*: Where is he?
> *Gunn*: He's not at the buffet.
> *Giordino*: Damn it!
> *Gunn*: Do you want another kebab?

The same is true of a conversation Pitt and Giordino have two days later as they sit in an outdoor café after visiting the home of the man who originally found the Confederate dollar in Mali. Pitt hoped to get more information about where the coin was found, but the man has died, and as he ponders where to search next Giordino offers him some honest advice:

> *Giordino*: Hey, you know, my dad collected ancient coins. From Rome, China, Siam, Persia. Somehow they all ended up in a shoebox in New Jersey.
> *Pitt*: Meaning?
> *Giordino*: Coins travel, Dirk. Even if that poor guy was still alive, it could have been nothing.
> *Pitt*: Yeah, but the coin traveled from somewhere, Al. And unless it hitched a ride on the back of a dolphin, I'm gonna guess that its jumping off point was a little bit closer to where we're sitting.

Crusader's *Sahara* also demonstrates a familiarity with other novels in the Pitt series, as well as the real-life NUMA. For instance, the film introduces Pitt in the same manner he is introduced in many of his adventures, from another character's perspective. Like Cussler's *Sahara*, most of the action during Eva's rescue is seen from her point of view, including the first close-up of Pitt, with his black wavy hair and green eyes.[80] Another instance takes place aboard the *Calliope* when Giordino pulls a stash of cigars from a compartment and Gunn asks if they belong to the admiral, a reference to the running gag about Giordino stealing Sandecker's expensive handmade cigars. Crusader's *Sahara* was intended to be the first in a series of Pitt films, and it pays homage to Cussler's first Pitt novel by naming NUMA's salvage vessel *Martha Ann*, which is also the name of a navy salvage vessel in *Pacific Vortex*.[81] Pitt drives a bright red AC Cobra in *Pacific Vortex*,[82] and during the film's opening credits (a nonstop tour through Pitt's cabin aboard the *Martha Ann*) there is a model of a silver 1967 Shelby Cobra (AC) Mk II.[83] The opening credits also feature a newspaper clipping with the headline "NUMA Digs Deep in Kurile Trench" and a subhead "Team claims they detected [the next few words are obscured by a shadow] moving fast at a depth of 14,000 feet." In *Pacific Vortex* Pitt recounts a recent incident, during underwater acoustical testing in the Kurile Trench off Japan, when instruments seemed to detect the sound of a vessel traveling at a speed of 110 miles an hour at a depth of 19,000 feet.[84] The opening credits also include photographs of Pitt with classic cars, trophies from car shows, an ashtray with one of Sandecker's smoldering cigars, a variety of photographs of lifelong pals Pitt and Giordino through the years, a football and helmet (Pitt and Giordino played on their high school and college teams), a Jolly Roger key chain (in Cussler's *Sahara* Pitt orders the Jolly Roger flown from the *Calliope*) and a clipping of an article with the headline "NUMA Unfathomed: the Men Who Raised the Titanic" and the subhead "We Meet the American Divers Who Raised the Titanic."[85] Another clipping from the fictional French newspaper *Nouvelles de Monde*[86] features the headline "*L'Osseau Blanc Retrouvé par NUMA*" ("*White Bird* Found by NUMA"), an homage to three attempts made by Cussler's 501(c)(3) non-profit, NUMA, to locate the remains of the *White Bird*, the first plane believed to have crossed the Atlantic, from east to west, only to crash somewhere in Maine.

Not every change made by Crusader has anything to do with Cussler's *Sahara* or any Pitt novel, in particular NUMA's transformation from a government agency to a private organization.[87] In many ways this change seems dramatically correct as it does not violate the focus of Cussler's novel; it has very little influence on the focus of the film and it appears to be temporary. At the end of *Sahara* Polidori extends an offer to Sandecker from the U.S. Government to fully fund NUMA "in exchange for the occasional side job for the good guys," and the admiral accepts after Polidori agrees to several concessions, including a promise that NUMA will only do jobs approved by Sandecker. However, this change *does* violate the film's source material because, in this movie at least, Pitt is not a bureaucrat, and being a series hero who is also a public administrator is one of the series' most innovative core attributes. This change also rewrites NUMA's origin. Showing how NUMA becomes a government agency is not out of line for the first film in a series, but there is no mention in a Cussler novel that part of NUMA's charter is to do any sort of side jobs. There is no denying that NUMA occasionally, albeit begrudgingly, performs side jobs for the government,[88] but most of the adventures NUMA gets involved in evolve from its maritime operations.

Another big difference between Cussler's *Sahara* and Crusader's adaptation is a missing character from the *Texas* prologue, President Abraham Lincoln, a prisoner-of-war abducted during a carriage ride.[89] With the war all but lost, the Confederate government had hoped to use Lincoln as leverage to coerce favorable surrender terms from the Union government. The plan soured, however, when Lincoln's secretary of war, Edward Stanton, refused to negotiate and then faked Lincoln's assassination at Ford's Theater to cover up the kidnapping as well as Stanton's own plot to eliminate some political rivals.[90] Conspiracy theories like this can be fun (and it would have been interesting to see Lincoln in the film), but deleting this subplot served to streamline the film and the change does not violate the source material since the President's kidnapping has even less impact on the novel's focus than the *Texas* and the gold. Crusader further streamlined the film by deleting the novel's second prologue, "Lost." *Sahara* is Cussler's first novel to feature two prologues, and "Lost" shows Kitty Mannock and her Fairchild FC-2W crashing during a sandstorm in the southwest Sahara in October 1931. This second prologue was filmed with Dana Cussler as Mannock,[91] but according to director Breck Eisner in his commentary on the *Sahara* DVD, test audiences were confused by it, so it was deleted along with scenes showing Pitt and Giordino discovering Kitty's skeleton near her plane.[92]

Other Cussler characters and subplots Crusader deleted or streamlined involved reoccurring characters Yaeger, Perlmutter and UN secretary General Hala Kamil, along with Hala's former lover Ismail Yerli, a French intelligence agent working for WHO but spying for Massarde. Also missing is the nasty pair of Chief Engineer Selig O'Bannon and overseer Melika from Tebezza, a mine where Mali's political prisoners (and anyone Massarde wants eliminated) are condemned to dig for gold until they die. In the film, Tebezza and Fort Foureau, the site of the caverns where Massarde is dumping toxic waste in the novel, are blended into toxic storage caverns beneath Massarde's plant. A last-second rescue during the climactic battle at Fort Foureau by Giordino and members of the U.S. Special Forces that saves Pitt, Eva, soldiers from UNICRATT (United Nations International Critical Response and Tactical Team) and several Tebezza survivors is replaced in the film by a nick-of-time rescue of Pitt, Giordino and Eva at the *Texas* by Modibo and his Tuareg. In the novel, Pitt and Giordino twice end up as prisoners of Massarde, but the film prunes these captures to one. The film also keeps a clandestine train ride by Pitt and Giordino into the detoxification plant, but adds Eva, to whom Massarde holds on after capturing them and shipping Pitt and Giordino off to Kazim.

One change from the novel that has no easy explanation is the role of the Tuareg. In Crusader's *Sahara* the Tuareg are sympathetic characters. Many are dying from contamination sickness, and the prisoners working in the caverns beneath Massarde's detoxification plant are Tuareg. In Cussler's *Sahara* most of the Tuareg characters work for Massarde and Kazim, including the guards at Tebezza. For Massarde, the Tuareg fill much the same functions as the Chigros (Jamaican Chinese-Negroes) do for the titular villain in Fleming's *Doctor No* (1958),[93] while Kazim employs Tuareg because the general is also Tuareg.[94] When Pitt rescues Eva in the novel he kills all but one of her attackers, identified as a Tuareg by his indigo headdress, but the film replaces this elusive assailant with Massarde's towering henchman Zakara (Maurice Lee), who wears a black headdress and thawb.[95] In the novel the Tuareg attacker swallows poison to escape Pitt, but Zakara escapes after being wounded, setting up a final battle with Pitt at the detoxification plant.[96]

There are no obvious reasons for these changes, which makes it tempting to blame Hollywood's preoccupation with political correctness. If so, then these changes cannot be dramatically correct, even though having Kazim go from being a Tuareg to fighting them is plausible as the Tuareg tend to be nomadic warriors rather than professional soldiers. It also calls into question if NUMA's decision to give the Confederate gold to the Tuareg is dramatically right. In Cussler's novel Perlmutter assumes the Tuareg carted off the gold from the *Texas* after the ironclad's crew and President Lincoln passed away during the siege, a far less sympathetic scenario than what happens in Crusader's *Sahara*. These changes likewise alter the focus of the source material regarding the *Texas* and its cargo. In Crusader's *Sahara* the *Texas* escapes the American Civil War only to play a part in the end of a distant civil war over a century later, but there is no Malian civil war in the novel. In Cussler's *Sahara* the Tuareg unintentionally end any chance the Confederacy (a government fighting for the right to enslave people from Africa) has of setting up a government in exile when they cart away the gold from the *Texas*, but, in the film, the gold gives the Tuareg a chance to start a better government in one of the most violent areas of Africa.

Cussler's Kazim is a dictator operating behind the façade of an honest government. A Princeton graduate who needs to be constantly complimented on his genius, Kazim is pompous, oozes self-importance and looks like a benign villain from an old Warner Bros. cartoon. The film drops Cussler's power-behind-the-throne subplot to streamline its story, but, for no apparent reason, it also eliminates Kazim's pompous self-importance and makes him a Malian army colonel who promotes himself by shooting the president. Crusader's Kazim is astute, ruthless, even more erudite (although we are never told where he was educated) and is in no way cartoonish in his impeccably tailored Western clothes. Kazim is also the dominant member of his partnership with Massarde, a necessary reversal from the novel given these changes in character. In the film, Mali is Kazim's country (or at least half of it is) and the general calls the shots, so while the film's Massarde is not intimidated by Kazim, he is always diplomatic when speaking to the general. In contrast, Cussler's Massarde, known as The Scorpion in the business community,[97] can be manipulative with Kazim[98] but there is never any doubt that he does what he wants when he wants. Another difference between Cussler's and Crusader's Massarde is their reason for storing the toxic waste. In the film, Massarde is hiding the waste because his plant is experiencing technical problems and cannot keep up with the shipments coming by train each day; in the novel, Massarde simply wants a bigger profit, and it is cheaper to hide toxic waste than to destroy it.

Kazim and Massarde are not the only major characters to undergo a makeover in the film. Pitt, Giordino, Sandecker and Gunn also get some tweaking. In the novels none of these men have intelligence or Special Forces training. Pitt and Giordino are officers and graduates of the Air Force Academy with degrees in marine engineering, while Sandecker and Gunn are career sailors, although all four men are combat veterans or have performed admirably under fire while working for NUMA. Crusader's *Sahara* (like Marble Arch's *Raise the Titanic*) transfers Pitt to the navy, does likewise for Giordino, and makes them and Sandecker SEALs[99] apparently to explain Pitt and Giordino's fighting skills and proficiency with firearms. In Cussler's novels Pitt and Giordino can take care of themselves, but their skills have limits. After Pitt rescues Eva on the beach he tells her that, if her attackers had been professional assassins, they would both be dead,[100] but in the film Kazim can tell Pitt and Giordino have military training after they rescue Eva from a handful of Malian soldiers in Asselar: "The two unarmed men who did this ... they were not amateurs, Yves."[101] Sandecker is still a retired admiral, but conversations between he and Carl, in Niger, suggests he also has a history in covert intelligence, whereas Cussler's Sandecker has connections but no intelligence experience.[102] As for Gunn, the film never makes it clear if he served in the navy.[103] Gunn is also shaky when it comes to shooting a flare during the battle on the *Calliope*, but in Cussler's *Sahara* he has no problem shooting two modified M-16 automatic rifles and a Remington TR870 automatic shotgun. Gunn still wears glasses and is intelligent in the film, but there is nothing in the novels to suggest he has medical training; however, when Eva wakes up on the *Martha Ann*, Gunn tells her, "You had an edema of the upper tracheal track."

One last element of the film that many Pitt fans might find dramatically incorrect is its soundtrack, which includes several rock songs from the sixties and seventies. Doctor Hook's "Right Place Wrong Time" might seem an odd choice for the opening credits as Pitt's musical tastes run along the lines of the Great American Songbook. But a case can be made that many of these songs are dramatically right since they were released at the same time that Pitt was created and his early adventures were published. A case could also be made that music like Glenn Miller's "American Patrol" or Max Steiner's "Adventures of Don Juan" would not have had the same impact as Steppenwolf's "Magic Carpet Ride" in the scene with Pitt and Giordino sailing the land yacht.

Crusader's *Sahara* was not a financial success, but its gross box-office sales and projected revenues suggest the studio might want to blame itself rather than Cussler for its failure. Anschutz is right when he said, "At the end, we spent, in my view, too much money." However, when it comes to Cussler's comment that the film "tore the heart" out of his novel, this review has hopefully been thorough enough to support that many of the changes Crusader made are dramatically correct. Crusader tampered with Cussler's novel, but, unlike Marble Arch's *Raise the Titanic*, many of the changes in *Sahara* contain the essence of scenes from its source material. Crusader's *Sahara* is also much more respectful in its translation of Cussler's novel to the screen. Despite the changes to NUMA, Pitt, Giordino, Sandecker and Gunn, the agency and these characters resemble their literary counterparts more than Her Majesty's Secret Service and Agent 007 do in the Bond films, which often use little else except the titles, a few characters and some settings from Fleming's novels.[104] Crusader's *Sahara* also features Pitt's audacious style of adventure. History reaches out from the past in the glitter of Pitt's Confederate gold dollar and the weathered riveted hull of the *Texas* under the African sun. Coincidence manifests itself like a fateful guide to keep heroes on the right course when they need it most by bouncing a soccer ball down a stairway into an out-of-the-way cave in the Tuareg's secret camp. Pitt and Giordino are brothers-in-arms who venture where other men with more common sense but thinner blood fear to tread, ready to risk it all. When Admiral Sandecker says, "I can't ask you boys to go this alone," Pitt tells him, "That's the great part, sir. You know you never have to." And Pitt is still extremely dangerous to enemies, extremely loyal to friends and the ever-smiling Samaritan to strangers. These are trademarks of a Clive Cussler Dirk Pitt adventure, none of which can be found in Marble Arch's *Raise the Titanic*, and that may explain why filmgoers rejected that movie but went to see *Sahara*.

"Coins travel, Dirk."
"Yeah, but the coin traveled from somewhere, Al."

It is a mystery, and it does not matter if this mystery makes no sense. Pitt will never quit until he discovers the answer, and wherever the journey takes him, Giordino will be by his side, and like a tag-along little brother we want to come, too. Crusader's *Sahara* is not Cussler's *Sahara*, but Crusader did get a lot of things right and the studio and the film deserve credit for that.

Oregon Files Television Series (2010)

> Juan Cabrillo takes to the seas after the bad guys in his amazing ship the *Oregon*. With a crew of X-CIA [sic] and special ops warriors his corporation becomes an unbeatable extension to our government as well as others to make sure that the world stays safe.—Logline for *Oregon Files* television series[105]

In 2010, two sizzle reels were produced to try to raise funding for an *Oregon Files* television series. According to an accompanying press release, the estimated $42 million series was to be produced by 5 Pictures Entertainment in association with Mix Entertainment Holding. The plan was to release a two-hour pilot worldwide in late 2011, with the series premiering the following spring.[106]

The first reel features Cussler and executive producers Daniel Tibbets (*Rome*) and Scott Ross, former senior vice-president at Industrial Light and Magic and former chief operating officer at Digital Domain, discussing the *Oregon Files*' potential. The reel also features a number of concept paintings, including two showing the *Oregon* under construction and in action on the high seas, emphasizing its size and firepower. Other concept paintings show Dubai, which, if the series had been produced, would have been the location for The Corporation's headquarters.[107] According to Cussler, "I think Dubai being the home port would be very exotic rather than just have San Francisco, you know, or Marseilles, or something like that. But this is a class act. The *Oregon* is a very class act. So putting it in Dubai, I think, works out very well. They complement each other."[108]

The second reel is an action montage featuring Gregg Sargeant's 911 Stunts company.[109] No acting, creative or production credits are presented and none of the characters in the reel are identified, but it appears that Sargeant plays Cabrillo, and most of The Corporation's prominent members also appear. A loose story unfolds in a series of disjointed images showing the abduction of an accountant; the apparent torture of an unidentified man by a nasty-looking fellow holding a circular power saw; the rescue of an unconscious female (possibly Linda Ross) from a mini-sub; the chase of a Middle Eastern parkour traceur; and Dubai (including the Atlantis Hotel) and some of the less exotic areas inside the *Oregon*. Binding these images together is a voice-over by Cabrillo, who explains, "We began our careers with youthful and naive enthusiasm. Joined organizations that promised to make the world a safer place. But it didn't take long to realize that governments would never allow for those promises to be delivered. That's why we created this. This Corporation." Cabrillo explains to The Corporation that their latest contract has exceeded their original mission and is now about the Earth's most precious commodity: "human life." Cabrillo's voice-over picks up again as he explains, "And it is our duty as members of a civilized society to stand up and be counted among those who believe what is right." Back in the meeting with The Corporation, Cabrillo explains that in less than an hour they will engage an unknown force with the fate of untold lives depending upon them. The reel concludes with this unknown force assaulting the *Oregon* in Zodiacs and helicopters only to be dispatched by a single member of The Corporation (possibly Eric Stone) using the *Oregon*'s sophisticated weaponry, leaving the tramp steamer to sail off as Cabrillo says in a final voice-over, "I need to know who's in."

As slick and exciting as this second reel is, it suffers from a lack of Cussler's signature audacity and old fashion adventure, which may explain why the series failed to find funding. Nothing about the characters or action stands out. Cabrillo's speech, for example, could have just as easily been given by Jack Ryan, Jr., to the Campus's strike team. When the traceur is cornered on a rooftop by a member of The Corporation (possibly Franklin Lincoln), he steps off after taunting, "You have no idea who we are. I am just a pawn. And there are a thousand of us." After the traceur hits the roof of a car, The Corporation member cracks, "Nine hundred and ninety-nine to go," a quip that could have come from Schwarzenegger, Willis, Stallone, Chuck Norris or virtually any action hero. Worst of all, there is no clear shot of the *Oregon* in the reel. Revealing the shabby exterior of the *Oregon* after the assault would have been an absurdly wonderful Cussleresque moment, but when the ship passes by the camera its image speeds up and does not return to normal until the *Oregon* is too far away for a good view of her hull.

In the first reel, Ross comments how he believes the *Oregon Files* is "an Indiana Jones-plus. The combination of Indy and James Bond in the most unbelievable environment with some of the most unbelievable technology." A press release states the same thing but also lists what makes *Oregon Files* unique. "[The *Oregon*] is run like a business, with its crew being actual shareholders, taking jobs for Interpol, the CIA, business, and wealthy individuals to help stop international crimes and catastrophic terrorism. They are modern-day privateers, sailing the high seas taking on ultra-covert and ultra-dangerous missions for the right cause and the right price. The crew is adept at disguises, combat, advanced technologies, covert actions and much more to aid in their missions." In other words, *Mission: Impossible* meets *Star Trek* on the high seas, and it is disappointing that some of this good stuff did not make its way into the second reel.

Cussleresque Adventures

> We still shall require very loud and violent physical action to resolve the story.—
> William Foster-Harris[110]

Raise the Titanic and *Sahara* are the only film adaptations of Cussler's novels, but there are many movies that contain enough of the same elements that appear in Cussler's adventures that they could be called Cussleresque, much in the same way movies like *Alien* (1979), *In the Mouth of Madness* (1995) and *The Mummy* (1999) can be called Lovecraftian, even though they are not adaptations of anything written by H. P. Lovecraft.[111]

Cussler was not even two years old when *F.P.1 Does Not Answer* (*F.P.1 antwortet nicht*), a co-production of Gaumont British Pictures and Germany's UFA (*Universum Film Aktien Gesellschaft*), was released on December 12, 1932.[112] Curt Siodmak wrote the screenplay, based on his novel.[113]

F.P.1 is an acronym for "Flying Platform One," an artificial island in the middle of the Atlantic Ocean, which serves as an airplane fueling and repair station. The platform is the brainchild of Lieutenant Droste (Paul Hartman),[114] who gets the Lennartz-Werke corporation to finance F.P.1 with the aid of his friend, the famous aviator and adventurer Major Ellissen (Han Albers). During negotiations, Ellissen falls in love with the owner's sister Claire Lennartz (Sybille Schmitz), but when things get too serious Ellissen's Peter Pan syndrome kicks in and he hightails it for new adventures.

Over the next two years Claire falls in love with Droste, and F.P.1 develops as much into a resort as it does a waystation. F.P.1 is so successful that a rival corporation begins planting sleepers among the platform's crew, and during a storm these saboteurs subdue the rest of the crew with gas, destroy the power plant, scuttle the diesel for the turbines and wreck the escape planes. Droste tries to stop Chief Engineer Damsky (Hermann Speelmanns) from opening the sea valves and swamping the platform, and during their fight a radio transmits the sounds of gunshots and then screams to Lennartz-Werke. When the transmission ends, the Lennartz-Werke wireless operator is unable to re-establish contact and reports, "F.P.1 does not answer!"

Claire is hellbent on finding out what happened to Droste, so she goes to Ellissen. The aviator is still in love with her, and Claire promises to give herself to Ellissen if he flies her to the platform. Ellissen agrees, but crashes their plane as he lands. Ellissen and Claire escape the wreck, and, as Ellissen revives the crew, Claire finds Droste. Damsky has escaped, Droste has a broken shoulder, every radio on the platform has been destroyed and, with no fuel for the power plant, the sea valves cannot be closed. Droste retrieves salvageable parts from the remains of the escape planes to assemble one working plane that can be used to fetch help. But, when

Ellissen learns that Claire loves Droste, he refuses to fly it. Droste insists on trying to fly the makeshift plane despite his injury, but when a photographer (Peter Lorre)[115] berates the lovesick Ellissen for making Droste risk his life, the major steals the plane. Ellissen locates a steamship, but, with no radio, he is forced to make a dangerous parachute jump; once aboard the steamship, he dispatches a message for a supply ship to bring diesel to F.P.1 in time to rescue the platform. When Ellissen can see that F.P.1 will be saved, he asks where the steamship is heading. The answer: South America, to search for condors. Ellissen decides to tag along, resigned that his chance at happiness with Claire is gone.

F.P.1 Does Not Answer may be the first big-budget Cussleresque film. Besides being primarily set on the ocean, its heroes are similar to Cussler's heroes in many ways. Ellissen is an adventurer who needs to see what waits beyond the next horizon; Droste is an engineer who is unafraid to tackle projects other men deem impossible. Both men are in the military, or are veterans, and both are pilots. Any Cussler hero would have tried to stop Damsky from opening the sea valves, and the lieutenant's makeshift plane recalls MacGyver-like vehicles cobbled together by Pitt. No Cussler hero would accept Claire's proposition (much less throw a hissy fit, like Ellissen) when the major discovers Claire loves Droste, but Ellissen stealing the makeshift plane, and the perilous parachute jump,[116] are par for the course for a Cussler hero. Claire, meanwhile, could be Jessie LeBaron's younger sister, a wealthy woman doing what she has to do to discover what has happened to the man she loves. Like a traditional Cussler heroine, Claire is a classy woman (albeit with a strong sense of entitlement), who is tough enough to survive in a man's world, but never behaves like an amazon or warrior princess.

F.P.1 Does Not Answer and many of Cussler's adventures feature espionage, although political rather than the corporate variety is the norm for Cussler. The sabotage of the platform during the storm recalls Prevlov and his Russian marines taking command of the *Titanic* during Hurricane Amanda. Most Cussler adventures feature one or two prologues set in the past, while the majority of the story takes place a few years into the future, and while *F.P.1 Does Not Answer* begins in the present (1932), most of the story takes place two years in the future. Many Cussler adventures feature a monumental or futuristic engineering feat like F.P.1 (e.g., Kanoli, the Fyrie probe, the *Titanic* salvage, the Fort Foureau solar waste disposal plant, Soggy Acres, Edo City), although it is not always a prominent part of the story. Siodmak claims, in his autobiography, that F.P.1 is the prototype for the aircraft carrier,[117] but the platform seems to have more in common with the *Ocean Wanderer* luxury hotel from *Trojan Odyssey*. An aircraft carrier is a forward-deployed asset, its mobility and independence making it a much more difficult target for ballistic missile and terrorist attacks than fixed land-bases and ground forces.[118] The *Ocean Wanderer* can be mobile but only when five tugboats are pulling it, and even then the hotel is primarily stationary, spending most of its time moored at one of five locations.

F.P.1 Does Not Answer is an A-picture, but several successful B-movies in a variety of genres from the thirties through the fifties also qualify as Cussleresque films, with perhaps the best (yet oddest) example being *The Mummy's Hand* (1940). This unofficial sequel[119] to *The Mummy* (1932), starring Boris Karloff, features two prologues, the first set in the recent past. Professor Andoheb (George Zucco) arrives in Egypt to replace the dying high priest of Karnak (Eduardo Ciannelli), a cult dedicated to protecting the ancient burial site of Princess Ananka in the Hills of the Seven Jackals. This prologue wraps around the second prologue as the high priest tells Andoheb about Ananka's death and a sacrilege committed by her grieving lover,

Kharis (Tom Tyler), a priest caught stealing sacred tana leaves from the Temple of Karnak. Tana leaves possess the power to restore life, and, as punishment for his misdeed, Kharis is tasked with being the eternal guardian of Ananka's tomb. Kharis is buried alive, minus his tongue, but with a bountiful supply of the now-extinct tana leaves. One of the most sacred tasks of the high priest of Karnak is to brew three tana leaves each night during the cycle of the full moon, and administer the fluid to Kharis to keep his dormant mummy alive. If necessary, the high priest can brew nine leaves to give Kharis motion, but under no condition is Kharis ever to receive more than nine tana leaves or he will become an uncontrollable monster.

The film jumps to the present (1940), where we meet our heroes in a Cairo bazaar. Down-on-their-luck Americans Steve Banning (Dick Foran) and Babe Jenson (Wallace Ford) are brothers-in-arms in the Pitt and Giordino tradition, Banning the tall, athletic leader who looks and talks like someone from California, and Jenson the shorter, burly sidekick from Brooklyn.

Banning is an educated young Pitt archetype hero who has accomplished several impressive feats in his field of archaeology, an occupation that often finds him straying from the highroads and bringing back secrets from lost places and from the past. Banning is also intuitive, trusting his feelings enough to risk the last of his and Jenson's money to buy a potshard which he is convinced contains a clue to the location of the legendary lost tomb of Ananka. Even when Andoheb, who is now the head of the Cairo Museum and one of the world's most respected authorities on Egyptian archaeology, insists that the potshard is a forgery and refuses to finance an expedition, Banning remains confident that he is right.[120] Banning is honest but willing to bend the rules if the end result satisfies his moral compass, like letting Jenson entice a stage magician and fellow Brooklynite Tom Sullivan, a.k.a. The Great Solvani (Cecil Kellaway), into a barroom conversation that leads to Sullivan financing their expedition.[121] Later, when Sullivan's daughter, Marta (Peggy Moran), tells Banning her father spent the last of their money on the expedition, Banning confesses he and Jenson thought Sullivan was wealthy. It is obvious that Banning would return the Sullivans' money if he could, but it has been spent on buying equipment and hiring men. Banning is also resourceful. The potshard leads the expedition to a mountain and what appears to be a dead end, a small cave where they find a man's mummy (Kharis) and an urn filled with strange leaves (the tana leaves). Later, after Sullivan is nearly strangled and Marta is carried off by Kharis, Banning remains calm and works the problem, discerning more clues from the potshard that point to a secret passage leading from the cave to Ananka's tomb. Although the results are more supernatural than what happens in Cussler's novels, Banning's convenient discovery of the potshard in the bazaar is reminiscent of numerous convenient discoveries in many of Cussler's adventures, as well as an example of the past reaching out from history to affect the present.

The number of Cussleresque movies declined during the sixties and most of the seventies, but the same year Marble Arch released *Raise the Titanic*, a lesser-known British adventure film set in the North Atlantic, *ffolkes*,[122] demonstrated some better ways to adapt an adventure novel. Whereas Marble Arch hired the untested Kennedy and Jameson, Cinema Seven Productions hired veteran adventure screenwriter Jack Davies to adapt his novel *Esther, Ruth, and Jennifer*, and director Andrew V. MacLaglen, whose credits included *McLintock!* (1963), *Shenandoah* (1965) and *Hellfighters* (1968). Cinema Seven also cast a number of dependable actors with experience making adventure films: James Mason (*North by Northwest, 20,000 Leagues Under* the Sea, *Journey to the Center of the Earth*) and David Hedison (*The Son of Robin Hood, The Lost World, Lie and Let Die*, and television's *Voyage to the Bottom of the Sea*). The casting director took a risk by hiring actors against type: Anthony Perkins, best known as *Psycho*'s Norman Bates, plays ruthless mastermind Lou Kramer, Roger Moore, then at the pinnacle of his James Bond popularity, plays eccentric and hirsute Rufus Excalibur ffolkes. The film also revels in the same kind of classic movie banter and audacious action that Marble Arch ignored in its adaptation of Cussler's novel.

The straightforward plot of *ffolkes* will never be confused with any of Cussler's complicated adventures. The film focuses on the hijacking of the world's largest oil platform, *Jennifer*, and its oil-drilling rig, *Ruth*, by extortionists demanding £25 million. If the bad guys do not get their money they will blow up *Jennifer* and *Ruth* at prearranged schedules with limpet mines. There are no prologues set in the past, history never reaches out to affect the present, and no secrets or treasures are recovered from lost places, but many of the film's elements are Cussleresque. Even though the plot takes place in a relatively short period of time in a relatively small location it behaves like Cussler's Structure-B plot by following several VP characters, including ffolkes, Kramer, and a brave young member of *Jennifer's* crew named Sanna (Lea Brodie). Cussler enjoys giving characters and vehicles unusual or endearing names, like Perlmutter and *The Wallowing Windbag*, and, in *ffolkes*, we have the titular hero and his private band of aquatic commandos known as "ffolkes' ffusiliers." As for ffolkes, at first glance he may not seem to fit the Pitt archetype. A misogynistic Scottish lord who prefers cats to people, he drinks Scotch whiskey out of the bottle at almost any time of the day, does needlepoint in order to concentrate, and is anything but self-effacing or humble.[123] In fact, he is as belligerent and brash as Conan Doyle's Challenger and Nigel Kneal's Professor Bernard Quatermass. But, at second glance, it is hard to deny that ffolkes resembles what Sandecker's gruffer cousin from Great Britain might look like; he is also as colorful and eccentric as Perlmutter or Pitt's uncle Percy. Very little is revealed about ffolkes's past, but it is obvious that he is educated, intuitive[124] and honorable,[125] as well as a realist and a cynic who is self-reliant and patriotic. Like Pitt, ffolkes may have difficulty behaving himself around authority figures and does not approve of everything his government does, but he loves his country and will defend it with his life. He is also a master strategist and, as Kramer finds out, an indefatigable adversary.

Although it is a solid adventure film, *ffolkes* did not perform well enough at the box office to qualify as a success, and the same could be said for Disney's animated adventure[126] *Atlantis: The Lost Empire* (2001). Helmed by Kirk Wise and Gary Trousdale, whose credits include *Beauty and the Beast* (1991), the first animated movie to be nominated for Best Picture by the Academy Awards, *Atlantis: The Lost Empire* is an even bigger production than *F.P.1 Does Not Answer*, with a budget of over $100 million and five-year production schedule. When production was in full swing, 350 animators, artists and technicians were involved. Among these specialists were John Emerson, who created a boustrophedon alphabet for Atlantis (including a letter "A" that serves as a treasure map) and linguist Marc Okrand, who created an Atlantean language and also served as a model for the film's bookish hero, Milo Thatch (Michael J. Fox). Disney planned to launch an animated television series based on the film and incorporate elements from Atlantis into a new version of its Disneyland Submarine Voyage, which had closed in 1998, but when the movie grossed only $84 million, work on both the series and the ride were cancelled.[127]

Except for a prologue, *Atlantis: The Lost Empire* is set in 1914, a fitting time that demonstrates the creators' familiarity with classic adventure literature, being only two years removed from the introduction of Challenger in *The Lost World* and taking place during the same decade that heroes such as John Carter, Tarzan, O'Rourke and Moore first appeared in the early pulp magazines.[128] The creators also appear to be familiar with Cussler's adventures. *Atlantis: The Lost Empire* contains many Cussleresque elements, including several ingredients from Cussler's Structure-A formula, a Pitt archetype hero and at least part of the adventure takes place under the sea. There are no government agencies like NUMA, but, as on the *Seaview*, the Atlantis expedition starts off operating with crewmen in uniforms and commanders designated by rank. The expedition also includes a colorful collection of supporting characters that excel at B-movie dialogue. The Atlantis expedition's answer to the *Seaview*, a steampunk submarine called the *Ulysses*, is a stunning technological achievement that would have made Frank Reade, Jr., proud, and rivals Cabrillo's *Enterprise* on the high seas.

Examining a couple of these elements more closely, in the film's Structure-A plot Milo is introduced immediately and is the story's VP character. Milo is drawn into the adventure (although not by the Villain) and there is at least one traitor in the expedition. There is a dark descent wherein the riddle of Atlantis's greatest secret is revealed, Milo defeats the Villain, and the plot's loose ends are tied up in an epilogue.

Like Crusader's *Sahara*, two prologues were created for *Atlantis: The Lost Empire*, but only one appears in the theatrical release. This prologue, set in an unspecified ancient past, shows the near-destruction of Atlantis by a massive tidal wave. Instead of being caused by a comet, as in *Atlantis Found*, this wave is triggered by a massive energy blast. But just before Atlantis is flooded a force field created by a huge crystal, called the Heart of Atlantis, shields it as it vanishes underwater. In contrast, the deleted prologue, which is set aboard a Viking ship in AD 977, is less fantastic and, therefore, more traditionally Cussleresque. In a scene that recalls how the captain of the *Flying Dutchman* got himself in trouble, the leader of a Viking war party berates his ship's crew as they search for Atlantis and an incredible treasure. The captain is following directions in a codex called *The Shepherd's Journal*[129] but ignores its warnings that the gate to Atlantis is guarded by a monster. As a Gothic storm rages, a Leviathan[130] attacks the Vikings, dragging everyone beneath the water with its tentacles just before an energy blast obliterates the vessel. Somehow, the codex survives incineration and is hurled miles away before splashing in the water to float off to parts unknown.[131]

As for the film's hero, there is no denying that Milo looks more like Rudi Gunn than Pitt. Thin and not particularly tall, Milo wears glasses, is brilliant and can be resourceful in a pinch. Milo works in Languages and Cartography at the Smithsonian Institution, which makes him a public servant, but he is neither in the military nor a veteran. Like Casey and Lacey Nicefolk, Milo has a shadow side in his lineage, his late grandfather Thaddeus Thatch,[132] an explorer dismissed by the academic community because he believed Atlantis actually exists and that its remains can be found beneath the Earth. Inspired by his grandfather, Milo does not hesitate to stray from the highroads when Thaddeus's wealthy (and possibly eccentric) college friend Preston B. Whitmore (John Mahoney) asks him to join an expedition to find Atlantis. Whitmore, the story's Wise Old Man, is reminiscent of Sandecker in many ways. Both are shorter than average and bearded, although Whitmore has white hair and is a few years older than the admiral.[133] But, like Sandecker, he keeps fit through regular and strenuous exercise, in Whitmore's case, yoga. Whitmore can also be as charming and devious as Sandecker, and, like the admiral, there is never any doubt that he is in command of any situation at which he is present.

Years earlier, Whitmore bet Thaddeus that if *The Shepherd's Journal* was ever located then Whitmore would finance a search for Atlantis, but by the time Thaddeus found the *Journal* his spirit had been broken by the scientific community and he refused to lead the expedition. Thaddeus bequeathed the *Journal* to Milo, and now Whitmore wants Milo to help vindicate Thaddeus.[134] (In this way, *The Shepherd's Journal* represents the past reaching out to affect the present.) Milo never has an opportunity to demonstrate if he is a patriot; however, he is clearly an optimistic dreamer as opposed to a cynic or realist, and it is just as obvious that he is no manhunter. But when Atlantis and his new love, Princess Kida (Cree Summer), are threatened by the traitors in the expedition, Milo becomes a worthy adversary to stop them.

Even with these Cussleresque elements and elements borrowed from Verne,[135] Burroughs,[136] Grell,[137] *Star Trek*[138] and *Stargate*,[139] *Atlantis: The Lost Empire* begins to lose steam after a rousing Act One, when the expedition arrives in Atlantis, and never regains this momentum, a common complaint of Lost World stories.[140] The same cannot be said for Disney's next Cussleresque adventure, *National Treasure*. With worldwide earnings totaling approximately $347 million,[141] this blockbuster demonstrates just how successful a Cussler film could be at the box office.

The film starts with two prologues, one wrapped around the other like *The Mummy's Hand*, and, in the best Gothic tradition, both begin on dark and stormy nights. The first prologue takes place in 1974, in the attic of John Adams Gates (Christopher Plummer), father of Patrick Henry Gates (Jon Voight) and grandfather of ten-year-old Benjamin Franklin Gates (Hunter Gomez). The past wastes no time reaching out to affect the present as Ben seems drawn to the attic to look for a scrapbook about his family's history. The Gates have been notorious for searching for the legendary Knights Templar treasure since young Thomas Gates (Jason Earles) supposedly received a clue as to its whereabouts ("The secret lies with Charlotte") on a rainy night from a dying Charles Carroll, a Freemason[142] (a brotherhood founded by the Knights Templar) and the last surviving signer of the Declaration of Independence. John finds Ben in the attic with the scrapbook and, to the accompaniment of a thunderstorm, first tells his inquisitive grandson about Thomas and then about the Templar treasure, the historical events appearing in a second prologue made up of a montage of flashbacks that span from ancient Egypt to the Revolutionary War. Patrick finds his father and son in the attic and tells Ben that the only thing the family's search for the treasure has accomplished is to curse the Gates with poverty and shame. Six generations have tried to locate the treasure, including Patrick, who hunted 20 years until, like Thaddeus Thatch, ridicule from academia broke his spirit. After Patrick leaves the attic, an undaunted Ben asks his grandfather if the Gates are knights, like the Templars who swore to defend the ancient treasure. A delighted John asks, "Would you like to be?" The prologues conclude with John dubbing Ben a knight.

The story jumps ahead 30 years. Ben (Nicolas Cage) has grown up to become a Pitt archetype hero. A cryptologist with degrees in mechanical engineering from MIT and American history from Georgetown, Ben is a navy veteran who attended the Naval Diving and Salvage Training Center. He is also self-reliant, self-effacing, self-sacrificing, educated, intuitive, wisecracking and adept at MacGyverisms (examples include using a bottle of water for a magnifying glass, using the bulletproof case housing the Declaration of Independence for a body shield and using household products to concoct a reagent to view an Ottendorf cipher on the back of the Declaration). Ben is a Boy Scout and, contrary to what his critics believe, he is a realist, but his faith and determination in finding the treasure demonstrates that he has some Peter Pan in him. A walking encyclopedia of American history, Ben may also be more of an old soul than Pitt.[143] Ben does not work for the government, nor is he a manhunter or a nemesis, but he is a patriot who admires the best attributes of the founding fathers,[144] and is as much a defender of the realm as Pitt.[145] Perhaps the best comparison between the two can be found in *Vixen 03*, in which Pitt joins Giordino, Sandecker, Steiger and Bass in destroying the Quick Death organism, even though they all know they will probably be arrested and branded as traitors. In *National Treasure*, Ben risks the same fate when he steals the Declaration of Independence so his former benefactor, Ian Howe (Sean Bean), cannot steal it first.[146] If things go awry, Pitt and his compatriots will only be able to take comfort in knowing that public and moral opinion will stand on their side,[147] but Ben takes comfort in recalling the courage of men like Carroll who "did what was considered wrong, in order to do what they knew was right." With one important exception, Ben, like Pitt, does not care what people think about him, and that exception is that Ben wants to vindicate his family by finding the treasure and removing its curse of shame. Ben's search for the treasure also takes him from the highroads to uncover secrets found in places that have become lost to history: a merchant vessel (the *Charlotte*) shipwrecked in the polar ice cap along Canada's Atlantic coast; and a cavernous secret chamber excavated by Freemasons, beneath the crypts of New York City's Trinity Church.

The colorful supporting cast is also Cussleresque, beginning with Ben's sidekick Riley Poole (Justin Bartha), a computer whiz Ian hired to help search for the *Charlotte*. Riley is no brother-in-color but he is as sarcastic as Giordino and Zavala, and, like Giordino and Zavala, will *kvetch* but still willingly follows his friend into any situation, even when all he has to go on is his blind faith in Ben.

Dr. Abigail Chase (Diane Kruger) is every inch a Cussler heroine. A blonde rather than a redhead, Abigail is a beautiful, classy, independent and likable professional working at the National Archive. Abigail is also more than capable of holding her own in a man's world. When the FBI apprehends Ben it is Abigail who thinks outside the box to broker a deal with Ian to rescue him. Abigail has no noticeable physical imperfections, but she does have one distinctive tag. A German native who immigrated to America while still a child, she has a light but noticeable accent.

Ian Howe is a Janus villain in the Rondheim tradition, a corporate businessman with a shady past that includes activities of "questionable legality," and with his British accent, blond good looks, wealth and active lifestyle he is also reminiscent of Sir Richard Branson. Ian is not as educated as Ben, but he is clever enough to keep one step behind him during the search for the treasure, and unlike Rondheim, whose expertise in poetry gives him a patina of civility, Ian has a genuine decent side. When the arduous search for the *Charlotte* turns up more clues instead of the treasure, Ian not only remains upbeat but gives Ben a pep talk. Later, during a visit to the Franklin Institute, in Philadelphia, Ian watches a schoolboy (Yves Michel-Beechen) jotting down notes while leaving the museum, as-yet-unaware that the boy is not working on a school assignment but actually helping Ben. While Ian's henchmen grumble about visiting a museum, Ian takes the time to smile at the boy. Moments like these make Ian much more frightening when his dark side gets the better of him, especially after his best friend, Shaw (David Dayan Fisher), is killed during the dark descent beneath Trinity Church. Grieving for Shaw, Ian makes it clear to Ben, Riley, Abigail and Patrick (whom Ian has abducted) that he is in a murdering mood and will kill anyone giving him even the slightest provocation.

Several thematic preoccupations and plot elements that appear in Cussler's stories also appear in *National Treasure*, beginning with history reaching out to affect the future. There is the scrapbook in John Gates's attic but also the clues left by the Freemason members of

America's founding fathers.[148] These clues, the history of the Templar treasure and Ben's hunt for the treasure imbue the film with motifs from fairy tales (e.g., knights, quests, kingdoms), myths and legends (e.g., the purported origins of the Freemasons, the Templar treasure itself, lost artifacts from places like the Library of Alexandria scattered among the treasure) and the classic hero cycle (e.g., Ben's call to adventure in the attic; his passing tests along the road of trials by solving the riddle of the Freemasons' clues; the dark descent beneath Trinity Church), including Jungian archetypes like the Wise Old Men (first John Gates, and, eventually, the Father figure Patrick Gates), a trickster (Riley) and a benign Goddess figure (Abigail). There are also Gothic elements, such as inclement weather underscoring situations (e.g., the storms in the prologues), allusions to tombs and graves (e.g., frozen corpses of the *Charlotte*'s crew found in the shipwreck; the crypt beneath Trinity Church; a chase through an old Philadelphia cemetery) and several settings that may not be medieval but are historical (e.g., Independence Hall, Trinity Church, Old North Church), some of which even contain secret passages. There are also ancient riddles and, if Patrick is to be believed, a curse. As in Cussler's adventures there are a number of clever hairbreadth escapes, such as Ben knowing enough about Revolutionary-era American shipbuilding to locate and flee through a smuggler's hold in the *Charlotte* before some gunpowder, ignited during a showdown with Ian and his henchmen, explodes. Finally Ben, like Pitt and the Fargos, is not hunting the treasure for either wealth or fame.[149] He believes that the treasure and all it has to offer "belongs to the world,"[150] which makes him a true knight.

Parodies

With an estimated worldwide readership of 250 million[151] and an average of four to five new novels appearing on bestseller lists each year, Cussler's adventures and his most famous hero have become a fixture of contemporary popular culture. When historical treasures are recovered, especially on shipwrecks, it is often referred to as being like something in a Clive Cussler novel.[152] These distinctive adventures have been lampooned in parodies, including *Moby Dick II: Raise the Pequod!*, the centerpiece of the anthology *The Book of Sequels* (1990),[153] and in "Daus Mouse," the premiere episode of the Warner Bros.–Steven Spielberg cartoon series *Pinky and the Brain* (1995–1998).[154]

Moby Dick II: Raise the Pequod! is purported to be "the first of a projected multivolume collection of fast-paced, edge-of-your-seat sequels to classic but sometimes stuffy works by our nation's greatest writers." Its hero is Commander Dipp Schmidt, a "rugged, 40-year-old former Navy SEAL commando" who takes orders from Admiral Charles "Chuck" Chairweather, who tells Schmidt, "You're insubordinate, Dipp, but you have a way of getting results." Dipp comes to the aid of a Woods Hole scientist named Ishmael (the great-great-great grandson of the narrator of *Moby-Dick*) trying to unlock the alphabet to communicating with whales, which in turn could give the United States a way of detecting Russian submarines. This alphabet is carved on a broken piece of whalebone that was part of Captain Ahab's peg-leg, and the only way to recover that broken piece is to raise the *Pequod*. Dipp succeeds against all odds (and the best efforts of the Russians to stop him) thanks to Queequeg (descendant of the Queequeg from *Moby-Dick*) and his beautiful daughter Sheequeg, who is first heard speaking in "a husky female voice." Cussler's references to Pitt's tags and the author's endearing but sometimes awkward choice of words are also lampooned. After a sexual interlude with Petty Officer Doris

Chestley, "Dipp winked at her with one of his cold, gray eyes and then blew her a kiss that neatly snapped off both of her earrings." Later, Chestley ponders Dipp's "two men" personality. "She had seen Dipp's warm side; she never wanted to see the cold side that she knew lay hidden beneath the surface, brutally defying the elementary rules of heat transfer between adjacent layers." As for Dipp's ability for beating the odds, he admits, "I'll concede it's a long shot—hell, it would be like winning Monopoly with one house each on Baltic and Mediterranean, the Waterworks, and a single railroad." The adventure also includes a clever cameo by Cussler, not in person but as a salvage vessel, the USS *Clive Cussler*. The parody concludes with an invitation to read Dipp's next adventure *Moby Dick III: Resink the Bismarck!*

None of Cussler's characters appear in "Daus Mouse," but it is so reverential it borders on being an homage. The series *Pinky and the Brain* features a pair of genetically altered lab mice that have gained consciousness. Pinky (Rob Paulsen) is good-natured but dimwitted, while Brain (Maurice LaMarche) is a demented genius bent on taking over the world. In "Daus Mouse," Brain concocts a plan to create an army of human slaves by feeding them pancakes laced with the secretion of the Peruvian Gaokin frog mixed with meat from a rare deep-water white crab. A massive number of these crabs reside inside the wreck of the *Titanic*, so Pinky and Brain confiscate a submarine "to raise the hull of that sorrowful ship!" Their trip is picked up by the CIA, which enlists the aid of Captain Jack MacGuire (James Belushi) to destroy the submarine. In a nice tip-of-the-hat to reality and to Cussler, the *Titanic* is in one piece when Pinky and Brain arrive, but as the ship begins to rise it breaks in half, with the stern half falling back to the ocean floor.

Recap

The history of adaptations of Cussler's adventures is brief and has not always been satisfying, but it is definitely not discouraging. While there is little to recommend the film *Raise the Titanic* besides John Barry's music and the scenes with Bigalow and the raising of the White Star liner, the *Best Seller Show Case* adaptation is quite good when its medium's restraints are taken into consideration. As for the film *Sahara*, it is not only better than its detractors insist, but performed well enough to justify a more modestly budgeted sequel. If that seems far-fetched compare the numbers for *Sahara* with *Star Trek: The Motion Picture*, which had a budget of $35 million (a substantial amount in 1979, as Marble Arch can attest) and earned $85 million,[155] a disappointing profit when contrasted with the film that inspired its production, *Star Wars*, which earned $307 million.[156] Nevertheless, *Star Trek: The Motion Picture* did enough things right to prompt the production of a sequel, *Star Trek II: The Wrath of Khan*, which had a smaller budget, of $11.2 million, earned nearly $79 million, and is considered one of the most successful films in the *Star Trek* franchise.[157]

There are also many successful Cussleresque movies that are not adaptations of any of his adventures, but feature many of the same elements. These include big-budget motion pictures as well as B-movies and serials from the thirties, forties and fifties, including *F.P.1 Does Not Answer* and *The Mummy's Hand* to modern films, such as *Atlantis: The Lost Continent* and *National Treasure*. The success of *National Treasure* and its Cussleresque sequel *National Treasure: Book of Secrets* (budget = $130 million, worldwide gross = $457 million)[158] demonstrate, like *Sahara*, that there is a market for adaptations of Cussler's adventures when they are faithful to their source material.

Afterword
A Review of the Review

> I may surprise you.—Dirk Pitt[1]
>
> Women loved him; enemies respected him; associates idolized him.
> —Robert Sampson[2]

When it comes to adventure heroes Cussler gets it, and the Pitt archetype hero is proof of this.

The Pitt archetype hero is a Boy Scout who fixes a stranger's flat tire on a rainy night, or sticks his neck out for them when no one else will, and he is a patriotic hero in the southwestern American folk tradition, brave and cool under pressure, ready to save civilization while treasuring the time he spends away from it.

The Pitt archetype hero can be a grand adventure hero, accomplishing Herculean tasks, an action hero going toe to toe with brutal and merciless enemies, and a wisecracking hero, à la Groucho Marx or Bugs Bunny, capable of cutting smarmy know-it-alls down to size with the right remark at the right moment. He is also a human hero capable of poor judgment calls. Boneheaded plays make the Pitt archetype fallible and more believable than intimidating and less-accessible heroes, like Holmes and Doc Savage. Cussler's adventures may be incredible, but his heroes are never larger than life.

The Pitt archetype hero lives in a world where anachronisms can reach out from the past to affect the present, like a World War I German airplane strafing an air force base, a treasure ship rotting away in the green hell of a South American jungle, or the remnants of a Viking colony turning up inside a New England cavern.[3] And while other action heroes occasionally do the least predictable thing to escape death or save the day, Pitt will almost always do something totally unpredictable. As he himself confesses in *Sahara*, "I have an aversion to pursuing the expected."[4]

Dirk Pitt is a hero in the best pulp tradition, a wonder of accomplishment, financially well to do and physically astounding, although these attributes are tempered when compared to the likes of Zorro, The Shadow and Doc Savage,[5] and that is no accident. Pulp adventures were "rooted in the immediate past" and "influenced by Stevenson and Kipling, [Conan] Doyle, Old Sleuth, Haggard, [and] Buffalo Bill,"[6] but they also evolved to suit their times. Pulp heroes became a little more adult, the settings a little more exotic, and the action a little more violent. Today, when Cussler creates a thrilling story with a modern setting and contemporary characters in the old fashion adventure tradition, he is changing the adventure story to suit his times. Adventure stories are the oldest type of story, and Cussler's novels are the most recent development of this perennial genre that has been "polished by accumulated centuries of story telling."⁷

One can find traces of Pitt in classic films and B-movie serials from Hollywood's Golden Age. People respond to Cussler's novels because his adventures feature many of the same components that Gianetti lists as hallmarks of American movies:

> [They are] profoundly democratic ... overtly hostile toward rank, privilege, and authority. Almost invariably its sympathies are with the underdog and the oppressed. Conflicts between the individual and society are usually resolved in favor of the individuals.... [Protagonists] are often rebels, outsiders, and inner-directed loners ... and their morality is often based on a private code rather than a consensus.... A romantic yearning for the extraordinary is the rule rather than the exception, and this theme is frequently expressed with lyrical fervor ... encumbered by few traditions of restraint, decorum, or "good taste"; genres are mixed with casual nonchalance; the fantastic and the real are fused with matter-of-fact facility. Impatient of nuances, our filmmakers prefer bold, sweeping themes and strident clashes.⁸

That said, Cussler's best and most famous hero, Dirk Pitt, is unique among Cussler's other creations, a knight-errant and a defender of the realm, unafraid to stray from the highroads to bring back secrets from lost places, as well as an indefatigable nemesis and a merciless manhunter. Sometimes, Austin will stray from the highroads and bring back a secret, but, as head of NSAT, he is primarily a defender of the realm. The same is true for Cabrillo, an EMT for a troubled world. Bell is a manhunter who will occasionally defend the realm, as will Sam and Remi Fargo, but the Fargos are primarily looking to take any detour they can that strays from the highroads. As for the nice folks twins, they are after pure adventure in their own fantasyland, although in the process they do learn one secret (the machine that turns toys into life-size anthropomorphic vehicles) and they have been known to do a little realm defending.

This archetype has been popular for over 40 years, but, as stated in the preface, critics ignore the adventures of Pitt and Cussler's other heroes in spite of this success because Cussler writes popular fiction.

Entertaining readers has never been enough to satisfy the dictates of some critics, even when a story has other virtues. *The Woman in White* is one of the early masterpieces of detection literature,⁹ an accomplishment deserving of some critical attention. But, when it was first published, a *Dublin University Magazine* reviewer declared that, without the plot, there "was nothing left to examine,"¹⁰ while a reviewer for the *Saturday Review* dismissed Collins as just an "admirable story-teller" with a line of reasoning that contemporary critics might level at Cussler:

> He is ... a very ingenious constructor; but ingenious construction is not high art, just as cabinet-making and joining is not high art. Mechanical talent is what every great artist ought to possess. Mechanical talent, however, is not enough to entitle a man to rank as a great artist. When we have said that Mr. Wilkie Collins succeeds in keeping up our excitement by the happy way in which he interweaves with mystery incident just sufficiently probable not to be extravagant, and that he is an adept at administering continual stimulants to our attention, we have said all.¹¹

Collins's critics considered novels to be manufactured products, and a "sensation novel," like *The Woman in White*, carried "the scent of industry and trade" and "blurred stylistic distinctions" by drawing "on melodrama, the new journalism, penny dreadfuls, blending 'high' and 'low' art to create a wider audience for the novel."¹² Times change, however, and today most reviewers no longer consider the novel to be a manufactured product, but Cussler does. He is, in fact, a proud commercial writer who believes he is creating a product that relies as much on his marketing experience as it does on his writing talents to succeed.[13] To accomplish this, Cussler draws on the same sources that Collins and other Victorian sensation writers did, along with dime novels, pulp magazines, motion pictures and B-movie serials, and in the process he has created a worldwide audience of fans that are as enthusiastic as Baker Street Irregulars are about Holmes.

These fans demonstrate their enthusiasm in more ways than just reading Cussler's adventures. Many frequent the numerous websites about Cussler and his works such as:

- clivecussler.com: the official Clive Cussler website
- clivecusslerbestsellers.com: an official website for Clive Cussler's novels
- clive-cusslerbooks.com: an official website about Cussler and his novels
- www.cusslermen.com: a website for collectors of Cussler's books and memorabilia
- www.cusslersociety.com: official website for the Cussler Collector's Society, sponsor of the annual Adventure Writers Competition and Clive Cussler Convention
- www.doxawatches.com: where fans can buy their own Clive Cussler edition SUB 1200T Doxa diver's watch like Pitt wears
- fanfiction.net: hosts a fan fiction library including many Dirk Pitt pieces
- numa.net: official website for Cussler's 501(c)(3) non-profit organization dedicated to the preservation of maritime history

Fans can also become friends on Cussler's Facebook page, and read about the man and his many novels on Wikipedia.

A few fans have even taken to writing books about Cussler and his works. Wayne Valero is the most proficient to date, with *The Collector's Guide to Clive Cussler* (2000), *From The Mediterranean Caper to Black Wind: A Bibliography of Clive Cussler* (2005), *The Adventure Writing of Clive Cussler* (2007) and *Collecting Cussler: An Ethical Approach* (2012). Tony Krome and Sean Ellis delve deep into the secrets buried in Cussler's writing, in *The Clive Cussler Code* (2005), and, as of this writing, Stuart Leuthner, author of *Wheels: A Passion for Collecting Cars* (2005), has completed a Cussler biography and is looking for a publisher.

The Clive Cussler Society's annual convention is a three-day event, where fans have the chance to meet Cussler, members of his family, and his collaborators. During the convention, people can hear guest speakers, attend book signings, purchase books and memorabilia, and enjoy dinners as well as special events. For example, the 2007 convention in Charleston, South Carolina, included a tour of the *Hunley*. The convention began in 2005 and, except for the 2007 and 2009 conventions in San Diego, it has been held in either Scottsdale, Arizona, or Denver, Colorado.

The Cussler Museum (www.cusslermuseum.com) in Arvada, Colorado, was founded by the author, and is open to the public from May to September. The museum is dedicated to the preservation of classic automobiles and displays more than a hundred cars, built from 1906 to 1965. A few of these have been showcased in Pitt's adventures and many appear in the coffee-table book, *Built for Adventure: The Classic Automobiles of Clive Cussler and Dirk Pitt*.

When all is said and done, Cussler's readers are fans of his adventures and his heroes because Cussler gets it. Cussler gets what people want to read and he gives it to them. Cussler admits as much at the end of *Shock Wave* when Sandecker tells Loren, "To Dirk, every hour has a mystery to be solved, every day a challenge to conquer." Sandecker and Loren envy Pitt, and when Loren wonders why that is, Sandecker tells her, "There's a little of Dirk Pitt in all of us."[14]

Cussler tells people that he is an advertising copywriter who got lucky,[15] and that is true. There is no denying he was at the right place with the right book like *Raise the Titanic!* at the right time, but anyone can decide they want to write modern versions of old fashion adventure stories, and anyone can perform market research, but not everyone has the empathy to understand what readers want and the talent to manufacture that product. More than that, not everyone has what it takes to create a hero like Dirk Pitt.

Cussler does.

Cussler not only gets it, he can do it.

Cussler calls that luck, but maybe, just maybe, it is Fate or coincidence (take your pick).

Chapter Notes

Preface

1. Herman Melville, *Moby-Dick* (New York: Bantam Books, 1986), p. 283.
2. "Introduction," *Moby-Dick*, pp. viii, xii.
3. Ibid., p. viii.
4. "Herman Melville's *Moby-Dick*," *Moby-Dick*, pp. 581–582.
5. Robert Sampson, *Yesterday's Faces: Vol. III, From the Dark Side* (Bowling Green, OH: Bowling Green State University Popular Press, 1983), p. 179.
6. An observation made in regard to the adventure literature of Rafael Sabatini in "Swashbuckling Hero the World Forgot," http://icliverpool.icnetwork.co.uk/expats/localhistory/tm_objectid=14211800%26method=full%26siteid=50061%26page=1%26headline=swashbuckling-hero-the-world-forgot-name_page.html.
7. Sampson, *Yesterday's Faces: Vol. III*, p. 179. In *Toxic Feedback: Helping Writers Survive and Thrive* (Lebanon, NH: University Press of New England, 2005), p. 2, freelance writer and editor Joni B. Cole alludes to this type of material when she describes the work of a fiction teacher who "had all the markings of a genius, literary and otherwise. His novels broke ground and enjoyed dismal sales."
8. Brian Dochtery, "Grace Under Fire: Reading Alistair MacLean," *Twentieth Century Suspense* (1990), p. 203.
9. Ibid.
10. According to Cussler's bio page at the Penguin Group website, he is considered the "dean of adventure writers" and his novels have sold more than 125 million copies in over a hundred countries and been translated into 40 languages ("Clive Cussler/About the Author," http://us.penguingroup.com/static/packages/us/clivecussler/bio.html). These figures may not be accurate, having been called into question in 2007 during a trial between Cussler and the producers of the film adaptation of *Sahara* (http://www.variety.com/article/VR117958535.html?categoryid=22&cs=1), but by all accounts they appear to be accurate enough to support Cussler's popularity as an adventure writer. For instance, in the review book *Action Figures* (New York: Palgrave Macmillan, 2006), pp. 114–15, Mark Gallagher writes that Cussler's novels are "enormously popular works" and Cussler remains "among the most popular authors of contemporary fiction."
11. In *Twentieth Century Suspense*, p. 205, British scholar and critic Brian Dochtery writes, "Unlike crime writers such as [Raymond] Chandler or [Agatha] Christie, or thriller writers such as Ian Fleming, MacLean does not have a recurring named hero or central character with known attributes and characteristics who solves the case or averts the threat by employing his special or unique faculties." However, MacLean's heroes tend to be similar. So similar, in fact, that Docherty points out (on p. 223), "It would perhaps have been preferable if MacLean had acknowledged this, and used a series hero, rather than giving several different heroes a limp or a scarred face, or both." MacLean did have one hero appear in two books—Keith Mallory of *The Guns of Navarone* and *Force 10 from Navarone*—and, near the end of his life, MacLean was commissioned by an American film production company to write story outlines for a series about a fictional United Nations organization called UNACO.
12. Robert Sampson, *Yesterday's Faces: Vol. IV, The Solvers* (Bowling Green, OH: Bowling Green State University Popular Press, 1983), p. 15; Gallagher, *Action Figures*, p. 113. Gallagher adds (on p. 116) that Cussler's novels are "indebted to popular-fiction conventions" but "repeatedly reference cinematic masculinity as well."
13. In an email to the author, dated August 30, 2009, Mike Grell might have been talking about Pitt when he described his character Jon Sable as someone "capable of brutal violence and gentle humor."
14. Arlene Schmuland, "The Archival Image in Fiction: An Analysis and Annotated Bibliography," *The American Archivist* (Spring 1999): p. 26.
15. Norman J. Argyle and Gerald A. Merwin, "Fuzzy Lines: Using the Best-Selling Novel to Illustrate the Blurring Boundaries of 'Public,'" *Public Voices* IX, no. 2, pp. 46–60.
16. William G. Brozo and Ronald V Schmelzer, "Wildmen, Warriors and Lovers," *Journal of Adolescent & Adult Literacy* (September 1997): p. 5.
17. See author's questions to Cussler, August 2009.
18. Clive Cussler and Craig Dirgo, *Dirk Pitt & Clive Cussler Revealed!* (New York: Pocket Books, 1998), p. 74.
19. Gallagher, *Action Figures*, pp. 114–9, 144-6.
20. "Cussler's Writing Is Taken to Task," *Los Angeles Times*, April 11, 2007.
21. Gallagher, *Action Figures*, p. 146.
22. Peter Haining, *The Classic Era of Crime Fiction* (Chicago: Chicago Review Press, 2002), p. 193. This is how Richard Hannay's creator, John Buchan (*Prester John, 39 Steps, The Three Hostages*), describes dime novels, or what the British call "shockers."

23. Gallagher, *Action Figures*, pp. 144–5.
24. Bunting, "Cussler's Writing Is Taken to Task," *Los Angeles Times*, April 11, 2007.
25. Louis Gianetti, *Masters of American Cinema* (Upper Saddle River, NJ: Prentice Hall, 1981), Chapter 12, p. 9.
26. Ibid., p. 5.
27. Haining, *The Classic Era of Crime Fiction*, p. 125. Spillane actually did not mind bad reviews, saying that "if the critics blow me apart, that's fine. Every time they do, I just sell more millions of copies."
28. Letter to author, April 7, 2009.
29. George N. Dove, *Suspense in the Formula Story* (Bowling Green, OH: Bowling Green State University Popular Press, 1989), p. 2.
30. Note to author, September 14, 2009.
31. Camille Paglia, "My Conversation with Camille Paglia," *Limbaugh Letter*, October 1999, p. 10.
32. Ibid. In other words, the artist creates while "the commentator stands in a kind of a media role, in between the artwork and the audience, which is either the general audience or the students in the classroom. We're there to comment, to kibitz, to observe." There might be some people, including Cussler, who scoff at the idea of any adventure series creator working in a creative ferment, but I beg to differ. Allow me to pass along the following apocryphal incident as an example. In 1989, I approached Cussler about the idea of adapting his Pitt adventures into the comic-book medium. He was open to the idea and, at one point, sent me a letter, asking me to call him to discuss the topic. I called him the same morning I received his letter and happened to catch him while he was in the middle of writing. At first, he sounded dazed and did not recall my name or why I was calling, but after a few moments he remembered and apologized, explaining that when he is really into writing a scene he forgets about everything else going on around him. While this might not be the same degree of tension and mania Paglia was referring to while discussing Bob Dylan's "Desolation Row," such intense tunnel-vision certainly sounds like a good example of creative ferment.
33. Stephen King, *Danse Macabre* (Corunna, Spain: Everest House, 1981), pp. 19, 291–2.
34. Cussler thinks there is a chance. When I asked him this question, he replied, "I think Pitt will be around for a long time" (author's questions to Cussler, August 2009, p. 13).
35. From the 1890s to 1920, British author Thomas Hall Caine (the "Hommy-Beg," to whom Bram Stoker dedicated *Dracula*) was popular enough to earn a fortune and a knighthood, but less than ten years after his death, Caine's books, including *The Bondman* (1890), had become discarded relics of the bygone Victorian era (see Clive Bloom, *Bestsellers: Popular Fiction Since 1900* [New York: Palgrave Macmillan, 2002], p. 2). At about the same time, Robert W. Chambers was as popular in America as Stephen King is today, and while Chambers's *King in Yellow* (1895) continues to influence horror writers because it influenced H.P. Lovecraft (a virtually unknown writer until several years after his death in 1937), Chambers and his bestsellers are also forgotten today (see Alden Norton, ed., *Masters of Horror* [New York: Berkley, 1968], p. 88). Even MacLean, whose "work remains the epitome of the adventure story" (Bloom, *Bestsellers*, p. 176) and died in 1987, would have probably already followed Caine and Chambers into obscurity if not for such film adaptations as *The Guns of Navarone* (1961), *The Satan Bug* (1965), *Ice Station Zebra* (1968) and *Where Eagles Dare* (1968).
36. To give credit where credit is due, I am borrowing the term "negative evidence of scholarly production" from economist and author Thomas Sowell ("My Conversation with Thomas Sowell," *Limbaugh Letter*, June 2007, p. 9).
37. Cussler and Dirgo, *Clive Cussler & Dirk Pitt Revealed!*, p. 45.

Chapter 1

1. Charles Foley, Jon Lellenberg, and Daniel Stashower, "To Charlotte Drummond, Southsea, April 12, 1888," in *Arthur Conan Doyle: A Life in Letters* (New York: Penguin, 2007), p. 254.
2. Clive Cussler, *Valhalla Rising* (New York: Berkley, 2002) p. 476.
3. Dolores Johnson, "The Man Who Raised the Titanic—and a Small Fortune," *Reader's Digest*, May 1978, p. 32.
4. Jacqueline A. Jaffe, *Arthur Conan Doyle* (Boston: G. K. Hall, 1987), pp. 5–8. See also John Dickson Carr, *The Life of Sir Arthur Conan Doyle* (New York: Carroll & Graf, 1987), pp. 44–6.
5. Marilyn Cannaday, *Bigger Than Life: The Creator of Doc Savage* (Bowling Green, OH: Bowling Green State University Popular Press, 1990), pp. 6–16.
6. Wayne Valero, *The Adventure Writing of Clive Cussler* (Kearney, NE: Morris Publishing, 2007), p. 62.
7. Clive Cussler and Craig Dirgo, *Sea Hunters* (New York: Simon & Schuster, 1996), p. 17. See also Cussler and Dirgo, *Clive Cussler & Dirk Pitt Revealed!*, pp. 16, 20.
8. Clive Cussler, ed., "Introduction," *Thriller 2: Stories You Just Can't Put Down* (West Yorkshire, UK: Mira, 2009), pp. i–ii. See also Cussler and Dirgo, *Clive Cussler & Dirk Pitt Revealed!*, p. 46.
9. Wayne Valero points out in *The Adventure Writing of Clive Cussler* (p. 23) that during the late sixties, it was easier for Cussler to write an adventure tale than to actually get it published. "When I started out," he recalls, "people in publishing would say, 'Don't waste your time. Nobody buys adventure.'" Valero adds (p. 73) that, in the seventies, American publishers "believed that after the surfeit of such novels following World War II and the Korean War, [the adventure genre] was dead. Now it is again a booming market in all its varied forms. Cussler was one of those who helped revive interest in adventure novels."
10. Johnson, "The Man Who Raised the Titanic—and a Small Fortune," p. 32. In 2004, author and reviewer Douglas Winter (*Run, Revelations*) got a round of applause during his introduction of Cussler at the National Book Festival when he turned the famous Ajax slogan on its head and said, "We know there is nothing stronger than Dirk."
11. Ibid., p. 46.
12. Ibid., pp. 45–6.
13. Cussler and Dirgo, *Sea Hunters*, p. 17. Cussler writes, "Since I'm a Cancer, I've always had an affinity for water."

14. Cussler and Dirgo, *Clive Cussler & Dirk Pitt Revealed!*, pp. 26–8.
15. Ibid., p. 25.
16. Cussler and Dirgo, *Sea Hunters*, p. 1; Cussler and Dirgo, *Clive Cussler & Dirk Pitt Revealed!*, pp. 29, 32.
17. Foreword to Cussler, *Pacific Vortex* (New York: Bantam, 1979), p. v.
18. Cannaday, *Bigger Than Life*, pp. 173–181.
19. Carr, *The Life of Sir Arthur Conan Doyle*, pp. 45–6. It is also hard to imagine Dr. John Watson going by Conan Doyle's first choice of a name for his character: Ormond Sacker.
20. Philip Lisa and Lee Pfeiffer, *The Incredible World of 007: An Authorized Collection of James Bond* (New York: Citadel Press, 1992) p. 12.
21. Valero, *The Adventure Writing of Clive Cussler*, pp. 21–2.
22. From "Clive Cussler and *The Chase*," *Radioed Houston*, interview by Olivia Flores Alvarez, http://blogs.houstonpress.com/hairballs/2007/11/radio_houstoned_clive_cussler.php#more. Cussler contradicts this in a 1978 *Writer's Digest* article when he says, "I tried to analyze everything before I started the series.... I wanted a hero with one-syllable first and last names (like Bond), someone tall and dark because I think this type still makes the best hero" (Johnson, "The Man Who Raised the Titanic—and a Small Fortune," p. 32).
23. See Cussler and Dirgo, *Clive Cussler & Dirk Pitt Revealed!*, p. 73. Cussler claims that when he started writing, he and Pitt were both 36 years old, but in Pitt's third adventure, *Iceberg*, Lillie announces that Pitt is 32 (see p. 192).
24. Ibid. Cussler adds that he imagines there is more of himself in Pitt than Pitt would care to admit.
25. Ibid.
26. Ibid., pp. 39–41. Calling upon his knack for finding angles, Cussler got the job by overstating his qualifications.
27. Ibid., p. 51. Cussler's advertising work also won a first-place prize at the Chicago Film Festival.
28. Ibid., p. 44.
29. Valero, *The Adventure Writing of Clive Cussler*, p. 23. In between *Sea Dwellers* and *Pacific Vortex*, the book was given a variety of different titles. "It turned out that *Sea Dwellers* was rejected by every major publishing house he sent it to, so Cussler decided that maybe the title wasn't catchy enough. He sent it out again as *Rape of the Sea Dwellers*. After six months, when that didn't work, Cussler went with the even more lurid *Rape of the Perverted Sea Dwellers*. Needless to say, that didn't have them banging on his door either."
30. Ibid., pp. 22–3.
31. Cussler and Dirgo, *Clive Cussler & Dirk Pitt Revealed!*, pp. 28, 41. Pitt is also a lifelong body-surfer, a skill that saves his life in *Pacific Vortex* (see p. 4) and *Treasure of the Khan* (New York: Putnam, 2006), see p. 93.
32. Valero, *The Adventure Writing of Clive Cussler*, p. 24.
33. Cussler and Dirgo, *Clive Cussler & Dirk Pitt Revealed!*, p. 48.
34. Valero, *The Adventure Writing of Clive Cussler*, p. 27; "Interview with Dr. Clive Cussler," http://www.numa.net/articles/interview_with_dr_clive_cussler.html. Prior to wearing the Doxa, Pitt wears an Omega watch (see *The Mediterranean Caper*, p. 20).
35. Clive Cussler, *Iceberg* (New York: Berkley, 2006), p. 192.
36. RobertI, *Faces: Vol. IV, The Solvers* (Bowling Green, OH: Bowling Green State University Popular Press, 1983), p. 15. Prior to Drummond, it was not rare (but it was uncommon) for adventure series heroes to be military men or veterans. For example, Dr. John H. Watson is a veteran, but Sherlock Holmes never formally served in the military.
37. See Chapter 3 for more details about this innovation, one Clancy incorporated into his Jack Ryan character nearly a decade later. See also Argyle and Merwin, "Fuzzy Lines: Using the Best-Selling Novel to Illustrate the Blurring Boundaries of 'Public.'"
38. And McGee is middle-class right down to the houseboat he lives on, *The Busted Flush*, named after the poker hand with which he won it.
39. Foreword to Cussler, *Pacific Vortex*, p. v.
40. Clive Cussler, *Sahara* (New York: Pocket Star Books, 1992), p. 95.
41. Cussler even commends Pitt for this trait in his short story "The Reunion," when Pitt nearly misses meeting him because Pitt has been busy fixing a flat tire for another guest (see Cussler and Dirgo, *Clive Cussler & Dirk Pitt Revealed!*, p. 17).
42. Robert Sampson, *Faces: Vol. VI, Violent Lives* (Bowling Green, OH: Bowling Green State University Popular Press, 1983), p. 20.
43. Cussler and Dirgo, *Clive Cussler & Dirk Pitt Revealed!*, pp. 48–50. Six years later, Cussler finally confessed what he had done to Lampack, who had told the author that he had always assumed Winthrop was somebody he had met after drinking too much at a cocktail party (see p. 63).
44. Ibid., p. 57.
45. Paul Leggett, *Terence Fisher: Horror, Myth and Religion* (Jefferson, NC: McFarland, 2002), pp. 182–3. See also Michael Allen and Larry Schweikart, *A Patriot's History of the United States* (New York: Sentinel, 2004), pp. 667, 732.
46. Jaffe, *Arthur Conan Doyle*, p. 71.
47. Allen and Schweikart, *A Patriot's History of the United States*, p. 700. Many of these revisionists were Marxist-Leninists who were so hypersensitive to any message that may be viewed as positive about America that during a 1968 conference of the Free Speech group Students for a Democratic Society (SDS) suburban "radicals such as Tom Bell of Cornell faced harassment and taunting form the audience ... when members of the Progressive Labor wing howled curses at him for being too anticommunist. Here was a revolutionary who wanted to destroy, or at the very least, fundamentally eviscerate the foundations of American democracy and capitalism being called a 'red baiter.'"
48. In Joseph Keeley's study of political bias in television, *The Left-Leaning Antenna* (New York: Arlington House, 1971), p. 180, the author writes how one of John Wayne's last films, *The Green Berets*, was "produced only because of Wayne's dogged determination. When it was finally screened, certain liberal critics went into a frenzy of denunciation. Probably the worst denunciation was the one published by the *New York Times*. However, the *Times* reported

that as of January 1969 *The Green Berets* is 'turning into one of the most successful movies released by Warner Bros.–Seven Arts in the last five years.'" Keeley adds that *U.S. News & World Report* did a comparison of *The Green Berets* with another box-office smash, *The Graduate*. While the latter was popular with college students—many who saw it two or three times—Wayne's unabashedly patriotic film was a hit with working-class youngsters, many of whom "saw it two or three times." *The Green Berets* is an occasionally humorous, occasionally heartbreaking film about heroes and war, one anti–American critics of the Vietnam War like to chide as unrealistic. Even Tom Clancy and John Grisham point out in their nonfiction *Special Forces* that while the film is "the best movie ever made about the Special Forces ... it is little more than a World War II–era propaganda film wrapped in a Vietnam suit of clothes." But Clancy and Grisham add, "Despite the unrealistic portrayal of Vietnam, it is something of a Special Forces tradition that Special Forces units on a mission or training exercise have a copy of this movie in their traveling video library. Special Forces soldiers respect the image of the Duke, and often show the movie to their foreign hosts" (p. xv). What is true for Special Forces soldiers is true for most Americans, even 30 years after Wayne's death, as testified by the continued popularity of his movies, including *The Green Berets*.

49. Valero, *The Adventure Writing of Clive Cussler*, p. 32.

50. Cussler and Dirgo, *Clive Cussler & Dirk Pitt Revealed!*, pp. 59–60. See also Valero, *The Adventure Writing of Clive Cussler*, pp. 33–4. This turned out to be a good investment, but Cussler was so anxious to recover his rights that he mailed a $5,000 check to Dodd, Mead before all the loans had been approved, and the check bounced. To his credit, Jonathan Dodd could have nixed the deal, but waited for the check to clear and returned the rights to Cussler (see Valero, *The Adventure Writing of Clive Cussler*, p. 34).

51. Cussler and Dirgo, *Clive Cussler & Dirk Pitt Revealed!*, pp. 60–1. Bantam originally purchased *The Mediterranean Caper* and *Iceberg* to keep them off the market, but, after reading the manuscripts, an editor convinced Bantam to publish them.

52. Valero, *The Adventure Writing of Clive Cussler*, p. 32. One can only wonder what James Cameron would have called his Oscar-winning film if this change had not been made.

53. Ibid., pp. 36, 39.

54. Possibly with Maureen O'Hara substituting for Summer Moran?

55. According to Cussler, it was not his idea to name the non-profit after NUMA (*Sea Hunters*, p. 24). Cussler may be too humble to name an organization NUMA, but that has not prevented him from dropping the name of ships found or being searched for by NUMA in his adventures. *Valhalla Rising* alone mentions the Confederate submarine *H.L. Hunley* (see p. 349), the *Bonhomme Richard* (see p. 352) and the accidental discovery of a Russian spy trawler in 1988 by Pitt and Captain Jimmy Fleet of the *Arvor III* (see p. 445). Cussler's NUMA organization located the *Hunley* off the coast of South Carolina, and has made several searches for the *Bonhomme Richard*. And, in his introduction to *The Sea Hunters*, Cussler recounts NUMA's accidental discovery of a Russian spy trawler while searching for the *Bonhomme Richard* in England, aboard the *Arvor III*, whose captain was Jimmy Fleed (see p. 25).

56. Valero, *The Adventure Writing of Clive Cussler*, pp. 107–8. Cussler and Dirgo's collaboration is explained thusly: "Work on *The Sea Hunters* progressed for which Cussler did a majority of the research. He wrote each narrative introduction from a historical perspective with Dirgo filling in some of the research and adding pertinent information regarding the modern ending of each story. Cussler would then finish up at the point where NUMA came into the picture, detailing the search for that particular shipwreck."

57. Ibid., p. 116.

58. Ibid., pp. 159–60.

59. Ibid., p. 192.

60. Robert Sampson, *Yesterday's Faces: Vol. I, Glory Figures* (Bowling Green, OH: Bowling Green State University Popular Press, 1983), p. 27.

61. See "Introduction" to *Century of Thrillers* (New York: President Press, 1937), pp. v–vi. According to the uncredited author of this piece, "It is exciting and fascinating to participate in adventures of murder, arson, theft, intrigue, spies, danger, horror—when the reader is safely and comfortably at home reading about them, and all these things involve someone else."

Chapter 2

1. Sampson, *Yesterday's Faces: Vol. I, Glory Figures*, p. 3.

2. Martin Greenberg, ed., *The Tom Clancy Companion* (New York: Berkley, 1992), p. 9.

3. Ibid.

4. Cussler, "Introduction," *Thriller 2*, pp. i–ii.

5. One of the first and most influential pulp magazine scientific detectives, Craig Kennedy of Columbia University, was created by Arthur Benjamin Reeve and appeared in a series of short stories published in *Cosmopolitan* beginning in 1910.

6. Cannaday, *Bigger Than Life*, p. 15. Lester Dent, who wrote most of the Doc Savage novels, often listed the first three characteristics when describing his main character, while Doc's co-creator, Street & Smith business manager Henry Ralston, added Lincoln's messianic qualities.

7. Beginning in the sixties, all 181 novels (along with an unpublished novel *The Red Spider*) were reprinted as paperbacks by Bantam Books, with covers by James Bama. This made Doc one of the few pulp serial heroes to have his adventures reprinted in their entirety. More recently, Nostalgia Ventures has been publishing all of Doc's adventures, two at a time, in their original pulp-magazine size on high-quality paper and accompanied by many of the original pulp magazine covers.

8. Cannaday, *Bigger Than Life*, p. 19.

9. Ibid., p. 27. Dent claimed he received 780 letters from writers who had tried the formula and sold their first story. "That was one of the most awful things I ever did," Dent complained, "building up a helluva lot of competition for myself!" Dent's article is reviewed in relation to Cussler's plot and structures in Chapter 7.

10. All Dent quotes in this section are from Cannaday, *Bigger Than Life*, pp. 173–181. Cussler often gives

the same type of advice to writers (see Cussler and Dirgo, *Clive Cussler & Dirk Pitt Revealed!*, pp. 46–7, for an example).

11. Clive Cussler, "Do Your Characters Fit Their Roles?" *The Writer* (April 1982): p. 10. In *Basic Formulas of Fiction* (Norman: University of Oklahoma Press, 1944), pp. 96–7, Professor William Foster-Harris defines tags as "the signs of character" that "offer a swift, sharply focused method of presenting as complete a picture of your character each and every time he enters the story." Foster-Harris breaks tags into four categories: appearance, expression, mannerism, and habit of thought. For example, President Theodore Roosevelt's teeth and glasses were appearance tags, "Bully!" an expression tag, shaking his fist beside his head a mannerism tag, and vigorous, direct thinking a habit of thought tag. "Like the identification tags, or the collar insignia of soldiers, these story tags serve to identify the wearers anywhere and keep them separated in the minds of readers."

12. Ibid., p. 97. Foster-Harris writes: "It is good practice to use at least two different kinds of tags, e.g., of appearance and of mannerisms, or of appearance and habit of thought, for all significant characters. For your principal characters, use tags in all four classes if you can."

13. Clive Cussler, "Make Your Story 'Fly,'" *The Writer* (March 1979): p. 13. Cussler goes on to explain that he believes a hero dying in an adventure novel is unacceptable to readers unless the hero makes a noble sacrifice (e.g., being killed at the Alamo) and the reader is pre-conditioned during the story that this may happen. For more about how sacrificial heroes and happy endings, see Foster-Harris's *Basic Patterns of Plot*, p. 63.

14. Cussler and Dirgo, *Clive Cussler & Dirk Pitt Revealed!*, p. 47.

15. Ian Fleming, *You Only Live Twice* (New York: Signet, 1964), pp. 150–2.

16. Clive Cussler, *Dragon* (New York: Pocket Star Books, 1990), p. 527.

17. Clive Cussler, *Flood Tide* (New York: Pocket Star Books, 1998), p. 141. Qin Shang also peruses a summary written by one of his agents in the U.S. government about Pitt through April 2000, which is more detailed than the summation in the *Dragon* obituary (see pp. 141–2).

18. Cussler, *Pacific Vortex*, p. 4. Drinking and smoking were not always guilty pleasures for heroes. Even that paragon of virtue, dime-novel detective Nick Carter, drank wine and regularly enjoyed cigars.

19. If this seems far-fetched, a real-life comparison can be found in Humphrey Bogart. People unfamiliar with Bogart's life are often surprised that this classic tough guy with the snarling voice and curled upper lip grew up in Manhattan's upper-class society, or that his father was a surgeon and his mother an illustrator who used baby Humphrey as a model for some of her advertisement work. Bogart was also one of Broadway's most dependable juveniles before creating a new image for himself in films.

20. Valero, *The Adventure Writing of Clive Cussler*, p. 46. Depending on the novel, Pitt's height varies, but this may not entirely be Cussler's fault. According to Valero, the author "cannot be responsible when typos occur, causing, say, Pitt to inadvertently vary in statute [sic] from six-foot-two inches to six-foot-four."

21. According to *Valhalla Rising*, Pitt inherited his features and green eyes from his mother (see p. 100).

22. Qin Shang's report says Pitt was promoted to lieutenant colonel (see *Flood Tide*, p. 141), but since this rank is never mentioned again, perhaps Qin Shang's informants were mistaken.

23. Unlike many adventure heroes, Pitt ages during his series, and is in his early forties by Cussler's last solo effort.

24. Exactly how many years is never mentioned in *Pacific Vortex*, but, in *Treasure*, Pitt has been on loan from the U.S. Air Force to NUMA almost six years (see p. 47), and that adventure is set in 1991. The first Pitt adventure that provides any sort of specific dating is *Raise the Titanic!* (New York: Bantam, 1976) which is set in 1987 and seems to take place within one to two years of *Pacific Vortex*.

25. Clive Cussler, *Night Probe!* (New York: Bantam, 1982), p. 344.

26. Cussler, *Flood Tide*, p. 536.

27. Cussler, *Dragon*, p. 198.

28. Clive Cussler, *Deep Six* (New York: Pocket Books, 1984), p. 277. Pitt tries to drown his sorrows with Manhattans after his 1948 Talbot-Lago is destroyed by a bomb. When a waitress asks Pitt if he has lost his wife or his girlfriend, he sadly replies, "Worse ... my car."

29. Cussler, *Flood Tide*, p. 261. Wealth is one of "those requirements of personal excellence and accomplishment from which [a series hero] dare not deviate" (Sampson, *Yesterday's Face:, Vol. I, Glory Figures*, p. 94).

30. Clive Cussler, *Cyclops* (New York: Pocket Books, 1986), p. 49.

31. To find out more about the Cussler Museum, see www.cusslermuseum.com.

32. There are also several ship models in glass cases (see *Vixen 03*, p. 254, and *Deep Six*, pp. 147–8).

33. Clive Cussler, *Vixen 03* (New York: Bantam, 1978), p. 254.

34. Cussler, *Night Probe!*, p. 331, *Treasure*, p. 48, and *Inca Gold* (New York: Pocket Books, 1994), p. 350.

35. Cussler, *Shock Wave*, p. 281.

36. A few of the many other old songs mentioned, hummed or sung in Pitt's adventures include "Fly Me to the Moon" in *Treasure*, "Moon River" in *Shock Wave*, and "Up a Lazy River in the Noonday Sun" and "Waiting for the *Robert E. Lee*" in *Flood Tide*.

37. Cussler, *Vixen 03*, p. 23. There are numerous other references to old movies in the Pitt series, including *Gone With the Wind* in *Treasure*, *Song of the Desert* in *Sahara*, and the Laurel & Hardy comedies in *Inca Gold*.

38. Cussler, *Pacific Vortex*, p. 30.

39. Clive Cussler, *Valhalla Rising* (New York: Berkley, 2002), p. 198.

40. Clive Cussler, *The Mediterranean Caper* (New York: Pocket Books, 1973), p. 11. This can be a difficult juxtaposition to carry off, as the two Pitt movie adaptations have shown. While Matthew McConaughey handles the action scenes well, and is excellent in his portrayal of Pitt as a scamp in *Sahara* (2005), he shows only glimpses of Pitt's cynical side. In *Raise the Titanic!* (1980), Richard Jordan is given few opportunities to be good-natured and none at all to flex his fighting muscles, but he is excellent at presenting Pitt's cynicism.

41. Clive Cussler, *Shock Wave* (New York: Pocket Star Books, 1996), p. 322.

42. Valero, *The Adventure Writing of Clive Cussler*, p. 125.
43. Cussler and Dirgo, *Clive Cussler & Dirk Pitt Revealed!*, p. 9.
44. Cussler, *Pacific Vortex*, pp. 150, 169–170.
45. Cussler, *Iceberg*, pp. 61–2, 75.
46. Cussler and Dirgo, *Clive Cussler & Dirk Pitt Revealed!*, p. 73.
47. For examples, see Cussler, *Pacific Vortex*, pp. 39–45, *Iceberg*, pp. 104–6, *Vixen 03*, p. 47, and *Deep Six*, pp. 183–4.
48. For examples, see Cussler, *Raise the Titanic!*, p. 345, and *Valhalla Rising*, p. 110.
49. For an example, see Cussler, *Cyclops*, p. 256.
50. Quote from Ken Darby, *The Brownstone House of Nero Wolfe* (New York: Little, Brown, 1983), p. 138.
51. Cussler, *Iceberg*, p. 306. Not that a secure man might not sneak a peak. Richard "Rick" Blaine (Humphrey Bogart) in *Casablanca* is one of the most secure heroes in Hollywood history, but he still glances at Major Strasser's (Conrad Veidt) notes from a dossier the Nazi have on him and quips, "Are my eyes really brown?"
52. Perhaps even more commendable, a few hours later Pitt does the NIA's job for them by foiling an assassination scheme, and it never dawns on him that he showed the rude NIA agents that they made a mistake in snubbing him.
53. Cussler, *Vixen 03*, pp. 34–5. See also "The Reunion," in Cussler and Dirgo, *Clive Cussler & Dirk Pitt Revealed!*, p. 17.
54. Cannaday, *Bigger Than Life*, pp. 90–4. Compare what Giordino writes (on p. 93) about Pitt to the Doc Savage code: "Let me strive every moment of my life to make myself better and better, to the best of my ability, that all may profit by it. Let me think of the right and lend all my assistance to those who need it, with no regard for anything but justice. Let me take what comes with a smile, without loss of courage. Let me be considerate of my country, of my fellow citizens and my associates in everything I say and do. Let me do right to all, and wrong no man."
55. Ibid., p. 85. Zweig adds that an adventurer may also be fascinated by evil and cites Beowulf as an example. Beowulf is fascinated with the demonic world and "longs to plunge into it for nothing but the exaltation of adventure itself" (*The Adventurer*, p. 39).
56. Ibid., pp. 86–7.
57. Ibid., p. 86.
58. Cussler, *Pacific Vortex*, p. xii.
59. At this moment, the submarine's name turns tragically ironic. In *Moby-Dick*, Starbuck is the first mate aboard the *Pequod*, a ship whose crew pays a hefty price for following its captain on a foolhardy adventure.
60. Combine the lure of the unknown with Pitt's passion for history and he is a goner. As he tells an acquaintance in *Night Probe!* (p. 181), he is a sucker for historical mysteries.
61. See *Treasure*, p. 48, and *Inca Gold* (New York: Pocket Books, 1994), pp. 128–9.
62. We see this same moral component with Sam and Remi Fargo. Cussler underscores this theme in *Pacific Vortex*, with the legend of Kanoli, a fable about the heavy price men pay for hubris (see pp. 51–2), but the contrast between hubris and serving others is not an uncommon theme in adventure stories. As diverse characters as Fred C. Dobbs in *The Treasure of the Sierra Madre* (1948) and Indiana Jones in *Indiana Jones and the Temple of Doom* (1984) learn the hard way that seeking fortune and glory will end in self-destruction. Pitt and the Fargos already know this, whereas while Indy learns this lesson in time, but Dobbs does not.
63. Cussler, *Deep Six*, p. 347. Larimer's stellar behavior seems ironic when compared to a character like Paul Beaumont, who was created by the ship's namesake. In *He Who Gets Slapped* (1914), Beaumont, a prototypical Andreyev character, destroys himself and a young woman he loves because of his own self-pity.
64. To see just *how* patriotic, see Cussler, *Dragon*, p. 163.
65. Allen and Schweikart, *A Patriot's History of the United States*, pp. 229–30.
66. Ibid., pp. 121–2.
67. Ibid., p. 120.
68. Cussler, *Iceberg*, p. 59. Ironically, when this observation is put to the test in Pitt's final showdown with Fyrie, it proves to be as accurate as it is cynical (see Chapter 7).
69. Allen and Schweikart, *A Patriot's History of the United States*, pp. 122–3.
70. Ibid., pp. 106, 111–2, 120, 122. Schweikart and Allen point out (on p. 120): "Washington had to look no further than his own life to realize the error of his position: he was on track to gain a general officer's commission in the British army, replete with additional land grants for dutiful service to His Majesty. Instead, Washington threw it away to lead a ragtag army of malcontents into the snow of Valley Forge and the icy waters of the Delaware. Self-interest indeed!" To appreciate Washington's sacrifice, compare him to Robert E. Lee, who agreed to become the commander of the forces for his home state of Virginia during the American Civil War, even though he did not agree with secession and was offered a command position in the Union army. If the Colonies had lost the Revolutionary War, the British would likely have punished Washington more severely than the North punished Lee, who lost the right to vote and some property. One can but wonder if Lee might not have followed in Washington's footsteps if the South had been victorious and become president of the Confederate States of America instead of just president of Washington College (now known as Washington and Lee University).
71. Ibid.
72. Cussler, *Sahara*, p. 431.
73. Cussler and Dirgo, *Clive Cussler & Dirk Pitt Revealed!*, p. 70. According to Cussler, when he used himself as a character for the first time, in *Dragon*, his editor, Michael Korda, told him that he "found it unconventional, but knowing you as an unconventional guy, I thought, oh, well, it's pure Cussler."
74. Cussler, *Deep Six*, p. 424. Where Cussler hid alcohol in the same sort of violin case in which gangsters used to carry machine guns, in *Deep Six* Pitt actually carries a Thompson machine gun in a violin case.
75. Cussler, *Shock Wave*, p. 290.
76. Cussler, *Iceberg*, p. 261, and *Sahara*, p. 353.
77. Cussler, *Sahara*, p. 455.
78. Cussler, *Dragon*, p. 392.
79. Cussler, *Sahara*, pp. 378–80.
80. Cussler, *Shock Wave*, pp. 431–2, 434–5.

81. Cussler, *Cyclops*, p. 207.
82. See Chapter 8.
83. Cussler and Paul Kemprecos use this delay-and-rescue characterization trick when they introduce Kurt Austin in the first *NUMA Files* adventure, *Serpent*. Austin's first appearance does not occur until p. 76, when he rescues marine archaeologist Nina Kirov; Austin's buddy-in-color, Zavala, is introduced immediately afterwards, on p. 77.
84. For more on this, see Valero, *The Adventure Writing of Clive Cussler*, p. 125.
85. Cussler, *Pacific Vortex*, 208.
86. Cussler, *Sahara*, pp. 75–6.
87. For example, in *Deep Six* the friends do not appreciate being ordered about by Julie Mendoza, who wants them to abandon a NUMA salvage operation but is not as forthcoming as to why. Pitt and Giordino banter like high school boys until Mendoza is all but forced to beg that they come with her (see p. 37).
88. In *Raise the Titanic!*, Sandecker is seen at a White House party smoking a Churchill cigar (see p. 35), but in *Night Probe!*, he has switched to Cuban cigars (see p. 285). Later, Sandecker is smoking cigars made by a family in Latin America (see *Flood Tide*, p. 71).
89. For more about the epic "Cigar Saga," see http://sh1.webring.com/people/xh/hn4dpitt/cigarsaga.htm.
90. Cussler, *Vixen 03*, p. 34.
91. "So Enkidu and Gilgamesh embraced and their friendship was sealed." See Editorial Board of the University Society (Supervisors), *Epic of Gilgamesh* (New York: Penguin, 1986), p. 69.
92. Cussler is not always consistent about just when Giordino and Pitt met. For instance, in *Raise The Titanic!*, Giordino and Pitt have been friends since high school (see p. 171), but in *Vixen 03* Giordino tells Steiger the playground fight that launched their friendship happened in the first grade (see p. 34). For a breakdown of the different versions of how Dirk met Al, see http://sh1.webring.com/people/xh/hn4dpitt/algiordino.htm.
93. Cussler, *Dragon*, p. 528.
94. Cussler, *Valhalla Rising*, p. 119.
95. Clive Cussler, *Trojan Odyssey* (New York: Berkley, 2004), p. 197.
96. Cussler, *Inca Gold*, p. 562.

Giordino's recollection is evocative of the famous reminiscence by Mr. Bernstein's (Everett Sloane) in *Citizen Kane* (1941): "A fellow will remember a lot of things you wouldn't think he'd remember. You take me. One day, back in 1896, I was crossing over to Jersey on the ferry, and as we pulled out, there was another ferry pulling in, and on it there was a girl waiting to get off. A white dress she had on. She was carrying a white parasol. I only saw her for one second. She didn't see me at all, but I'll bet a month hasn't gone by since that I haven't thought of that girl."
97. Ibid., p. 563. With characteristic cynicism, Girodino concludes his recollection by telling Loren that he and the girl might have gotten married, had ten kids and found out they hated each other.
98. Cussler, *Treasure*, p. 215.
99. Cussler and Dirgo, *Clive Cussler & Dirk Pitt Revealed!*, p. 21. Unlike Cussler, Pitt's humorous outlook on life was inherited from his father's side of the family (see *Valhalla Rising*, p. 100).
100. Cussler, *Inca Gold*, pp. 50–1. This becomes a running gag (see pp. 97, 158), concluding when Pitt survives a harrowing journey and a showdown with the villain along a subterranean river. He finds Giordino waiting for him with a mariachi street band playing "Waiting for the Robert E. Lee" (see p. 564).
101. Ibid., p. 117.
102. Cussler, *Flood Tide*, p. 151.
103. See *Deep Six*, p. 34, for an example.
104. Cussler, *Inca Gold*, p. 92.
105. Cussler, *Pacific Vortex*, 183, *Vixen 03*, p. 46.
106. Cussler, *The Mediterranean Caper*, p. 171, and *Pacific Vortex*, 188.
107. See *Trojan Odyssey*, p. 480. In a June 2001 interview for AudioBooksToday.com, Cussler was asked why he gave Pitt a sidekick; he does not disagree with the term as he answers: "I wanted to be different. All the rest of [Pitt's peers] are single heroes and I thought this way Pitt and Giordino could play off each other" (http://www.cusslermen.com/Characters.htm).
108. Richard B. Schwartz, *Nice and Noir* (Columbia: University of Missouri Press, 2002), p. 73.
109. Joseph Campbell, *Hero with a Thousand Faces* (Princeton: Princeton University Press, 1949), p. 79. See Chapter 7 for more on Campbell and the initiation quest pattern in relation to the Pitt series.
110. Schwartz, *Nice and Noir*, p. 73.
111. This is the same kind of friendship forged through shared adventure and adversity that exists between the human Captain James T. Kirk and Vulcan Mr. Spock in *Star Trek*. It is a friendship, as an older Mr. Spock (Leonard Nimoy) tells his younger self (Zachary Quinto) in the 2009 reboot film *Star Trek*, which "will define you both."
112. Cussler, *Valhalla Rising*, p. 287. Giordino is so conditioned to saving Pitt's life that when he rescues him a second time in *Valhalla Rising*, he jokingly complains how monotonous his interventions are becoming (see p. 329).
113. See *Pacific Vortex*, p. 40, *Vixen 03*, p. 41, and *Valhalla Rising*, p. 132. Girodino is not always thrilled about following Pitt into such stunts, however; for an example, see *Sahara*, p. 165.
114. Schwartz, *Nice and Noir*, p. 74.
115. Ibid., pp. 57–8. Schwartz adds, "In some ways the two are inseparable."
116. To cite the most obvious example, few if any of Pitt's fans complain about Giordino's absence in *Iceberg*, and many seem to agree with Valero when he states, on p. 95 of *The Adventure Writing of Clive Cussler*, "In the physical sense, Dirk Pitt is more than capable of handling the circumstances that are randomly thrown in his direction. Of course—at times—he is greatly aided in these efforts by Al Giordino."
117. For a list of the times Giordino saves Pitt's life, from *Pacific Vortex* to *Valhalla Rising*, see http://sh1.webring.com/people/xh/hn4dpitt/moments.htm.
118. Author's questions to Cussler, August 2009.
119. According to *Webster's New World Dictionary*, pp. 753–4, James is a masculine name. James was also the name of a Christian apostle, a brother of Jesus, several kings and, ironically (considering Sandecker's personality), the last name of William James, an exponent of pragmatism.
120. See *Deep Six*, p. 27, *Cyclops*, pp. 96, 130, and *Night Probe!*, p. 86.

121. Cussler, *Raise the Titanic!*, p. 144.
122. Cussler, *Flood Tide*, p. 60.
123. Cussler, *Cyclops*, p. 130.
124. Clive Cussler and Paul Kemprecos, *Fire Ice* (New York: Berkley, 2003), p. 255.
125. See, for example, Cussler, *Night Probe!*, p. 86.
126. *Webster's New World Dictionary*, p. 366.
127. Cussler, *Deep Six*, p. 27.
128. Cussler, *Iceberg*, p. 104. But height can be an inconsistent trait for Cussler's characters; in *Night Probe!* (p. 87), Sandecker is just over five feet tall.
129. Cussler, *Raise the Titanic!*, p. 34.
130. See *Raise the Titanic!*, p. 136, *Night Probe!*, p. 87, and *Iceberg*, p. 23.
131. For examples, see Cussler, *Deep Six*, p. 39, and *Sahara*, p. 99.
132. Cussler, *Night Probe!*, p. 86.
133. Cussler, *Shock Wave*, p. 350.
134. Cussler, *Trojan Odyssey* (p. 362).
135. Cussler, *Cyclops*, p. 249.
136. Cussler, *Shock Wave*, p. 351.
137. See *Night Probe!*, p. 87, and *Trojan Odyssey*, p. 362.
138. See *Cyclops*, p. 174, and *Deep Six*, p. 39.
139. See *Cyclops*, p. 249. Apparently, Sandecker was not as respected in the navy as he is at NUMA. In *Raise the Titanic!* Sandecker tells Kemper that he heard people were dancing in the corridors of the Pentagon when he left (see p. 144). The reason for Sandecker's retirement is never explained, although, in *Vixen 03*, we are told it was forced upon him. After this, Sandecker connived his way to the top job at the fledgling NUMA (see p. 177).
140. See *Raise the Titanic!*, p. 131, and *Fire Ice*, p. 78, 271.
141. Cussler, *Sahara*, p. 188.
142. Cussler and Kemprecos, *Fire Ice*, p. 355.
143. Cussler, *Sahara*, p. 142.
144. Cussler and Kemprecos, *Fire Ice*, p. 108. Sandecker always arrives one minute before a meeting, a habit he picked up during his days in the navy.
145. Ibid., p. 352.
146. For an example, see Cussler, *Flood Tide*, pp. 36, 70–1.
147. Cussler and Kemprecos, *Fire Ice*, p. 108.

148. Sandecker's tenure as VP is hard to pin down. *Trojan Odyssey* is set in 2006, and he is still the VP in *Artic Drift*, which is set in April 2011. But, in *Corsair*, apparently set in 2009, someone else is VP.
149. See Clive Cussler and Dirk Cussler, *Arctic Drift* (New York: Putnam, 2008), pp. 32–3, and *Trojan Odyssey*, p. 461.
150. See *Shock Wave*, p. 490.
151. See *Dragon*, p. 528, and *Cyclops*, p. 249. Also, in *Night Probe!* (p. 254), Sandecker silently demonstrates fatherly concern for Pitt; later (pp. 314, 316), he voices concern for Pitt's safety before a dangerous night probe (or dark dive) into an underwater cave. As for Pitt, he admits in *Iceberg* (p. 103) that he respects Sandecker, and that the admiral is more than a friend or boss. In *Vixen 03* (pp. 342–51) both Pitt and Giordino put their lives at risk by refusing to abandon Sandecker as he sails out over the Atlantic, on what appears to be a suicide mission, to save Washington, DC.
152. Sandecker also gets embarrassed when it comes to displaying personal feelings; a good example of this occurs in *Sahara* (p. 150).
153. Cussler, *Cyclops*, p. 249.
154. Ibid., p. 96.
155. See *Iceberg*, p. 134, and *Raise the Titanic!*, pp. 299–301.
156. See *Pacific Vortex*, p. 183, *Iceberg*, p. 150, and *Raise the Titanic!*, pp. 302–14.
157. See *Vixen 03*, p. 340.
158. See *Night Probe!*, pp. 165–6, *Flood Tide*, p. 52, *Sahara*, p. 80, *Inca Gold*, p. 159, *Shock Wave*, p. 141, *Serpent*, p. 146, *Atlantis Found*, p. 131, and *Trojan Odyssey*, pp. 45, 461.
159. Cussler, *Sahara*, pp. 116–7.
160. See *Flood Tide*, p. 536.
161. Cussler, *Treasure*, p. 287. Another example occurs in *Cyclops* (p. 101), wherein Pitt agrees to search for a missing entrepreneur, but only if Giordino and Gunn join him.
162. Cussler, *Sahara*, p. 81.
163. Cussler, *Cyclops*, p. 173.
164. Cussler, *Night Probe!*, p. 166.
165. See *Night Probe!*, pp. 165–6, *Sahara*, pp. 80–1, *Treasure*, pp. 338–9, *Atlantis Found* (New York: Berkley, 1999), pp. 131–2, and *Raise the Titanic!*, p. 117. Gunn's exact height is never given, but, in *Trojan Odyssey* (p. 45) he is less than an inch taller than Sandecker.

166. Cussler, *Night Probe!*, pp. 165–6. Regarding his brown eyes, perhaps Gunn had to start wearing tinted contacts under his glasses in later adventures as his eye color inexplicably changes to blue (see *Cyclops*, p. 126, and *Atlantis Found*, p. 131).
167. This facet of Gunn's character may be a reflection of the author's love of research.
168. See *The Mediterranean Caper*, p. 195, *Flood Tide*, p. 52, and *Serpent*, p. 152.
169. Cussler, *Sahara*, pp. 204, 242.
170. Cussler, *Pacific Vortex*, p. 10.
171. Cussler, *The Mediterranean Caper*, p. 186.
172. Ibid., p. 184.
173. See *Treasure*, p. 421, and *Sahara*, p. 181.
174. See *Cyclops*, pp. 212, 333.
175. *Webster's New World Dictionary*, p. 664.
176. See http://en.wikipedia.org/wiki/Chuck_Yeager.
177. Yaeger is the father of three daughters (see *Valhalla Rising*, p. 197), but during his first appearance in *Deep Six* (p. 250), he lives alone in an apartment.
178. Cussler, *Atlantis Found*, pp. 378–391.
179. Cussler and Kemprecos, *Fire Ice*, p. 367.
180. Cussler, *Valhalla Rising*, p. 197.
181. Cussler, *Shock Wave*, p. 177.
182. http://en.wikipedia.org/wiki/St_Julien.
183. http://en.wikipedia.org/wiki/Saint_Julian.
184. *Webster's New World Dictionary*, p. 764.
185. http://en.wikipedia.org/wiki/Perlmutter. Perhaps in tribute to his German father, Cussler has given other prominent supporting characters in his series German surnames, including Joseph Van Dorn from the Isaac Bell Detective series.
186. Cussler, *Flood Tide*, p. 472.
187. Ibid., pp. 473–4.
188. See Chapters 5 and 6. A possible tribute to Felix Mulholland could be Perlmutter's chauffeur, Hugo Mulholland, a taciturn man with bloodhound eyes who first appears in *Shock Wave* (see p. 176).
189. Cussler, *Inca Gold*, pp. 135–40.
190. Senator Pitt's party affilia-

tion is not revealed until *Trojan Odyssey* (see p. 452).

191. See *Iceberg*, pp. 86–7, and *Shock Wave*, p. 290.

192. See *Pacific Vortex*, p. 9, and *Cyclops*, p. 62.

193. Cussler, *Treasure*, p. 382.

194. Cussler, *Iceberg*, p. 159.

195. Ibid., p. 59.

196. The extortion involves exposing explicit photos of Loren with Dirk. The elder Pitt is so unimpressed by this plot that he jokingly asks for a set of photos as a memento (see *Vixen 03*, pp. 246–8).

197. Cussler, *Iceberg*, p. 128.

198. Barbara (Nash) Pitt is the name most often associated with Pitt's mother, but, in *Flood Tide*, her maiden name is Knight (see p. 142), the same as Cussler's first wife, Barbara; in Pitt's obituary his mother's first name is Susan (see *Dragon*, p. 527).

199. Cussler, *Treasure*, pp. 177–8.

200. Cussler, *Shock Wave*, p. 322.

201. Cussler, *Valhalla Rising*, p. 100.

202. This is not the first time Pitt realizes he is getting older. See *Shock Wave*, pp. 121–2, which is set three years before *Valhalla Rising*.

203. This recollection is inexplicable considering Pitt is just shy of 50 in the year 2000, and the U.S. Naval Station Tutuila closed operations on June 25, 1951. See http://en.wikipedia.org/wiki/United_States_Naval_Station_Tutuila.

204. Cussler, *Valhalla Rising*, p. 195

205. Ibid., pp. 514–6.

206. This is the same age as Cussler when he first saw the Pacific Ocean.

207. Cussler, *Valhalla Rising*, p. 516.

208. Cussler received his honorary doctorate of letters from the New York Maritime College four years before *Valhalla Rising* was published.

209. Or asks for a second date when he rescues the girl after their first date (see *Crescent Dawn*, p. 161).

210. In *Trojan Odyssey*, for example, Summer boils lobsters she captured during a dive and makes Bananas Foster for dessert (see p. 410).

211. Dirk competed in track-and-field at the University of Hawaii. See *Trojan Odyssey*, p. 410.

212. Pitt also competed in fencing at the Air Force Academy, and still works out when given an opportunity (see *Dragon*, p. 270).

213. For an example, compare *Trojan Odyssey*, p. 411, with *Crescent Dawn*, pp. 148–161.

214. Clive Cussler and Dirk Cussler, *Treasure of Khan* (New York: Putnam, 2006), pp. 438–40.

215. Cussler, *Pacific Vortex*, pp. 248–9.

216. Ibid., p. 235.

217. Cussler lists this comment as one of his favorite reviews about the Pitt series. (Quoted in Cussler and Dirgo, *Clive Cussler & Dirk Pitt Revealed!*, p. 77.)

218. Colorado's seventh district did not exist when *Vixen 03* was published, in 1978. It was created after the 2000 census and, as of this writing, includes the city of Arvada.

219. See *Vixen 03*, pp. 1–3.

220. Time is kind to Loren during these years. She is 37 in 1989 (*Deep Six*), so she should be almost 60 when she walks down the aisle. However, Loren's age is never mentioned in *Trojan Odyssey*, and, judging by her description in this novel (see p. 150), she has not changed a bit since *Vixen 03*.

221. Loren does this in *Deep Six* (p. 116), *Inca Gold* (p. 261), *Atlantis Found* (p. 254), *Valhalla Rising* (p. 341) and *Trojan Odyssey* (p. 150), greeting Pitt each time with "Welcome home, voyager," or "Welcome home, sailor."

222. Cussler, *Inca Gold*, p. 263.

223. Loren is not only independent in character but in her politics. (See *Vixen 03*, p. 4.)

224. Gianetti, *Masters of American Cinema*, Chapter 7, p. 6. Many of Hawks's heroes are as traditionally American as Cussler's, but Hawks and Cussler's heroines have little in common with the heroines from many of America's earliest adventure novels, especially those by America's first adventure writer, James Fenimore Cooper, whose "heroines are commonly but lay-figures for the development of his plots." Quoted in Henry S. Pancoast, *Introduction to American Literature* (New York: Henry Holt, 1898), p. 138. Cussler heroines are active participants who may not be able to extricate themselves from danger but do try whenever possible.

225. Cussler, *Vixen 03*, p. 3

226. Ibid., p. 130.

227. Ibid., p. 170.

228. Ibid., pp. 256–7.

229. Cussler, *Deep Six*, p. 116.

230. Cussler, *Dragon*, p. 531.

231. Cussler, *Inca Gold*, p. 577.

232. Cussler, "The Reunion," pp. 16–7.

233. Author's questions to Cussler, August 2009.

Chapter 3

1. Clive Cussler and Jack Du Brul, *Skeleton Coast* (New York: Berkley, 2006), p. 134.

2. That said, Pitt not only writes but signs the introduction to *Serpent* and appears in a cameo with Giordino (see pp. 142–3). Fair is fair, though, and *Serpent*'s heroes, Austin and Zavala, have a cameo appearance in *Trojan Odyssey* (see p. 155). These scenes are very similar, right down to the dialogue as the men bump into each other outside Sandecker's office at NUMA headquarters. They ask each other about their latest adventures, make mention of Pitt's automobile collection and promise to get together for dinner. Also, in a bit of nifty planning or serendipity, these cameos appear in Chapter 15 of both books.

3. Interview with Clive Cussler, June 2001, http://www.cusslermen.com/Characters.htm.

4. Valero, *The Adventure Writing of Clive Cussler*, pp. 159–60.

5. Clive Clusser and Paul Kemprecos, *Serpent* (New York: Pocket Books, 1999), p. 81, and Cussler, *Fire*, pp. 87–8.

6. Valero, *The Adventure Writing of Clive Cussler*, pp. 157–8.

7. Cussler and Kemprecos, *Serpent*, p. 81. "Zavala, in fact, was a professional in every kind of propulsion."

8. As of this writing, Gamay is the only regular cast member of a Cussler adventure series not to have her eye color identified.

9. This may not always have been intended to be the case. In *Trojan Odyssey* Austin is Pitt's counterpart at NUMA, a fellow director of special projects (see p. 155).

10. The *Star Trek* example is an obvious comparison. For another example, see Valero, *The Adventure Writing of Clive Cussler*, p. 161.

11. The television series *Stargate SG-1* was a spin-off of the 1994 film *Stargate*.

12. And woe to any series that strays too far from the parent series. The spin-off *Stargate Universe* (2009–2011) failed to find an audience when it ignored the heroic and humorous elements that made *Stargate SG-1* and its first spin-off *Stargate: Atlantis* so popular with viewers.

13. For information on Solar Pons, see http://en.wikipedia.org/wiki/Solar_Pons.

14. For information on Dr. Gregory House, see http://en.wikipedia.org/wiki/House_(TV_series)#References_to_Sherlock_Holmes.

15. See Chapter 9.

16. George Pitt crewed on a lumber ship while in college and made ten runs between San Diego and Portland before he graduated. According to Dirk, his father keeps a picture of that lumber ship on his office wall (see *Flood Tide*, p. 157).

17. Dirk Pitt did work in a Leadville, Colorado, silver mine one summer during semester break while at the Air Force Academy (see *Trojan Odyssey*, p. 270).

18. Austin did not love Cabral, having even less opportunity to spend time with her than Pitt did with Summer Moran in *Pacific Vortex* before her apparent demise, but his feelings were strong enough to be a concern to Sandecker (see *Fire Ice*, p. 45).

19. Austin's name may have been borrowed from the city of Austin, Texas, where Cussler's 501(c)(3) NUMA was headquartered at the time, in the law offices of NUMA's president Wayne Gronquist (see *Sea Hunters*, p. 70). Originally, Cussler suggested the name Maximilian Kane ("Max" for short) for NSAT's leader, but the publisher, Simon & Schuster, was unimpressed; they also balked at Cussler's suggestion that Max have a beard. It is tempting to wonder if Cussler might have been inspired to make this suggestion to show up the bearded Dirk Pitt (Richard Jordan) from the lackluster film adaptation of *Raise the Titanic!* In an example of what-goes-around-comes-around, Kemprecos's newest adventure novel, *The Emerald Scepter* (2013), features hero and team leader Matinicus "Matt" Hawkins, an ex–Navy SEAL who is working as an undersea robotics engineer at Woods Hole. For more information, see http://www.paulkemprecos.com/Home_Page.html.

20. Cussler, *Iceberg*, 261.

21. Cussler and Kemprecos, *Fire Ice*, p. 60.

22. The theme of chess versus poker runs throughout *Fire Ice*.

23. Cussler and Kemprecos, *Fire Ice*, pp. 70–1.

24. Ibid., p. 214.

25. Soc, the hero of *Cool Blue Tomb* and five other mysteries published between 1991 and 1997, is a part-time diver, part-time fisherman, and part-time private investigator. While imbuing Austin with Soc's philosophical bent was Kemprecos' idea, it was Cussler's idea to have Austin, like Soc, live on a houseboat (see *The Adventure Writing of Dirk Pitt*, p. 159, http://www.paulkemrecos.com/About_Paul.html, and http://www.paulkemprecos.com/NUMA_Files_Series.html) and the titular Pitt archetype hero from the television adventure series *MacGyver*.

26. Cussler and Kemprecos, *Fire Ice*, pp. 138–9.

27. "Tuckerization" is a term coined by science fiction and mystery fans, and is usually attributed to writer Arthur Wilson "Bob" Tucker (*The Long, Loud Silence*; *The Lincoln Hunters*), who frequently named characters in his novels and stories after real people.

28. The late Leigh Hunt was one of Cussler's close friends; after Hunt passed away, Cussler dedicated *Arctic Drift* to him.

29. Foss Gly is also one of the most unusual names of any Cussler villain. I asked the author if the name might have been a pun for the words "false guy," since Gly twice pretends to be someone he is not in *Night Probe!*, but Cussler replied, "No, sorry" (author's questions to Cussler, August 2009). Valero provides more details about the origin of Gly's name on pp. 130–1 in *The Adventure Writing of Clive Cussler* when he recounts how Cussler found the name "Fos Gly" (with only one "s") on a gravestone in a Boot Hill–type cemetery in east central Utah.

30. Cussler, *Sea Hunters*, pp. 63–75. Cussler usually does not name people after ships but he does name ships after places he has lived, including the U.S.S. *Arvada* in *Night Probe!* Cussler also apparently has no qualms about naming ships after his book titles, such as the NUMA vessel *Sea Hunter* in *Fire Ice*.

31. See *Trojan Odyssey*, p. 127.

32. See *Fire Ice*, p. 263, *Sea Hunters*, p. 75, and *Dragon*, p. 193.

33. In a June 2001 interview with AudioBooksToday.com Cussler mentions the series that became the *Oregon Files*, explaining how his publisher wanted him to come up with a third adventure series, this one "a spin-off on a few chapters from a book where I had these mercenaries with this old derelict ship. It was loaded with missiles and it could do fifty knots and had big engines. It was run like a corporation; the captain was the chairman of the board. They want to take this concept of this ship and have it going around the world, getting into mischief."

34. Yes, that's Taft, not Shaft, and Dirgo's hero also seems to be influenced as much by Bond as Pitt. Besides being the tiniest government agency, the NIA headquarters operates behind the façade of the Capco Mining Corporation of Bethesda, Maryland; in the Bond series, Her Majesty's Secret Service operates behind the façade of Universal Exports. The 50 operatives within the NIA know one another only by numbers, and Taft is number 7. Bond, of course, is Agent 007. Almost as secret an organization as CURE from the *Destroyer* series, the NIA's budget is buried within the budget of its big brother, the National Security Agency; its directors are answerable solely to the National Security Council, but, in large part, the NIA exists to follow orders from the president. Taft, like Bond, has a scar on his face, except his is on the left side, whereas Bond's is on the right; both men are good at their jobs, and they know it. Like Pitt, Taft is slightly over six feet tall, in good physical shape and frequently accomplishes missions that are considered impossible, but, unlike Pitt, he has blond hair and blue eyes. Also like Pitt, Taft's adventures are triggered upon events set in the past. Instead of searching for items lost to history, however, Taft's adventures involve great scientific discoveries believed never to have been proven, including Albert Einstein's Unified Field The-

ory and Nikola Tesla's atmospheric transmission of electricity. For information on John Taft, see http://www.spyguysandgals.com/sgShowChar.asp?ScanName=Taft_John.

35. Cussler, *Flood Tide*, p. 167.
36. Ibid., pp. 159–237.
37. Clive Cussler and Jack Du Brul, *Plague Ship* (New York: Berkley, 2008), p. 30.
38. Cussler, *Flood Tide*, p. 235.
39. When Pitt and Giordino first board the *Oregon*, Cabrillo informs them that this is the third ship with that name (see *Flood Tide*, p. 167). One can only wonder if the first two ships were as similar to the ship in *Flood Tide* as this fourth one is, and, if so, why bother to change the ships at all unless each successive model has been upgraded.
40. In *Flood Tide* (p. 207), Cabrillo explains that the *Oregon* carries "flags and ensigns of every maritime country in the world," but flies the flag of Iran because (as it is explained on p. 167) it is "the last country any port authority would identify with the United States."
41. Clice Cussler and Craig Dirgo, *Golden Buddha* (New York: Berkley, 2003), p. 14.
42. This is one of the rare times that futuristic technology from one Cussler adventure is employed again in a later novel.
43. Cussler and Du Brul, *Plague Ship*, p. 34–5. As discussed in Chapter 6, the *Oregon* is, in many ways, reminiscent of the *Whirlwind*, another disguised ship with sophisticated weaponry and propulsion system designed by its captain, John Fury, the hero of *The Skipper* pulp adventure series.
44. See Foreword, *Golden Buddha*.
45. Ibid., pp. 20, 34.
46. Ibid., p. 20.
47. See *Flood Tide*, p. 169. Perhaps in an attempt to trim The Corporation's roster to a more manageable number, Manley's replacement as vice-president of operations in *Golden Buddha* and *Sacred Stone*, Richard "Dick" Truitt, retires for reasons unknown and is replaced by Linda Ross (see *Dark Watch*, pp. 36 and 38).
48. See Cussler and Dirgo, *Golden Buddha*, "Cast of Characters," and Cussler and Du Brul, *Plague Ship*, pp. 31–3.

49. Cabrillo's father also insists that his family is descended from the historical Cabrillo (see *Flood Tide*, p. 166). The captain of Cussler's version of the *Enterprise* has being named after a historical figure in common with Captain Jean-Luc Picard from *Star Trek: The Next Generation*, who is named after a real chemist and aeronautical engineer, Jean Felix Piccard (1884–1963).
50. See Cussler and Dirgo, *Golden Buddha*, p. 50.
51. See Cussler and Du Brul, *Skeleton Coast*, pp. 75 and 342. Amy Cabrillo's death takes place 11 years prior to the events in *Skeleton Coast* (see p. 342).
52. See *Skeleton Coast*, p. 342.
53. Ibid., pp. 133–4.
54. Ibid., pp. 131–9.
55. Clive Cussler, *The Adventures of Vin Fiz* (New York: Philomel), pp. 3–5.
56. Ibid., p. 2. Cussler never mentions if Knot Nicefolk ever did anything comparable to returning punitive taxes to the poor, as did Sir Robert of Locksley.
57. Ibid., p. 1. Further emphasizing the contradictory nature of artichokes is that they are edible flower heads that are cooked and eaten as vegetables.
58. Ibid., p. 2. Living a life that follows the beat of a different drummer is a recurrent trait with Cussler and his fictional heroes.
59. Artichokes and herbs might also represent the incongruous nature of conformity and nonconformity. Raising artichokes and living a life of conformity can provide security, but both can be flavorless on their own, whereas herbs and nonconformity are more flavorful but provide far less security.
60. Cussler, *The Adventures of Vin Fiz*, p. 5, and Cussler and Dirgo, *Clive Cussler & Dirk Pitt Revealed!*, pp. 27–8.
61. See Don Swaim interview with Clive Cussler, January 30, 1986 (http://wiredforbooks.org/clivecussler/index.htm).
62. See Cussler and Dirgo, *Clive Cussler & Dirk Pitt Revealed!*, p. 29.
63. Ibid., pp. 42, 54, and 76–7.
64. When Cussler "meets" Perlmutter in "The Reunion," he confesses to being envious of the gourmand's lifestyle and appreciation of the finer things (see p. 4).

65. Cussler, *The Adventures of Vin Fiz*, p. 3.
66. Cussler and Dirgo, *Clive Cussler & Dirk Pitt Revealed!*, p. 36
67. Cussler, *The Adventures of Vin Fiz*, p. 3
68. Note to author, September 14, 2009.
69. Cussler, *The Adventures of Vin Fiz*, p. 9
70. In "The Reunion," Loren inquires about Mr. Periwinkle, and Cussler tells her that the last time he saw the donkey he was running free with a herd in the Mojave Desert (see Cussler and Dirgo, *Clive Cussler & Dirk Pitt Revealed!*, p. 16).
71. Cussler, *The Adventures of Vin Fiz*, p. 13
72. See Chapter 7 and Carl Jung, *Psyche and Symbol*, ed. Violet S. de Laszlo (New York: Doubleday Anchor, 1958), p. 75.
73. Cussler, *The Adventures of Vin Fiz*, pp. 17 and 19–20.
74. See "Children's Bookshelf Talks with Clive Cussler," http://www.publishersweekly.com/pw/by-topic/authors/interviews/articles/9380-children-s-bookshelve-talks-with-clive-cussler.html.
75. See *The Adventures of Vin Fiz*, pp. 165–7.
76. See http://en.wikipedia.org/wiki/Chitty_Chitty_Bang_Bang_(novel).
77. Cussler, *The Adventures of Vin Fiz*, p. 115. This simple advice could serve as Pitt's motto.
78. See "Children's Bookshelf Talks with Clive Cussler," http://www.publishersweekly.com/pw/by-topic/authors/interviews/articles/9380-children-s-bookshelve-talks-with-clive-cussler.html.
79. See "The Gold Cup Class Revisited," http://www.thunderboats.org/history/history0160.html.
80. See Chapter 7 for more information concerning microcosmic and macrocosmic adventures.
81. Cussler also dedicated *The Adventures of Vin Fiz* to his children and grandchildren, and dedicated *The Adventures of Hotsy Totsy* to his great-grandchildren.
82. The superhero mother Helen Parr (Holly Hunter) from *The Incredibles* (2004) makes much the same point from the opposite spectrum of adventure when she warns her superhero children Violet (Sarah Vowell) and Dash (Spencer Fox),

"Remember the bad guys on the shows you used to watch on Saturday mornings? Well, these guys aren't like those guys. They won't exercise restraint because you are children. They *will* kill you if they get the chance. Do *not* give them that chance."

83. Clive Cussler, *The Adventures of Hotsy Totsy* (London: Puffin, 2010), p. 156.

84. Ibid., pp. 58–9.

85. Gothic stories often feature ancient castles with subterranean dungeons, which certainly inspired this chapter's title, "Locked in a Dungeon."

86. See "The Gold Cup Class Revisited," http://www.thunderboats.org/history/history0160.html.

87. Cussler, *The Adventures of Hotsy Totsy*, p. 11.

88. One of the central characters in *Golden Buddha* is the Dalai Lama, and while it is not unusual for historical leaders to appear in Cussler's novels, the Dalai Lama is the first historical religious leader. He is also the first supernatural character to appear in a Cussler novel, experiencing visions and astral projections while he meditates. Another prominent historical character is the Dalai Lama's elderly oracle, also known as Dorje Drakden, who makes eerily accurate predictions based on what are reportedly actual predictions made prior to the Dalai Lama's exile in 1959. The oracle makes these predictions while in the grip of a dervish and, at such times, he is able to perform amazing physical feats, despite his advanced age. After seeing the Dalai Lama and his oracle in action, it is difficult to pooh-pooh corrupt art dealer Winston Spenser when he looks at a Golden Buddha he has stolen and finds it hard not to believe it is mocking him. (Although it is not supernatural, there is a nice allegorical moment earlier in the story, when Spenser first visits the A-Ma Temple to hide the Golden Buddha in plain sight. Someone lights a coil firecracker to chase away evil spirits, and Spenser instinctively ducks [see Cussler and and Dirgo, *Golden Buddha* p. 58]). Granted, mocking is hardly in keeping with Buddhist philosophy, but, then, Spenser is not a Buddhist; he is a Westerner, whose apprehensions are borne from a Biblical point of view: he fears that his immoral scheme for selling a *faux* Buddha is being frustrated by a spiritual and moral authority represented by the genuine Buddha he has stolen. And, at times in *Golden Buddha*, it is difficult to tell if Spenser's assumption is correct or not. Things are not so cut and dry in *Corsair*, wherein Cabrillo mentions to Hunley that human blood was found inside a Middle Eastern jewel made between 50 BC and 80 AD. While the analysis could not be conclusive because the blood was so degraded, it appeared to contain traces of female DNA. According to the woman who ran the analysis, this would be exactly how she would imagine the blood work to look like from a person produced by a virgin birth (see p. 437).

89. Even in the *Harry Potter* adventures, Harry and his companions, Hermoine Granger and Ron Weasley, do very little exploring beyond Hogswarts, its immediate grounds or the nearby village of Hogsmeade until they are in their teens. This is also true during Harry's summer holidays, when he lives with his aunt's family.

90. Haining, *The Classic Era of Crime Fiction*, p. 46.

91. Ibid., pp. 46, 50. This irascible character, created by Harlan Page Halsey, first appeared in the *New York Fireside Companion* in 1872. Halsey was the first detective referred to by the term "sleuth," which means a bloodhound. Old Sleuth was also the first dime-novel detective to appear in a continuing series; he became so popular that he inspired a host of imitators, including Old Cap Collier and Old King Brady.

92. Perhaps the greatest of the dime-novel detectives, the amazing Nick Carter was created by John Russell Coryell and first appeared in the *New York Weekly* in 1886.

93. Drew and Sant, both created by William Tufnell Le Queux, were the first two series characters in spy fiction. The setting for *The Chase* is also contemporaneous with the first modern high adventure espionage novel, Robert Erskine Childers's *The Riddle of the Sands: A Record of Secret Service* (1903).

94. Haining, *The Classic Era of Crime Fiction*, p. 46.

95. Stories involving characters working as intelligence agents or spies have been a part of American literature since James Fenimore Cooper's first successful novel, *The Spy* (1821), which introduces Harvey Birch and is set during the War of Independence. Like Cooper's Hawkeye, Birch possesses many of the requirements for a southwestern folk hero, and, in many ways, he sounds like a Revolutionary War–era Dirk Pitt. Tall, powerfully built, intelligent, intuitive and able to handle himself and his drink with accomplished skill, Birch "is seen as an outcast roaming the parts of New York State that are a no-man's-land in the colonial days. He is self-sufficient, carrying what he needs with him, and employing his expertise, his wits and his agility to avoid capture by the enemy. He has a slightly cynical attitude towards the Establishment—such as it is—and avoids its restrictions, occasionally even breaking them to help his missions. His clandestine existence makes him a figure of mystery, brave in the eyes of men and appealing to women, whom he charms and leaves as easily as he meets them. In an amusing episode, Birch disguises himself as a woman to fool a British colonel, revealing 'herself' when the necessary information has been extracted from the blustering lecher" (see Haining, *The Classic Era of Crime Fiction*, p. 184). Some 50 years later, books about secret invasions (also known as the "future war genre") became popular in England, starting with Sir George Chesney's *The Battle of Dorking* (1871) and followed by popular titles such as Le Queux's *The Great War in England in 1897* (1894), both of which are credited with playing major roles in the development of the spy story (see Haining, *The Classic Era of Crime Fiction*, pp. 186–7).

96. Clive Cussler, *The Chase* (New York: Berkley, 2007), pp. 23–4.

97. Genesis 21:6. If referring to the Hebrew meaning for Bell's first name seems a bit of a stretch, consider the fact that when Bell visits Denver he looks at the Mizpah Arch and knows *mizpah* means watchtower in ancient Hebrew (see *The Chase*, p. 39).

98. For an excellent overview of this period see "Chapter Thirteen: 'Building Best, Building Greatly,'

1896–1912," in Allen and Schweikart, *A Patriot's History of the United States*, pp. 457–491.

99. See *The Chase* p. 50.

100. Ibid., p. 60. Unlike his fellow detectives Arthur Curtis and Glenn Irvine, Bell is familiar with the term sociopath.

101. Cussler and Dirgo, *Clive Cussler & Dirk Pitt Revealed!*, pp. 26–9.

102. Ibid., p. 22.

103. See *Treasure*, p. 48.

104. See *The Chase*, p. 40, 447.

105. Sampson, *Yesterday's Faces: Vol. I, Glory Figures*, pp. 70–1.

106. Cussler, *The Chase*, p. 30.

107. In the Fargos' first adventure, they are even confronted by a puzzle involving a gold bug (specifically a cicada) and cryptograms (see *Spartan Gold*, pp. 124 and 177–9).

108. As of this writing, Disney has a third *National Treasure* film in development, and between 2007 and 2009 Disney Press released a novelization of *National Treasure: Book of Secrets*, followed by six original books written by Catherine Hapka about ancestors of the film's hero, Benjamin Franklin Gates (Nicolas Cage), and their quest for the Knights Templar treasure.

109. The city was named after William Fargo, founder of Wells Fargo and director of the Northern Pacific Railroad. Wells Fargo helped Western expansion, first by investing in the pony express, and then in stagecoaches, merging with other companies to form the Overland Mail Company. The Red River, which separates North Dakota and Minnesota, runs along Fargo's eastern border; during the 1870s and 1880s the town was a stopping point for steamboats. The Northern Pacific Railroad arrived about this time, and this is when Fargo became known as the Gateway to the West for the northern United States.

110. Although Remi is more common in France than America.

111. This is stated in *Dragon* (p. 527), but in *Flood Tide* (p. 142), Pitt graduated 35th in his class.

112. Clive Cussler and Grant Blackwood, *Spartan Gold* (New York: Berkley, 2009), p. 35.

113. Ibid., p. 37.

114. Again, this is evocative of Lacey and Casey Nicefolk, whose differences balance their relationship and make them as effective a team as the Fargos.

115. In a possible case of repetition, this argon laser scanner sounds like a somewhat more sophisticated variation of the Fyrie probe, from *Iceberg*.

116. Dashiell Hammett, *The Big Knockover: Selected Stories and Short Novels by Dashiell Hammett* (New York: Vintage, 1972), p. xvii.

117. Author's questions to Cussler, August 2009.

118. Valero, *The Adventure Writing of Clive Cussler*, pp. 157–8.

119. In spite of these examples, Gallagher writes in *Action Figures*, on p. 118: "Cussler's novels introduce the recurring figure of the exceptional woman, defined according to masculine categories such as candor and rationality and set apart from conventions of femininity such as domesticity and desire for romantic commitment." Many of Cussler's heroines are exceptional women who are candid and rational and may not be as keen on domesticity, but it is hardly accurate to say they are set apart from the desire of romantic commitment.

120. For examples, see Clive Cussler and Grant Blackwood, *Lost Empire* (New York: Putnam, 2010), pp. 43, 138, and *Spartan Gold* (New York: Berkley, 2009), pp. 43, 51, 116–7.

121. For example, see *Spartan Gold*, p. 51.

122. As of this writing, the closest the Fargos come to being manhunters takes place in *The Kingdom*, when they are hired to find a missing archaeologist.

123. See Chapter 5.

124. See http://en.wikipedia.org/wiki/Enchanted_forest.

125. For an example, see *Spartan Gold*, p. 66.

Chapter 4

1. Robert Sampson, *Yesterday's Faces: Vol. V, Dangerous Horizons* (Bowling Green, OH: Bowling Green State University Popular Press, 1983), p. 131.

2. O. F. Snelling, *007 James Bond: A Report* (New York: Signet, 1964), pp. 35–7.

3. See Chapter 5 for more about Pitt's behavior towards women, as well as Cussler's thematic preoccupation with the differences between the sexes.

4. If Pitt never has sex with Summer Moran, how do we explain their twin children? We cannot, except to admit that such things happen in literature. For example, in *The Big Sleep* Raymond Chandler never explains who kills the Sternwood family's chauffer, Owen Taylor, and Howard Hawks had no concerns about carrying this oversight over in his 1946 film adaptation. See also Chapter 6.

5. Snelling, *007 James Bond: A Report*, pp. 35–7.

6. Cussler, "Make Your Story Fly," p. 13.

7. Sampson, *Yesterday's Faces: Vol. V, Dangerous Horizons*, p. 67.

8. Cussler, "Make Your Story Fly," p. 13.

9. Cussler, "Do Your Characters Fit Their Roles?" p. 10.

10. See unpublished 1985 interview, pp. 16–7.

11. See "Do Your Characters Fit Their Roles?" p. 10.

12. All we are told about Summer's mother is that she is dead and lies buried in the seamount of Kanoli (*Pacific Vortex*, p. 265).

13. "Introduction," *The Mediterranean Caper and Iceberg* (New York: Simon & Schuster, 1995), p. 9.

14. Summer's clothes are in keeping with the novel's Hawaiian setting, but could her Oriental dress be a tip-of-the-hat to Fah Lo Suee? Anything is possible, but according to Cussler, the inspiration for Summer's look (as well as her green sheath dress) is an 18-year-old girl he saw trying on a similar dress in a shop in Hawaii in 1965. See http://www.facebook.com/clivecussler?ref=ts#!,/photo.php?v=10100497096865792.

15. Fleming, *You Only Live Twice*, p. 18.

16. Pitt intends to marry Maeve, and does marry Loren, but when he finally visits Summer Moran's grave in *Treasure of Khan* (p. 543), we are told that Summer is Pitt's first, and deepest, love.

17. Arthur Dorsett is Australian, so the choice of Irish names for his daughters, Maeve, Deirdre and Boudicca, is curious. The names Maeve and Deirdre can be found in the Ulster Cycle of Irish mythology from the First Century AD. Boudicca is a

historical figure, but all three were queens. Medb (Maeve is derived from Medb) is a warrior queen; Deirdre of the Sorrows is a commoner forced to marry a king she does not love; and, sometime around 60 AD, Boudicca led a revolt of the British Iceni against the Romans. Of Dorsett's three daughters, Maeve's name is the most prescient. The sociopathic Deirdre is named after Irish mythology's most tragic character, and the brutal Boudicca's namesake was so noble that Queen Elizabeth I was compared to her.

18. Cussler, *Shock Wave*, p. 372.
19. Cussler, *Pacific Vortex*, p. 24.
20. Cussler, "Introduction," *The Mediterranean Caper and Iceberg*, pp. 9–10.
21. While we are on topic of similar scenes, Pitt and Giordino abduct Teri by tying her negligee over her head. In *Casino Royale*, Vesper Lynd is apparently abducted by having her dress tied over her head, revealing that she is nude underneath. Fleming plays the scene straight, but Cussler has a little fun at Teri's expense after she is supposedly rescued from Pitt and Giordino by Inspector Zacynthus's men, Zeno and Darius; Zeno tells Giordino to release Teri so they can look at her other end (see *The Mediterranean Caper*, p. 120).
22. Cussler, *Deep Six*, p. 78.
23. Cussler, *Treasure*, p. 24.
24. Ibid., p. 456.
25. Why Yerli and not Pitt? See *Sahara*, p. 200, for Cussler's explanation.
26. Stacy is cunning and crafty and her covert cover as a photographer makes her a bit of a trickster. Perhaps it is not a coincidence that one of literature's most famous tricksters is Reynard the Fox, the hero of several European poems and fables, beginning around the 12th century.
27. Other redheaded women include the anonymous woman Pitt meets at Newport Beach, in *Iceberg*; the anonymous receptionist at the Winthrop Nursing Home, in *Cyclops*; Deirdre Dorsett (if you count copper hair) the "sisterhood" from *Trojan Odyssey*; and the anonymous NUMA marine biologist who speaks with Kelly Egan aboard the *Deep Encounter*, in *Valhalla Rising*.
28. Cussler, *Dragon*, p. 41.
29. Cussler never describes Summer as having high cheekbones, but since Maeve has this facial feature and (by Pitt's own admission) Maeve and Summer look so much alike, it seems safe to assume that Summer has high cheekbones as well.
30. Cussler, *Sahara*, p. 507.
31. Cussler, *Atlantis Found*, p. 122.
32. Cussler, *Inca Gold*, p. 31.
33. Ibid.
34. Ibid., p. 572.
35. See *Night Probe!*, p. 101.
36. See *Valhalla Rising*, p. 206.
37. From Snelling, *007 James Bond: A Report*, p. 114: "Ernst Stavro Blofeld is one of the most engaging criminals in sensational fiction. He bids air to rival villains like [Bulldog Drummond's arch-enemy] Carl Peterson and [Sherlock Holmes's nemesis] Professor Moriarty."
38. The Blofeld Trilogy is an unofficial part of Fleming's Bond series. If there is an equivalent of it in the Bond films it would be *You Only Live Twice* (1967), *On Her Majesty's Secret Service* (1969) and *Diamonds Are Forever* (1971).
39. Cussler, "Introduction," *The Mediterranean Caper and Iceberg*, pp. 9–10. When Cussler was asked if he ever considered bringing back Moran, perhaps in a spin-off series, he simply answered, "No" (author's questions to Cussler, August 2009).
40. Sampson, *Yesterday's Faces: Vol. V, Dangerous Horizons*, pp. 7–8.
41. Campbell, *Hero with a Thousand Faces*, pp. 15–6.
42. It does not matter if a villain is tyrant-monster or antagonist so long as he is, like Captain Blackbeard from *Pirates of the Caribbean: On Stranger Tides* (2011), a bad man, and in adventure literature, the more villainous the adversary the more memorable he becomes. This is why Chester Gould, creator of *Dick Tracy*, made the bad guys who battled Tracy, including Flaptop Jones, Pruneface, and The Brow so memorable, and why Bob Kane and Bill Finger, creators of The Batman, followed Gould's example. In Kane's autobiography, *Batman and Me* (Buenos Aires: Eclipse Books, 1989), p. 105: "Along with Chester Gould's *Dick Tracy*, *Batman* has the most bizarre and unique villains in comics. Indeed, it was *Dick Tracy* which inspired us to create an equally weird set of villains for *Batman*." Stan Lee and Steve Ditko, creators of Spider-Man, and Fleming may have also followed Gould's example by creating some of the adventure genre's most impressive Rogue's Galleries.
43. Unlike Rondheim, though, Blackwood has to contend with being upstaged by one of the most memorable of monster-tyrants, Professor Moriarty (uncredited), who appears only briefly in the film. Even though he sticks to the shadows, Moriarty's malevolence overshadows Blackwood's, even though Blackwood has supposedly risen from the dead, is prone to making scene-stealing Lugosi-esque speeches, and may be in league with the Devil. Blackwood is a maniacal opponent, but Moriarty is a force of evil whose mastery over England's underworld (including an unwitting Blackwood) must be rooted out, lest untold numbers of innocents suffer.
44. This is just as true when the main character of a series is a villain. Fu Manchu is known worldwide, but how many people recognize the name of the series' hero, Sir Denis Nayland Smith?
45. Campbell, *Hero with a Thousand Faces*, pp. 15–6.
46. Sampson, *Yesterday's Faces: Vol. III, From the Dark Side*, p. xii. This list also includes the Criminal with a Cause, and the Bent Hero.
47. Ibid., p. 1.
48. Ibid.
49. Originally, Delphi Moran was called Delphi Ea, but before Bantam Books published *Pacific Vortex* in 1982, Cussler did a quick rewrite, and in the process Delphi's last name was changed to Moran. Cussler was unaware of this until it was brought to his attention in 1997 (see *Clive Cussler and Dirk Pitt*, p. 91), which explains why he refers to the villain as Delphi Ea in an introduction to a Simon & Schuster reprint of *The Mediterranean Caper and Iceberg*, published in 1995 (see pp. 9–10).
50. See Sampson, *Yesterday's Faces: Vol. V, From the Dark Side*, p. 4.
51. See author's questions to Cussler, August 2009.
52. Pitt's eyes can also affect people. In *Valhalla Rising* (p. 100), for example, we are told that his eyes have a hypnotic quality that seems to reach into people's souls, especially women.
53. Cussler and Dirgo, *Clive Cussler & Dirk Pitt Revealed!*, p. 47.

54. Cussler, *The Mediterranean Caper*, p. 122, and *Night Probe!*, pp. 26–7.

55. Cussler, *The Mediterranean Caper*, p. 122.

56. Another parallel between these fights takes place at their conclusions. In *The Mediterranean Caper* Pitt and Giordino finally take down Darius when Pitt kicks Darius in the groin; in *Cyclops* Pitt mortally injures Gly, but he refuses to die until Jessie LeBaron shoots him in the groin.

57. Sampson, *Yesterday's Faces: Vol. V, From the Dark Side*, p. 2.

58. See Ian Fleming, *From Russia, With Love* (New York: Signet, 1967), pp. 15–8.

59. Ibid., pp. 172–82.

60. What are the odds of this happening? Sampson (*Yesterday's Faces: Vol. I, Glory Figures*, p. 237) puts his tongue firmly in check and advises, "If the coincidences bother you, breathe slowly and think of calm thoughts."

61. Fleming, *From Russia, With Love*, p. 16. Fleming adds a supernatural touch, or at least hearkens back to the original definition of a "lunatic"—that is, someone affected by the moon (*luna*)—when the adolescent Grant begins getting violent homicidal compulsions during a full moon.

62. Cussler, *Night Probe!*, p. 26.

63. See *Cyclops*, pp. 194–6 and 202. Even the title, *Cyclops* (the name of a collier sunk by a giant wave near Cuba in the prologue), recalls a monster like Gly, the one-eye giant from Greek mythology; he is described by Homer, in *The Odyssey*, as living in a cave and devouring human beings; it is also possible that the sink-throwing scene was inspired by that epic poem. In *The Odyssey* the Cyclops is blinded by Ulysses and is so angry when Ulysses and his men escape his island that the monster rips a boulder out of the ground and hurls it at their boat (see *Bulfinch's Mythology*, pp. 237–40). Cussler may have also been inspired by this scene to have Pitt partially blind Gly by jamming a thumb into one of his eyes, turning Gly into a genuine cyclops. It is also interesting to note that, from this point in the Pitt series, Cussler increasingly alludes to legends and creatures from ancient Greek mythology and Homer's epics to such an extent that they almost become their own thematic preoccupation.

64. Corrupt businessmen are also a favorite villain type with Fleming (see Snelling, *007 James Bond: A Report*, p. 97).

65. Min and Lee Tong are not the masterminds behind the plot to brainwash the president and other U.S political figures, but *Deep Six* is Cussler's first adventure with a scientific (or science fiction) threat rather than a purely political or criminal threat. The second scientific threat does not appear until *Shock Wave*, after which they appear more frequently (e.g., *Atlantis Found*, *Treasure of Khan*), though not as frequently as criminal clans. For more about the scientific threats in Cussler's adventures, see the "Science Fiction" sub-section in Chapter 5.

66. For some reason, Epona is the only major supporting character in the Pitt series whose eye color is never stated.

67. See chapters 5 and 7.

68. Spectre is an appropriate name for a person who does not really exist, although, in an adventure series, it is hard to hear the name and not think of the international crime organization SPECTER from the James Bond novels and films. Epona is almost as shadowy and formidable as Blofeld, the head of SPECTER.

69. See Eternal Return, http://en.wikipedia.org/wiki/Eternal_return_(Eliade).

70. Similar "exposing" scenes take place in less ostentatious surroundings in *Iceberg* (see p. 339) and *Shock Wave* (see p. 528).

71. Cussler, *Trojan Odyssey*, p. 455.

72. No relation to Epona Eliade's alter-ego or SPECTER.

73. Both first names start with "C," their middle names have two syllables and six letters, and their last names have one syllable and four letters, with the second letter being "a" and the last letter "e."

74. Cussler, *Valhalla Rising*, pp. 312–3.

75. Kane's denouement is not as public as Zale's, although it happens in front of a large group of people, after which Kane loses the will to live, whereas Zale takes the coward's way out.

76. This truism is driven home with unusual effectiveness in the film *Unbreakable* (2000), in which the villain Elijah Price (Samuel L. Jackson), a man who suffers from a condition that makes his bones as brittle as glass, explains it to David Dunn (Bruce Willis), an otherwise-average man who discovers he has tremendous strength and is nearly invulnerable after surviving a train wreck caused by Price:

> Elijah Price: You know what the scariest thing is? To not know your place in this world. To not know why you're here. That's just an awful feeling.
> David Dunn: What have you done?
> Elijah Price: I almost gave up hope. There were so many times I questioned myself.
> David Dunn: You killed all those people.
> Elijah Price: But I found you. So many sacrifices, just to find you.
> David Dunn: Jesus Christ.
> Elijah Price: Now that we know who you are, I know who I am. I'm not a mistake!, It all makes sense!, In a comic, you know how you can tell who the arch-villain is going to be? He's the exact opposite of the hero. And most times they're friends, like you and me!, I should've known way back when. You know why, David? Because of the kids. They called me Mr. Glass.

77. http://en.wikipedia.org/wiki/Rat_(zodiac).

78. http://en.wikipedia.org/wiki/Cancer_(Zodiac_sign), and Cussler and Dirgo, *Sea Hunters*, p. 17.

79. Cussler, *Flood Tide*, p. 135.

80. Ibid., p. 142. That master plotter Conan Doyle succinctly presents the classic pattern for conflict between a hero and his opposite in "The Final Problem." Moriarty recites the dates of the conflict going on between himself and Holmes: "You crossed my path on the 4th of January.... On the 23rd you incommoded me; by the middle of February I was seriously inconvenienced by you; at the end of March I was absolutely hampered in my plans; and now, at the close of April, I find myself placed in such a position through your continual persecution that I am

in positive danger of losing my liberty" (see Sir Arthur Conan Doyle, *The Annotated Sherlock Holmes*, Vol. II, p. 305). Pitt and Qin Shang even have a face-to-face comparable to Moriarty's famous visit to Holmes's Baker Street rooms (see *Flood Tide*, pp. 279–83). Cussler also delays Qin Shang's first scene until late into the story (see p. 133) after other characters have had time to talk about the villain and his activities, just as Conan Doyle does with Moriarty in "The Final Problem."

81. After Yaeger presents an initial rundown about Qin Shang, Pitt jokes that the man may be a reincarnation of Fu Manchu (see *Flood Tide*, p. 44), which is a lovely thought, but based on his accomplishments Qin Shang is no more a reincarnated Fu Manchu than Suma or Delphi.

82. See *Dragon*, p. 140. This is where similarities between Suma and Qin Shang end. Suma, at 49, is older; he is approximately five-foot-seven, which makes him a bit taller than the average Japanese but shorter than Qin Shang; he is also in excellent physical shape, having been a dedicated weightlifter since the age of 15. Suma also has white hair, which makes him look older than his age since most Japanese men have black hair, and has indigo blue eyes (see p. 139). Suma is also spiritual, unlike Qin Shang. Suma is first seen visiting the Shokonsha shrine; he later he explains to Giordino how the Japanese have combined Shintoism with their culture (see p. 360).

83. See Schultz and Wielde, "Wonks and Warriors," pp. 66, 74.

84. Historical former presidents also appear in the Pitt series, even though their appearances are inexplicable if their terms are compared to those of Cussler's fictional chief executives. For example, President Ronald Reagan appears with President Jimmy Carter in *Cyclops* (see p. 251), but Cussler's first fictional president is in office during the years 1987–8 (see *Raise the Titanic!* and *Vixen 03*). Another example is a reference to the Clinton Administration in *Flood Tide* (see p. 58) even though two different fictional presidents are serving during the years 1991–1996 (see *Treasure*, *Dragon* and *Sahara*).

85. In *Flood Tide* Sandecker is 65, but by *Trojan Odyssey* he is somehow 61 again.

86. See *Flood Tide*, pp. 52 and 312, and *Fire Ice*, p. 350.

87. See *Flood Tide*, pp. 59 and 542–4.

88. Ibid., p. 543.

89. It also helps that, this time, it is not Wallace aiding a foreign enemy; it is his vice-president, Sid Sparkman. When Sandecker finds out, he insists that Sparkman resign or have these activities exposed. Whereas Wallace would have been delighted to fire Sandecker, the admiral is angry at the prospect of destroying a man's career (see *Fire Ice*, pp. 361–3).

90. Cussler and Cussler, *Treasure of Khan*, pp. 321–3.

91. "What Is It That We Love in Sherlock Holmes?" in Sir Arthur Conan Doyle, *The Annotated Sherlock Holmes*, Vol. 1, p. 103.

92. See Chapter 4 and http://www.cusslermen.com/Characters.htm.

93. See Sampson, *Yesterday's Faces: Vol. I, Glory Figures*, pp. 79 and 82–3.

94. Ibid., p. 95.

Chapter 5

1. Sampson, *Yesterday's Faces: Vol. III, From the Dark Side*, p. 107.

2. See Cussler and Dirgo, *Clive Cussler & Dirk Pitt Revealed!*, p. 72, and Valero, *The Adventure Writing of Clive Cussler*, p. 57. In a list of questions I submitted to Cussler in 2009, I asked if he still took pride in the quality of his plots and characters. Cussler replied: "Yes, that I do. The fact that so many people and children have enjoyed my books and been influenced by them is a great source of satisfaction and joy." See also Don Swaim nterview with Clive Cussler, January 30, 1986, and "Clive Cussler Biography: BookRags.com."

3. "Foreword," Stephen King, *Night Shift* (Garden City, NY: Doubleday, 1976), p. xiii. King may seem an odd choice to compare with Cussler in any manner, but in *Sea Hunters II* (New York: Simon & Schuster, 1996, p. 345) Cussler recounts how he stopped by King's home while searching with NUMA for the missing French plane *White Bird*. King never answered the door, and Cussler never found out if King was home.

4. Ibid., pp. xxiii–xiv.

5. Cussler, *Treasure*, p. 520.

6. Foreword in *Pacific Vortex*, p. v.

7. Valero, *The Adventure Writing of Clive Cussler*, p. 23.

8. See Schultz and Wielde, "Wonks and Warriors," pp. 63–5. When Cussler was asked if he agrees that Pitt is the first (or among the first) series heroes who are also pubic administrators, he replied: "Yes, he preceded [Jack] Ryan by several years" (author's questions to Cussler, August 2009).

9. See Schultz and Wielde, "Wonks and Warriors," p. 65. Sandecker, Giordino, Gunn and Yeager are public administrators with NUMA, as are Austin and Zavala. Loren Smith, a congresswoman, and Pitt's father, a senator, were both elected to their posts. A president's chief of staff, like the self-important Harrison Moon (*Night Probe!*), is an appointed official.

10. See Gallagher, *Action Figures*, p. 116.

11. Argyle and Merwin, "Fuzzy Lines," pp. 52, 57. Argyle and Merwin also spotlight Tom Clancy's Jack Ryan and Jack Ryan, Jr.

12. According to its indicia, *Public Voices* is a magazine "concerning public administrators and the public service."

13. Argyle and Merwin, "Fuzzy Lines," p. 52. Again, Argyle and Merwin include Clancy's novels about Ryan and Ryan, Jr., in this discussion.

14. Ibid., p. 52; Argyle and Merwin cite the phrase "what the U.S. can't" from Robert Ludlum's *The Amber Warning* (p. 190). Argyle and Merwin also include Clancy's novels about Jack Ryan, Jr., Hendley Associates and the Campus as other examples of private organizations in fiction which work outside the state to do what they believe is best for the citizenry (see Argyle and Merwin, "Fuzzy Lines," p. 57).

15. Gallagher, *Action Figures*, p. 148. Gallagher adds that this rejection of authority is "a sign of the hero's innate curiosity and his willingness to court danger."

16. Sampson, *Yesterday's Faces: Vol. VI, Violent Lives* (Bowling Green, OH: Bowling Green University State Popular Press), p. 43.

17. Ibid., p. 100. Such rebels have always been and, will likely always be, a part of the American tradition, a fact made apparent in movies and

other forms of media. In *Masters of American Cinema*, film historian and reviewer Louis Gianetti writes: "American movies have repeatedly glorified nonconformists and outsiders. Romantics of all periods advocate the overthrow of stultifying convention and decorum. Social institutions are portrayed as antihuman and tyrannical. Above all, romantic art is an art of revolt against the Establishment, and its characteristic hero is the rebel."

18. From *The Council of Justice* (Ward, Lock & Co., Ltd., 1916), p. 190; quoted in Sampson, *Yesterday's Faces: Vol. I, Glory Figures*, p. 165.

19. Schultz and Wielde, "Wonks and Warriors," pp. 61–82.

20. Ibid., p. 61. To support this claim, Wielde and Schultz cite "Synthetic History and Subjective Reality: The Impact of Oliver Stone's *JFK*," in David A. Schultz, ed., *It's Show Time: Media, Politics, and Popular Culture* (New York: Peter Lang, 2000), pp. 171–96.

21. Schultz and Wielde, "Wonks and Warriors," p. 62.

22. Ibid., p. 65. Wielde and Schultz define a public servant as "anyone employed to carry out the policies or duties set forth by the elected body."

23. Ibid., p. 70. Wielde and Schultz's list also includes a fifth species of public servant, the Hyper Loyalists. Neither heroes nor villains, Hyper Loyalists are a rare breed, basically public servants dedicated to their job and to serving the public to the best of their abilities.

24. Ibid., p. 71.
25. Ibid., p. 72.
26. Ibid., pp. 71–3.
27. See *The Mediterranean Caper*, p. 12.
28. Cussler, *Iceberg*, p. 24.
29. Schultz and Wielde, "Wonks and Warriors," pp. 71–3.
30. Ibid., p. 66.
31. Ibid.
32. Ibid., p. 72. According to Schultz and Wielde, the Action Hero, by his very presence and nature, counteracts the general public's negative opinion of bureaucrats. Wilde and Schultz discovered during their research that "the negative connotation of the term 'bureaucrat' is a way to set the stage for discussion of negative portrayals. If this terminology holds fast, then the Action Hero essentially becomes an Anti-Bureaucrat by not fitting the criteria of a typical paper-pushing automaton."

33. Ibid., p. 74.

34. Such distrust is complex in its philosophy and explanation. For an overview of this American perspective of people and government, see "A Nation of Laws: 1776–89," in Allen and Schweikart, *A Patriot's History of the United States* (pp. 88–126).

35. Author's questions to Cussler, August 2009.

36. Cussler, *Night Probe!*, p. 149.

37. Sources for these descriptions are http://en.wikipedia.org/wiki/Janus, and *Webster's Encyclopedic Unabridged Dictionary of the English Language*, p. 763.

38. See *The Big Knockover*. This short story begins with the memorable opening line: "It was a wandering daughter job." The Op explains, "The Hambletons had been for several generations a wealthy and decently prominent New York family. There was nothing in the Hambleton history to account for Sue, the youngest member of the clan. She grew out of childhood with a kink that made her dislike the polished side of life, like the rough."

39. Cussler, *Iceberg*, p. 339.

40. See Chapter 7 for more about the trickster elements of Emma's character.

41. For an example, see *Vixen 03*, p. 322. Emma using a female name while encouraging people to believe she is a man is the single time in *Vixen 03* that she hides in plain sight instead of using a disguise.

42. We can deduce a few things. Calling herself Emma and encouraging misunderstandings allows the clever and bold Emma to hide her gender in plain sight. Selling doctored files, attempting to assassinate Fawkes, and helping with Operation: Wild Rose demonstrates that she has little compassion for her fellow human beings, although it is hard to say if aligning with De Vaal suggests a prejudice against Negroes. Emma's firearm proficiency, tactical planning skills, fighting abilities, and mastery of disguises suggest extensive professional training, possibly as a covert operative in the military or in an intelligence agency. Emma primarily works in South Africa and surrounding countries, so she may be a native or was raised in South Africa. As notable a villain as Emma is, it is interesting to note that this master of disguise does not appear in "The Reunion."

43. Paul and Robert Capesterre might be considered transitional characters, borderline Janus villains who belong to an international crime family.

44. In what might have been a subtle indication of Cromwell's divided personality, Cussler quotes Robert Louis Stevenson when he describes Nob Hill and Cromwell's home as a "hill which is covered with palaces (*The Chase*, p. 114)." Stevenson, of course, is the creator of the most famous of Janus villains, Dr. Henry Jekyll and Mr. Edward Hyde. Jekyll also lives in a respectable home on a prosperous London bystreet, but he feels most alive when releasing Hyde in the shabby rear quarters of the house that faces a sinister block of building. For a good examination of the Gothic duality of Jekyll's house and the duality which such a house can represent in its owner, see footnotes 13 and 15 in Leonard Wolf's *The Essential Dr. Jekyll & Mr. Hyde* (N.p: ibooks, 2005), pp. 33–4.

45. Cussler, *The Chase*, p. 188.

46. Bruce A. Rosenberg, *Ian Fleming* (Woodbridge, CT: Twayne, 1989), pp. 115–6.

47. Cussler, *The Chase*, p. 188.

48. Ibid., p. 101. When we first see Cromwell he is wearing a tailored black conservative suit with a yellow rose in the buttonhole and a cocked derby hat. When we first see Massey he is fastidiously dressed and has a cocked Panama straw hat (see *Night Probe!*, p. 10).

49. When a newspaper reporter tries to prove that Massey is Dapper Doyle, Massey's influential friends cover up the scandal (see *Night Probe!*, pp. 265–6).

50. *Night Probe!*, pp. 265–6.

51. Just the opposite was true barely a century ago. While there have been plenty of homosexual or bisexual poets, it was common for masculine heterosexual authors like Poe, Conan Doyle and Stoker to write and study poetry. Associating poetry as strictly feminine or homosexual is a perplexing (and historically recent) trend.

52. Cussler plays against this stereotype with Kristjan Fyrie. Prior to his sex change, the adventurous entrepreneur Kristjan was the antithesis of the homosexual stereotype Pitt pretends to be.

53. See *Iceberg*, pp. 214–6. Rondheim is a walking search engine of poetry, able to name the title and author of any poem after hearing only one line.

54. Ibid., pp. 238–43.

55. When Cussler was asked if reader identification was the reason for the many pairs with physical differences that appear in his stories, he replied, "No reason. Just whatever characters fit the story" (author's questions to Cussler, August 2009).

56. Helen Wheatley, *Gothic Television* (Manchester: Manchester University Press, 2006), p. 3.

57. For more details, see "Introduction," Wilkie Collins, *The Woman in White* (Hertfordshire, UK: Wordsworth Classics, 2002), p. xiii.

58. The concept of someone impersonating the president is hardly new. Films like *G. I. Joe: The Rise of Cobra* (2009), *Vantage Point* (2008), *Dave* (1993) and *The Phantom President* (1932) have featured presidential impostors in their plots.

59. Wallace never possesses Arta in the traditional sense, but as a point of comparison readers might debate if Dr. Henry Jekyll remains Jekyll by any definition when he becomes Hyde, even though Jekyll's account of his first transformation into Hyde is described from the doctor's perspective (see Wolf, ed., *The Essential Dr. Jekyll & Mr. Hyde*, pp. 119–22). By the end of the novella, Jekyll writes that he will lose total control of his body and mind during his next transformation into Hyde (see p. 136), but the fact remains that Hyde and Jekyll are never two people. Jekyll may become oblivious of his fate on earth after his final transformation, but not of his ultimate fate, a point Sherlock Holmes makes to Jekyll in my and Gary Reed's pastiche *The Strange Case of Dr. Jekyll & Mr. Holmes* (San Diego: IDW, 1996), p. 27. Hyde is wanted for murder, and Jekyll is increasingly unable to prevent himself from transforming into Hyde. Jekyll is also running out of the draft that causes the transformation, but as Holmes tells him, "Of course, if Hyde is Hyde, then no matter what you do, you have nothing to fear besides the same extinction that confronts all God's creatures. If, however, there is only Jekyll, then sir, you have the gallows to look forward to, as well as whatever awaits beyond for the chief of sinners."

60. Cussler, *Vixen 03*, p. 98.

61. Ibid., p. 248.

62. L. Burzrlova, "The Spy Novel in English Literature," thesis, Masaryk University Faculty of Education, p. 33.

63. "Humanity thrives on thrills," writes the anonymous editor of the 1937 anthology *Century of Thrillers* (p. v), and fairy tales, like all forms of adventures, generally feature a hero who undergoes a set of adventures to reach a goal. This set of adventures, which Campbell refers to as the "monomyth" or "hero cycle," also appears in myth and legends, and is explored in relation to the Pitt series, in Chapter 7.

64. Rosenberg, *Ian Fleming*, p. 95.

65. A less famous variation of the Prince Charming fairy tale, also from 17th century France, is Charles Perrault's "Toads and Diamonds," in Editorial Board of the University Society (Supervisors), *Bookshelf for Boys and Girls*, Vol. III (New York: University Society, 1972), pp. 147–9.

66. Umberto Eco, *The Role of the Reader: Explorations in the Semiotics of Texts* (Bloomington: Indiana University Press, 1979), pp. 161–3. Essayist and author Eco (*The Name of the Rose*, *Foucault's Pendulum*) writes that Fleming "decides to rely upon the most secure and universal principles and puts into play precisely those archetypal elements that proved successful in fairy tales.... M is the King and Bond is the Knight entrusted with a mission; Bond is the Knight and the Villain is the Dragon; that Lady and Villain stand for Beauty and the Beast; Bond restores the Lady to the fullness of spirit and to her senses—he is the Prince who rescues Sleeping Beauty; between the Free World and the Soviet Union, England and the non–Anglo-Saxon countries is realized the primitive epic relationship between the Privileged Race and the Lower Race, between White and Black, Good and Bad.... Fleming also pleases the sophisticated reader who here distinguish, with a feeling of aesthetic pleasure, the purity of the primitive epic impudently and maliciously translated into current terms and who applaud in Fleming the cultured man, whom they recognize as one of themselves, naturally the most clever and broadminded."

67. See Rosenberg, *Ian Fleming*, pp. 95–6.

68. See *Night Probe!*, pp. 39–41, 46–7. Also see Chapter 7 for a detailed look at Heidi's rebirth.

69. Other famous sleeping ladies or heroes include Brynhild, Charlemagne, Muchukunda, Rip Van Winkle and Tubber Tintye (see Campbell, *Hero with a Thousand Faces*, p. 413). Cussler hints at the Lady in the House of Sleep motif with Summer Moran, Teri Von Til, and, in a bit of role reversal, with Pitt in *Shock Wave* (see pp. 130–6) and Cabrillo in *Skeleton Coast* (see p. 341).

70. Campbell, *Hero with a Thousand Faces*, pp. 110–1. The *Titanic* is the only supporting character in the Pitt series that outshines the protagonist.

71. In a nice touch, Cussler names the submersible after the 7th century Greek lyric poetess of Lesbos.

72. Cussler, *Raise the Titanic!*, pp. 169–70.

73. Ibid., p. 132.

74. Ibid., p. 141. There is more going on here than perhaps even Pitt realizes. For NUMA, the search for the *Titanic* could be called a treasure hunt, but it is motivated by their respect and admiration for the ship. Her spell is undeniable to them, unlike Seagram, who is only after the supposed boon the *Titanic* holds. It is the Sicilian Project that captivates him, not the *Titanic*, not even God and country. Seagram indicates this when he tells his wife, Dana, that he believes his ideas are the project's sperm (see p. 24). Seagram may have been the one who suggested that the *Titanic* be raised, but, unlike Pitt and NUMA, his motivation for the salvage is based in pure hubris. This is why in the film adaptation it is Pitt who suggests the salvage. There is no hubris theme in the film, but in Cussler's novel it takes someone with so much riding on the Sicilian Project as to dare suggest such a seemingly impossible feat. As explained in the Gothic subsection of this chapter, Seagram's hubris ultimately costs him everything.

75. This is the one time in the Pitt series that Cussler includes an insert chapter, an unprecedented occurrence that underscores the unprecedented nature of the ship's discovery. When Cussler was asked what inspired him to do this, he answered, "I merely thought it was a scene the readers would enjoy" (author's questions to Cussler, August 2009).

76. A similar interlude for a famous ship occurs in *Star Trek: The Motion Picture* (1979), as Admiral James T. Kirk views the recommissioned *Enterprise* in orbital dry-dock. The scene lasts over four minutes and serves no other purpose than to showcase the iconic starship's premiere appearance on the big screen. Thanks to Douglas Trumbull's special effects and Jerry Goldsmith's musical score, it is worth every second.

77. Editorial Board of the University Society (Supervisors), "Sleeping Beauty," *The Bookshelf for Boys and Girls*, Vol. III, p. 7.

78. Unfortunately the same cannot be said for the real *Titanic*.

79. Editorial Board of the University Society (Supervisors), "Sleeping Beauty," *The Bookshelf for Boys and Girls*, Vol. III, p. 8.

80. See *Raise the Titanic!*, pp. 177–8.

81. Ibid., p. 178. The waiting bridal motif may seem more apt if we remember that the *Titanic* never completed her "maiden" voyage.

82. Ibid., pp. 21–4.

83. Magic mirrors can do more than reveal the inner person; they can also be used to explore the vagaries of society or explore "bigger questions," such as humanity's place in the cosmos, as witnessed in perhaps the most famous mirror fairy tale of all, *Through the Looking-Glass*, Lewis Carroll's follow up to *Alice's Adventures in Wonderland*. In this story, Alice is a virtual pawn in a chess game that transpires as she explores the bizarre world on the other side of her looking-glass. During her exploration, Alice is told by the characters Tweedledee and Tweedledum that she is merely a figment in a dream of a slumbering character called the Red King.

84. See "Forty-four Turkish Fairy Tales: 'The Snake-Peri and the Magic Mirror,'" http://www.sacred-texts.com/asia/ftft/ftft34.htm. Another variation on this revelation theme in magic mirrors appears in Steven Philip Jones's *Talismen: The Knightmare Knife* (Cincinnati: Mundania Press, 2009). In this story, four boys are given a glimpse into one of the other boys' future when they stare into the pieces of a broken mirror (see pp. 78–84). This glimpse not only reveals something important about the reflected boy but about the boy looking into the mirror, both by how that boy reacts immediately and then throughout the course of the *Talismen* novels. Magic mirrors can be found in fairy tales around the world, such as the Chinese fairy tale "The Maid in the Mirror" (Editorial Board of the University Society (Supervisors), *The Bookshelf for Boys and Girls*, Vol. III, pp. 307–9).

85. Cussler, *Raise the Titanic!*, p. 29. Cussler slips in other military terms to describe Dana and Seagram's relationship whenever the mood turns tense (see pp. 22 and 24 for examples).

86. Characters being haunted by something from the past that threatens to reach out and destroy them is also a favorite theme in Gothic stories, such as Edgar Allan Poe's "The Fall of the House of Ushers and H. P. Lovecraft's *The Case of Charles Dexter Ward*. See the "Gothic" subsection in this chapter for more details.

87. See *Raise the Titanic!*, pp. 30–1.

88. Ibid., p. 33.

89. Even more tragic and ironic, Seagram's project will succeed, making him a savior of sorts for America, but it is Dana who gets all the credit in the Beltway as the supposed heroine of the *Titanic* rescue.

90. Cussler, *Raise the Titanic!*, p. 162. In some ways, Marie is a mirror image of Dana in that Marie is many of the things Dana wants to be. Marie is a truly liberated, no-nonsense woman who is comfortable in her own skin and makes no excuses for her actions or desires, something Dana does frequently (see pp. 164 and 352 for examples). When Dana tries to explain her indecision by claiming nothing has seemed to go right for her lately, Marie points out that this has been the case since Dana left Seagram. When Dana snaps that she does not need a sermon, Marie calmly but firmly replies that if Dana wants to vent her wrath on somebody, she should "stand in front of the mirror."

91. Ibid., p. 188. In most of her early scenes Dana dresses and acts like actress/singer Doris Day. But, as her metamorphosis continues, this becomes less noticeable.

92. Ibid., p. 350.

93. Ibid., p. 352.

94. See Sir Arthur Conan Doyle, *The Strange Case of Dr. Jekyll & Mr. Hyde* (New York: Bantam, 1985), pp. 83–4. A case could also be made that Cussler uses mirrors in relation to Dana as a symbol of her self-centeredness and self-delusions since, like the hypocritical Jekyll looking at Hyde, Dana consistently looks at in the mirror and only sees what she wants to see.

95. Cussler, *Raise the Titanic!*, pp. 350–2.

96. Cussler, *Deep Six*, pp. 4–8.

97. See *Shock Wave*, p. 528.

98. Stolen children are a common motif in fairy tales, from "Hansel and Gretel" to the Lost Boys of *Peter Pan*, as well the myths and legends of trolls and leprechauns. There are also fairy tales, myths and legends such as *Beowulf*, wherein a protector-dragon guards fabulous treasures, and there are fairy tales like Henry C. Brunner's "Casperl and the Princess," in which protector-dragons guard a princess (Editorial Board of the University Society (Supervisors), *The Bookshelf for Boys and Girls*, Vol. III (New York: University Society, 1972), pp. 194–200. The dragon-guarding-the-princess motif is also used in the film *Shrek* (2001), although in William Steig's book *Shrek!* (1993), the basis for the film, the protector is a knight and the dragon ends up performing the marriage between the ogre Shrek and an even more hideous ogress. When the stolen child and protector motifs are combined it recalls the famous legend involving St. George, who defeated a dragon that was living in a pond near the Libyan town of Silene (see Leonard Wolf, ed., *The Annotated Dracula* [. New York: Clarkson N. Potter, 1975], pp. 7–8, 27n). A variation on the stolen child/protector motif appears in *Iceberg*, wherein Rondheim represents a dragon/guardian for Kirsti Fyrie, who is

both a damsel and a temptress (see Chapter 7 for more details), and in *Cyclops*, wherein Gly represents the dragon/guardian, and Giordino, Gunn and Jessie LeBaron are, in essence, the stolen children.

99. Cussler, *Shock Wave*, p. 523.
100. Cussler, *Iceberg*, p. 299.
101. Ibid. p. 304.
102. See *Shock Wave*, pp. 532–3. Pitt's confrontations with these mirrors are less like "Snow White" and more like Steig's *Shrek!* Shrek enters a room filled with mirrors on his way to rescue the princess. This is the first time the monstrous creature sees himself, and it is also the first time he feels fear. But, then, Shrek becomes proud of the fear he ignites in himself; he not only accepts what he is, but grows happy to be who and what he is, much like Pitt normally feels about himself.
103. See http://en.wikipedia.org/wiki/Enchanted_forest.
104. See Editorial Board of the University Society (Supervisors), *Epic of Gilgamesh*, pp. 70–84.
105. Professor Dumbledore warns students in J. K. Rowling's *Harry Potter and the Sorcerer's Stone* (New York: Scholastic, 1999), p. 127, that the forest on the Hogwarts grounds is forbidden to all pupils because, as Percy Weasley explains, it is "full of dangerous beasts," including such magical creatures as centaurs, unicorns and giant spiders. Harry's first friend and guide in the wizardy world, Rubeus Hagrid, is part magical creature since his mother was a giant, which may explain why he is fond of dangerous beasts and lives on the forest's edge. The forbidden forest is the site of an important scene in each of Harry's adventures.
106. The young apprentice Luke Skywalker is studying under Jedi master Yoda on this swampy planet when, during one training session, Yoda lures Luke to a giant tree, inside which Luke has a face-to-face encounter with his shadow side.
107. See *Spartan Gold*, pp. 1–11. A similar trek occurs in *Indiana Jones and the Last Crusade* (1989) wherein Indy (Harrison Ford) travels through a cavern guided by the teachings of his father Henry (Sean Connery). Eventually, Indy must cross a treacherous bridge over a bottomless gorge and enter a small cavern on the other side, where he finds a lost treasure and the answer to an ancient secret.
108. See Julian Symons, *A Pictorial History of Crime* (New York: Bonanza Books, 1966), pp. 60–1.
109. "Dream-Land," in *The Complete Tales and Poems of Edgar Allan Poe* (New York: Barnes & Noble, 1992), p. 70.
110. Machen quotes from T.E. Klein, "A Dreamer's Tales," in H.P. Lovecraft, *Dagon and Other Macabre Tales* (Sauk City, WI: Arkham House, 1987), p. lii.
111. Cussler, *Pacific Vortex*, p. 218.
112. Cussler, *Night Probe!*, p. 127.
113. Klein, "A Dreamer's Tales," in Lovecraft, *Dagon and Other Macabre Tales*, p. lii.
114. See *Night Probe!*, pp. 127–30. Pitt's showdown with this spectral train is also one of the best Gothic moments in the series; it is filled with wonderfully evocative phrases and descriptions (see pp. 129–30).
115. Klein, "A Dreamer's Tales," in Lovecraft, *Dagon and Other Macabre Tales*, p. lii.
116. See Thomas Bulfinch, *Bulfinch's Mythology: The Age of Fable, The Age of Chivalry, Legends of Charlemagne* (New York: Thomas Y. Crowell, 1970), pp. 348, 904.
117. "Maybe" because time alone will tell if Pitt ever finds that lost city.
118. Cussler, *Pacific Vortex*, p. 62.
119. Much the same could be said for Fleming (see Eco, *The Role of the Reader*, p. 165). When Cussler was asked if he was influenced by Gothic stories, mysteries with Gothic overtones (e.g., *The Moonstone*, *The Hound of the Baskervilles*) or pulp adventures that used Gothic techniques, he replied, "I probably was since I read all that material when I was young" (author's questions to Cussler, August 2009).
120. See *Vixen 03*, p. 24.
121. Ibid., p. 163.
122. Ibid., pp. 264–5.
123. Shelley Costa Bloomfield, PhD, *The Everything Guide to Edgar Allan Poe* (Avon, MA: Adams Media, 2007), p. 156. *Webster's New World Dictionary* (p. 604) defines Gothic as "of or in a style of literature using a medieval setting, atmosphere, etc., esp. to suggest horror and mystery." A good description of the attitude behind Gothic's style, setting and atmosphere may be "imagination for the sake of imagination." Gothic literature was a response to the Age of Reason and the 18th century's rational climate of opinion, an appeal to imagination when science was producing facts and demanding logical explanations. Horace Walpole specifically wrote the first Gothic novel, *The Castle of Otranto* (1764), as an escape from life's unpleasant realities. An antiquarian and conservative, Walpole was inspired by his fellow antiquarians' romantic recreations of the past (Tobias Smollett's novel *Ferdinand Count Fathom*, the Graveyard School of poets, and a revival of interest in Tarquato Tasso and Ludovico Ariosto's romances) to create a story that reveled in its mixture of Jacobean, medieval, graveyard and mock–Renaissance setting. Twelve years passed before another conservative, Clara Reeve, produced the second Gothic, *The Old English Baron*, written as an expression of her opposition to authority. But, this time, a procession of Gothic stories immediately followed, all written by conservative writers, including Ann Radcliffe. H. P. Lovecraft wrote that Radcliffe "made terror and suspense a fashion" and "closely approached genius" ("Supernatural Horror in Literature," in Lovecraft, *Dagon and Other Macabre Tales*, p. 375). At one point, Gothic literature became so popular it helped spark the English Romantic Movement. As author and essayist Dr. Ronald Donald Spector writes in his introduction to *Seven Masterpieces of Gothic Horror*: "An age obsessed by the rational arguments of deists and French Encyclopedists required an emotional release," and Gothic literature became one of the most important avenues for that release. The genre simultaneously underwent its first major change during this time, brought about by the influence of German folk tales. The first (and one of the most enduring) German Gothics is Matthew Gregory Lewis's *The Monk* (1796). Because Radcliffe and her fellow conservative English Gothic writers were constrained by the orthodox mindset of the 18th century and Horace's demand that literature must entertain and instruct, they had to include logical explanations for their stories' otherworldly events ("the dead body proves to be a wax image; the mysterious sounds turn

out to be the lover's lute; and the supernatural happenings are the tricks of pirates"), and see that moral retribution guided their plots as well as counterbalanced their villains' terrible deeds, while their characterizations had to be marked by clear distinctions between good and evil. Lewis was anything but a conservative, and in *The Monk* he "unleashed all the horror of the German fancy, born of ghost tales, necromancy, and folklore." Some of Lewis's scenes were so sensational in their immorality that he was forced to revise them after being threatened with legal prosecution. But that did not prevent *The Monk* from becoming an extremely popular novel, its influence noticeable in Radcliffe's most excessive work, *The Italian* (1797).

124. See "Introduction," Robert Donald Spector, *Seven Masterpieces of Gothic Horror* (New York: Bantam, 1971), p. 1.

125. Clive Bloom, *Gothic Horror: A Reader's Guide from Poe to King and Beyond* (New York: St. Martin's Press, 1998), p. 1. Bloom adds, "*Dracula* is both a synthesis and a nostalgic revival of gothic themes."

126. Seminal examples of this include Edgar Allan Poe's "The Murders in the Rue Morgue" (1841), Wilkie Collins's *The Woman in White* (1860), and Sir Arthur Conan Doyle's *The Hound of the Baskervilles* (1901).

127. See Spector, *Seven Masterpieces of Gothic Horror*, p. 11, and Bloom, *Gothic Horror*, p. 2.

128. See Spector, *Seven Masterpieces of Gothic Horror*, p. 2.

129. Bloom, *Gothic Horror*, p. 9. Lovecraft also broaches this subject in "Supernatural Horror in Literature" (see p. 388).

130. Ibid., p. 14. Because the genre has been absorbed into so many other genres, there is always a danger of getting lost in a labyrinth of esoteric meanderings, such as the differences between horror fiction and supernatural fiction, the emphasis of the sentimental and the sublime in Gothic fiction, or the "feminist approaches to the analysis of bodily functions and to boundary and identity transgressions." In *Gothic Television* (p. 2), scholar Helen Wheatley adds, "A singular definition of the Gothic as a genre of fiction has, throughout the history of Gothic studies, been difficult to isolate, due in no small part to the fact that the Gothic has been alternately described as an aesthetic, mode or style, as a set of particular themes and narrative conventions, as a subgenre of fantasy, and, initially, as an isolated historical movement."

131. Lenora Ledwon, "*Twin Peaks* and the Television Gothic," *Literature/Film Quarterly* 21, issue 4 (1993): p. 261.

132. Wheatley, *Gothic Television*, p. 3.

133. Cussler and Dirgo, *Clive Cussler & Dirk Pitt Revealed!*, p. 106.

134. Even writers and writing instructors who warn against stereotypes cannot deny that a twist or variation can turn a stereotype into an interesting character or plot. For an example, see Constance Nash and Virginia Oakey, *The Screenwriter's Handbook: What to Write, How to Write It, and Where to Sell It* (New York: Barnes & Noble Books, 1974), p. 4.

135. Lovecraft, "Supernatural Horror in Literature," pp. 374–5.

136. Ibid., p. 375.

137. Bond is the son of wealthy (but hardly noble) European parents and rarely appears in "humble disguise," while Jack O'Neill is really just "humble." Pitt, the son of a U.S. senator (but not a true noble), is so humble in his ways that people are often surprised to find out about his privileged background.

138. Campbell, *Hero with a Thousand Faces*, p. 3. In *Gothic Horror*, p. 4, Bloom states that Gothic "is *the* genre against which critics attempted to separate serious fiction from such popular entertainment and escapism [as detective fiction and science fiction]."

139. In *Action Figures*, p. 146, Gallagher recognizes that Cussler's novels regularly "invoke history," but he fails to recognize this subtle Gothic element. Instead, Gallagher focuses on Cussler's borrowing "from pulp tradition, his novels reconceive historical events and cultures as sites of vigorous present-day action."

140. A variation of the past affecting the future in a Gothic story appears as early as *The Castle of Otranto*. A usurper prince, Manfred, divorces his wife, Hippolita, so he can wed Isabella, the intended bride of his only son, Conrad, who is apparently killed as part of a prophecy that foretells the end of Manfred's line. Supposedly supernatural events, many involving oversized artifacts and body parts (e.g., a gigantic helmet falls and crushes Conrad), get in the way of his plans and, in the process, he accidentally kills his daughter, Matilda, and loses his estate to her beloved, Theodore, who turns out to be the son and heir of the true prince, Alfonso.

141. Spector, *Seven Masterpieces of Gothic Horror*, p. 6.

142. Bloom, *Gothic Horror*, p. 4.

143. In a strange case of life imitating Cussler, in 2008 U.S. diplomats tried and failed to trade Spanish gold recovered from the wreck of the *Nuestra Señora de las Mercedes*, a Spanish galleon that sank off the coast of Portugal in 1804 while battling four Royal Navy ships, in exchange for a painting, Camille Pissarro's "Rue St Honoré. Après-midi. Effet de Pluie" (1897), which, as of this writing, hangs in Madrid's Thyssen-Bornemisza Museum. In 1939, Pissaro's painting was sold by a Jewish woman named Lilly Cassirer to raise money to flee Nazi Germany. In 1958, Cassirer received a DM 120,000 restitution payment for the disappearance and provisional dispossession of the painting, but retained full rights to it. In 1976, Baron Hans Heinrich Thyssen-Bornemisza acquired the painting, then sold it in the early 1990s to the Spanish government. Cassirer's heirs have been attempting to recover the painting, but the museum has refused to release it. A December 9, 2010 report on the attempted trade on WikiLeaks.com begins: "An underwater treasure. A looted Impressionist masterpiece. Diplomatic intrigue. Nazis. It all sounds like the plot of a Clive Cussler novel" ("WikiLeaks Art Exposé: U.S. Tried to Trade Sunken Gold for Nazi Loot").

144. This is one of the most popular scenes in the Pitt series, but *NUMA Files* presents an almost equally exciting (and even more audacious) sequel of sorts, involving a historical ship in *Fire Ice*. Austin and the crew of the three-masted frigate USS *Constitution* not only engage in a battle with assassins working for Razov, but successfully prevent the bad guys from boarding the ship.

145. In the prelude for *Raise the Titanic!*, p. 2, Brewster is the passen-

ger in Deck A, Stateroom 33, and, like more than a few anonymous protagonists of Gothic stories, he is going insane after surviving a recent terrible episode, yet not so far gone that he does not realize the liner is in danger. Cussler employs Gothic language as he describes how Brewster's insanity has his five senses working overtime; he is therefore able to recognize that the ship is in peril from the moment it strikes the iceberg. This statement is reminiscent of the opening paragraph of one of the world's most famous Gothic stories, Poe's testament of madness, "The Tell-Tale Heart," wherein the unidentified narrator insists his insanity has its advantages: "The disease had sharpened my senses—not destroyed—not dulled them." See *Great Tales of Horror by Edgar Allan Poe* (New York: Barnes & Noble Books, 1992), p. 13.

146. Cussler, *Raise the Titanic!*, p. 372. Pitt even comments on how Seagram's hubris links him with Brewster after the byzanium is finally discovered.

147. Ibid., p. 349. It is disappointing that Gothic scenes like this and the theme of hubris are missing in the film *Raise the Titanic*, especially since Seagram is played by David Selby, best known for playing Quentin Collins on the cult Gothic soap opera *Dark Shadows* (1966–1971). Selby's fine performance in the film *Night of Dark Shadows* (1971), which features both themes, suggests how powerfully he could have brought Cussler's troubled Seagram to life on the screen. Almost as disappointing is the fact that Selby, a tall, dark-haired, athletic man with mesmeric eyes, was not selected to play Pitt in *Raise the Titanic*.

148. See H.P. Lovecraft, *Supernatural Horror in Literature & Other Literary Essays* (Rockville, MD: Wildside Press, 2008), pp. 394–400. Along with "Ligeia," Poe's "The Fall of the House of Usher," "The Tell-Tale Heart" and "The Black Cat" are some of the finest fictional accounts of insanity, as well as excellent examples of the past reaching out to affect the present.

149. Cussler, "Writing the Suspense-Adventure Novel," p. 233

150. Dr. Scott Brewster, of the University of Central Lancashire, writes on p. vi of his introduction to the Wordsworth Classic edition of *The Woman in White*: "A common feature of these texts is their use of first-person accounts and multiple narratives rather than omniscient narration. They are constructed from a series of reports, letters, documents, journal and diary entries, a web of stories that attempts to net and explain perplexing, frightening or estranging stories."

151. Lyn Pykett, *The Sensation Novel: From* The Woman in White *to* The Moonstone (Devon, UK: Northcote House, 1994), p. 5.

152. Brewster, "Introduction," Collins, *The Woman in White*, p. vii.

153. Wheatley, *Gothic Television*, p. 3.

154. Eve Sedgwick, *The Coherence of Gothic Conventions* (New York: Arno Press, 1986), p. 13.

155. See *Pacific Vortex*, p. 66.

156. Examples include Hurricane Amanda in *Raise the Titanic!*, and the rainstorm in *Vixen 03*, pp. 261, 264.

157. See *Iceberg*, p.146, and *Pacific Vortex*, p. 261 for but two examples.

158. A few examples include *Raise the Titanic!*, p. 358, *Vixen 03*, p. 26, 77–80, and *Night Probe!*, p. 141.

159. A few examples include Carzo Butera/Oskar Rondheim and Kristjan/Kirsti Fyrie in *Iceberg*; Marcus Somala and the younger (and slightly lighter) version of himself in *Vixen 03* (see p. 63); Hiram Jones/ Hiram Lusana in *Vixen 03*; Henry Villon/Foss Gly in *Night Probe!*; and Arta Casilighio/Estelle Wallace, as well as the president and Jack Sutton, in *Deep Six*.

160. Examples include *Raise the Titanic!*, p. 326, and *Vixen 03*, p. 163.

161. A few examples include *Iceberg*, pp. 54–6, 153, *Pacific Vortex*, pp. 202–3, and *Flood Tide*, pp. 49–50.

162. Pitt's macabre discovery in Orion Lake remains one of Cussler's most chilling moments (see *Flood Tide*, pp. 49–50).

163. See *Raise the Titanic!*, pp. 177–8 and compare this to a similar scene (with a near- lack of Gothic descriptions) in *Fire Ice*, p. 224.

164. This is not to say that these other adventures are totally devoid of Gothic imagery. For instance, *Serpent*, *Blue Gold* and *Treasure of Khan* do feature exciting climaxes set in a tomb, much like a similar scene in *Treasure*; *Golden Buddha* showcases a harrowing journey through a flooding labyrinth of sewers during a nighttime storm in Macau.

165. Cussler and Blackwood, *Spartan Gold*, p. 17.

166. Author's questions to Cussler, August 2009.

167. Cussler, *Pacific Vortex*, p. 82. Pitt maintains this realistic outlook even in the face of what appears to be the supernatural.

168. Ibid., p. 121.

169. John Clute, *Science Fiction: The Illustrated Encyclopedia* (New York: Dorling Kindersley, 1995), pp. 24–5, 299.

170. "An Interview with Tom Clancy," in Greenberg, ed., *The Tom Clancy Companion*, pp. 61–2.

171. The concept of staking a claim for the Moon was broached by Robert A. Heinlein in "The Man Who Sold the Moon" (1949); Heinlein also predicted what a battle for a lunar colony could be like in *The Moon Is a Harsh Mistress* (1966). A lunar battle between the USA and USSR is the subject of Martin Caiden's *No Man's World* (1967).

172. A little inconsistency here: in *Cyclops*, set in 1989, the embargo is lifted at the end of the novel, but in *Night Probe!* (p. 285) we are told that the Cuban embargo had been lifted in 1985.

173. These changes fall into the "no decision is a decision" category.

174. Even though Clancy rejects the title "techno-thriller," Marc A. Cerasini does an excellent job of breaking down the evolution of the techno-thriller in "Tom Clancy's Fiction: The Birth of the Techno-Thriller" in Greenberg, ed., *The Tom Clancy Companion*, pp. 5–9. Cerasini begins with "proto" techno-thrillers, including H. G. Wells's "The Land Leviathans" (1903), *The War in the Air* (1908), and *The World Set Free* (1914); it also discusses Childers's *The Riddle of the Sand* (1903), and Le Queux's *The Invasion of 1910* (1906), and follows the subgenre's development through the writings of Heinlein, Jerry Pournelle, and David Drake, and the George Lucas film *Star Wars* (1977). As Cerasini explains that Childers and Le Queux's proto techno-thrillers were also warnings against an invasion by Ger-

many, it seems inexcusable that he left out Conan Doyle's *Danger!, Being the Log of Captain John Sirius* (1914), which predicted the use of U-boats against England. Cerasini also fails to mention Martin Caiden's considerable contributions, including the novels *No Man's World* (1964), *Marooned* (1967) and *Cyborg* (1972), the last book serving as the basis for the TV series *The Six Million Dollar Man* (1974–1978).

175. Ibid., p. 9.

176. Ray Bradbury, "Science Fiction: Before Christ and After 2001, An Introduction by Ray Bradbury," *Science Fact/Fiction*, ed. dir Leo B. Keener (Glenview, IL: Scott Foresman, 1974), p. xiv.

177. The Shadow is perhaps the best-known supernatural purveyor of mind control from the pulps, but one of Pitt's inspirations, Doc Savage, is not far behind. As Cannady writes in *Bigger Than Life*, on p. 93, "Bad guys were ... taken away to the 'college' where Doc performed a delicate operation on them to remove all memory of their criminal past; they were rehabilitated, given jobs and returned as productive members of society." This sounds quite similar to the fate that befalls the president in *Deep Six*.

178. Prior to the publication of *Deep Six* in 1984, these chestnuts had been featured in separate bestsellers: Charles Templeton's *The Kidnapping of the President* (1975) and Richard Condon's *The Manchurian Candidate* (1959). In Templeton's novel, the president gets handcuffed to a terrorist while shaking hands at an outdoor ceremony and is dragged into an armored car wired with explosives; in *The Manchurian Candidate*, a Korean War Medal of Honor winner is brainwashed by Communists into becoming a sleeper assassin. Much like *The Manchurian Candidate*, the Communist plot in *Deep Six* is at least partially thwarted by a nasty maternal figure. Whether either of these novels inspired Cussler is unknown. Interestingly, the film adaptations of *The Kidnapping of the President* and *Raise the Titanic!* were both released in 1980. Unfortunately for Cussler's fans, the more modestly budgeted *Kidnapping of the President* starring William Shatner (who might have made a fine Dirk Pitt) is the more faithful adaptation and a more enjoyable film to watch.

179. Pitt and Giordino are actually fascinated by the robot sentries that possess limited artificial intelligence. Giordino even begins calling one sentry, assigned to watching the men in their cell, McGoon (see *Dragon*, pp. 350–1).

180. Such advanced technology supports Foster-Harris's claim on p. 9 of *Basic Patterns of Plot*: "The science-fiction story is essentially the detective story, or an effort to write fantasy, the magical or fairy tale, in objective terms. Equip Jack with a super plant-food, give the beanstalk a scientific name, and make the giant an inhabitant of an unknown planet in outer space, and you have transformed the familiar fairy story into quite acceptable science fiction."

181. "An Interview with Tom Clancy," in Greenberg, ed., p. 75.

182. Unpublished 1985 interview, p. 1. One of the few exceptions to this rule is Dr. Elmore Egan's quantum teleportation device from *Valhalla Rising* (pp. 484–6, 503).

183. See *Night Probe!*, pp. 94, 100.

184. See *Vixen 03*, pp. 203, 284, *Night Probe!*, pp. 87, 207, *Cyclops*, p. 129, and *Sahara*, p. 385, for examples.

185. See *Trojan Odyssey*, pp. 228, 313, and (with Paul Kemprecos) *Medusa* (New York: Putnam, 2009) p. 443. Also see http://www.geocities.ws/hn4dpitt/numa.htm.

186. See *Night Probe!*, pp. 74, 111, 259.

187. See *Raise the Titanic!*, pp. 17, 149.

188. See *Night Probe!*, pp. 17–8.

189. In *Atlantis Found*, on p. 149, Yaeger says that he originally programmed his own voice into Max.

190. Early science-fiction stories did not pay much attention to computers, even though Ada Lovelace, the daughter of Lord Byron, wrote the first software manual in 1842 (see Clute, *Science Fiction: The Illustrated Encyclopedia*, p. 74). Until the 1980s science-fiction writers seemed to prefer concentrating on ray guns, dynamos, robots and other scientific marvels that were easier than circuitry and microchips for readers to visualize. When computers did appear in science-fiction stories they were often presented as challengers who enslaved *Homo sapiens*, or became God. "The computer was not imagined [in science fiction] simply because to do so was to welcome into our bosoms the ultimate enemy."

191. See http://en.wikipedia.org/wiki/HAL_9000.

192. See *Trojan Odyssey*, p. 314. *Flood Tide* was published in 1997, and *Atlantis Found* in 1999, but, in 2002, Grell gave Cussler's fans a glimpse of Max in action on the comic book page, with an AI computer named Friday, in *Iron Man #398*. Max and Friday have similar personalities, but where Max changes wardrobe to fit her mood or topic of discussion, Friday changes her entire "physical" appearance.

193. See *Atlantis Found*, p. 152, *Trojan Odyssey*, pp. 313–16, and (with Paul Kemprecos) *White Death* (New York: Berkley, 2004), pp. 262–4.

194. See the following Jack Du Brul collaborations: *Skeleton Coast* (New York: Berkley, 2006), pp. 30, 40–1, *Corsair* (New York: Putnam, 2009), p. 44; and *The Jungle* (New York: Putnam, 2011), p.123. The *Oregon* is not the only ship in a Cussler adventure that evokes comparisons with the *Enterprise*. In *Valhalla Rising* (p. 29) the superstructure of the *Emerald Dolphin* resembles the *Enterprise*, and the helm of Cussler's futuristic yacht, *Periwinkle*, is supposedly more elegant than the starship's bridge (see p. 157). Adding elements like these to a ship is presaged by the *Martha Ann*'s Flash Gordon room (see *Pacific Vortex*, pp. 93–5).

195. For examples, see *Skeleton Coast* pp. 41–50, 98–105.

196. See Cussler and Dirgo, *Clive Cussler & Dirk Pitt Revealed!*, p. x. It may be just a coincidence, but in *Shock Wave* (p. 140) we find out that, among a gallery of paintings of naval actions hanging in Sandecker's favorite meeting room in NUMA, there is one showing dive bombers roaring off of the carrier *Enterprise* during the Battle of Midway.

197. "Science Fiction: Before Christ and After 2001, An Introduction by Ray Bradbury," p. xiv. [NOT IN BIB]

198. Cussler, *Night Probe!*, p. 339.

199. Warp refers to "that which is thrown across" and weft (horizontal threads) refers to "that which is woven" (http://en.wikipedia.org/wiki/Loom).

200. For instance, in *Night Probe!*,

Ansel McGee tells Pitt about interviewing ticket agent Sam Harding about the *Manhattan Limited* disaster, and McGee's description of the interview is as immediate and vibrant (see pp. 134–7), as Harry Potter seeing the past with Dumbledore's Pensieve in J. K. Rowling's *Harry Potter and the Goblet of Fire* (New York: Scholastic, 2002), pp. 581–604.

201. Unlike many real-life government environmental agencies, NUMA's conservation practices do not discourage the harvesting of natural resources (see *Iceberg*, p. 122).

202. Cussler, *The Adventures of Vin Fiz*, p. 1.

203. See *Raise the Titanic!*, pp. 12–4, and *Night Probe!*, p. 159.

204. See *Night Probe!*, pp. 136–7.

205. Foster-Harris, *Basic Patterns of Plot*, p. 97.

206. Cussler, *Iceberg*, p. 246.

207. See Rowling, *Harry Potter and the Deathly Hallows*, pp. 706–23, 737–44.

208. See Fleming, *On Her Majesty's Secret Service*, pp. 189–9, and *You Only Live Twice*, pp. 16–20, 144–149.

209. In reality, there has never been a presidential yacht named *Eagle*; the current presidential yacht is the USS *Sequoia*.

210. Ribonucleic acid, which is used to transmit genetic instructions (see *Deep Six*, p. 178).

211. Cussler, *Deep Six*, p. 180.

212. Clute, *Science Fiction: The Illustrated Encyclopedia*, pp. 74–5.

213. Keith Douglas, "How to Kill," *Keith Douglas: The Complete Poems*, 3d ed. (Oxford: Oxford University Press, 1998), p. 119.

214. Pitt's rebirth in *Iceberg* is also echoed in *Shock Wave* (p. 333, 526), when Pitt is brutally beaten by John Merchant's guards after he partially blinds Arthur Dorsett. When Pitt awakens, Giordino says, "Praise be, Lazarus is back from the dead." Pitt manages to rescue Giordino and Maeve, so they can all return to Gladiator Island, where Boudicca is surprised to see him. Then, upon seeing Giordino, Boudicca says, "So you came back from the dead, too."

215. Or, like Heidi Milligan in *Vixen 03* and *Night Probe!*, and James Bond in *On Her Majesty's Secret Service* and *You Only Live Twice*. In Fleming's novels, Bond's rebirth is capped by 007 suffering amnesia after defeating Blofeld; so, in a way, Bond really *is* reborn into a new identity and a new way of life, as a Japanese fisherman with Kissy Suzuki. In Pitt's case, this rebirth is capped by returning to his old self after he kills the villain Qin Shang in *Flood Tide*.

216. Bell is metaphorically washed in the blood or baptized during his rebirth.

217. Cussler, *Iceberg*, p. 244.

218. Clute, See *Science Fiction: The Illustrated Encyclopedia*, p. 84.

219. A personal thought about exceptions: Science teaches that mutations improve a species, so social mutants deserve respect. That said, societies which accept exceptions into its fold are not axiomatically required to change their morals and rules to accommodate misfits. Being different means you are different, which is the inescapable curse and blessing of being a social misfit. Society develops morals and rules that work for the majority of its citizens (i.e., normal people), so these morals and rules will not always fit well when applied to mutants, but that is why social misfits occasionally require exceptions, or at least some patience and understanding from normal people. The problem is, if you treat the exceptions as normal you ignore the wonderful fact that misfits are different. Trying to change a society to accommodate all the needs of the exceptions relegates mutants to run-of-the-mill status and damages (if not destroys) the foundations of society by forcing it to operate in counterintuitive ways.

220. For an example involving abortion, see *Shock Wave*, p. 132.

221. In *Shock Wave* Maeve is a guide showing tourists an old whaling station on Seymour Island, near Antarctica. When one tourist feels a sample of whale oil and comments on its extraordinary lubricant qualities, Maeve warns him not to tell the oil companies or whales will be extinct by Christmas (see p. 60). Later, Pitt and Giordino spend several paragraphs discussing the Antarctic ozone hole and global warming (Ibid., see pp. 92–3). Other examples include America's space race with the USSR for the moon and Mars (see *Cyclops*, erpp. 205–6, 264, 280–93), America's late–20th-century trade policies with Japan, war crimes committed by the Japanese during World War II (see *Dragon*, pp. 198, 364), and illegal immigration into the United States (see *Flood Tide*, pp. 61–64, 542).

222. Cussler, *The Mediterranean Caper*, p. 29.

223. Cussler, *Iceberg*, p. 103.

224. Cussler, *Raise the Titanic!*, p. 282.

225. Ibid., p. 162.

226. Cussler, *Inca Gold*, p. 84.

227. Cussler, *Trojan Odyssey*, p. 361–2. Another character is described as being "shocked at seeing Pitt brutally strike the woman," and asks why he did not just gag the woman. Pitt replies, "Because she would have bitten my hand, and I didn't feel in a chivalrous mood to let her do it."

228. Cussler, *Valhalla Rising*, p. 79.

229. Ibid., p. 109.

230. Cussler, *Iceberg*, p. 125.

231. Cussler, *Valhalla Rising*, pp. 343–2.

232. Cussler, *Shock Wave*, p. 158.

233. In *Science Fiction: The Illustrated Encyclopedia* (p. 84), Clute offers an alternate (and more rational) explanation for the exclusion of women, at least when it comes to science-fiction adventure: "During the 19th century Western Civilization believed that it understood about women: they were essentially emotional creatures, vulnerable, passive, revered, and hearth-bound. By definition [science fiction] occupied other realms: it was all about adventure, exploration and penetration of the unknown, warfare, combat, hard science, and the end of the world in tracts of ice or fire. It was only *natural*, it was assumed, that the protagonists who acted out the leading roles in these scenarios were most likely to be male."

234. Something Rondheim finds out, to his apparent shame, when it comes to Kirsti.

235. Cussler, *Shock Wave*, p. 132.

236. Cussler, *Raise the Titanic!*, p. 337.

237. Cussler, "Make Your Story 'Fly,'" *The Writer*, pp. 13, 45.

238. For just a few examples, see *The Mediterranean Caper*, pp. 11–2, 28, 126, 149, *Iceberg*, pp. 103, 122, 134, 210–1, and *Flood Tide*, pp. 104, 113–4.

239. Cussler, *Iceberg*, p. 173.

240. Cussler, *Dragon*, p. 193.

241. Cussler, *Valhalla Rising*, p. 103.
242. Ibid., pp. 414–16.
243. For examples, see *Night Probe!*, pp. 152, 248.
244. Cussler, *Cyclops*, p. 128. Later during the search (p. 132), Jessie panics as a storm overtakes the blimp *Prosperteer* that she is piloting, but Pitt reminds her that she wanted to be one of the boys, so she can just hang in there.
245. Cussler, *Sahara*, p. 71.
246. Cussler, *Shock Wave*, p. 281. Pitt is not the only character in Cussler's adventures that exhibits chauvinistic behavior one moment and seems enlightened the next. Sandecker, for example, is in lockstep with Pitt's condescending way of thinking in *Iceberg* (see p. 173), but, in *Deep Six* (p. 38), he selects Mendoza to be the on-scene coordinator for the Regional Emergency Response Team to Alaska because she is one of the world's best biochemists. In *Sahara* (p. 71), after Hala convinces a secret conference of the United Nations about the danger of the red plague, Sandecker admits, "It took a woman's foresight to recognize the danger."
247. Cussler, *Sahara*, p. 200. Yerli comes off as heartless, but what does this say about women in general? In *Deep Six* (p. 28), Sandecker, normally a decent sort when it comes to the opposite sex, is described as a man who "possessed an aloofness and coarse personality that appareled to women."
248. Cussler, *Shock Wave*, p. 132.
249. Cussler, *Raise the Titanic!*, p. 163.
250. Cussler, *Sahara*, p. 160.
251. Cussler, *Flood Tide*, pp. 304–5.
252. Cussler, *Sahara*, p. 146.
253. Cussler, *Raise the Titanic!*, p. 283. In *Action Figures* (p. 137), Gallagher takes a big-picture view of this when he writes: "Women's presence accentuates the danger of narrative events; threats to women simply produce stronger emotional reactions than do those to men. Correspondingly, the presence of women transforms the male protector role from an abstraction—with men facing danger to protect women and children who are removed form the action—into a palpable necessity."

254. Cussler, *Sahara*, p. 75.
255. Cussler, *Vixen 03*, pp. 89–90.
256. See Jaffe, *Arthur Conan Doyle*, pp. 92, 98–9. Several years before writing *The Lost World*, Conan Doyle began thinking about "trying a Rider Haggardy kind of book" that would be "dedicated to all the *bad boys* of the Empire" (my emphasis). When he finally followed through with his idea, he gave *The Lost World* this dedication: "I have wrought my simple plan, if I give one hour of joy to the boy who's half a man, or the man who's half a boy."
257. See Chapter 6.
258. One of these scenes includes Pitt rescuing Loren from Daggat (*Vixen 03*, pp. 245–8), but, because it is a rescue, Pitt is operating on his own, without Loren's aid.
259. Alan Dundes, ed., "The Hero Pattern and the Life of Jesus: Protocol of the Twentyfifth Colloquy 12 December 1976," Center for Hermeneutical Studies in Hellenistic and Modern Culture, digitized September 30, 2009, p. 28.
260. See comments about Jung's anima archetype in Chapter 7.
261. *Vixen 03*, p. 4. One of the great unanswered mysteries of the Pitt series is the fate of Ichabod, who is never mentioned again.
262. Cussler emphasizes this element of Loren's character when she uses the sexual slang "hanky-panky" while describing her chaste political career to Pitt (see *Vixen 03*, p. 3).
263. For example, read Pitt and Loren's conversation about Sawyer in *Vixen 03*, p. 130.
264. Jaffe, *Arthur Conan Doyle*, pp. 92, 98–9, 117–8. Gallagher takes an opposite (and even less complimentary) view of this attitude in the works of Clancy and Cussler: "In their novels, women appear principally as dutiful mates, sexual temptresses, or token figures against which male expertise can be judged. Women tend to weaken or inhibit male characters' homosocial relations.... While women characters represent the social world the heroes are sworn to protect, they more frequently impede rather than aide the heroes' goals."
265. Cussler, *Vixen 03*, pp. 256–7. Baldwin and Sawyer are little men as well as dupes, but Leeson is a dupe who is also a refreshingly rugged and goodhearted Texas rancher who has no intention of being tamed and will only settle for a wife who can live with him on his terms.

266. Jaffe, *Arthur Conan Doyle*, pp. 98–9. Ironically, Maeve (in *Shock Wave*, p. 284) expresses her affection for Pitt by comparing him to Huckleberry Finn and quoting Johnny Mercer's references to "my Huckleberry friend" in the lyrics to "Moon River" from the 1961 film *Breakfast at Tiffany's*.
267. Cussler, *Vixen 03*, pp. 256–7.
268. Ibid., p. 109.
269. See *Shock Wave*, p. 120.
270. See unpublished 1985 interview, p. 16. Cussler adds, "I have often been told men want to be like Pitt and Pitt is the man women want. [Approximately] 50% of my readers are women" (author's questions to Cussler, August 2009).
271. Cussler, "Writing the Suspense-Adventure Novel," p. 235.
272. Author's questions to Cussler, August 2009.
273. Gallagher, *Action Figures*, p. 114.
274. Ibid., p. 155.
275. Neither Cussler nor Gallagher cite the sources for their claims about the percentage of men and women among Cussler's readers.
276. Quoted in Gallagher, *Action Figures*, p. 155.
277. Gallagher, *Action Figures*, p. 155. Also see p. 151.
278. Cussler, *Valhalla Rising*, p. 343.

Chapter 6

1. See unfinished manuscript.
2. See Snelling, *007 James Bond: A Report*, pp. 11–6. Snelling admits that, by the sixties, the Terrible Trio appeared archaic: "The generation that separates Bond from the Clubland Heroes has made all the difference. The code of honour and the morality that bred Buchan and his contemporaries in late Victorian days did not obtain during the Edwardian and Georgian era that produced Ian Fleming," and so "James Bond is a latter-day member of their Set who has Gone Off The Rails, a renegade Etonian type who has been mixing with the Townies."
3. Robert Lesser, *Pulp Art* (Baltimore: Metro Books, 2009), pp. 48–9.

4. Cussler and Dirgo, *Clive Cussler & Dirk Pitt Revealed!*, p. 46. When Cussler talks about pulp magazines he refers to "The days of Doc Savage and Alan Quartermain [sic]."

5. Yellow-backs took their name from the primarily yellow cover on strawboard covered by glazed paper that graced *Experiences of a Lady Detective* by Anonyma (1861). The cover's illustration shows Anonyma's purportedly real-life heroine, Mary Paschal, tracking a suspected killer through a bustling London park (Haining, *The Classic Era of Crime Fiction*, p. 26).

6. The founder of Illustration House in New York is quoted in "The Pulps and Their Illustrators: A Brief Survey," in Lesser, *Pulp Art*, p. 50, as saying: "With an ancestry going back to the chapbooks and the penny dreadfuls, the pulps were carrying on a venerable tradition of exploiting the sensational adventures of pirates and notorious highwaymen or fights with Indians on the western frontier. The pulps simply updated the old subject matter and put it in a cheaply produced pulp paper package with a gaudy cover."

7. In *String of Pearls* (1846), by Thomas Preskett Prest.

8. In *The Old House of West Street* (1846), by Thomas Preskett Prest.

9. Whether or not the novel was written by Prest or Rymer, or both, or even someone else, remains a subject of debate. The cover for the first issue of *Varney the Vampire; or, The Feast of Blood* lists no author, only that it is "By the Author of *Grace Rivers; or, The Merchant's Daughter*," but this does not settle the matter. While some contend that Prest wrote *Grace Rivers*, at least one treatise argues: "The British Museum has a copy of [*Grace Rivers*] which, in turn, is advertised as by the author of *Ada, the Betrayed*. James Malcolm Rymer is that author ("Scrutinizing Varney the Vampire: Making Sense," http://www.onthevampire.com/On_The_Vampire/Scrutinising_Varney_the_Vampire%3A_Making_Sense.html). I leave it to others to hash out who wrote *Varney the Vampire*, but there is no debating that Sir Francis Varney was one of the most popular literary vampires before Count Dracula even serving as an influence on Bram Stoker (see Devendra P. Varma's "The Vampire in Legend, Lore, and Literature," and Margaret L. Carter's "A Preface from Polidori to Prest," in Rymer and Prest, *Varney the Vampire*, vol. I (pp. xii–xlii).

10. Haining, *The Classic Era of Crime Fiction*, p. 12.

11. Valero, *The Adventure Writing of Clive Cussler*, pp. 72–3.

12. Haining, *The Classic Era of Crime Fiction*, pp. 26, 33.

13. Although it has never been proven, Savage is believed to have been the inspiration for the character, or at least the source of the name (see Cannaday, *Larger Than Life*, pp. 15–6).

14. Pancoast, *Introduction to American Literature*, p, 380. All modern American children fiction, of course, owes its greatest debt to Mark Twain's "twin epics of boyhood, *The Adventures of Tom Sawyer* and *The Adventures of Huckleberry Finn*, [which] are, of a kind, unsurpassed."

15. Sampson, *Yesterday's Faces: Vol. I, Glory Figures*, p. 41.

16. See *Raise the Titanic!*, inside jacket cover.

17. *The Skipper*, "The Man Who Makes His Own Laws," appeared in 52 stories from Street & Smith starting with 12 issues of his own magazine, between 1936 and 1937, before low sales forced the series to move to *Doc Savage Magazine*.

18. From the cover of *The Skipper* #10.

19. See *Cyclops*, p. 271. Hans Kronberg, the ill-fated partner of Raymond LeBaron, is described as a more realistic version of Matt Burden.

20. See Cannaday, *Larger Than Life*, pp. 110–1. Sail also shares many of these similarities with John D. MacDonald's Travis McGee, resident of the *Busted Flush*.

21. Wallace confesses in his autobiographical *People*: "My idea was to convey to America a picture of English soldiers and English [war] effort which would create an atmosphere of sympathy, if not for our cause, for the men who were fighting our battles.... When I was in New York four years later, an American editor told me that Tam was the inspirer of the American Flying Corps spirit" (quoted in Sampson, *Yesterday's Faces: Vol. VI, Violent Lives*, pp. 233–4).

22. Lesser, *Pulp Art*, p. 128.

23. Cussler, *Pacific Vortex*, p. 193. *Sahara* features a remix of this when Pitt hits upon a scheme to sneak into a heavily guarded solar detoxification plant in Mali, by hiding on a train with Giordino (see p. 290).

24. Lesser, *Pulp Art*, p. 135.

25. Sampson, *Yesterday's Faces: Vol. I, Glory Figures*, p. 226.

26. This is particularly noticeable in Pitt. Valero writes in *The Adventure Writing of Clive Cussler* (p. 62): "By reading through the books from their beginnings in serial order, one can see that Pitt has traded in his chain-smoking, take-advantage-of-women mode for a more long-term approach to life. In doing so he has even resurrected some of the chivalry of old. As [Cussler's] readers 'grew-up,' so did his hero."

27. See, for example, *Iceberg*, pp. 196, 307, and *Vixen 03*, p. 13.

28. Wilbur C. Tuttle, "The Cross in a Box Mystery," *Adventure* 82, no. 1 (March 15, 1932): 24.

29. Wilbur C. Tuttle, "The Buckaroo of Blue Wells," *Adventure* 60, no. 4 (November 23, 1926): 50.

30. Sampson, *Yesterday's Faces: Vol. V, Dangerous Horizons*, pp. 178–9.

31. Cussler, *Vixen 03*, p. 19.

32. Cussler, *Cyclops*, p. 75.

33. "Interview with Clive Cussler, June 2001," AudioBooksToday.com. In *Action Figures*, p. 85, Gallagher alludes to one important reason for this when he talks about what he calls "avowedly hardened, authentic male stars of the 1960s." A talent agent notes, "We have a lot of pretty guys running around with six-pack abs, but they lack authenticity and credibility.... In the 1950s a lot of men had been in the war; some of them became actors. They lived hard lives. There was a weight that came out of it.... When Steve McQueen took his shirt off, he's thin, he's not ripped. There's a hardness and danger about him because of who he was." Gallagher points out, "By the early 1970s, there were no young veterans of World War II and Korea, so Hollywood necessarily modeled male stars' personae on different attributes."

34. I asked Cussler if he had been influenced by Capra, Ford or Hawks, and he replied, "I enjoyed their movies, but I can't say they influ-

enced me" (author's questions to Cussler, August 2009).

35. Populism champions American traditions such as "good neighborliness, decent and responsible leadership, and social improvement on the community level" as well as "such middle-class values as hard work, frugality, and healthy competition, but also generosity, compassion, and social purpose" (Gianetti, *Masters of American Cinema*, Fig. 5.9). These traditions are also championed in Cussler's adventures, most often by deed, not words. Occasionally, however, such views are given voice (see *Raise the Titanic!*, p 354).

36. Gianetti, *Masters of American Cinema*, Chapter 5, p. 10.

37. Cussler admits in *Sea Hunters* (p. 74): "Politicians are not my favorite people. I always take great pride in marking "No" on my IRS return where it asks if I would donate a dollar to my favorite party. I recall voting in an election where I couldn't stand any of the candidates. So I wrote in John Dillinger, Baby Face Nelson, Pretty Boy Floyd, and Ma Barker for the nation's highest offices." In *Flood Tide* (p. 236) Pitt finds himself musing on how the world "may be a place that is scarce of honest politicians, white buffalo, unpolluted rivers, saints and miracles."

38. As Dirgo writes in *Clive Cussler & Dirk Pitt Revealed!* (p. 101), starting with *Vixen 03*, "The theme of governmental corruption is one Clive will continue to use in future novels."

39. Gianetti, *Masters of American Cinema*, Chapter 5, p. 5.

40. Ibid., Fig. 5.3.

41. Morris Dickstein, "It's A Wonderful Life, But...," *American Film* (May 1980): p. 44.

42. Gianetti, *Masters of American Cinema*, Chapter 5, p. 12.

43. Dickstein, "It's A Wonderful Life, But...," p. 47.

44. Ibid., p. 44.

45. Gianetti, *Masters of American Cinema*, Chapter 5, p. 10.

46. Ibid., Chapter 5, p. 6.

47. Ibid., Fig. 5.8. These last two differences could have been what Capra was referring to during an interview, during which he admitted that his heroes lack a pragmatic sense of reality. Yet he believes that his naïve heroes are necessary for a basic reason: "Between the idealist and the pragmatist—somewhere in between—lies the truth, and they are often rubbing against each other."

48. Ibid., Chapter 5, p. 10. This "twin ordeal, this mutual conversion from experience to innocence and innocence to experience, is the key to Capra's surprisingly ambivalent vision" (Dickstein, "It's A Wonderful Life, But...," p. 44).

49. Ibid.

50. See Gianetti, *Masters of American Cinema*, Chapter 5, p. 6.

51. For the premier example of this, see *Raise the Titanic!*, pp. 345–6.

52. See Gianetti, *Masters of American Cinema*, Chapter 6, p. 9, and Cussler and Dirgo, *Clive Cussler & Dirk Pitt Revealed!*, p. 17.

53. Cussler, *Raise the Titanic!*, p. 21.

54. For examples in Pitt's case, see *Pacific Vortex*, p. 9, *Raise the Titanic!*, pp. 99–100, *Vixen 03*, p. 4, and *Night Probe!*, p. 149.

55. See *Raise the Titanic!*, pp. 99–100, *Vixen 03*, p. 4, *Night Probe!*, p. 149, *Treasure*, p. 48, and *Dragon*, p. 527.

56. See Gianetti, *Masters of American Cinema*, Chapter 6, p. 10. Especially when it comes to matters of vengeance, as Wayne demonstrates in *The Searchers* and *Stagecoach*, and Pitt demonstrates in *Iceberg* and *Deep Six*.

57. Perhaps it is not a coincidence that one of Cussler's favorite adventure heroes, Horatio Hornblower, also ages during the course of his adventures. Aging heroes are not rare but they are uncommon in most adventure series. Aging is one element that Pitt shares with Clancy's heroes Jack Ryan and John Clark.

58. See Gianetti, *Masters of American Cinema*, Chapter 6, p. 10.

59. This is not to overlook a certain over-the-hill "Kid" (a.k.a. Clive Cussler) who makes cameos in several of the novels, and, coincidentally, could pass for the brother of Senator George Pitt (see Cussler and Dirgo, *Clive Cussler & Dirk Pitt Revealed!*, p. 14).

60. Gianetti, *Masters of American Cinema*, Chapter 6, p. 10.

61. This is one more similarity shared by Pitt and Ryan. Ryan has a father-son relationship with Admiral James Greer and technically replaces Greer for a time as acting deputy director of intelligence (CIA) when Greer is diagnosed with cancer in *Clear and Present Danger* (1990).

62. Clancy does something very similar when he turns Ryan into the president of the United States, and later, has Ryan's son, Jack, Jr., go on adventures like his father did.

63. "Critic Michael Dempsey goes so far as to deplore what he refers to as Ford's Victorian pedestalism of women" (Gianetti, *Masters of American Cinema*, Chapter 6, p. 10).

64. Cussler, *The Mediterranean Caper*, p. 11.

65. See Gianetti, *Masters of American Cinema*, Chapter 7, p. 5.

66. Ibid., Chapter 7, p. 8.

67. Journalist-turned-author Ben Hecht is perhaps best remembered as the co-author (with Charles MacArthur) of the play *The Front Page* (1928) which he helped Hawks transform into *His Girl Friday* (1940).

68. Gianetti, *Masters of American Cinema*, Chapter 7, p. 9. Hawks was one of the first to champion Faulkner's work.

69. Ibid. Hawks also made some excellent contributions to many of his films' screenplays, including Lauren Bacall's whistle speech in *To Have and Have Not* (1944).

70. See Don Swaim interview with Clive Cussler (January 30, 1986).

71. See Walter Wagner, *You Must Remember This* (New York: G.P. Putnam and Sons, 1975), p. 61. This also brings to mind Alfred Hitchcock, who spent months intricately preparing to make a movie, from the script to creating storyboards to the art direction, so that when it came time to actually film the story Hitchcock would appear bored (see David Freeman, *The Last Days of Alfred Hitchcock* [New York: Overlook Press, 1999], pp. 3–68).

72. See Gianetti, *Masters of American Cinema*, Chapter 7, p. 6. The most infamous example may be Owen Taylor's unsolved murder in *The Big Sleep*.

73. Gianetti, *Masters of American Cinema*, Chapter 7, p. 8.

74. Ibid., Chapter 7, p. 7.

75. Ibid., Chapter 7, p. 5.

76. Ibid., Chapter 7, p. 2.

77. Ibid., Chapter 7, p. 8

78. Ibid., Chapter 7, p. 6.

79. Not that Yaeger was always a family man. In his debut in *Deep Six*

(p. 250), Yaeger appears to be a single man living alone.

80. This is in stark contrast with Cussler's peer Clancy, who shows his hero Ryan's family life starting with Clancy's first novel, *Patriot Games* (1987).

81. According to Bloom, Harold Robbins "used male pulp genres and turned them into women's romance. He was the first of the so-called 'blockbuster' novelists and his books ... are long, complicated, and filled with the sex and violence that seem to accompany his rich jet-setters" (*Bestsellers: Popular Fiction Since 1900*, pp. 179–80).

82. See Gianetti, *Masters of American Cinema*, Chapter 7, p. 5.

83. Ibid., Chapter 5, p. 1.

84. Ibid., Chapter 12, p. 9.

85. Ibid., Chapter 13, p. 10.

86. A good example of this in a Ford film *Fort Apache*'s Silas Meachum (Grant Withers), a cowardly and greedy agent whose exploitation of American Indians leads to unrest between the Apaches and the U.S. Calvary; a good example in a Cussler novel is Hunnewell.

87. A minor but notable difference between this new archetype and earlier television heroes is his inherent style of humor. Westerns were the dominant adventure genre in television in the fifties and early sixties, and, during this time, humor was used to break up the action or vary the mood; it was rarely an extension of the adventure. For example, one of television's most popular westerns, *Bonanza* (1959–1973), features several comedic episodes, but these are painted with broad strokes: Ben Cartwright (Lorne Greene) and his three adult sons, Adam (Pernell Roberts), Hoss (Dan Blocker) and Little Joe (Michael Landon) come across as ineffectual doppelgängers of their normally capable selves. Another popular western, *Gunsmoke* (1955–1975), rarely featured comedic episodes, but comic relief was supplied by supporting characters Doc Galen Adams (Milburn Stone) and Fester Haggen (Ken Curtis), who seemed to bicker with each other constantly. Comic relief can also be found on *Wagon Train* (1957–1965), *Rawhide* (1959–1966) and Disney's *Zorro* (1957–1959).

88. Bloom, *Bestsellers: Popular Fiction Since 1900*, p. 202.

89. Author's questions to Cussler, August 2009.

90. I am particularly indebted to the following Wikipedia entries and Internet sources for fact-checking material on *Voyage to the Bottom of the Sea*: "Voyage to the Bottom of the Sea (TV Series)," "Harriman Nelson," and the "Episode Guide: "Voyage to the Bottom of the Sea."

91. USOS is an acronym for "United States Oceanographic Survey," and, in the film, the *Seaview* is under the authority of the Bureau of Marine Exploration (BME). As the series progresses, the submarine's designation changes to *SSRN* for "Submarine Ship Research Nuclear," which indicates the *Seaview* is a radar picket submarine.

92. *Polidor* and *Neptune* are destroyed during the program's first season.

93. Although the *Oregon* is not subject to being drafted into service like the *Seaview*, when the ship is introduced in *Flood Tide* (p. 167), its crew—The Corporation—is made up of a few ex-intelligence agents but mostly retired naval officers who will work for any U.S. government agency requiring their services.

94. *Voyage to the Bottom of the Sea* even features an alloy as fictional as the mineral byzanium and man-made element celtinium–279 (see *Iceberg*, p. 109), which is responsible for an important part of the *Seaview*. The transparent windows of the submarine's distinctive bow (which is shaped like a manta ray) are made from X-tempered herculite, which is created by a top-secret process invented by Nelson.

95. I am particularly indebted to the following articles from *Amazing Heroes*# 95 for reference material on *Jonny Quest*: "Interview: Doug Wildey" by David Olbrich (pp. 34–47) and "Quest for Adventure" by Jim Korkis (pp. 17–25).

96. See Korkis, "Quest for Adventure," p. 19.

97. See Olbrich, "Interview: Doug Wildey," p. 36. Wildey, who served as the model for the irascible aerial mechanic Peevey from Dave Stevens's comic-book series *The Rocketeer* (1982, 1988, 1989, 1991), refers to this as "projections."

98. Norman M. Klein, *Seven Minutes: The Life and Death of the American Animated Cartoon* (New York: Verso, 1996), pp. 197–8.

99. The show's creator touches upon this in Olbrich, "Interview: Doug Wildey," p. 37, when he mentions that Joe Barbera "had gone to see a movie called *Dr. No* and wanted to get in stuff like '007'-numbers. Which we included, by the way, in the first *Jonny Quest*. It was called something like 'Jonny Quest File 037' or something. We dropped that later; it didn't work. But that was his father's code name as he worked for the government as a scientist and that kind of thing."

100. Ibid., p. 38.

101. Ironically, insofar as titles are concerned, Cussler's homage to Richard Connell's famous man-hunting-man story occurs in *Dragon* (see Chapter 8).

102. See Craig Reid, "The Wild, Wild West," *Cinefantastique* 31, no. 8, p. 47.

103. While humor plays a big part in *The Wild, Wild West*, the tone of each episode is—like the tone in the Bond films that helped inspire the series—played straight, despite the outlandishness of the plots. While there is some occasional tongue-in-cheek humor, generally the acting is serious, which adds to the series' appeal. This is a difficult balancing act to pull off, but similar examples can be found in *The Green Hornet* (1967–68) and in the straight adventure moments from the best episodes of *Batman* (1966–68).

104. Reid, "The Wild, Wild West," p. 47.

105. Loveless first appeared in the third episode of *The Wild, Wild West*, "The Night the Wizard Shook the Earth," and was so popular that the character appeared in a total of ten of the series' 104 episodes.

106. See Cussler and Dirgo, *The Sea Hunters*, p. 17; Valero, *The Adventure Writing of Clive Cussler*, p. 20; and "Captain James T. Kirk," http://en.wikipedia.org/wiki/James_T._Kirk#cite_note-21.

107. See J.J. Dillard, *Star Trek: "Where No Man Has Gone Before"— A History in Pictures* (New York: Pocket Books, 1994), p. 26.

108. Cussler's heroes are not above making *Star Trek* references in their banter. For examples, see *Dragon*, p. 351, and *Serpent*, p. 169.

109. See *Sahara*, p. 95.

110. Bloom, *Bestsellers: Popular Fiction Since 1900*, p. 201.
111. Pitt owns a 1938 Packard Towncar in *Valhalla Rising*.
112. Here are a few examples:
- A wise man never plays leapfrog with a unicorn.
- Though the hippopotamus has no sting, the wise man would prefer to be sat upon by the bee.
- If a wolf is after your sleigh throw him a raisin cookie, but don't slow down to bake him a cake.

113. For an example in *NUMA Files*, see *Serpent*, pp. 126–9.
114. Bloom, *Bestsellers: Popular Fiction Since 1900*, p. 201.
115. See Sampson, *Yesterday's Faces: Vol. V, Dangerous Horizons*, p. 178, and Sampson, *Yesterday's Faces: Vol. I, Glory Figures*, p. 4.
116. Sampson, *Yesterday's Faces: Vol. I, Glory Figures*, p. 3.
117. Cussler and Dirgo, *Clive Cussler & Dirk Pitt Revealed!*, p. 75.
118. Cannel created *Baretta* after another program he was working on, *Toma* (1973–1974), based on real-life New Jersey undercover detective David Toma, shut down when its star, Tony Musane, left the series after one season. Cannell borrowed elements from *Toma*, created a colorful supporting cast, added some unique comedic touches (the most famous of which is Baretta's pet cockatoo, Fred) and created a show that was more popular than its inspiration.
119. *Battlestar Galactica* (1978–1979) tried to bring the space opera of *Star Wars* to television. It featured a cast in the new heroic archetype mold, including Commander Adama (Lorne Greene, from *Bonanza*) and Dirk Benedict as the series' Han Solo character, Starbuck. The show's creator, Glen A. Larson, had better luck as far as finding an audience with *Buck Rogers in the 25th Century* (1979–1981), starring Gil Gerard as Philip Francis Nowlan's pulp hero.
120. Like Cannell, Bellisario, a Marine sergeant-turned-scriptwriter-and producer, has created (or co-created) several series featuring some of the best of the new heroic archetype mode. These include the techno-thriller *Airwolf* (1984–1987), the time-travel adventure *Quantum Leap* (1989–1993), the military-legal adventure *J*A*G* (1995–1996 on NBC; 1997–2005 on CBS) and *Tales of the Golden Monkey* (1982–1983), an aviation-adventure series with overtones of *Raiders of the Lost Ark*.
121. Magnum also has two memorable brothers-in-arms in his colorful cast, fellow Vietnam veterans Theodore Calvin or "T.C." (Roger Molsey) and Rick Wright (Larry Manetti).
122. One more thing MacGyver has in common with Pitt is discovering that he is the father of a full-grown child. In the series' final episode, "The Stringer" (1992), MacGyver learns that a photojournalist named Sean "Sam" Angus Malloy is his biological son. Sean's mother, Kate Malloy, a photojournalist MacGyver met soon after graduating college, was murdered several years earlier while on an assignment in China.
123. This spin-off of the film *Stargate* (1994) became the most popular American science-fiction television series (second only to *Star Trek*) by creating its own brand of space opera, good-naturedly winking at its fantastic elements while treating its characters and adventures seriously. *Stargate SG-1*, like *Star Trek*, inspired its own animated series, *Stargate Infinity* (2002–2003), and live-action television spin-offs, *Stargate Atlantis* (2004–2009) and *Stargate Universe* (2009–2011).
124. *Torchwood* is an anagram of *Doctor Who*.
125. One of Gibbs's most famous attributes is a willingness to trust his intuition, although Gibbs typically refers to this as "going with his gut."
126. Although there has never been any confirmation of this, Bellisario may have acknowledged the possible debt *NCIS* owes to Cussler by having Special Agent Timothy McGee (Sean Murray) write best-selling mystery-crime novels under the series' title, *Deep Six*.
127. Bloom, *Bestsellers: Popular Fiction Since 1900*, p. 202.
128. Cussler and Dirgo, *Clive Cussler & Dirk Pitt Revealed!*, pp. 45–6.

Chapter 7

1. Joseph Campbell and Bill Moyers, *The Power of Myth*, edited by Betty Sue Flowers (Garden City, NY: Doubleday, 1988), p. xv.
2. "Introduction," *The Mediterranean Caper and Iceberg*, p. 211. Also see Cussler and Dirgo, *Clive Cussler & Dirk Pitt Revealed!*, p. 47.
3. See Campbell, *Hero with a Thousand Faces*, pp. 38–9, for a comparison of tribal or local heroes with universal heroes.
4. Ibid., p. 3. Also see p. 39, 43n.
5. Adapted from Elliott Gose, *Mere Creatures* (Toronto: University of Toronto Press, 1988), p. 86.
6. Jaffe, *Arthur Conan Doyle*, pp. 43–44.
7. Ibid., p. 44. Jaffe (on p. 31) goes so far as to call Holmes a "cliché whose time has come," something that is true for Pitt and all iconic adventure heroes.
8. Ibid., p. 52.
9. This scene also contains overtones of Fleming's "M" sending Bond on another mission.
10. In an ironic bit of heroic underscoring, Pitt's helicopter is a Ulysses Q-55.
11. See Campbell, *Hero with a Thousand Faces*, pp. 196–7.
12. Ibid., p. 30. Campbell borrows the term monomyth from James Joyce's 1939 novel *Finnegans Wake* (ibid., p. 120), but not everyone agrees with his approach, including some of his fellow academics in the field of folklore (see Dundes, "The Hero Pattern and the Life of Jesus," p. 8, for an example).
13. Ibid., pp. 30, 35.
14. Ibid., p. 246.
15. Jung, *Psyche and Symbol*, p. 75.
16. Ibid., p 76. Also see Campbell, *Hero with a Thousand Faces*, pp. 9–10.
17. See Gose, *Mere Creatures*, pp. 86, 149–50.
18. For a pair of excellent descriptions of shadow elements in an adventure story, see George Lucas, *Star Wars: From the Adventures of Luke Skywalker* (New York: Ballantine), pp. 58, 82.
19. Campbell, *Hero with a Thousand Faces*, pp. 10–1, 30.
20. J.M. Barrie, *Peter Pan* (London: Puffin Classics, 2002), p. 206.
21. Ibid., pp. 38, 158, 220, 221, 230.
22. In "When Wendy Grew Up," Peter visits the Darlings' nursery 20 years after Wendy and her brothers have returned from Neverland, only to find that Wendy is now a real

mother with her own child, a daughter named Jane. Peter, the little bird that has broken out of the egg, is heartbroken to have lost another mother. Earlier in the novel, Peter tells Wendy about returning to his home in London to find the window barred and his mother tending another baby. It never occurs to Peter that his mother has moved on with her life but would welcome him in if he only knocked on the window. A mother has room in her heart for more than one child. Peter, a child, can only feel hurt, and because he never grows older he never discovers he could have misjudged the situation, remaining childishly blind forever to the fact that he has only himself to blame for this ostracism. It is Peter who refuses to return home and it is Peter who stubbornly continues to stay in Neverland, where he never has to grow up. See Barrie, *Peter Pan*, p. 153 and p. 225. Bradbury also touches on many of these topics in his 1953 short story, "Hail and Farewell" (see *The Golden Apples of the Sun* (New York: Bantam, 1970), pp. 157–64.

23. This realization is at the heart of the 1991 film *Hook*. In this original sequel to *Peter Pan*, Peter (Robin Williams) decides to leave Neverland and marry Wendy's granddaughter on one of his visits to the Darling household. Over time Peter forgets his enchanted past, grows up and becomes a workaholic lawyer. When Captain Hook (Dustin Hoffman) abducts Peter's son and daughter, Peter returns to Neverland, where he remembers his past and learns to be like a child again so he can defeat Hook to rescue his children. After this last great battle, Peter leaves Neverland forever to return to his family, where he proclaims, "Life. Now there's a *real* adventure."

24. Campbell, *Hero with a Thousand Faces*, p. 29.

25. And it may not be a coincidence that sales of the Pitt novels dramatically improved after *Iceberg*, perhaps due in no small part to its hero's exploits graduating from the microcosmic to the macrocosmic, à la the best Bond novels, such as like *Thunderball* and *Dr. No*, and MacLean adventures including *The Guns of Navarone* and *Ice Station Zebra*.

26. See Jaffe, *Arthur Conan Doyle*, p. 39. In *Hero with a Thousand Faces*, p. 53, Campbell writes, "Typical of the circumstances of the call are the dark forest, the great tree, the babbling spring."

27. Cussler, *Iceberg*, p. 44.

28. Ibid., 23, 45. Cussler's spectral description of Pitt watching ships in Newport Beach before Sandecker's call foreshadows Pitt's first glimpse of the imbedded ship.

29. Campbell, *Hero with a Thousand Faces*, p. 78.

30. Cussler, *Iceberg*, p. 52.

31. Campbell, *Hero with a Thousand Faces*, p. 83.

32. Ibid., pp. 51, 55. In *The Hobbit* the herald is the theft of Thorin the dwarf's treasure by Smaug the dragon. In *Star Wars* the herald is Princess Leia's mayday to Obi-Wan Kanobi. In *Harry Potter and the Philosopher's Stone* the herald is Harry turning 11, making him the requisite age to attend Hogwarts.

33. Ibid., p. 51.

34. Ibid., p. 52.

35. Ibid., p. 16.

36. Ibid., pp. 52–3.

37. Ibid., pp. 51, 53. As an example of a blunder, Campbell cites the four signs that rouse Prince Gautama Sakyamuni out of his secluded life and put him on the path of his predestined journey to become the Buddha (see pp. 56–8).

38. Ibid., p. 55.

39. Pitt is not always this suggestible. In *Pacific Vortex* (p. 92), he calls legends about lost civilizations such as Kanoli, Mu and Atlantis "drivel," but in *Night Probe!* (p. 116) he tells his friend Joe Epstein, "Let's just say I'm a sucker for historical mysteries." In *Atlantis Found* Pitt actually locates Atlantis.

40. Jaffe, *Arthur Conan Doyle*, pp. 39–40.

41. See *Iceberg*, pp. 51–2. Take particular notice of how Hunnewell and Pitt talk after the rescue, a conversation that could have come from a modern adventure film, directed by Ford or Hawks.

42. Campbell, *Hero with a Thousand Faces*, p. 90.

43. Cussler, *Iceberg*, p. 54.

44. See *The Mediterranean Caper*, p. 76, and *Iceberg*, p. 53. The crossing of the threshold into the belly of the whale is a form of self-annihilation. The hero literally goes inward to be born again, an image so prevalent around the world that for millennia it has been associated with a worshipper passing into a temple where the visitor is reminded that, unlike his Creator, a man came from dust and to dust he must return (see Campbell, *Hero with a Thousand Faces*, p. 91).

45. Cussler, *Iceberg*, p. 56. Pitt sounds a little like Holmes talking to Watson as he points this out to Hunnewell.

46. Ibid., p. 58.

47. Ibid., p. 110.

48. Ibid., p. 59. Ironically, Pitt seems to have changed his mind about Fyrie during his final scene with Kirsti (see p. 339).

49. Edgar Rice Burroughs is a bit more forgiving when he touches upon this point about humanity in *People That Time Forgot* (1918), the second novel of his Caspak trilogy. Near the end of the story (p. 124), the hero-narrator, Tom Billings, alone and nearly naked in a savage world, experiences a brief sensation of cowardice: "I was immediately filled with shame; but in thinking the matter over I have come to the conclusion that my state of mind was influenced largely by my approximate nakedness. If you have never wandered about in broad daylight garbed in a bit of red-deer skin in inadequate length, you can have no conception of the sensation of futility that overwhelms one. *Clothes, to a man accustomed to wearing clothes, impart a certain confidence; lack of them induces panic*" (my emphasis).

50. Cussler, *Iceberg*, pp. 61–62.

51. Cussler, *Iceberg*, p. 75. Pitt says as much as Hunnewell and he depart the *Catawaba*. Later on (p. 185), an Air Force mechanic named Sam Cashman makes a similar attitude adjustment towards Pitt, demonstrating that Pitt has grown enough to inspire the same sort of mature respect in others that Koski inspired in him.

52. Ibid., p. 78.

53. Ibid., p. 79. To underscore Pitt's Peter Pan shadow, Cussler refers to this life-and-death battle as a game.

54. See Campbell, *Hero with a Thousand Faces*, p. 97. The road of trials is so popular that it has inspired literature around the world about miraculous tests and ordeals.

55. Ibid., p. 58.
56. Cussler, *Iceberg*, p. 73.
57. See Campbell, *Hero with a Thousand Faces*, p. 89. This motif of opposites, like the image of the belly of the whale, has many other examples, including the Greek legend of Symplegades, the clashing rocks that will crush travelers, but, between which, heroes always pass.
58. Cussler, *Iceberg*, p. 73.
59. Ibid., p. 84.
60. Ibid., p. 206.
61. See Campbell, *Hero with a Thousand Faces*, p. 69. See also 63n (old crone).
62. Ibid., p. 72–3.
63. Jonsson's effective counsel is succinct if not piquant (see *Iceberg*, p. 86) in contrast to Boland's brief but bland advice when Pitt bemoans March's death (see *Pacific Vortex* p. 137).
64. See *Iceberg*, p. 99.
65. Cussler, *Iceberg*, pp. 86–7.
66. Considering that Pitt works for NUMA it is likely he is already living in D.C.; however, the first time his home is mentioned is in *Raise the Titanic!*
67. Campbell, *Hero with a Thousand Faces*, p. 121.
68. Gose, *Mere Creatures*, p. 78.
69. Bulfinch, *Bulfinch's Mythology*, pp. 635–7.
70. Editorial Board of the University Society (Supervisors), *Epic of Gilgamesh*, pp. 97–103.
71. See *Iceberg*, pp. 152, 154. Compare this to Bilbo's descent into Smaug's cave, which he describes as "a nasty clockless, timeless hole" (quoted in Gose, *Mere Creatures*, p. 176).
72. Ibid., pp. 153, 155. The metaphor "engulfed" is apt since Pitt just escaped the belly of a dragon, only to be devoured again by the fog that is hiding the hydrofoil.
73. Cussler, *Iceberg*, p. 166. Cussler emphasizes this hunt by comparing the *Grimsi* to a frightened impala.
74. Ibid., p. 172. Pitt has a more callous feeling towards killing, in *Dragon* (p. 305).
75. See Campbell, *Hero with a Thousand Faces*, p. 101.
76. Ibid., p. 19.
77. Ibid., p. 111.
78. See Gose, *Mere Creatures*, p. 86, and Jung, *Psyche and Symbol*, p. 11.
79. See http://www.jcjc.cc.ms.us/faculty/humanities/pwedgeworth/JungArchetypes.htm.
An Earthmother is symbolic of fruit, abundance and fertility. She offers spiritual and emotional nourishment (e.g., Mother Nature, Mother Country, alma mater).
A Platonic Ideal is a source of inspiration and a spiritual ideal for which the protagonist or author will have an intellectual attraction (e.g., Dante's Beatrice, Petrarch's Laura, most of Shelley's heroines). A Temptress is a sensual beauty for whom the protagonist or author is physically attracted, and who may ultimately bring about his downfall (e.g., Delilah, the Sirens, Cleopatra). An Unfaithful Wife is a woman married to a man she sees as dull and unimaginative, and is physically attracted to a more virile and desirable man (e.g., Guinevere, Madam Bovary, Anna Karenina, Lady Chatterley).
80. Cussler, *Iceberg*, pp. 100, 102.
81. Ibid., pp. 99–100.
82. Ibid., pp. 102–3.
83. Ibid., pp. 124, 126, 212–3, 339.
84. Nowhere in the story does anyone mention if Kristjan Fyrie had flashes.
85. A most effective representation of this can be found in the Book of Job 38:1–42:5.
86. Campbell, *Hero with a Thousand Faces*, p. 147. Also see pp. 130, 136–7.
87. Cussler, *Iceberg*, pp. 103, 105. Pitt confesses to Tidi that Sandecker is more like a boss or a friend to him. Perhaps this is why Pitt sounds like a petulant son when he tells Sandecker how unhappy he is that the admiral did not trust him enough to confide everything about the *Lax* mission to him from the start.
88. Ibid., 108. Pitt defeats Sandecker to stay in Iceland when he refuses to follow the admiral's orders to return home.
89. Ibid., p. 130.
90. (Baroness) Emma Orczy, *The Scarlet Pimpernel* (Garden City, NY: International Collectors Library, n.d.) p. 41. The Scarlet Pimpernel is actually Sir Percy Blakely, Baronet, one of the richest men in England, taller than average, powerfully built and good-looking, but also "leader of all the fashions" and "the sleepiest, dullest, most British Britisher that had set a pretty woman yawning."
91. Cussler, *Iceberg*, p. 131.
92. In the gym, Rondheim tells Pitt that Kirsti doubts he is really so effeminate. While we are on the topic, however, there is an intriguing possibility that Pitt based his gay performance after a close family member. Pitt tells Kirsti that an uncle of his is the leading bon vivant of San Francisco, and, in some ways, Pitt is trying to follow in his footsteps (see *Iceberg*, p. 128). Could this comment (see p. 133) be Cussler's way of hanging a lantern on what Sandecker refers to as Pitt's "little homo act?" Is it so hard to believe that San Francisco's leading bon vivant is a homosexual who behaves more like Oscar Wilde than John Barrowman? When Pitt's uncle Percival "Percy" Nash is introduced in *Dragon* (see p. 170), he is clearly heterosexual, and there is no mention of his ever living in San Francisco. Could the San Francisco uncle be someone other than Nash?
93. Gose, *Mere Creatures*, pp. 87–8.
94. See *Iceberg*, p. 212.
95. Ibid., p. 214. Cussler does not refer to Pitt's vision as a dream, but a "fantasy."
96. Campbell, *Hero with a Thousand Faces*, p. 101.
97. Cussler, *Iceberg*, p. 100.
98. Ibid., p. 83.
99. This is an inversion of the three tests Pitt has to face along the road of trials.
100. Cussler, *Iceberg*, p. 216.
101. Gose, *Mere Creatures*, p. 152.
102. Ibid., p. 153.
103. Ibid., p. 86.
104. Ibid., pp. 152–3.
105. Just like the images in Pitt's nightmares, Gollum and Bilbo's riddles deal with symbols that represent elements of the hero's quest. Dark descents also happen to Luke Skywalker and Harry Potter. For Luke, his dark descent comes during *Star Wars: The Empire Strikes Back* when he enters the interior of a sinister and shadowy tree where he must face the riddle of his own destiny. Once inside, he battles a symbolic Darth Vader whom he decapitates, only to find his own face beneath Vader's mask. For Harry, his dark descent comes while trying to win the Triwizard Cup inside a maze in *Harry Potter and the Goblet of Fire*. Harry first encounters a sphinx with a rid-

dle, and then, along with the unfortunate Cedric Diggory, confronts the regenerated Lord Voldermort, whose real name is Tom Riddle (see pp. 605–669).

106. Cussler, *Iceberg*, p. 130.
107. Ibid., p. 110.
108. Ibid., p. 131.
109. Ibid., p. 229.
110. Ibid., p. 237.
111. Ibid., p. 130.
112. Ibid., p. 243.
113. Ibid., pp. 240–3.
114. Campbell, *Hero with a Thousand Faces*, p. 109.
115. Ibid., p. 193.
116. Cussler, *Iceberg*, pp. 245–6. Similar comments are made by Tidi earlier in *Iceberg* (see p. 98), and by Giordino in *Shock Wave* (see p. 333).
117. Cussler, *Iceberg*, 247. Cussler also circles back to Tidi's Earth-mother qualities by again describing her hair color.
118. Ibid., p. 246.
119. John 19:34. Interestingly, this spear plays a major role in *Atlantis Found*.
120. See Matthew 16:17, Luke 24:16, John 20:14, 21:4. Being unrecognized is not unusual for heroes after rebirth. A more pedestrian example of this is Rip Van Winkle, who is not recognized after his rebirth because he has aged and has not been seen in his township for many years (see Editorial Board of the University Society (Supervisors), *Bookshelf for Boys and Girls,* Vol. VIII: Bookland Classics [New York: University Society, 1972], pp. 339–40).
121. Cussler, *Iceberg*, p. 247.
122. Campbell, *Hero with a Thousand Faces*, pp. 150–1.
123. Ibid., pp. 196–7, 199.
124. In another ironic touch, the helicopter that appears to have crashed is a Titan class.
125. Cussler, *Iceberg*, p. 248.
126. Ibid., pp. 253–5.
127. Ibid., p. 256.
128. Ibid., p. 257. Cussler makes a point of separating the ascended hero from those he is leaving behind by switching perspectives from Pitt to the people in the ravine.
129. Ibid., pp. 273–4.
130. Ibid., p. 294. Cussler never completely abandons value-neutrality when it comes to technology, not even during Pitt's battle with Hermit Limited's computers. Pitt uses a radio transmitter owned by the river warder, Golfur Andursson, to request help from Sandecker, but he chooses his words carefully in case anyone from Hermit Limited might overhear (see pp. 267–8). Apparently, Pitt learned his lesson after causing a tragedy in *Pacific Vortex* when he used the radio on the *Starbuck* to contact the *Martha Ann* (see pp. 118–38). Like Hermit Limited's and the NSA computers, the radio transmitter is value-neutral because it can cause beneficial or detrimental results, depending on how it is used.
131. Gose, *Mere Creatures*, pp. 84–5.
132. Ibid., p. 84. This is a psychic rather than a physical journey; it is clear that Pitt is equipped for it when he talks about his and Kirsti's flashes (see *Iceberg*, p. 26).
133. See *Iceberg*, p. 259.
134. Ibid., p. 260.
135. Ibid., pp. 259–63. Cussler adroitly transforms the fog into symbols working against Pitt.
136. Ibid., pp. 263–4. The description of Pitt's trek echoes Gilgamesh's travels through the mountain Mashu in *The Epic of Gilgamesh* (p. 99): "Two hours became three. Three hours became four. Each minute was an infinite unit of misery and suffering, of aching cold, of intense burning pain, of fighting for control of his mind." The narrator also states how Gilgamesh travels one league, then two, then three, and all the way through 12.
137. Cussler, *Iceberg*, pp. 264–5.
138. This is also the moment Pitt reaches what Foster-Harris calls "the hero's dark moment," a story's most essential plot point (see *Basic Patterns of Plot*, p. 63).
139. Campbell, *Hero with a Thousand Faces*, p. 147.
140. Gilgamesh gets this same glimpse of the universe (see *Epic of Gilgamesh*, p. 102), and the introduction to Ecclesiastes in the *New Oxford Annotated Bible* (p. 805) explains how the Biblical author offers advice which is much in keeping with this germinal secret glimpsed by Pitt and Gilgamesh.
141. See *Iceberg*, p. 265–6. The inclusion of the cosmos is suggested while Pitt muses on the miraculous nature of his salvation, which is followed by another miracle during his return flight to the ravine (see p. 279).

142. See Campbell, *Hero with a Thousand Faces*, p. 207.
143. See *Iceberg*, p. 265. As befits a protective figure, Andursson is described with a mixture of natural and supernatural language, topped off by a historical martial comparison for good measure (see *Iceberg*, p. 265–6).
144. Ibid., p. 266.
145. Ibid., p. 273. Cussler leaves no doubt that this scene is an echo of the earlier one with Jonsson, by having Pitt joke that he has another poet on his hands. Unfortunately, we may never know the name of the poet responsible for the advice quoted by Andursson. In a list of questions I submitted to Cussler in August 2009 I confessed I could not locate the source of the quote and asked if Cussler remembered if he wrote it or, if not, the source. Cussler answered, "No, and no" (p. 6).
146. Ibid., p. 273.
147. Ibid.
148. Ibid., p. 276.
149. Ibid., p. 98.
150. Ibid., p. 108. Quite the contrary! See Sandecker's curse about Pitt.
151. See Campbell, *Hero with a Thousand Faces*, pp. 9–10. When Pitt leaves Iceland with Kippmann, Sandecker behaves less like a Wise Old Man than a grumpy (albeit concerned) father (see *Iceberg*, p. 298).
152. See *Iceberg*, pp. 273–4. This could almost be Pitt's heroic credo, and for the first time in the series, he pulls off a heroic feat using a historical implement.
153. Ibid., p. 280.
154. Ibid., pp. 282–3.
155. Ibid., p. 283.
156. Ibid., p. 284. Sandecker may not be one for public displays of sentimentality, but the admiral can be as compassionate as his surrogate son. Before the Tri-Motor takes off for the ravine, Sandecker uses his considerable clout to get the vodka and cigars stocked on the airplane. When Pitt slips the cigar in Kelly's breast pocket, he is pleasantly surprised to see that it is Sandecker's special brand.
157. Pitt is an adventure hero in the tradition of Holmes, not a transcendental hero like Richard Bach's Jonathan Livingston Seagull or Donald Shimoda, so the Master of the Two Worlds (see Campbell, *Hero*

with a Thousand Faces, pp. 229–37) and Freedom to Live (ibid., pp. 238–43) parts of the monomyth play a minor role at best in *Iceberg*.

158. Pitt and Kippmann know this is untrue, even though they approach the topic of how to defeat evil from completely different perspectives (*Iceberg*, pp. 293–4). Cussler often uses terms like "game" and "sport" to refer to adventures, so it may not be a coincidence (considering that Pitt is on a hero's quest) that, here, he uses terms like "fantasy" and "make-believe" when Pitt describes Kippmann's views on how good must battle evil. This is especially significant when Pitt uses the term "make-believe" when Kirsti the Temptress tries to seduce him into replacing Rondheim by her side (p. 338). Pitt's other comments about good and evil are also recollected during this seduction scene, during which he confesses that evil triumphed over good too often (p. 336).

159. Gose, *Mere Creatures*, p. 85.

160. Cussler, *Iceberg*, p. 304. As discussed in Chapter 5, magic mirrors are among the thematic preoccupations in Cussler's adventures, and in *Iceberg* Pitt examines himself in his costume in a full-length mirror (much like Dana Seagram examines herself at pivotal moments in *Raise the Titanic!*) and decides that the Big Bad Wolf costume is in keeping with his character.

161. For an example, see *Iceberg*, p. 287. This is hardly unusual when it comes to men, though. Lou Costello points this out in *Abbott and Costello Meet Frankenstein* (1948) when lycanthrope Larry Talbot (Lon Chaney, Jr.) says, "When the moon is full, I turn into a wolf," to which Costello replies, "You and twenty million other guys."

162. Rondheim may even sense this when Pitt wins the boon during the poetry challenge (see *Iceberg*, p. 216).

163. Rondheim is just Butera's latest alias. Before Rondheim there were at least three others: Max Rolland, Hugo von Klausen and Chatform Marazan (see *Iceberg*, p. 305).

164. The power of Pitt the Big Bad Wolf is likewise intensified because he finds the assassins when no one else can.

165. Cussler, *Iceberg*, pp. 321. Harry Potter experiences a similar moment in *Harry Potter and the Deathly Hollows* (pp. 699–700) when the personified memories of his parents, James and Lilly, his godfather, Sirius Black, and surrogate uncle, Remus Lupin, not only talk to him before he puts his ego to death, but remain by his side up through Harry's "death."

166. Ibid., p. 329. Rondheim's hotel room is reminiscent of Count Dracula's English hideaways in Piccadilly and Carfax Abbey, both dark, cool and odorous places (see Wolfe, ed., *The Annotated Dracula*, pp. 222–6, 266).

167. Ibid., 331. Cussler hangs a lantern on Kristjan's (Christian's) rebirth as Kirsti by identifying the surgeon who performs the operation as Dr. *Jesus* Ybarra (see p. 332).

168. Ibid., pp. 332–3.

169. Ibid., p. 339. The Temptress makes her intentions clear to the hero at this moment. Before offering herself to Pitt, she tells him that she will do all he demands of her, but she must extract a small cost in return. Although this seems to imply something sexual, she is, in truth, hoping to tempt Pitt into relinquishing his soul by forsaking NUMA and everything he believes in to join her.

170. Ibid., p. 339. This can also be viewed as yet another magic mirror scene.

171. Ibid., p. 59. In this instance, considering Kirsti really is naked, this cynical observation becomes as ironic as it is accurate.

172. Ibid., p. 340. This blessing brings Pitt full circle, to Hunnewell's death, but it also demonstrates his atonement as he uses the same weapon he used to steal a boon from the Father (Rondheim) to win the Woman (Kirsti).

173. Ibid., p. 23.

174. Ibid.

175. Ibid., p. 301.

176. Ibid., p. 340.

177. Ibid. As the novel concludes, Pitt cannot see—or refuses to see—that he is not the same man he was at the beginning.

178. Campbell, *Hero with a Thousand Faces*, p. 251.

179. Frederick Pierce, *Dreams and Personality: A Study of Our Dual Lives* (New York: D. Appleton, 1931), p. 109.

180. These allusions are among the many stylistic and structural changes that Cussler introduces to the Pitt series in this novel; they are explored in more detail in Chapter 8.

181. Most notably on pp. 54–7. Another reason for this delay may be because, while Pitt certainly has investigative skills, in this novel he is a man of action, and with his arrival the story moves from its investigative stage (researching where the byzanium went after Brewster and his men left Novaya Zemlya) to an active stage (locating and salvaging the *Titanic*).

182. However, starting with *Raise the Titanic!*, Pitt never appears throughout an entire book again. In a 1986 interview, Cussler says that he thinks this is why his Pitt adventures are referred to as Clive Cussler books, while Fleming's 007 adventures are referred to as Bond novels. Cussler then cites *Vixen 03* as an example of what he means. Pitt appears in the first 80 pages of the novel, then disappears for approximately the next 120 pages (see http://wiredforbooks.org/clivecussler/index.htm).

183. See *Raise the Titanic!*, pp. 20–1. This is daring imagery for the counter-culture seventies, when most authors and publishers shied away from unabashed heroic descriptions, but Cussler has made a career out of following his instincts. Another newcomer to the bestseller list in the seventies, Stephen King, also benefited from reveling in imagery most authors of the period were avoiding when he wrote *Salem's Lot*, a novel about vampires. One key difference between Cussler and King, however, is that Cussler was told that adventure was a dead genre, but the horror genre was enjoying great success, even if vampires were considered passé. The horror genre of the time included such titles as William Peter Blatty's *The Exorcist* (1973), Thomas Tryon's *The Other* (1971) and King's *Carrie* (1974).

184. Pitt is a ruthless hero who takes no joy in killing, the kind of hero that women can love. Like Beast (Robby Benson) in *Beauty and the Beast* (1991), Pitt can save a heroine from wolves and then take her dancing.

185. A paraphrase of Stanley's quote appears in several Cussler adventures, though not always spoken

by Pitt. For examples, see *Sahara*, p. 91, *Serpent*, p. 162, *Valhalla Rising*, p. 141, and *White Death*, p. 324.

186. See *Raise the Titanic!*, p. 21. Pitt demonstrates this same strength with Loren in their first scene together, in *Vixen 03* (see p. 2).

187. Ibid., p. 54.

188. Ibid., pp. 87–8.

189. See Exodus, 14:21.

190. *Raise the Titanic!*, p. 260. Cussler adds a little more irony that Melville might have approved of by having this same character also say (on p. 194), "Only God can make a storm." In an earlier scene (on p. 170) Sandecker, the Wise Old Man and dominant father figure of the Pitt series, suggests the same is true when it comes to knowing if Man possesses the ability to raise the *Titanic*.

191. Ibid., p. 320. The novel's central antagonist, Captain André Prevlov, warns Pitt about this. America has escaped the threat of nuclear missile attack, but, as *Vixen 03* demonstrates, there are plenty of other weapons in the world.

192. For an example of Pitt's cynicism see *Deep Six*, p. 184. The golden calf story appears in Exodus 32, a story that, on the surface, appears to be about a failed test of the Hebrew people, but, on closer reading, it concerns a test passed by Moses. After the golden calf is created, God orders Moses to leave Him alone so His wrath can consume the Hebrews, but "of you I will make a great nation." This high honor parallels the one God made to Father Abraham in Genesis 17:4–6, but Moses has long-term faith in his people, and defends them. However, God did not need Moses to leave Him alone to destroy the Hebrews. Nevertheless, Moses is given a tempting offer but refuses, in essence sticking with his imperfect people instead of reaping some hard-won glory for himself. As a parallel, Pitt passes a similar test each time he puts his life on the line for America and its citizens. Pitt knows America's system of government and its citizens are not perfect, but his long-term faith allows him to continue to defend his country.

193. See Pancoast, *Introduction to American Literature*, pp. 136–9.

194. Cussler, *Raise the Titanic!*, p. 88.

195. Ibid., p. 91.

196. Ibid., p. 90. This rebuttal could count as a third heroic allusion as Pitt's self-confidence seems noble when contrasted with Seagram's hubris.

197. The movie's only other memorable lines come during Pitt's visit with John Bungalow (Sir Alec Guinness), the last living crew member of the *Titanic*. Bungalow tells Pitt, "What a lovely thing she was.... Standing as high in the water as one of your skyscrapers, longer than two rugby fields, and furnishings to match the finest mansions in England. She was one of a kind, no question about it, and God Himself, they said, couldn't sink her. Then in two hours she was gone ... and fifteen hundred souls with her."

Pitt and Bungalow also have this Cussleresque exchange:

Bigalow: It's an odd thing, you know. I've had a few ships shot out from under me. More than my share. Three in the 1914 to '18 fracas, and two in '39 to '45. But all anybody ever asks me about is the *Titanic*.

Pitt: And now I'm doing the same thing.

Bigalow: And you're lucky you came to the right man!

198. See Pancoast, *Introduction to American Literature*, pp. 133 & 275.

199. One of the secrets of success for an adventure story like *Raise the Titanic!* is that the hero, more often than not, is going to save the day, so the author has to make the events leading up to the hero's success interesting and entertaining enough to make the reader want to follow along, even if the author cannot convince the reader that failure is a possibility. And Cussler is a master at this. We *know* Pitt is going to save the day; we just cannot figure out *how* he is going to do it.

200. See Chapter 8.

201. A 1978 article for *Writer's Digest* reports that, after the lukewarm sales of *The Mediterranean Caper* and *Iceberg*, "Cussler wanted a gimmick that would make his next Pitt book a success everywhere, so he started playing his *what if* game again. *What if ... what if* someone decided to raise the *Titanic*."

202. Which is not to say that these other challenges are unimportant (see Campbell, *Hero with a Thousand Faces*, p. 173).

203. "The course of the narrative is to chart the actions of the perpetrators who have overturned or are at least threatening the status quo, block or blunt them, and, ultimately, exile them, so that the society they are undermining or obstructing can be returned to its previous, happy condition" (Schwartz, *Nice and Noir*, p. 5).

204. *Raise the Titanic!*, p. 110. Brewster writes that the Coloradans "raped" the byzanium from the land.

205. Ibid., p. 25. Like Seagram, Prevlov ends up a victim of his own hubris, but, in another ironic twist, the Soviet intelligence officer comes off better than the American responsible for the Sicilian Project. Where Seagram loses his marriage and his mind, Prevlov realizes his vanity has caused his downfall and accepts it (see p. 340), and this acceptance saves his life. After his capture, he is offered the chance to defect to America, but he refuses. However, when he is informed by chief CIA director Warren Nicholson that he has been put on the Soviet liquidation list, the proud Russian again accepts the inevitable and agrees to Warren's offer of a new identity, plastic surgery and a lucrative paycheck. Nicholson would appear to be correct when he suggests that Prevlov might learn to enjoy Western-style decadence, but, as they shake hands to close the deal, Nicholson sees tears in Prevlov's eyes. His choice might seem an easy one, but, to his credit, it is not (see pp. 341–2).

206. Ibid., p. 25. Cussler adds to this "opposite number" role for Prevlov by giving him and Pitt other similarities. Both are military officers assigned to an agency outside of their branch of service; both have powerful fathers in their country's governments; and both are considered untouchable because of their brilliance and their father's rank.

207. Cussler underscores this element of the adventure by naming the defense shield project after a chess strategy, the Sicilian Defense.

208. The *First Attempt* makes her debut in *The Mediterranean Caper* and is named after a speedboat Cussler converted into an outboard (see Cussler and Dirgo, *Clive Cussler & Dirk Pitt Revealed!*, pp. 42–3). *Raise*

the *Titanic!* also marks the first (but not the last) time Cussler incorporates the name of his California boyhood home into a story, in this case as the U.S. Navy vessel *Alhambra*.

209. Cussler, *Raise the Titanic!*, p. 299. Dana's stripping is admirable, but there is more going on here than defiance. As discussed in Chapter 5, Dana is teetering on becoming a more respectable version of her mother, and in Dana's final scene she muses how her stripping will linger in the minds of the men on the *Titanic* that night (see p. 351). Compare this to a similar scene from another bestseller published in 1976, Peter Benchley's *The Deep*. In that book a beautiful young woman, Gail Berke, removes some of her clothes to prove she is not hiding morphine ampules on her person while members of a Caribbean drug gang hold her fiancé, David Saunders, at knifepoint (see pp. 80–1). Berke stands half-naked in front of a small group of dangerous men to save the man she loves, a stark contrast to Dana's perverse satisfaction.

210. It is never explained why Pitt feels compelled for the first time in his series to bed another man's wife. Until now Pitt has shown no interest in Dana, except for one brief moment immediately after the *Titanic* is reduced to a skeletal crew. As the *Alhambra* sails away, Pitt searches for a glimpse of Dana among the journalists and sailors gathered at the *Alhambra*'s rails for what may be the world's last look at the resurrected *Titanic*.

211. Cussler, *Raise the Titanic!*, p. 337.

212. Campbell, *Hero with a Thousand Faces*, p. 113.

213. Ibid., pp. 118–9. "And if she has shunned him, the scales fall from her eyes; if she has sought him, her desire finds its peace." Dana has certainly sought the president, but, by bedding him, Dana will replace Fleming as Washington's most sophisticated divorcée and glorified hooker, in essence succumbing to her family curse.

214. This is the one of the few times this happens in the Pitt series, where love scenes are usually seen, at least in part, from the woman's point of view.

215. See *Raise the Titanic!*, p. 337.

216. Ibid., p. 339.

217. Ibid., p. 207. Pitt is also not the first man Dana has been with since her separation, but her other dates have been platonic.

218. Ibid., p. 375.

219. The prologue is also more in line with Pitt's past adventures because it is set in the recent past, only 34 years before the main adventure in 1988.

220. *Webster's New World Dictionary*, p. 509. If not Fate than this power could be Destiny (p. 383), a "succession of events that may either be caused by necessity or a supernatural agency."

221. See Campbell, *Hero with a Thousand Faces*, p. 109, 121.

222. And coincidences, however absurd they may be, are an accepted part of any adventure story.

223. See *Vixen 03*, p. 1, and *Pacific Vortex*, p. 218. A vision similar to Summer appears in *The Mediterranean Caper* when Pitt finds Teri asleep on a sofa in Von Til's study wearing a negligee that hides nothing (see p. 115).

224. Summer and Botticelli's Venus are similar in appearance, right down to their long red hair; Summer is even holding a hand over one breast.

225. When it comes to fishing scenes in other Pitt adventures they are usually a cover for something more important, such as the dive on the black jet in *Iceberg* (pp. 147–50, 152–6) or the meeting between Sandecker, Seagram, and Kemper in *Raise The Titanic!* (pp. 143–52). Even in *Vixen 03* Fawkes pretends to be fishing while actually taking notes about ship traffic at Walnut Point, Virginia (pp. 192–3).

226. Cussler, *Vixen 03*, p. 96.

227. Ibid., p. 110.

228. Ibid., pp. 170–1.

229. Ibid., p. 176. Later (on p. 247), when Pitt forces his way into Daggat's limousine to rescue Loren, he fixes "Daggat with a stare that would have frozen a shark."

230. Ibid., pp. 115–9.

231. Ibid., p. 171. Pitt has more faith in Loren's constituency (see p. 247).

232. Ibid., p. 113.

233. Ibid., pp. 112, 327.

234. Ibid., p. 99.

235. Ibid., p. 136.

236. See Matthew 13:47–50.

237. See Matthew 14:13–21 and 15:32–39, Mark 6:30–44 and 8:1–10, and Luke 9:10–17. All three Synoptic Gospels recount the Feeding of the Five Thousand, but only Matthew and Mark recount another incident where Jesus feeds the Four Thousand (see Matthew 15:29–39 and Mark 8:1–10).

238. See Matthew 17:24–27 and Mark 1:16–20.

239. See Reader's Digest Books, *The Story of Jesus*, edited by Gardner Associates (Bath, UK: Reader's Digest Association, 1993), p. 244.

240. John 1:29.

241. A redeemer hero is "the defending hero who is prepared to take on the power of evil at the cost of his own life in order to save the world. The Babylonians called him Marduk. The Canaanites called him Baal; the Egyptians, Osiris. He is the precursor of Hercules and Achilles, along with King Arthur, Charlemagne and Robin Hood. In modern culture he is found in many examples from Harry Potter to TV science fiction shows like *First Wave*. Some would argue that Jesus Christ is simply another variation on this mythical hero" (Leggett, *Terence Fisher*, p. 142). Seen in this light, Sherlock "Holmes is another version of [the] Redeemer Hero. He is putting his life on the line in a cosmic struggle. Like his predecessors he is not only unrewarded in his efforts but actually rebuffed" (ibid., p. 150).

242. Unlike the fish symbol, this image of Jesus does appear in the Gospels. For example, in John 1:29, John the Baptist calls Jesus the Lamb of God when he first sees the Christ, and 1 Corinthians 5:7 states, "Christ, our paschal lamb, has been sacrificed."

243. Cussler may be displaying his fondness for Bass or emphasizing that Bass is a true hero by making Bass's middle name Horatio. While it is always possible that this middle name could have been inspired by Hamlet's confidant, it seems more likely that it could have been a tip-of-the-hat to Captain Horatio Hornblower. Whatever the case may be, Bass's middle name, Horatio, remains a noble name, one Bass honors by his actions.

244. The first character introduced in *Vixen 03* is the doomed plane's pilot, Air Force major Raymond Vylander.

245. See *Vixen 03*, pp. 146–59, 177–82.

246. Millions of lives depend upon the information Bass can tell Pitt, but at one point Bass's lover, Heidi Milligan, begs Pitt to stop; he is tempted until Bass orders him to wait until he can continue (see *Vixen 03*, p. 276). It is interesting to compare Pitt's reaction here to Lusana's callousness in a similar situation earlier in the story (see pp. 86–7).

247. Shortly before the last QD missile is neutralized, the president is informed that Bass has died, and POTUS opines how strong Bass must have been to carry the terrifying secret alone for 30 years. Ironically, a few moments later, POTUS gets a sample of the weight of Bass's burden when he is forced to put his own career on the line for the good of mankind when he orders a secret nuclear strike on tiny Rongelo Island, in the Pacific, the site of the only test of the QD organism (see *Vixen 03*, pp. 351–2).

248. In this sense, Bass can also be seen as this adventure's Father figure, from whom the hero wins a boon for his society (the secrets about the release mechanisms) by atoning with the Father. In a way, Pitt also wins the bride from the Father by bedding Bass's mourning lover and liberating Heidi in *Night Probe!*

249. See *New Oxford Annotated Bible with Apocrypha* (New York: Oxford University Press, 1977), 22:28–31.

250. In a telling scene, Ness (Kevin Costner) makes this confession to a corrupt judge he is about to extort into running an honest courtroom during the trial of public enemy number one Al Capone (Robert DeNiro): "I have foresworn myself. I have broken every law I have sworn to uphold, I have become what I beheld and I am content that I have done right!" It is a scene rich in irony, not the least of which is that Ness's extortion threat turns out to be a bluff.

251. See Sampson, *Yesterday's Faces: Vol. I, Glory Figures*, p. 19. De Vaal's most trusted advisor, Colonel Joris Zeegler, the director of Internal South African Defense, provides evidence of Fawkes's extraordinary gifts when he tells De Vaal that a month-long computer search of experienced military veterans has verified that Fawkes is the best man to offer an opinion on Operation: Wild Rose (see *Vixen 03*, pp. 69–70).

252. See *Vixen 03*, p. 62.

253. Ibid., p. 61. Unlike Bass, whose name is a direct reference to a fish, there are no such direct references associated with Fawkes; however, we are told that he was also an Aberdeen sea captain, so it is possible that he has experience as a commercial fisherman.

254. An old-fashioned adventure hero that may have influenced Cussler, Allan Quatermain, lives in Durban, in the South African province of Natal.

255. Cussler, *Vixen 03*, p. 71. During his Pembroke meeting Fawkes makes a second religious reference about the bush kids when he tells De Vaal, "God only knows what devil inspired them to go on a killing spree." This sentence is echoed when Fawkes returns home (see p. 81) to discover the slaughter and shouts, "God in hell!"

256. The name De Vaal sounds like "devil," and this is a classic Gothic technique. In *Dracula*, Stoker's Vampire King buys one of several safe houses in London, using the alias Count de Ville (see Wolf, ed., *The Annotated Dracula*, p. 241). That said, perhaps it is no coincidence that Fawkes sounds a little like "Faust."

257. See *Vixen 03*, p. 84 and 1 Kings 19:19–21. Elisha, like Fawkes, does not always follow his moral compass (e.g., 2 Kings 2:23–25) and so, unlike the Hebrew Bible's two other God-men, Moses (whose body was buried by God in a secret place in the land of Moab) and Elijah (who never died, but ascended to Heaven), he dies and is cast into a grave like any other man. Ironically, during Elisha's funeral the body of another man is tossed into his grave when a band of attackers ride over a hill. That dead man is resurrected, but in *Vixen 03* De Vaal's body is tossed in Fawkes's grave after he is executed to bury the truth behind Operation: Wild Rose for all time.

258. See *Vixen 03*, p. 102.

259. Ibid., p. 70. An example of this occurs when De Vaal suggests that Scotsmen have trouble learning a new language; Fawkes brushes off the insult.

260. Ibid., p. 74. An example occurs after the meeting with De Vaal. Fawkes, who is a very large man, gets drunk at a Pembroke bar and takes some infantile glee in intimidating the bartender.

261. Ibid., p. 71.

262. Ibid., p. 86.

263. Ibid., pp. 71–2.

264. Ibid., pp. 96–7. Also see pp. 141, 244.

265. Ibid., p. 135.

266. Ibid., p. 116.

267. Jumana's satanic expression in this scene symbolically links him to Lusana's major outside threat, the "Devil" De Vaal.

268. Matthew 3:16–17, Mark 1:9–11, Luke 3:21–26.

269. Reader's Digest Books, *The Story of Jesus*, p. 129.

270. Ibid., p. 128.

271. Matthew 4:1–11, Mark 1:12–13, Luke 4:1–13.

272. As Daggat told Collins, Lusana is adored by Bible-beaters (see *Vixen 03*, pp. 96–7).

273. Lusana's reference also alludes to his earlier sin of trading Collins to Daggat. In the Hebrew Bible, 30 pieces of silver is the price of a slave (see Reader's Digest Books, *The Story of Jesus*, p. 28).

274. If Machita does not save Lusana's soul by way of baptism, at least he is saving him physically.

275. This may be seen as a mockery of the Old Man archetype. Emma calls Machita to this place far from her home with the AAR, but there is nothing genuine about this, starting with Emma's disguise and ending with the package Machita gets from her.

276. In "Little Red Riding Hood" a treacherous male wolf wears old lady clothing and waits to devour Red. In contrast, Emma, the wolf in *Vixen 03*, is disguised as an old man.

277. This unexpected burst of light echoes the breeze that brought Loren and Pitt together at the secretary's party.

278. The concept of Satan being Emma's helper turns out to be a visual pun after it is discovered Emma is helping De Vaal. When it comes to Operation: Wild Rose, in particular, Emma is a devil who sells secrets and death to anyone foolish enough to pay the informer's and the Satan De Vaal's price.

279. See Matthew 4:3–11 and Luke 4:3–13.

280. Campbell, *Hero with a Thousand Faces*, pp. 142–3.
281. See *Vixen 03*, pp. 135–6.
282. Here Lusana exhibits the same common-sense myopia Fawkes does when volunteering to lead Operation: Wild Rose.
283. This moment also serves as a point of comparison between Machita and the disciple Peter, who tells Jesus during the Last Supper that he is ready to follow him into prison and death, only to deny him not once but three times when the moment of truth arrives. Peter's denial is foretold by Jesus in Matthew 26:30–35, Mark 14:26–31, and Luke 22:31–34, and Peter denies being a disciple of Jesus three times in Matthew 26:57–75, Mark 14:53–72, and Luke 22:54–71. Unlike Peter, Machita follows through on his oath (see *Vixen 03*, p. 216).
284. Lusana's injuries and imprisonment (see *Vixen 03*, p. 220) are more than a little comparable with the Passion of the Christ. According to the Gospel of Luke (22:54), Roman guards "seized him and led him away" (22:63–64), "mocked him and beat him, they also blindfolded him," and while Jesus was dying on the cross (23:34) Roman soldiers "cast lots to divide his garments."
285. See *Vixen 03*, pp. 220–4. Overlooking Machita proves to be a terrible miscalculation for the white South African government. De Vaal is aware of Machita's potential as a redeemer when he tells Zeegler during the colonel's after-action report of the attack that Machita is the only person capable of succeeding Lusana in the AAR (see p. 223).
286. Ibid., pp. 221–4.
287. In the process of avenging Lusana, Machita finally defeats Satan or the Devil (or dragon) when he helps slay the corrupt De Vaal.
288. See *Vixen 03*, pp. 173–175.
289. Cussler never uses the word "apartheid" in *Vixen 03*, perhaps to distance his fictional South African government from the real-life government ruling in that country.
290. See Chapter 7, 283n.
291. See *Vixen 03*, pp. 216–9. Daggat, like De Vaal, has no problem furthering his career by assigning blame to other innocent parties or recommending that others do likewise.
292. Ibid., p. 250. Comparing Fawkes to a giant is one of the few outright fairy-tale touches in this story.
293. Ibid., p. 250.
294. Ibid., p. 311.
295. Ibid., p. 261.
296. Ibid., pp. 261–5.
297. Ibid., p. 279. As Fawkes sails on, we realize his fate is sealed when he hears the mournful sound of a buoy's bell calling to him.
298. Ibid., pp. 273, 275, 289. Even after plowing over the *Molly Bender*, Fawkes has moments when he can do the right thing and quit instead of pressing on (for example, see *Vixen 03*, p. 301).
299. See Campbell, *Hero with a Thousand Faces*, p. 249, n3. The belly of Hell is an even more fitting description of the place the trio find themselves when it is overlaid with the words of the prophet Jonah as he prays from the stomach of leviathan and compares his plight to being in the "belly of Sheol." This also wraps back to Fawkes's exclamation about the Lord in Hades, on p. 81.
300. *Vixen 03*, p. 321.
301. Ibid., p. 320.
302. Ibid., p. 328–9. Fawkes's most poignant realization of the hell his ship has become occurs when he communicates via radio with a young crewman named Obasi in the turret officer's booth after the Satan missile attack (see p. 315).
303. Ibid., p. 311.
304. Ibid., p. 318. While this is the first time Lusana admits it, the reader already knows about the robbery; it is revealed in an earlier scene (on p. 138) when Loren tells the congressman that she has read Hiram Jones's FBI file, which lists several crimes including the armored truck robbery.
305. Ibid., pp. 327–8.
306. Ibid., p. 322.
307. Ibid., p. 326. Cussler provides no motivation for Emma employing this deception, if indeed it *is* a deception. We have no way of knowing if this was a misunderstanding that arose from Emma's disguises or if she just took advantage of the mistake. Logically, it would benefit an informer to have your buyers and your enemies thinking you are a man when you are a woman. The individual reader can give Emma the benefit of the doubt and assume she did this on purpose, although this remains speculative.
308. Ibid., p. 333.
309. Ibid., p. 356. This is the first time we see Machita since his resurrection, and considering what he is about to do, perhaps it is fitting that he looks more like the Grim Reaper than a redeemer.
310. Ibid., p. 358.
311. As Robert Young Pelton points out in *World's Most Dangerous Places*, 5th ed. (New York: HarperCollins, 2003), p. 896: "The principal reason that post-apartheid South Africa didn't drown in a sea of blood" is the leadership of Nelson Mandela. "As president, Mandela strove for reconciliation with the white minority rather than revenge against them, and the moral authority lent by his suffering at the hands of the apartheid regime brought his country along with him. One needs only look north to Zimbabwe to see how badly it could have turned out." Unfortunately for Zimbabwe (and Mike Grell's hero Jon Sable, who suffers a similar tragedy there as Fawkes does in South Africa) they had Robert Mugabe, whose "rule is one of pettiness, vanity, and extreme violence" (Ibid., p. 983).
312. Schwartz, *Nice and Noir*, p. 5.
313. See *Vixen 03*, p. 122.
314. Ibid., pp. 301–5. In an oddly inspirational moment, the building splits apart instead of crumbling inward, which leaves the statue of the seated Lincoln exposed but unscathed.
315. Ibid., p. 273. Some small solace can be found in the prevention of letting the QD organism survive as a weapon. When Jarvis and Pitt first unite to track down the QD missiles, Pitt insists Jarvis promise that they will be destroyed, but Jarvis cannot do that. At least Jarvis is honest with Pitt, who does not trust the government to do the right thing when it comes to the QD organism (see pp. 287–8), but when one of the president's advisors recommends the organism be preserved as a weapon, it is Jarvis who argues against it because the QD organism is too dangerous to control, as the situation with the *Iowa* proves (see p. 293).
316. Ibid., p. 359.
317. Cussler has never denied that Shaw is Bond, and in *Night Probe!* Pitt even implies that Shaw is Bond (see p. 344). Nevertheless Dirgo plays

sly in *Clive Cussler & Dirk Pitt Revealed!* (see p. 238), and Cussler is just as sly in "The Reunion" (see pp. 9–10). In *The Adventure Writing of Clive Cussler* (pp. 129–39), Valero writes, "At the time [Cussler] wrote the passage comparing Shaw to Bond, Cussler honestly thought it wouldn't pass with his editor, and if it did that the Fleming estate would be upset at Cussler for using Bond's name without their permission. So far, not a word from anyone except the speculative reader who believes that Shaw *really* is Bond." I asked Cussler how he felt Pitt stacked up against Bond in *Night Probe!* and if it was an interesting experience comparing the individual strengths and weaknesses of these heroes when pitted against each other. Cussler replied that it was "just a fun idea" (author's questions to Cussler, August 2009).

318. This is not the last time Pitt takes up a quest for someone else (see *Cyclops*, p. 277).

319. See *Vixen 03*, p. 154.

320. See *Night Probe!*, *03*, pp. 40–3.

321. Ibid., p. 44. This is also the first of three game-changing events involving Heidi that transpire at the very last moment. During the first event Heidi does not even choose the restaurant, but goes to one at a cab driver's recommendation (ibid., p. 44). The second is Pitt's appearance at the restaurant (see p. 45). The third involves her decision to pass along her research to Pitt just before she boards a plane for San Diego to return to duty (see p. 60). The first event also involves Cussler's magic-mirror thematic preoccupations (see Chapter 5). Before going out, Heidi examines herself in the hotel mirror, but unlike Dana Seagram before the White House dinner party (see *Raise the Titanic!*, p. 24), Heidi likes what she sees. She even likes a pie-shaped splash of gray she has in her right eye that her school classmates used to call an evil eye, whereas Dana agonizes over crow's feet. The difference between Heidi and Dana is also underscored by Heidi's research into the North American Treaty. When she hands her research material over to Pitt she tells him she thinks it may be important, and by that she means important for her society (America) rather than for herself. Finally, this first event includes a visual cue involving lights reflected in rivers (or on water) that is repeated during other game-changing events in *Night Probe!* (see pp. 44, 111, 142, 303, 317–8, and 341). The novel ends with Pitt driving home after rain has stopped falling on Washington, and the city's lights are reflected on low-hanging clouds (see p. 345).

322. Ibid., pp. 149–55. It could be argued that Heidi's quest actually begins with Pitt, playing the role of an Old Man, calling her out of her comfortable home by his need to talk to Bass at Anchoprage House.

323. Ibid., pp. 40 and 42.

324. Ibid., p. 45.

325. Campbell, *Hero with a Thousand Faces*, p. 101.

326. Cussler, *Night Probe!*, pp. 46–8.

327. Ibid., p. 212. Shaw's role as the Father figure gets playfully pointed out during his first meeting with Pitt.

328. *Night Probe!* begins in February 1989, so Shaw retried in 1964, the year Fleming wrote the last Bond novel, *The Man with the Golden Gun*, which was posthumously published in 1965.

329. Shaw tells Huston that he originally retired to the West Indies, but moved home after living in the Caribbean became unsafe (*Night Probe!*, p. 47). The West Indies was a favorite locale for Bond and Fleming.

330. Ibid., pp. 46–8. Before going to the zone unknown, Shaw crosses the threshold of adventure by answering the call to return to his old offices, but he swiftly realizes that things are not what they appear to be (see pp. 64, 67).

331. Ibid., pp. 317–9, 323–4. To reach the limestone quarry where the *Manhattan Limited* rests, Pitt makes a dive through a flooded shaft while Shaw lowers himself through another shaft excavated by miners and explosives (see pp. 324–6). Along their separate descents, Pitt almost drowns and Shaw fractures a wrist.

332. Ibid., p. 214. Purists may argue that Pitt engages in a bit of verbal fencing when Shaw inquires if he is armed; Pitt does not lie when he says that it did not occur to him to bring a gun to the quarry.

333. Ibid., p. 65.

334. Ibid., p. 71.

335. Ibid., p. 215.

336. Ibid., p. 260.

337. The truth is, Heidi is not the right woman for Pitt, even though she does look quite a bit like Maeve Fletcher.

338. Cussler, *Night Probe!*, p. 344.

339. See *Vixen 03*, p. 149, and *Night Probe!*, pp. 39, 44.

340. The president of the United States and Canadian prime minister Sarveux might have dreamed of uniting their two countries (see *Night Probe!*, pp. 339–41), but if Heidi had not uncovered the secret of the North American Treaty their dream may never have become a reality. Despite this, in *Night Probe!* the treaty is never ratified, and in *Arctic Drift* the two countries find themselves on the brink of war.

341. Could Danielle Sarveux have been partially inspired by Margaret Trudeau, the young, beautiful and adulterous wife of Pierre Trudeau, Canada's prime minister from 1968 to 1979? The couple divorced in 1980, after separating in 1977. *Night Probe!* was published in 1981.

342. Cussler, *Night Probe!*, pp. 31–3.

343. Ibid., p. 36.

344. See "A Brief Outline of Jungian Psychology with Some Archetypal Images, Themes, and Symbols" (http://www.csulb.edu/~csnider/jungian.outline.html).

345. For examples, see *Night Probe!*, p. 38.

346. See Chapter 5.

347. Even Villon in unable to recognize the disguised Gly (*Night Probe!*, p. 304).

348. Bloomfield, *The Everything Guide to Edgar Allan Poe*, pp. 158–9.

349. See *Night Probe!*, p. 306.

350. Ibid., p. 308.

351. At one point Seagram even confesses that the *Titanic* means nothing to him (see *Raise the Titanic!*, p. 347).

352. Campbell, *Hero with a Thousand Faces*, pp. 120–1.

353. Cussler, *Vixen 03*, p. 130.

354. Campbell, *Hero with a Thousand Faces*, pp. 120–1.

355. Cussler, *Inca Gold*, p. 577.

356. Cussler, *Atlantis Found*, pp. 529–30.

357. Cussler, *Trojan Odyssey*, p. 445.

358. Ibid., p. 456. Pitt is so sure that the time is right that he does not even bother to propose. He asks Loren if next Sunday will work for her because he has reserved the Washington Cathedral for their wedding and then leaves the room before she can answer. To see how far Pitt has come, in *Inca Gold* he confesses that he cannot picture himself and Loren walking down the aisle of the Washington Cathedral (see p. 316).

359. Campbell, *Hero with a Thousand Faces*, pp. 120–1.

Chapter 8

1. Unpublished 1985 interview, p. 12.

2. Ibid., pp. 10 and 12–3. See also "Cussler, Writing the Suspense-Adventure Novel," p. 232.

3. Foster-Harris, *Basic Patterns of Plot*, pp. 18 and 40. In "Writing the Suspense-Adventure Novel," p. 232, Cussler notes that using the Formula-A structure "is a common practice among new writers because of its basic simplicity."

4. Some might argue that *Pacific Vortex* features a Heroine (Adrian Hunter) and a Villainess (Summer), but Adrian hardly qualifies as a Heroine, and she only gets caught up in Delphi Moran's plans because she is Admiral Hunter's daughter. As conflicted as Summer is, she is the Heroine of this novel.

5. Readers are used to Pitt doing reckless things, like diving on the *Starbuck* and using its radio to contact the *Martha Ann*, or invading Von Til's villa and kidnapping Teri, so this helicopter landing seems in character for him. The only difference is that, in *Iceberg*, Pitt is actually doing something reckless while following orders from Sandecker. A reckless act done without just cause can often result in tragedy (e.g., using the radio on the *Starbuck* to contact the *Martha Ann*), but a reckless act performed for a good cause usually benefits a situation (e.g., violently rocking the *Starbuck* to free it from the ocean floor). Such recklessness is often underscored by frequent gambling and game references.

6. In *Basic Patterns of Plot* (p. 44), Foster-Harris explains that when a hero reaches a great decision point in his life he symbolically dies and experiences "a rebirth in a new and finer form."

7. See *Pacific Vortex*, pp. 183, 235, *The Mediterranean Caper*, pp. 126, 207, 215–6, and *Iceberg*, pp. 38, 151–2, 267, 271–3, 279, 286, 299, 305, 313–4.

8. In *Action Figures* (p. 146), Gallagher writes that Cussler's "novels recurringly invoke history" and that he "mobilizes history to legitimate his hero's adolescent-style activity." That may or may not be true, but Gallagher fails to explain how Cussler does this. Gallagher also appears to contradict himself when he comments earlier that "Cussler uses contemporary settings rather than historical or mythological ones" (p. 145).

9. See Cussler, "Writing the Suspense-Adventure Novel," p. 233.

10. This is an extreme example but during one four-page span in the prologue to *Raise the Titanic!*, Bigalow and Brewster switch VP roles five times.

11. Cussler, "Writing the Suspense-Adventure Novel," p. 233. Cussler lists Leon Uris, Robert Ludlum and Harry Patterson (writing as Jack Higgins) as masters of Formula-B (see Unpublished 1985 Interview, p. 9).

12. Cussler admits to borrowing the concept of the MacGuffin from Hitchcock, but in Cussler's adventures the MacGuffin is a pivotal clue or a central riddle that must be solved (see unpublished 1985 interview, pp. 4 and 13); Hitchcock (quoted in Gianetti, *Masters of American Cinema*, Chapter 12, p. 11) describes a MacGuffin as "something the characters in the film care a lot about, but the audience doesn't worry about it too much." David Freeman, who collaborated on Hitchcock's final unproduced screenplay "The Short Night," adds, "The point is, a MacGuffin is something that's nothing. In a film or a story, it's the pretext for the plot" (Freeman, *The Last Days of Alfred Hitchcock*, p. 51).

13. "There is nothing new under the sun," to quote Ecclesiastes 1:9, and that is true when it comes to structure. Variations of Cussler's Formula-B Structure can be found in other popular but very different kinds of stories, such as the 1968 film *2001: A Space Odyssey*. This visceral science-fiction epic begins with a prologue set in the historical past ("The Dawn of Man" sequence), followed by a main story that is set a few years in the future from the film's release date. Several characters come together to solve a mystery: a monolith has been discovered that was buried four million years ago in Tycho Crater on the Moon. (Unknown to the characters, a monolith like this appears in the prologue to a group of protohumans on Earth and provides the spark to move them up the evolutionary ladder towards becoming *Homo Sapiens*, an echo of a popular current myth that aliens played a hand in the creation of Humanity.) The characters confront a second mystery when the monolith inexplicably sends a radio signal to Jupiter. More characters are introduced in the second section of the film, astronauts sent to Jupiter who are unaware of their true mission, which is the macrocosmic feat of learning why the monolith sent the radio transmission to Jupiter and, hopefully, discover who buried the monolith on the Moon, and why. The Villain, Hal 9000, attempts to stop the mission because the computer discovers the astronauts are planning to deactivate him after it appears to be malfunctioning. HAL murders all but one astronaut, the hero Dr. David Bowman (Keir Dullea), who defeats HAL and then discovers what his true mission to Jupiter has been. In the third and final section of the film Bowman solves both mysteries by entering a monolith waiting in orbit over Jupiter, and (like the protohumans in the prologue) is transformed, moving up the evolutionary ladder in the film's epilogue to become the Star Child, Humanity's next step on its journey through the universe.

14. "A Clive Cussler/Dirk Pitt Adventure" is included in the film's opening credits.

15. See *Raise the Titanic!*, p. 8. Cussler not only concocts a way to get a character to insist on going down into the *Titanic* while everyone else is doing whatever it takes to get off the ship, he also mentions a classic automobile that actually went down with the White Star liner, a Renault town car (see p. 7). For more details, and to see photographs of this beautiful car (which also appears in James Cameron's 1997 film *Ti-*

tanic), see *Sea Dweller Magazine*, June 2003, pp. 12–13.

16. This list does not include the "Regenesis" chapter in the novel's epicenter.

17. See Cussler, "Make Your Story 'Fly,'" p. 12.

18. See unpublished 1985 interview, p. 11. Because *Raise the Titanic!* is set in the future, Cussler includes some technological and historical predictions, none of which have turned out to be accurate (e.g., the first manned flight to Mars is scheduled for 1990; a breakthrough in the successful treatment of cancer; the gas shortages of the seventies have continued into the eighties; the Soviet Union has an economic, as well as a military, edge over the United States).

19. See unpublished 1985 interview, p. 13, and Valero, *The Adventure Writing of Clive Cussler*, p. 68.

20. See *Raise the Titanic!*, p. 55.

21. Since Pitt fulfills many of the antagonist's duties in *Raise the Titanic!*, and Prevlov is not the sort of man to be haunted by anyone, it falls to Seagram to be tormented in this way.

22. These first two appearances introduced Pitt to many thousands of readers who were unfamiliar with his earlier adventures, *The Mediterranean Caper* and *Iceberg*. Speaking as a reader who first met Pitt in *Raise the Titanic!*, these mythic introductions had a tremendous impact and made a lasting impression.

23. In a refreshing change of pace, Prevlov's human flaws turn out to have as much to do with his defeat as anything Pitt does in the story.

24. A case could be made that Cussler was able to make *Vixen 03* more complex because the financial success of *Raise the Titanic!*, gave him more time and, therefore, more liberty while writing. For the sake of accuracy, though, it should be restated that Cussler wrote *Pacific Vortex* at home each night after he put his children to bed; he penned *The Mediterranean Caper* during his ample free time while working at a dive shop; *Iceberg* was written during a sabbatical; and most of *Raise the Titanic!* was completed after he was dismissed from a Denver advertising firm.

25. The plot pattern for the Lacey and Casey Nicefolk Adventures are simplified variations of the Formula-A plot pattern from *Pacific Vortex*, *The Mediterranean Caper* and *Iceberg*. Lacey and Casey use a magic machine given them by the mysterious Sucoh Sucop to transform toys into apparently sentient life-size vehicles. After their adventure Lacey and Casey return home, and the vehicle returns to toy size. Their exploits also feature a recurring villain, The Boss, whom the children help put behind bars in *Vin Fiz*, but who returns to exact vengeance in *Hotsy Totsy*.

26. "The Reunion," in Cussler and Dirgo, *Clive Cussler & Dirk Pitt Revealed!*, p. 17

27. Cussler,, *Pacific Vortex*, p. 8.

28. Cussler, *Sahara*, p. 348.

29. Cussler, *The Mediterranean Caper*, p. 191.

30. Cussler, *Raise the Titanic!*, p. 268.

31. Cussler, *Night Probe!*, p. 98.

32. Foster-Harris, *Basic Patterns of Plot*, p. 16. When Cussler (in "Make Your Story 'Fly'") recommends that new writers study "the successful authors and you'll find they've all stumbled upon and utilized similar tactics," he is referring to all tactics of writing, including the plot. In *Basic Patterns of Plot* (p. 103), Foster-Harris also advises new writers to "dissect other people's stories to learn your plot anatomy, but have a respect for the life of your own."

33. See Cannaday, *Bigger Than Life*, p. 172. In each of these four parts Dent advises the writer to ask if each individual part has suspense ("Does the menace grow like a black cloud?") and if everything happens in a logical manner.

34. This is not a crucial difference. As Foster-Harris points out in *Basic Patterns of Plot* (pp. 102–3), a story can be divided into three or four parts (i.e., "triangular" or "square form") so long as a problem is introduced in the first part, with a further complication arising in each part thereafter.

35. Valero, *The Adventure Writing of Clive Cussler*, p. 124.

36. Cussler does not delay introducing the heroes in *Golden Buddha* and *Spartan Gold*, the debut adventures for *Oregon Files* and *Fargo Adventures*. He also introduces Casey and Lacey Nicefolk immediately in both of their stories. Perhaps because *NUMA Files* is analogous to the Pitt series, Cussler felt comfortable delaying Austin and Zavala's introductions until Chapter 6 of their debut, *Serpent*.

37. See unpublished 1985 interview, p. 4. To be fair, there have always been differences in Cussler and MacLean's styles. Most notably, MacLean's novels feature little (if any) romance or sex, and very few techno-thriller elements.

38. MacLean started blending these elements with his fifth novel *Night Without End* (1959). For more about this, see http://en.wikipedia.org/wiki/Alistair_MacLean.

39. Orl Cinana, in *Pacific Vortex*, and Captain Darius, in *The Mediterranean Caper*.

40. For reasons known only to him, Cussler decided to utilize the same third-person narrative style MacLean uses in his earliest novels, *HMS Ulysses*, *The Guns of Navarone*, *South by Java Head* and *The Last Frontier* rather than the first-person narrative MacLean uses in many later novels, beginning in 1959 with *Night Without End*. It may also be an interesting coincidence that MacLean and Cussler made a major switch in their writing styles early in their respective careers: in MacLean's case, on his fifth book; in Cussler's, his fourth.

41. See Eco, *Role of the Reader*, p. 144. This appears to be a case of influence by diffusion. It seems likely that Fleming borrowed this plot tactic from Spillane for Bond, and then Cussler, who admits to studying the Bond series but never mentions Spillane, borrowed it from Fleming.

42. Also in *Deep Six*, Sal Casio is haunted by the disappearance of his daughter, and the president is haunted by the memories of Oskar Belyaka.

43. *The Chase*, p. 246.

44. See "Preface," *Hamlet*, 14th ed., *The Temple Shakespeare*, p. xiv and "Preface," *Macbeth*, 13th ed., *The Temple Shakespeare*, pp. ix–x.

45. According to the About.com biography on Alexandre Dumas: "Dumas grasped at any possible subject; he borrowed plots and material from all periods and all countries, then transformed them with ingenuity" (http://www.answers.com/topic/alexandre-dumas).

46. See King, *Danse Macabre*, pp. 37–8.

47. An extreme example of this is

the film *The Sting* (1973) and the November 23, 1951, episode "Horse Play" from the radio series *The Adventures of Harry Lime*. Both stories use the same real-life con game. The details of this con appear in the book *The Big Con: The Story of the Confidence Man* (1940) by David Mauer. In the *Harry Lime* episode, Lime (Orson Welles) is trying to raise some quick cash between bigger capers and ends up netting about $2.50 for his efforts. In *The Sting* semi-retired conman Harry Gondorff (Paul Newman) makes the con an elaborate scheme to help young grifter Johnny Hooker (Robert Redford) avenge the murder of his mentor, Luther Coleman (Robert Earl Jones) by the gangster Doyle Lonnegan (Robert Shaw).

48. Jeff Thompson, *The Television Horrors of Dan Curtis* (Jefferson, NC: McFarland, 2009), pp. 63 &and130. Later in his book (on p. 82), Thompson discusses Curtis's 1971 film *Night of Dark Shadows*, which borrows from Daphne Du Maurier's *Rebecca* (1938) and Roger Corman's 1963 film *The Haunted Palace*, an adaptation of H. P. Lovecraft's 1927 novel *The Case of Charles Dexter Ward*. "Just as *Dark Shadows* borrowed classic devices, *Night of Dark Shadows* also turns eclecticism into originality."

49. This is Roger Moore's second Bond film, and Moore's Bond finds himself the elusive prey of yet another manhunter, in *Octopussy* (1983).

50. The name Ship Trap Island calls to mind Captain Jack Sparrow (Johnny Depp) in *Pirates of the Caribbean: At World's End* (2007) commenting to a companion after arriving at Shipwreck Cove," You know, for all that pirates are clever-called, we are an unimaginative lot when it comes to naming things."

51. The result, as Dirgo states in *Clive Cussler and Dirk Pitt Revealed!* (p. 112), is "a scene reminiscent of 'The Most Dangerous Game,' the classic story of a hunter whose prey is humans. Ingeniously, Pitt foils the hunter."

52. Mike Grell, *Jon Sable, Freelance*, No. 3–5.

53. Cussler and Grell do have similar writing styles, and in their younger days even looked a lot alike, as Grell explained to me in an email, dated August 30, 2009. Cussler is taller, but, in the seventies, they had similar hair color and wore goatees. It does not take a lot of imagination to look at Cussler's author photo from *Raise the Titanic!*, and any photo of Grell from the same period, and think they could be cousins. Back at this time I used to show Cussler's author photo to friends familiar with Grell and ask, "You don't think Mike is writing novels under a pen name, do you?"

54. In the same email Grell writes, "I was trying to create a character who was the opposite of the standard comic book hero of the day—no secret identity; he works for MONEY, not some deep moralistic ideal; he's capable of brutal violence and gentle humor. Above all, I wanted to be able to do stories ranging from mystery to thriller to just plain high adventure and *Sable* gave me that very liberal framework."

55. Author's questions to Cussler, August 2009.

56. Cussler hangs a lantern on the fact that he is repeating a plot element he has used before by having Pitt tell Maeve about the earlier adventure (see *Shock Wave*, p. 355).

57. This is not the only example of Cussler possibly borrowing plot elements from James Bond adventures in *Shock Wave*.

58. Bond's physical wounds are healed, but his mental recovery is lagging. All he suffered was "a crack on the head," but "all his zest had gone ... he wasn't interested in his job any more, or even his life (Fleming, *You Only Live Twice*, p. 18)." Pitt is suffering a similar problem in *Flood Tide* (see pp. 33–4).

59. Fleming, *You Only Live Twice*, p. 19. In *Flood Tide* Sandecker comes to a similar conclusion (see p. 70), although Pitt is not so far gone that he needs an impossible mission to keep from going completely off the rails. Another advantage Pitt has over Bond is Pitt's indefatigable urge to explore the unknown, a spark that drives him through the darkest of times (see *Flood Tide*, p. 34). It is also interesting to note that, in contrast to Gothic heroes like Victor Frankenstein, whose life is destroyed because he pursues the unknown, adventure heroes like Pitt can have their lives salvaged by following this desire.

60. See Chapter 1 and Cussler and Dirgo, *Clive Cussler & Dirk Pitt Revealed!*, pp. 45–6.

61. See *Shock Wave*, p. 545.

62. Fleming, *On Her Majesty's Secret Service*, pp. 189–90.

63. http://en.wikipedia.org/wiki/On_Her_Majesty%27s_Secret_Service_(soundtrack).

64. See "Journey to Nowhere," in *The Sea Hunters*, pp. 223–235.

65. Cussler, *Night Probe!*, pp. 284–5.

66. Lernac is not only as arrogant as Cromwell (see "The Lost Special," in Conan Doyle, *The Original Illustrated Arthur Conan Doyle* [Secaucus, NJ: Castle Books, 1980], p. 47–8) but as cold-blooded. One chilling example takes place when Lernac describes his casual fascination at watching the train slam into a deep pit inside the mine (see p. 50).

67. "The Lost Special," in Conan Doyle, *The Original Illustrated Arthur Conan Doyle*, p. 47.

68. A modern variation of this plot element appears in Stephen King's "Dolan's Cadillac," in King's anthology *Nightmares & Dreamscapes* (New York: Signet, 1994), pp. 9–56.

69. See Cussler and Dirgo, *Clive Cussler & Dirk Pitt Revealed!*, pp. 45–6.

70. In "The Lost Special," the narrator refers to "an amateur reasoner of some celebrity at that date, [who] attempted to deal with the matter in a critical and semi-scientific manner." This story was published during the years known as the "Great Hiatus," when Conan Doyle had stopped writing Holmes adventures. Conan Doyle seems to have been having some fun at Holmes's expense by having a solution to the train's disappearance suggested by this amateur reasoner turn out to be utterly wrong.

71. In *The Last Days of Alfred Hitchcock*, p. 37. Freeman writes, "On the surface [*Psycho* is] really a rather straightforward melodrama."

72. Author's questions to Cussler, August 2009.

73. Cussler, *Deep Six*, p. 161. The passport is only mentioned once after the prelude. During their first meeting Casio tells Pitt that Wallace's passport was stolen. Nothing specific is ever mentioned about Estelle.

74. Ibid., p. 5.

75. Which is creepy, but not as disturbing as Norman dressing up like his dead mother or Scottie Fer-

guson (Jimmy Stewart) getting Judy Barton (Kim Novak) to dress as the dead Madeleine Elster in *Vertigo* (1958).

76. Perhaps no scene from any type of thriller film has had such a lasting impact on America's popular psyche since the unveiling of Lon Chaney's Eric from *The Phantom of the Opera* (1925). In *Masters of American Cinema*, Chapter 12, p. 17, Gianetti explains that one of the reasons for this is that "an unquestioned convention of American movies of that era was that a star character stays in the picture until the final reel, at which point it's permissible—though seldom advisable—to kill him or her off. But in *Psycho*, the Janet Leigh character is brutally murdered in the first third of the film, a shocking violation of convention which jolted audiences out of their coziness." Only a few thriller films have dared to break this convention since *Psycho*, one of the most recent and effective being the death of Lieutenant Colonel Austin Travis (Steven Segal) in the first half of *Executive Decision* (1996).

77. See *Deep Six*, p. 4.

78. Fu Manchu's poison paralyzes his victims, leaving them alive as they are presumed dead and eventually buried.

79. Gianetti, *Masters of the American Cinema*, Chapter 12, p. 4. One would like to think that a veteran self-promoter like Cussler appreciates Hitchcock's skill in this arena.

80. However, the final irony belongs to Arta and to Marion: their murders play at least some part in the capture of their killers. Pitt and Casio track down Min Koryo because of her insatiable desire to avenge her family, and Norman Bates completely succumbs to his Oedipal desire after he is arrested. In another bit of Hitchcockian irony, Casio, who has been trying to bring Arta's killer(s) to justice for over 20 years, is denied the satisfaction of completing his quest when Min kills him. Only Pitt, the one person on the scene who is not out to avenge a family member (Mendoza was a new friend and potential lover), escapes Min's lair (the World Trade Center) after disposing of him (see pp. 464–9).

81. Gianetti, *Masters of American Cinema*, Chapter 12, p. 1. Hitchcock is even quoted as saying, "The fact is I practice absurdity quite religiously."

82. Ibid., p. 6.

83. Ibid., p. 22.

84. Ibid., p. 16.

85. Ibid., p. 9.

86. *The Last Days of Alfred Hitchcock*, p. 40. Freeman writes: "Is it possible that the maestro will ask us to identify with this man? And that we will? Yes on both counts.... As Norman is carefully mopping up the blood and stashing the body in Marion's car, we begin to hope that he can cover his mother's crime."

87. Ibid., p. 39. Freeman explains that Hitchcock piles up details about his protagonist "until a viewer first watched, then began to associate and identify with the character."

88. Cussler, *Deep Six*, p. 7.

89. The closest any other prologue in the Pitt series comes to *Deep Six* in regards to intimacy is *Raise the Titanic!*, but there are some significant differences. Arta is the star of the *Deep Six* prologue while Brewster has to share the spotlight with Bigalow and the *Titanic*. There are no more mysteries about Arta (that is, if we don't count her father) when her prologue ends, but Brewster is as much of an enigma when the *Raise the Titanic!* prologue ends as when it started. The epic atmosphere of the sinking of the ship also prevents Brewster's story from feeling as intimate as Arta's story.

90. Gianetti, *Masters of American Cinema*, Introduction, p. 50.

91. Cussler, *Deep Six*, p. 5. This is not the first time a character in a Pitt adventure has his or her perspective of a dilapidated ship affected by their sinister purpose. Fawkes does the same thing when he first sees the battleship *Iowa* in *Vixen 03* (see p. 122).

92. As of this writing Cussler has not used a manmade biological weapon again in any of his adventures, although in *Plague Ship* he uses a similar plot tactic from Clancy's *Executive Orders* and *Rainbow Six*, in which villains create a weapon out of an existing disease, in this case hemorrhagic fever.

93. Cussler also gives his ship-in-an-iceberg gimmick an inspired twist in *Treasure* by camouflaging a hijacked cruise ship, the *Lady Flamborough*, inside an artificial iceberg.

94. Another example of this conceit includes the ferryboat *Alhambra* in *Inca Gold*.

95. See Holstmark, *Edgar Rice Burroughs*, pp. 39–40.

96. In the Pitt series (as of this writing) Loren Smith holds the records for most abductions and most consecutive abductions by one character besides Pitt, Giordino, and Gunn, with three (*Deep Six*, *Dragon*, *Inca Gold*) after she is introduced in *Vixen 03*.

97. It is one thing to abduct a despicable character like Spenser, but the abduction of the Samuelsons is more disturbing than Dirgo and Cussler seem to acknowledge in *Golden Buddha* (p. 186). The abduction comes off like a home invasion, with the couple drugged by the use of hypodermic needles and bound with plastic ties. The Corporation leaves music playing, to entertain the Samuelsons, and a note of apology, but the Samuelsons' home and sense of security are violated, which seems odd for a group that, in Cabrillo's words (on p. 215), exist "to make right from wrong."

98. Author's questions to Cussler, August 2009.

99. Cussler, *Raise the Titanic!*, p. 352.

100. Cussler, *Trojan Odyssey*, p. 202.

101. Cussler, *Dragon*, p. 502.

102. Cussler, *Sahara*, p. 82.

103. In the kea's first appearance Charles "Bully" Scaggs, captain of the *Gladiator*, sounds a little like one of the Mariner's crew when he suggests the Almighty sent the bird as a message (see *Shock Wave*, p. 32). In the kea's second appearance Maeve mentions that some sailors in Southwestern waters believe the bird will lead them to a safe harbor and then recalls that a kea led her ancestors to Gladiator Island (see p. 377).

104. Cussler and Kemprecos, *Fire Ice*, p. 47.

105. Cussler and Kemprecos, *Blue Gold*, p. 256.

106. Cussler and Kemprecos, *Lost City*, p. 140.

107. *Flood Tide*, 221. Cabrillo is a bit off base here: The Ancient Mariner is a person, not a ship.

108. See *Iceberg*, p. 54, and compare the rhythm of this description to Coleridge's description of the arrival of the skeletal ship carrying a Spectre-Woman and her two Death mates, in lines 168–171.

109. Ibid., pp. 129–30.

110. There is quite a bit of symbolism surrounding the hydrofoil attack, but the color gray also seems to saturate every description in this scene. The *Grimsi* is owned by Rondheim, who has blue-gray eyes (see *Iceberg*, p. 130), and the word *grimsi* means "grayish." The sunlight is a yellow-gray (see p. 151) aboard the *Grimsi* as Pitt wakes up and prepares to make a second dive on the sunken black jet, and after he descends the colors around him turn a soft gray (see p. 152). When the hydrofoil arrives it is a large gray form (see p. 165), and, during the battle, a red-and-yellow light can be seen pulsating from the hydrofoil through the gray mist (ibid.).

111. Cussler, *Iceberg*, p. 259.

112. Samuel Taylor Coleridge, "The Rime of the Ancient Mariner," lines 121–122 (http://www.bartleby.com/101/549.html).

113. Cussler, *Iceberg*, p. 259. Later in this scene Cussler turns mist into a metaphor as Pitt struggles to recall something from his Boy Scout days; the memory finally breaks through the fog of time (see p. 261).

114. Ibid., p. 258. This scene with the snipe also underscores that (1) Pitt is re-establishing the paradisal situation that takes place during a shamanistic spirit quest, and (2) visually signifies he is Rondhiem's shadow by contrasting his "gay" clothing against the tundra's green background, with Rondheim's corporate emblem of a white albatross against a red background.

115. See *Valhalla Rising*, p. 210.

116. Ibid., p. 151. In another example, a castaway Giordino can hear *Tales from the Vienna Woods* coming across the ocean from Cussler's high-tech yacht *Periwinkle*.

117. Cussler includes Barry's music in *Cyclops* as a "tip-of-the-hat to the *Raise the Titanic* score" (author's questions to Cussler, August 2009).

118. John Ford often includes "Garry Owen," the unofficial marching tune of General George Custer's Seventh Cavalry, on the soundtrack of his cavalry films. The song is often attributed to Jackson of Cork, and its lyrics seem almost more appropriate for Cromwell than cavalrymen.

119. The real Minutemen have been paid to stay away from Ho's party so Cabrillo and other members of The Corporation can gain entrance as part of their plan to steal the Golden Buddha; this has its own counterfeit floating around, due to the machinations of the unscrupulous Spenser.

120. Released in 1973, this easy-listening chart-topper is more recent than most songs referenced in Cussler's adventures, but Pitt soon sets things right when he arrives in the nick of time to save the crew of *Old Gert* while singing the American Songbook standard "Minnie the Mermaid" in *Big John*.

121. Cussler and Kemprecos, *Fire Ice*, p. 344. Austin and his helpers have an added problem in that that they must prevent the bad guys from boarding their ship because no enemies (except for prisoners of war) have ever come aboard the *Constitution*.

122. This scene ends with Pitt proposing to Loren, who finally accepts (see *Trojan Odyssey*, pp. 387–90).

123. For example, see *Skeleton Coast*, p. 373, and *Fire Ice*, p. 402.

124. A few examples include *Night Probe!*, p. 125, *Vixen 03*, p. 1, *Cyclops*, p. 62, and *The Chase*, p. 52.

125. See unpublished 1985 interview, p. 9.

126. See *The Carpetbaggers*, pp. 240, 518. For further evidence that Cussler may have borrowed this from Robbins, see *Deep Six*, p. 34.

127. Cussler, *Night Probe!*, p. 142.

128. Other Cussler women with gray eyes include Heidi Milligan (whose Castilian brown right eye has that small pie-shaped splash of gray) and an anonymous nursing home receptionist with gray-blue eyes (see *Cyclops*, p. 273).

129. Cussler, *Iceberg*, p. 126.

130. Cussler, *The Chase*, p. 54.

131. Cussler, *Pacific Vortex*, p. 155.

132. Cussler, *Iceberg*, p. 339.

133. Cussler, *Raise the Titanic!*, p. 290.

134. Cussler, *Night Probe!*, p. 180.

135. Ibid., p. 174.

Chapter 9

1. "A Novel Comic Strip Idea Starts Today," *Toronto Star*, August 15, 1977.

2. "Interview with Frank Bolle," *The Sea Dweller* 1, Issue 2, p. 10, and *Strippers Guide: Obscurity of the Day: Best Seller Show Case*, June 2, 2010. http://strippersguide.blogspot.com/2010_06_01_archive.html. *Best Seller Show Case* ran for about two years and during that time Bolle generally split art chores with Gray Marrow (*Tarzan, Buck Rogers*), the pair alternating on each adaptation.

3. According to the June 2, 2010, installment of *Strippers Guide* the complete list of novels that appeared in *Best Seller Show Case* during its run are:

- *Raise the Titanic* by Clive Cussler, art by Frank Bolle, August 15–October 9, 1977.
- *Storm Warning* by Jack Higgins, art by Gray Morrow (or possibly Winslow Mortimer or Jack Sparling), October 10–December 4, 1977.
- *The Chancellor Manuscript* by Robert Ludlum, art by Frank Bolle, December 5, 1977–February 12, 1978 (ten weeks).
- *The Sword of Shannara* by Terry Brooks, art by Gray Morrow, February 13–April 9, 1978.
- *The Second Deadly Sin* by Lawrence Sanders, art by Frank Bolle, April 10–June 18, 1978 (ten weeks).
- *Illusions* by Richard Bach, art by Gray Morrow, June 19–August 13, 1978.

4. Each Sunday a review of the previous week's events appeared in an expanded strip, featuring eight panels in three tiers, and printed in color. These Sunday reviews also incorporated other visual storytelling devices, including split panels within panels to add more motion and information (see *Strippers Guide: Obscurity of the Day: Best Seller Show Case*, June 2, 2010). Unfortunately, some newspapers (such as the *Los Angeles Times*) did not print all eight panels in their Sunday comic sections, deleting the first two panels that regularly appeared in the top tier and printing only the six panels in the bottom two tiers (see *The Sea Dweller* 1, issue 2, pp. 12 and 16).

5. *Strippers Guide*, June 2, 2010.

6. See *Best Seller Show Case—Featuring* "Raise the Titanic!," August 17, 1979.

7. Ibid., August 22, 1979.

8. Ibid., September 24, 1979.

9. Ibid., October 7, 1979.

10. Further attempts to be faithful to Cussler's novel can be also seen in some little details, such as giving the president a mustache, and making the U.S. agent aboard the *Mikhail Kurkov* a lieutenant (the same rank as Pavel Marganin).

11. Caplin and Bolle demonstrate considerable skills as comics creators by succinctly encapsulating the novel's prologue into six exciting panels using approximately 200 words in the August 15th and 16th strips. Perhaps this scene, more than any other, demonstrates Caplin and Bolle's knack for knowing what to show and what to leave to a reader's imagination.

12. This scene appears in the September 19th and 20th strips, and the full impact of Bolle's cinematography cannot be appreciated unless the strips are stacked one on top of the other. Pitt's helicopter tumbles off the *Titanic* and gets snagged by cables on the deck, giving Pitt time to extract himself and climb back on the ship. During these six panels Bolle's camera never stops moving, panning in and out as it rotates what seems like 360° while the hurricane lashes the *Titanic* and the helicopter, creating a dizzying effect that accentuates the difficulty of Pitt's peril.

13. *Best Seller Show Case—Featuring* "Raise the Titanic!," October 8, 1979.

14. See *Raise the Titanic!*, p. 174.

15. Cussler and Dirgo, *Clive Cussler & Dirk Pitt Revealed!*, p. 75.

16. See *Guts and Glory*, pp. 416, 418.

17. See Paul Heyer, *Titanic Legacy* (Westport, CT: Praeger, 1995), p. 143.

18. See *Guts and Glory*, p. 418.

19. http://www.supershadow.com/star_wars/production_budget_how_much_cost_to_make_costs/starwars_budget_cost_make.html.

20. http://www.imdb.com/title/tt0082971/trivia.

21. Heyer, *Titanic Legacy*, p. 143.

22. Barry's score was unavailable as a soundtrack release until 1999, but this did not prevent it from acquiring a well-respected reputation in the interim. The restrained score is grand, elegant and compelling even during the movie's most glacial moments, in particular the needlessly lengthy underwater search and salvage scenes that add up to nearly a half hour of the movie's 115-minute running time.

23. Heyer, a professor of communications at Simon Fraser University, writes in *Titanic Legacy* (p. 143) that "the surfacing of the *Titanic* is one the most spectacular salt-water sequences since the parting of the Red Sea in *The Ten Commandments*."

24. "Raise the Titanic, Her Cargo is Dangerous," *New York Times*, August 1, 1980, p. C8.

25. Or did they? In *Guts and Glory: The Making of the American Military Image in Film* (Lexington: University Press of Kentucky, 2002), military historian Lawrence Suid breaks down the 1979 negotiations between Marble Arch and the U.S. government. Suid states, "Without full Navy support, including a flotilla of salvage vessels and a submersible, Marble Arch had no way to make *Raise the Titanic*" (p. 416), but in the novel all of the salvage vessels and all but two submersibles, the navy's *Sea Slug* and *Modoc*, belong to NUMA or private corporations. The only navy ships are the salvage tugs *Thomas J. Morse* and *Samuel R. Wallace*. At Sandecker and Seagram's request, the navy does provide NUMA's salvage operation protection from possible Russian interference, but the submarine *Dragonfish*, which warns off the *Mikhail Kurkov*, is never seen. If Marble Arch had followed suit, it could have used private vessels outfitted to look like NUMA's vessels and the navy's tugs and submersibles.

26. See Suid, *Guts and Glory*, p. 415. The State Department did not limit its concern to movies: even chief executives had to deal with it. Ronald Reagan touches upon such interference in his autobiography *An American Life* (p. 594): "Whenever I wanted to send a message to a foreign leader, for example, copies of my message were usually first circulated to a half-dozen or more agencies at the State Department, the Pentagon, the Commerce Department, and elsewhere for comment and suggestions. And often the bureaucrats down the line (I'm sure in good faith) would try to add or change something—whether it was needed or not. The result: often a blurring of my original intentions."

27. Suid, *Guts and Glory*, p. 416.

28. Ibid., p. 402. Suid reports that the U.S. Air Force also practiced this public-relations tactic, except it exploited such footage to acquire long-range bombers and intercontinental ballistic missiles.

29. Ibid., pp. 402–423.

30. Two directors who come immediately to mind are Bond veterans Guy Hamilton (*Goldfinger*) and Lewis Gilbert (*You Only Live Twice*).

31. Kramer was interested in producing and directing an adaptation of *Raise the Titanic!*, and mentioned the book to Martin Starger at Marble Arch, which got that company interested in the project. Kramer remained attached to it even after Marble Arch purchased the film rights, but eventually left, citing creative differences (see Valero, *The Adventure Writing of Clive Cussler*, pp. 47–50). Kramer's near participation is also mentioned in an August 1980 article in *On Location* magazine (see "The Forgotten Titanic," http://www.allatsea.co.za/santarosa).

32. Lisa and Pfeiffer, *The Incredible World of 007*, p. 7.

33. Suid, *Guts & Glory*, p. 413. According to Suid, part of these costs include hiring four writers who took over two years to fashion a final screenplay, but, according to Valero, it took over two and a half years and nine writers (see *The Adventure Writing of Clive Cussler*, p. 55).

34. Tom Stemple, *Screenwriter: The Life and Times of Nunnally Johnson* (San Diego: A.S. Barnes, 1980), pp. 80–1.

35. Ibid., p. 81.

36. Perhaps this oversight is not an impossible one in a world where the potential computer problems that threatened international economies and infrastructures during Y2K were overlooked, but Gene comes off a tad myopic here, especially when journalists at a NUMA press conference are able to foresee this possibility.

37. As Sandecker tells Gene in the film, "I am just saying that somewhere in the world, in some think tank, right now, they're *figuring out* a way to build a byzanium bomb (my emphasis)." In other words, the only practical application at present for the mineral is the Sicilian Project. A moment later Robard's Sandecker sounds like Cussler's Sandecker when he adds, "I believed in what we were

trying to do, and if it didn't defensively ... if somebody was going to make a byzanium bomb ... I wanted it to be us."

38. Suid, *Guts and Glory*, p. 418.

39. Another change that puts the Soviet Union in a bad light occurs when Pitt tells Sandecker and Gene that Brewster's miners were killed by Russian agents instead of assassins from the French Société des Mines de Lorraine.

40. It is Pitt's natural reaction to stick his neck out and do what is right. In contrast, a Byronic hero like Pierce will do the same, but only when—in Pierce's words in "The Sniper"—he is "tired enough, cold enough, and hungry enough not to give a damn." For more about the classic Byronic hero, see Rosenberg, *Ian Fleming*, pp. 16–7.

41. The talented Archer was nominated as Best Supporting Actress for *Fatal Attraction* (1987), but she is wasted in *Raise the Titanic*. Ironically, Archer bears more than a passing resemblance to Cussler's descriptions of Lauren Smith and could have been excellent in the role if given a better script.

42. We can only assume Pitt wanted to change the world for the better, but the film never explains how he planned to do it or why he felt the world needed changing.

43. Cussler's Pitt is not one to back down from a challenge, even when it is he alone against the world, but Dana's comment is an important key to understanding his character in the film. As Gene and Pitt leave Southby Cemetery Pitt contentedly mentions his conversation with Dana, without identifying her by name. The implication appears to be that he has finally succeeded in changing the world (by saving it from a byzanium weapon) as well as picked up a recruit (or "number") for his side in Gene.

44. Perhaps Marble Arch wanted to make the Seagrams more sympathetic characters, which seems nonsensical given the number of dysfunctional families then hugely popular on television (e.g., *Dallas*, *All in the Family*, *Soap*).

45. In a subtle demonstration of how much Seagram craves acceptance from East Coast intellectuals, Cussler gives him an Ivy League haircut, even though it has been out of style for years (see *Raise the Titanic!*, p. 23).

46. Cussler, *Raise the Titanic!*, p. 129.

47. Ibid., p. 352.

48. The *Washington Star* went out of business on August 7, 1981, about a year after the release of *Raise the Titanic*, and many of the newspaper's staff went to work for the *Washington Times*. http://en.wikipedia.org/wiki/Washington_Star.

49. Cussler, *Raise the Titanic!*, p. 111. Because of the film's changes to Gene's character, it falls to Pitt to recommend that the ship be raised.

50. Ibid., p. 129.

51. Ibid., p. 362. The hubris that links Seagram with Brewster is dramatically played out in the hold as Seagram bashes in the head of the man who identifies the mineral in Brewster's boxes as gravel, then strangles Brewster's corpse until its head comes off in his hands.

52. Ibid., p. 319.

53. Ibid., p. 147.

54. Ibid., p. 319.

55. "Raise the *Titanic*!" Chris Tookey's Movie-Film-Review.

56. Cussler, *Sahara*, p. 64.

57. During a phone conversation I had with Cussler in 1989, he discussed Hollywood's continued interest in the Pitt series, and he mentioned that he had been offered as much as $10 million for the film rights, but turned it down.

58. Cussler and Dirgo, *Clive Cussler & Dirk Pitt Revealed!*, p. 75.

59. See "Crusader Entertainment Acquires the Rights to Clive Cussler's Best-Selling Dirk Pitt Book Series," http://us.penguingroup.com/static/packages/us/clivecussler/news3.html.

60. In a September 11, 2001, interview with Bookreporter.com (http://www.bookreporter.com/authors/au-cussler-clive.asp), Cussler says, "I'm sitting here today working on the screenplay. I sold it to Hollywood finally, and they are going to do *Sahara* first.... You know, they messed up *Raise the Titanic* twenty-some years ago. They made such a botch of it I held off for all these years, but finally they gave me script and casting approval. So that's why I'm reading the script the screenwriter came up with. If it fails this time, it's my fault." Also see "Sahara's Cussler Draws Line in Sand: Author Takes Stand in Crusader Case" (http://www.variety.com/article/VR1117959458?refCatId=13), "$78 Million in Red Ink" (http://www.latimes.com/business/la-fi-movie15apr15,0,6005119.story) and "The Blame Game on the Sahara Movie Bomb Begins in the Land of Dreams!" (http://doomandgloomnews.com/home.html).

61. Janet Shprintz, "Sahara's Cussler Draws Line in Sand: Author Takes Stand in Crusader Case," Variety.com.

62. Glen F. Bunting, "$78 Million in Red Ink," http://www.latimes.com/business/la-fi-movie15apr15,0,6005119.story.

63. Ibid. Anschutz seems to have a point when the budget for *Sahara* is compared to more ambitious adventure films from 2005 like *The Dark Knight* ($150 million according to http://boxofficemojo.com/movies/?id=batmanbegins.htm) and Walden Media's *The Chronicles of Narnia: The Lion, The Witch and the Wardrobe* ($180 million, according to http://www.the-numbers.com/movies/2005/LWWRB.php). The *Times* article also cites a $10 million fee to Cussler as one of the exorbitant costs, but fails to mention that this was the payment for the film rights to the Pitt series, not just *Sahara*, and therefore would have been part of the film's original $80 million budget. It should also be pointed out that it was Anschutz's decision, not Cussler's, to let *Sahara*'s budget balloon to $160 million.

64. Ibid. These budget records were made public due to the Cussler-Crusader lawsuits, and as Bunting explains, "The records offer insights into the economics of modern-day moviemaking and industry practices that seldom are disclosed." This is because "movie budgets are one of the last remaining secrets in the entertainment business, typically known to only high-level executives, senior producers and accountants.

"'The studios guard that information very, very carefully,' said Phil Hacker, a senior partner in a Century City accounting firm that audits motion pictures. 'It is a gossip industry. Everyone wants to know what everyone else is getting paid.'"

According to the budget records *Sahara* earned the following in revenues:

• net box office = $79.5 million

- home video = $68.8 million
- pay television = $16.5 million
- network television = $9.5 million
- British subsidy = $20.4 million
- other = $8.2 million

The records also show expenses of $281.2 million: production = $160 million, prints and advertising = $61.0 million, home video = $21.9 million, distribution fee = $20.1 million, other ... $18.2 million. The result is a net loss of $78.3 million.

65. An apparent mistake in the film comes when Pitt is checking out local history with an imam, who tells him about "a dark ship [that] rode without sails under the banner of a single star." This banner sounds more like the state flag of Texas than the second Confederate Navy Jack or second Confederate Navy Ensign, both of which would have been flown by the *Texas* in 1865 and feature a prominent blue star with thirteen smaller white stars inside it.

66. See *Sahara*, p. 543.

67. In the novel *Sahara* the cave paintings Pitt and Giordino discover are created by the different cultures over a period of ten to twelve thousand years, beginning when the desert had a tropical climate. As the pair examines the paintings Pitt lectures Giordino on the different cultures and how four millennia of uncontrolled grazing forced the lands and then the river to dry up, which stranded the *Texas* (see pp. 366–7). The film distills Pitt's lecture into an exchange between Pitt and Giordino as the men and Eva examine the cave paintings:

> *Pitt:* At one time much of this desert was farmland and there were rivers everywhere. The ironclad obviously came from this river and stopped at this structure. Which is a fort, a castle, I don't know. So the climate changed, the water level dropped, and the boat became stranded.
>
> *Giordino:* Yeah. Or sailed away.
>
> *Pitt:* Or the land dried up. The soil turned to dust. The sands blew in and the ship is still there to this day. Right here, next to the structure.

68. In Crusader's *Sahara*, Pitt hopes that killing Kazim will get his army to break off their attack on the *Texas* ("Cut the head off the snake..."). After Kazim is killed the Mali army does not back down until they are surrounded by hundreds of Tuareg warriors, who can start a new life now that Kazim's war against them is at an end. In Cussler's *Sahara*, Kazim's death opens the way for a new government to form in Mali (see *Sahara*, p. 511).

69. During the film's climax Pitt tells Massarde, "I've seen sick Tuareg women and kids and I saw the dead in Asselar." It could be these victims did the same thing as their counterparts in the novel, who, according to Kazim, slaughtered and devoured themselves (see *Sahara*, p. 88). One image in the film of a damaged toy in the house with the bloody handprint also recollects a scene in the novel wherein Eva finds evidence in a home of parents possibly eating their children (see p. 153).

70. See *Sahara*, pp. 85–6.

71. Ibid., p. 73.

72. In Cussler's *Sahara*, NUMA does not recover the pharaoh's barge but presents its location to the Egyptian Organization of Antiquities (see p. 68).

73. This is one of the subtlest characteristic moments in the film. In the novels, Sandecker could not have built NUMA into one of the largest historical-environmental preservation agencies if he did not share Pitt's knack for running a con, a skill aptly demonstrated in the film at the museum party as the admiral considers Pitt's deal for borrowing the *Calliope*. Sandecker pauses and puffs on his cigar, and it appears he is merely weighing the possibilities that the coin could have been carried to Africa aboard the ironclad, but when Pitt, Giordino and Gunn find Eva and Hopper waiting for them the next morning it becomes obvious that the admiral had also been weighing how he could use Pitt's offer to help the WHO doctors.

74. Cussler, *Sahara*, p. 101.

75. Ibid., p. 238.

76. In yet another tense conversation with Modibo, Pitt tries to convince the Tuareg leader to help him shut down Massarde's plant to stop the toxins causing the contamination sickness. Modibo refuses to lead the Tuareg in a suicide attack, so Pitt comes up with another plan, and in a scene-ending line on par with some of the best spoken by Pitt in Cussler's novels, he tells Modibo he has another plan and asks, "Can I borrow your car?"

77. The 1936 Voisin C28 seen in the film is actually two cars. Plusfilm Services constructed two special convertibles ("special" because the original Voisin C28 never existed as a convertible) with four-wheel drive to handle desert conditions. http://plusfilm.com/credits.php?c=2005%20SAHARA#credits/2005SAHARA/1SAH.jpg.

78. See *Sahara*, p. 120.

79. Ibid., p. 377.

80. Pitt is first glimpsed in Cussler's and Crusader's *Sahara* from a distance while spearfishing, but the novel has Pitt swim ashore and smile at Eva on his way to his Jeep, while the film shows Pitt hauling himself out of the water into an inflatable motormount boat, with the Logos lighthouse prominent in the background. This establishing shot shows where Pitt comes from when he rescues Eva.

81. Cussler, *Pacific Vortex*, p. 86. As mentioned earlier (see Chapter 5), Cussler's ultra-modern but decrepit-looking clandestine salvage ship *Martha Ann* presages the *Oregon*, but, in Crusader's *Sahara*, the Martha Ann is just old.

82. Ibid., p. 6.

83. Emails to author from Cussler Society members Peter Slater (February 7, 2011) and Mike "Captain Sparrow" Scheulen (February 12, 2011). According to Scheulen, a hood scoop on the model "denotes the 427 side oiler in 1967."

84. Cussler, *Pacific Vortex*, p. 83. Pitt adds to the mystery by saying another NUMA research vessel working over the Cayment Trench off of Cuba experienced a similar incident.

85. In this instance Crusader is being more reverential to the Pitt novels than Cussler. In *Valhalla Rising* Giordino mentions that the *Titanic* broke in half (see p. 121), although by *Crescent Dawn* Pitt has again raised the *Titanic* (see p. 35). Valero offers an interesting possible explanation for this that involves the alternate timelines created by Cussler in his adventures eventually catching up with current events (see Valero, *The Adventure Writing of Clive Cussler*, pp. 76–9). Only Cussler knows if Valero's theory is cor-

rect, and while a case can be made that Cussler does create alternate timelines in his books by altering facts (e.g., the *Titanic* has never been raised), these events never become a prominent part of the plot in any future Pitt adventures. Generally, if any mention is made of them in later novels they are usually cited among Pitt's accomplishments and then filed away so they do not get in the way of his current adventure. Considering the importance that raising the *Titanic* had on Pitt and Cussler's careers, however, it is good to see it being mentioned again in the series.

86. From IMDb.com's entry for *Sahara*: "During the opening credits (after approx 4.5 minutes) a newspaper titled *Nouvélles de Monde* (French) appears. *Nouvelles* (news) is misspelled (there should be no accent). Moreover *Nouvelles de Monde* is not correct, the adequate form is *Nouvelles du Monde*" (http://www.imdb.com/title/tt0318649/trivia?tab=gf).

87. During Sandecker's presentation of King Bateen's sarcophagus to the Lagos Museum he says, "With the help of museums, with the help of governments, private organizations like ours can work in partnership to make sure that history, history that has been lost to the tides of time, can be returned to its people."

88. Pitt admits as much to Seagram in *Raise the Titanic!* (see p. 90).

89. Lincoln was the target of several kidnapping schemes from the start of his first term, in 1860. Even John Wilkes Booth became involved when he and some compatriots plotted to kidnap Lincoln by ambushing his carriage after the president attended a play on the evening of March 17, 1865. The attempt failed when the president instead delivered a speech at Booth's own hotel, the National. See James L. Swanson's *Manhunt: The 12-Day Chase for Lincoln's Killer* (New York: William Morrow, 2006), pp. 24–6.

90. See *Sahara*, p. 557. There are holes in the *Sahara* conspiracy theory but, for what it is worth, Stanton *did* take full command of the manhunt for Booth and his fellow assassins (see Swanson, *Manhunt*, pp. 110–1).

91. The crash was filmed in England at a cost of $2 million and runs for 46 seconds (see "Sahara: $78 Million in Red Ink").

92. Mannock's mummified hand can be glimpsed in the foreground of one shot, and her remains can be seen poking out of the sand in front of Pitt and Giordino after they tumble down a dune. Mannock's remains can also be seen in front of Pitt and Giordino in a picture on the back of DVD case for the current release of *Sahara*.

93. See Fleming, *Dr. No*, p. 139, and Rosenberg, *Ian Fleming*, pp. 89–90 and 114.

94. When Kazim is introduced he is even wearing a *litham*, a traditional indigo Tuareg veil (see *Sahara*, p. 59).

95. Zakar might have also been inspired, in part, by O'Bannon. Zakar's headdress hides most of his face, but enough of his features can be seen, revealing a few ceremonial scars. O'Bannon wears a Tuareg headdress to cover his face, which was disfigured during a mining explosion in Brazil (see *Sahara*, p. 422).

96. Pitt has no climactic battles in Cussler's novel, only a run-in with O'Bannon (see *Sahara*, pp. 422–3), but Giordino has his death-match with Melika (see pp. 425–6).

97. Massarde is known as The Scorpion because many of his competitors and business partners have vanished over the years. Unbeknown to most of the world, this list also includes employees and their family members who know too much.

98. See *Sahara*, pp. 85 and 209, for examples. Massarde does not like Kazim in the novel, but the existence of his solar detoxification plant depends upon the general's cooperation, so Massarde treats Kazim to trips on his private yacht.

99. A clipping from *USA Today* in the opening credits features the headline "From Navy SEALs to Salvage Kings—Sandecker, Pitt and Giordino Profiled." A photograph of Pitt and Giordino elsewhere in the opening credits shows them in navy white dress uniforms. Giordino has the rank of junior lieutenant (O-2) and Pitt is a lieutenant (O-3), with both men wearing ribbons for commendation and a Purple Heart along with the National Defense medal and the expert pistol medal (February 7, 2011, email to author from Peter Slater). While aboard the *Calliope*, Hopper asks Giordino how long Pitt and Al have known each other. Al answers, "Oh, since kindergarten. College. Navy. NUMA. Poor guy's always been in my shadow. Always the Al's-maid, never the Al." As for Sandecker, along with the *USA Today* clipping there is a photograph in the opening montage in which he is wearing fatigues and speaking to combat troops preparing to board a helicopter.

100. See *Sahara*, p. 50.

101. Compare this to Pitt's admission about his combat skills to Colonel Ramon Kleist, U.S. Marine Corps, Retired, in *Cyclops* (p. 267).

102. See *Sahara*, p. 195. In Crusader's *Sahara*, Sandecker coerces Carl into finding out what happened to Pitt, Giordino and Gunn in Mali by calling in an unexplained debt from October 27, 1982.

103. During the battle with the Malian gunboats Pitt decides they need to do a Panama, and when Gunn asks "What's a Panama?" Giordino tells him, "Navy thing." Later, when the three men have to split up with Gunn on the way back to the *Martha Ann* so he can warn Eva and Hopper that Kazim is looking for them, Gunn asks, "How am I going to get across the border? I never took survival training."

104. From Rosenberg, *Ian Fleming*, p. 9: "For their $100,000 a film, [Harry] Saltzman and [Albert R. "Cubby"] Broccoli bought a title, a few characters, and an occasional exotic setting. The plots, the witty dialogues, the gimmickry, the very character of James Bond, all were made in England's Pinewood Studios and Hollywood."

105. Clive Cussler Forum: "Trailer for *The Oregon Files*."

106. Ibid.

107. According to the press release, Oregon Production, LLC, the corporate umbrella created for the series' production, had a partnership with Kerzner International. Kerzner had recently opened an Atlantis Hotel on Dubai's Palm Island that is prominently featured in one of the paintings. The press release also mentions, "Established long term relationships with business partners across the globe have played a vital role in presenting unprecedented opportunities to the production company for locations such as the pioneering global city of Dubai or the historic sixteenth century city of

Cartagena, Colombia, as well as Cape Town, South Africa, and for product placement with high profile Fortune 500 companies" (Clive Cussler Forum: "Trailer for *The Oregon Files*").

108. "Trailer for *The Oregon Files*," (http://z4.invisionfree.com/CLIVE_CUSSLER/index.php?s=93f9817d37f7efd12507ec4e73196abf&showtopic=5131&st=12&#last).

109. See http://www.stunts911.com/images/Oregon_files_New_09.mov.

110. *Basic Formulas of Fiction*, p. 66.

111. http://en.wikipedia.org/wiki/Lovecraftian_horror; http://www.denofgeek.com/movies/18189/hp-lovecraft-and-his-lasting-impact-on-cinema.

112. Gaumont and UFA released two other versions of *F.P.1 Does Not Answer* in 1933, one in English starring Conrad Veidt (*The Cabinet of Dr. Caligari, The Man Who Laughs, Casablanca*), the other in French starring Charles Boyer (*Algiers, Love Affair, Gaslight*), with all three versions directed by Karl Hartl (*The Countess of Monte Cristo, Gold, The Man Who Was Sherlock Holmes*).

113. Siodmak's later works include the screenplay for Universal's *The Wolf Man* (1941) and the novel *Donovan's Brain* (1942). *F.P.1 Does Not Answer* was Siodmak's last film before fleeing Germany in the wake of Adolf Hitler's rise to power. Before coming to America, Siodmak worked in England, where he wrote the screenplay for *Transatlantic Tunnel* (1935), based on a 1913 science-fiction novel by Bernhard Kellerman. *Transatlantic Tunnel* has the potential to be a Cussleresque film but is missing too many elements to qualify. Like *F.P.1 Does Not Answer, Transatlantic Tunnel* is primarily set a few years in the future and takes place around a colossal engineering feat: digging a tunnel from England to the United States. Like more than a few Cussler adventures *Transatlantic Tunnel* also features corrupt businessmen, but its engineer protagonist Robert "Mack" McAllan (Richard Dix), a married man who forsakes his wife and loses his son while accomplishing the project, does not fit the Pitt hero archetype. *Transatlantic Tunnel* also contains no espionage.

114. The filmmakers designed F.P.1 from plans by Albert Berthold Henninger, a German engineer who wanted to build a real platform; he also served as the film's technical advisor (see http://www.dieselpunks.org/profiles/blogs/fp-1-doesnt-respond?xg_source=activity).

115. *F.P.1 Does Not Answer* was also Lorre's last German film before he fled the country, but he returned after World War II to direct and star in *Der Verlorene* (1951).

116. Pitt performs a somewhat similar feat in *Treasure of the Khan* with a helicopter and a ship's mast (pp. 80–1), and Austin, in an impressive display of derring-do in *Fire Ice*, leaps from a helicopter to get aboard the *Sea Hunter* (p. 250).

117. See *Wolf Man's Maker*, pp. 17, 273.

118. See "Foreword," *Carrier*, pp. xi, xiii.

119. *The Mummy's Hand* was successful enough to spawn its own sequel, *The Mummy's Tomb* (1942), two follow-ups, *The Mummy's Ghost* (1944) and *The Mummy's Curse* (1944), and the sendup *Abbott and Costello Meet the Mummy* (1955). *The Mummy's Hand* also served as an inspiration for Universal's 1999 blockbuster *The Mummy*.

120. Even after the mummy Kharis murders a member of the expedition and Banning has no choice but to return his party to civilization, he makes it clear that he will return and keep searching for Ananka's tomb.

121. In a demonstration of turnabout is fair play, Banning does not try too hard to stop Sullivan from turning the tables on a con Jenson is running in the bar to scam free drinks.

122. The film is also known as *Assault Force* and *North Atlantic Hijack*.

123. When Admiral Sir Francis Brindsen (Mason) spies ffolkes working on the *London Times* crossword puzzle and comments that he is probably one of those fellows who completes the puzzle in ten minutes, ffolkes huffs, "I have never taken ten minutes." Later, after ffolkes' ffusiliers thwart the extortionists despite some comical Cussleresque complications (e.g., ffolkes is forced to wear a vermilion wetsuit during the night assault and then forced to toss an overzealous member of his commandos into the ocean to save his own life), ffolkes radios news that the rescue has been completed: "As planned, naturally."

124. In a videotape ffolkes produces for Lloyd's of London, he accurately predicts how extortionists will hijack *Jennifer* and *Ruth*.

125. In a neat little scene, ffolkes exits a cab, realizes he has only a £10 note, grabs a coin from his pocket and tells the driver they will have to flip for it. The driver calls heads but expects to be cheated out of his fare only to have ffolkes say, "Heads it is. Must be your lucky day."

126. Lost World adventures, wherein pockets of lost civilizations like Atlantis exist out of place or time, date back at least to the early 18th Century, but the genre's heyday was between 1871 and the First World War, when Haggard's *King Solomon's Mines* and Conan Doyle's *The Lost World* were published. See *Science Fiction: The Illustrated Encyclopedia*, pp. 38–9, and http://en.wikipedia.org/wiki/Lost_World_(genre).

127. I am indebted to *The Animated Movie Guide* and the Wikipedia and Wikiquote entries for *Atlantis: The Lost Empire* for much of the production information about this film. According to these sources, three episodes were produced for the canceled series and released direct-to-video as *Atlantis: Milo's Return* (2003). Also according to http://en.wikipedia.org/wiki/Submarine_Voyage, the Submarine Voyage ride opened again in 2007 as Finding Nemo Submarine Voyage, based upon the Disney-Pixar film *Finding Nemo* (2003).

128. It is also only a few years in the future from *The Chase*.

129. According to one of the screenwriters, Tad Murphy, he introduced *The Shepherd's Journal* because he needed a map for the characters to follow throughout their journey (see http://en.wikipedia.org/wiki/Atlantis:_The_Lost_Empire). The *Journal* also calls to mind Snorri Sturluson's runic manuscript from *Journey to the Center of the Earth* (1864); see http://en.wikipedia.org/wiki/Journey_to_the_center_of_the_earth.

130. Sea monsters may not be typical of Cussler's adventures but they are not unprecedented, as Basil

the sea serpent demonstrates. Given that a sea serpent is not a supernatural monster his presence is not out of line with the otherwise-realistic tone of Cussler's adventures. In fact, the battle between Basil and the shark in *Shock Wave* is reminiscent of a documented fight between a sea serpent and a sperm whale seen from the barque *Pauline* and reported in an 1875 edition of the *Illustrated London News*. Historian Edward Rowe Snow also gives an account of this battle in *Supernatural Mysteries and Other Tales*. That said, the Leviathan in *Atlantis: The Lost Empire* turns out not to be a genuine monster but an Atlantean machine.

131. This was scrapped because the producers felt it did not give viewers enough of an emotional involvement with the Atlanteans, but it does appear on the DVD release of *Atlantis: The Lost Empire*. As of this writing, the deleted prologue can also be seen on YouTube at http://www.youtube.com/watch?v=fV21Qtt6qW0.

132. Originally, Milo was going to be a descendant of the pirate Edward Teach, but this was changed so Milo could discover his talent for exploration (http://en.wikipedia.org/wiki/Atlantis:_The_Lost_Empire).

133. Whitmore tells Milo that he attended Georgetown with Milo's grandfather, "Class of '66." This would make Whitmore approximately 70 years old in 1914.

134. Whitmore sounds a little like Sandecker when he tells Milo, "Your grandfather was a great man, Milo. You probably don't realize how great. Those buffoons at the museum tracked him down, made a laughing stock of him. He died a broken man. If I could bring back just one shred of proof that'd be enough for me."

135. The *Ulysses* is an impressive submarine but more than a little reminiscent of Captain Nemo's *Nautilus*; Verne's *20,000 Leagues Under the Sea* (1870) includes a dramatic glimpse of the submerged ruins of Atlantis.

136. Perhaps more than any other author Burroughs solidified Atlantis as an established part of the Lost World genre, with the city of Opar. This colony first appears in *The Return of Tarzan* (1913) and reappears throughout the Tarzan series.

137. Grell's fantasy series *The Warlord* features the exploits of U.S. Air Force pilot Travis Morgan in a hollow-earth setting called Skartaris (after the mountain peak Scartaris, from *Journey to the Center of the Earth*). Skartaris is reminiscent of Burroughs's hollow-earth setting Pellucidar, but Grell also incorporates elements from Atlantis, such as ruined cities and super-science artifacts.

138. Martin Goodman lists several connections to *Star Trek* in *The Animated Movie Guide* (see pp. 26–7) beginning with Orkrand, who created the Klingon language for the film *Star Trek: The Motion Picture* (1979). The voice of King Kashekim Nedakh of Atlantis is Leonard Nimoy, who played Mr. Spock on the original television series and in several motion pictures. The expedition's leader, Captain Lyle Tiberius Rourke, has the same distinctive middle name as Captain James T. Kirk, and the name of one of the Smithsonian's directors, Fenton Q. Harcourt (David Ogden Stiers), is an inversion of the name of the series' popular con man character Harcourt Fenton Mudd (Roger C. Carmel). Finally, the film's production designer, Jim Martin, also designed spacecraft for the *Star Trek* spin-off *Deep Space 9* (1993–1999).

139. A common complaint leveled against *Atlantis: The Lost Empire* is that its plot is too similar to the film *Stargate* (1994) and that Milo is too similar to Dr. Daniel Jackson, played by James Spader in the film, and by Michael Shanks in the television spin-off *Stargate SG-1*. Jackson is a civilian linguistic professor working for the United States military; in the television series it is revealed that Jackson has an archaeologist grandfather, Nick Ballard (Jan Rubeš), who has been institutionalized because of his study into crystal skulls and his insistence that he has met "giant aliens." In the film Jackson journeys to another planet, where he falls in love with Sha'uri (Mili Avital), the daughter of her tribe's leader, Kasuf (Erick Avair). Jackson and Milo also trap their respective expeditions far from home, both become leaders against a force threatening to destroy the natives of the faraway land, and, in the end, both Jackson and Milo decide to remain in the Lost World they discovered rather than return home with their expeditions. Some critics have complained that the story is also reminiscent of the Japanese *anime* series *Nadia: The Secret of Blue Water* (1990–1), which, like *Atlantis: The Lost Empire*, was inspired, at least in part, by *20,000 Leagues Under the Sea*.

140. In classics such as *She* and *The Lost World*, Haggard and Conan Doyle never forget that "what is discovered in the forbidden valley is more important than the valley itself, or the journey undertaken to get there." As Clute points out in *Science Fiction: The Illustrated Encyclopedia*, p. 38, "There is not much point in traveling if the destination is not worth the trip," but "some of the finest passages in most Lost World [stories] tend to be those concerned with the perils and mysteries of the long journey to the interior of the island, or the mountain, or the gorge, or the continent, or the submarine, or subterranean world." Disney's Atlantis, however, is a feast for the eyes. Instead of the usual Greek ruins, the film's graceful ancient architecture is influenced by Plato's writings and Southeast Asian and Indian cultures. Producer Don Hahn also states that the creators frequently referenced Egypt to describe the people of Atlantis: "When Napoleon wandered into Egypt, the people had lost track of their once-great civilization. They were surrounded by artifacts of their former greatness but somehow unaware of what they meant" (http://en.wikipedia.org/wiki/Atlantis:_The_Lost_Empire). The creators also co-opted elements from Edgar Cayce's prophesies about the lost continent into their designs, most notably the Heart of Atlantis, but, ironically, the creators may have done too good a job of world-building. Act II focuses on sightseeing rather than building on the excitement and suspense of Act I, so even the satisfying conclusion comes too late to reignite the opening's rousing atmosphere.

141. http://www.the-numbers.com/movies/2004/NATTR.php; http://boxofficemojo.com/movies/?id=nationaltreasure.htm.

142. In real life, Carroll could not and did not belong to the Freemasons because he was Catholic (see http://en.wikipedia.org/wiki/Charles_Carroll_of_Carrollton).

143. In the film's conclusion Ben is living in a new home that once belonged to Charles Carroll.

144. *National Treasure* is unabashedly patriotic. The founding fathers are not recalled as rich, white slave-owners (as they have been depicted in some Hollywood films), but as courageous men who risked their fortunes and their lives to defy British tyranny.

145. Another trait Ben shares with Pitt is his lack of skills when it comes to poker. Pitt confesses in *Iceberg* (on p. 126) that he always loses at the game because he has never learned to read his opponent's cards or mind; in *National Treasure* Ben claims that he is unable to bluff.

146. This is a crucial difference between Ben and Ian. Ben knows a clue is somewhere on the Declaration of Independence but will only continue his search if he can find a legitimate means of examining the document, which he knows is probably never going to happen. Ian, on the other hand, immediately begins plotting to steal it. When Ben makes it clear he will not permit this, Ian does not hesitate to try to kill him.

147. See *Vixen 03*, p. 180.

148. John Gates elegantly expresses this thematic preoccupation when he shows his grandson the back of a dollar bill and explains, "The Freemasons among our Founding Fathers left us clues like these. The unfinished pyramid, the all-seeing eye. Symbols of the Knights Templar, guardians of the treasure. They are speaking to us through these."

149. After the treasure is recovered, Ben refuses a 10 percent finder's fee and has to practically be forced to accept a 1 percent finder's fee, which he splits with Riley.

150. Ben is not the only Gates who feels this way. In the attic prologue, Patrick becomes so frustrated with his grandfather and son that he equates the family's quest as a chase for fool's gold. This analogy does not sit well with John, who snaps, "It's not about the *money*, Patrick! It's *never* been about the money!" Patrick demonstrates that he feels the same way near the end of the film when it appears the treasure is not in Trinity Church. A disappointed Ben confesses to his father, Abigail and Riley, "I just really thought I was going to find the treasure." Patrick relents: "Okay. Then we just keep looking for it." This is reminiscent of an earlier scene, aboard the *Charlotte*, where Ian gives Ben a pep talk when it appears that his son's quest has reached a dead end. Ian sounds a little like Whitmore talking to Milo about Thaddeus in *Atlantis: The Lost Empire* when he tells Ben that he wants him to be able to prove the arrogant naysayers wrong; he does not, however, tell Ben that he also wants the treasure for the staggering wealth it will provide. Patrick's motivation for joining the quest again has no such deceitful qualities. After telling Ben that they will keep looking for the treasure, Patrick explains, "We're in the company of some of the most brilliant minds in history because you found what they left behind for us to find, and understood the meaning of it. You did it, Ben, for all of us. Your grandfather, and all of us. And I've never been so happy to be proven wrong." Up until this time, Patrick and Ben's relationship has been strained by the quest because Patrick believed there was no treasure and that his son was wasting his life. But, by realizing he was wrong and joining the quest, Patrick repairs his relationship with Ben and both men gain something greater than any treasure could buy.

151. See "Trailer for *The Oregon Files*." In an unpublished 1985 interview Cussler estimates that number to be much lower, somewhere between ten to twenty million readers worldwide (see p. 2). The sizzle reel was produced in 2010, so if both it and Cussler are correct, then Cussler's readership experienced an impressive growth in a 25-year period.

152. See "WikiLeaks Art Exposé: U.S. Tried to Trade Sunken Gold for Nazi Loot."

153. *Book of Sequels*, pp. 93–122.

154. This series features a pair of genetically altered lab mice. Pinky (Rob Paulsen) is good-natured but dimwitted, while Brain (Maurice LaMarche) is a demented genius bent on taking over the world. In "Daus Mouse," Brain concocts a plan to create an army of human slaves by feeding them pancakes laced with the secretion of the Peruvian Gaokin frog mixed with meat from a rare deep water white crab. A massive number of these crabs reside inside the wreck of the *Titanic*, so Pinky and Brain confiscate a submarine "to raise the hull of that sorrowful ship!" Their trip is picked up by the CIA, which enlists the aid of Captain Jack MacGuire (James Belushi) to destroy the submarine. In a nice tip-of-the-hat to reality and to Cussler the *Titanic* is in one piece when Pinky and Brain arrive, but as the ship begins to rise it breaks in half, with the stern half falling back to the ocean floor.

155. See http://boxofficemojo.com/movies/?id=startrek.htm.

156. See http://boxofficemojo.com/movies/?id=starwars4.htm. As of this writing *Star Wars* has gone on to earn a gross domestic box office of $460 million (http://boxofficemojo.com/movies/?id=starwars4.htm); http://en.wikipedia.org/wiki/National_Treasure:_Book_of_Secrets#cite_note-BOM-1.

157. http://boxofficemojo.com/movies/?id=startrek2.htm.

158. http://en.wikipedia.org/wiki/National_Treasure:_Book_of_Secrets#cite_note-BOM-1.

Afterword

1. Cussler, *Atlantis Found*, p. 53.
2. Sampson, *Yesterday's Faces: Vol. I, Glory Figures*, p. 94.
3. Cussler is one of the few writers capable of creating consistently engrossing fiction in which an event will reach out from the past to affect the future. As outlandish as finding Atlantis or the *Nautilus* might seem, we are ready to follow his heroes into one more adventure with every new book.
4. Cussler, *Sahara*, p. 431.
5. Sampson, *Yesterday's Faces: Vol. I, Glory Figures*, p. 94.
6. Sampson, *Yesterday's Faces: Vol. V, Dangerous Horizons*, p. 178.
7. Ibid.
8. Gianetti, *Masters of American Cinema*, Introduction, Figure I.40.
9. Haining, *The Classic Era of Crime Fiction*, p. 16.
10. "Introduction," Collins, *The Woman in White*, p. ix.
11. Ibid.
12. Ibid., pp. ix–x.
13. See unpublished 1985 interview, pp. 4–5.
14. Cussler, *Shock Wave*, p. 537.
15. See unpublished 1985 interview, p. 20.

Bibliography

Articles

Argyle, Norman J., and Gerald A. Merwin. "Fuzzy Lines: Using the Best-Selling Novel to Illustrate the Blurring Boundaries of 'Public.'" *Public Voices* IX, no. 2 (n.d.): pp. 46–60.

Berg, Charles M. "Stagecoach." In *Magill's Survey of Cinema*, edited by Frank N. Magill. Englewood Cliffs, NJ: Salem Press, 1980.

Bradbury, Ray. "Science Fiction: Before Christ and After 2001: An Introduction by Ray Bradbury." *Science Fact/Fiction*, ed. dir. Leo B. Keener. Glenview, IL: Scott Foresman, 1974.

Brozo, William G., and Ronald V Schmelzer. "Wildmen, Warriors and Lovers." *Journal of Adolescent & Adult Literacy* 41, no. 1 (September 1997): pp. 4–11.

Collins, Robert. "The Last Word on the Lost Locomotive of Kiowa Creek." *Territorial Magazine* 30, no. 1 (February 21, 2010): pp. 27–33.

Conklin, Gary. "1912 Renault Town Car." *Sea Dweller Magazine*, June 2003, pp. 14–15.

Cussler, Clive. "Do Your Characters Fit Their Roles?" *The Writer*, April 1982, pp. 9–10.

_____. "Finding His Way Home." In *Chicken Soup for the Ocean Lover's Soul*, edited by Chrissy Donnelly, Jack Canfield, and Mark Donnelly. Deerfield Beach, FL: Health Communications, 2003.

_____. "Hero for the Day." In *Chicken Soup for the Baseball Fan's Soul*, edited by Chrissy Donnelly, Jack Canfield, and Mark Donnelly. Deerfield Beach, FL: Health Communications, 2001.

_____. "Make Your Story 'Fly.'" *The Writer*, March 1979, pp. 11–13, 45.

_____. "Nothing Comes Easy." In *Chicken Soup for the Writer's Soul*, edited by Chrissy Donnelly, Jack Canfield, and Mark Donnelly. Deerfield Beach, FL: Health Communications, 2000.

_____. "Writing the Suspense-Adventure Novel." In *The Writer's Handbook 1987*, edited by Sylvia K. Burack. N.p.: Writer, Inc., 1987.

Dickstein, Morris. "It's a Wonderful Life, But…" *American Film*, May 1980, pp. 43–47.

Dochtery, Brian. "Grace Under Fire: Reading Alistair MacLean." *Twentieth Century Suspense*, 1990.

Dundes, Alan, ed. "The Hero Pattern and the Life of Jesus: Protocol of the Twentyfifth Colloquy 12 December 1976." Center for Hermeneutical Studies in Hellenistic and Modern Culture, digitized September 30, 2009, pp. 1–30.

Johnson, Dolores. "The Man Who Raised the Titanic—and a Small Fortune." *Writer's Digest*, May 1978, pp. 32–33.

Kenfield, Bruce. "Raise the Titanic Newspaper Comic Strips." *Sea Dweller Magazine*, June 2003, pp. 12–13.

Klein, T. E. "A Dreamer's Tales." In H.P. Lovecraft, *Dagon and Other Macabre Tales*. Sauk City, WI: Arkham House, 1987, pp. xiii–lii.

Korkis, Jim. "Quest for Adventure." *Amazing Heroes* 95 (May 15, 1986): pp. 17–25.

Lawrence, D.H. "Herman Melville's *Moby Dick*." *Moby-Dick*. New York: Bantam, 1986, pp. 581–7.

Ledwon, Lenora. "*Twin Peaks* and the Television Gothic." *Literature/Film Quarterly* 21, issue 4 (1993): pp. 260–70.

"A Novel Comic Strip Idea Starts Today." *Toronto Star*, August 15, 1977.

Olbrich, Doug W. "Interview: Doug Wildey." *Amazing Heroes* 95 (May 15, 1986): pp. 34–47.

Reid, Craig. "The Top 20 *Wild, Wild West* Episodes Guide." *Cinefantastique* 31, no. 8 (n.d.): p. 46.

_____. "The Wild, Wild West." *Cinefantastique* 31, no. 8: pp. 47–8.

Schmuland, Arlene. "The Archival Image in Fiction: An Analysis and Annotated Bibliography." *The American Archivist* 62, no. 1 (Spring 1999): pp. 24–73.

Schultz, David, and Beth A. Wielde. "Wonks and Warriors: Depictions of Government Professionals in Popular Film." *Public Voices* IX, no. 2 (n.d.): pp. 61–82.

Smith, Edgar W. "What Is It That We Love in Sherlock Holmes?" In Sir Arthur Conan Doyle, *The Annotated Sherlock Holmes*, edited by William S. Baring-Gould, vol. 1, pp. 103–4.

Books (Fiction)

Adams, Richard. *The Plague Dogs*. New York: Knopf, 1978.

_____. *Watership Down*. New York: Avon, 1972.

Bach, Richard. *Illusions*. New York: Dell, 1977.
_____. *Jonathan Livingston Seagull*. New York: Avon, 1970.
Barrie, J.M. *Peter Pan*. London: Puffin Classics, 2002.
Benchley, Peter. *The Deep*. Garden City, NY: Doubleday, 1976.
_____. *Jaws*. New York: Bantam, 1974.
Blackwood, Grant. *An Echo of War*. New York: Jove, 2003.
_____. *The End of Enemies*. New York: Jove, 2001.
_____. *The Wall of Night*. New York: Jove, 2002.
Blackwood, Grant, and Tom Clancy. *Dead or Alive*. New York: Berkeley, 2012.
Brown, Graham. *Black Rain*. New York: Dell, 2010.
_____. *Black Sun*. New York: Bantam, 2010.
_____. *The Eden Prophecy*. New York: Bantam, 2012.
Burroughs, Edgar Rice. *The Land That Time Forgot*. New York: Ballantine, 1992.
_____. *Out of Time's Abyss*. New York: Ballantine, 1992.
_____. *The People That Time Forgot*. New York: Ballantine, 1992.
Century of Thrillers. New York: President Press, 1937.
Clancy, Tom. *The Bear and the Dragon*. New York: Putnam, 2000.
_____. *Debt of Honor*. New York: Putnam, 1994.
_____. *Executive Orders*. New York: Putnam, 1996.
_____. *Hunt for Red October*. Annapolis: Naval Institute Press, 1984.
_____. *Rainbow Six*. New York: Putnam, 1998.
_____. *The Teeth of the Tiger*. New York: Putnam, 2003.
Collins, Wilkie. *The Moonstone*. New York: Barnes & Noble, 1993.
_____. *The Woman in White*. Hertfordshire, UK: Wordsworth Classics, 2002.
Conan Doyle, Sir Arthur. *The Annotated Sherlock Holmes, Vol. 1-2*. Edited by William S. Baring-Gould. New York: Clarkson N. Potter, 1979.
_____. *The Historical Novels, Vol. I & II*. London: New Orchard Editions, 1986.
_____. *The Lost World & Other Stories*. Hertfordshire, UK: Wordsworth Editions, 1995.
_____. *The Original Illustrated Arthur Conan Doyle*. Secaucus, NJ: Castle Books, 1980

1. The Pitt Novels

Cussler, Clive. *Atlantis Found*. New York: Berkeley, 1999.
_____. *Cyclops*. New York: Pocket Books, 1986.
_____. *Dragon*. New York: Pocket Star Books, 1990.
_____. *Deep Six*. New York: Pocket Books, 1984.
_____. *Flood Tide*. New York: Pocket Star Books, 1998.
_____. *Iceberg*. New York: Berkeley, 2004.
_____. *Inca Gold*. New York: Pocket Books, 1994.
_____. *The Mediterranean Caper*. New York: Pocket Books, 1973.
_____. *The Mediterranean Caper* and *Iceberg*. New York: Simon & Schuster, 1995.
_____. *Night Probe!* New York: Bantam, 1982.
_____. *Pacific Vortex*. New York: Bantam, 1979.
_____. *Raise the Titanic!* New York: Bantam, 1976.
_____. *Sahara*. New York: Pocket Star Books, 1992.
_____. *Shock Wave*. New York: Pocket Star Books, 1996.
_____. *Treasure*. New York: Pocket Books, 1988.
_____. *Trojan Odyssey*. New York: Berkeley, 2004.
_____. *Valhalla Rising*. New York: Berkeley, 2002.
_____. *Vixen 03*. New York: Bantam, 1978.
Cussler, Clive, and Dirk Cussler. *Arctic Drift*. New York: Putnam, 2008.
_____. *Black Wind*. New York: Putnam, 2004.
_____. *Crescent Dawn*. New York: Putnam, 2010.
_____. *Poseidon's Arrow*. New York: Putnam, 2012.
_____. *Treasure of Khan*. New York: Putnam, 2006.

2. The Non-Pitt Novels

Cussler, Clive. *The Adventure of Hotsy Totsy*. London: Puffin, 2010.
_____. *The Adventures of Vin Fiz*. New York: Philomel, 2006.
_____. *The Chase*. New York: Berkeley, 2007.
Cussler, Clive, and Grant Blackwood. *Fargo Adventures: The Kingdom*. New York: Putnam, 2011.
_____. *Fargo Adventures: Lost Empire*. New York: Putnam, 2010.
_____. *Fargo Adventures: Spartan Gold*. New York: Berkeley, 2009.
Cussler, Clive, and Graham Brown. *The NUMA Files: Devil's Gate*. New York: Putnam, 2011.
_____. *The NUMA Files: The Storm*. New York: Putnam, 2012.
_____. *The NUMA Files: Zero Hour*. New York: Putnam, 2013.
Cussler, Clive, and Craig Dirgo. *The Oregon Files: Golden Buddha*. New York: Berkeley, 2003.
_____. *The Oregon Files: Sacred Stone*. New York: Berkley, 2004.
Cussler, Clive, and Jack Du Brul. *The Oregon Files: Corsair*. New York: Putnam, 2009.
_____. *The Oregon Files: Dark Watch*. New York: Berkley, 2005.
_____. *The Oregon Files: The Jungle*. New York: Putnam, 2011.
_____. *The Oregon Files: Mirage*. New York: Putnam, 2013.
_____. *The Oregon Files: Plague Ship*. New York: Berkley, 2008.
_____. *The Oregon Files: The Silent Sea*. New York: Berkley, 2010.
_____. *The Oregon Files: Skeleton Coast*. New York: Berkley, 2006.
Cussler, Clive, and Paul Kemprecos. *The NUMA Files: Blue Gold*. New York: Pocket Books, 2000.
_____. *The NUMA Files: Fire Ice*. New York: Berkley, 2003.
_____. *The NUMA Files: Lost City*. New York: Berkley, 2005.

_____. *The NUMA Files: Medusa*. New York: Putnam, 2009.
_____. *The NUMA Files: The Navigator*. New York: Berkley, 2008.
_____. *The NUMA Files: Polar Shift*. New York: Berkley, 2005.
_____. *The NUMA Files: Serpent*. New York: Pocket Books, 1999.
_____. *The NUMA Files: White Death*. New York: Berkley, 2004.
Cussler, Clive, and Thomas Perry. *Fargo Adventures: The Mayan Secrets*. New York: Putnam, 2013.
_____. *Fargo Adventures: The Tombs*. New York: Putnam, 2012.
Cussler, Clive, and Justin Scott. *The Bootlegger*. New York: Putnam, 2014.
_____. *The Race*. New York: Berkley, 2011.
_____. *The Spy*. New York: Berkley, 2010.
_____. *The Striker*. New York: Putnam, 2013.
_____. *The Thief*. New York: Putnam, 2012.
_____. *The Wrecker*. New York: Berkley, 2009.
Cussler, Clive, ed. *Thriller 2: Stories You Just Can't Put Down*. West Yorkshire, UK: Mira, 2009.
Dickens, Charles. *A Christmas Carol*. New York: Washington Square Press, 1967.
Dirgo, Craig. *The Einstein Papers*. New York: Atria, 1999.
_____. *Tremor*. Memphis: Onyx, 2008.
Douglas, Keith. *Complete Poems*, 3d ed. Oxford: Oxford University Press, 1998.
Du Brul, Jack. *Charon's Landing*. Memphis: Onyx, 2006.
_____. *Deep Fire Rising*. Memphis: Onyx, 2003.
_____. *Havoc*. Memphis: Onyx, 2007.
_____. *The Medusa Stone*. Memphis: Onyx, 2010.
_____. *Pandora's Curse*. Memphis: Onyx, 2001.
_____. *River of Ruin*. Memphis: Onyx, 2002.
_____. *Vulcan's Forge*. Memphis: Onyx, 2005.
Editorial Board of the University Society (Supervisors). *Bookshelf for Boys and Girls*, Vol. I, "Nursery Favorites Old and New." New York: University Society, 1972.
_____. *Bookshelf for Boys and Girls*, Vol. II, "Happy Hours in Storyland." New York: University Society, 1972.
_____. *Bookshelf for Boys and Girls*, Vol. III, "Folk and Fairy Tales." New York: University Society, 1972.
_____. *Bookshelf for Boys and Girls*, Vol. IV, "Stories and Songs form Many Lands." New York: University Society, 1972.
_____. *Bookshelf for Boys and Girls*, Vol. V, "Things to Make and Things to Do." New York: University Society, 1972.
_____. *Bookshelf for Boys and Girls*, Vol. VI, "Art and Music." New York: University Society, 1972.
_____. *Bookshelf for Boys and Girls*, Vol. VII, "Nature and Science." New York: University Society, 1972.
_____. *Bookshelf for Boys and Girls*, Vol. VIII, "Bookland Classics." New York: University Society, 1972.
_____. *Bookshelf for Boys and Girls*, Vol. IX, "Great Events and Famous People." New York: University Society, 1972.
_____. *Bookshelf for Boys and Girls*, Index, "Bookshelf Parents Guide." New York: University Society, 1972.
_____. *Epic of Gilgamesh*. New York: Penguin, 1986.
Fleming, Ian. *Casino Royale*. New York: Signet, 1953.
_____. *Diamonds Are Forever*. New York: Signet, 1956.
_____. *Dr. No*. New York: Signet, 1958.
_____. *Live and Let Die*. New York: Signet, 1954.
_____. *For Your Eyes Only*. New York: Signet, 1959, 1960.
_____. *From Russia, With Love*. New York: Signet, 1957.
_____. *Goldfinger*. New York: Signet, 1959.
_____. *The Man With the Golden Gun*. New York: Signet, 1965.
_____. *Moonraker*. New York: Signet, 1955.
_____. *Octopussy*. New York: Signet, 1967.
_____. *On Her Majesty's Secret Service*. New York: Signet, 1963.
_____. *The Spy Who Loved Me*. New York: Signet, 1962.
_____. *Thunderball*. New York: Signet, 1961.
_____. *You Only Live Twice*. New York: Signet, 1964.
Grell, Mike. *Sable*. New York: Forge Books, 2000.
Hammett, Dashiell. *The Big Knockover: Selected Stories and Short Novels by Dashiell Hammett*. New York: Vintage, 1972.
Jones, Steven Philip. *As Time Goes By* (unfinished manuscript).
_____. *Bushwhackers*. New York: Avalon, 2004.
_____. *Henrietta Hex: Shadows From the Past*. Chandler, AZ: Actionopolis, 2011.
_____. *King of Harlem*. Cincinnati: Mundania Press, 2005.
_____. *Talismen: The Boy in the Well*. N.p.: Aelthorne Press, 2005.
_____. *Talismen: The Knightmare Knife*. Cincinnati: Mundania Press, 2009.
_____. *Wizard Academies: House with the Witch's Hat*. N.p.: Wizard Academies LLC, 2009.
_____, ed. *Re-Animator: Tales of Herbert West, Six Stories by H.P. Lovecraft*. Calabasas, CA: Malibu Graphics, 1991.
Kemprecos, Paul. *Cool Blue Tomb*. New York: Bantam, 1991.
_____. *Bluefin Blues*. New York: St. Martin's Press, 1997.
_____. *Death in Deep Water*. Garden City, NY: Doubleday, 1992.
_____. *Feeding Frenzy*. Garden City, NY: Doubleday, 1993.
_____. *The Mayflower Murder*. New York: St. Martin's Press, 1996.

_____. *Neptune's Eye*. New York: Bantam, 1991.
King, Stephen. *Night Shift*. New York: Doubleday, 1976.
_____. *Nightmares & Dreamscapes*. New York: Signet, 1994.
Kneer, Leo B, ed. *Science Fact/Fiction*. Glenview, IL: Scott Foresman, 1974.
Lovecraft, H.P. *The Best of H.P. Lovecraft: Bloodcurdling Tales of Horror and the Macabre*. New York: Del Rey, 1982.
_____. *Dagon and Other Macabre Tales*. Sauk City, WI: Arkham House, 1987.
_____. *Re-Animator: Tales of Herbert West*. Calabasas, CA: Malibu Graphics, 1992.
Lucas, George. *Star Wars: From the Adventures of Luke Skywalker*. New York: Ballatine, 1976.
Melville, Herman. *Moby-Dick*. New York: Bantam, 1986.
Mitchell, Margaret. *Gone With the Wind*. New York: Macmillan, 1936.
Norton, Alden. *Horror Times Ten*. New York: Berkley, 1967.
_____. *Masters of Horror*. New York: Berkley, 1968.
Norton, Alden, and Sam Moskowitz. *Ghostly By Gaslight: Fearful Tales of a Lost Era*. Buffalo, MN: Pyramid Books, 1971.
_____. *Hauntings and Horrors: Ten Grisly Tales*. New York: Berkley, 1969.

1. The Butcher's Boy Series
Perry, Thomas. *The Butcher's Boy*. New York: Random House, 2003.
_____. *The Informant*. New York: Mariner Books, 2012.
_____. *Sleeping Dogs*. Raleigh, NC: Ivy Books, 1993.

2. Jane Whitefield Series
Perry, Thomas. *Blood Money*. New York: Ballantine, 2002.
_____. *Dance for the Dead*. Raleigh, NC: Ivy Books, 1997.
_____. *The Face-Changers*. Raleigh, NC: Ivy Books, 1999.
_____. *Poison Flowers*. Walterville, ME: Thorndike, 2012.
_____. *Runner*. New York: Mariner Books, 2010.
_____. *Shadow Woman*. New York: Ballantine, 1998.
_____. *Vanishing Act*. New York: Fawcett, 1996.

3. Other Novels
Perry, Thomas. *Big Fish*. New York: Macmillan, 1985.
_____. *The Boyfriend*. New York: Mysterious Press, 2013.
_____. *Dead Aim*. New York: Random House, 2006.
_____. *Death Benefits*. New York: Ballantine, 2001.
_____. *Fidelity*. New York: Mariner Books, 2009.
_____. *Island*. New York: Avon, 1989.
_____. *Metzger's Dog*. New York: Random House, 2003.

_____. *Nightlife*. New York: Ballantine, 2007.
_____. *Pursuit*. New York: Random House, 2006.
_____. *Silence*. New York: Mariner Books, 2008.
_____. *Strip*. New York: Mariner Books, 2011.
Poe, Edgar Allan. *Complete Tales & Poems of Edgar Allan Poe*. New York: Barnes & Noble Books, 1992.
_____. *Great Tales of Horror by Edgar Allan Poe*. New York: Bantam Pathfinder Edition, 1964.
Rohmer, Sax. *Sax Rohmer's Collected Novels: The Hand of Fu Manchu, The Return of Dr. Fu Manchu, The Yellow Claw, Dope*. Secaucus, NJ: Castle Books, 1983.
Rowling, J.K. *Harry Potter and the Chamber of Secrets*. New York: Scholastic, 2000.
_____. *Harry Potter and the Deathly Hollows*. New York: Scholastic, 2007.
_____. *Harry Potter and the Goblet of Fire*. New York: Scholastic, 2002.
_____. *Harry Potter and the Half-Blood Prince*. New York: Scholastic, 2005.
_____. *Harry Potter and the Order of the Phoenix*. New York: Scholastic, 2003.
_____. *Harry Potter and the Prisoner of Azkaban*. New York: Scholastic, 2001.
_____. *Harry Potter and the Sorcerer's Stone*. New York: Scholastic, 1999.
Rymer, J.M., and Thomas Preskett Prest. *Varney the Vampire, Vol. I–III*. New York: Arno Press, 1970.
Scott, Justin. *The Auction*. New York: Jove, 1985.
_____. *The Cossack's Bride*. N.p.: Grafton, 1988.
_____. *Frost Life: A Ben Abbott Mystery*. London: Collins Crime, 1997.
_____. *Hardscape: A Ben Abbott Mystery*. New York: Viking, 1994.
_____. *Many Happy Returns*. New York: David McKay, 1973.
_____. *Mausoleum: A Ben Abbott Mystery*. Scottsdale, AZ: Poisoned Pen Press, 2007.
_____. *McMansion: A Ben Abbott Mystery*. Scottsdale, AZ: Poisoned Pen Press, 2006.
_____. *A Pride of Royals*. New York: HarperCollins, 1983.
_____. *Rampage*. New York: Simon & Schuster, 1986.
_____. *The Shipkiller*. Asheville, NC: Pegasus, 1978.
_____. *Stonedust: A Ben Abbott Mystery*. New York: Viking, 1995.
_____. *Treasure for Treasure*. New York: David McKay, 1974.
_____. *Treasure Island*. New York: St. Martin's Press, 1994.
Scott, Justin [Paul Garrison, pseud.]. *Buried at Sea*. New York: Harper Torch, 2002.
_____. *Fire and Ice*. New York: Avon, 1998.
_____. *Red Sky at Morning*. New York: Harper Torch, 2001.
_____. *The Ripple Effect*. New York: William Morrow, 2004.
_____. *Sea Hunter*. New York: HarperCollins, 2003.

Scott, Justin, and Robert Ludlum. *The Janson Command*. New York: Grand Central, 2012.
Shakespeare, William. *Hamlet*. London: J.M Dent, 1907.
_____. *Macbeth*. London: J.M Dent, 1904.
_____. *A Midsummer Night's Dream*. London: J.M Dent, 1905.
_____. *The Sonnets*. London: J.M Dent, 1905.
Spector, Robert Donald, ed. *Seven Master Pieces of Gothic Horror*. New York: Bantam, 1971.
Stevenson, Robert Louis. *The Strange Case of Dr. Jekyll & Mr. Hyde*. New York: Bantam, 1985.
Stoker, Bram. *Dracula*. Stamford, CT: Longmeadow Press, 1991.
_____. *Five Novels*. New York: Barnes & Noble, 2006.
_____. *The Jewel of Seven Stars*. New York: Carroll & Graf, 1989.
Wolf, Leonard, ed. *The Annotated Dracula*. New York: Clarkson N. Potter, 1975.
_____. *The Essential Dr. Jekyll and Mr. Hyde*. N.p.: ibooks, 2005.

Books (Nonfiction)

Allen, Michael, and Larry Schweikart. *A Patriot's History of the United States*. New York: Sentinel, 2004.
Beck, Jerry, ed. *The Animated Movie Guide*. Chicago: Chicago Review Press, 2005.
Belford, Barbara. *Bram Stoker: A Biography of the Author of Dracula*. New York: Alfred Knopf, 1996.
Bloom, Clive. *Bestsellers: Popular Fiction Since 1900*. New York: Palgrave Macmillan, 2002.
_____. *Cult Fiction: Popular Reading and Pulp Theory*. New York: St. Martin's Press, 1996.
_____. *Gothic Horror: A Reader's Guide from Poe to King and Beyond*. New York: St. Martin's Press, 1998.
_____. *Reading Poe Reading Freud: The Romantic Imagination in Crisis*, New York: Macmillan, 1988.
_____. *Spy Thrillers: From Buchan to le Carré*. New York: St. Martin's Press, 1990.
_____. *Twentieth-Century Suspense*. New York: Macmillan, 1990.
_____, ed. *Creepers: British Horror and Fantasy in the Twentieth Century*. London: Pluto Press, 1993.
Bloom, Clive, Brian Cocherty, Jane Gibb, and Keith Shand. *Nineteenth-Century Suspense*. New York: Macmillan, 1988.
Bloomfield, Shelley Costa, PhD. *The Everything Guide to Edgar Allan Poe*. Avon, MA: Adams Media, 2007.
Bulfinch, Thomas. *Bulfinch's Mythology: The Age of Fable, The Age of Chivalry, Legends of Charlemagne*. New York: Thomas Y. Crowell, 1970.
Campbell, Joseph. *The Hero with a Thousand Faces*. Princeton: Princeton University Press, 1949.
_____. *The Hero's Journey*. Edited by Phil Cousineau. New York: Harper & Row, 1990.
Campbell, Joseph, and Bill Moyers. *The Power of Myth*. Edited by Betty Sue Flowers. Garden City, NY: Doubleday, 1988.
Cannaday, Marilyn. *Bigger Than Life: The Creator of Doc Savage*. Bowling Green, OH: Bowling Green State University Popular Press, 1990.
Carr, John Dickson. *The Life of Sir Arthur Conan Doyle*. New York: Carroll & Graf, 1987.
Chesterton, G.K. *What I Saw in America*. New York: Dodd, Mead, 1922.
Clancy, Tom. *Carrier*. New York: Berkley, 1999.
Clancy, Tom, and John Grisham. *Special Forces: A Guided Tour of U.S. Army Special Forces*. New York: Berkeley, 2001.
Clute, John. *Science Fiction: The Illustrated Encyclopedia*. New York: Dorling Kindersley, 1995.
Cole, Joni B. *Toxic Feedback: Helping Writers Survive and Thrive*. Lebanon, NH: University Press of New England, 2005.
Comentale, Edward P., Stephen Watt, and Skip Wellman. *Ian Fleming and James Bond: The Cultural Politics of 007*. Bloomington: Indiana University Press, 2005.
Cray, Ed. *The Erotic Muse: American Bawdy Songs*. Champaign: University of Illinois Press, 1999.
Cussler, Clive. *Built For Adventure: The Classic Automobiles of Clive Cussler and Dirk Pitt*. New York: Putnam Adult, 2011.
Cussler, Clive, and Craig Dirgo. *Sea Hunters*. New York: Simon & Schuster, 1996.
_____. *Clive Cussler & Dirk Pitt Revealed!* New York: Pocket Books, 1998.
_____. *Sea Hunters II*. New York: Simon & Schuster, 2002.
D'Ammassa, Don. *Encyclopedia of Adventure Fiction*. New York: Infobase, 2009.
D'Souza, Dinesh. *Ronald Reagan: How an Ordinary Man Became an Extraordinary Leader*. New York: The Free Press, 1997.
Darby, Ken. *The Brownstone House of Nero Wolfe*. New York: Little, Brown, 1983.
Dillard, J.J. *Star Trek: "Where No Man Has Gone Before"—A History in Pictures*. New York: Pocket Books, 1994.
Dougall, Alastair. *James Bond: The Secret World of 007*. New York: Dorling Kindersley, 2000.
Dove, George N. *Suspense in the Formula Story*. Bowling Green, OH: Bowling Green State University Popular Press, 1989.
Eerdmans Analytical Concordance to the Revised Standard Version of the Bible. Grand Rapids: Wm. B. Eerdmans, 1988.
Eco, Umberto. *The Role of the Reader: Explorations in the Semiotics of Texts*. Bloomington: Indiana University Press, 1979.
Eliot, Alexander. *The Universal Myths: Heroes, Gods, Tricksters and Others*. New York: Truman Talley Books/Meridian, 1990.
Foley, Charles, Jon Lellenberg, and Daniel Stashower.

Arthur Conan Doyle: A Life in Letters. New York: Penguin, 2007.

Foster-Harris, William. *Basic Formulas of Fiction*. Norman: University of Oklahoma Press, 1944.

_____. *Basic Patterns of Plot*. Norman: University of Oklahoma Press, 1959.

Freeman, David. *The Last Days of Alfred Hitchcock*. New York: Overlook Press, 1999.

Gallagher, Mark. *Action Figures: Men, Action Films, and Contemporary Adventure Narratives*. New York: Palgrave Macmillan, 2006.

Gianetti, Louis. *Masters of American Cinema*. Upper Saddle River, NJ: Prentice-Hall, 1981.

Gose, Elliott. *Mere Creatures*. Toronto: University of Toronto Press, 1988.

Greenberg, Martin, ed. *The Tom Clancy Companion*. New York: Berkley, 1992.

Haining, Peter. *The Classic Era of Crime Fiction*. Chicago: Chicago Review Press, 2002.

Heyer, Paul. *Titanic Legacy: Disaster as Media Event and Myth*. Westport, CT: Praeger, 1995.

Holstmark, Erling B. *Edgar Rice Burroughs*. Woodbridge, CT: Twayne, 1986.

Jaffe, Jacqueline A. *Arthur Conan Doyle*. Boston: G.K. Hall, 1987.

Joshi, S.T. *A Dreamer and a Visionary: H.P. Lovecraft in His Time*. Liverpool: Liverpool University Press, 2001.

Jung, Carl. *Psyche and Symbol*. Edited by Violet S. de Laszlo. New York: Doubleday Anchor, 1958.

_____. *Symbols of Transformation*. Princeton: Princeton University Press, 1956.

Kane, Bob, and Tom Andre. *Batman and Me*. Buenos Aires: Eclipse Books, 1989.

Keeley, Joseph. *The Left-Leaning Antenna*. New York: Arlington House, 1971.

Klein, Norman M. *Seven Minutes: The Life and Death of the American Animated Cartoon*. New York: Verso, 1996.

King, Stephen. *Danse Macabre*. Corunna, Spain: Everest House, 1981.

Kreimeier, Klaus. *The UFA Story: A History of Germany's Greatest Film Company, 1918–1945*. Berkeley: University of California Press, 1999.

Leibfried, Philip. *Rudyard Kipling and Sir Henry Rider Haggard on Screen, Stage, Radio and Television*. Jefferson, NC: McFarland, 2000.

Leggett, Paul. *Terence Fisher: Horror, Myth and Religion*. Jefferson, NC: McFarland, 2002.

Lesser, Robert. *Pulp Art*. Baltimore: Metro Books, 2009.

Lisa, Philip, and Lee Pfeiffer. *The Incredible World of 007: An Authorized Celebration of James Bond*. New York: Citadel Press, 1992.

Lord Raglan (Fitzroy Richard Somerset). *The Hero: A Study in Tradition, Myth, and Drama*. New York: Vintage, 1956.

McNally, Raymond T., and Radu Florescu. *In Search of Dracula: A True History of Dracula and Vampire Legends*. New York: Warner Paperback Library, 1973.

Mitchell, Charles P. *The Complete H.P. Lovecraft Filmography*. Westport, CT: Greenwood Press, 2001.

Nash, Constance, and Virginia Oakey. *The Screenwriter's Handbook: What To Write, How To Write It, Where To Sell It*. New York: Barnes & Noble Books, 1974.

New Oxford Annotated Bible with Apocrypha. New York: Oxford Univesity Press, 1977.

Orczy, (Baroness) Emma. *The Scarlet Pimpernel*. Garden City, NY: International Collectors Library, n.d.

Pancoast, Henry S. *Introduction to American Literature*. New York: Henry Holt, 1898.

Pierce, Frederick. *Dreams and Personality*. New York: D. Appleton, 1931.

Punter, David. *The Literature of Terror: A History of Gothic Fictions from 1765 to the Present Day*. New York: Longman, 1980.

Pykett, Lyn. *The Sensation Novel: From* The Woman in White *to* The Moonstone. Devon, UK: Northcote House, 1994.

Reagan, Ronald. *An American Life*. New York: Pocket Books, 1990.

Reader's Digest Books. *The Story of Jesus*. Edited by Gardner Associates. Bath, UK: Reader's Digest Association, 1993.

Robbins, Harold. *The Carpetbaggers*. New York: Forge Books, 2007.

Rosenberg, Bruce A. *Ian Fleming*. Woodbridge, CT: Twayne, 1989.

Rumbelow, Donald. *The Complete Jack the Ripper*. New York: New American Library, 1976.

Sampson, Robert. *Yesterday's Faces: Vol. I, Glory Figures*. Bowling Green, OH: Bowling Green State University Popular Press, 1983.

_____. *Yesterday's Faces: Vol. II, Strange Days*. Bowling Green, OH: Bowling Green State University Popular Press, 1983.

_____. *Yesterday's Faces: Vol. III, From the Dark Side*. Bowling Green, OH: Bowling Green State University Popular Press, 1983.

_____. *Yesterday's Faces: Vol. IV, The Solvers*. Bowling Green, OH: Bowling Green State University Popular Press, 1983.

_____. *Yesterday's Faces: Vol. V, Dangerous Horizons*. Bowling Green, OH: Bowling Green State University Popular Press, 1983.

_____. *Yesterday's Faces: Vol.VI, Violent Lives*. Bowling Green, OH: Bowling Green State University Popular Press, 1983.

Sedgwick, Eve. *The Coherence of Gothic Conventions*. New York: Arno Press, 1986.

Senf, Carol A. *Bram Stoker*. Cardiff, Wales: University of Wales Press, 2010.

Siodmak, Curt. *Wolf Man's Maker: Memoirs of a Hollywood Writer*. New York: Scarecrow Press, 2001.

Smith, Don G. *H.P. Lovecraft in Popular Culture: The Works and Their Adaptations in Film, Television,*

Comics, Music and Games. Jefferson, NC: McFarland, 2006.
Snelling, O.F. *007 James Bond: A Report*. New York: Signet Books, 1964.
Snow, Edward Rowe. *Supernatural Mysteries and Other Tales*. New York: Dodd, Mead, 1974.
Stemple, Tom. *Screenwriter: The Life and Times of Nunnally Johnson*. San Diego: A.S. Barnes, 1980.
Stoker, Bram. *Bram Stoker's Notes for* Dracula. Annotated and transcribed by Robert Eighteen-Bisang and Elizabeth Miller. Jefferson, NC: McFarland, 2008.
Suid, Lawrence H. *Guts & Glory: The Making of the American Military Image in Film*. Lexington: University Press of Kentucky, 2002.
Swanson, James L. *Manhunt: The 12-Day Chase for Lincoln's Killer*. New York: William Morrow, 2006.
Symons, Julian. *Conan Doyle: Portrait of an Artist*. New York: Mysterious Press, 1979.
_____. *A Pictorial History of Crime*. New York: Bonanza Books, 1966.
Thompson, Jeff. *Television Horrors of Dan Curtis:* Dark Shadows, The Night Stalker *and Other Productions, 1966–2006*. Jefferson, NC: McFarland, 2009.
Thoms, Peter. *Detection & Its Designs: Narrative & Power in 19th-Century Detective Fiction*. Athens: Ohio University Press, 1998.
Throckmorton, Jr., Burton H., ed.. *Gospel Parallels: A Synopsis of the First Three Gospels*. Nashville: Thomas Nelson, 1979.
Webster's Encyclopedic Unabridged Dictionary of the English Language. Houston: Portland House, 1989.
Webster's New World Dictionary of the American Language, 2d ed. Emeryville, CA: World Publishing, 1972.
Wheatley, Helen. *Gothic Television*. Manchester: Manchester University Press, 2006.
Wildcat Books Staff. *The Pulp Hero*. Wildcat Books, 2007.
Valero, Wayne. *The Adventure Writing of Clive Cussler*. Kearney, NE: Morris Publishing, 2007.
Wagner, Walter. *You Must Remember This*. New York: G.P. Putnam and Sons, 1975.
Young, Robert Pelton. *The World's Most Dangerous Places*, 5th ed. New York: HarperCollins, 2003.
Zweig, Paul. *The Adventurer: The Fate of Adventure in the Western World*. New York: Basic Books, 1974.

Comics/Graphic Novels

Grell, Mike. *Green Arrow: The Long-Bow Hunters*. Burbank: DC Comics.
_____. *Green Arrow*, vol. 2, issues 1–80. Burbank: DC Comics.
_____. *James Bond: Permission to Die* Issues 1–3. Staten Island: Acme Press/Eclipse Comics.
_____. *Jon Sable, Freelance*, vol. 1, issues 1–5. Chicago: First Comics.
_____. *Starslayer: The Log of the Jolly Roger*, 1–6. San Diego: Pacific Comics, 7–8. Chicago: First Comics.
_____. *The Warlord*, vol.1. 1–52, v.2 1–6. Burbank: DC Comics.
Goodwin, Archie & Simonson, Walt. *Manhunter: The Complete Saga*. Edited by Roger Slifer. New York: Excalibur Enterprises, 1979.
Jones, Steven Philip and Gary Reed. *Curious Cases of Sherlock Holmes*. San Diego: IDW, 2012.

Internet Sources

Al Giordino. http://sh1.webring.com/people/xh/hn4dpitt/algiordino.htm.
Alistair MacLean. http://en.wikipedia.org/wiki/Alistair_MacLean.
Alvarez, Olivia Flores. Radioed Houston: Clive Cussler and *The Chase*. http://blogs.houstonpress.com/hairballs/2007/11/radio_houstoned_clive_cussler.php#more.
Angus Dei. http://en.wikipedia.org/wiki/Agnus_Dei.
Atlantis: The Lost Empire. http://en.wikipedia.org/wiki/Atlantis:_The_Lost_Empire.
Atlantis: The Lost Empire Viking Prologue. http://www.youtube.com/watch?v=fV21Qtt6qW0.
Banacek. http://en.wikipedia.org/wiki/Banacek.
Banacek, Thrilling Detective Website. http://www.thrillingdetective.com/banacek.html.
Batman Begins. http://boxofficemojo.com/movies/?id=batmanbegins.htm.
Benjamin Franklin Gates. http://www.enotes.com/topic/Benjamin_Franklin_Gates#Fictional_biography.
"The Blame Game On the *Sahara* Movie Bomb Begins In the Land of Dreams!" http://doomandgloomnews.com/home.html.
Bunting, Glen F. "Cussler's Writing Taken to Task." April 11, 2007. http://articles.latimes.com/2007/apr/11/business/fi-mckee11.
_____. "$78 Million of Red Ink." April 15, 2007. http://www.latimes.com/business/la-fi-movie15apr15,0,6005119.story.
Cancer (zodiac sign). http://en.wikipedia.org/wiki/Cancer_(Zodiac_sign).
Captain James T. Kirk. http://en.wikipedia.org/wiki/James_T._Kirk#cite_note-21.
Charles Carroll. http://en.wikipedia.org/wiki/Charles_Carroll_of_Carrollton.
Charters, David. "Swashbuckling Hero the World Forgot." http://www.thefreelibrary.com/Swashbuckling+hero+the+world+forgot%3B+Once+his+stories+thrilled...-a0116221155.
Checklist, Mike Grell. http://www.mikegrell.com/checklist.jsp.
"Children's Bookshelf Talks with Clive Cussler, January 5, 2006." http://www.publishersweekly.com/pw/by-topic/authors/interviews/article/9380-children-s-bookshelf-talks-with-clive-cussler.html.
Chitty Chitty Bang Bang: The Magical Car. http://

en.wikipedia.org/wiki/Chitty_Chitty_Bang_Bang_(novel).

The Chronicles of Narnia: The Lion, The Witch, & The Wardrobe. http://www.the-numbers.com/movies/2005/LWWRB.php.

Chuck Yaeger. http://en.wikipedia.org/wiki/Chuck_Yeager.

Cigar Saga. http://sh1.webring.com/people/xh/hn4dpitt/cigarsaga.htm.

"Clive Cussler/About the Author." http://us.penguingroup.com/static/packages/us/clivecussler/bio.html.

"Clive Cussler/Crusader Entertainment Acquires the Rights to Clive Cussler's Best-Selling Dirk Pitt Book Series." http://us.penguingroup.com/static/packages/us/clivecussler/news3.html.

Clive Cussler Forum. "Trailer for *The Oregon Files*": http://z4.invisionfree.com/CLIVE_CUSSLER/index.php?s=93f9817d37f7efd12507ec4e73196abf&showtopic=5131&st=12&#last.

Clive Cussler's *Oregon Files*: http://www.stunts911.com/images/Oregon_files_New_09.mov.

Cussler, Clive. http://www.bookreporter.com/authors/au-cussler-clive.asp.

_____. Interview. June 2001. http://www.cusslermen.com/Characters.htm.

"Dale Messick—Adding My Voice to the Many." http://www.mikegrell.com/feature-messick.jsp.

Davis, John Renfro. "Gary Owen." http://www.contemplator.com/ireland/gowen.html.

Dick Foran. http://en.wikipedia.org/wiki/Dick_Foran.

Dirk Pitt Is Saved by Al Giordino. http://sh1.webring.com/people/xh/hn4dpitt/moments.htm.

Doppelgänger. http://en.wikipedia.org/wiki/Dopelg%C3%A4nger.

Drew's Script-o-rama. http://www.script-o-rama.com.

Dumas, Alexandre. http://www.answers.com/topic/alexandre-dumas.

Enchanted Forest. http://en.wikipedia.org/wiki/Enchanted_forest.

"Episode Guide: *Voyage to the Bottom of the Sea*." http://www.vttbots.com/episode_central.html.

Farley, Fred. "Gold Cup Class Revisited." http://www.thunderboats.org/history/history0160.html.

F.P.1 Doesn't Respond. http://www.dieselpunks.org/profiles/blogs/fp-1-doesnt-respond?xg_source=activity.

Fargo, ND. http://en.wikipedia.org/wiki/Fargo,_North_Dakota.

ffolkes. http://www.imdb.com/title/tt0081809/.

Forgotten Titanic. http://www.allatsea.co.za/santarosa.htm.

"Forty-Four Turkish Fairy Tales: 'The Snake-Peri and the Magic Mirror.'" http://www.sacred-texts.com/asia/ftft/ftft34.htm.

HAL 9000: http://en.wikipedia.org/wiki/HAL_9000.

"Harriman Nelson." http://en.wikipedia.org/wiki/Harriman_Nelson.

Hollow Earth. http://en.wikipedia.org/wiki/Hollow_Earth.

"H.P. Lovecraft and His Lasting Impact on Cinema." http://www.denofgeek.com/movies/18189/hp-lovecraft-and-his-lasting-impact-on-cinema.

"I Spy—The Museum of Broadcast Communication." http://www.imdb.com/title/tt0058816/.

I Spy. http://en.wikipedia.org/wiki/I_Spy_(1965_TV_series).

I Spy. http://www.imdb.com/title/tt0058816/.

International Thriller Writers. http://thrillerwriters.org/join-itw/uso-tour/.

Janus. http://en.wikipedia.org/wiki/Janus.

Journey to the Center of the Earth. http://en.wikipedia.org/wiki/Journey_to_the_center_of_the_earth.

"Jung Archetypes." http://www.jcjc.cc.ms.us/faculty/humanities/pwedgeworth/JungArchetypes.htm.

"Just Tell Him Irv Sent You: In Memory of Irv Novick." http://www.mikegrell.com/feature-novick.jsp.

Kemprecos, Paul. About. http://www.paulkemprecos.com/About_Paul.html.

_____. Home Page: http://www.paulkemprecos.com/Home_Page.html.

Lady Paget Walburga. http://en.wikipedia.org/wiki/Walburga,_Lady_Paget.

Levesque, Marc. "Interview with Dr. Clive Cussler." http://www.time2watch.net/cusslerinterview.htm.

Looms. http://en.wikipedia.org/wiki/Loom.

Lost World (genre). http://en.wikipedia.org/wiki/Lost_World_(genre).

Lovecraftian Horror (genre). http://en.wikipedia.org/wiki/Lovecraftian_horror.

Marquis de Rarignac. "Scrutinizing Varney the Vampire, Making Sense." http://www.onthevampire.com/On_The_Vampire/Scrutinising_Varney_the_Vampire%3A_Making_Sense.html.

Michael Dunn. http://en.wikipedia.org/wiki/Michael_Dunn_(actor).

National Treasure. http://boxofficemojo.com/movies/?id=nationaltreasure.htm.

National Treasure. http://en.wikipedia.org/wiki/National_Treasure_(film).

National Treasure. http://www.imdb.com/title/tt0368891/.

National Treasure. http://www.the-numbers.com/movies/2004/NATTR.php. http://nationaltreasure.wikia.com/wiki/Benjamin_Franklin_Gates#Biography.

National Treasure: Book of Secrets. http://en.wikipedia.org/wiki/National_Treasure:_Book_of_Secrets#cite_note-BOM-1.

National Treasure: Book of Secrets. http://www.box

officemojo.com/movies/?id=nationaltreasure2.htm.
North Sea Hijack. http://en.wikipedia.org/wiki/Ffolkes_(film).
NUMA Files Series. http://www.paulkemprecos.com/NUMA_Files_Series.html.
On Her Majesty's Secret Service (Soundtrack). http://en.wikipedia.org/wiki/On_Her_Majesty%27s_Secret_Service_(soundtrack).
Perlmutter. http://en.wikipedia.org/wiki/Perlmutter.
Plusfilm Services. http://plusfilm.com/credits.php?c=2005%20SAHARA#credits/2005 SAHARA/1 SAH.jpg.
Quipu. http://en.wikipedia.org/wiki/Quipu.
Raiders of the Lost Ark. http://www.imdb.com/title/tt0082971/trivia.
Rat (zodiac). http://en.wikipedia.org/wiki/Rat_(zodiac).
"Redheads." http://www.facebook.com/clivecussler?ref=ts#!/photo.php?v=10100497096865792
Richards, Casey. Tvdvdreviews.com: *Banacek*: http://en.wikipedia.org/wiki/Banacek.
"The Rime of the Ancient Mariner." http://www.bartleby.com/101/549.html.
Sabatini, Rafael. "Swashbuckling Hero the World Forgot" by David Charters. http://icliverpool.icnetwork.co.uk/expats/localhistory/tm_objectid=14211800%26method=full%26siteid=50061%26page=1%26headline=swashbuckling-hero-the-world-forgot-name_page.html.
Sacrificial Lamb. http://en.wikipedia.org/wiki/Sacrificial_lamb.
"Soc" Series. http://www.paulkemprecos.com/Soc_Series.html.
Sahara. http://www.imdb.com/title/tt0318649/&http://www.imdb.com/title/tt0318649/trivia?tab=gf.
Saint Julian.http://en.wikipedia.org/wiki/Saint_Julian.
Saint-Julien. http://en.wikipedia.org/wiki/St_Julien.
Senses of Cinema. "Howard Hawks." http://archive.sensesofcinema.com/contents/directors/02/hawks.html
Shprintz, Janet. "Sahara Trial Heating Up: Cussler Camp Accused of Inflating Sales Figures." http://www.variety.com/article/VR1117958535.html?categoryid=22&cs=1.
_____. "Sahara's Cussler Draws Line in Sand: Author Takes Stand in Crusader Case." http://www.variety.com/article/VR1117959458?refCatId=1.
Site Map, Dirk Pitt. http://sh1.webring.com/people/xh/hn4dpitt/sitemap.htm,
Skartaris. http://en.wikipedia.org/wiki/Skartaris.
The *Skipper*. http://www.reocities.com/jjnevins/pulpss.html.
The *Skipper* #10. http://tricky-manofbronze.blogspot.com/2011/05/12-skipper-cap-fury.html.
Snider, Clifton. "A Brief Outline of Jungian Psychology with Some Archetypal Images, Themes, and Symbols." http://www.csulb.edu/~csnider/jungian.outline.html.
Spy Guys & Gals. "John Taft." http://www.spyguysandgals.com/sgShowChar.asp?ScanName=Taft_John
"Star Trek." http://en.wikipedia.org/wiki/Star_Trek.
Star Trek: The Motion Picture. http://boxofficemojo.com/movies/?id=startrek.htm.
Star Trek: The Wrath of Khan. http://boxofficemojo.com/movies/?id=startrek2.htm.
Star Wars: A New Hope (Episode IV). http://boxofficemojo.com/movies/?id=starwars4.htm.
Submarine Voyage. http://en.wikipedia.org/wiki/Submarine_Voyage.
http://www.supershadow.com/star_wars/production_budget_how_much_cost_to_make_costs/starwars_budget_cost_make.html.
Swaim, Don. Interview with Clive Cussler (January 30, 1986). http://wiredforbooks.org/clivecussler/index.htm.
Trickster. http://en.wikipedia.org/wiki/Trickster.
Unbreakable. http://www.imdb.com/title/tt0217869/quotes.
U.S. Naval Station Tutuila. http://en.wikipedia.org/wiki/United_States_Naval_Station_Tutuila.
Voyage to the Bottom of the Sea. http://en.wikipedia.org/wiki/Voyage_to_the_Bottom_of_the_Sea_(TV_series).
Walter Siegmeister. http://en.wikipedia.org/wiki/Raymond_W._Bernard.
Washington Star. http://en.wikipedia.org/wiki/Washington_Star.
WikiLeaks.
"WikiLeaks Art Exposé: U.S. Tried to Trade Sunken Gold for Nazi Loot." http://www.artinfo.com/news/story/36553/wikileaks-art-expos-us-tried-to-trade-sunken-gold-for-nazi-loot/.
The Wild, Wild West. http://en.wikipedia.org/wiki/The_Wild_Wild_West.
"*The Wild, Wild West*: A Title & Episode Guide." http://epguides.com/WildWildWest/.

Interviews

Cussler, Clive. Unpublished interview, 1985.
Grell, Mike. "Mike Grell," COMICS INTERVIEW #69, pp. 22–44.
_____. "Mike Grell, Freelance: Jon Sable's Creator On His Days of Independence," from *Comic Book Artist* #8, http://twomorrows.com.comicbooksartist/articles/08grell.html.
Jones, Steve Philip. *Dracula: An Illustrated Adaptation*. Calabasas, CA: Malibu Graphics, 1990.
_____. *Curious Cases of Sherlock Holmes*. San Diego: IDW, 2012.
_____. *Sherlock Holmes: The Case of the Twisted Minds*. Detroit: TransFuzion, 2009.
_____. *Worlds of H.P. Lovecraft, Vol. I & II*. Detroit: TransFuzion, 2008, 2009.

Paglia, Camille. "My Conversation with Camille Paglia," *Limbaugh Letter*, Vol. 8, #10, October 1999, pp. 10–14.

Sowell, Thomas. "My Conversation with Thomas Sowell," *Limbaugh Letter*, Vol. 16, #6, June 2007, pp. 8–12.

Parodies

Beard, Henry and Christopher Cerf. "Moby-Dick II: Raise the Pequod!"

Book of Sequels. New York: Random House, 1990, pp. 93–122.

Short Stories

Bradbury, Ray. "Hail and Farewell." *The Golden Apples of the Sun*. New York: Bantam, 1970.

Tuttle, Wilbur C. "The Buckaroo of Blue Wells," *Adventure*, Vol. 60, No. 4, November 23, 1926.

_____. "The Cross in a Box Mystery," *Adventure*, Vol. 82, No. 1, March 15, 1932.

_____. "The Ranch of the Tombstone," *Adventure*, Vol. 38, No. 3, December 30, 1922.

Thesis

Burzrlova, Leoná. "The Spy Novel in English Literature." Masaryk University Faculty of Education, 2010.

Correspondence

Cussler, Clive
Grell, Mike
Legget, Paul A.
Murray, Will
Scheer, Andy
Scheulen, Mike (a.k.a., Captain Sparrow)
Slater, Pete
Smith, Jonathan
Valero, Wayne

Index

The A-Team (TV series) 109
Abbott and Costello Meet Frankenstein (film) 227n161
abduct 32, 36, 45, 46, 58 82, 87, 89, 138, 152, 160, 177, 181, 188, 208n21, 236n96, 236n97
Abraham (Biblical patriarch) 48, 228n192
AC Cobra 176
Academy Awards 185; *see also* Oscars
Achilles (legend) 88, 229n241; *see also* Hector; Paris
acoustic waves 82
Action Figures: Men, Action and Contemporary Adventure Narratives (book) 5, 66
action hero 67–8, 211n32; *see also* criminals, bureaucratic; ethics hero; power monger; "Wonks and Warriors: Depictions of Government Professionals in Popular Films"
adaptation 5, 6, 17, 59, 154, 155, 164–182, 185, 190, 195n10, 196n35, 199n40, 204n19, 207n4, 212n74, 217n178, 235n48, 237n2, 238n31
Admiral Byrd 83
Admiral Heibert 72; *see also* Von Til, Bruno
adventure 1, 3, 7, 9, 10, 16, 18, 19, 20, 21, 23, 24, 26, 27, 28, 29, 31, 32, 33, 34, 44, 45, 46, 47, 48, 49, 50, 52, 57, 58, 72, 73, 79, 80, 81, 86, 89–91, 95, 96, 97, 98, 99, 103, 104, 105, 106, 107, 108, 109, 110, 111–28, 130, 144, 145, 146, 149, 151, 152, 158, 160, 166, 167, 169, 171, 173, 177, 180, 181, 182, 184, 185–6, 191, 192, 194, 195n6, 196n35, 196n9, 199n13, 200n62, 201n111, 203n224, 205n82, 206n89, 206n93, 208n42, 212n63, 214n105, 218n233, 220n6, 221n62, 222n87, 222n103, 223n123, 223n18, 224n23, 226n157, 227n158, 227n183, 228n199, 229n222, 235n54, 235n59, 239n63, 242n126
adventure hero 4, 9–10, 11, 15, 95, 102, 170, 191, 199n 23, 221n57, 223n7, 226n157, 230n254, 235n59; creation in the 1960s and 1970s 12, 20, 21, 47, 103–8, 164; progression through generations 107–10; as proxy for reader 17, 64, 198n61; reflection of generation 91, 94–5, 97, 112, 219n2
The Adventure Writing of Clive Cussler (book) 22, 193, 196n9, 197n29, 198n50, 198n52, 198n56, 199n20, 201n116, 203n10, 204n29, 210n2, 220n26, 231–2n317, 238n31, 238n33, 240n85
adventurer 10, 13, 18, 20, 23–4, 51, 67, 69, 132, 182, 183, 200n55
The Adventurer: The Fate of Adventure in the Western World 23
adventurers to places close and far 96
"Adventures of Don Juan" (music) 179
Adventures of Hotsy Totsy (book) 45–47, 96, 150
The Adventures of Robin Hood (1938 film) 113
Adventures of Vin Fiz (book) 17, 43–47, 95, 150
Aegean Sea 87
Aegis-missile cruiser 41
affair (adultery) 57, 70, 170
Afghanistan 17
Africa 86, 100, 136, 137, 138, 139, 140, 172, 173, 174, 175, 178, 180, 240n73
African Army of Revolution (AAR) 70, 133, 134, 135, 136, 137, 138, 139, 140, 153, 230n275, 231n285
Age of Reason 80, 214n123
Agnus Dei 134, 141, 229n242; *see also* Bass, Adm. Walter Horatio; Jesus Christ; martyr; redeemer
aide-mémoires 121
Air Force Academy 12, 20, 26, 50, 179, 203n212, 204n17
Airport (film) 102, 167
Airport '77 (film) 167
Ajax 94, 196n10; White Knight campaign 10, 12, 94
Alain-Fournier 3
Alamo 39, 199n13
Alaska 55, 219n246; Cook Inlet 158
Albatross (airplane) 75, 147, 160
albatross 75, 160–1, 237n114
Albers, Han 182
Alcatraz Island 45, 46, 47
Alda, Alan 169
Alderaan 114
Alexander the Great 126
Alexandria, Egypt 174
Alexandria, Virginia 26
Álfheim 78
Alfred Hitchcock's The Birds (book) 6
Alhambra, California 10, 11; tuckers 159, 228–9n208, 229n210, 236n94
alias 39, 69, 71, 157, 227n163, 230n256

Alien (film) 182
All-Story Magazine (magazine) 47
All the President's Men (film) 67
Allard J2X (1953) 35
Allen, Irwin 103
Allen, Michael 24, 200n70; *see also* Schweikart, Larry
"Already Gone" (song) 161
alternate history (genre) 105
America 15, 23, 24, 45, 47, 48, 51, 55, 59, 61, 68, 71, 80, 83, 84, 88, 102, 103, 104, 105, 106, 112, 129, 130, 131, 136, 137, 138, 140, 141, 162, 165, 166, 167, 168, 169, 171, 175, 184, 187, 188, 189, 192, 197n47, 197–8n48, 203n224, 207n110, 210n17, 218n221, 220n21, 221n35, 222n86, 223n123, 228n191, 228n192, 228n205, 232n321, 236n76, 242n113; aristocracy and privileged class 12, 20, 215n137; troubles of 1960s and 1970s 14, 16, 17; *see also* North America; United States
American (U.S.) government 12, 21, 38, 40, 41, 48, 50, 59, 62, 66, 67, 68, 69, 104, 109, 126, 143, 168, 169, 171, 173, 175, 177, 180, 185, 186, 188, 199n17, 204n34, 211n34, 213n89, 218n201, 222n93, 222n99, 228n192, 228n206, 231n315, 238n25; chain of command 82, 87
American folklore 43
American Indian 24, 220n6, 222n86
American literature 28, 91, 95, 206n95, 220n14
"American Patrol" (song) 179
American Samoa 33, 96; *see also* Pago Pago; Tutuila Naval Station
Amie Marie (ship) 158, 159
Amity Island 170
amor fati 132
Ananka, Princess 183–4, 242n120
Ancient Mariner (submersible) 160
Anderson, Richard Dean 109
Andes 28, 89, 104
Andoheb (Professor) 183–4
Andursson, Golfur 125–6, 127, 226n130, 226n143, 226n145
Angel, Heather 27
USOS *Angler* 103, 222n92
anima 119, 128
Animated Movie Guide 242n127, 243n138
Annapolis 30
Anschutz, Philip 172, 180, 239n63

255

Index

Antarctic Snow Cruiser 83
Antarctica 28, 218n221; Antarctic Peninsula 159
Anthony, Bruno 157
anthropology 51, 55
anti-American 197–8n48
anti-Bureaucrat 211n32
anti-Communist 6
anti-hero 14, 108
anti-McCarthyism 6
antique 11, 21, 34, 39, 49, 83, 85, 106, 147
Antonov, Georgi 66
Apartheid 70, 140, 231n289; post-apartheid 231n311
The Apartment (film) 102
Apartment 3-G (newspaper strip) 164
Apollo 13 (film) 130
Apophis 80
apotheosis 111, 113, 117, 124, 127, 128, 129, 130; see also Iceberg
Apple (corporation) 103
Aquatic Dive Center 12
Arabic language 42
archaeology 27, 34, 55, 56, 74, 85, 170, 184, 201n83, 297n122, 243n139
archenemy 57, 104, 208n37
Archer, Anne 169, 239n41
archetypes 35, 44, 114, 119, 142, 144, 189; see also Jung, Carl
Archibald, Dana 169–71; see also Seagram, Dana
"Archival Image in Fiction: An Analysis and Annotated Bibliography" (article) 4
Arctic 100, 101, 103, 104, 167
Argo (ship) 39
argon laser scanner 51, 207n115
The Argosy (magazine) 47
Argyle, Nolan J. 4, 66–7, 197n37, 210n11, 210n13, 210n14; see also Merwin, Gerald A.
Arizona 60, 156, 165, 193
Arlington, Virginia 133
Armstrong, Louis 155
Army and Navy Club 29
Arsenic and Old Lace (film) 98
Arthur, King 144, 229n241
Arthur Conan Doyle (book) 91
artificial intelligence 84, 217n179
USS *Arvada* 204n30
Arvada, Colorado 14, 21, 193, 203n218
As Time Goes By (unfinished manuscript) 94
Ashkenazi Jewish 31–2
Asian 62, 154, 243n140
Asquith, Herbert Henry 141–2
assassin 14, 60, 61, 68, 87, 104, 124, 127, 144, 150, 177, 179, 200n52
Asselar Oasis 174, 179, 240n69; see also cannibal; Gollum
At the Mountains of Madness (book) 79
Ataman Explorer I (ship) 31
Atlantic Ocean 74, 95, 115, 128, 130, 149, 166, 173, 177, 182, 188, 202n151; North Atlantic 71, 112, 128, 165, 184
Atlantis 78, 82, 86, 95, 150, 185, 186, 187, 224n39, 242n126, 243n135, 243n136, 243n137, 243n138, 243n140, 244n3; see also lost civilization; Opar; Skartaris; *The Warlord*
Atlantis Found (book) 17, 25, 26, 28, 31, 36, 37, 56, 57, 61, 83, 103, 145, 150, 160, 186, 224n39, 226n119, 244n150
Atlantis Hotel (Dubai) 181, 241n107
Atlantis: Milo's Return (film) 242n127
Atlantis: The Lost Empire (film) 164, 185–7, 190, 242n127, 243n131, 243n138, 243n139; see also Heart of Atlantis; leviathan; *The Shepherd's Journal*
Atomic Energy Commission 33
Atonement (monomyth) 113, 120, 124, 135, 145, 227n172
Auburn limousine (1925) 11
audaciousness 37, 39, 156, 180; style of Cussler's adventures 96, 104, 107, 108, 180, 185, 215n144; see also unpredictability
AudioBooksToday.com 37, 204n33
Augustine Island 158, 159
Aurora, Illinois 10
Austin, Kurt 16, 26, 31, 38–9, 40, 42, 43, 48, 49, 50, 52, 64, 66, 67, 68, 71, 85, 96, 97, 99, 105, 107, 160, 162, 192, 201n83, 203n2, 203n9, 204n18, 204n19, 204n25, 210n9, 215n144, 234n36, 237n121, 242n116; Doe, John 39; special projects director 203n9
Australia 159, 173, 175, 207n17
"Autumn" (song) 73
The Autumn Garden 51
Avions Voisin (1936) 175
Awakening of the Self (monomyth) 115–6
The Awful Truth (1937 film) 91
Axis 80, 96

Baby the RSV (remote-search vehicle) 83, 160
backgammon 143
bad boy adventures 52, 105, 147, 219n256
bad guy 25, 46, 71, 89, 98, 130, 141, 147, 180, 185, 206n82, 208n42, 215n144, 217n177, 237n121
bad seed 69
badinage 26; see also banter
Baggins, Bilbo 114, 121–2, 225n75, 225n105
Baker Street 116, 210n80
Baker Street Irregulars 193
Balaam's talking ass 135
"Balance of Terror" (TV episode) 106
Balboa, Rocky 86
Balboa Club 129
Balboa Island, California 26, 65
Baldwin, Bruce 91, 219n265
ballistic missiles 103, 183, 238n28
Banaceck (TV series) 32, 109
Banaceck, Thomas 32, 107
Bandit 104
Bank of America 94
Banning, Steve 184, 242n121
Bannon, Roger "Race" 104

Bantam 29
Bantam Books 15, 198n51, 198n7, 208n49
banter 26, 40, 52, 97, 105, 106, 169, 176, 185, 201n87, 222n108; see also badinage
banty 29
baptism 136, 218n216, 230n274
Barbera, Joseph 104, 222n99; see also Hanna, William; Hanna-Barbera
Barbie doll 89
Baretta (TV series) 109
Baretta, Anthony Vicenzo "Tony" 109, 223n118
Barracus, Sgt. First Class Bosco "B.A." 109
Barry, John 155, 161, 166, 190, 237n117, 238n22; see also Raise the Titanic (film)
Bartha, Justin 188
Barton, Judy 157, 235–6n75
Barton, Prof. Preston 70
Barton gang 49
Basehart, Richard 103
Basic Patterns of Plot (book) 86, 199n13, 217n180, 226n138, 233n6, 234n32, 234n34; see also Foster-Harris, William
Basil 105, 150, 242–3n130; see also sea serpent
Bass, Adm. Walter Horatio 134, 135, 139, 140, 141, 144, 145, 188, 229n243, 230n246, 230n247, 230n248, 230n253, 232n322; see also Agnus Dei; Jesus Christ; martyr; redeemer
The Bat People (film) 167
Bateen, King 174, 241n87
Bates, Norman 156, 157, 185; see also Perkins, Anthony
Bates Motel 156
bathysphere, renovated 83
Batman (comic book series) 208n42
Batman (TV series) 222n23
The Batman 62, 98, 120, 130, 208n42
Batman and Me (book) 208n42
Battlestar Galactica 109, 223n119
Bay of Monterrey 174, 175
Bay of Pigs 14
Beacon Hill 107
Bean, Sean 188
"Beauty and the Beast" (fairy tale) 115, 212n66
Beauty and the Beast (1991 film) 185, 227n184
Beijing, China 41
Belford, Christine 107
Bell, Dr. Joseph 9
Bell, Isaac (Isaac Bell Detective series) 17, 47–50, 51, 52, 62, 64, 70, 71–2, 81, 85, 88, 96, 97, 99, 100, 105–6, 150, 152, 163, 192
Bell (Morgan), Marion 49, 51
Bellamy, Ralph 91
Bellisario, Donald P. 109, 223n120, 223n126
belly of Hell 138–40, 231n299; see also Hades
Belly of the Whale (monomyth) 112, 113, 116, 224n44, 225n57

Belmont, Hurricane Dan 86
Belushi, James 190, 244n154
Belyaka, Oskar 87, 234n42
Ben Abbott series 17
Benchley, Peter 168, 170, 229n209
Bender, John 77
Bender, Kate 77
benefit others 23, 122, 132, 139
Benin Navy 176
USS *Benjamin Franklin* 31
Bennedict, Dirk 223n119, 109
bent heroes 67, 208n46
Beowulf 118, 200n55
Beowulf (poem) 213n98
Berlin Wall 14
Bermuda Triangle 23
Bernice Pauahi Bishop Museum of Polynesia Ethnology and Natural History 85
Bernstein, Carl 67
Bernstein, Mr. 201n96
Best Seller Show Case 164, 165
Bestgen, Leo 11–2, 51
Bestgen & Cussler 11–2
Big Bad Wolf 77, 126, 227n160, 227n164; *see also* spirit quest, shamanistic
Big Jake (film) 47
Big John Deep Sea Mining Vehicle (DSV) 21, 83, 105, 237n120
Bigalow 65, 80, 149, 165, 166, 171, 190, 228n197, 233n10, 236n89; *see also* Ross, Sandra
Bigger Than Life: The Creator of Doc Savage 23
Bilko, Ernie 11
Birch, Harvey 206n95
Birds of the West Indies 11
"Black Cat" (short story) 80, 216n148
Black Rain (book) 16
Black Sea 39
Black Sun (book) 16
Black Wind (book) 17, 56, 81, 102, 160, 193
Blackwood, Grant 17, 50
Blackwood, Lord Henry 50, 208n43
Blake, Robert 109
Blakeney, Sir Percey 69
Blaylock, Winston Lloyd 52
bless 124, 125–6, 127, 227n172
Blofeld, Ernst Stavros 57, 80, 154, 208n37
Blofeld Trilogy 57, 208n38
Blood, Capt. Peter 96
bloods 95
Bloom, Clive 79, 103, 106, 107, 110, 196n35, 215n125, 215n138, 222n81
Bloomfield, Dr. Shelley Costa 79, 214n123
Blue Gold 39, 46, 150, 160, 162, 216n164
BMW 740 il (automobile) 31
The Body Snatchers (book) 6
Bogart, Humphrey 11, 98, 199n19, 200n51
Boland, Paul 22, 225n63
Bolle, Frank 164, 166, 237n2, 237n3, 238n11, 238n12
Bolshevik 126
Bombay Gin 11

bon vivant 32, 33, 225n92
Bonaparte, Napoleon 77, 243n140; wine bottles 52; *see also* Grand Army
Bond, James (007) 1, 10, 11, 12, 19, 20, 25, 37, 51, 53, 57, 60, 62, 73, 80, 83, 86, 94, 105, 106, 107, 110, 130, 141, 143, 152, 154, 164, 167, 180, 181, 185, 212n66, 218n215, 219n2; *see also* Fleming, Ian; Shaw, Brian
Bond (Di Vicenzo), Teresa "Tracy" (Countess) 73, 86, 154
Bond films 167, 180, 208n38, 222n3
Bones, Dr. Leonard "Bones" 106
The Book of Sequels (book) 189
Boone, Daniel 24
The Bootlegger (book) 47
Borjin, Tolgoi 162
Borneo Jungle Incepus 11
borrowing 60, 76, 88, 152, 153, 154, 156, 157, 161, 163, 187, 215n139, 233n12, 234n32, 234n45, 235n57
bosom 53, 217n190; breasts 36, 123, 131, 229n224; cleavage 75
The Boss 45, 46, 234n25
Boston, Massachusetts 49, 70, 106
Boston College 50
Botticelli, Sandro 133, 229n224; *see also* Venus
bougainville (flower) 140; 153
Bougainville, (Madam) Min Koryo 69; *see also* Koryo, Min
Bougainville Maritime Lines Incorporated 69
Bowden, Mark 17
"The Bowmen" (short story) 78
box office 108, 164, 166, 167, 172, 179, 185, 187, 217n7–8n48, 239–40n64, 244n156
boxer 40, 60, 162; boxing 20, 50
Boy Scout 4, 39, 90, 98, 125, 169, 197, 191, 237n113
Boyd, Felix 95
boyhood 10, 52, 159, 228–9n206
boy's adventure tale 46
Brackett, Leigh 101
Bradbury, Ray 33, 82, 84, 223–4n22
Brady Air Field 112, 147, 160
Brain 190; *see also* Pinky
brainwash 59, 104, 209n65, 217n178; memory transfer process 87–8
Branson, Sir Richard 188
brass pounder 9, 96; *see also* telegrapher
Bravo, Danny 104
Breakfast at Tiffany's (1961 film) 155, 219n266
Brennan, Walter 101
Brewster, Joshua Hays 76, 80, 149, 165–6, 168, 215–6n45, 216n146, 227n181, 228n204, 233n10, 236n89, 239n39, 239n51
Briar-rose, Princess 73–4
Brickley, Lt. John "Brick" 16, 100
Briggs, Marlin "Spike" 96
Briggs Tanner series 17, 50
Britain/British 15, 24, 66, 95, 184, 188, 195n22, 200n70, 206n93, 207–8n17, 225n90, 239–40n64, 244n144; field marshal 148; government 66, 143; penal colony 159;

prime minister 87, 143; *see also* Kitchener, Lord H.H.
British club man 12
British Museum 220n9
British Prime Minister 87, 143
British Royal Navy 42, 135, 215n143
British Secret Service 21, 37, 87, 142, 143
Broccoli, Albert R. "Cubby" 167, 241n104
Brodie, Lea 185
Brody, Ellen 170
Brody, Martin (Sherriff) 67, 108, 170
Brogan, Martin 66
Bronson, Charles 108
Brontë, Emily 80
Brooklyn, New York 71, 184
Brosnan, Pierce 67
brother 26, 29, 31, 34, 35, 45, 57, 72, 74–5, 88, 95, 97, 104, 118, 124, 144, 180, 201n119, 221n59, 223n22
brother-in-arms 80, 105, 106, 147, 180, 184, 223n121; brothers from different mothers 26; brotherhood 27, 28, 91, 187; *see also* buddy-in-color
Brown, Graham 16, 37
Brown, Sandra 17
Brozo, William G. 4, 5
Brundin, Bo 168
Brunhilda 83; *see also* computers and supercomputers; Hermit Limited's computers; Hope; Max
Buchan, John 94, 195n22
Buckley Field, Colorado 134
buddy-in-color 27–8, 38, 40, 91, 104, 188; avenging angel 28; *see also* brother-in-arms
Budweiser 94
Buenos Aires, Argentina 31
Bugs Bunny 191
Built for Adventure: The Classic Automobiles of Clive Cussler and Dirk Pitt (book) 21, 193
Bulfinch's Mythology (book) 209n63, 214n116
Bulldog Drummond's Revenge (film) 27
Bulldog Drummond's Secret Police (film) 27
Bunting, Glenn F. 172, 239n64
bureaucrat 12, 14, 21, 42, 63, 66, 67, 68, 104, 106, 177, 211n32, 238n26
Burr, Raymond 157
Burroughs, Edgar Rice 7, 153, 160, 187, 224n49, 243n136, 243n137
Bushido code 95
Butcher Boy series 17
Butera, Carzo 71, 127, 215n159, 227n163; *see also* Rondheim, Oskar
Butera, Comm. Scotty 71
Byronic hero 169, 170, 239n40
byzanium 76, 80, 100, 105, 129, 130, 131, 132, 140, 149, 161, 165, 167, 168, 170, 171, 216n146, 222n94, 227n181, 228n204, 238–9n37, 239n43
Byzantine plan 58

Cabral, Francesca 160, 204n18
Cabrillo, Amy 42, 205n51

Cabrillo, Juan (historical figure) 42, 205n49
Cabrillo, Juan Rodriguez ("Chairman") 16, 37, 40–3, 48, 49, 50, 52, 64, 67, 77, 96, 99, 107, 160, 162, 180, 181, 186, 192; *see also* Flood Tide; Oregon Files
Cadillac 83
Caesarea, Israel 148
Cage, Nicolas 108, 187, 207n108
Cagney, James 98
Caiden, Martin 216n171
Cairo, Egypt 56, 184
Cairo Museum 184
Calais, France 45
"Calcutta Adventure" (TV episode) 105
Calhoun, Jack 95
California 12, 21, 23, 32, 42, 43, 49, 50, 52, 56, 70, 113, 126, 128, 159, 184, 228–9n208
call to adventure 111, 112, 113, 114, 115, 123, 189
Callahan, "Dirty" Harry 14, 108
Calliope (ship) 175, 176, 177, 179, 240n73, 241n99
Caltech 50, 52
Cambridge University 148
Cameron, James 1, 233n15
Camp Perry 50
Campbell, Joseph 27, 57, 58, 73, 80, 111, 113, 115, 116, 119, 120, 145, 201n109, 212n63, 212n69, 223n3, 223n12, 224n26, 224n37, 224n44, 224n54, 225n57, 226n151, 226n157, 228n202, 231n299; *see also* The Hero with a Thousand Faces
Campbell, Louise 27
The Campus 181
Canada 68, 70, 188; *see also* North America
Canadian Parliament 61, 66, 144
Canadian television 16
Cancer (zodiac) 62, 196n13
cancer 17, 62
cane 32, 106
Caniff, Milton 104
Cannady, Marilyn 23
Cannell, Stephen J. 108, 109, 223n118, 223n120
cannibal 3, 84, 121, 174; *see also* Asselar Oasis; Gollum; *28 Days Later*; zombie
Cannon, Patty 77–8
Cape Cod, Massachusetts 39
Čapek, Karel 82
Capernaum 134
Capesterre, Paul 211n43
Capesterre, Robert ("Topiltzin") 65, 162, 211n43
Capesterre family 59, 61
capitalism 16, 197n47; not wicked in Cussler's adventures 63
Capitol Hill 36, 133
Caplin, Elliot 164, 166, 238n11
Capone, Al 45, 46, 230n250
Capra, Frank 98, 102, 103, 220n34, 221n47, 221n48; Capra hero 98–9; Capra heroine 99
Capricorn (ship) 165

Capstick, Peter 153
Captain Ahab 189
Captain Hook 115, 125, 127, 224n23
Caratal, Monsieur Louis 155
Caribbean Joint Task Force 28
Caribbean 104, 229n209, 232n329
Carl (*Sahara* film) 175, 179, 241n102
carnival 137
The Carpetbaggers (book) 163
Carr, Paul 167
carriage house, renovated 32
Carrier Pigeon (helicopters) 83
Carroll, Charles 187, 243n142, 244n143
cartel 59, 71, 90
Carter, John 186
Carter, Nick 47, 64, 96, 107, 199n18, 206n92
Casablanca (film) 21, 98, 200n51
The Case of Charles Dexter Ward (book) 80, 213n86, 235n48
The Casey and Lacey Nicefolk adventures (fiction series) 43, 45, 85, 150, 234n25
Cash, Johnny 3
Casilighio, Arta 72, 76, 80 155–8, 212n59, 216n159, 236n80, 236n89; *see also* Crane, Marino; Wallace, Estelle
Casino Royale (book) 94, 152, 208n21
Casio, Sal 37, 79, 80, 234n42, 235n73, 236n80
"The Cask of Amontillado" 80
Cassidy, Hopalong 79, 97
Castle of Otranto 79, 214n123, 215n140
Castro, Fidel 55, 66
Castroville, California 43
catamaran 34, 44
Catawaba (Coast Guard supercutter) 22, 71, 112, 147, 158, 159, 224n51
cathedral, Romanesque 3, 7
Catherick, Anne 72; *see also* Fairlie, Laura
Caulden, Albert 148
Cavanah, Robert 173
Cayo Santa María (Cuba) 60, 83
Celt 61
celtinium–279 161, 222n94
Central America 155
Central Park, New York 100
Cerberus Corporation 62, 90
Chairweather, Adm. Charles "Chuck" 189
Challenger, Prof. George Edward 82, 185, 186; *see also* Conan Doyle, Sir Arthur; *The Lost World*
Chambers, Robert W. 80, 196n35
Chan, Jackie 26
Chance (*Rio Bravo* film) 101
Chaney, Lon, Jr. 227n161
chaos and order 157
character blueprint 18, 19, 64; *see also* Dent, Lester; "The Pulp Paper Master Fiction Plot"; "Wave Those Tags!"
characterization trick 18, 19, 25, 129, 201n83
Charles, Nick 20, 51–52
Charles, Nora 51–52

Charles Winthrop Agency 13, 197n43
Charleston, South Carolina 193
Charlotte (ship) 187, 188, 189, 244n150
Charon's Landing 16
Charteris, Leslie 5
Chase, Dr. Abigail 188, 189, 244n150
The Chase (book) 17, 46, 47–50, 53, 69, 70, 71, 72, 88, 105, 106, 152, 206n93, 206n97, 211n44, 242n128
chauvinism 89–91, 219n246
cheekbones: high 54, 56, 57, 208n29; prominent 35
Chengdo (Chinese destroyer) 41
Chesapeake Bay bugeye 96
chess 39, 131, 204n21, 213n83, 228n207
Chestley, Petty Officer Doris 189–90
Chevy Chase, Maryland 33
Chicago, Illinois 45
Chief of Staff (U.S. Navy) 28, 134
Chief of Staff (White House) 66, 210n9
The Chief 45, 46
Chigros (Jamaican Chinese-Negroes) 178
The Children's Hour (play) 51
China 26, 62, 63, 100, 176, 223n122
Chinese dynasty 62
Chinese slave smuggling 35, 63, 101, 160, 213n84
Chingachgook 28
Chitty Bang Bang 45; *see also* Chitty-Chitty-Bang-Bang: The Magical Car; Paragon Panther
Chitty-Chitty-Bang-Bang 45
Chitty-Chitty-Bang-Bang: The Magical Car (book) 45; *see also* Chitty Bang Bang; Paragon Panther
chivalry 9, 29, 218n227, 220n26; Code of Chivalry 94
cholera 49
Christianity 14, 28, 130, 134, 160, 201n119, 227n167
Christie, Agatha 1, 195n11
Chronicles of Narnia (fiction series) 45
Chronicles of Narnia (film series) 174, 239n63
Chrysler, Dr. Elmer 71
CIA 16, 39, 40, 41, 42, 50, 66, 67, 84, 131, 165, 167, 175, 180, 182, 190, 221n61, 228n205, 244n154
Ciannelli, Eduardo 183
Cinana, Capt. Orl 72, 234n39
"Cinderella" (fairy tale) 73
Cinema Seven Productions 184
Citizen Kane (film) 62, 201n96
"City Beneath the Sea" (TV episode) 103
Civil War (American) 105, 173, 178, 200n70; ironclad 86; reenactors 25, 80, 162
civilization 14, 17, 24, 27, 58, 83, 86, 105, 191, 218n233, 224n39, 242n120, 242n125, 243n140
Clancy, Tom 5, 18, 50, 82, 83, 197n37, 197–8n48, 210n11, 210n13, 210n14, 216n174, 219n264, 221n57, 221n62, 222n80, 236n92
Clandestine Service (CIA) 50

Index 259

Clark, John 221*n*57
Clarke, Arthur C. 84
classic automobiles 1, 5, 11, 175, 233*n*15
Clavering, Phyllis 27
cliché 21, 102, 106, 223*n*7
cliffhanger 5, 95, 165
Clift, Montgomery 101
CLIO Award 12
Clipperton Island 175
Clive, Colin 87
Clive, E.E. 27
USS *Clive Cussler* 190
Clive Cussler & Dirk Pitt Revealed 16, 37, 40, 84, 155, 197*n*41, 231–2*n*317
The Clive Cussler Code (book) 193
Clive Cussler Convention 193
Clive Cussler Society 193
Clubland Heroes (book) 94
clubmen 12, 94, 107, 219*n*2
Clute, John 82, 88, 218*n*233, 243*n*140
Coast Guard 28, 63, 71, 112, 158
code of conduct 135
Code of Courtly Love 94
code of honor 94, 95
codex 186
Cody, William "Buffalo Bill" 95–6
coincidence 32, 99, 133, 135, 136, 169, 180
Cold War 4, 39, 107, 130, 166, 167, 169
Coleridge, Samuel Taylor 160, 236*n*108
Collecting Cussler: An Ethical Approach (book) 193
collection 12, 20, 21, 26, 30, 35, 39, 42, 49, 51, 57, 73, 85, 176, 203*n*2; restoration 10, 38, 45, 49, 73
The Collector's Guide to Clive Cussler (book) 193
Collins, Felicia 36, 56, 65, 72, 92, 133, 136–8, 147
Collins, Quentin 216*n*147
Collins, Wilkie 72, 81, 192, 212*n*56, 215*n*126
Colorado 13, 133, 134, 154, 158, 172, 193, 204*n*17; seventh district 35, 203*n*218
Colorado Supreme Court 172
"The Colour Out of Space" (short story) 79
Colt .45 97, 139
Columbus, Christopher 39
comic books 64, 98, 153
communism and communists 14, 28, 124, 217*n*178
computers and supercomputers 31, 32, 83–4, 85, 87, 88, 107, 217*n*190, 230*n*251, 233*n*13, 238*n*36; *see also* Brunhilda; Hermit Limited's computers; Hope; Max
Conan Doyle, Sir Arthur 7, 11, 14, 38, 64, 82, 112, 155, 185, 191 *see also* Challenger, Prof. George Edward; Holmes, Sherlock; "The Lost Special"; *The Lost World*
Confederacy (U.S. Civil War) 32, 173, 175, 176, 177, 178, 180, 198*n*55, 200*n*70, 240*n*65
Confederate Navy 240*n*65
Congress 30, 62, 63, 92, 175

Connell, Richard 152–4, 222*n*101; *see also Dragon*; Ivan; "The Most Dangerous Game" Rainsford, Sanger; Ship Trap Island; Zaroff, General
Connery, Sean 214*n*107
Conrad, Robert 105
USS *Constitution* 162, 215*n*144, 237*n*121
Continental Op 12, 25, 69, 95
Continental slope 81
Cool Blue Tomb 16, 204*n*25
Cooney, Adm. David 168
Cooper, Gary 11, 98
Cooper, Jackie 104
Cooper, James Fenimore 24, 28, 203*n*224, 206*n*95
Corden, Wendy 52; *see also* Jeffcoat, Peter; Wondrash, Selma
The Corn-fed Amigos 94
Cornwell, Bernard 108
coronet 30, 73, 148
corporation 39, 41, 59, 67, 69, 76, 182, 204*n*33, 238*n*25
The Corporation 40, 41, 42, 67, 96, 150, 180, 181, 204*n*33, 205*n*47, 222*n*93, 236*n*97, 237*n*19; *see also Oregon Files*
Corrigan, Secret Agent 164
corruption: businessmen 61, 62, 63, 68, 69, 98, 129, 209*n*64, 242*n*113; clan corporations 69; governmental 98, 221*n*38; politicians 33, 61, 62, 63, 98, 129, 132; pubic servants 68
Corsair (book) 47, 202*n*148, 206*n*88, 217*n*194
corsair (ship) 127
Corvette split window (1963) 26
Cosby, Bill 28, 105
Costa Mesa, California 11, 12
Costain, Thomas B 10
Costello, Lou 227*n*161
Costner, Kevin 135, 230*n*250
Cotton, Joseph 102, 157
The Count of Monte Cristo (book) 135
countdown 147, 149, 152
cowboys 14, 33, 79, 96, 97, 101, 107, 108; *see also* pilot
Crabtree, Monica 41
Crack in the World (film) 82
Crane, Marion 156, 157, 158, 236*n*80, 236*n*86; *see also* Casilighio, Arta; Wallace, Estelle
creative ferment 6, 196*n*32
Crescent Dawn (book) 66, 147, 203*n*209, 203*n*213, 240*n*85
criminal clan 61, 62, 76, 209*n*65
Criminal Investigation Department (CID) 48
Criminal Mastermind 59, 62, 63, 106; *see also* Emperor of Crime; Grand Single; villain types
criminals, bureaucratic 67, 68; *see also* action hero; ethics hero; power monger; "Wonks and Warriors: Depictions of Government Professionals in Popular Films"
critic 4, 5, 6, 23, 27, 66, 79, 92, 93, 157, 166, 192, 195*n*11, 196*n*27, 197*n*48, 215*n*138, 221*n*63, 243*n*139; critical review 5, 6, 91, 172

Crockett, Davy 24
Cromwell, Jacob ("The Butcher Bandit") 62, 69–70, 71–2, 84, 88, 106, 152, 155, 157, 161, 211*n*44, 211*n*48, 237*n*118; *see also* Massey, Clement ("Dapper Doyle")
Cromwell, Margaret 69, 163
"Cross in the Box Mystery" (short story) 97
Crossing of the Return Threshold (monomyth) 111, 113, 126; *see also* Threshold of Return
Crossing of the Threshold (monomyth) 111, 116, 142, 224*n*44
Crusader Entertainment 17, 171–80, 186, 239*n*64, 240*n*68, 240*n*80, 240*n*81, 240*n*85, 241*n*102; Bristol Bay Productions 172, 174; Walden Media 172, 174, 239*n*63
Cruz, Penélope 174
cryptograms 52, 207*n*107
CSI (TV series and franchise) 38
Cub Scout 39
Cuba 28, 30, 40, 66, 82, 88, 128, 201*n*88, 209*n*63, 216*n*172, 240*n*84
Cuban Missile Crisis 14
Culp, Robert 28, 105, 109
"Curse of Anubis" (TV episode) 104
curses 74–6, 80, 187–9, 229*n*213
Curtis, Arthur 71, 207*n*100
Curtis, Dan 152
Cussler, Amy 10, 26
Cussler, Barbara (Knight) 9, 11, 15, 17, 203*n*198
Cussler, Clive 1, 4–7, 9–17, 18–31, 32, 34, 35, 36, 37, 38, 39, 40, 41, 42, 43, 44, 45, 46, 47, 47, 48, 49, 50, 51–2, 53, 54, 55, 56, 57, 58, 59, 60, 61, 62, 63, 64, 65, 66, 67, 68, 69, 71, 72, 74, 75, 76, 77, 78, 79, 80–2, 83, 84, 85, 86, 87, 88, 89, 90, 91, 92–3, 94, 95, 96, 97, 98, 99, 100, 101, 102, 103, 104, 105, 106, 107, 108, 110, 111, 112, 115, 116, 117, 118, 120, 122, 124, 125, 126, 127, 128, 129, 130, 131, 140, 143, 145, 146, 147, 148, 149, 150, 151, 152, 153–8, 159, 160, 161, 163, 164, 166, 167–8, 169, 170, 171, 172, 173, 174, 175, 176, 177, 178, 179, 180, 181, 182, 183, 184, 185, 186, 187, 188, 189, 190, 191, 192, 193, 194, 195*n*10, 195*n*12, 196*n*32, 196*n*34, 196*n*10, 196*n*13, 197*n*22, 197*n*23, 197*n*24, 197*n*26, 197*n*29, 197*n*41, 197*n*43, 198*n*50, 198*n*55, 198*n*56, 198*n*9, 198–9*n*10, 199*n*13, 199*n*20, 199*n*23, 200*n*62, 200*n*73, 200*n*74, 201*n*83, 201*n*92, 201*n*99, 201*n*107, 202*n*128, 202*n*185, 203*n*198, 203*n*206, 203*n*217, 203*n*224, 203*n*8, 204*n*19, 204*n*25, 204*n*28, 204*n*29, 204*n*30, 204*n*33, 205*n*42, 205*n*49, 205*n*56, 205*n*58, 205*n*64, 205*n*70, 205*n*81, 206*n*88, 207*n*119, 207*n*3, 207*n*14, 208*n*21, 208*n*29, 208*n*49, 209*n*63, 209*n*65, 209–10*n*80, 210*n*84, 210*n*2, 210*n*3, 210*n*8, 211*n*44, 212*n*52, 212*n*55, 212*n*69, 212*n*71, 212*n*74, 213*n*75, 213*n*85, 213*n*94, 214*n*119, 215*n*139, 215*n*143, 215–6*n*145,

260 Index

216n147, 216n162, 217n178, 217n192, 217n194, 219n246, 219n262, 219n264, 219n270, 219n275, 220n4, 220n26, 220-1n34, 221n35, 221n37, 221n57, 222n80, 222n86, 222n101, 222n108, 223n126, 224n28, 224n53, 225n73, 225n92, 225n95, 226n117, 226n128, 226n135, 225n145, 227n158, 227n160, 227n167, 227n180, 227n182, 227n183, 227–8n185, 228n190, 228n197, 228n199, 228n201, 228n206, 228n207, 228–9n208, 229n243, 230n254, 231n289, 231n307, 231–2n317, 232n231, 233n3, 233n8, 233n11, 233n12, 233n13, 233–4n15, 234n18, 234n32, 234n36, 234n37, 234n41, 235n56, 235n57, 236n79, 236n92, 236n93, 236n97, 237n113, 237n116, 237n117, 237n120, 237n126, 237n128, 237n3, 238n10, 238–9n37, 239n41, 239n43, 239n45, 239n57, 239n60, 239n63, 239n64, 240n68, 240n72, 240n76, 240n80, 240n81, 240–1n85, 241n96, 242n113, 242n123, 242–3n130, 244n151, 244n154, 244n3; Air Force service 11, 25; awards 9, 11, 12, 14, 94, 197n27; cameos 5, 44, 52, 150, 173, 190, 221n59; collaboration 16, 17, 37–8, 40, 46, 47, 50, 53, 82, 108, 145, 151, 193, 198n56, 217n194; education and honorary Ph.D. 10, 16, 34, 43–4, 48, 203n208; entertainer 65, 101; influence on modern heroes 107–110, 210n2; influences 23, 26, 53, 94–107, 110, 151, 156, 214n119, 220n34, 230n254, 234n41; The Kid 173; knee surgery 17; marketing 10, 11–2, 14, 51, 94, 103, 193, 194, 196n9, 197n22, 197n27, 234n24; Operation Thriller II 17; quintuple bypass operation 17; simpleminded at heart 6, 44; strong work ethic 10, 48; writing style 21, 79, 81, 151, 189, 234n40, 235n53
Cussler, Dana 9, 46, 177, 205n81; *see also* Mannock, Dana
Cussler, Dirk 9, 11, 17, 46, 56, 102, 205n81
Cussler, Eric 10, 26, 44, 48, 49, 202n185
Cussler, Teri 9, 46, 205n185
Cussler heroine 5, 35, 53, 54, 56, 93, 183, 188, 203n224, 207n119, 237n128; imperfection as character tag 54–6, 188; independent 36, 45, 51, 92, 94, 96, 98, 102, 163, 188, 203n223
Cussler Museum 21, 193, 199n31
Cussler villain 55, 57–63, 68, 69–72, 204n29
Cussleresque adventures 164, 182–9, 190, 242n113, 242n123
Cusslermen 193
Custom Super 8 convertible Packard 49
Cutty Sark 11, 136
cybernetics 87

Cyborg (book) 216n171
Cyclops 16, 24, 25, 28, 29, 30, 31, 55, 60, 61, 71, 73, 78, 81, 83, 85, 88, 128, 144, 150, 159, 162, 202n161, 202n166, 208n27, 209n56, 209n63, 210n84, 214n98, 216n172, 219n244, 220n19, 237n117
cynic 4, 22, 24, 33, 39, 43, 96, 99, 106, 129, 169, 185, 187, 199n40, 200n68, 201n97, 206n95, 227n171, 228n192

Daedalus 119
Daggat, Congressman Frederick 61, 66, 68, 72, 92, 132–4, 136–8, 145, 157, 219n258, 229n229, 230n272, 230n273, 231n291
Dagobah 77
Daily Variety (newspaper) 171
The Dain Curse (book) 79
Daley, Brian 108
Dalton, Harry 67
Daly, John Carroll 95
damsels in distress 14, 24, 79, 131, 213–4n98
Damsky (Chief Engineer) 182, 183
dandy 48, 69, 70, 71
Daniels, Norman 96
Danse Macabre (book) 6
Dantès, Edmund 135
Dante's Peak (film) 67
Danzler, Col. Henry 48, 49
D'arcy 12
Darius (Captain) 60, 208n21, 209n56, 234n39; *see also* Gly, Foss
dark descent 86–8, 118, 122, 131, 143, 146, 147, 186, 188, 189, 225–6n105; descent into darkness and disintegration 120
The Dark Knight Returns (film) 239n63
Dark Shadows (1966–1971 TV series) 152, 216n147, 235n68
Dark Watch (book) 40, 205n47
DARPA (Defense Advanced Research Projects Agency) 50
Darth Vader 114, 225n105
data mining 32
"Daus Mouse" (TV episode) 189–90, 244n154
David, Hal 155
David, Ziva 19–20
Davies, Jack 184
Davis, Frederick W. 95
DC Comics 1
Dead or Alive (book) 50
Death Eater 85
death ships 159
Declaration of Independence 187–8, 244n146
Deeds, Longfellow 98, 102
The Deep (book) 229n209, 237n126
Deep Encounter (ship) 160, 162, 208n27
Deep Fathom (submersible) 30, 149, 169
deep ocean geology 38
Deep Six (book) 13, 16, 21, 23, 35, 36, 51, 55, 66, 72, 73, 76, 80–4, 87–8, 92, 104, 150, 152, 159–61, 200n74,

201n87, 202n177, 203n220, 203n221, 209n65, 217n177, 217n178, 218n210, 219n246, 219n247, 223n126, 235n73, 236n89, 236n91, 236n96; parallels with *Psycho* 155–8
deep water white crab 190, 244n154
The Defiant Ones (film) 167
de Havilland, Olivia 113
de la Mare, Walter 80
Delaware-Maryland border 77
delay introduction 19, 25, 147, 150, 151, 201n83, 209–10n80, 227n181, 234n36
de Lernac, Herber 155, 235n66
Deliverance (film) 108
Delmarva Peninsula 77
DeMille, Cecil B. 173
democractic 106, 192
Democrat (political) 61, 98
Denny, Reginald 27
Dent, Lester 9–10, 18–19, 23, 64, 96, 151, 198n6, 198n9, 198–9n10, 234n33; *see also* character blueprint; "The Pulp Paper Master Fiction Plot"; Robson; Kenneth; Savage, Doc Clark; "Wave Those Tags!"
Denver, Burdette 30
Denver, Colorado 193
Denver Post 154–5
Department of Defense 167
Departure (monomyth) 113, 114–7, 118, 126, 131
Depp, Johnny 108, 235n50
derelict 41, 158, 159, 204n33
derringer 48
"Desolation Row" (song) 6, 196n32
detective 10, 14, 19, 48, 50, 66, 72, 95, 107, 108, 109, 198n5, 199n18, 206n91, 206n92, 223n118
detective fiction 9, 20, 47, 69, 72, 217n180; genre 79, 95, 98, 152, 215n138
"Detour to Nowhere" (TV episode) 107
Deuville-Hudson River bridge 78
De Vaal, Pieter 61, 66, 69, 132, 135–6, 138, 139, 140, 153, 211n42, 230n251, 230n255, 230n256, 230n257, 230n258, 230n260, 230n267, 230n278, 231n285, 231n287, 231n291
Devil (Satan) 135, 136, 137, 139, 208n42, 230n256, 230n267, 230n278, 231n287
Devil's Gate (book) 37
Devine, Phil 71, 98
diamonds 76; *see also* gemstones
Diaz, Sen. Mike 66
Dick Tracy (newspaper strip) 208n42
Dickstein, Morris 98–92, 221n48
Die Hard (film) 16
Die Hard (film franchise) 108
Digital Domain 181
dime novel 46, 47–8, 49, 50, 95–6, 193, 195n22, 206n91, 206n92
DiNozzo, Tony 19
Dionysus 137
Dirgo, Craig 16, 40, 41, 198n56, 204n34, 221n38, 231–2n317, 235n51, 236n97

dirigible 81
Dirk Pitt series (fiction series) 4, 7, 10, 15, 16, 17, 21, 22, 26, 30, 31, 32, 35, 38, 46, 52, 56, 57, 61, 62, 77, 100, 102, 105, 106, 108, 119, 125, 132, 140, 141, 145, 147, 150, 159, 160, 162, 171, 176, 177, 197n22, 199n23, 199n37, 201n109, 203n17, 209n63, 209n66, 210n84, 210n8, 212n63, 212n70, 213n75, 214n114, 215n144, 219n261, 221n57, 226n152, 227n180, 228n190, 229n210, 229n214, 234n36, 236n89, 236n96, 239n57, 239n59, 239n63, 240–1n85
Discovery 84
disguise 41, 42, 49, 60, 61, 62, 63, 69, 96, 105, 135, 137, 144, 175, 182, 205n43, 206n95, 211n41, 211n42, 215n137, 230n275, 230n276, 231n307, 232n347
Disney (film studio) 50, 158, 164, 185, 187, 207n108, 222n87, 243n140; Disney-Pixar 242n127
Disney, Walt 158
Disneyland 58, 77, 113, 126, 127
Disneyland Hotel 127, 128, 147, 160
Disneyland Submarine Voyage 185, 242n127
Distinguished Flying Cross 114
dithyrambs (choral songs) 137
Ditko, Steve 208n42
diver, professional 96
Divercity (ship) 71
Divine Star (ship) 159
Dixieland band 27
"Do Your Characters Fit Their Roles?" (article) 19, 199n11
Doc Ford series 108
Doc Savage (magazine) 18, 23
Doc Savage (radio series) 18
Doctor Hook 179
Dr. Jonsson *see* Jonsson, Dr.
Dr. Lavella *see* Lavella, Dr.
Doctor No 57, 70
Doctor No (book) 178
Dr. Robleman *see* Robleman, Dr.
Doctor Solar (comic book series) 164
Doctor Who (TV series) 109, 223n124
Dr. Zin *see* Zin, Dr.
Dodd, Jonathan 15, 198n50
Dodd, Mead 14, 15, 198n50
Dolan, Harvey 71
"Dolan's Cadillac" (short story) 236n68
The Domino Principle (book) 167
The Domino Principle (film) 167
Donavan, Guns 15
Donovan's Reef (film) 15, 94
Donner, Mel 71, 129,
Donovan's Brain (book) 242n113
Doodlebug (submersible) 83
Doom, Peter 96
The Doomfarers of Coramonde (book) 108
doppelgänger 72, 79, 81, 155
Dorsett, Arthur 22, 46, 54, 58, 76, 157, 207n17, 218n214
Dorsett, Boudicca 76, 140, 161, 162, 207–8n17, 218n214

Dorsett, Deirdre 76, 89, 92, 147, 207n17, 208n27
Dorsett Consolidated Mining Company 76
Dorsetts (family) 80, 154, 159
007 James Bond: A Report (book) 94, 208n37, 209n64, 219n2
doubles 144, 157; *see also* opposites
doubting Thomas 123
Douglas, Keith 88
Dove, George N. 6, 7, 196n29
Dover, Lt. Amos 22, 71
Downey, Robert, Jr. 105
Doxa dive watch 12, 25, 34, 49, 193, 197n34
Dracula (book) 19, 79, 81, 152, 168, 196n35, 215n125, 230n56
Dracula (1931 film) 168
Dracula, Count 58, 220n9, 227n166; Count de Ville 230n256
Dracula's castle 120
dragon 3, 7, 61, 111, 112, 118, 119, 122, 132, 212n65, 213n98, 224n32, 225n72, 231n287; artificial dragons 104
Dragon (book) 16, 20, 25, 26, 28, 33, 36, 56, 63, 80, 83, 90, 99, 103, 148, 150, 153, 155, 159, 160, 162, 199n17, 200n64, 200n73, 203n198, 203n212, 207n111, 210n82, 217n179, 218n221, 222n101, 222n108, 225n74, 225n92, 236n96, *see also* Dragon Center; "The Most Dangerous Game"
Dragon Center 26, 148, 153, 154; *see also* Dragon; Suma, Hideki
Dragonfish (submarine) 162, 238n25
"Dragons of Ashida" (TV episode) 104
Drake, Sir Francis 32; *see also Nuestra Señora de la Concepción*
dramatically right 168, 170
"Dreadful Doll" (TV episode) 104
dreads 95
dream landscape of symbolic figures 119, 121, 125, 135, 138
dreams 100, 119, 120–1, 142, 213n83, 214n109, 225n95; dream state 117
Dreams and Personality: A Study of Our Dual Lives (book) 128
Drew, Nancy 46
Dreyfus, Richard 108
Droste, Lt. 182-3
drugs 35, 46, 55, 106, 138, 156, 158, 236n97; drug smuggling 70, 136, 229n209
Druids 35, 61
Drummond, Bulldog 10, 12, 25, 27, 53, 94, 107, 110, 197n36, 208n37
Drummond, Florence (The Flame) 95
drunks 23, 49, 60, 101, 260n230; drunk driving 42
Drury, Jay 107
Dubai 181, 241n107
Dublin University Magazine 192
Du Brul, Jack 16, 17, 40, 42, 108, 217n194
Duckworth Drew 47; *see also* Sant, Gerry

"Ducky" Mallard 19
Dude 101; *see also* Martin, Dean
dueling pistols 39, 85
duets 51
Duke family (*Dukes of Hazzard* TV series) 46
Dumas, Alexandre 7, 152, 234n45
du Maurier, Daphne 79, 235n48
Dumbledore, Albus 86, 114, 214n105, 217–8n200
Dunn, Christopher 66
Dunn, Michael 106
Dunson, Thomas 101–2
Dupin, Chevalier C. August 38, 110
Dupree, Comm. Felix 23
DXS 109
Dylan, Bob 6, 196n32

The Eagle (ship) 81, 87, 218n209
Eagle Scout 10, 13
The Eagles 161
Earhart, Amelia 97
Earles, Jason 187
earth crust displacement 82
Earthmother (monomyth) 119, 123, 143, 225n79, 226n117
East Potomac Park 80
eastern European superstitions 79
Eastwood, Clint 108, 169
eccentric 19, 32, 38, 96, 105, 109, 162, 185, 186
Eclipse Comics 1
Eco Nova productions 16
Eden 135
Eden, Barbara 84
Edgar, Marnie 157-8
Edgar Award 50
Edison brass lamp 49
Edison cylinder phonograph 161
Edith Heron (book) 95
Edith the Captive (book) 95
Edo City 83, 183
Edwardian Era 112, 219n2
Edwards, Ethan 16, 100
Eeyore 135
Egan, Dr. Elmore 41, 162, 217n182
Egan, Kelly 56–7, 89, 90, 162, 208n27
ego 22, 23, 58, 123, 227n165; egocentric 34, 75, 85; egomaniac 62, 76; egotism 24, 34, 71
Egypt 55, 56, 59, 129, 174, 183, 184, 187, 229n241, 240n72, 243n140
The Einstein Papers (book) 40
Eisenhower, Dwight D. 66, 134
Eisner, Breck 177
El Dorado 78; *see also* La Dorada
Elcar, Dana 109
electrical-chemical engineer 96
"Eleven Days to Zero" (TV episode) 103
Eliade, Epona 61–2, 162, 209n66, 209n68; *see also* Spectre
Eliade, Mircea 61–2
Elisha 135, 230n257
Ellis, Sean 193
Ellissen (Major) 182-3
Elster, Madeline 157, 235–6n75
Emerald Dolphin (ship) 41, 217n194
Emerson, John 185
Emma 61, 69–70, 133, 136-7, 139–40,

211n40, 211n41, 211n42, 230n275, 230n276, 230n278, 231n307
Emperor of Crime 54, 59, 60, 62, 104; *see also* Criminal Mastermind; Grand Single; villain types
EMT 43, 192
enchanted forests and fairylands 46, 52, 72, 77–8; *see also* Neverland; Oz
Encyclopedia Brown 47
The End of Enemies (book) 50
England 14, 32, 43, 95, 112, 113, 132, 155, 165, 198n55, 206n95, 208n43, 212n66, 216–7n174, 225n90, 228n197, 241n91, 241n104, 242n113; *see also* Great Britain
English Channel 45
English Reformation 51
Enkidu 26, 201n91; *see also Epic of Gilgamesh*; Gilgamesh
USS *Enterprise* 41, 84, 106, 186, 217n194, 119n4
entomologist 7
environmental and conservation issues 89
Environmental Protection Agency 55
Epic of Gilgamesh (poem) 26, 77, 201n91, 226n136, 226n140; *see also* Enkidu; Gilgamesh
epidemiology 56
epilogue 47, 49, 114, 115, 146, 148, 149, 150, 152, 186, 233n13; *see also* prologue
episodic fiction 95
erotic 35, 57, 90, 127, 133
Escape (radio series) 155
Eskimo 160
espionage 47–8, 50, 82, 105, 110, 143, 183, 206n93, 242n113
Essex, Richard 66, 143, 162
Estes Park, Colorado 13
Esther, Ruth, and Jennifer (book) 184
the eternal return 61
ethics hero 63, 67, 68; *see also* action hero; criminals, bureaucratic; power monger; "Wonks and Warriors: Depictions of Government Professionals in Popular Films"
European stock market 49
Eurydice 86, 88
The Everything Guide to Edgar Allan Poe 214n123
evil empire 58, 76
Executive Decision (film) 236n76
Exodus, Book of 129, 229n192
The Exorcist (film) 108, 227n183
The Expendables (film) 67
external tags 18, 19, 20, 25, 30, 31, 32, 35, 42
eyes 11, 20, 26, 29, 30, 32, 33, 34, 35, 39, 40, 42, 43, 44, 48, 49, 54, 55, 56, 57, 59, 61, 62, 63, 65, 75, 76, 77, 95, 112, 118, 119, 121, 123, 127, 129, 133, 143–4, 151, 164, 176, 190, 199n21, 200n51, 202n166, 202n188, 203n8, 204n34, 208n52, 209n63, 209n66, 210n82, 216n147, 228n205, 229n213, 232n321, 237n110, 237n128; flashes 120, 122, 163, 225n84, 226n132

fabled guardians 76
Fabre, Jean-Henri 7
Facebook 193
Fah Lo Suee, Lily Blossom 54, 207n14
Fahrenheit 451 (book) 33
Fairchild FC-2W 177
Fairlie, Laura 72; *see also* Catherick, Anne
Fairvale, California 156
fairy tale elements and motifs 52, 58, 65, 72–8, 115, 118, 126, 134–5, 141, 142, 155, 158, 189, 212n63, 212n65, 212n66, 213n83, 213n84, 213n98, 217n180, 231n292
fairylands 46, 52, 78
Falcons football team (Air Force Academy) 20
"Fall of the House of Usher" (short story) 213n86, 216n148
Fall of the White Ship Avatar (book) 108
fantasy 35, 44, 72, 78, 92, 114, 121, 131, 215n130, 217n180, 225n95, 227n158, 243n137
fantasyland 192
Fargo, Eunice 50
Fargo, Remi 26, 45, 50–2, 56, 64, 77–8, 81, 82, 85, 97, 189, 192
Fargo, Sam 26, 45, 48, 50–2, 64, 77–8, 81, 82, 85, 97, 189, 192
Fargo, North Dakota 50; *see also* Gateway to the West
Fargo Adventures (fiction series) 17, 50–2, 81, 150, 234n136
Fargo Foundation 52
Fargo Group 51
Farley, Graham 73, 148
Fate 117, 129, 132, 133, 134, 138, 139, 140, 142, 159; fate 75, 86, 115, 138, 156, 159, 170, 180, 181, 188; or coincidence 14, 22, 55, 85, 97, 126, 147, 152, 194
father 17, 21, 24, 26, 30, 32–3, 34, 35, 39, 40, 42, 43, 44, 48–9, 50, 51, 54, 57, 60, 73, 74, 75, 76, 80, 81, 88, 89, 90, 100, 102, 104, 107, 114, 117, 120, 122, 126, 127, 132, 145, 159, 162, 174, 184, 187, 199n19, 201n99, 202n151, 202n177, 202n185, 204n16, 205n49, 210n9, 214n107, 221n61, 221n62, 222n99, 223n122, 226n151, 228n190, 228n206, 236n89, 244n150; second or surrogate 27, 29, 75, 80, 86, 99, 100, 103, 107, 109, 119, 120, 126, 145, 147
Father archetype 86, 113, 120, 122, 126, 127, 128, 132, 142–3, 145, 189; *see also* Goddess archetype
Fathom mind control project 84
Faulkner, William 71, 101, 221n68
Faust 139
Fawcett, Dan 66
Fawkes, Myrna 140, 153
Fawkes, Capt. Patrick McKenzie 69, 91, 132, 135–6, 137, 138–41, 145, 153 211n42, 229n225, 230n251, 230n253, 230n255, 230n256, 230n257, 230n259, 231n282, 231n291, 231n297, 231n298, 231n299, 231n302, 231n311, 236n91

FBI 20, 188
"The Fear-Makers" (TV episode) 103–4
Federal Reserve Bank 76, 156, 158
fem jep 79, 95
female readers 11, 92–3
feminine attributes 5, 38, 43, 70, 75, 89, 90–1, 92, 120, 123
femme fatale 95
Fergus, Lt. Alan 139
Ferguson, Adm. Dale 28
fetch help 31, 134, 182
ffolkes (film) 184–5
ffolkes, Rufus Excalibur 185, 242
"ffolkes' ffusiliers" 185, 242n123
Fields, W.C. 98
The Final Countdown 167
Finch, Atticus 67
Finding Nemo (film) 242n147
Finding Nemo Submarine Voyage 242n147
fine dining 44, 50
Finn, Huckleberry 28, 92, 219n266
Finney, Jack 6–7
Fire Ice (book) 31, 39, 40, 63, 148, 160, 162
Firefox (book) 82
First Attempt (ship) 55, 131, 228–9n208
First Comics 153
first-refusal rights 15
fish and fishing 42, 50, 81, 133–4, 136–8, 161
Fisher, Carrie 108
Fisher, David Dayan 188
Fitzhugh, Alacrity 108
5 Pictures Entertainment 180
Fizzbin 106
Flagstaff, Arizona 60
Fleming, Ashley 75
Fleming, Ian 7, 11, 20, 54, 57, 59, 60, 66, 70, 73, 80, 83, 86, 94, 95, 152, 154, 178, 180; *see also* Bond, James
Fletcher, Betsy 159, 160, 236n103
Fletcher (Dorsett), Maeve 35, 58, 76, 88, 89, 90–1, 92 101, 147, 154, 162, 207n17, 218n214, 218n221, 219n266, 232n337, 235n56, 236n103; rebirth; 159–60; similar to Moran, Summer, 54, 56, 207n16, 208n29
Fletcher, Michael 76, 88, 92, 159, 160
Fletcher, Sean 76, 88, 92, 159, 160
flight, magic 124, 161
flight and pursuit 111, 113
The Flight of the Phoenix (book) 176
The Flintstones (TV series) 104
flood 34, 40–2, 103, 165, 186; Great Flood 86
Flood Tide (book) 13, 16, 20, 31, 56, 63, 66, 71, 72, 81, 83, 88, 99, 101, 154, 160
Floopy 44, 45
floozy 74, 75, 145
Florida 81, 128
Florida Atlantic Engineering 34
Floyt, Hobart 108
fly-casting 133, 136
"Fly-Paper" (short story) 69
Flying Dutchman (legend) 131, 138, 159, 160, 186

Flynn, Errol 11, 98, 113, 169
Flynn, Vince 67
Fodouop, Paulin 175
fog 81, 112, 119, 124, 132, 225*n*72, 226*n*135, 237*n*113
folk tale 24, 43, 58, 79, 86, 111, 135, 191
Fonda, Henry 99, 100
football 11, 20, 25, 34, 39, 107, 177
Foran, Dick 184
Ford, Glenn 98
Ford, Harrison 92, 108, 214*n*107
Ford, John 15–6, 94, 98, 101, 102, 103, 176, 220*n*34, 221*n*63, 222*n*86, 237*n*188; Ford heroes 99–100
Ford, Wallace 184
Ford Tri-Motor 126
Ford's Theater 177
Foreign Correspondent (film) 157
foreign enemies and threats 24, 48
Forester, C.S. 10, 96, 106
Formula-A Structure 146–8, 186, 233*n*3, 234*n*25; *see also* Formula-B Structure; structure
Formula-B Structure 18, 148–51, 233*n*11, 233*n*13; *see also* Formula-A Structure; structure
Fort Apache (1948 film) 15, 222*n*86
Fort Foureau 56, 173, 178, 183
fortune and glory 23, 200*n*62
Foster-Harris, William 86, 146, 182, 199*n*11, 199*n*12, 199*n*13, 217*n*180, 226*n*138, 233*n*6, 234*n*32, 234*n*34
founding fathers 188, 189; view of humanity 24, 188
The Four Just Men (book) 67
Fourth Reich 61
Fox, Michael J. 185
Fox, Stacy 56, 90, 161, 208*n*26
F.P.1 Does Not Answer (*F.P.1 antwortet nicht*) 182–3, 185, 190, 242*n*112, 242*n*113, 242*n*114, 242*n*115
France 7, 31, 73, 80, 90, 130, 172, 155, 173, 175, 176, 177, 178
franchise 38, 108, 154, 190; *see also* spin-off series
Frankenstein (1931 film) 87
Frankenstein, Henry 87
Frankenstein, Victor 235*n*58
Frankenstein monster 84
Frankenstein, or The Modern Prometheus (book) 81
Franklin Institute 188
Free Quebec Society 61, 70
Freemason 187, 188, 189, 243*n*142, 244*n*148
The French Connection (film) 108
French Foreign Legion 173
Friend, Dr. Timothy 31
friendship 10, 11, 21, 52, 58, 97, 124, 201*n*91, 201*n*92, 201*n*111
From Russia with Love (film) 60
From The Mediterranean Caper *to* Black Wind: *A Bibliography of Clive Cussler* (book) 193
frontiersmen 24, 26, 50
Frost, Walter Archer 95
Frostline (book) 47
Fu Manchu, Dr. 54, 59, 79, 156; poison of living-death 156; the Devil Doctor 54

fuel cell technology 61
fugitive wanderers 107
Fury, Capt. John 96, 205*n*43
future bride 128, 141
future 7, 33, 81, 82, 83, 86, 103, 129, 145, 147–50, 158, 173, 183, 188, 234*n*18
"Fuzzy Lines: Using the Best-selling Novel to Illustrate the Blurring Boundaries of 'Public'" (article) 4, 66–7
Fyrie, Kirsti 46, 54, 55, 65, 117, 127, 140, 144, 162, 200*n*68, 213*n*98, 216*n*159, 224*n*48
Fyrie, Kristjan 24, 46, 69, 87, 112, 116–7, 123, 126, 127, 140, 162, 212*n*52, 216*n*159, 224*n*48, 225*n*84
Fyrie Limited 127
Fyrie probe 83, 113, 124, 161, 183, 207*n*114

G-8 and His Battle Aces 96
gadgeteer 105
galactic Empire 114
Gale, Dorothy 47
Gallagher, Ian 68
Gallagher, Mark 5, 66–7, 92–3, 195*n*10, 195*n*12, 207*n*119, 210*n*15, 215*n*139, 219*n*253, 219*n*264, 219*n*275, 220*n*33, 233*n*8
galleon 32, 86, 215*n*143
Gandalf 114
gangster 11, 25, 45, 61, 98, 200*n*74, 235*n*47
Gant, Mitchell 108
Gardner, Mildred 85, 142
Garin, Katie 81
Garner, James 108
Garrison, Paul 47
"Garry Owen" (song) 161, 237*n*118
Garth, Matt 101–2
gas crisis 83
Gaskill, Davis 66
Gates, Benjamin Franklin 4, 108, 187, 188, 189, 207*n*108, 244*n*143, 244*n*145, 244*n*146, 244*n*149, 244*n*150
Gates, John Adam 187, 188, 189, 244*n*148
Gates, Patrick Henry 187, 189, 244*n*150
Gates, Thomas 187
Gateway to the West 50; *see also* Fargo, North Dakota
Gaumont British Pictures 182, 242*n*112
Gavin, John 156
gay 25, 71, 89, 127, 161, 225*n*92, 237*n*114; *see also* homosexual
gemstones 58; *see also* diamonds
Genesis, Book of 48, 152, 206*n*97, 228*n*192
Genghis Khan 162
genie 74
Georgetown (Washington, D.C.) 32
A German Requiem (book) 108
Germany/German 32, 39, 48, 49, 60, 80, 97, 148, 168, 182, 188, 191, 202*n*185, 214*n*123, 215*n*143, 242*n*113, 242*n*114, 242*n*115
gers 63

"The Ghost of the Canyon" (short story) 79
ghost 79, 82, 87, 88, 118, 131, 155, 160; specter 80, 129; tutelary spirit 161
ghost ride 137
ghost ship 81, 160
ghost town 46
G.I. Joe (doll) 89
Gianetti, Louis 98, 101, 157, 192, 210–11*n*17, 236*n*76
Gibbs, Leroy Jethro 4, 19, 109, 223*n*125
Gibson, Mel 28, 108
Gilbert, Lewis 230*n*30
Gilgamesh 26, 188, 201*n*91; *see also* Enkidu; *Epic of Gilgamesh*
gin rummy 29
Giordano, Al 25; *see also* Girodino, Albert Cassius; South Vineland, New Jersey
Giordino, Albert Cassius 12, 13, 20, 22, 23, 25–8, 28, 29, 30, 31, 35, 40, 44, 52, 54, 56–7, 60, 63, 64, 65, 66, 68, 72, 73–4, 76, 80, 81, 83, 88, 90, 91, 97, 100, 101, 105, 106, 128, 131, 134, 140, 145, 147, 150, 151, 153, 161, 162, 164, 169, 171, 173, 174, 175, 176, 177, 178, 179, 180, 184, 188, 200*n*54, 201*n*87, 201*n*92, 201*n*96, 201*n*100, 201*n*107, 201*n*117, 202*n*151, 202*n*161, 203*n*2, 205*n*39, 208*n*21, 209*n*56, 210*n*82, 210*n*9, 213–4*n*98, 217*n*179, 218*n*214, 218*n*221, 220*n*23, 226*n*116, 236*n*96, 237*n*116, 240*n*67, 240*n*73, 240–1*n*85, 241*n*92, 241*n*96, 241*n*99, 241*n*102, 241*n*103; absence in *Iceberg* 29, 201*n*116; assistant special projects director 26, 29; purloining Sandecker's cigars 26, 176, 201*n*89; sidekick 27, 201*n*107; *see also* Girodano, Al
Gisbourne, Sir Guy of 113
Giza, Egypt 174
Gladiator (ship) 159
Gladiator Island 76, 88
global warming 61, 218*n*221
Glover, Danny 28, 108
Gly, Foss 40, 55, 60–1, 62, 68, 72, 83, 87, 88, 140, 144, 163, 204*n*29, 209*n*56, 209*n*63, 232*n*347, 213–4*n*98; *see also* Darius, Captain
God 3, 43, 48, 118, 125, 133, 134, 135, 137, 151, 155, 188, 212*n*59, 217*n*90, 229*n*190, 229*n*192, 229*n*197, 229*n*242, 230*n*255, 230*n*257; blessings 121, 124, 125–6, 129
"God save thee" 121, 125–6, 127
Goddess archetype 113, 119–20, 127, 131–2, 141, 144, 145; *see also* Father archetype
godfather 31
Gogstad Corporation 39
"The Gold Bug" (short story) 50, 207*n*107
Gold Cup Grand National 45, 46, 47
Golden Buddha 206*n*88, 237*n*119
Golden Buddha (book) 16, 40, 41, 42, 47, 67, 205*n*47, 206*n*88, 216*n*164, 234*n*36, 236*n*97

Index

Golden Dawn (ship) 159
golden-eyed giant 76
Golden Marlin (aubmarine) 28, 41, 162
Goldfinger (book) 59
Goldfinger (film) 59, 166
Goldfinger, Auric 57, 58, 59
Goldmill, Mickey 86
Golgotha 137, 138
Gollum 121–2, 225n105; *see also Asselar Oasis;* cannibal; *28 Days Later;* zombie
Gomez, Hunter 187
Good Samaritan 13, 62
Goodwin, Archie 11, 20, 22, 25
Goodyear, Julie 148
Gooney (ultralight) 160
Gordian Knot 126
Gordon, Artemus 105–6
Gordon, Commissioner James 19
Gordon, Flash 217n194
Gorgon 127
Gose, Elliot 122, 124, 223n5, 225n71
gothic 36, 46, 65, 72, 76, 78–82, 87, 95, 127, 129, 138, 151, 152, 154, 155, 186, 187, 189, 206n85, 211n44, 212n74, 213n86, 214n114, 214n119, 214–5n123, 215n130, 215n138, 215n139, 215n140, 215–6n145, 216n147, 216n163, 216n164, 230n256, 239n59
Gothic Television (book) 79, 215n130
Gould, Chester 208n42
Gourmand 19, 32, 33
gourmet cook 12, 55, 56
government employee 48, 66, 68
government official 38, 59, 66
Grade, Lord Lew 166
Graham, Misty 44
Grand Army 77; *see also* Bonaparte, Napoleon
Grand Funk 174
Le Grand Meaulnes (book) 4
Grand Single 59, 60; *see also* Criminal Mastermind; Emperor of Crime; villain types
Grand St. Bernard Pass 77
grandfather 21, 34, 49, 60, 186, 187, 243n133, 243n134, 243n139, 144n150
grandparents 42
grandson 42, 58, 61, 69, 187, 244n148
Granger, Farley 157
Grant, Cary 11, 102
Grant, Donovan "Red" 57, 60, 62, 209n61
Grant, Ulysses S. 105
The Grapes of Wrath (film) 99
gravel 168, 239n51
Gray Lady Down (film) 167
Grayson, Dick 19
Great American Songbook 179, 237n120
Great Britain 95, 141, 185; *see also* England
"The Great God Pan" (short story) 78, 80
Great Pokomoke Swamp 77
great-grandfather 34, 49
great-grandmother 59
great-great-great grandson 189

The Greatest American Hero (TV series) 109
Greece/Greek 20, 60, 80, 86, 127, 148, 209n63, 212n71, 225n57, 243n140
Greek mythology 127, 209n63
Green Arrow: The Longbow Hunters (graphic novel) 1
Greenberg, Martin H. 18
Greer, Adm. James 221n61
Grell, Mike 1, 108, 153, 195n13, 217n192, 231n311, 235n53, 235n54, 243n137
Grendel 118
Grendel's dam 118
Griffith, D.W. 41
Grimm Brothers 73, 76
Grimsi (ship) 119, 161, 225n73, 237n110
"Guantanamera" (song) 40
Guess Who's Coming to Dinner? (film) 167
Guinevere 144, 225n79
Guinness, Sir Alec 108, 166, 228n197
Gulf of Alaska 55
Gunn, Rudolph "Rudi" 29, 30–1, 38, 52, 68, 73–4, 81, 88, 91, 100, 106, 128, 131, 147, 150, 162, 164, 171, 173, 175–6, 179, 180, 186, 202n161, 202n165, 202n166, 202n167, 210n9, 214n98, 236n96, 240n73, 241n102, 241n103
The Guns of Navarone (book) 4, 195n11, 224n25, 234n40
The Guns of Navarone (film) 196n35
Gunther, Bernie 108
Gutman, Casper 18
gypsy 25, 118; *see also* Spanish Gypsies

Hades 138, 231n299; *see also* belly of Hell
Hadji 104
Haggard, H. Rider 7, 96, 191, 219n256, 242n146, 243n140
"Hail to the Chief" (TV episode) 104
Haines, Guy 157
HAL 9000 (Heuristically programmed ALgorithmic computer) 84, 233n13
half-a-crown 60
Hall, Wes 71
Ham 20; *see also* Savage, Doc Clark
Hambleton, Sue 69, 211n38
Hamill, Mark 108
Hamilton, Alexander 24
Hamilton, Guy 238n30
Hamlet 22, 229n243
Hamlet (play) 152, 234n44
Hammer, Mike 1, 37, 152
Hammett, Dashiell 12, 18, 20, 51, 69, 79, 95
HMS *Hampshire* 148
handkerchief 90
Hanley, Max 40, 42
Hanna-Barbera 104; *see also* Barbera, Joseph; Hanna, William
Hanna, William 104; *see also* Barbera, Joseph; Hanna-Barbera
Hannay, Richard 94, 107, 195n22
Hardscape (book) 47

Hardy Boys 46
Harker, Jonathan 120
Harkness, Capt. Jack 4, 109
harlots 91
Harmon, Mark 109
Harris, Quint 92
Harry Potter adventures (fiction series) 45, 77, 85, 206n89
Harry Potter and the Deathly Hallows (book) 86, 227n165
Harry Potter and the Goblet of Fire (book) 217–8n200, 225n105
Harry Potter and the Philosopher's Stone (book) 114, 214n105, 224n32
Harry the peddler 157
Hartley, Hashknife 97; *see also* Stevens, Dave "Sleepy"
Hartman, Paul 182
Harvard 70
Hatari (film) 101
Hawaii 20, 25, 33, 57, 82, 109, 149, 207n14, 20, 25, 30, 33
Hawaii Five-O (TV series 1968–1980) 71
Hawk 28; *see also* Parker, Robert B.; Spenser
Hawkeye 24, 28, 206n95
Hawks, Howard 98, 100–3; Hawks hero 36, 100; Hawks heroine 36, 50, 91, 203n224, 207n3, 220n34, 221n67, 221n68, 221n69, 224n41
Hawthorne, Nathaniel 3, 80
Hayes, Gabby 98
Heart of Atlantis 186; *see also Atlantis: The Lost Empire*
The Heart of Juliet Jones (newspaper strip) 164
Heartease mine 155
Heathcliffe 22
Hebrew 31, 124, 129, 135, 206n97, 228n192, 230n257, 230n273
Heche, Anne 92
Hecht, Ben 101, 221n101
Hector (legend) 88; *see also* Achilles; Paris
Hedison, David 103, 185
Hedren, Tippi 92
Heidelberg University 49
Heinlein, Robert A. 84, 216n171, 217n174
Heinrick, Papa 42–3, 77
Helen of Troy 127
Hellfighters (film) 184
Hellman, Lillian 51
helper 52, 85, 101, 111–2, 116, 117–8, 119, 120, 121, 126, 138, 147
Hemingway, Ernest 3–4
Hepburn, Audrey 54
Her Majesty's Secret Service 141, 180, 204n34
herald 70, 115–6, 142, 143, 224n32
herbs 43–4, 205n59
Hercules 88, 229n241
Herero chief 162
heritage 20, 32, 39, 40, 55, 72, 140
Hermit Limited 59, 113, 122, 124, 126
Hermit Limited's computers 124–5, 226n130; *see also* Brunhilda; computers and supercomputers; Hope; Max
Hermosa Beach 52

hero and adventurer, difference between 23
The Hero with a Thousand Faces 27, 73; see also Campbell, Joseph
Hickam Air Force Base 25
Higgins, Jonathan Quayle, III 109
High Priest of Karnak 183–4
high priestesses 35
highwaymen 43, 95, 220n6
Hillerman, John 109
Hills of the Seven Jackals 183
hippocampus 87; see also RNA
His Girl Friday (film) 36, 91, 221n67
history 16, 17, 22, 23, 32, 46–7, 50–1, 61, 65, 70, 85–6, 108, 180, 185, 187–9, 193, 200n60, 204n34, 211n20, 215n139, 233n8, 240n65, 241n87, 244n150; see also past
Hitchcock, Alfred 5, 6, 102–103, 155–8, 221n71, 236n79, 236n80, 236n81, 236n86, 236n87; Hitchcock hero 102; Hitchcockian whimsy 156; Master of Suspense 5, 156; see also MacGuffin
Hitler, Adolf 242n113
HMS Ulysses (book) 10, 234n40
Ho, Stanley 161
Hobart, Adeline 99
Hobart, Jake 168
The Hobbit, or There and Back Again (book) 114, 121, 224n32; "Riddles in the Dark" 121–2
Hoffman, Dustin 67, 224n23
Hogan, Robert J. 97
Hogg, James 81
Hogwarts's Great Hall 86
Hogwarts School of Witchcraft and Wizardry 85, 114, 214n105, 224n32
Holes (film) 174
Hollywood 1, 16, 36, 98, 101, 102, 108, 170, 171, 172, 178, 192, 200n51, 220n33, 239n57, 239n60, 241n104, 244n144
Holmes, Mycroft 104
Holmes, Sherlock 9, 10, 11, 12, 18, 25, 38, 58, 62, 94, 110, 115–116, 155, 191, 193, 197n36, 208n37, 209–10n80, 212n59, 223n7, 224n45, 226n157, 229n241, 235n70; initiation quest pattern in Holmes adventures 112; see also Conan Doyle, Sir Arthur; "The Lost Special"
Holmes, Sherrinford 11
HOLMES IV (High-Optional, Logical, Multi-Evaluating Supervisor, Mark IV) computer Mike (a.k.a Mycroft) 84
holocaust 34, 58
holograms 83; holographic images 31
Holy Saturday 138
homage 49, 104, 106–7, 190, 222n101
homosexual 71, 120, 122, 123, 211n51, 212n52, 225n92; see also gay
Hong Kong, China 29
honor suicide 60
Hook (film) 224n23
Hooper, Matt 108, 170
Hope 83; see also Brunhilda; computers and supercomputers; Hermit Limited's computers; Max

Hopper, Dr. Frank 174–6, 240n73, 241n99, 241n103
Hornblower, Horatio 10, 96, 106, 221n57, 229n243
Horror of Dracula (1958 film) 168
Hotsy Totsy (powerboat) 45–46, 96
House, Dr. Gregory 38, 204n14
House of Seven Gables (book) 80
Hovarth, Janet 17
hovercraft 45, 83
Howard, John 27
Howe, Ian 188, 189
hubris 23, 74, 76, 80, 138, 170, 200n62, 212n74, 216n146, 216n147, 228n196, 228n205, 239n51
Hudson River 159
Hudson River Valley 78
Huggins, Roy 108
Hughes, Howard 97
Hull/Medford Agency 14, 98
human hero 124, 129–30, 191
human sacrifice 92
humanity 24, 33, 34, 68, 85, 96, 119, 212n63, 213n83, 224n49, 233n13; humanity's past 114, 122, 124
humble 23, 26, 62, 71, 87, 125–7, 136–7, 139, 185; humility 24
humiliation 77, 99
humor 22, 48, 100, 106, 198n48; humorous outlook 32, 34, 201n99
CSS *Hunley* (submarine) 1, 193, 198n55
Hunnewell, Dr. William 24, 115–21, 123, 125–6, 127, 147, 152, 160, 222n86, 224n41, 224n45, 224n51, 227n172
Hunt, Leigh 204n28, 40; Wandering Buccaneer 81
Hunt for Red October (book) 5, 15
Hunted Past Reason (book) 153
Hunter, Adrian 21, 54, 60, 86, 76, 160, 163, 233n4
Hunter, Ian 113
Hunter, Adm. Leigh Hunter 22, 40, 76
Hunton Gazelle (RS43) 175
hurricane 165, 166, 238n12
Hurricane Amanda 129, 131, 149, 167, 169–71, 183, 215n169, 224n156
husband 26, 33, 48, 51, 55, 70, 73, 75, 78, 81, 90, 92, 100, 102, 140, 144; ex-husband 142
husband and wife team 38, 51
Huston, Mrs. Graham 142
Hutton, Wilbur 66
Hyde, Edward 72, 75, 211n44, 212n59, 213n94, 72, 75; see also Jekyll, Dr. Henry
hydrofoil 43, 77; *Iceberg* (book) 112, 119, 122, 161, 225n72, 237n110; see also leviathan
Hyperion nuclear missiles 86
hypocritical 72, 170, 213n94

I Dream of Jeanie (TV series) 84
I Spy (TV series) 28, 105
I, the Jury (book) 5, 152
"I Want a Girl (Just Like the Girl That Married Dear Old Dad)" (song) 21
I Went to Denver but It Was Closed 15
IBM 103

Ice Station Zebra (book) 4, 10, 224n25
Ice Station Zebra (film) 167, 196n135
Iceberg 13, 14–5, 22, 23, 24, 25, 29, 33, 46, 55, 56, 57, 58, 62, 66, 71, 73, 76, 81, 82, 83, 87, 88, 90, 98, 99, 105, 111–128, 129, 130, 140, 146, 147, 151, 152, 157, 158, 159, 160, 161, 162, 163, 169, 201n116; see also apotheosis
Iceland 23, 81–2, 117–8, 129, 159, 225n88, 226n151; contrary nature 118, 125, 127
Ichabod (Loren Smith's cat) 91, 219n261
ichthyologist 108, 170
idealized masculinity 5
ideals, ancient Eastern 91
identity theft 72
"If Max Is So Smart, Why Doesn't He Tell Us Where He Is?" (TV episode) 107
imagination 10, 40, 58, 126, 156, 171, 214n123, 235n53, 238n11
immaturity 22, 84, 118
immigration 218n221
Immigration and Naturalization Service 35, 37, 56, 66
impatience 192
In the Mouth of Madness (film) 182
Inca Gold 16, 26, 27, 28, 32, 35, 36, 44, 52, 56, 62, 83, 145, 160, 199n37, 201n100, 233n358, 236n94, 236n96
Incas 83
incubus 144; see also succubus
Independence Hall 189
Independent (political) 98, 203n223
India 243n140
Indiana Jones and the Kingdom of the Crystal Skulls (film) 108
Indiana Jones and the Last Crusade (film) 108
Indiana Jones and the Temple of Doom (film) 108
individualism 6, 98, 192
Industrial Light and Magic 180
inferiority complex 22, 122
influences 3, 6, 53, 59, 153, 191, 196n35, 204n34, 214–5n123, 220n9, 234n41
The Informant (book) 50
Information Technology (IT) 31
informer 60, 61, 69, 133, 230n278, 231n307
ingenuity 10, 45, 151–2, 234n45
inheritance 21
Initiation Quest Pattern (monomyth) 27, 80, 111–128, 135; see also spirit quest, shamanistic
Inner Mongolia, China 63
insanity 80, 174, 215–6n145, 216n148; see also sanity
insecurity 22, 74
Insidious Dr. Fu Manchu 19
Intelligence I 104
Internal South Africa Defence 136, 230n251
Invasion of the Body Snatchers (1957 film) 6
USS *Iowa* (BB-61) 138–41, 231n315, 236n91
Iran 41, 205n40

Irish mythology 207–8*n*17
ironclad 32, 86, 173, 178, 240*n*67, 240*n*73
irony 3, 48, 59, 68, 75, 80, 85, 126, 127, 129, 156, 161, 163, 200*n*59, 200*n*63, 200*n*68, 213*n*89, 223*n*10, 226*n*24, 227*n*171, 228*n*190, 228*n*205, 230*n*247, 230*n*250, 236*n*80
IRS 30
Irvine, Glenn 71
Isaac Bell Detective series (fiction series) 17, 47–50, 81, 150, 202*n*185
Ishmael 28, 189
Isle of Wright 143
Italian 26, 27, 77, 91, 130, 169
Ivan 153; *see also* Connell, Richard; Dragon; "The Most Dangerous Game"; Rainsford, Sanger; Ship Trap Island; Zaroff, General
Ivy League 170, 239*n*45

Jack Armstrong, All-American Boy (radio series) 104
jack-of-all-trades 38, 96
Jackson, Dr. Daniel 243*n*139
Jackson, Samuel L. 208*n*76
Jaffe, Jacqueline 91, 112, 223*n*7
J*A*G (TV series) 109, 223*n*120
Jaguar XK-One-twenty 33
Jamaica Inn (1939 film) 157
James, Frank 96
James, Jesse 55, 96
James, Lennie 174
James, Pete 41; *see also* Jones, Pete
James Bond: Permission to Die (graphic novel) 1
James River 173
Jameson, Jerry 167, 184
Jane Whitefield series 17, 50
Janus 68, 69, 86
Janus cloth 69
Janus villain 61, 65, 68–71, 188, 211*n*43, 211*n*44; alternating moods 69; deceit 69
Janus-faced 69
Japan 28, 40, 63, 66, 80, 138, 152, 153, 177, 210*n*82, 218*n*221
Jarvis, Dale 66, 138, 231*n*315
Jaws (book) 168, 170
Jaws (film) 67, 108, 168, 170
jazz 30, 39, 51, 52, 154
Jedi knight 114
Jeffcoat, Peter 52; *see also* Corden, Wendy; Wondrash, Selma
Jekyll, Dr. Henry 72, 75, 211*n*44, 212*n*59, 213*n*94; *see also* Hyde, Edward
Jenkins, Leroy 148
Jennifer (oil platform) 184, 185, 242*n*124
Jenson, Babe 184, 242*n*121
Jersey Colony 82
Jessie LeBaron 24, 55, 56, 65, 88, 91, 128, 161, 183, 209*n*56, 213–4*n*98, 219*n*244
Jesus Christ 86, 123, 134, 136, 137, 138, 139, 201*n*119, 227*n*167, 229*n*237, 229*n*241, 229*n*242, 231*n*283, 231*n*284; Jesus Fish (Ichtus) 134; Lamb of God 134, 229*n*242, see also Agnus Dei; Bass, Adm. Walter Horatio; martyr; redeemer
Jimmie Dale, the Gray Seal 79
Jinx on a Terran Inheritance (book) 108
Joe the Monster 45
John Paul Jones Club 29
Johnny 20; *see also* Savage, Doc Clark
Johnson, Hildy 36
Johnson, Nunnally 168
Johnson, Samuel 121
The Joker 58, 62, 130
Jolly Roger 177
Jon Sable, Freelance (comic book series) 1, 108, 153, 235*n*54; *see also* "The Origin"
Jonah 116, 231*n*299
Jones, Casey 43
Jones, Henry, "Indiana," Jr. 108, 181, 200*n*62, 214*n*107
Jones, Henry, Sr. 214*n*107
Jones, Pete 42; *see also* James, Pete
Jones, Peter 80
Jonny Quest (TV series) 104–5
Jonsson, Dr. 99, 118–9, 125, 126, 142, 225*n*63, 226*n*145
Jordan, Raymond 66
Jordan, Richard 167, 199*n*40, 204*n*19
Journey to the Center of the Earth (book) 242*n*129, 242*n*137
Journey to the Center of the Earth (film) 185
Juan Julio tequila 90
Judas 134, 136, 137
Judgment Day 131
Judo 50, 56
Julius Caesar 31
Jumana, Col. Randolph 133, 136, 137, 138, 230*n*267
Jung, Carl 35, 44, 114, 119, 144, 189
Jungian Devil 144; *see also* Shadow archetype
Jungian fantasy archetype 35, 44, 114, 189, 232*n*344
jungle 27, 86, 153, 159, 191
The Jungle (1906 book) 67
Junshiro, Ueda 66
justice figures 67, 95

Kaena Point, Hawaii 20
Kamatori, Moro 153
Kamil, Hala 55–6, 59, 90, 160, 178, 219*n*246
Kanai, Ono 62
Kane, Bob 208*n*42
Kane, Charles Foster 62, 209*n*75; *see also* Zale, Curtis Merlin
Kane, Margo 89
Kane, Maximillian 204*n*19
Kanoli 34–5, 54, 59, 76, 78, 86–7, 88, 133, 149, 183, 200*n*62, 207*n*12, 224*n*39
Kasim, Hali 41
katana 153
Kauai, Hawaii 34
Kazim, Gen. Zateb 172–5, 178–9, 240*n*68, 240*n*69, 241*n*94, 241*n*98, 241*n*103
kea 160, 236*n*103

Keflavik airport 126
Kellaway, Cecil 184
Kelley, DeForest 106
Kelly, F. James 122, 124
Kelly, Lt. 169; *see also Kelly's Heroes* (film)
Kelly, Sam 124, 126, 127, 226*n*156
Kelly's Heroes (film) 169; *see also* Kelly (Lt.)
Kelsey, Shannon 27, 56, 57, 89
Kemper, Adm. Joseph 28, 171, 202*n*139, 229*n*225
Kemprecos, Paul 16, 37, 39, 201*n*83, 202*n*144, 204*n*19, 204*n*25
Kennedy, Adam 167–8, 184
Kennedy, Craig 18, 198*n*5
Kennedy, John 14
Kennedy, Robert 14
Kenobi, Obi-wan "Ben" 108, 114
Kentucky 10
Kenya 153; *see also* Zimbabwe
Kerr, Phillip 108
Kersey, Paul 14, 108
Key West, Florida 50
Keystone Kops 40
Kharis 184, 242*n*120
Kida, Princess 187
Killer's Wake (book) 108
King, Rev. Martin Luther, Jr. 14
King, Stephen 6, 65, 152, 196*n*35, 210*n*3, 227*n*183, 235*n*68
King in Yellow (book) 196*n*35
"King in Yellow" (short story) 80
King Solomon's Mines (book) 52, 242*n*126
The Kingdom (book) 50, 207*n*122
King's Cross Station 86
Kiowa Creek, Colorado 154–5
Kipling, Rudyard 77, 191
Kippmann, Dean 23, 25, 112, 124, 126, 128, 226*n*151, 227*n*158
Kirk, Capt. James Tiberius 106, 213*n*76, 243*n*138
Kirk chair 84; *see also The Oregon*
Kirkland, Carlie 107
Kiss Me Deadly (book) 5
Kitchener, Lord H.H. 148; *see also* Britain/British, field marshal
Klein, Dick 11
Klingon 84, 243*n*138
Kneal, Nigel 185
knight-errant 13, 14, 24, 38, 43, 49, 52, 94, 95, 97, 192; *see also* samurai
knights 9, 72, 118, 187, 189, 212*n*66, 213*n*98
Knights Templar 187, 189, 207*n*108, 244*n*148; treasure 207*n*108
Knox Inn 162
komondor 129
Koplin, Sid 129, 130, 132, 149, 159, 167
Koryo, Min 13, 69, 59, 61, 158, 236*n*80; *see also* Bougainville, (Madam) Min Koryo
Koski (Commander) 22, 71, 112, 116, 117, 123, 147, 224*n*51
Kradzik, Melo 46
Kradzik, Radko 46
Kramer, Lou 185; *see also* Bates, Norman; Perkins, Anthony
Kramer, Stanley 167, 238*n*31

Krome, Tony 193
Kronberg, Hans 58, 78, 220*n*19
Kronberg, Hilda 55, 78; *see also* Wise Old Woman
Kruger, Diane 188
Kudo, Toshie 63
Kurile Trench 176–7

La Dorada 78, 150; *see also* El Dorado
La Jolla, California 52
Labell, Skye 160
Labette County, Kansas 77
labyrinth 60, 77, 81, 87, 88, 116, 119, 148, 215*n*130, 216*n*164; interrogation room six 60; Pit of Hades 87; *see also* maze
lacrosse 50
Lady Chatterley's Lover (novel) 3
Lady in Her House of Sleep 73–4, 140, 145, 212*n*69; *see also* "Sleeping Beauty"
Lagos, Niger 174
Lagos Museum 174, 176, 241*n*87
LaMarche, Maurice 190, 244*n*154
Lampack, Peter 13, 14, 15
Lancelot 95, 144
Land Rover 117
land yacht 17, 25, 179
Lane, Lois 89
Lang, Fritz 83
Lang, James "Clubber" 86
language, melodramatic 79, 81
lapel microphone 83
Larmier, Sen. Marcus 23–4, 66, 200*n*63
Larson, Glen A. 109, 223*n*119
The Last of the Mohicans (book) 24
Latin America 33, 201*n*88
Lavella, Dr. 34
Law & Order (TV series and franchise) 38
Lawrence, D.H. 3
Lax (ship) 81, 112, 116–7, 123, 126, 149, 160, 225*n*87
Leadville, Colorado 204*n*17
LeBaron, Raymond 55, 61, 78, 160, 220*n*19
Lee, Christopher 168
Lee, Crane 103
Lee, Harper 3
Lee, Julia 13, 21, 37, 56, 91, 101, 163
Lee, Maurice 178
Lee, Robert E. 200*n*70
Lee, Stan 208*n*42
Lee Tong 61, 69, 156, 157, 162, 209*n*65
Leeson, Dan 91, 219*n*265
legend 27, 58, 73, 74, 76, 78, 81, 86, 88, 95, 116, 118, 119, 126, 147, 150, 155, 166, 184, 187, 189, 200*n*62, 209*n*63, 212*n*63, 213*n*98, 224*n*39, 225*n*57
Leigh, Janet 156, 236*n*76
Leiter, Felix 19, 80
Lennartz, Claire 182
Lennartz-Werke 182
Leonid Andreyev (ship) 24, 36
Lesser, Richard 94, 97, 220*n*6
Lethal Weapon (1987 film) 28
Lethal Weapon (film series) 108
"Let's Hear It for a Living Legend" (TV episode) 107

Leuthner, Stuart 193
leviathan 116, 231; *Iceberg* (book) 119; *see also Atlantis: The Lost Empire*; hydrofoil
Lewis, C.S. 45
Lewis, Francis 24
Lexington, Virginia 135
Liberia 136
Liberty ship 76, 156, 158–9
Library of Alexandria 55, 78, 82, 95, 150, 162, 189, 193
library 31, 32, 39, 85, 107
"Ligeia" (short story) 80; 216*n*148
Lighthouse jazz club 51, 52
Lillie, Jerome P., III 37, 86, 112, 123–4, 126–7, 151, 197*n*23
Lillie Beer 37
Lima, Peru 32
liminality 77
limpet mines 185
Lincoln, Abraham 18, 177, 178, 198*n*6; assassination conspiracy 150, 241*n*89
Lincoln, Franklin 42, 181
Lincoln Memorial 141, 231*n*314
Lindbergh, Charles "Lucky Lindy" 97
Lindo, Delroy 175
linguist 185, 243*n*139
literature 3, 4, 9, 19, 20, 26, 28, 38, 46, 51, 53, 58, 66, 71, 79, 86, 91, 103, 108, 160, 169, 186, 192, 195*n*6, 206*n*5, 207*n*4, 208*n*26, 208*n*42, 214*n*123, 224*n*54
little Eva 22
little men 91–2, 219*n*665
Little Orphan Annie (newspaper strip) 164
The Little Rascals (film series) 10
Little Red Riding-hood 116, 137, 230*n*276
Live at San Quentin (album) 3
Liverpool, England 155
L.L. Bean 109
Lloyd's of London 242*n*124
Locomobile race car 49
locus in quo 116
London, England 12, 15, 143, 211*n*44, 220*n*5, 223–4*n*22, 230*n*256
London Bridge 58
London Times crossword 242*n*123
Long Tom 20; *see also* Savage, Doc Clark
Longworth, Algy 27
Loomis, Sam 156, 157
Lorre, Peter 183, 242*n*115
Los Angeles, California 10, 12, 60, 76, 156
Los Angeles Times 172, 237*n*4
"Lost" (prologue for *Sahara* book and film) 177
Lost Boys 114, 125, 213*n*98
lost civilization 105, 224*n*39, 242*n*126; *see also* Atlantis; Lost World adventures; Opar; Skartaris
The Lost Special (film) 155
The Lost Special (1932 movie serial) 155
"The Lost Special" (radio adaptation) 155
"The Lost Special" (short story) 154–

5, 235*n*70; 1949 radio adaptation 155; *see also* Conan Doyle, Sir Arthur; Holmes, Sherlock
The Lost World (book) 52, 94, 186, 219*n*256, 242*n*126, 243*n*140; *see also* Conan Doyle, Sir Arthur
The Lost World (1925 film) 130
The Lost World (1960 film) 185
The Lost World (1960 film) 185
Lost World adventures 187, 242*n*126, 243*n*136, 243*n*139, 243*n*140; *see also* Atlantis; lost civilization; Opar; Skartaris
The Love Bug (1968 film) 64
Lovecraft, H. P. 79, 80, 182, 196*n*35, 213*n*86, 214*n*123, 215*n*129, 235*n*48
Loveless, Dr. Miguelito 71, 106, 222*n*105
Lowery, George 156
Loy, Myrna 51
loyal 5, 20, 23, 29, 34, 42, 54, 60, 69, 98, 103, 137, 180
Lucas, Carolyn 51; *see also* Lucas, Oscar
Lucas, George 108, 114, 216*n*174, 223*n*18
Lucas, Oscar 51; *see also* Lucas, Carolyn
Luftwaffe 80
Lugosi, Bela 168, 208*n*43
Lugovoy, Dr. Aleksei 87–8
Luigi 19; *see also* video games
lumber hauler (ship) 32, 41, 204*n*16
lure of the unknown 23, 200*n*60
Lusana, Hiram 61, 70, 71, 72, 84, 92, 132–40, 145, 160, 230*n*246, 230*n*267, 230*n*272, 230*n*273, 230*n*274; Jones, Hiram 70, 216*n*159
lycanthrope 104, 227*n*161

"M" 80, 86, 142, 143, 154, 223*n*9
M-16 automatic rifle 176
Macbeth (play) 152
MacGuffin 130, 148, 156, 158, 161, 233*n*12; *see also* Hitchcock, Alfred
MacGuire, Capt. Jack 190
MacGyver (TV series) 25
MacGyver, Angus 4, 109, 125, 223*n*122
MacGyverism 25, 34, 46, 103, 125, 161, 183, 187
Mach 1 31
Machen, Arthur 78, 80, 214*n*110
machinations 31, 146, 237*n*119
Machita, Maj. Thomas 133–4, 136–41, 230*n*275, 231*n*283, 231*n*285, 231*n*287, 231*n*309
Macintyre, Sloan 42–3, 77, 147, 162
MacLaglen, Andrew V. 184
MacLean, Alistair 4, 10, 25, 60, 66, 152, 195*n*11, 196*n*35, 224*n*25, 234*n*37, 234*n*38, 234*n*40
MacMillan Books 15
macrocosmic (universal) adventure and hero 45, 59, 62, 82, 87, 111, 115, 119, 125, 127, 128, 129, 130, 141, 145, 148, 150, 151, 157, 205*n*80, 223*n*3, 224*n*25, 233*n*13; Herculean 115, 128, 191
Macy, William H. 171
Madison, James 24

Magee, Annie 71
Magee, Ansel 71, 85, 217–8n200
"Magic Carpet Ride" (song) 179
magic 45, 46, 47, 52, 76, 77, 85, 87, 112, 115, 116, 124, 158, 184, 215n105, 217n180, 234n25; *see also* flight, magic; mirrors, magic
Magic Shop 42, 158
magnet 25, 42, 153
magnetohydrodynamics technology (MHD engines) 42
Magnum, Thomas 109, 223n121
Magnum P.I. (TV series) 109
Mahoney, John 186
"The Maid in the Mirror" (fairy tale) 213n84
Maid Marian 113
maiden 74, 132
Maine 177
MAIT Team Stutz 153
"Make Your Story Fly" (article) 19
Malahide, Patrick 175
Mali 173–6, 178–9, 220n23, 240n68, 241n102, 241n103
Mali Navy 176
Mamet, David 135
The Man Who Shot Liberty Valance (film) 47, 99
The Man with the Golden Gun (film) 152, 232n328
Mancini, Henry 154
Mandela, Nelson 140, 231n311
Manhattan, New York 13, 134, 199n19, 199n28
Manhattan Limited (train) 78, 81, 85, 143, 154–5, 160, 217–8n200, 232n331; *see also* Pacific Railroad Engine 51
Manhattan Project 20, 33
Manhunter (1973–1974 comic book series) 153
Manila Bay, Philippines 40
Mannock, Kitty 173, 176, 177, 241n92; *see also* Cussler, Dana
Mansel, John 94, 107
Manza, Ralph 107
Marble Arch Productions 15, 166–169, 171, 172, 179, 180, 184–5, 190, 238n25, 238n31, 239n44
March, Arabella 58
March, Lt. 117–8, 152, 225n63
March Violets (book) 108
Marcus Maxentius 148
Marganin, Lt. Pavel 130, 238n10
Marinda Park 33
marine antiques 21
marine archaeologist 74, 201n83
marine biology 38, 208n27
marine conservation 4
marine engineer 12, 16, 25, 26, 38, 40, 96; marine engineering 20, 34, 50, 179
marine life 159
marine research 103
marine salvage 39
marine science 83
marine technology 105
Mario 19; *see also* video games
maritime archives or library 85, 116
maritime history 16, 32, 85, 193

marksman 51
Marnie (film) 157–8
Marooned (book) 216–7n174
Marooned (film) 167
marriage 17, 51, 73, 74, 132, 141, 144, 145, 149, 213n98; happily married couples 51–2, 102; troubled 51–2
Marseilles, France 181
Martha Ann 161, 176, 217n194, 226n130, 233n5, 240n81; in *Sahara* film 174, 176, 179, 241n103
martial arts 20
The Martian Chronicles (book) 33
Martin, Dean 101; *see also* Dude
Martin, Ross 105
Martinez, Larry 40; *see also* Taft, John
martyr 31, 84, 139, 145; *see also Agnus Dei*; Bass, Adm. Walter Horatio, Jesus Christ; redeemer
Marx, Groucho 40, 191
Maryland 31, 33, 77, 138
M*A*S*H (TV series) 169
Mashu 119
The Masked Venus (book) 95
Maslin, Janet 166
Mason, James 184–5, 242n123
Massachusetts senate 70
Massarde, Yves (The Scorpion) 172, 174, 178, 179, 240n69, 240n76, 241n97, 241n98; differences between book and film 173, 174, 175, 178, 179
Massey, Clement ("Dapper Doyle") 70, 155, 157, 162, 211n48, 211n49; *see also* Cromwell, Jacob
Master, Robin 109
Master Bra'tac 80
master's degree 34, 39, 50, 57, 96
Masters of American Cinema 98, 203n224, 210–1n17, 221n35, 221n50, 221n52, 221n56, 221n58, 221n63, 221n65, 221n68, 221n72, 222n82, 233n12, 236n76, 236n81
mathematical formula 81
Matheson, Richard 153
Matheson, Tim 104
Matos, Ferdinand 66
Matt Burden 96, 220n19
Maturin, Charles 81
Maurice (*Oregon* steward) 42
Mausoleum (book) 47
Maverick (TV series) 108
Maverick, Brett 108–9
Max 31, 83–4, 217n189, 217n192; *see also* Brunhilda, computers and supercomputers; Hermit Limited's computers; Hope
Maxwell, Bill 109
The Mayan Secrets (book) 17, 50
maze 60, 87, 88, 225n105; *see also* labyrinth
McCarey, Leo 91
McCarthy, Kevin 6
McClane, John 4, 108
McConaughey, Matthew 171, 199n40
McCoy, Leonard "Bones" (Dr.) 106
McDonald, Gil 108
McDonald, John D. 12
McGarrett, Steve 71
McGee, Tim 19, 223n126

McGee, Travis 12, 25, 197n38, 220n20
McHale, Quentin 10
McKee, Robert 5
McLintock (film) 184
McQueen, Steve 106, 220n33
Meadows, Bob 41
mechanical engineering 187
The Mediterranean Caper (book) 12, 13, 14, 66, 98, 103, 106, 111, 112, 117, 121, 132, 146–7, 151, 152, 154, 157, 160, 164, 198n51, 208n21, 208n39, 208n49, 209n56, 224n44, 228n201, 228n208, 229n223 234n22, 234n24, 234n25, 234n39; nominated for Best Mystery of 1973 by Mystery Writers of America 14; second-place short story trophy from Orange Coast Community College 12
Medusa 127
Medusa (book) 83, 217n185
Melika 40, 161, 178, 241n96
Melmouth the Wanderer (book) 81
Melville, Herman 3, 28, 228n190
memory 32, 107, 217n177, 237n113
memory transfer process 84, 87
men and women, differences between 51, 65, 88–93
Mendoza, Dr. Julie 55, 65, 152, 159, 201n87, 219n246, 236n80
Menkura 174; *see also* Mycerinus
mens sana in corpore sano ("strong mind in a healthy body") 64
mercenaries 16, 40, 41, 62, 204n33
Mercer, Chuck 160
Mercer, Johnny 154, 219n266
Mercer, Philip 16
merchant vessel 188
Mercier, Alan 83–4
Meredith, Burgess 86
Merker, Ron 12
Merrick, Geoffrey 160
Merriwell, Dick 96; *see also* Merriwell, Frank
Merriwell, Frank 96; *see also* Merriwell, Dick
Merwin, Gerald A. 4, 66–7, 197n37, 210n11, 210n13, 210n14; *see also* Argyle, Nolan J.
Mesoamerican 27
Mesopotamian 124
Messick, Don 104
Meta Section 71, 74, 164, 170, 171
Metropolis (film) 83
Mexican National Affairs Department 66
Mexico/Mexican 40, 42, 59, 162
Miami, Florida 96
Michel-Beechen, Yves 188
microcosmic (local) adventure and hero 46, 62, 87, 111, 115, 127, 128, 145, 147, 157, 205n80, 223n3, 224n25
Middle East/Middle Eastern 181, 206n88
Mighty Casey at the Bat 43
Mikhail Kurkov (ship) 165, 238n10, 238n25
military 4, 24, 38, 39, 48, 50, 66, 83,

99, 100, 101, 106, 135, 147, 166, 167, 168, 171, 179, 183, 186, 197*n*36, 211*n*42, 213*n*85, 223*n*120, 228*n*206, 230*n*251, 234*n*18, 238*n*25, 243*n*139; garbage removal 137; protocol 22; science and technology 83, 103, 161; vessel 106
military fiction 82
Military Police Non-Commission Officer (NCO) 109
Miller, Glenn 179
Milligan, Heidi 37, 55, 73, 87, 141–4, 145, 162, 218*n*215, 230*n*246, 230*n*248, 232*n*321, 232*n*322, 232*n*337, 232*n*340; heterochromia iridis 163, 237*n*128
"A Million the Hard Way" (TV episode) 107
Milne, A.A. 135
mind filter 7, 65, 156
mine 39, 80, 81, 96, 104, 105, 148, 155, 161, 167, 178, 204*n*17, 235*n*66, 238*n*37
miner 49, 76, 165, 232*n*331, 239*n*39
mineral 76, 80, 239*n*51; fictional 161, 222*n*94
mineralogist 129
minicars 83
mini-sub 41, 104, 105, 181
Minnesota 10, 207*n*109
"Minnie the Mermaid" (song) 22, 237*n*120
Minotaur 61, 119
The Minutemen 161
Mirage (book) 17
mirrors, magic 72, 74, 75, 213*n*83, 213*n*84, 227*n*160, 232*n*321
misandrists 61
mischief 97, 204*n*33; mischievous 29, 30
Mission: Impossible (TV series) 40, 182
mission statement 41
Missouri 18, 49
Mr. Deeds Goes to Town (film) 98
Mr. Periwinkle (donkey) *see* Periwinkle, Mr.
Mr. Roberts (film) 99
Mr. Smith Goes to Washington (1939 film) 98
Mr. Spock *see* Spock, Mr.
Mr. T *see* T, Mr.
Mr. Wu *see* Wu, Mr.
misuse of technology 82, 84
MIT 187
Mitchell Gant series 82
Mix Entertainment Holding 180
Mobile Oil 11
Moby-Dick (book) 3, 189, 200*n*59
Moby Dick II: Raise the Pequod! (parody) 189
Moby Dick III: Resink the Bismarck! (parody) 190
modern adventure 10, 64, 73, 224*n*41
Modibo 175, 178, 240*n*76
Modoc (submersible) 238*n*25
modus operandi 39
Molly Bender (ship) 138, 231*n*298
Molony, Sir James 154
Monfort, Adm. Clyde 28

Mongol herdsman 63
Mongolia 63, 162
Monk 20; *see also* Savage, Doc Clark
monomyth 113–127, 128, 131, 212*n*63, 223*n*12, 226–7*n*157
Monopoly (board game) 190
Monroe, Robin 92
monster 3, 60, 69, 83, 84, 87, 88, 104, 118–9, 124, 126, 127, 141, 161, 163, 184, 186, 209*n*63, 214*n*102, 242–3*n*130
"Monsters in the Monastery" (TV episode) 104
Montgomery, Robert 16
Moon 84, 87, 100, 184, 209*n*61, 216*n*171
Moon, Harrison 66, 85, 210*n*9
The Moon Is a Harsh Mistress (book) 84, 216*n*171, 218*n*221, 227*n*161, 233*n*13
The Moon Is Down (1943 film) 168
Moon of the Wolf (film) 152
moon pool 41
"Moon River" (song) 154, 199*n*36, 219*n*266
Moondragon Hook 155
Moore, Henry 52; *see also* Moore, Micki
Moore, Micki 52; *see also* Moore, Henry
Moore, Peter 96
Moore, Roger 185
moral component 23, 200*n*62
moral purpose 23–4
morality 9, 14, 67, 81, 100, 114, 135, 136, 145, 153, 157, 184, 192, 219*n*219, 219*n*2, 230*n*257, 235*n*54
Moran, Congressman Alan 66, 68
Moran, Delphi 33, 34, 54, 57, 59–60, 76, 80, 86, 140, 152, 154, 161, 208*n*39, 208*n*49, 219*n*81, 233*n*4; Delphi Ea 59, 208*n*49
Moran, Dr. Frederick 34, 76; Oracle of Psychic Unity 34
Moran, Peggy 184
Moran, Summer 22, 33, 34, 35, 49, 54, 56, 65, 73, 76, 78, 80, 87, 88, 133, 145, 163, 198*n*54, 204*n*18, 207*n*4, 207*n*12, 207*n*14, 207*n*16, 208*n*29, 212*n*69, 229*n*223, 229*n*224, 233*n*4
Morgan, Lt. Col. Travis 243*n*137
Morgan-Trout, Dr. Gamay 38, 51, 56, 160, 203*n*8
Moriarty, Prof. James 58, 62, 106, 208*n*37, 208*n*43, 209–10*n*80
Moros 48
Morse, Sally 90
Moscow, Russia 149
Moses 129, 228*n*192, 230*n*257; Moses figure 70
Mosses from an Old Manse (book) 3
"Most Dangerous Game" (short story) 104, 152, 154, 235*n*51; *see also* Connell, Richard; *Dragon*; Ivan; Rainsford, Sanger; Ship Trap Island; Zaroff, General
mother 22, 26, 33, 34, 39, 46, 50, 51, 54, 56, 57, 62, 74–5, 76, 89, 91, 92, 114–5, 145, 156, 199*n*19, 199*n*21,

203*n*198, 205*n*82, 207*n*12, 214*n*105, 223*n*122, 223–4*n*22, 229*n*209, 235–6*n*75, 236*n*86
mother-destroyer 145
motion picture and B-movie adventure heroes 98–103
movie references 21, 98
Moyers, Bill 111, 223*n*1
Ms. Moneypenny 19, 142–3
Mu 224*n*39
Mulford, Clarence E. 79, 97
Mullholland, Felix 32, 107; *see also* Wise Old Man archetype
Mulholland's Rare Books and Prints 32, 107
mummy 104, 184, 242*n*120
The Mummy (1932 film) 183
The Mummy (1999 film) 182
The Mummy's Hand 183–4, 187, 190, 242*n*119
Munk (film character) 169
Munk, Henry 169
murder 35, 43, 60, 61, 62, 77, 80, 86, 90, 92, 102, 114, 136, 147, 151, 152, 154, 157, 166, 169, 188, 198*n*61, 212*n*59, 221*n*72, 223*n*122, 233*n*13, 234–5*n*47, 236*n*76, 236*n*80, 242*n*20; mass murder 63, 70
Murder, She Wrote (TV series) 40
Murdock, Capt. H.M. "Howling Mad" 109
Murphy, Mark 42
Murtaugh, Roger 28, 108
Muslim 56
"The Mutiny" (TV episode) 103
Mutt and Jeff 25, 71
"My Bonnie Lies Over the Ocean" (song) 119
Mycerinus 174; *see also* Menkura
The Mysteries of London (book) 95
mystery 1, 3, 6, 11, 12, 13, 16, 20, 22, 25, 32, 37, 44, 73, 77, 79, 81, 90, 93, 95, 97, 103, 107, 112, 115–6, 122, 126, 129, 141, 142, 146, 148–52, 155, 158, 180, 192, 193, 200*n*60, 204*n*25, 205*n*27, 206*n*95, 214*n*119, 214–5*n*123, 219*n*261, 223*n*126, 224*n*39, 233*n*13, 235*n*25, 235*n*54, 236*n*89, 240*n*84, 243*n*140
"Mystery of the Lizard Men" (TV episode) 104
Mystery Writers of America 14
myth and mythology 27, 58, 62, 73, 74, 75, 78, 86, 99, 111, 112, 113, 116, 117, 118, 119, 126, 127, 128, 131, 144, 147, 149, 150, 152, 158, 189, 207–8*n*17, 209*n*63, 212*n*63, 213*n*98, 223*n*12, 226–7*n*157, 229*n*241, 233*n*8, 233*n*13, 234*n*22
mythological series hero 111

N Street 32
Namibia 77
naming characters 40
nanotechnology 82
Nantucket, Massachusetts 3
Narcotics Drug Committee 32
Nash, Percival "Percy" (Payload Percy) 33, 185, 225*n*92
Natal Province 35, 230*n*254

National Aeronautic and Space Administration (NASA) 50
National Archive 188
National Intelligence Agency (NIA) 23, 25, 37, 40, 200n52, 204n34
National Meridian Insurance 107
National Space Headquarters 82
National Treasure (film) 50, 108, 164, 187–9, 190, 207n108, 244n144, 244n145
National Treasure: Book of Secrets (film) 50, 108, 190, 207n108
National Underwater and Marine Agency (NUMA) 1, 4, 21, 113, 118, 124, 127, 131, 145, 147, 148, 150, 160, 161, 164, 169, 170, 172, 173, 174, 175, 176, 177, 178, 179, 180, 186, 198n55, 199n24, 201n87, 202n139, 203n2, 203n9, 204n30, 208n27, 210n9, 212n74, 217n196, 218n201, 225n66, 227n169, 238n25, 238n36, 240n72, 240n73, 240n84, 241n99
National Underwater and Marine Agency (NUMA) 501(c)(3) 1, 16, 176, 177, 193, 198n55, 198n56, 204n19
nautical library 32
Nautilus (submarine) 95, 159, 162, 243n135, 244in3
USS *Nautilus* (SSN-571) 103
Naval Appropriations Committee 32
Naval Criminal Investigative Service 109
Naval Diving and Salvage Training Center 187
Naval reserve vessel 103
Naval reserve 103
Navy SEAL 31, 38, 41, 42, 83, 109, 139, 140–1, 167, 169, 179, 189, 204n19, 241n99; *see also* Special Forces
Navy Weather 130
Nazi 80, 104, 200n51, 215n143, 244n152; air base 148; swastika 161
NCIS (TV series and franchise) 19, 38, 109, 223n126
"Nearer My God to Thee" (song) 73
necromancy 58, 214–5n123
Nefertiti 6, 55
negative evidence of scholarly production 3, 7, 196n36
Negro 28, 178, 211n42
Nelson, Adm. Harriman 103, 222n94
Nelson Institute of Marine Research 103–4
Nemo, Captain 95, 243n135
USOS *Neptune* 103
Nerve Agent S 55, 103, 158–9, 161
Ness, Eliot 135, 230n250
neurologist 154
Nevada 45, 158
Neverland 5, 52, 78, 114–5, 125, 223–4n22, 224n23; *see also* enchanted forests and fairylands; Oz
New England 3, 51, 170, 191
New Jersey 25, 176, 223n118
New Mexico 40
New Testament 134–5, 136–7
New York City, New York 13, 14, 15, 32, 44, 45, 59, 71, 76, 80, 96, 100, 140, 162, 165, 166, 188
New York Harbor 128, 145
New York Maritime College 16, 34, 203n208
New York Times 166, 197–8n48; bestseller list 16
Newport Beach, California 12, 82, 99, 113, 129–30, 208n27, 224n28
Newton, Charlotte "Charlie" 102, 157
Nicaragua 95; Sandinistas 42
Nice and Noir: Contemporary American Crime Fiction 27, 228n203
Nicefolk, Casey 43–7, 50, 52, 53, 64, 96, 186, 207n114, 234n25, 234n36
Nicefolk, Ever 43, 44, 45
Nicefolk, Knot 43, 205n56
Nicefolk, Lacey 43–7, 50, 52, 53, 64, 96, 186, 207n114, 234n25, 234n36
Nicefolk family 44, 45
Nicefolk Landing 43, 44
Nichols, Dale 66
Nicholson, Nikki 36
Nicholson, Warren 165, 167, 228n205
Nielson, Col. J.A. 27
Niger 172, 174, 175, 179
Niger River 172, 173, 175, 176; Oued Zarit tributary 173
night elves 78
Night of Dark Shadows (film) 216n147, 235n48
"Night of the Winged Terror" (TV episode) 105
Night Probe! 16, 29, 55, 57, 60–1, 68, 70, 71, 72, 73, 78, 81, 83, 85, 87, 140, 141–4, 145, 154–5, 160, 162, 163, 200n60, 201n88, 202n128, 202n151, 202n166, 204n29, 204n30, 210n9, 211n48, 211n49, 214n114, 215n159, 216n172, 217–8n200, 218n215, 224n39, 230n248, 231–2n317, 232n321, 232n328, 232n329, 232n340, 232n341, 237n124; *see also* North American Treaty; United States of North America
Nightingale, Florence 119
Nile River 174
Nimoy, Leonard 106, 201n111, 243n138
911Stunts 181; *see also* Sargeant, Gregg
Nixon, Kevin 42
No Man's World (book) 216n171
Nobel Prize 154
noble savage 28, 97
non-elected public servant 67
nonfiction humor 15
Nordic god 117
Norris, Chuck 181
Norse mythology 78, 129, 130
North America 95, 115, 143, 150; *see also* America; Canada; United States
North American Treaty 115, 141, 142, 143, 155, 162, 232n321, 232n340; *see also Night Probe!*; United States of North America
North Atlantic 71, 112, 128, 165, 184
North by Northwest (film) 102, 184
North Sea 39
North Vietnamese regulars 21
Northern Pacific Railroad 207n109
nose gear 35
Nosferatu (1922 film) 168
Nouvelles de Monde 117, 241n86
Novak, Kim 157, 235–6n75
Novaya Zemlya, Russia 129, 131, 159, 165, 167, 169, 227n181; *see also* Seymour Island; Svlardala
novel (medium) 79, 168
NR-1 (submarine) 160
nuclear aircraft carrier 167
nuclear arsenal 23, 86 130
nuclear devices 33
nuclear holocaust 34
nuclear missile 86, 141; nuclear missile attack 168, 228n191
nuclear power 41
nuclear strike 230n247
nuclear submarine 23, 81, 103, 167
nuclear threat 80, 141
nuclear weaponry 33, 86, 130
Nuestra Señora de la Concepción 32, 159, 215n143; *see also* Drake, Sir Francis
NUMA Files (fiction series) 150, 201n83, 203n2, 204n30, 210n3, 215n144, 223n113, 234n36; *see also* NUMA's Special Assignments Team (NSAT)
NUMA's Special Assignments Team (NSAT) 16, 38, 39, 192, 204n19; *see also NUMA Files* (fiction series)
Numbers, Book of 135

O. Henry 158
Oahu, Hawaii 23, 33
Oakey, Charles ("Uncle Charlie") 62, 102, 157
Oates, Douglas 66
O'Bannon, Selig 178, 241n95, 241n96
obsessions 65; *see also* thematic preoccupation
ocean 10, 25, 28, 31, 74, 78, 100, 159, 165, 166, 173, 183, 237n116, 242n123
ocean engineering 34
ocean floor 165, 166, 190, 233n5, 244n154
ocean science 34, 38
Ocean Wanderer (luxury hotel) 183
oceanic missing link 104
oceanic science organization 29
oceanography 12, 30, 34; oceanographer 38, 73
O'Connell, Megan 160
O'Connell, Dr. Patricia 26, 56, 160
O'Connor, Richard 168
Odin (ship) 148
Odysseus 95, 150
Odysseus (ship) 159
The Odyssey (epic poem) 209n6
Odyssey syndicate 59, 61, 62, 65, 89, 162
officials, appointed 66, 210n9
Ohio 45
oil rig 39, 185
Okrand, Marc 185
Old Gert (submersible) 83, 161, 237n120
The Old Man and the Sea (book) 4
Old North Church 189
Old Sleuth 47, 96, 191, 206n91

O'Meara, Dr. Raphael 85, 98
omnipotent narrator 25, 81
On Her Majesty's Secret Service (book) 57, 73, 86, 154 218*n*215
"One and Twenty" (poem) 121
101st Salvage Fleet 22, 161
O'Neill, Col. Jonathan "Jack" 4, 80, 109, 215*n*137
Opar 243*n*136; *see also* Atlantis; lost civilization; Skartaris
Operation Wild Rose 133, 135–40, 153, 211*n*42, 230*n*251, 230*n*257, 230*n*278, 231*n*282
opposite number 39, 131, 228*n*206; *see also* Vixen 03
opposites 31, 39, 40, 62–3, 65, 71–2, 112, 117–8, 147, 209*n*76, 209*n*80, 225*n*57, 228*n*206; *see also* doubles
Orange Coast Community College 12
Orange County, California 42
orchids 19, 32
The Oregon 16, 41, 42, 67, 77, 84, 96, 106, 151, 152, 161, 162, 180, 181, 186, 205*n*39, 205*n*40, 205*n*43, 217*n*194, 222*n*93; *see* also Kirk chair
Oregon Files (fiction series) 16, 17, 40–43, 46, 66–7, 81, 106, 150, 164, 181, 204*n*33, 234*n*36; *see also* The Corporation
Oregon Files (TV series) 180–2, 241–2*n*107, 244*n*151
Organa, Princess Lea 108, 224*n*32
organized crime 71
"The Origin" (graphic novel) 153–5; *see also Jon Sable, Freelance*
Orion Lake 63, 81, 101, 216*n*162
Orkney Islands, Scotland 148
O'Rourke, Terence 96, 186
orphan 57, 62, 114
Orpheus 86, 88
Oscars 104, 198*n*52; *see also* Academy Awards
O'Shaughnessy, Brigid 127
Ottendorf cipher 187
Ottoman Empire 148
Oval Office 68, 133; *see also* White House
Overholt, Langston, IV 42
Oz 78; *see also* enchanted forests and fairylands; Neverland

pace 41, 81, 89, 95, 101, 149, 166, 167, 173, 189
Pacific Grove, California 174
Pacific Ocean 3, 10, 21–2, 34, 76, 78, 97, 104, 134, 140, 141, 175, 203*n*206, 230*n*247
Pacific Railroad Engine 51 154–5; *see also Manhattan Limited*
Pacific Vortex 23
Pacific Vortex (book) 12, 21, 22, 23, 25, 26, 30, 32, 37, 48, 53, 54, 60, 71, 72, 73, 78, 79, 80, 81, 82, 85, 86, 98, 111, 112, 117, 127, 133, 145, 146, 147, 151, 152, 157, 160, 161, 176, 197*n*31, 199*n*24, 200*n*47, 200*n*62, 201*n*113, 201*n*117, 202,*n*156, 203*n*192, 204*n*18, 207*n*12, 208*n*49, 216*n*155, 216*n*157, 216*n*161, 216*n*167,

217*n*194, 220*n*23, 221*n*54, 224*n*39, 225*n*63, 226*n*130, 229*n*223, 233*n*4, 233*n*7, 234*n*24, 234*n*25, 234*n*39, 240*n*81, 240*n*84; parallels with *Shock Wave* 76, 88, 154, 235*n*56; *The Sea Dwellers* 12, 15, 197*n*29
packaging machines 47
Packard, Frank L. 79
Packard One-Eighty limousine (1942) 107
Packard Towncar (1938) 223*n*11
Paglia, Camille 6, 196*n*32
Pago Pago 33; *see also* American Samoa; Tutuila Naval Station
pajamas 32
The Pale Criminal (book) 108
Palm Key Island, Florida 104
Panama 32, 159
Panama (a Navy thing) 241*n*103
Panama City, Panama 32
Panama hat 50, 211*n*48
Papaaloa, George 85
paperback 16, 198*n*7; rights 15; series 7, 10
Parable of the Net 134
Paragon Motor-Car Company 45
paragon 64, 73, 199*n*19
Paragon Panther 45; *see also* Chitty Bang Bang, *Chitty-Chitty-Bang-Bang: The Magical Car*
paramedic 43
parent 10, 29, 35, 40, 44, 46, 51, 76, 89, 114, 117, 130, 215*n*137, 227*n*165, 240*n*69
parent series 38, 204*n*12
Paris (legend) 88; *see also* Achilles; Hector
Paris, France 155
Parker, Robert B. 28; *see also* Hawk; Spenser
parkour traceur 181
parodies 189–90
partner 11, 37, 42, 51, 55, 105, 106, 122, 179, 220*n*19, 239*n*64, 241*n*87, 241*n*97, 241*n*107
Pasadena Community College 44
Pasha Peddler 105
passport 72, 76, 156, 158, 235*n*73
past 14, 21, 23, 27, 33, 35, 43, 47, 49, 52, 69, 72, 78, 85–6, 97, 114, 118, 121, 122, 133, 138, 142, 147, 148, 149, 150, 158, 171, 183, 184, 185, 186, 188, 191, 204*n*34, 213*n*86, 214*n*123, 217*n*177, 217–8*n*200, 224*n*23, 229*n*219, 233*n*13; *see also* history
past affecting future 80, 126, 147, 184, 185, 187, 188, 191, 215*n*140, 215*n*148, 244*n*3
Pataki, Michael 169
patience 35
patient 9, 43
patriarch 28, 43, 48
Patton (film) 16
Paulsen, Rob 190, 244*n*154
Pearl Harbor, Hawaii 23, 138
Peck, Gregory 67
Peck, Lt. Templeton "Face" 109
Pecos River 97
pediatrician 51

Peel, Mrs. Emma 89; *see also* Ripley, Ellen
peignoir 35
Pembroke 135, 230*n*255, 230*n*260
The Penguin 58
Pennine Alps 77
Pennsylvania 188–9
penny bloods 95
penny dreadful 95, 97, 192, 220*n*6
Pennyworth, Alfred 19
penthouse 29, 61
Penthouse (magazine) 133
Peppard, George 106, 109
Pequod (ship) 3, 189, 200*n*59
Periwinkle (ship) 44, 217*n*194, 237*n*116; *see also* Mr. Periwinkle
Periwinkle, Mr. (donkey) 44; *see also* Periwinkle
Perkins, Anthony 156, 185; *see also* Bates, Norman; Kramer, Lou
Perlmutter, St. Julien 20, 31–2, 85, 107, 178, 185, 202*n*188, 205*n*64; parallels with Nero Wolfe 32
Perry, Thomas 17, 50
Perseus 127
Persia 176
Person of Interest (TV series) 67
personal combat 31
personal secretary 20, 57, 119
Peru 32, 190
Peruvian Gaokin frog 190, 244*n*154
Peter Gunn (TV series) 30
Peter Pan 4, 22, 35, 39, 49, 56, 105, 106, 109, 114, 115, 117, 123, 125, 127, 143, 145, 182, 187, 223–4*n*22
Peter Pan and Wendy 114–5, 223–4*n*22
Petersen, Herman 96
Peterson, Andrew 17
Petrov, Viktor (a.k.a. Ivan) 39
Ph.D. 38, 54, 55, 170
Philadelphia, Pennsylvania 188–9
Philadelphia's University of the Arts 6
Philippines 16, 48
philosophy/philosophical 24, 39, 43, 104, 204*n*25, 206*n*88, 211*n*34
Phoenix, Arizona 165
Phoenix Foundation 109
phoniness 48
photographer 56, 183, 208*n*26
physical fitness 29
piano 51
Picard, Cap. Jean-Luc 106, 205*n*45
Piccard, Jean Felix 205*n*45
Pidgeon, Walter 103
"A Piece of the Action" (TV episode) 106
Pierce, Capt. Benjamin Franklin "Hawkeye" 169, 239*n*40
Pierce, Frederick 128
Pierre Hotel 100
pilot 12, 21, 23, 33, 38, 50, 77, 96, 97, 100, 101, 114, 121, 147, 169, 180, 183, 219*n*244, 229*n*244, 243*n*137
Pilottown 55, 81, 158, 159; *see also* San Marino
Pinky and the Brain (TV series) 189–90
Pinky 190; *see also* Brain
pinto 97
piracy 69

pirate 10, 34, 59, 92, 96, 115, 127, 156, 214–5n123, 220n6, 235n50, 243n132
Pirates of the Caribbean (Disneyland ride) 58, 127
Pirates of the Caribbean (film series) 108, 208n42, 235n50
Pisces (NUMA underwater laboratory) 40
Pisces Corporation 59
Pisces Metal Company 176
Pisces Pacific Company 176
pit crew 30
Pitt (Nash), Barbara 33, 203n198; observation that all life is a gift 22, 46
Pitt, Dirk Eric 1, 4, 6, 7, 9, 10–17, 19, 20–5, 26, 27, 28, 29, 30, 31, 32, 33, 34, 35, 36, 37, 38–9, 40, 41, 42, 43, 44, 46, 47, 48–9, 50, 51, 52, 53, 54, 55, 56–7, 58, 59, 60, 62–3, 64, 65, 66–7, 68, 71, 72, 73–4, 76–7, 78, 80, 81, 82, 83, 84, 85, 86–7, 88, 89, 90, 91, 92, 93, 94, 96–7, 98, 99–100, 101, 102, 103, 105, 106, 107, 108, 109, 111, 112–3, 114, 115, 116, 117–8, 119, 120–1, 122, 123–5, 126, 127, 128, 129, 130–1, 132, 133, 134–5, 136, 138–9, 140, 141, 142, 143, 144–5, 146, 147, 148, 149, 150, 151, 152, 153, 154, 155, 158–9, 160, 161, 162, 163, 164–6, 167–71, 172–80, 183, 184, 185, 186, 188, 189, 191, 192, 193, 194, 195n13, 196n32, 196n34, 197n23, 197n24, 197n31, 197n34, 197n41, 198n55, 199n17, 199n20, 199n21, 199n22, 199n23, 199n24, 199n28, 199n36, 199n40, 200n52, 200n54, 200n60, 200n62, 200n68, 200n74, 201n87, 201n92, 201n99, 201n100, 201n107, 201n112, 201n113, 201n116, 201n117, 202n151, 202n161, 203n198, 202n202, 203n203, 203n212, 203n221, 203n2, 203n9, 204n17, 204n18, 204n19, 204n34, 205n39, 205n77, 206n95, 207n3, 207n4, 107n16, 208n21, 208n25, 208n27, 208n29, 208n52, 209n56, 209n63, 209–10n80, 210n81, 210n8, 210n9, 212n52, 212n69, 212n74, 214n102, 214n114, 214n117, 215n137, 216n146, 216n147, 216n162, 216n167, 217n177, 217n178, 217n179, 217–8n200, 218n214, 218n215, 218n221, 218n227, 219n244, 219n246, 219n258, 219n262, 219n263, 219n266, 219n270, 220n23, 220n26, 221n37, 221n56, 221n57, 221n61, 223n111, 223n122, 223n7, 223n10, 224n25, 224n28, 224n39, 224n41, 224n45, 224n48, 224n51, 224n53, 225n63, 225n66, 225n72, 225n74, 225n87, 225n88, 225n92, 225n95, 225n99, 225–6n105, 226n128, 226n130, 226n135, 226n136, 226n138, 226n140, 226n141, 226n145, 226n150, 225n151, 226n152, 226n156, 226–7n157, 227n158, 227n160, 227n162, 227n164, 227n169, 227n172, 227n177, 227n181, 227n182, 227n184, 227–8n185, 228n186, 228n191, 228n192, 228n196, 228n197, 228n199, 228n201, 228n206, 229n210, 229n217, 229n219, 229n223, 229n229, 229n231, 230n246, 230n248, 230n277, 231n315, 231–2n317, 232n318, 232n321, 232n322, 232n327, 232n331, 232n332, 232n337, 233n358, 233n5, 234n21, 234n22, 234n23, 235n51, 235n56, 235n58, 235n59, 235n73, 236n80, 236n96, 237n110, 237n113, 237n114, 237n120, 237n122, 238n12, 239n39, 239n40, 239n42, 239n43, 239n49, 240n65, 240n67, 240n68, 240n69, 240n73, 240n76, 240n80, 240n84, 240–1n85, 241n88, 241n92, 241n96, 241n99, 241n101, 241n102, 241n103, 242n116, 244n145; disrespect to authority figures 13, 26; driven to rediscover the past 23, 49, 85; Giordino's assessment of Pitt 23; grandfather 21; gypsy ancestors 25, 32, 118; hangar home 21, 33, 37, 41, 57, 84, 90, 145, 161, 162; ideal of a man 23–4; no patience for fools 48; obituary 20, 199n17, 203n198; old school 90, 129; prefers old look 21; Purple Heart 114, 241n99; selfish with his emotions with women 13, 36, 145; special projects director 4, 12, 21, 29, 38, 68, 99, 165, 203n9; star quarterback 34; tags 20–2, 189; "two men" personality 22, 27, 48, 100, 106, 129, 147, 190, 199n40; *see also* Pitt archetype hero
Pitt, Dirk, Jr. 17, 20, 34, 46, 54, 148, 223n122; special projects director 34
Pitt, Sen. George 21, 32–3, 49, 66, 68, 160, 202–3n190, 203n96, 204n16, 210n9, 215n137, 221n59; observations about humanity 24, 33, 117, 126, 127, 224n49; the Socrates of the Senate 32
Pitt, Summer 17, 20, 34–5, 46, 54, 57, 76, 148, 163, 203n210
Pitt, William, the Elder 11
Pitt archetype hero 4, 10, 16, 39, 40, 46, 48, 50, 107–109, 111, 184, 185, 186, 187, 191–2; bureaucrat/public-sector employee 4, 12, 21, 42, 48, 63, 65–8, 104, 106, 177, 211n22, 211n32, 238n26; defender of the realm 13, 24, 39, 43, 46, 49, 52, 188, 192; descendants 107–10; manhunter 13, 22, 43, 46, 49, 52, 77, 153, 187, 188, 192, 207n122, 235n49; need to see beyond horizon 46, 48, 50, 92, 118, 183; nemesis 13, 22, 43, 49, 52, 57, 188, 192, 208n37; old soul 21, 27, 32, 85, 107, 187; patriotic 4, 24, 39, 42, 48, 105, 106, 185, 187, 188, 191, 200n64; realist 4, 24, 33, 39, 43, 48, 62, 126, 185, 187; self-effacing 4, 39, 48, 103, 105, 106, 109, 185, 187; self-reliant 4, 39, 48, 50, 56, 103, 105, 106, 109, 185, 187, 206–95; self-sacrificing 4, 39, 48, 50, 54, 103, 105, 106, 109, 185, 187; stray from the highlands or highroads 13, 23, 39, 49, 78, 184, 186, 192; strong work ethic 10, 48; wisecracking 4, 39, 48, 187, 191; *see also* Pitt, Dirk Eric
Pitt literary descendants 107–11
Pivet, Barbe 96
places lost to history 13, 49, 52, 188
plague 59, 172, 174, 219n246
Plague Ship (book) 159, 205n43, 205n48, 236n92
Planet of the Apes (1968 film) 167
Platonic Ideal 119, 225n79
play angles (gimmick) 10, 25, 30, 125
Playboy Books 15
plays 51, 71, 83, 221n67, 241n89
plot 1, 4, 16, 18, 38, 38, 42, 44, 79, 98, 101, 102, 146–63, 166, 167, 185, 186, 192, 209n80, 210n2, 215n143, 225n138, 234n32; complex plots 81, 150; elements and repeating elements 7, 60, 76, 88, 95, 158–63, 235n36, 235n68; plot tactics 151–8, 234n34, 236n92; stereotypical plots 80, 215n134
Plummer, Christopher 187
pocket watch 21, 49
Poco Bonito (ship) 81, 161
Poe, Edgar Allan 9, 38, 50, 78, 80, 121, 144, 211n51, 213n86, 215n126, 216n145, 216n148
poet 88, 118, 211n51, 212n71, 214n123, 226n145
poetry 71, 188, 211n51, 212n53
poetry reading 119–23, 147, 227n162
Poison Flower (book) 50
poison missile attack 29
poker 39, 197n38, 204n22, 244n92
Polar Queen (ship) 92, 159
police 9, 66, 67, 95, 96, 107, 109, 118, 170
USOS *Polidor* 103, 222n92
Polidori (Ambassador) 175, 177
Polish Americans 106
Polish proverbs 107, 223n112
political correctness 57, 178
political science 4, 42
politicians (elected government officials) 14, 20, 33, 40, 61–3, 66, 68, 91, 98, 129, 132, 221n37
politics 18, 63, 170, 203n223
Pons, Solar 38, 204n13
Poole, Riley 188–9, 244n149, 244n150
popular culture 21, 28, 67
popular fiction 3–4, 7, 9, 67, 94, 192
popular fiction writer 192
popular hero 4, 13, 49, 97, 98
Popular Mechanics (magazine) 104
Popular Science (magazine) 104
populist 98–9, 102
postindustrialism 14
post-war adventure hero 4, 12, 53, 94, 107
Potomac River 81, 138
Pott, Comm. Caractacus 45

Pott, Jemimah 45
Pott, Jeremy 45
Pott, Mimsie 45
Potter, Harry 86, 114, 206n89, 217–8n200, 225n105, 227n165, 229n241
Powell, William 51
power monger 63, 67, 68, 85; see also "Wonks and Warriors: Depictions of Government Professionals in Popular Films"
powerboat 34, 45
prairie church 3, 7
prayer 123, 125
prediction 74, 206n88, 234n18; see also premonition
pregnant 34
premonition 79, 81; see also prediction
preservation 4, 16, 85, 118, 193, 240n73
President of the United States 29, 55, 59, 85, 87–8, 92, 104, 132, 139, 160, 165, 166, 209n65, 210n84, 212n58, 216n159, 217n177, 229n213, 230n247, 231n315, 232n340, 234n42, 238n10
press secretary 36, 66
Prest, Thomas Preskett 95, 220n9
Prevlov, Capt. André Prevlov 57, 130–1, 140, 143, 149, 163, 165, 166, 168, 169, 171, 183, 228n191, 228n205, 228n206, 234n23; performs protagonist duties 130–1, 234n21
"The Price of Doom" (TV episode) 104
Prime Minister of the United Kingdom 141, 143
prince 73–4, 212n65, 215n140, 224n37
Prince Charming 72–3, 76, 77, 212n65
princess 213n98, 214n102, 183
Princess (Mario Bros.) 19; see also video games
A Princess of Mars (book) 160
Princeton University 85, 142, 178
prison colony 84, 159
prisoner 24, 127, 150, 152, 177, 178, 237n121
private and public sectors 4, 24, 66
private detective 1, 10, 14, 17, 30, 37, 47, 96, 108–9, 204n25
The Private Memoirs and Confessions of a Justified Sinner (book) 81
Prober 105
producer 17, 102, 104, 164, 167, 168, 180, 195n10, 223n120, 239n64, 243n131, 243n140
progression of adventure heroes 94–5, 107–8, 110
Prohibition 11, 25
prologue 23, 47, 76, 77, 85, 132, 146, 149, 150, 152, 155, 158, 173, 177, 183, 185, 186, 187, 189, 209n63, 229n219, 233n10, 233n13, 236n89, 238n11, 243n131, 244n150; see also epilogue
promiscuity 53
prop master 42
proposal 17, 46, 91–2, 145, 233n358, 237n122
propulsionist 38, 203n7
Prosperteer (dirigible) 81, 219n244
Prosperteer (magazine) 55
prosthetic leg 42

protective figure 118, 125, 142, 226n143
prototype 23, 81, 95, 96, 104, 183
protracted adolescence 5, 233n8
Providence, Rhode Island 70
Psyche 22, 58, 236n76
Psycho (1960 film) 185, 235n71, 236n76; parallels with *Deep Six* 156–8
PT boat 16
public administrator 66–8, 210n9, 210n12
Public Voices (magazine) 66–7, 210n12
Publisher's Weekly (magazine) 45
publishing industry 10
puer aeternus (eternal boy) 115
Pullman car 57, 81, 84, 143
pulp magazines 9–10, 13, 18, 19, 20, 23, 27, 47, 53, 82, 89, 94–7, 107, 110, 151, 160, 161, 163, 186, 191, 193, 198n7, 205n43, 214n119, 215n139, 220n4, 220n6, 222n81
"The Pulp Paper Master Fiction Plot" 18, 151; see also character blueprint; Dent, Lester; "Wave Those Tags!"
pulp series adventure heroes 18, 58, 59, 67, 94–7, 110, 153, 191, 198n5, 198n7, 205n43, 217n177, 220n4, 223n119
punch cards 88
punctual 29
pure adventures 10, 192
Putnam 15
Pyramid Books 14, 15, 16, 66, 164
pyramids of Giza 174, 244n148
Pyrotech 610 161

"Q" 19
Q Branch 84
QD (Quick Death or Doomsday) organism 83, 84, 103, 134–5, 139–41, 159, 161, 168, 230n247, 231n315
Qin Shang Maritime 63
quarantine 55
quartermaster 41
Quatermain, Allan 96, 230n254
Quatermass, Prof. Bernard 182
Quebec, Canada 68, 70
Queequeg 3, 28, 189
quest 27, 73, 78, 80, 96, 100, 111, 112, 115, 119, 122, 124, 125, 126, 128, 135, 137, 141–2, 143, 144–5, 173, 189, 207n107, 225n105, 227n158, 232n318, 232n322, 236n80, 237n114, 244n150
Quest, Dr. Benton 104–5, 222n99
Quest, Jonny 104–5
The Quiet Man (film) 15
Quint 170
quipu ("talking knots") 83

The Race (book) 47
Rafferty, Lee 52, 102
Rafferty, Maxine 52, 102
Raiders of the Lost Ark (film) 16, 108, 166
Rainbow Six (book) 5
Rainsford, Sanger 153
Raise the Titanic! (book) 1, 15–6, 23, 25, 26, 55, 66, 68, 71, 73, 74–5, 81–2, 83, 87, 91, 99, 100, 105, 115, 128–32, 140–1, 143, 144–5, 146, 148–50, 152, 159, 160, 161, 162, 164, 165, 166, 167, 171, 194, 199n24; 201n88, 201n92; 202n139, 210n84, 213n85, 213n90, 215–6n145, 216n146, 216n147, 216n156, 219n253, 221n35, 225n66, 227n160, 227n182, 227n183, 228n190, 228n199, 228n201, 228n204, 229n209, 229n225, 232n321, 232n351, 233n10, 233n15, 234n18, 234n21, 234n22, 234n24, 235n53, 236n89, 239n45, 241n88; "Regenesis" 73–4, 81, 234n16
Raise the Titanic (film) 1, 166–71, 172, 179, 180, 182, 184, 190, 199n40, 204n19, 217n178, 237n117, 238n25, 238n31, 239n41, 239n60; alternative ending 168; see also Barry, John
Raise the Titanic (newspaper strip) 164–6, 190, 237n3
Rampage (book) 47
Rathbone, Basil 113
Razov, Mikhail 31, 148, 162, 215n144
Reade, Frank, Jr. 96, 186
Reagan, Ronald 24, 210n84, 238n26
Rear Window (film) 157
Rebecca (book) 79, 235n48
rebirths & resurrections 60, 65, 86–8, 115, 116, 123–4, 126, 137–8, 142, 147, 154, 159, 166, 171, 212n68, 218n214, 218n216, 226n120, 227n127, 231n309, 233n6
recipes 43–4
recombination and reinterpretation 152–58
Recover a Boon (monomyth) 86, 112, 113, 115, 121, 122, 123, 128, 130, 132, 143, 212n74, 227n162, 227n172, 230n248
red algae 106; see also red tide
The Red Lion 95
Red Menace 6
Red River (film) 101–2
Red Sea 129, 238n23
red tide 159, 172, 173, 175; see also red algae
Reddale, Frederic 96
redeemer 134, 136, 137, 138, 139, 140, 229n241, 231n285, 231n309; see also *Agnus Dei*; Bass, Adm. Walter Horatio, Jesus Christ; martyr
Redford, Robert 67
redheads (women) 38, 54, 55, 56, 57, 61, 109, 128, 163, 188, 208n27, 229n224
Reeves, John 11
Refusal of the Call (monomyth) 113, 115
Regional Emergency Response Team 55, 246n246
rehabilitation, of characters 170–1
Reichs, Kathy 17
religion 27, 35, 61, 111, 125
Remington TR870 automatic shotgun 176
Renny 20; see also Savage, Doc Clark
repetition (Gothic) 72, 79
reprint libraries 95

Republic of Texas Navy 40
Republican (political) 98, 202–3n190
Requiem for a Ruler of Worlds (book) 108
rescue 5, 14, 21, 22, 25, 27, 28, 29, 33, 35, 36, 39, 44, 54, 56, 57, 60, 72, 73, 76, 79, 80, 86, 88, 89, 111, 112, 113, 114, 116, 119, 120, 125, 126, 128, 129, 131, 139, 140, 141, 144, 148, 149, 150, 151, 152, 160, 162, 165, 166, 167, 172, 174, 175, 176, 178, 179, 181, 183, 188, 201n83, 201n112, 208n21, 212n66, 213n89, 214n120, 218n214, 219n258, 224n23, 224n41, 229n229, 240n80, 242n123; her asks damsel out to dinner 34, 39, 174, 203n209
Rescue from Without (monomyth) 113, 125, 159
retirement 12, 33, 37, 40, 42, 51, 62, 87, 95, 103, 107, 134, 135, 169, 179, 202n139, 205n47, 222n93, 232n329, 234–5n47, 241n101
Return (monomyth) 111, 113, 120, 123–7, 131
The Return (book) 80
The Return of Tarzan (book) 243n136
"The Reunion" (short story) 16, 22, 36, 103, 150, 197n41, 200n53, 205n64, 205n70, 211n42, 231–2n317
Revolutionary War 78, 187, 200n70, 206n95
Reykjavik, Iceland 71, 125
Reynolds, George W.M. 95
Rhode Island 70
Richard the Lionheart 113
Richard's Lido Market 11
Richmond, Virginia 173
riddle 52, 186, 189, 233n12
riddle clues 52, 189
riddle contest 52, 122, 139, 225–6n105
Riddle of Submission (monomyth) 115–6, 120, 123; see also Submission
"Riddle of the Gold" (TV episode) 105
Riggs, Martin 28, 108
"Right Place Wrong Time" (song) 179
"Rime of the Ancient Mariner" 121, 160–1, 236n107
Rio Bravo (film) 101
Rio Grande (film) 99
Ripley, Ellen 89; see also Peel, Mrs. Emma
The Ripple Effect (book) 47
"Rita Hayworth and the Shawshank Redemption" (short story) 6
River Jordan 136
river warder 125, 226n130
RNA 87; see also hippocampus
Road, Mike 104
Road of Trials (monomyth) 113, 117, 118, 119, 121, 125, 128, 132, 135, 138, 141, 189, 224n54, 225n55
Robards, Jason 168
Robbins, Harold 102, 163, 222n81, 237n126
Robert Ludlum's The Janson Command 47

Robin Hood (Robin, earl of Locksley) 67, 113, 185, 229n241
Robinson, Kelly 28, 105
Robinson R44 (helicopter) 41
Robleman, Dr. 34
robots: dogs 153; sentries 83
Robson, Kenneth 18; see also Dent, Lester; Savage (Doc) Clark
The Rocketeer 222n97; see also Stevens, Dave
Rockford, Jim 108–9
The Rockford Files (TV series) 108–9
"The Rocking-Horse Winner" (short story) 3
Rocky III (film) 86
Rogers, Rosemary 92
Rogers, Will 98
Rohmer, Sax 54, 59, 79
Rojas, Dr. Eva 13, 35, 56, 90, 163, 171, 172
Rollins, Grump 96
romance 27, 56, 57, 89, 92, 111, 142, 172, 222n81, 234n37
Romance (genre) 14, 79, 214n123
Rome 176
Rome (TV series) 180
Romulans 84
USS *Ronald Reagan* 84
Rondheim, Oskar 58, 59, 61, 71, 88, 112–3, 119–23, 127, 147, 149, 160, 161, 163, 188, 208n43, 212n53, 213–4n98, 216n159, 218n234, 225n92, 227n158, 227n162, 227n163, 227n166, 227n172, 237n110, 237n114; see also Butera, Carzo
Rondheim Industries 59, 71, 161
Rongelo Island 141, 230n247
Rooney, Dr. Calvin 71
Roosevelt, Theodore 48, 199n11
Ross, Linda 41, 181, 205n47
Ross, Sandra 65; see also Bigalow
Ross, Scott 180–1
ROTC 42
Rove (ship) 162
Rowling, J.K. 45, 114, 214n105, 217–8n200
Royal, Tidi 55, 56, 57, 89, 90, 112, 119–20, 123–4, 126, 127, 147, 161, 225n87, 226n116, 226n117
Royal Crown Cola 94
Royal Hawaiian Hotel 54
Ruark, Robert 153
rude 22, 98, 122, 200n52
rugged 11, 20, 25, 92, 101, 122, 189, 219n265
Ruggles 96
The Running Man (film) 152
R.U.R. (play) 82–3
Rush Hour 3 (film) 26
Russia 24, 31, 35, 39, 42, 60, 80, 124, 129, 130, 131, 165, 167, 169, 189, 198n55, 228n205, 238n25, 239n39; Soviet Union 167; USSR 59, 88, 130, 167, 169, 216n171, 218n221
Russian marines 131, 140, 167, 183
Ruth (oil-drilling rig) 185
Ryan, Jack 4, 25, 50, 58, 108, 197n37, 210n8, 210n11, 210n13, 221n57, 221n61, 221n62, 222n80

Ryan, Jack, Jr. 181, 210n11, 210n13, 210n14, 221n62
Ryan, Marcus 160
Ryan, "Rusty" (LTJG) 100
Ryder, H.A. 162
Rymer, Malcolm James 95, 220n9

Sabatini, Rafael 7, 96, 195n6
saber 20, 153
Sable, Elise (McKenna) 153
Sable, Jon 4, 108, 153, 195n13, 231n311
Sacred Stone (book) 40, 41, 205n47
sacrifice 24, 29, 39, 72, 75, 84, 91, 99, 123, 134, 135, 139, 141, 199n13, 200n70, 229n242
sage 32, 85; see also Wise Old Man
Sahara (book) 5, 13, 16, 31, 32, 40, 44, 56, 104, 159, 160, 161, 162–3, 172, 173, 174, 175, 176, 177, 178, 179
Sahara (2005 film) 5, 17, 28, 164, 171–80; budget 171–2; DVD 177; lawsuit 172; "Lost" (prologue in book and film) 177; opening credits 176–6
Sahara desert 17, 28, 173, 175, 177
Sail (ship) 96
Sail, Oscar 96, 220n20
The Saint 5
Saint Julian 31
Saint-Julien 31
St. Louis, Missouri 37
Salem, Lee 165
Salem's Lot (book) 6, 152, 168, 227n183
Saltzman, Harry 241n104
salvage 4, 12, 21, 30, 39, 73, 75, 81, 83, 85, 96, 100, 130, 131, 134, 138, 149, 150, 154, 161, 165, 169, 174, 176, 182, 183, 190, 201n87, 212n74, 235n59, 238n22, 238n25, 240n81, 241n99
salvation 75, 137, 144, 226n141
Sampson, Robert viii, 13, 18, 49, 53, 57, 58–9, 64, 65, 96, 97, 107, 191, 195n7; see also villain types; *Yesterday's Faces*
Samuel R. Wallace (shop) 71, 238n25
Samuelson, Paul (and wife) 160, 236n97
samurai 94–5, 97; see also knight-errant
San Diego, California 142, 143, 162, 193, 204n16, 232n321
San Francisco, California 33, 69, 181, 225n92; Nob Hill 69
San Marino 76, 156, 158, 159; see also Pilottown
San Quentin (prison) 108
sanctuary 35, 125, 162
Sandecker, Adm. James 12, 16, 17, 20, 21, 22, 26, 28–9, 30, 31, 41, 53, 55, 57, 63, 68, 69, 73, 75, 76, 80, 85, 89, 90, 91, 98, 99–100, 104, 105, 112, 113, 114, 115, 117, 118, 119, 120, 121, 122, 126, 131, 134, 140, 145, 147, 160, 161, 164, 168, 169, 170, 171, 173, 174, 175, 176, 177, 179, 180, 185, 186, 188, 193, 194, 201n88, 201n119, 202n202, 202n139, 202n144, 202n148, 202n151,

202n152, 202n165, 203n2, 210n85, 210n89, 217n196, 219n246, 224n28, 225n87, 225n92, 226n130, 226n150, 226n156, 228n190, 233n5, 235n59, 238n25, 238n37, 239n39, 240n73, 241n87, 241n99, 241n102, 243n134
Sanibel Flats (book) 108
sanity 23, 71, 76, 80, 145; *see also* insanity
Sanna 185
Sant, Gerry 47; *see also* Drew, Duckworth
Santa Fe Railroad 21
Sapper 27, 94
Sappho I (submersible) 73, 83, 165, 166
Sappho II (submersible) 169
Sarah 48
Sargasso Sea 104
Sargeant, Gregg 181; *see also* 911 Stunts
Sarveux, Prime Minister Charles 60, 61, 66, 68, 70, 87, 232n340, 232n341
Sarveux, Danielle 70, 144, 232n341
Satan missiles 83, 139, 231n302
satellites 83
Saturday Review (magazine) 192
Saudi Arabia 22
Savage, Doc Clark 9–10, 18, 19, 20, 23, 58, 64, 96, 107, 191, 198n6, 200n54, 217n177, 220n4, 220n17; *see also* Dent, Lester; Ham; Long Tom; Monk; Johnny; Renny; Robson, Kenneth; Savage, Patricia
Savage, Patricia 20; *see also* Savage, Doc Clark
Savage, Richard Henry 95, 220n13
Sawatch mountain range 132
Sawyer, Phil 36, 66, 91–2, 219n263, 219n265
Sawyer, Tom 10
The Scarlet Pimpernel 69, 120, 225n90
Scheider, Roy 67, 108
Schiller, Julius 66
Schmelzer, Ronald V. 4, 5
Schmidt, Comm. Dipp 189
Schmitz, Sybille 182
Schmuland, Arlene 4
Schofield, Penrod 47
Schreck, Max 168
Schultz, David 67, 68, 211n20, 211n22, 211n23, 211n32
Schultz, Dwight 109
Schwartz, Robert B 27, 28, 140, 201n115, 228n203
Schwarzenegger, Arnold 95, 181
Schweikart, Larry 24, 200n70; *see also* Allen, Michael
Science Digest (magazine) 104
science fiction 18, 65, 79, 82–6, 204n27, 209n65, 215n138, 217n180, 217n190, 218n233, 223n123, 229n241, 233n13; *see also* technothriller
Science Fiction: The Illustrated Encyclopedia 88, 101, 105
Scientific American (magazine) 104
Sciuto, Abby 19
Scooby-Doo 46; *see also* Shaggy

Scorpions (Mesopotamian monster) 119
Scotland 148
Scotland Yard 27
Scott, Alexander "Scotty" 28, 105
Scott, Justin 17, 47, 108
Scottsdale, Arizona 193
scout sniper 109
scow 119
screenplays and scripts 13, 166, 167, 168 169, 171, 172, 182, 221n69, 221n71, 233n12, 238n33, 239n41, 239n60, 242n113
screwball comedy 101
Scripps Institute of Oceanography 34
Scrooge, Ebenezer 79
scuba diving 12, 50, 51
sculling 39, 107
sea captains 96, 230n253
Sea Dog II (submersible) 41
sea farming 9
"The Sea Haunt" (TV episode) 104–5
The Sea Hawks (film) 169
The Sea Hunters (book) 16, 37, 40, 154, 155
The Sea Hunters (TV series) 16
The Sea Hunters II 16, 40
sea serpent 76, 105, 150, 242–3n130; *see also* Basil
Sea Slug (submersible) 74, 238n25
sea spider 74
Seagram, Dana 54, 55, 74–5, 76, 80, 89, 91, 100, 102, 131, 132, 144–5, 149, 157, 160, 164, 169, 170–1, 212n74, 213n85, 213n89, 213n90, 213n91, 213n94, 216n147, 227n160, 229n209, 229n210, 229n213, 229n217, 232n321, 239n43, 239n44; *see also* Archibald, Dana; Seagram, Gene
Seagram, Gene 23, 24, 71, 74, 75–6, 80, 82, 85, 100, 102, 129, 130, 132, 134, 145, 149, 152, 157, 164, 168, 169, 170, 171, 212n74, 213n85, 213n89, 213n90, 216n146, 228n196, 228n205, 229n225, 232n351, 234n21, 238n25, 238n36, 238n37, 239n39, 239n43, 239n44, 239n45, 239n49, 239n51, 241n88; *see also* Seagram, Dana
SEAL assault boat 41
Seals & Crofts 161
The Searchers 16, 100, 221n56
Seattle, Washington 39
USOS *Seaview* 103–4, 186, 222n91, 222n93, 222n94
Second Italian Campaign 77
secret agent 10, 11, 21, 66, 107, 109, 141, 165
secret of enchantment 44, 46, 47
Secretary of the Environment 132
Sedgwick, Eve 81
seduce 35, 56, 75, 120, 127, 227n158
Segal, Steven 236n76
Selby, David 168; 216n147
self-preservation 26, 68
Selleck, Tom 109
Senate committee for oil exploration on government lands 32
Senate Foreign Relations Committees 32

Seng, Eddie 40
sensation novel 192
sequel 9, 17, 28, 47, 84, 108, 183, 189, 190, 215n144, 224n23, 242n119
serial killer 77, 102, 157
series adventure hero 4, 11, 10, 47, 95, 96, 110, 111, 131, 177, 195n11, 197n36, 199n29, 205n43, 206n91, 206n93, 208n44, 210n8
series literature 1, 7, 9, 10, 19–20, 38, 40, 53, 58, 79, 81, 96, 110, 130, 150, 196n32, 204n12, 209n68, 210n8, 220n17, 221n57, 234n41, 243n136, 243n137
Serpent 16, 37, 39, 150, 160, 162, 201n83, 203n2, 203n7, 216n164, 222n108, 227–8n185, 234n36
sex 36, 46, 53, 56, 69, 72, 73, 89, 90, 91, 92, 120, 123, 126, 128, 131–2, 140, 162, 163, 189, 207n4, 212n52, 219n247, 219n262, 219n264, 222n81, 227n169, 234n37
Sexual Personae: Art and Decadence from Nefertiti to Emily Dickinson (book) 6
Seymour Island 159, 218n221; *see also* Novaya Zemlya
Shadow archetype 35, 43, 52, 114–5, 118, 121–3, 139–40, 144, 186–7, 214n106, 223n18, 224n53, 225n105, 237n114; *see also* Jungian Devil
Shadow of a Doubt (film) 102, 157
"Shadow of the Condor" (TV episode) 104
Shadow Over Innsmouth (book) 79
The Shadow 10, 18, 58, 191, 217n177
Shaggy 46; *see also* Scooby-Doo
Shakespeare, William 14, 71, 152
Shamus award 16
Shang, Qin 13, 20, 21, 41, 56, 72, 101, 157, 160, 199n17, 199n22, 209–10n80, 210n81, 210n82, 218n215; similarities and differences with Dirk Pitt 62–3
Shanks, Michael 243n139
shark 3, 27, 96, 170, 229n229, 243n130
Sharp, Lily 35, 55–6
Sharpe, Jim 164
Sharpsburg, Maryland 31
Shatner, William 106, 217n178
Shaw, Brian 21, 37, 60, 87, 99, 141–5, 154, 155, 162, 231n317 *see also* Bond, James; Fleming, Ian
Shaw, Robert 60, 170, 234–5n47
She Wore a Yellow Ribbon (film) 99
Sheequeg 189
Shelby Cobra (AC) Mk II (1967) 176
Sheldon, Marie 75, 91
Shellaburger, Samuel 10
Shelley, Mary Wollstonecraft 81
Shenandoah (film) 184
Sheol 124, 231n299
The Shepherd's Journal 242n129, 243n130; *see also* Atlantis: The Lost Empire
Sherlock Holmes (2009 film) 58
Shields, Harvey 66
shiftiness 55, 69
The Shining 6

Ship Trap Island 153; *see also* Connell, Richard; *Dragon*; Ivan; "The Most Dangerous Game"; Rainsford, Sanger; Zaroff, General
The Shipkiller (book) 47
shipwreck 12, 16, 55, 106, 148, 158, 188, 189, 198n56
Shock Wave 16, 22, 33, 54, 56, 90, 101, 105, 140, 145, 147, 159, 160, 161, 162, 193, 199n36, 202n150, 202n158, 202n188, 203n191, 203n202, 209n65, 209n70, 212n69, 213n97, 214n102, 217n196, 218n214, 218n220, 218n221, 219n246, 219n266, 219n269, 226n116, 235n57, 325n61, 236n103, 242–3n130; parallels with *Pacific Vortex* 76–7, 88, 154, 235n56
The Shootist (film) 47
Shrek! (book) 213n98, 214n102
Si Fan 59, 62
Siam 176
Sicilian Defense 228n207; *see also* Sicilian Project
Sicilian Project 23, 71, 76, 149, 165, 168, 170, 171, 212n74, 228n205, 238–9n37; Project Sicilian 129, 130, 131, 132, 140–1, 161; *see also* Sicilian Defense
Siduri 119
Siegel, Don 6
The Sign of Four (book) 9
Sigurd, Brynhild 39, 162, 212n69
Silicon Valley, California 31
silver mine 104, 204n17
Silverstein, Dr. Murray 73
Simmons, George 66
Simon 134
Simon & Schuster 38, 204n19, 208n49
sine quo non 89
Singh, Khan Noonien 84
Sinn-Feiners 60
Siodmak, Curt 182–3, 242n113
Sir Nigel 14
sister 29, 34, 56, 62, 69, 72, 91, 92, 103, 117, 119, 156, 182, 183, 208n27
Six Days, Seven Nights (film) 92
six-shooters 97
Sixth Louisiana Regiment 102
sizzle reel 180, 244n151
Skartaris 243n137; *see also* Atlantis; lost civilization; Opar; *The Warlord*
Skeleton Coast (book) 42, 67, 77, 147, 160, 162, 205n51, 212n69, 217n194
The Skipper (magazine) 96
"Skull and Double-Crossbones" (TV episode) 104
Skywalker, Luke 108, 114, 214n106, 225n105
slang 29, 84, 219n262
slave 35, 72, 67, 77, 129, 133, 178, 190, 217n190, 230n273, 244n144, 244n154
"Sleeping Beauty" (fairy tale) 73, 74, 76, 77, 158, 212n66; *see also* Lady in the House of Sleep
Slick Sixty-six 161
Sloane, Everett 201n96
SMERSH 60
Smith, Charlie 132, 133

Smith, Edgar W. 64
Smith, Jefferson 98, 102
Smith, Col. John "Hannibal" 109
Smith (Pitt), (Congresswoman) Loren 17, 20, 24, 26, 31, 33, 35–6, 50, 51, 54, 55–7, 65, 66, 68, 87, 89–93, 100, 132, 133, 141, 145, 147, 162, 193–4
Smith & Wesson 30
Smithsonian Institution 186
smoking 20, 29, 42
smuggling 11, 25, 33, 63, 70, 115, 136, 189
"The Snake Peri and the Magic Mirror" (fairy tale) 74, 213n84
Snelling, O.F. 94, 208n37, 209n64, 219n2
snorkeling 50
"Snow White" (fairy tale) 74, 75, 214n102
Snow White and the Seven Dwarves (1937 film) 158
Socarides, Aristotle "Soc" 39, 204n25
socialist 144
Société des Mines de Lorraine 239n39
sociopath 27, 60, 62, 69, 76, 92, 157, 207n100, 207–8n17
Sodom and Gomorrah 137
Soggy Acres (underwater colony) 83, 103, 183
solar detoxification plant 172, 183, 220n23, 241n98
soldier 78, 135, 136, 153, 165, 167, 178, 179, 197–8n48, 199n11, 220n21, 231n284
Solo, Han 108, 223n119
Somala, Marcus 135, 216n159
Some Like It Hot (film) 102
Something Wicked This Way Comes (book) 33
Somewhere in Time (film) 166
The Son of Robin Hood (film) 185
songs and lyrics: old 21, 40, 73, 161, 199n36, 237n118, 237n120
Sonora, Mexico 42
Soseki Island, Japan 28, 153
A Sound of Thunder (film) 174
South Africa 61, 70, 133, 135, 136, 137, 138, 139, 140, 211n42, 230n254, 241–2n107; government 69, 137–8, 231n285, 231n289, 231n311
South Africa Defense Forces 61
South Africa Defense Minister 139
South Africa Defense Ministry 69
South America 59, 86, 183, 191
South Vineland, New Jersey 25; *see also* Giordano, Al
Southby, England 149, 165, 168, 239n43
Southern California 21, 26
southwestern America folk hero 24, 39, 48, 50, 130, 191, 206n95
Soviet American 84
Soviet intelligence 165, 228n205
Soviet Navy 167; Department of Foreign Intelligence 130; naval intelligence 39
Soviet secret base on Cuba 30, 60, 88
Soviets 60, 61, 66, 83, 84, 87, 126, 130, 131, 165, 167
spaceship 83, 84

Spad (airplane) 97
Spade, Sam 18, 95
Spader, James 243n139
Spain/Spanish 40, 42, 104
Spanish American War 48
Spanish galleon 86, 215n143
Spanish Gypsies 32; *see also* gypsies
Spanish treasure 104, 215n143
Sparrow, Capt. Jack 108, 235n50
Spartan Gold (book) 46, 50, 52, 77, 82, 207n107, 214n107, 234n36
Special Forces 42, 62, 178, 179, 197–8n48; *see also* Navy SEALs
special projects director 4, 12, 21, 29, 34, 38, 68, 99, 165, 203n9; *see also* Girodino, Albert Cassius; Pitt, Dirk; surface security officer
special-purpose undersea transport (SPUT) 83
The Specter 62; *see also* Zolar, Charles
Spectre 162; *see also* Eliade, Epona
SPECTRE 130, 209n68
Speelmanns, Hermann 182
spell 72, 73, 92, 212n74
Spencer, Don 12
Spenser 28; *see also* Hawk; Parker, Robert B.
Spenser, Winston 160, 206n88
Sphere (British publisher) 15
sphinx 55, 56, 225–6n105
Spielberg, Steven 108, 166, 189
Spillane, Mickey 1, 5, 95, 152, 153, 196n27, 234n41
spin-off series 16, 38, 106, 204n11, 204n12, 204n33, 208n39, 223n123, 243n138, 243n13; *see also* franchise
spirit quest, shamanistic 120, 124, 126, 237n114; *see also* Big Bad Wolf; initiation quest pattern
Spock, Mr. 106, 201n111, 243n138
spokesperson 75
The Spy (book) 206n95
Stagecoach (film) 99, 221n56
Stalag 17 (film) 102
Stallone, Sylvester 86, 181
standard bearers of adventure 91
Stanley, Sir Henry Morton 129, 227–8n185
Stanton, Edward 177
Stapleton, Jack 58
Stapleton Airport 35
Star Trek (2009 film) 201n111
Star Trek (TV series) 38, 84, 106, 152, 182, 187, 222n108, 243n138, 201n111, 203n10
Star Trek: Deep Space 9 (TV series) 243n148
Star Trek: Generations (film) 106
Star Trek: The Motion Picture (film) 167, 190, 213n76, 222n108, 223n123, 243n138
Star Trek: The Next Generation (TV series) 38, 205n49
Star Trek II: The Wrath of Khan (film) 106, 190
Star Wars (Strategic Defense Initiative or SDI) 83
Star Wars (film) 16, 73, 108, 167, 190, 216–7n174, 223n119, 223n18, 224n32, 244n156

Star Wars: The Empire Strikes Back (film) 77, 225n105
Starbuck (submarine) 23, 59, 81, 86, 147, 160, 226n130, 233n5
Starbuck, Chief Mate 200n59
Starbuck, Lt. 223n119
The Starfollowers of Coramonde (book) 108
Stargate (film) 204n11, 223n123, 243n139
Stargate Atlantis (TV series) 38, 187, 204n12, 223n123
Stargate Infinity (TV series) 223n123
Stargate SG-1 (TV series) 38, 80, 109, 204n11, 204n12, 223n123, 243n139
Stargate Universe (TV series) 204n12
starship 41, 84, 106, 213n76, 217n194
starship captains 107
State Department 167–9, 238n26
stealth technology 83
steam locomotives 47, 85
steampunk 105, 186
steamships 40, 47, 80, 162, 183, 207n109
Steig, William 213n98, 214n102
Steiger, Abe 23, 29, 72, 91, 134, 140, 188, 201n92; wife 51
Steinbeck, John 168
Steiner, Max 179
Stephenson, John 104
stepmother, wicked 74, 75, 158
Steppenwolf 179
stereotypes 38, 71, 79–80, 91, 112, 212n52, 215n134; plots 80
Stern, Alan 84
Stevens, Blake 30
Stevens, Craig 30
Stevens, Dave 222n97; see also The Rocketeer
Stevens, Dave "Sleepy" 97; see also Hartley, Hashknife
Stevenson, Robert Louis 7, 191, 211n44
Stewart, Jimmy 98, 235–6n75
Stewart, Patrick 106
stockholders 42
Stockton, Judge Richard 24
Stoker, Bram 79, 81, 168, 196n35, 211n51, 220n9, 230n56
Stone, Eric 42, 181
stonemason 25
Stonewall Jackson (ship) 80, 162
Stormchild (book) 108
story 1, 3, 5, 6–7, 12, 16, 18–9, 22, 37, 38, 43, 45, 49, 53, 60, 69, 72, 79, 80–2, 85, 86, 87, 89, 91, 95, 97, 111, 125, 128, 130, 132, 139, 141, 146, 148–55, 158, 161, 165, 170, 173–4, 178, 181–3, 186, 187, 189, 191–2, 195n11, 196n35, 197n41, 198n56, 198n9, 198–9n11, 199n13, 206n88, 206n95, 209–10n80, 211n38, 212n15, 213n83, 213n84, 214–5n123, 215n140, 217n180, 221n71, 222n101, 223n18, 226n138, 227n181, 228n192, 228n199, 229n222, 233n12, 234n33
story papers 95
Stout, Rex 11
The Strand (magazine) 9
Strangers on a Train (film) 157

Strauss, Johann 161
Street & Smith 9, 18
The Striker 17, 47
string saws 46
Strong, Mark 50
"Stronger than dirt!" 10; "Stronger than Dirk!" 196n10
structure 6, 38, 79, 81, 146–51, 223n13; see also Formula-A Structure; Formula-B Structure
A Study in Scarlet (book) 9
Stumpy 101
style 6, 7, 21, 24, 38, 79, 103, 105, 106, 120, 152, 176, 180, 214–5n123, 215n130, 222n87, 234n37, 234n40, 235n53
subgenre 72, 82, 105, 215n130, 216–7n174
submarine 1, 23, 28, 30, 31, 39, 81, 82, 83, 96, 103, 160, 165, 167, 185, 186, 189, 190, 198n55, 200n59, 222n91, 222n92, 222n94, 238n25, 242n147, 243n135, 243n140, 244n154
submersible 30, 40, 41, 73, 74, 148, 160, 161, 165, 166, 167, 169, 212n71, 238n25; bathysphere 83
Submission (monomyth) 86–7, 112, 142; see also Riddle of Submission
succubus 92, 144; see also incubus
Sucop, Sucoh 44–7, 234n25
suffering 57
Sullivan, Marta 184
Sullivan, Tom ("The Great Solvani") 184, 242n121
Suma, Hideki 26, 63, 148, 153, 162, 210n82; see also Dragon Center
summa cum laude 70
Summer (concerto) 51
Summer, Cree 187
supercutter (ship) 71, 112
superheroes 98, 205n82
superhuman 67, 117, 132; supermen 19
Superman 98, 129
the supernatural 47, 77, 79, 81, 131, 136, 144, 184, 206n88, 209n61, 214–5n123, 215n130, 215n140, 216n167, 217n177, 226n143, 229n220, 242–3n130
Supernatural Aid (monomyth) 113, 118
"Supernatural Horror in Literature" 79, 214–5n123, 215n129, 216n148
supporting character 23, 25, 53, 64, 85, 87, 98, 105, 118, 141, 144, 151, 186, 202n185, 209n66, 212n70, 222n87
Supreme Being (shamanic quest) 124, 126
surface security officer 68; see also Pitt, Dirk; special projects director
surfboards 34
surveillance analyst 41
suspense-adventure 4, 67, 78, 94, 97, 110, 155
Suspense in the Formula Story (book) 6
Sussex, England 142
Sutton, Jack 72, 216n159
Svlardala 167, 169; see also Novaya Zemlya
swamp 52, 77, 82, 155, 214n106
Swear, Sherriff Tyler 71

Sweeny Todd 95
Swiss Army knife 109
symbol 1, 6–7, 27, 48, 64, 69, 86, 90, 115, 116, 119, 121, 124, 127, 128, 131, 134, 136, 137, 141, 142, 145, 160, 161, 213n94, 225n79, 225–6n105, 226n135, 229n242, 230n267, 233n6, 237n110, 244n148
systems management 39, 96

T, Mr. 86, 109
Table Lake, Colorado 134, 136, 138
Taft, John 40, 204n34; see also Martinez, Larry
Talbot, Larry 227n161
Talbot-Lago Grand Sport coupe (1948) 90, 199n28
"Tales of the Vienna Woods" (waltz) 161
Tam O' The Scoots 96, 220n21
Tamareztov 124, 126
tana leaves 184
tanker 60, 96
Tarzan 18, 58, 58, 186, 243n136
Tarzan (newspaper strip) 1, 237n2
Tarzan of the Apes (book) 160
Taylor, Vaughn 156
Tazareen, South Africa 137–8
teacher 6, 98, 118, 195n7
Teal'c 80
Tebezza mine 161, 178
technology 9, 18, 25, 31–2, 41, 49, 61, 82–3, 84, 85, 104, 105, 106, 124, 161, 167, 181, 205n42, 217n180, 226n130
techno-thriller 18, 82–6, 104, 216n174; value-neutral technology 83, 84, 124, 226n130; see also science fiction
telegrapher 9; see also brass pounder
telephone 47, 101, 142, 166
teleportation device 162, 217n182
television adventure heroes 25, 103–7, 204n25
Television Horrors of Dan Curtis (book) 152, 235n48
"The Tell-Tale Heart" (short story) 80, 215–6n145, 216n148
Templar, Simon 5
Templar treasure 187, 189, 244n148
Temple of Karnak 184
Temple of the Four Orders 58
temptress 36, 69, 87, 113, 119–20, 122, 123, 127, 213–4n98, 219n264, 227n158, 227n169; temptress of geniality (dark temptress) 91–2
"Tenny" Tennison 27
tequila 11, 90
Term Limits (book) 67
Terrible Trio 94, 107, 219n2
terrorist 32, 133, 183, 217n178
Terry and the Pirates (newspaper strip) 104
Test (monomyth) 111, 112, 118–27, 132, 137–40, 145, 189, 224–5n54, 225n99, 228n192
Texas 40, 60, 240n65
CSS *Texas* (submarine) 32, 173, 175, 177, 178, 180, 240n65, 240n67, 240n68

Thames River, England 96
Thatch, Milo 185–7, 243n132, 243n133, 243n134, 243n139, 244n150
Thatch, Thaddeus 186–7, 244n150
thematic preoccupations 7, 60, 65–93, 101, 102, 147, 159, 160, 188, 207n3, 209n63, 227n160, 232n321, 244n148; *see also* obsessions; themes
themes 6, 67, 79, 101, 107, 108, 192, 200n62, 204n22, 212n74, 213n84, 213n86, 215n125, 215n130, 216n147, 221n38
thermonuclear fusion bomb 171
Theseus 119
thesis 6, 16, 66, 79, 142
They Were Expendable (film) 15–6, 100
The Thief (book) 47, 48, 49
thieves 27, 62, 95 157
The Thin Man (book) 20, 51, 52
The Thin Man (film) 20, 52
The Thin Man (1934–1947 film series) 51
The Thing from Another World (film) 36, 101
thirty pieces of silver 133, 134, 136
Thomas, Craig 82
The Thomas Crown Affair (1968 film) 106
Thomas J. Morse (ship) 71, 238n25
Thompson, Jeff 152, 235n48
Thorndyke, Richard 102
Thornton, James 165
Thornton, Peter 109
Thornton, Sean 15
Thorpe, Capt. Geoffrey 169
Thorwald, Lars 157
three-masted frigate 162, 215n144
threshold guardian 115, 117
threshold of adventure 27, 111, 115, 135, 142, 232n330
threshold of consciousness 137, 138
Threshold of Return (monomyth) 111, 113; *see also* Crossing of the Return Threshold
Thunderball (book) 57, 224n25
Tibbets, Daniel 180
tidal wave 32, 86, 103, 186
tiger fish 133, 136–7
Time 147, 149
Time Agent 109
time machines 83
tintype days 43
Titanic (1953 film) 98
Titanic (1997 film) 1, 198n52, 233n15
Titanic (original title for *Raise the Titanic!*) 14, 15
RMS *Titanic* 12, 23, 30, 57, 73–4, 75, 76, 80, 99, 100, 111, 115, 128, 129, 130, 131, 132, 134, 144, 148, 149, 160, 162, 163, 165, 166, 167, 168, 169, 170, 171, 177, 183, 190, 212n70, 212n74, 213n81, 213n89, 227n181, 228n190, 228n197, 228n201, 229n209, 229n210, 232n351, 233n15, 236n89, 238n12, 238n23, 240n85, 244n154; White Star liner 73, 115, 128, 129, 130, 131, 140, 165, 166, 190, 233n15
Titanic Legacy (book) 238n23

To Kill a Mockingbird (book) 3
To Kill a Mockingbird (film) 67
"To One in Paradise" (poem) 121
Toad 19; *see also* video games
tocsin 49
Tolkien, J.R.R. 114
Tom and Jerry (cartoon series) 104
The Tom Clancy Companion 18
Tombs, Capt. Mason 173
The Tombs: A Fargo Adventure 17, 50
Tonopah, Nevada 50
Took, Belladonna 114, 122
Topaz (film) 157
Torchwood (TV series) 109, 223n124
Torchwood Three 109
Torn Curtain (film) 157
torsion spring bow 25
torture 30, 31, 58, 79, 80
toxin 35, 134, 173, 175, 240n76; neuro-toxin 12
toxologist 174
track-and-field 34
tractor 47, 148
train 16, 44, 50, 112, 154–5, 178, 179, 214n114, 220n23, 235n66, 235n70
traitor 35, 60, 61, 84, 114, 117, 134, 140, 152, 186, 187, 188
tramp steamer 41, 181
Transatlantic Tunnel (film) 242n113
transformation 76, 77, 124, 158, 177, 212n59
transsexuals 162
transvestite 162
Travis, Lt. Col. Austin 236n76
treasure 5, 23, 50, 51, 52, 62, 78, 85, 87, 96, 101, 104, 105, 111, 113, 117, 122, 144, 148, 150, 158, 162, 166, 185, 186, 187, 188, 189, 191, 212n74, 213n98, 214n107, 215n143, 224n32, 244n150
Treasure 16, 31, 32, 33, 55, 56, 59, 61, 65, 69, 83, 150, 160, 162
Treasure of Khan 34, 63, 162
Tremor (book) 40
Trevor, Elleston 176
Trickster archetype 35, 69, 114, 122, 139–40, 144, 189, 208n26, 211n40
trimaran 25
Tri-Motor (Ford airplane) 126, 226n156
trinauxite 105
Trinity Church 188–9, 244n150
Trojan Odyssey (book) 17, 29, 33, 34, 35, 36, 52, 57, 61–2, 81, 100, 102, 145, 150, 160, 161, 162, 183, 202n148, 202n165, 202–3n190, 203n210, 203n211, 203n213, 203n220, 203n221, 203n2, 203n9, 204n17, 208n27, 210n85, 217n185, 217n192, 217n193, 218n227, 237n122
Trousdale, Gary 185; *see also* Wise, Kirk
Trout, Paul 38, 51, 160
Troy 78, 95
trust but verify 24
Tsengel 63
tsunami 162
Tuareg 173, 175, 178, 180, 240n68, 240n76, 241n94, 241n95

Tucker, Chris 26
tuckerization 40, 204n27
Tulsa, Oklahoma 9
Tunneling the English Channel (film) 130
Turkey 56, 74, 95, 147, 213n84
Turman, Glynn 174
"Turu the Terrible" (TV episode) 104
Tuttle, W.C. 97
Tutuila Naval Station 33, 203n203; *see also* America Samoa; Pago Pago
Twain, Mark 28, 220n14
28 Days Later (film) 174; *see also* Asselar Oasis; cannibal; Gollum
Twenty Thousand Leagues Under the Sea (book) 162
twins 17, 20, 34, 35, 43, 44, 45, 46, 54, 57, 64, 76, 88, 92, 159, 192
2001: A Space Odyssey (film) 84, 233n13
2010: Odyssey Two (book) 84
tycoon 98, 127, 129
Tyler, Tom 184
typhoid 49
tyrant-monster 57–8, 62, 63, 208n42, 208n43

UFA (*Universum Film Aktien Gesellschaft*) 182, 242n112
Ulysses 209n63
Ulysses (helicopter) 117, 147, 223n10
Ulysses (submarine) 186, 243n135
HMS *Ulysses* (book) 10, 234n40
Uncle Owen 114
Uncle Tom's Cabin (book) 67
undercover agent 37, 56
underworld 12, 63, 87, 95, 124, 126, 175
Unfaithful Wife (monomyth) 119, 120, 123, 144, 225n75
Union (U.S. Civil War) 173, 177, 200n70
Union Jack 53
Union Oil Company 11
United Nations 55, 178, 195n11, 219n246
United Nations International Critical Response and Tactical Team (UNICRATT) 178
United Press Syndicate 164–5
United States 13, 15, 33, 59, 63, 65, 66, 70, 77, 82, 85, 87, 95, 104, 141, 148, 160, 165, 167, 168, 171, 189, 205n40, 207n109, 218n221, 222n62, 232n340, 234n18, 242n113, 243n139; *see also* America
United States (ship) 41, 160
United States of North America 70; *see also* Night Probe!; North American Treaty
Universal Pictures vi
University of California 9
University of Colorado 55
University of Hawaii 203n211
University of Nottingham 5
University of Washington 39
the unknown 11, 20, 23, 27–8, 106, 115, 116, 200n60, 218n233, 235n59; *see also* wilderness
unpredictability 25, 30, 191; *see also* audacity

Index

unpretentiousness 3, 20, 22, 50, 100
unsung heroes 37
The Untouchables (1987 film) 135
Uphill, Lt. George 71
upper middle-class 42
U.S. Air Force 11, 12, 20, 21, 25, 26, 50, 64, 179, 191, 199n24, 203n212, 204n17, 224n51, 229n244, 238n28, 243n137
U.S. Army 24, 80, 158
U.S. Cavalry 47, 105, 237n118
U.S. Geological Survey 67
U.S. government officials 38, 59, 66
U.S. Marines 22, 38, 50, 109, 141, 223n120, 241n101
U.S. Navy 23, 28, 29, 41, 103, 109, 142, 167, 168, 176, 179, 187, 202n139, 202n144, 228–9n208, 238n25, 241n99, 241n103; using films to acquire appropriations 167
Usborne, Richard 94
USO 17

Valero, Wayne 22, 193, 196n9, 198n50, 198n56, 199n20, 201n116, 204n29, 220n26, 231–2n317, 238n33, 240–1n85
Valhalla Rising (book) 9, 17, 22, 26, 28, 32, 33–4, 41, 44, 56–7, 84, 90, 145, 150, 160, 161, 162, 198n55, 199n21, 201n99, 201n212, 202n177, 203n202, 203n208, 208n27, 208n52, 217n182, 217n194, 223n111, 240n85
value-neutral technology 83–4, 124, 226n130
vampire squid 74
Van Dorn Detective Agency 49, 88, 152
Vance, Louis Joseph 96
Vance, Philo 146, 148
Vanishing Act (book) 50
vanity 74, 228n205, 231n311
Varney the Vampire (book) 95, 220n9
vengeance 22, 45, 59, 60, 69, 113, 129, 135, 139, 145, 153, 154, 160, 221n56, 231n311, 234n25, 234–5n47, 236n80
Venice Film Festival 12
Venus 133, 229n224; *see also* Botticelli, Sandra
Verne, Jules 162, 187, 243n135
Vertigo (film) 157, 235–6n75
veterans 4, 12, 26, 31, 32, 48, 49, 100, 114, 164, 167, 179, 183, 184, 186, 187, 197n36, 220n33, 223n121, 230n251, 236n79, 238n30
Vice President of the United States 28
Vicenzo, Contessa Teresa "Tracy" 73, 86, 154
Victorian Era 89–90, 91, 106, 112, 155, 193, 196n35, 219n2, 221n63
video games 19; *see also* Luigi; Mario; Princess; Toad; Yoshi
Vietnam War 14, 21, 26, 31, 64, 66, 109, 114, 167, 169, 170, 197–8n48
viewpoint character (the VP) 25, 48, 129, 132, 146, 148–9, 176, 185, 186, 233n10
vigilante 108

Viking Press 15
Vikings 95, 162, 186, 191
villain types 58–61; *see also* Criminal Mastermind; Emperor of Crime; Grand Single
villainous cult 61
Vin Fiz (*Wright Flyer* airplane) 44–5
The Vipers 62
Vivaldi, Antonio 51
Vixen 03 (airplane) 134, 136–41, 142, 143; C-97 134
Vixen 03 (book) 16, 23, 25, 26, 29, 32, 35, 36, 51, 52, 55, 56, 57, 61, 66, 69, 71, 72, 78, 83, 84, 87, 91, 92, 102, 132–41, 142, 143, 145, 147, 150, 153, 155, 159, 161, 168, 188, 201n92, 202n139, 202n151, 203n196, 203n218, 203n220, 203n223, 210n84, 211n41, 216n156, 216n159, 216n160, 217n184, 218n215, 219n258, 219n261, 219n262, 219n265, 220n27, 221n38, 221n54, 221n55, 227n182, 228n186, 228n191, 229n223, 229n225, 229n244, 230n246, 230n247, 230n251, 230n255, 230n257, 230n272, 230n276, 231n283, 230n284, 230n285, 231n289, 231n291, 231n298, 234n24, 236n91, 236n96; *see also* Operation Wild Rose
voice, husky 120, 163, 189
"Voices of Spring" (waltz) 161
Voight, Jon 187
Voldemort (Lord) 85, 86, 114; Riddle, Tom 225–6n105
Von Til, Bruno 54, 59–60, 61, 72, 79, 80, 87, 116, 149, 152, 160, 161, 229n223, 233n5; *see also* Admiral Heibert
Von Til, Teri 54, 56, 73, 160, 162, 212n69; Amy 55, 72
voodoo 104
Voyage to the Bottom of the Sea (film) 103
Voyage to the Bottom of the Sea (TV series) 103–4, 105, 185, 222n90, 222n94
Vulcan's Forge (book) 16
vulpine 56

Wade, Lt. Smoke 97
"Waiting for the Robert E. Lee" (song) 27, 199n136, 201n100
Walker, Robert 157
The Wall of Night (book) 50
Wallace, Dean Cooper 28, 66, 210n89; Sandecker's opposite 63
Wallace, Edgar 67, 163
Wallace, Estelle 72, 76, 156, 212n59, 216n159, 235n73; *see also* Casilighio, Arta; Crane, Marion
Wallowing Windbag (hovercraft) 83
Walpole, Horace 79, 214n123
wanderlust 96, 118
War Birds (magazine) 96
Ware, Edward Parrish 95
The Warlord (comic book series) 1, 153, 253n137; *see also* Atlantis; Skartaris
Warner, H.B. 27

Warner Bros. 178, 189, 197–8n48
warped hero 132, 135, 136, 140
Washington (state) 101
Washington, George 24, 200n70
Washington, D.C. 14, 21, 28, 29, 57, 75, 90, 105, 112, 115, 117, 118, 132, 133, 139, 141, 149, 155, 170; Beltway 29, 33, 74, 75, 213n89, 202n151, 229n213, 232n321
Washington Cathedral 233n358
The Washington Star (newspaper) 170, 239n48
Watergate Apartments 29
Watergate scandal 14, 66
"Wave Those Tags!" 18–9; *see also* character blueprint; Dent, Lester; "The Pulp Paper Master Fiction Plot"
Wayne, Bruce 19
Wayne, John (The Duke) 14, 15–6, 98, 99, 100, 101, 197–8n48, 221n56
"We Have All the Time in the World" (song) 154
"We May Never Pass This Way Again" (song) 161
We, the People 24
weightlifter, professional 60
Weld, Therri 160
Wells, Orson 109, 234–5n48
Wendy 52, 114–5, 125, 223–4n22, 224n23
"We're an American Band" (song) 174
"Werewolf of the Timberland" (TV episode) 104
West, James 71, 105–6
West, Mae 54
West 35th Street 32
West Africa 56, 77, 172, 175
Western (genre) 16, 17, 24, 47, 98, 101, 105, 107, 108, 155, 222n87
Western allies 14
Western civilization 14, 59, 67, 75, 91, 179, 218n233, 228n205
Western enemies 130
Western Europe 33
Western literature 9
Westerners 62, 206n88
Whale, James 87
Wheatley, Helen 79, 215n130
Wheaton Security Bank 139
Wheels: A Passion for Collecting Cars (book) 193
"When the World Screamed" (short story) 82
Where Eagles Dare (book) 4
Where Eagles Dare (film) 196n35
Whirlwind 96, 205n43
white (color) 26, 33, 39, 44, 48, 75, 76, 87, 92, 107, 115, 122, 123, 142, 153, 157, 170, 186, 190, 201n96, 210n82, 221n37, 237n114, 240n65, 241n99, 244n154; Caucasian 5, 14, 28, 135, 136, 137, 138, 139, 140, 212n66, 231n285, 231n311, 244n144
White, Jesse 105
White, Randy Wayne 108
White Bird (*L'Osseau Blanc*, airplane) 177, 210n3
White Death (book) 84, 160, 217n193, 227–8n185

White House 36, 63, 66, 68, 69, 74, 75, 89, 101, 138, 201n88, 232n321; see also Oval Office
Whitmore, Preston B. 186–7, 243n133, 243n134, 244n150
widow 33, 55, 92
widower 29, 42
Wielde, Beth A. 67, 68, 211n20, 211n22, 211n23, 211n32
Wikipedia 193
Wilbanks, Ralph 71
The Wild, Wild West (TV series) 71, 105–6, 222n103, 222n105
Wilder, Billy 102–3; Wilder hero 102
wilderness 14, 24, 27–8, 136, 137, 138; see also the unknown
Wildey, Doug 104, 222n95, 222n97, 222n99
"Wildmen, Warriors, and Lovers: Reaching Boys through Archetypal Literature" (article) 4–5
Wildtrack (book) 108
will-o-the-wisp 69
William Morris Agency 13
"William Wilson" (short story) 144
Williams, Emlyn 157
Williams, Race 95
Willis, Bruce 108, 208n76
Wilson, Lambert 174
Wilson, Rainn 170
Wilson, Woodrow 48, 66, 141–2
Wingate, George, and wife 160
Wings (magazine) 96
Winnie-the-Pooh tales 135
Winthrop Manor Nursing Home 55, 78, 208n27, 237n128
USS *Wisconsin* 134
Wise, Kirk 185; see also Trousdale, Gary
Wise Old Man archetype 32, 44, 80, 114, 115, 119, 120, 122, 124, 142, 186, 226n151, 228n190, 232n322; see also Mulholland, Felix; sage
Wise Old Woman 78; see also Kronberg, Hilda
Wo Fat 71
wolf 116, 126–7, 227n161, 230n276
Wolf, Karl 61, 62
Wolf family 31, 59, 61, 62, 82
The Wolf Man (1941 film) 242n113

Wolfe, Nero 18, 19, 38; parallels with St. Julien Perlmutter 32
Woman in White 72, 81, 95, 192, 212n57, 215n126, 216n150, 215n151
women wearing green 65
Wondrash, Selma 52; see also Corden, Wendy; Jeffcoat, Peter
Wong, Maj. James 62
"Wonks and Warriors: Depictions of Government Professionals in Popular Films" (article) 67–7, 210n8, 210n9; see also action hero; criminals, bureaucratic; ethic hero; power monger
Wood, Omar 12
Woods Hole Oceanographic Institute 38, 189, 204n19
Woodward, Bill 67
World Health Organization (WHO) 35, 56, 172
World Trade Center 61, 236n80
World War I 49, 97, 104, 148, 191
World War II 16, 31, 32, 34, 50, 51, 59, 96, 101, 134, 152, 168, 196n9, 197–8n48, 218n221, 220n33, 242n115
Worts, George Frank 96
The Wrecker (book) 17, 47
wrestler, professional 60
Wright, Teresa 102, 157
Wright Flyer airplane 44, 45, 47
The Writer's Yearbook 18
Wu, Mr. 164
Wuthering Heights (book) 80, 81

Yaeger, Maj. Gen. Charles Elwood "Chuck" 31
Yaeger, Elsie 31, 83
Yaeger, Hiram 20, 22, 31–32, 51, 83, 84, 85, 102, 178, 202n177, 210n81, 217n189, 221–2n79; Communication and Information Network 31
Yankee 98, 126
Yates, Dornford 94
Year of the Rat 62
yellow 19, 32, 54, 161, 211n48, 237n10
yellow-backs 95, 220n5
Yerli, Ismail 56, 90–1, 178, 208n25, 219n247

Yesterday's Faces viii, 59, 94, 209n60
Yeti 104
yoga 35, 133, 186
York, Capt. Kirby 15
York, Dr. Raymond 71
Yoshi 19; see also video games
You Only Live Twice (book) 20, 57, 86, 154, 208n38, 218n215, 235n58
You Only Live Twice (film) 230n30
Young Mr. Lincoln (film) 99

Zacynthus (Inspector) 55, 151, 208n21
Zahn, Steve 171
Zakara 178
Zale, Curtis Merlin 62, 162, 209n75; see also Kane, Charles Foster
Zaroff, General 153; see also Connell, Richard; *Dragon*; Ivan; "The Most Dangerous Game"; Rainsford, Sanger; Ship Trap Island
Zavala (ship) 40
Zavala, Jose "Joe" 16, 26, 31, 38–40, 66, 68, 71, 83, 97, 105, 160, 161–2, 188, 201n83, 203n2, 203n7, 210n9, 234n36
Zhong, Su 20, 63
Zimbabwe 153, 231n311; see also Kenya
Zin, Dr. 104
zirconium 105
Zodiacs (SEAL assault boat) 41, 181
Zolar, Charles ("Oxley, Charles") 62; see also The Specter
Zolar, Joseph 62
Zolar, Mansfield (The Specter) 62
Zolar, Marla 62
Zolar, Samuel ("Sarason, Cyrus") 62
Zolar family 62
zombies 174; see also Asselar Oasis; cannibal; Gollum; *28 Days Later*
zone unknown 114, 117, 123, 125, 159, 232n330
zoologist 81
Zorro 120, 191
Zorro (TV series) 222n87
Zucco, George 183
Zweig, Paul 23, 200n55

www.ingramcontent.com/pod-product-compliance
Lightning Source LLC
Chambersburg PA
CBHW080801300426
44114CB00020B/2792